A COMPLETE GUIDE

THE HAMPTONS

Hook Windmill, East Hampton

SIXTH EDITION

THE HAMPTONS

A Great Destination

*Including the North Fork
and Shelter Island*

Suzi Forbes Chase

The Countryman Press
Woodstock, Vermont

To my late mother, who first encouraged my sense of curiosity, taught me the joy of discovery, and suggested I take my first trip to one of "the last great places"—the Hamptons.

Recommended by *National Geographic Traveler* and *Travel + Leisure* magazines

A crisp and critical approach, for travelers who want to live like locals.—*USA Today*

Great Destinations™ guidebooks are known for their comprehensive, critical coverage of regions of extraordinary cultural interest and natural beauty. Each title in this series is continuously updated with each printing to ensure accurate and timely information. All the books contain more than one hundred photographs and maps.

Current titles available:

THE ADIRONDACK BOOK

THE ALASKA PANHANDLE

ATLANTA

AUSTIN, SAN ANTONIO
  & THE TEXAS HILL COUNTRY

BALTIMORE, ANNAPOLIS & THE CHESAPEAKE BAY

THE BERKSHIRE BOOK

BIG SUR, MONTEREY BAY
  & GOLD COAST WINE COUNTRY

CAPE CANAVERAL, COCOA BEACH
  & FLORIDA'S SPACE COAST

THE CHARLESTON, SAVANNAH
  & COASTAL ISLANDS BOOK

THE COAST OF MAINE BOOK

COLORADO'S CLASSIC MOUNTAIN TOWNS

COSTA RICA: GREAT DESTINATIONS
  CENTRAL AMERICA

DOMINICAN REPUBLIC

THE FINGER LAKES BOOK

THE FOUR CORNERS REGION

GALVESTON, SOUTH PADRE ISLAND
  & THE TEXAS GULF COAST

GUATEMALA: GREAT DESTINATIONS
  CENTRAL AMERICA

THE HAMPTONS

HAWAII'S BIG ISLAND: GREAT DESTINATIONS
  HAWAII

HONOLULU & OAHU: GREAT DESTINATIONS
  HAWAII

THE JERSEY SHORE: ATLANTIC CITY TO CAPE MAY

KAUAI: GREAT DESTINATIONS HAWAII

LAKE TAHOE & RENO

LAS VEGAS

LOS CABOS & BAJA CALIFORNIA SUR:
  GREAT DESTINATIONS MEXICO

MAUI: GREAT DESTINATIONS HAWAII

MEMPHIS AND THE DELTA BLUES TRAIL

MICHIGAN'S UPPER PENINSULA

MONTREAL & QUEBEC CITY:
  GREAT DESTINATIONS CANADA

THE NANTUCKET BOOK

THE NAPA & SONOMA BOOK

NORTH CAROLINA'S OUTER BANKS
  & THE CRYSTAL COAST

NOVA SCOTIA & PRINCE EDWARD ISLAND

OAXACA: GREAT DESTINATIONS MEXICO

OREGON WINE COUNTRY

PALM BEACH, FORT LAUDERDALE, MIAMI
  & THE FLORIDA KEYS

PALM SPRINGS & DESERT RESORTS

PHILADELPHIA, BRANDYWINE VALLEY
  & BUCKS COUNTY

PHOENIX, SCOTTSDALE, SEDONA
  & CENTRAL ARIZONA

PLAYA DEL CARMEN, TULUM & THE RIVIERA MAYA:
  GREAT DESTINATIONS MEXICO

SALT LAKE CITY, PARK CITY, PROVO
  & UTAH'S HIGH COUNTRY RESORTS

SAN DIEGO & TIJUANA

SAN JUAN, VIEQUES & CULEBRA:
  GREAT DESTINATIONS PUERTO RICO

SAN MIGUEL DE ALLENDE & GUANAJUATO:
  GREAT DESTINATIONS MEXICO

THE SANTA FE & TAOS BOOK

THE SARASOTA, SANIBEL ISLAND & NAPLES BOOK

THE SEATTLE & VANCOUVER BOOK

THE SHENANDOAH VALLEY BOOK

TOURING EAST COAST WINE COUNTRY

TUCSON

VIRGINIA BEACH, RICHMOND
  & TIDEWATER VIRGINIA

WASHINGTON, D.C., AND NORTHERN VIRGINIA

YELLOWSTONE & GRAND TETON NATIONAL PARKS
  & JACKSON HOLE

YOSEMITE & THE SOUTHERN SIERRA NEVADA

The authors in this series are professional travel writers who have lived for many years in the regions they describe. Honest and painstakingly critical, full of information only a local can provide, Great Destinations guidebooks give you all the practical knowledge you need to enjoy the best of each region.

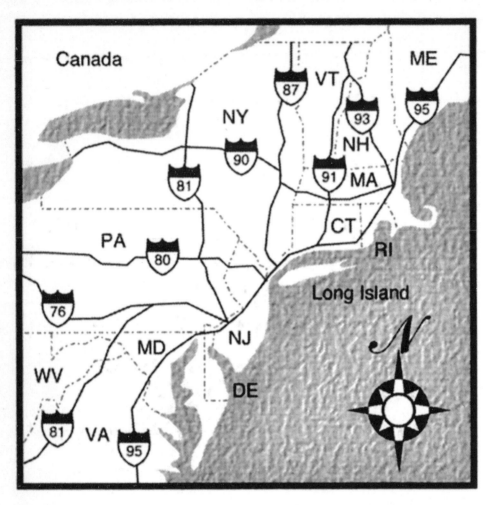

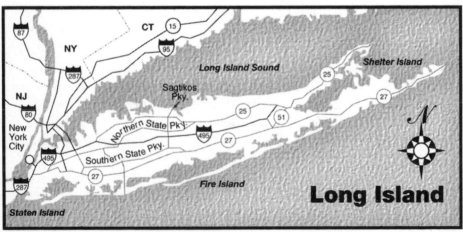

CONTENTS

ACKNOWLEDGMENTS 9

INTRODUCTION 11

HOW TO USE THIS BOOK 12

I

THE LAND & ITS PEOPLES
History
14

2

THE JOURNEY & THE VISIT
Transportation
33

3

HOSPITALITY, HAMPTONS STYLE
Lodging
45

4

FROM THE BOUNTY OF THE LAND
Restaurants & Food Purveyors
75

5

SHOP 'TIL YOU DROP
Shopping
140

6

DEVELOPING ARTISTRY
Culture
172

7

ONE OF THE LAST GREAT PLACES
Recreation
206

8

PRACTICAL MATTERS
Information
238

9

FROM VINES TO WINES
The North Fork
250

10

A CHARMING GREEN-CLAD ISLAND
Shelter Island
330

IF TIME IS SHORT   352

INDEX   367

LODGING BY PRICE   388

DINING BY PRICE   390

DINING BY CUISINE   392

SHOPPING BY DESTINATION   395

MAPS

Hamptons and North Fork Wineries   256
The East End   356
The South Fork   357
Westhampton Beach   358
Southampton   359
Bridgehampton   360

Sag Harbor   361
East Hampton   362
Amagansett   363
Montauk   364
The North Fork   365
Shelter Island   366

Acknowledgments

Writing and revising this book has been a privilege and a joy, and I am deeply indebted to those who have shared their expertise, knowledge, and time with me.

I wish to thank several people who read portions of my original manuscript in 1994. The late Robert Keene, former historian for the Town of Southampton, not only had an eagle eye for spelling, but always had dependable answers when I frequently called him with questions.

Carleton Kelsey, the late director of the Amagansett Free Library, unselfishly shared his vast wealth of historical knowledge with me on numerous occasions. His expertise went far beyond Amagansett. He had such a firm grasp of local history that each time I spoke with him I came away richer.

Dorothy Ingersoll Zaykowski, former historian at the John Jermain Library in Sag Harbor, was kind enough to make several suggestions about Sag Harbor that improved my manuscript, but her help didn't end there. She continued to verify my facts and called several weeks after we had completed our discussion, saying, "I've been researching this issue and believe if you stated it this way, it would more clearly reflect what actually happened." Thank you.

Most of all I wish to express my deep thanks to wonderful, marvelous Dorothy King, the former librarian of the Long Island Collection at the East Hampton Library. I feel as though I lived at the library while I was conducting my research. When I got to the writing stage, I called her over and over with obscure questions. She always knew exactly where to find the answers and often supplied me with additional information that helped fill out the book. Her wealth of knowledge was invaluable. Thank you, thank you, Dorothy.

Thanks also go to Marina Van, director of the East Hampton Chamber of Commerce, and to Millie Fellingham, director of the Southampton Chamber of Commerce, for their help. With their fingers on the pulse of the business community, they are always quick to tell me about new businesses or changes in existing ones. In addition, Steve Haweeli of Wordhampton and his staff offer expert insights into new restaurants and inns—often before they become public knowledge. And Steve Bate, director of the Long Island Wine Council, is an invaluable resource for what's happening in the rapidly evolving East End wine industry.

The first four editions of this book were published by Berkshire House Publishers, in Stockbridge, Massachusetts. I remain grateful to Jean Rousseau, Berkshire's former president, who agreed to publish this book in the first place and to underwrite the updates (we all know how rapidly things change in the Hamptons). During the production of the fifth edition, Berkshire House was acquired by W. W. Norton & Company. The Great Destinations series is now part of Norton's Countryman Press division. I wish to express my deepest thanks to Kermit Hummel, editorial director of Countryman Press, and Lisa Sacks, managing editor, for their commitment to this book, as well as to Melissa Dobson, my copyeditor for this edition. They have been a delight to work with.

Finally, thanks go to my husband, Dustin, who accompanied me to restaurants, inns, museums, and on bicycle and canoe rides, and who spent many nights on his own while I slaved over my manuscript. His encouragement and patience sustained me. I appreciate his belief in me.

Introduction

I'll never forget my first visit to the Hamptons. I was living in Seattle, and I was on my first trip alone to New York City. As much as I love the city, I really wanted to see the Hamptons. So I called for the train schedule. If I caught an early-morning train (around 7 AM at the time), I could be in East Hampton by 10 AM. That would give me time to see the village, spend time on the beach, and catch the afternoon train back.

Only it didn't work out that way. I fell in love with this idyllic place. It was one of those clear, blue-sky days, with the temperature hovering in the mid-70s. Luckily, I had packed a few essentials in my beach bag, so my first stop was the Maidstone Arms. What luck! One room had just been vacated. As the clerk took me up the back stairs, he explained that Joanne Woodward and her daughter Nell had just checked out. The room was very modest, with camp-style iron beds, and I believe the bath was down the hall. I couldn't have cared less. (The Maidstone has since undergone several renovations, and now operates under the name c/o The Maidstone.)

I freely admit that I am a beach zealot. If the sun is shining, I can't resist. So, without further ado, I walked to the most spectacular beach I had ever seen. I had lived in Hawaii, but nothing prepared me for the miles and miles of clean, broad, sparkling white sand, fringed by sea grass–covered dunes that I found in the Hamptons. I was hooked.

From that day on, I have returned to the Hamptons at every possible opportunity. While living in Seattle, it was generally once a year, but when I permanently moved to New York City, my visits became much more frequent. With the first hint of warm weather in the spring, I'd drive my 1966 MGB from Manhattan to the Hamptons to feast my eyes on all the budding trees. I came in the fall to take pumpkins and gourds home, and I came in the winter to sit at Main Beach to hear the waves crash and assure myself that it was all still here. Soon, I started spending summers here. At first I stayed in different inns, motels, or B&Bs every weekend (they were pretty funky then). Then I started renting houses or cabins for the summer, and eventually I moved here full-time. Although I don't currently live in the Hamptons, I live close enough to buzz out on a moment's notice.

I love the Hamptons when there's snow on the ground and the bluebird sky beams down. I love to see the first buds of spring burst into flower against the tapestry of the evergreen trees. I love to see the osprey return in the spring and to see their babies begin to fly, to observe the cranes and egrets on the marshy bays as they fish for dinner, and to watch the way anything planted in the garden blossoms forth. I love the kaleidoscope of autumn's oranges and reds, and I love the beach—that glorious, ever-changing, constant expanse of white sand. I love early-morning walks when the ocean spray lifts to meet the fog. The memories I cherish most are here. There's a peace and a tranquility, but it's also rejuvenating, relaxing, inspirational, and exhilarating, all at the same time.

Frankly, writing a guidebook about the Hamptons has presented a conflict for me. The public's opinion of the Hamptons is that it's the playground of the rich, so why would the rest of us want to come? Part of me says it's better to allow that belief to remain, because the roads and the beaches are too congested in the summer as it is. On the other hand, if more people learn the secret joys of a walk through Morton National Wildlife Refuge in the spring or a canoe trip on Georgica Pond, then perhaps more visitors will appreciate the precious resource we have and will help with its preservation.

I hope I have done justice to this "last great place." Each of us has our own favorite shop, restaurant, beach, and memory. There was so much more I would have liked to include, but space simply didn't permit it. I encourage you to make your own discoveries, using this book as an outline, to delve into and savor the Hamptons' rich history, to reflect on the paintings inspired by our scenery, to admire the picturesque windmills and the traditional and futuristic houses—to canoe on the ponds, fish in the ocean, trek across the nature trails, and soak up the sun on the beaches—with a spirit of new discovery. Stop to smell the fresh salt air, to watch the magnificent osprey in their nests, and to feel the sand sift through your toes. Then you'll reach beneath the surface and touch the spirit of the Hamptons.

—Suzi Forbes Chase
Long Island

HOW TO USE THIS BOOK

The Hamptons is divided into 10 chapters. Entries in each chapter are listed alphabetically by village. Most entries include such specific information as address, telephone number, Web site, hours of operation, and owners' or managers' names to ease your quest for a reservation or devise an itinerary. Although I checked all of the information as close to publication as possible, it's best to verify hours and prices, as changes inevitably occur.

Prices

You will note that specific prices are not listed, since they are likely to fluctuate. Instead, I have categorized them within various ranges. Lodging price codes are based on the average between the highest and lowest rate per room, double occupancy. If a continental or full breakfast is included, it will be noted under "Special Features." In general, these rates exclude local taxes and any service charges that may be added to your bill.

Dining price categories indicate the average cost of an individual meal, including appetizer, entrée, and dessert, but excluding cocktails, wine, tax, or tip. Similarly, rather than indicating the exact hours each restaurant is open, I have specified which meals are served.

Price Codes

Code	Lodging	Dining
Inexpensive	Up to $100	Up to $30
Moderate	$100–250	$30–50
Expensive	$250–400	$50–80
Very expensive	$400 or more	$80 or more

Credit Cards

The credit cards accepted at restaurants and lodging establishments are coded as follows:

AE: American Express; D: Discover; DC: Diner's Club; MC: MasterCard; V: Visa

Area Codes

The area code for the East End of Long Island is 631. All telephone numbers are within that area code, unless otherwise noted.

Towns in the Hamptons

The Hamptons are located in Suffolk County. Although on Long Island, town government is the predominant local lawmaker and enforcement agency, within each town, individual incorporated villages are also self-governing. The incorporated villages generally have legal and enforcement influence within their boundaries, including maintaining their own police force, but smaller hamlets depend on the town for these services. Most villages have a village hall where local business is conducted. Beach permits for the village beaches, for example, are issued by the village, while permits for the town beaches are issued at the town office.

There are two towns on the South Fork. Southampton Town takes in the villages of (traveling from west to east) Eastport, Remsenburg, Speonk, West Hampton Dunes, Westhampton, Westhampton Beach, Quogue, East Quogue, Hampton Bays, Southampton, Water Mill, Sag Harbor (although a portion of Sag Harbor is also in the town of East Hampton), Sagaponack, and Bridgehampton. East Hampton Town is composed of Wainscott, East Hampton, Amagansett, Springs, and Montauk.

There are also two towns on the North Fork. Riverhead takes in the villages of Aquebogue, Baiting Hollow, Calverton, Jamesport, Riverhead, South Jamesport, and Wading River. Southold Township encompasses the villages of Cutchogue, East Marion, Greenport, Laurel, Mattituck, New Suffolk, Orient, Orient Point, and Peconic.

Shelter Island is a separate township that incorporates three villages: Dering Harbor, Shelter Island village, and Shelter Island Heights.

1

THE LAND & ITS PEOPLES

History

The history of the Hamptons is laced with adventure, intrigue, and wisdom—a romantic tale of daring and enterprise, and of evolution. It's a region shaped by New England principles of hard work and thrift, stirred by strong religious convictions.

The Hamptons possess an unparalleled natural beauty—poets often rhapsodize about it, and artists spend lifetimes trying to capture it on canvas. The majestic Atlantic Ocean lies at its front door, while varied bays lie behind it. In between, the lakes and ponds are separated by hills and marshes, all interspersed with nature preserves, wildlife and bird sanctuaries, and hiking and nature trails.

NATURAL HISTORY

Long Island was formed some 15,000 years ago. It was shaped by the slow, relentless movement of ice during the last Ice Age—the forward thrust of massive boulders, soil, and accumulated debris formed valleys and crevices as they were pushed along in front of the ice, and as the ice receded and melted, it left deposits of rocks and dirt in its wake.

The resulting pile left on the South Fork of Suffolk County is known as the Ronkonkoma Moraine. It is submerged beyond Montauk Point, but surfaces again to form Block Island, Martha's Vineyard, and Nantucket. The moraine also disappears beneath the sandy surface of Napeague, indicating that Montauk itself may at one time have been an island. Even today, as the cliffs at Montauk Point continue their evolution through erosion, the residue is deposited at Napeague, creating an ever wider landmass. Probably about 4,000 years ago, after the ice receded and the soil began to nurture plant and animal life, the first humans arrived.

SOCIAL HISTORY

When the first English settlers landed on the shores of Long Island, they were greeted by tribes of peaceful Indians who were adept at farming and fishing. It is believed that these residents were descendants of tribes who had migrated to these shores after years of nomadic wandering, first across the Bering Strait, then east across North America, and eventually south to Long Island. The accounts of the earliest explorers indicate that the hills of eastern Long Island were well populated. "It was full of hilles, covered with trees, well

The Elias Pelletreau Goldsmith Shop was built in 1686. It's one of the few historical buildings that's still located on its original site, although it does face a different direction. Dustin Chase

peopled, for we sawe fires all along the coaste," recorded Giovanni da Verrazano as he sailed along the south shore of Long Island in 1524.

Unlike the native inhabitants, who were content to live within nature's protective cloak, the colonists viewed the bounty of natural resources as a challenge placed there for them to tame, control, and use. In the years to come, these settlers cut down trees for their homes and mills, created thriving fishing and whaling industries, and harnessed wind and water to grind corn and wheat and to saw wood.

Early Traders

In 1633, only 13 years after the landing at Plymouth Bay and 3 years after the settlement of Boston, John Winthrop, governor of the Massachusetts Bay Colony, sent a ship to the Connecticut coast on an exploratory expedition. Much to his surprise, the captain returned and reported "having made a further discovery of that called Long Island." This discovery was particularly interesting because he brought back "wampampeag, both white and blue, it being made by the Indians there."

Whereas Indians elsewhere made pottery, blankets, or beaded headdresses, the early residents of Long Island made wampum, which was highly prized. They searched through piles of clam, whelk, and other shells on the beach, selecting those of the right size and color and then boring a hole through the small, highly polished beads for stringing; a pointed wooden stick was used for this painstaking, skilled work. Those who bored the holes rapidly without breaking the shell were considered true artisans. When the English arrived, they introduced these artisans to the mux, or awl, a sharply pointed metal instrument that made the job much easier. Individual beads were strung on sinew and hung around the neck or woven into belts for transporting.

Wampum was the chief means of trade among the early colonists. They exchanged furs, coats, tools, and other implements with the natives for wampum, which the settlers then used to barter and buy goods among themselves. The value of wampum was as closely regulated by the colonists as United States currency is today.

Christopher R. Vagts described the importance of wampum in *Suffolk, A Pictorial History* (1983):

> The fur trade went something like this: A European trader brought cheap woven trade cloth (duffel) to coastal Indians on Long Island. The cheap cloth was traded for wampum at a good rate of exchange. The wampum was taken to inland Indians where it was highly valued. Lengths of beads were exchanged for beaver and other furs. The furs were shipped to Europe where they commanded high prices. Thus, at each step of this trade, enormous profits were possible. Long Island—the wampum "mine"—was of critical importance!

English Settlers and Settlements

One can only imagine the excitement generated in Massachusetts by the news of the wampum trade on Long Island. In order to get there before the Dutch, who had established a settlement at New York in 1625, Governor Winthrop encouraged Massachusetts residents to move to Long Island; several families from Lynn accepted the invitation. When the intrepid band of colonists landed at Conscience Point on Peconic Bay in 1640, they established the first English settlement in New York State, a village named Southampton in honor of the Earl of Southampton. These early colonists had received a land grant from James Farrett, the representative of the Earl of Stirling. Respectful of the Indians' claim to the land, the colonists also purchased the land from them.

The native residents were very helpful to the newcomers, sharing their agricultural and cooking techniques; teaching them to fertilize corn by placing a tiny, oily fish, the menhaden, in each seed hole; showing them how to use the bone and oil of beached whales; pointing out where to harvest an abundance of shellfish; and demonstrating how to make samp, a porridge that became a staple on colonial tables. In exchange, the English provided the Indians with protection against other marauding tribes, particularly the Pequots and Narragansetts of Connecticut.

Although there appear to have been few conflicts between the new English settlers and the native inhabitants, life apparently did hold a few aggravations. Edward Johnson, an early settler, wrote in 1640, "There are many Indians on the greatest part of this Island who at first settling of the English there did much to annoy their Cattel with the multitude of Doggs they kept, which ordinarily are young wolves brought up tame, continuing of a very ravening nature."

Of much more serious consequence was the scalping of Phebe Halsey, one of the earliest settlers of Southampton. It was proven that those who broke into her home were from one of the Connecticut tribes intent on starting trouble between the Long Island natives and the English. They were quickly captured and sent back to Connecticut, where they were executed.

The indigenous tribes who resided on the South Fork when the English arrived were the Montaukets, who lived in Montauk and had an influence that extended throughout much of

eastern Long Island, and the Shinnecocks, who lived in Southampton. With no immunity from English diseases, however, the Shinnecock population decreased rapidly until, in 1686, there were only 152 survivors. Today, however, the Shinnecocks count approximately 600 tribal members residing on their reservation in Southampton.

Although early colonial life must have been difficult, settlers on eastern Long Island were spared many of the tribulations encountered in other areas. The flat, treeless land with its rich soil was easy to till and produced bountiful crops; the sea yielded an abundance of seafood; and the freedom from attack encouraged the growth of stable, prosperous communities within a relatively short time.

The settlers from Lynn were New Englanders through and through. They built their houses and villages to reflect the styles of their northern neighbors, and their religion was strict Calvinist. Rev. Abraham Pierson was ordained minister of the Southampton Colony in 1640.

In his book, *The Early History of Southampton, L.I.* (1887), George Rogers Howell gives the following account of East End life:

An interesting question is that of the food and appliances of the table of the colonists
of the Puritan period. They raised on the farm Indian corn, wheat (both winter and
summer varieties), oats, barley, beans, and peas, but no potatoes.... The waters
abounded in fish, clams, and oysters, though the shellfish seem to have been used but
sparingly. Cows, oxen, goats, and sheep were raised in considerable numbers, both
for home consumption and for export. At a later period, many horses were shipped to
the West Indies. Tea and coffee were unknown.

Wine, cider, beer, homebrewed ale, milk, and water were the only drinks used by
the settlers upon the table. (Tea arrived in England about 1657.)

Heavy farmwork was done by oxen. The only vehicle in use for a long time was the two-wheeled oxcart. Men and women traveled on horseback, and when the horse was wanting, on one occasion at least, a bovine was pressed into service.

In Suffolk County, the governor authorized a fair to be held in Southampton in 1692. As in old England, fairs were an occasion when everybody offered their unwanted items for sale or exchange. The fairs were frequented by peddlers on whom the ladies depended for finery and light silk goods.

Although the settlers from Lynn are credited with establishing the first English colony in New York State, an English family was already in residence nearby when they arrived. In 1635, Lieutenant Lion Gardiner and his wife, Mary, sailed from London to the mouth of the Connecticut River. Mr. Gardiner was a military engineer who had been commissioned by Lords Say and Brook to build a fort in Connecticut where the town of Saybrook is now located. Upon completing his task in 1639, he received an entire 3,500-acre island located between the North and South Forks of eastern Long Island as a land grant. He also prudently purchased it from the native Indians and then changed its name from the Isle of Wight to Gardiner's Island. His daughter, Elizabeth, was the first English child born in New York State.

Lion Gardiner was both a diplomat and a statesman, and his influence extended throughout eastern Long Island and into Connecticut. He learned the Montauk language and befriended Chief Wyandanch, sachem (leader) of the Montauks, whom he had met at Saybrook—a friendship that proved to be mutually beneficial. At one point, Gardiner played an instrumental role in securing the release of the chief's daughter, Heather Flower, after she was kidnapped by the Pequots on her wedding day. In appreciation, Wyandanch gave Gardiner a large tract of land in what is now Smithtown.

Lion Gardiner and his descendants, the "lords of the manor," created a self-sufficient agrarian economy on Gardiner's Island. They grew and raised their own food, as well as that needed for barter, and they exercised total manorial control of their island from 1639 until 1788, when it was annexed to East Hampton. Today the island is still owned and managed by the Gardiner family—the only known English land grant in America to remain in the possession of the original family.

At the suggestion of Governor Winthrop, Lion Gardiner sponsored a young man in the new colony of East Hampton by the name of Thomas James. Arriving in 1650, Mr. James became the first pastor in East Hampton, where he soon established himself as a highly influential cleric and businessman. It is noteworthy that the first settlers here were staunch Puritans who were so fiercely independent of the British crown that it would be 200 years before any Episcopal church (which was closely affiliated with the Church of England) was established. On the other hand, even though they strongly advocated total

The Gardiner Windmill was built in 1771 and was in operation until the hurricane of 1938 incapacitated it. It was fully restored in 1999 and now sits on James Lane. Morgan McGivern

separation of church and state, the clergy were hired by the town fathers, paid out of the town coffers, and furnished with a house and pastureland at town expense.

In matters other than religious, the spread of ideas and commercial activity expanded rapidly throughout the East End. Word quickly reached Connecticut and Massachusetts that Long Island offered a mild growing climate with temperate winters and cool summers, as well as rich soil that yielded abundant crops; that congenial settlers had formed agreeable communities; and, best of all, that the native Indians were accommodating. By 1649, the census lists 45 heads of household in Southampton. Other settlements were soon established: East Hampton was settled in 1648, Wainscott and Springs in 1652, Bridgehampton and the village of Sagaponack in 1656, and Amagansett in 1680.

By 1644, the first crude post windmills were constructed to grind corn and wheat, saw wood, and perform other tasks. These early windmills were built on tall platforms supported by wooden frames. The structures were turned to catch the wind by means of long posts reaching to the ground. There are no remaining windmills of this type today, but the Hamptons can still claim the largest collection of windmills without posts in the U.S.

By the late 1600s, technology had advanced beyond the early post windmills, and mills were built with the machinery housed in a stationary octagonal tower capped by a revolving hood that held the sails and turned to allow the sails to catch the wind. Several of these so-called smock windmills, built in the early 18th century, remain and are open for public viewing in Hamptons villages.

The Dominy family of East Hampton built some of the finest windmills. They also were renowned for their finely handcrafted furniture, especially their extraordinary tall-case ("grandfather") clocks. In all, Nathaniel Dominy IV built six wind-powered gristmills and three wind-powered sawmills. The Hook Windmill in East Hampton is the finest example of his workmanship. Among the laborsaving devices in the Hook Windmill are a sack hoist, a grain elevator, a screener to clean the grain, and bolters to sift the flour and cornmeal.

The first gristmill in Water Mill was built in 1644 to provide the town of Southampton with grain. The town supplied the millstone and built the required dam. Edward Howell built the mill, which he powered with a huge waterwheel that depended on the ponds flowing into Mecox Bay. If there was an insufficient flow of water from the ponds to the bay, town law decreed that "...when the miller calleth, on three days warneing," the men of the village must gather to enlarge the water's passage into the bay.

This gristmill has retained its usefulness and dignity over the years. As the needs of Southampton changed, however, so did the mill. It has been used as a place to spin yarn, weave cloth, manufacture paper, and store ice; as a post office, an ice-cream factory, and a tearoom. Today the fully restored and functioning mill is known as the Water Mill Museum, where it's still possible to watch as corn is ground into cornmeal.

As early as 1656, the English settlers worried about Dutch expansion into their territory. In addition, they had learned of Dutch attempts to turn the neighboring Indians against them. They were therefore granted protection by their Connecticut neighbors to the north. Even when the Dutch surrendered New York to the English in 1664, the independent East Enders resisted association with the rest of Long Island. As far as

It is said that the childhood home of John Howard Payne was the inspiration for his famous poem and song, "Home, Sweet Home." Morgan McGivern

they were concerned, they were New Englanders, and their loyalties remained with Connecticut.

This attitude created considerable anxiety in New York. Lord Cornbury wrote in 1703 that "the people of the East End of Long Island are not very willing to be persuaded to believe that they belong to this province. They are full of New England principles. They choose rather to trade with the people of Boston, Connecticut, and Rhode Island than with the people of New York."

The architecture as well as the politics of the early villages followed New England examples. Wooden saltbox houses had steeply slanted roofs and were faced with shingles that were allowed to weather naturally. The houses were lined up on both sides of a grassy main road with dirt wagon tracks in the center; cows, pigs, sheep, and geese were allowed to graze on the grass. Eventually, villages required the residents whose homes bordered the road to build fences to contain their livestock. Most villages also set aside a common pasture for both cattle and sheep. The sheep pasture in East Hampton is still a public greensward, located opposite the post office.

By 1661, settlers had adopted the practice of collecting their cattle into one large herd and driving them to the hills of Montauk for summer fattening, along with sheep and horses. It's said that cattle joined these great drives from as far away as Patchogue. A description of the scene along the dusty Montauk route to pasture, which later became Montauk Highway, is contained in Madeline Lee's book, *Miss Amelia's Amagansett* (1976).

> *The high point of village life came twice a year when Main Street became the scene of immense cattle drives. Cattle and sheep raising was an important industry on Long Island from the seventeenth century through the nineteenth century, and the princi-pal grazing grounds were . . . Montauk. 1,200 to 1,500 head of cattle were driven "on" to the pastures at Montauk in the spring and "off" again in the fall. From miles around, they would be funneled through the Amagansett Street, which was at that time 150 feet wide to accommodate these herds.*

These great cattle drives continued until the 1920s. Second House, one of three houses where the cattle and sheep tenders lived during those languid summer months, now houses a fascinating museum. Third House serves as the headquarters of Suffolk County's Theodore Roosevelt County Park.

The sight of ships rounding Montauk Point would not have surprised the Montauk cattle tenders, but one ship that must have aroused suspicion was an unwelcome visitor to Gardiner's Island. Pirates often plied the waters off the Long Island shore and are known to have landed at Montauk several times. In 1699, Captain William Kidd, a respected New York captain who had been hired by the British to detain French vessels and confiscate their cargo during a French/British war, ran afoul of his sponsors. They declared him to be a pirate.

One of the ships that Kidd waylaid was a French pirate ship loaded with bounty. Kidd was on his way to deliver the spoils to his sponsors but, under the circumstances, rightly feared for his life. He stopped at Gardiner's Island and persuaded John Lyon Gardiner, the third lord of the manor, to give him food and drink. Gardiner also agreed to allow Kidd to bury his treasure on Gardiner's Island. Kidd then sailed on to Boston, where he had been assured of safety. Nevertheless, he was arrested. Gardiner was summoned to Boston to deliver the treasure and did so, but Kidd subsequently was taken to England and executed in spite of the treasure's return. Although the Gardiner family retains an ancient receipt for

The First Custom House in the state of New York was established in the village of Sag Harbor in 1790.

the bounty, a legend persists that a vast stash remains buried on Gardiner's Island, waiting to be unearthed by some future treasure seeker.

Revolutionaries

Fierce loyalty to New England principles of independence from the British prevailed on Long Island's East End at the onset of the American Revolution. Citizens were outraged at the heavy taxes imposed by England and by the events in Boston. In 1775 every eligible citizen of East Hampton signed a document that read, in part, "Shocked by the bloody scene now going on in Massachusetts Bay, do in the most solemn manner, resolve never to become enslaved and do associate under all the ties of religion, honor, and love to our country, to adopt whatever may be recommended by the Continental Congress."

That same year, Sag Harbor resident John Hulburt organized a company of minutemen. One of their first acts was to march to Montauk Point, as they had learned about a possible British invasion. On arrival, they discovered three British man-of-war ships and nine transports, all of which were preparing to land. Determined to protect their land and grazing cattle, Hulburt ordered his men to march down a hill in sight of the British ships. At the bottom, where they were hidden from view, they turned their jackets inside out and then paraded back up the hill—thereby fooling the British into thinking that there were twice as many troops. The British decided not to land.

Later Hulburt's men marched to Ticonderoga, taking with them a flag designed with 13 stars on a blue field and 13 alternating red and white stripes. It is believed that this flag was the model that Betsy Ross used to create her flag.

When General Washington was defeated in the Battle of Long Island in August 1776, all of Long Island fell under British rule, and those who had signed patriotic documents feared for their personal safety and possessions. Many families fled to Connecticut and lived there for the seven years of British occupation. Those who remained were required to sign an oath of allegiance to England, which they reluctantly did, knowing that a signature on a piece of paper could not eradicate what they felt in their hearts.

Henry P. Hedges addressed the Sag Harbor Historical Society in 1896 and attempted to describe those troubled times:

> The history of that seven years' suffering will never be told. Philosophy has no ade-
> quate remedy for silent, unknown, unpitied suffering.... Left to the tender mercies of
> the foe; plundered by countryman and stranger of their property and ripened harvest;
> robbed of the stores which they reaped and garnered; slandered by suspicious
> brethren; taunted and scoffed at by the mercenary victors; they never wavered. Their
> hearts were in their country's cause; and in the memorable language of their great
> compatriot, "sink or swim, live or die, survive or perish," they were true to their coun-
> try. Unterrified, unalterable, devoted Americans.

Although the ramifications of war affected those living on the East End, the only military action that actually took place occurred in Sag Harbor and made Colonel Return Jonathan Meigs a hero. The British had established a naval blockade and stationed a garrison there to prevent supplies from leaving Sag Harbor to aid American troops across Long Island Sound in Connecticut. On the night of May 23, 1777, Meigs sailed with his men across the sound from Connecticut to the North Fork of Long Island. They carried their boats over a narrow neck of land to Orient Harbor and then, hugging the coastline between Shelter Island and the North Fork, crossed Shelter Island Sound, arriving near Noyack about midnight. After hiding their boats, the men marched to Sag Harbor, killed 6 sailors, captured the British commander along with 90 of his troops, set fire to 12 British brigs and sloops, and appro-priated the needed supplies. Returning with their prisoners and the goods, Colonel Meigs miraculously accomplished his mission in 25 hours—and with no loss of American lives.

In 1783, at the end of the British occupation, most homeowners returned to their villages. Reconstruction was a slow, difficult process, however. Ground that had not been plowed had grown hard and unyielding. Family homes and possessions had been destroyed. Neverthe-less, residents were much more concerned with the future than with the past.

Dr. Samuel Buell became the third pastor of the Presbyterian church in East Hampton in 1746 (his ordination was presided over by the renowned cleric Jonathan Edwards). He took an active but conciliatory role in the British occupation of the East End during the Revolu-tion, and he made a lasting contribution by starting the first secondary school.

Although elementary schools had been organized shortly after East End villages were settled, Clinton Academy in East Hampton, which was established in 1784, was the first secondary school. One interesting facet of this academy is that although colleges, such as

Harvard and Yale, were open only to men, Clinton Academy was always coeducational. In addition to the classics, such practical subjects as accounting, navigation, and surveying were taught. For almost 100 years, students from faraway places and nearby homes received their education there. Many graduates went on to Harvard, Yale, and Princeton. In 1881, its school days came to an end. It subsequently became the site of town meetings, plays, and dances, and eventually housed the *East Hampton Star* newspaper and the library. This impressive building still stands on Main Street, where it is now a museum devoted to local history.

Whaling, Shipping, Manufacturing

Long before the arrival of the English, whaling was an important activity for the Indians. When, during the winter months, the ocean tempests tossed a whale on the shore, they raced to the beach to carve up the giant mammal. The English were quick to learn the many uses for whale carcasses, and they soon joined forces with the Indians on these great whaling expeditions. By agreement, the settlers reserved the fins and tail for the native residents, as these parts were cherished for religious ceremonies. The rest of the whale, however, was tryed-out (boiled) or boned and used for a variety of purposes.

By the 1660s, the colonists, not content to wait for whales to float onto their beaches, established whaling companies with ships that sailed the ocean coast, searching for whales. By 1687 the fleet had grown to seven ships. Captured whales were brought to East End beaches, where their blubber was boiled in giant black kettles called try pots to render the oil that was so highly valued for lamp fuel. Later, self-contained try works were constructed on the ships themselves. From the beginning, the colonists recognized the expertise of the native Indians and hired them as hands on the whaling vessels.

Sag Harbor, established in 1730, soon became an influential whaling and shipping port. The first wharf was built in 1753, and construction on the grand Long Wharf began in 1771. Although the American Revolution interrupted the growth of Sag Harbor and the whaling industry for some 10 years, in 1785 a Sag Harbor whaler returned from a voyage to Brazil with a load of 360 barrels of oil, and in 1789 Sag Harbor became the first port of entry in New York State.

Additions to Long Wharf in 1808 and 1821 increased its length to 1,000 feet, and Sag Harbor was poised on the brink of history. This bawdy, raucous seaport was the antithesis of the more elegant villages to the south. As the ports of call of Sag Harbor sailing ships became more diverse, so did the variety of men who returned to the home port.

James Fenimore Cooper came to Sag Harbor in 1818 and stayed on to purchase and outfit a whaling vessel. Later he wrote the whaling adventure *The Sea Lions* (1849), in which he described Sag Harbor's attitude toward whalers:

> *There was scarcely an individual who followed this particular calling out of the port of Sag Harbor, whose general standing on board ship was not as well known to all the women and girls of the place, as it was to his shipmates.... His particular merit, whether with the oar, lance, or harpoon is bruited about, as well as the number of whales he may have succeeded in "making fast to."*

A red-light district sprang up in Sag Harbor, and taverns thrived; an anchored ship served as a jail for drunken sailors. A variety of new occupations kept Sag Harbor men employed in shipbuilding and manufacturing supplies for the whaling ships. By 1839, the whaling fleet had grown to 31 ships, making Sag Harbor the third largest whaling port in the

Designed by Minard Lafever in 1845 for whaler Benjamin Huntting, this noble Greek Revival mansion now serves as the Sag Harbor Whaling and Historical Museum. Visitors enter the museum through the jaws of a right whale.   Morgan McGivern

world. Eighty businesses flourished there, including coopers, who made the barrels to store the whale oil, masons, boat builders, blacksmiths, and tool and rope manufacturers. The fleet had increased to 63 vessels by 1845, and the population had grown to approximately 4,000 residents. Sag Harbor became known the world over when a local whaler made the first voyage to the waters surrounding Japan.

In Herman Melville's *Moby-Dick* (1851), Queequeg comes to Sag Harbor to learn Christian ways:

> *But alas! the practices of whalemen soon convinced him that even Christians could be both miserable and wicked; infinitely more so than all his father's heathens. Arrived at last in old Sag Harbor, and seeing what the sailors did there, and then going on to Nantucket, and seeing how they spent their wages in that place also, poor Queequeg gave it up for lost. Thought he, it's a wicked world in all meridians. I'll die a pagan.*

People in nearby villages were fascinated by Sag Harbor and a bit envious as well. Business opportunities flourished in nearby communities. Shelter Island, for example, with its abundance of white oak, became an impressive shipbuilding center. In some quarters, however, the village generated nothing but dismay. From his pulpit in East Hampton, Reverend Lyman Beecher railed against the Infidels, a Sag Harbor society organized specifically to attack the Christians.

On lower Main Street, which was filled with taverns, shops, and warehouses, the selling of rum was widespread. The downtown atmosphere was that of an energetic, irrepressible seaport. On upper Main Street, however, the fashionable homes of the shipowners stood in stark contrast. Cosmopolitan society held sophisticated balls and social gatherings; worshipers were welcomed at the elegant Whaler's Church, which was completed in 1844 and boasted a spectacular 185-foot steeple; and amusing vaudeville shows entertained citizens in the fine music hall.

In 1845 a devastating fire raged through Sag Harbor's downtown, destroying 57 stores, shops, and warehouses, but merchants quickly rebuilt. The village's most productive year was 1847, when 32 vessels hauled in 3,919 barrels of sperm oil, 63,712 barrels of right whale oil, and 605,340 pounds of whalebone.

Then it was over. Petroleum products and gas lighting replaced whale oil. In 1849 only two whaling ships left the harbor. The discovery of gold in California in that same year created a mass exodus. The last recorded voyage of a Sag Harbor whaler was in 1871. In 1913 this village, which once had been designated New York State's first port of entry, was decommissioned.

Baymen, Trawlers, Bootleggers

Other industries replaced whaling on the East End. Fishing continued to yield a profit. Menhaden, the fish long used by the native Indians for fertilizer, was processed in large plants along Gardiner's Bay. At first the catches were hauled in from the ocean, but by the 1890s the shoreline of the bay was thick with ships using purse seines to gather the schools of fish. It was estimated that at one point over 230 sailing ships and 20 steam vessels were engaged in the trade. The last of these died out in the 1960s.

But East Enders continued to gather other varieties of fish, as well. A local Water Mill resident recalls his youth with a fishing crew:

> *When I was a kid, every so far along there were fishing crews on the ocean, and they had wood shanties on the beach with tar paper roofs. . . . A load of fish was a lot of fun. Men hung onto the net, while others crawled in to get the fish out of the net and throw them on the beach. We would load the fish onto handbarrows and carry them to the road. . . . We'd bring the fish home to pack them in wood boxes and ice them down. The trucks would come right to the house to pick up the fish and cart it to Fulton Street in New York. We always put a fish box out as a sign for the truck driver to stop, while another crew member tied a rag to a telephone pole to signal the driver.*

Fishing and shellfishing remain important industries on the East End today, although local baymen are finding it more and more difficult to prosper. Delectable tiny bay scallops, cherrystone and littleneck clams, lobsters, mussels, and oysters are gathered seasonally for markets locally and in New York. Commercial and sportfishing off Montauk Point yield striped bass, sturgeon, swordfish, white marlin, tuna, bluefish, and shark.

From 1920 to 1933 liquor was prohibited throughout the U.S., and enterprising East Enders found a new profit center. Sag Harbor, along with North Haven and Noyack, became part of the infamous "Rum Row" that attracted bootleg boats from Europe. By 1927, however, bootleg distilleries in the U.S. were producing such high-quality products that illegal imports were no longer necessary, and boat traffic dried up once more. During its heyday, however, the East End of Long Island was called the wettest place in the country—a bootlegger's paradise.

Travelers & Visitors

Passable roads were slow in reaching the Hamptons. Montauk Highway was paved to Amagansett in 1908, but not beyond to Montauk until 1921. Furthermore, the crude paths laid out in the area's earliest days to reach ports in Northwest, North Sea, and Fireplace, where passengers and goods were ferried to Gardiner's Island, were the only access to these areas for many years. Eventually, several of them were used by scheduled horseback riders who delivered messages and mail to the isolated villages.

In 1772 a stagecoach route was established from the Fulton Ferry in Brooklyn to Sag Harbor; from Sag Harbor travelers could take a boat to Connecticut or even to Boston. The stagecoach brought passengers who needed places to eat and stay, and soon inns were situated along the route. The trip from Brooklyn to Sag Harbor took three days. Travelers stopped on the first night at Samuel Nichols's inn on the Hempstead Plains. On the second night they rested at Benjamin Haven's inn in St. George's Manor, and on the final night they dined, supped, and slept at Duke Fordham's in Sag Harbor. This popular inn also housed James Fenimore Cooper while he wrote his novel *Precaution* (1820), and it inspired this classic poem by an unknown author:

> *Long ago at the end of the route*
> *The stage pulled up, the folks stepped out.*
> *They all passed under the tavern door,*
> *The Youth and his bride and the gray three-score,*
> *Their eyes so weary with dust and gleam,*
> *Three days gone by like an empty dream,*
> *Soft may they slumber and trouble no more*
> *For their dusty journey, its jolt and roar*
> *Has come to an end at Fordham's door.*

Even after the arrival of the stagecoach, distant Montauk had no official mail delivery. This oversight was remedied by a tall, colorful Native American, Stephen (Pharaoh) Talkhouse, who charged 25 cents to carry a letter from Montauk to the stage in East Hampton, stepping forth in the giant stride that allowed him to complete the round-trip, 35-mile journey in one day.

With the advent of the railroad, branch lines fanned out across the U.S., and eventually the Long Island Rail Road was established. The main line along the North Fork to Greenport was completed in 1844. Then the South Fork was added—first to Westhampton Beach, Bridgehampton, and Sag Harbor in 1870 and then to East Hampton, Amagansett, and Montauk in 1895. Before the easternmost extension was built, travelers would reach East Hampton and Amagansett by taking a stagecoach from the train station in Bridgehampton or Sag Harbor, or from the New York steamer pier in Sag Harbor. With the arrival of the railroad, the Hamptons began to change from a strictly rural and agricultural area to one that attracted leisure travelers.

All these new visitors needed places to stay, and village residents obliged by opening their homes. By the 1850s it was reported that all rooms in East Hampton were fully booked at $7 a night. Southampton soon built hotels to accommodate its many guests, notably the Canoe Place Inn and the grand Irving House, with its Terry Tavern annex. Due to the more remote location of East Hampton, however, boardinghouses remained the predominant accommodation there. It was reported that in 1895, when the railroad was completed to East Hampton, more than 800 summer visitors arrived to enjoy the balmy sea breezes and the beaches.

Julia Gardiner Tyler added a touch of glamour to the Hamptons in the mid-1800s. In 1844, at the age of 24, this beautiful, impetuous Gardiner married the tenth president of the United States, 54-year-old John Tyler. She brought the same style and elegance to East Hampton, where they summered, as she did to the White House. The vivacious heiress, who shared Tyler's life for 18 years and bore him seven children, never forgot her heritage and ancestry, reveling in her jewels, fine clothes, and exquisite manners. The house they occupied on Main Street is still standing, although it is privately owned.

As the summer season attracted more and more industrialists, doctors, lawyers, and wealthy tycoons, the building boom they created continued. Soon elegant mansions lined the beachfront from Westhampton Beach to Montauk.

The Hamptons Attract Artists

Lured by the rural quality of East Hampton, artists from New York began arriving in the 1870s. They were delighted with the bucolic charm, the seascape vistas, and the opportunity to congregate, to paint, and to live more economically than they could in New York City. Most of these artists were members of the Tile Club, an artists' organization founded to "preserve good fellowship and good talk." They gathered in Greenwich Village on long winter evenings to paint on 8-inch square Spanish tiles. Among the members of this group were Augustus Saint-Gaudens, Stanford White, Winslow Homer, William Merritt Chase, Thomas Moran, and Childe Hassam.

The Tilers at first stayed in East Hampton at the old house called Rowdy Hall, which was across the street from Clinton Academy, where they took their classes. Rowdy Hall was later moved to Egypt Lane, where it remains today. At one point it was the childhood summer home of Jacqueline Bouvier Kennedy, who was born at Southampton Hospital.

William Oliver Stevens described the artists' visits in his book *Discovering Long Island* (1939):

> The Tile Club made East Hampton their headquarters lured by the Lombardy poplars lined up like a regiment on each side of the street. . . .
>
> Naturally they sketched here with great zeal, not only along the street but also on the beach. The musicians (honorary members) loafed about and posed for their friends as quaint natives and old salts, whenever such figures were needed. . . .
>
> It was probably through these members of the Tile Club and their articles in Scribner's Monthly that word spread abroad regarding the artistic attractions of East Hampton, for within five years of their first visit, the village was being written up as the "American Barbizon." Thomas Moran (known for his paintings of the national parks) made his home here, and summer art classes flourished, especially large groups from the Art Students League of New York. This all ended, however, when a Tile Club member, William Merritt Chase, began his art school in Southampton in 1891, and suddenly everyone flocked there. . . .

Nevertheless, another wave of artists arrived in East Hampton to capture this spectacular landscape in 1945. When the abstract expressionist Jackson Pollock and his wife, Lee Krasner, established their home and studio on a site overlooking Accabonac Harbor in Springs in 1945, other artists soon followed. Robert Motherwell, Willem de Kooning, Fairfield Porter, Alfonso Ossorio, and others enlivened the artistic scene. In the 1950s New York's Museum of Modern Art held summer classes at Ashawagh Hall in Springs, and that firmly established the area's arts-oriented reputation. The Pollock-Krasner home is now an artistic study center and is open to the public.

Farming Takes on New Identities

In the 1920s small farms that grew a variety of crops gave way to large farms concentrating on single crops. The Hamptons' temperate climate, offering a growing season that begins in early April and lasts until mid-November, makes the area ideal for potato farming, and for a long time potatoes were the predominant local crop. Each June, fields of white potato blossoms stretch down the neat rows, announcing the anticipated arrival of a new crop in the fall.

Another crop that is still closely associated with Long Island gained nationwide popularity in the 1930s. White Pekin (Peking) ducks, which have more succulent meat than domestic ducks, were imported from China to Long Island in the 1870s. Gradually the famed Long Island duckling became a necessary item on fancy menus across the U.S. Eventually there were 80 duck farms on Long Island producing 6 million ducks a year, and by 1969 Suffolk County was raising fully 60 percent of the nation's ducks. The largest duck farm in the world was located on the Speonk River. A. J. Hallock's Atlantic Farm raised a quarter million ducks a year in the early 1930s. Although the number of duck farms on Long Island has declined to only four, duck farming is still big business. Crescent Duck Farm in Aquebogue has been in the Corwin family since the 1600s and is now one of the largest producers in the U.S. This 140-acre farm raises almost a million ducks a year in its 30 barns, which

accounts for 4.5 percent of the nation's entire production, according to a 2003 article by Richard Jay Scholem in the *New York Times.* Today, this farm and the Massey Duck Farm in Eastport are the only remaining duck farms on the North and South Forks, although there are two more on Long Island in the Moriches area—The Jurgielewicz farm, which raises 600,000 to 700,000 birds a year, and the Titmus Farm, which has an annual production of about 200,000.

The ducks gained fame off the table as well. In *Discovering Long Island* Stevens notes, "Its plumage is such a pure white that at a distance one of these duck farms looks like a field where patches of March snow have not yet melted. But he is something of a whited sepulcher, for all his angelic plumage. Each little White Pekin is a most active fertilizer factory, and

Carriages and buckboards parade at Mulford Farm in East Hampton. Morgan McGivern

when the wind is right, not all the perfumes of Araby could sweeten this little land of duck farms." Beginning in the mid-20th century, due to increasing land values, environmental concerns, and objections to the smell, the number of duck farms declined. Today about 10 percent of the nation's ducks are raised on Long Island. Yet, across the country, restaurant menus proudly continue to offer "Long Island duckling," a name that's become synonymous with tender, flavorful meat.

Although potatoes may still be the principal crop of the Hamptons, the burgeoning winery business is once again changing the face of farming. In 1979, following extensive research by Alex and Louisa Hargrave, the first vineyards were planted on the North Fork (see history of winemaking on Long Island in chapter 9). Their research paid off, and as the wines gained popularity, other growers were attracted to the area. Today more and more land on the North Fork, in particular, is being planted with grapevines, and there are currently 49 wineries on Long Island's East End.

Montauk's Special Place in History

Unlike the other Hamptons villages, Montauk has both an older and yet a younger history. It boasts the oldest cattle ranch in the U.S. Deep Hollow Ranch was built in 1658 and claims to be the birthplace of the American cowboy. A descendant of those early summer grazing pastures, it includes Third House, where the early cattle tenders lived.

In an article in *Scribner's Monthly* in 1879 titled "The Tile Club at Play," Montauk was described as follows:

> ... our tourists came out upon a scene of freshness and uncontaminated splendor, such as they had no idea existed a hundred miles from New York. The woods rolled gloriously over the hills, wild as those around the Scotch lakes; noble amphitheaters of tree-tufted mountains, raked by roaring winds, caught the changing light from a cloud-swept heaven; all was pure nature fresh from creation.

Walt Whitman, who was raised on Long Island, cherished Montauk's isolation. In celebration of its wild abandon, he wrote his acclaimed poem "Montauk Point" (1849).

MONTAUK POINT

I stand as on some mighty eagle's beak,
Eastward the sea absorbing, viewing (nothing but sea and sky),
The tossing waves, the foam, the ships in the distance,
The wild unrest, the snowy, curling caps—that inbound urge and urge of waves,
Seeking the shores forever.

—Walt Whitman

Until 1879 Montauk languished peacefully, with fishing and cattle ranching being virtually its only occupations. In that year, however, land developer Arthur Benson purchased much of Montauk for $151,000. Shortly thereafter he formed the Montauk Association and engaged the renowned architectural firm of McKim, Mead, and White and the landscape architect Frederick Law Olmsted. Benson invited several of his friends to join him in building houses on a bluff overlooking the ocean. McKim, Mead, and White built seven spectacular shingle-style houses with wraparound porches, gabled roofs, cupolas, and bay windows. Olmsted created roadways and gardens that enveloped the houses, as well as a clubhouse, laundry, and stables. The houses remain today and comprise a very private, exclusive compound.

In 1895 Austin Corbin, president of the Long Island Rail Road, extended the South Fork of his line to Montauk and laid plans to develop Fort Pond Bay as a transatlantic port of entry to New York City. It was a good idea—one that would have shortened the journey from Europe by at least a day and would have avoided the congestion of New York harbor. Due to his untimely death in a carriage accident in 1896, however, his dream was never realized.

In 1898 Teddy Roosevelt and 30,000 of his Rough Riders, fresh from the Spanish-American War, spent several months recuperating at Third House. A general breakdown of

A Bonaker

The history of the tiny village of Springs is one of the most interesting in the Hamptons, although, to the uninitiated, the hamlet may appear to be no more than a cluster of nondescript buildings randomly placed at the junction of Springs Fireplace Road and Old Stone Highway. It's the heart of Bonakerland, an area that claims, among other things, a language all its own.

The Nature Conservancy, in the *South Fork Shelter Island Preserve Guide* (1990), defines a Bonaker as "someone who descended from either the Bennett, King, Lester, or 'Green River' Miller families who lived in the area around the Springs and Three Mile Harbor. The Indian name Accabonac, however, means 'place where groundnuts are gathered.' This refers to a tuberous plant that once grew around the harbor, supplementing shellfish as the Indians' main source of protein."

Jason Epstein and Elizabeth Barlow in their excellent book, *East Hampton, A History & Guide* (1985), say, "'Bonaker,' the term often used to describe any East Hampton settler, originally meant a person who lived on Accabonac Harbor, particularly the baymen who made their living from the fish and shellfish in the harbor. When it first gained currency, 'Bonaker' was a derisive epithet akin to 'hick,' 'hayseed,' or more appropriately, 'lazy clamdigger.' Subsequently, it has become a chauvinistic badge."

It is unclear exactly how the longtime residents of Springs obtained their distinctive language, but recent scholarly studies indicate that it may be due to their relative isolation. This rural area of farmers, baymen, and fishermen seems to retain vowel pronunciations that hark back to the time of Shakespeare. Perhaps such pronunciations as "git" for "get," "yit" for "yet," "turrble" for "terrible," and "awchit" for "orchard" are simply the result of having so little contact with the rest of the population that they seldom heard the subtle changes. Local historian Stephen Taylor wrote in the chapter "Playing Hide and Seek with History," which was included in the pamphlet *Springs—A Celebration:* "For three centuries, the residents of the Springs . . . continue to speak the dialect that their forebears brought from post-Elizabethan England. . . . Above all else, history is change: freeze the world in place and there's no history. The Springs appears to want no part of it. It's as if the Springs engages history in a subtle game of hide-and-seek."

Change has occurred in Springs, however. Beginning in the 1950s, Springs was discovered by developers, and forested acres gave way to housing. Taylor concluded his paper by writing, "Where tradition was once the real architect of most of the structures in the Springs, the designers of these newer ones are 'creative' and 'imaginative.' Clusters of older Springs houses become de facto historic districts, enclaves of times past . . . (but) what might seem like a desecration of history isn't anything of the sort; it is history—history catching up with the Springs at last."

The first of these new residents were artists (illustrators, writers, designers) who were looking for a peaceful, quiet hideaway. They were soon joined by painters, sculptors, and artists of considerable acclaim. Springs is now recognized as a secluded community of artists who live side by side with the descendants of the original Bonakers.

Today the term Bonaker is often used with pride in recognition of a people who cling fast to old traditions. In fact, the East Hampton High School sports teams proudly call themselves the Bonakers, symbolizing a team that never gives up.

medical and sanitary conditions had left some of the men with yellow fever, malaria, or typhoid. Numerous casualties were taken ashore on litters and were detained at Montauk until the danger of contagion was past.

Another dreamer, in 1926, ventured to Montauk with a plan. Carl G. Fisher had developed Miami Beach and the Indianapolis Speedway. He reasoned that just as visitors flocked to Miami in the winter, they would flock to Montauk in the summer. He and his investors bought 10,000 acres, which included 9 miles of waterfront. High on Fort Hill he built Montauk Manor, a luxury hotel, and on Montauk's town square he built a seven-story office building. A golf course, polo grounds, a yacht club, and a pier followed. He filled his office building with salesmen, poised to find buyers to fulfill his grand scheme, but it was not to be. The stock market crash of 1929, a decline in the Florida real estate market, a hurricane in Florida, and the Great Depression conspired to bring an end to the "Miami of the North."

Recent History

The Great Hurricane of 1938 devastated the East End. The glorious steeple on the Whaler's Church in Sag Harbor came crashing to the ground, as did that of the Methodist church. Trees were uprooted; roofs and porches blew away. The turbulent sea cut a new inlet into the barrier reef, separating the ocean from Moriches Bay at Westhampton Beach. Another more recent storm in 1992 destroyed parts of Dune Road in Westhampton Beach, and washed away many houses, creating a new island. Yet, despite such devastation, the natural beauty of the Hamptons prevails.

And so history moves on—never ending, always evolving. After all, tomorrow's history is today's news event. The history of the Hamptons is as entwined with the baymen's efforts to eke out a living, the Nature Conservancy's land-preservation efforts, and the Peconic Land Trust's attempts to preserve farmland as it is with the glittering social scene and the sprawling estates. The latter lasts for two months each summer, but the former is the true heart of the Hamptons.

The Journey & the Visit

Transportation

Before the first settlers arrived, the Indians of eastern Long Island frequently crossed the great body of water now known as Long Island Sound. The 16 miles of water between Long Island and the Connecticut/Rhode Island shore offered a more hospitable and considerably shorter route than overland travel. In canoes they carved from trees that covered the hillsides, they traveled back and forth to hunt, fish, trade, and barter with other tribes.

It was natural, then, for the settlers to follow the Native Americans' example. They first arrived on Long Island via Connecticut, and transportation and communication were, at first, developed solely with Connecticut rather than with the western part of Long Island, which was settled by the Dutch rather than the English.

This strong link to New England created East End towns that looked and felt like New England towns. The English created common greens for grazing community cattle, built New England saltbox cottages, and constructed planned, strictly regulated communities in which only those settlers who possessed skills needed by the towns were invited to live.

Eastern Long Island became more and more English because overland communication was infrequent and slow. Western Long Island, on the other hand, developed strong loyalties and ties to the Dutch, who occupied New York City. As might be imagined, loyalty to New England caused East Enders considerable discomfort during the American Revolution.

Pony express mail routes were established in the early 1700s, but more sophisticated communication links were not forged until the first stagecoach route was initiated in 1772. This route from New York to the South Fork would serve as the only overland transportation link for almost 100 years. In 1844 the Long Island Rail Road built a rail line from New York to Greenport on the North Fork to connect with the steamers that departed from there to Boston. Finally, in 1870, the line was extended along the South Fork to Bridgehampton and Sag Harbor. It wasn't until 1895 that it reached East Hampton and Montauk.

The access provided by the railroad forever changed the face of eastern Long Island. At first, rail service provided a valuable transportation link for farmers, who could ship their produce by train to lucrative markets in New York, but as more and more people traveled to the East End, the permanent and summer populations mushroomed. Slowly, an economy that once had depended on the sea and the land evolved into one that supported a tourist and weekend population. Old main streets of dirt, sand, crushed shells, and rock were joined in a paved road of stone and tar called Montauk Highway, which reached Amagansett in 1908; it was extended to Montauk in 1921.

Transportation continues to play an important role in the life of the Hamptons. As road space becomes more and more scarce, alternatives to traveling by car are devised. Several excellent bus companies now relieve the congestion on the highways and augment the mass transportation services provided by the Long Island Rail Road. In addition, a number of airports offer charter services and landing space for small aircraft.

Today there are several options for getting to and from the Hamptons and for traveling around while here. Just remember, any travel difficulties will fade into dim memories once you arrive.

GETTING TO THE HAMPTONS

By Car

Let's go to the Hamptons! Get the kids, pack the car, and inevitably the question is, "What route do we take?" No matter how the conversation starts, if the destination is the Hamptons (a distance of about 100 miles from Manhattan), the quest for the elusive back roads that avoid the congested, bumper-to-bumper traffic on Montauk Highway becomes the hot topic.

A book titled *Jody's Shortcuts* lists a few secret back roads, and a librarian in East Hampton claims that the easiest way to reach the Hamptons is to "just turn right." There are old favorites that, if you are a true believer in back roads, will get you around all of the Montauk crawl. Those in the know, however, say you won't save time, just aggravation; and, generally, these roads are considerably out of the way, unless your destination happens to be the villages along the north shore of the South Fork—Noyack, Sag Harbor, or Springs, for instance.

In 1912, horse-and-buggies, automobiles, and bicycles were all typical forms of transportation in East Hampton.
C. Frank Dayton Collection, East Hampton Library Historical Collection

Personally, I think it's a shame to bypass the villages, because they're all so charming. I want to see what new shops have opened and what they have to offer; how the restaurants are doing; and what has happened since my last visit. If you're a weekender, one way to avoid the traffic is to leave for the Hamptons on Friday and return at dawn on Monday, although when I was doing that, I sometimes started for the Hamptons at dawn on Saturday and returned at 4 PM on Sunday, with no significant traffic problems. You never know.

With agreeable road conditions, the trip from New York City to Southampton should be an easy two-hour drive. As Timothy McDarrah put it, however, in the local weekly *Dan's Papers*, "One thing about roads: If you build them, cars will come. One thing about roads to the Hamptons: There are no shortcuts."

From New York City, most people head straight out on the Long Island Expressway

(Interstate 495). I must admit that my preference, however, is the Northern State Parkway, because generally it has fewer cars, and trucks are prohibited on all New York State parkways. Nevertheless, when the Northern State Parkway meets the Sagtikos Parkway, it's easy to drive the short distance south on the Sagtikos to hop onto the Long Island Expressway. Most drivers leave the expressway at Exit 70 in Manorville to take Route 111 on its straight diagonal course to Route 27, the Sunrise Highway. If your destination is Westhampton Beach, Hampton Bays, or another town west of these villages, you probably won't find many traffic problems at all. If, however, you're heading to Southampton or other towns east, it's an East End game to know secret byways that avoid the Hampton crawl. The following are a few suggestions, but most people find their own favorite route.

When you run into congestion on Route 27, on the outskirts of Southampton, you might find it easier to turn south onto Tuckahoe Road, which runs alongside the Southampton campus of Stony Brook University, and head for Route 27A, Montauk Highway. Turn left there and continue through the village of Southampton on that route, which is called Hill Street within the village. From there you might take several back roads, but you must reenter Montauk Highway just before Water Mill. After Water Mill, however, you have several options. You might take Scuttle Hole Road north through Noyac or Mecox Road south through Wainscott, sometimes jogging north or south on the eastward trek. Another option if traveling to Sag Harbor, East Hampton, or beyond, is to turn north in the village of Southampton onto Sandy Hollow Road, which becomes North Sea Road, and then travel east on Noyack Road to Sag Harbor along the northern route.

One difficulty with traveling by car from Southampton to Montauk is that all of the roads are two-lane; a tractor or a truck can slow traffic to a crawl for miles. Many residents prefer it that way, hoping to discourage further development. After all, the farmers were here first. Others join in a frustrated howl.

An alternative, of course, is to let someone else do the driving. We'll get to the train, bus, plane, and boat options in the following pages, but it's not that unusual to see limousines and chauffeured town cars stuck in the same traffic jams as everyone else, while their passengers work diligently on a laptop computer or relax with a good book. If this is a driving option that appeals to you, here are several suggestions. Otherwise, pack a selection of CDs and endure the inevitable summertime snags.

Archer Town Car 800-273-1505
Classic Coach and Hamptons Luxury Liner 631-567-5100 (outside NY State 800-666-
    4949; www.classictrans.com)
Colonial Limousine 631-728-0063
Beach Limousine 800-287-7820, 631-324-5466, 631-653-7820, 631-283-7820, or 631-
    324-0108
Hampton Jitney (limousines) 631-287-4000
Southampton Limousine, Ltd. 631-287-0001
Winston Limousine 631-924-1200

For information about rental cars and taxis, see the section "Getting Around Once You're Here" (page 43).

By Bus

Not long ago the only method of travel to the Hamptons was by car, train, or private plane, but now there are two excellent bus/coach alternatives.

HAMPTON JITNEY

631-283-4600 (Long Island); 212-362-8400 (New York)
www.hamptonjitney.com
Mailing Address: The Omni, 395 County Rd. 39A, Southampton, NY 11968
Price: All stops Southampton–Montauk $30 one way, $53 round trip; seniors and children (Tues., Wed., and Thurs. only) $26 one way, $49 round trip; Westhampton Line Fri–Mon. $30 one way, $53 round trip, seniors and children $22 one way, $45 round trip; lower mid-week rates to Westhampton Beach; Ambassador Service $38 one way, $65 round trip; value packs of 10–12 tickets reduce fares; pets $10 (in carriers only); bicycles $15
Credit Cards: AE, D, MC, V
Schedules: (summer hours) 5:30 AM–12:30 AM from NYC; 4:30 AM–10:30 PM from the Hamptons (varies by day of week)
Reservations: Strongly recommended

Hampton Jitney began service in 1974, and now has a large fleet of buses that ply the highways between New York City and the Hamptons many times a day. In addition to regular departure and pickup points in the Hamptons and on the North Fork, there are four pickup spots along Lexington Avenue in Manhattan, from 86th to 40th streets. Also, passengers can be dropped off at points on the Upper East Side on Third Avenue, as well as on the Upper West Side on selected trips. In general, the trip takes two hours from Manhattan to Southampton. There's Brooklyn and North Fork service (see chapter 9), as well as an airport connection, with pickup and drop-off service to several metropolitan airports. Package service and limousines can also be arranged. Hampton Jitney buses are modern, comfortable touring buses, with air-conditioning, wide seats, plenty of legroom, large windows, and restrooms. An attendant on each bus serves coffee, juice, or water with a muffin, peanuts, or chips, depending on the time of day; newspapers are provided as well. The newer fleet of Ambassador buses, which are deluxe coaches with leather seats and more legroom, offer computer hookups, free Wi-Fi, plus beer and wine (at an additional charge). Since the schedule does change according to requirements, it is prudent to call ahead. Reservations are often filled far in advance.

HAMPTON LUXURY LINER

631-537-5800
www.hamptonluxuryliner.com
231C Butter Ln., Bridgehampton
Mailing Address: P.O. Box 1438, Bridgehampton, NY 11932
Price: $36 one way, $69 round trip; value packs of 10 trips reduce price; no pets; bicycles $15
Credit Cards: AE, MC, V
Schedules: (summer hours) 8:25 AM–9:35 PM from NYC; 5:40 AM–7:25 PM from the Hamptons
Reservations: Required

Hampton Luxury Liner began operation in 2000. It provides an elegant alternative to the Hampton Jitney, by operating coaches with wide leather reclining seats and expanded legroom. Buses pick up passengers in New York City along Lexington Avenue between 85th and 40th streets, and they drop off passengers at locations along Third Avenue between 40th and 86th. In the Hamptons, buses pick up and drop off passengers from Amagansett to Southampton. There's hanging-garment storage, free Wi-Fi, personal power outlets,

Hampton Jitney offers an alternative to automobile travel to the Hamptons.   Courtesy Hampton Jitney

flat-screen TVs, DirecTV, and a restroom, as well as a galley where complimentary bottled water, soft drinks, and snacks are served. Furthermore, movies are shown on board, making the time pass quickly.

Suffolk Transit (631-852-5200; www.sct-bus.org) is discussed in more detail in the "Getting Around Once You're Here" section (see page oo). When traveling to the South or North Forks from points within Suffolk County, however, this local bus company is certainly an option. It serves the county from Massapequa to Montauk or Orient Point, with regular service daily except Sunday.

By Train

LONG ISLAND RAIL ROAD
718-217-5477 (NYC), 516-822-5477 (Nassau County), 631-231-5477 (Suffolk County), 718-558-8070 (parlor car reservations)
www.mta.info
Price: Peak $23 one way, $46 round trip; off-peak $16.75 one way, $33.50 round trip; Cannonball express parlor-car service (Thurs. and Fri. summer only) $23 additional; no charge for pets but must be in an approved AKC carrier; $5 permit required for bicycles (permit takes about 2 weeks to obtain)
Schedule: 7:49 AM–12:39 AM from NYC; 6:44 AM–7:34 PM from Montauk

The Long Island Railroad has an excellent reputation for dependability, and for many it's the only way to travel to the Hamptons. Now that Pennsylvania Station in Manhattan has been renovated, Manhattan departures and arrivals are much more pleasant than in the past. Clean, modern cars equipped with restrooms are now augmented by Hamptons Reserve Service. This consists of two special parlor cars (called The Cannonball) that whisk passengers nonstop from Jamaica to Westhampton Beach on Friday afternoons. These are carpeted cars with comfortable seats; an attendant serves light snacks and beverages ranging from beer, wine, and mixed drinks to soda and bottled water. A special parlor-car reservation is required. The trip takes about 2 hours from New York City to Westhampton Beach and 3.75 hours to Montauk, with about eight trains a day on summer weekends. For those traveling to the North Fork, three or four trains leave and arrive daily at Riverhead and Greenport during the week, but only two trains on the weekends. No reservations are taken on the Long Island Rail Road (except for the parlor cars). For fare and schedule information, consult local newspapers or call ahead.

Amtrak (800-523-8720; www.amtrak.com) travels from Penn Station (NYC) to New London, Connecticut, where Cross Sound Ferries (860-443-5281) provide transportation to Orient Point on the North Fork. (See ferry information below.) Pets are not allowed on Amtrak. Bicycles are permitted, as long as the train has a baggage car or a bicycle rack. If the bicycle is to be transported in the baggage car ($5 fee), it must be in a box, which can be purchased at Penn Station for an additional $15. The train station in New London is an easy walk from the ferry terminal.

By Ferry
Ferry service to Long Island is a pleasant option, especially if you're traveling from New England.

BRIDGEPORT & PORT JEFFERSON STEAMBOAT COMPANY
631-473-0286
www.bpjferry.com
330 Water St. Dock, Bridgeport, CT 06604 and 102 W. Broadway, Port Jefferson, NY 11777
Price: Car and driver $51 each way, $14.75 each additional passenger; motorcycles or mopeds $29.75 each way; walk-on $17 one way, $25 same-day round trip; seniors 60+ $12.50 one way, $17.00 same-day round trip; children 12 and under no charge: pets must be on leash or in a carrier and are not permitted in the cabin; bicycles OK
Credit Cards: AE, D, MC, V
Schedule: 6:30 AM–9:30 PM in summer from Bridgeport; 6 AM–9 PM in summer from Port Jefferson; shorter hours rest of year
Reservations: Required for cars

This ferry operates about 10 trips daily in summer for passengers and cars traveling between Bridgeport, Connecticut, and Port Jefferson on Long Island's North Shore, with fewer trips the rest of the year. The drive from Port Jefferson to Southampton takes about one hour. These are large ferries, with snack-bar service, a lounge where drinks are served, restrooms, and plenty of deck space on which to relax in the sun during the 90-minute trip. Pets are allowed on deck but not in the cabins, and bicycles are welcomed. A reservation is necessary for cars, especially during the summer months; cars are taken on a standby basis if you forget to call. It's advisable to go upstairs shortly after you get on the ferry to purchase the ticket from the purser, as standing in line can take a while. Tickets are collected when you reach the other side.

The North Ferry leaves Greenport for Shelter Island; note osprey nest in foreground.

CROSS SOUND FERRY

860-443-5281 (CT) or 631-323-2525 (NY)

www.longislandferry.com

2 Ferry St., New London, CT 06320 and 41720 Rte. 25, Orient Point, NY 11957

Mailing Address: P.O.Box 33, Orient, NY 11957

Price: Car ferries: car and driver $46 each way one way, $14 each additional adult one way,$24 round trip; children under 12 $6 one way, $10 round trip; motorcycle and driver $27 each way; no charge for pets but must be leashed; bicycles $4. Sea Jet: adults $19.50 one way, $31.50 same-day round trip; children under 12 one way $8.75, same-day round trip $14: pets in approved carriers only; no bicycles

Credit Cards: AE, D, MC, V

Schedule: Car ferries: 7 AM—8:30 PM from New London; 7 AM—8:30 PM from Orient Point. *Sea Jet:* 7 AM—9 PM from New London; 8 AM—9:45 PM from Orient Point

Reservations: Required for cars

Cross Sound Ferry travels between New London, Connecticut, and Orient Point on the North Fork. It is the most direct route from Boston, Cape Cod, Rhode Island, and points east. There are about 15 trips daily in the summer, but the ferry does run year-round. These are large ferries. The biggest accommodate up to 16 motor coaches. Car reservations are absolutely necessary to avoid a prolonged wait for space. The trip takes about 90 minutes, and there are outdoor and indoor spaces for relaxation, as well as restrooms and snack bars. On the largest boats, there are full-service lounges with drinks, televisions, a juke-box, and a video game room. Pets are allowed on deck. If you decide not to take your car, a high-speed boat (*Sea Jet*) has been added to the fleet; it makes six trips daily each way, and the crossing is only 40 minutes. This is a good option if you're bringing your bicycle, but there are no buses that meet these boats and few services at Orient Point. On the Connecticut side, however, there are connections to Foxwoods and Mohegan Sun casinos.

NORTH FERRY

631-749-0139
www.northferry.com
3 Summerfield Rd., Shelter Island Heights, NY 11965
Price: Car and driver $9 one way, $13 same-day round trip; $2 each passenger; bicycles $3 one way, $5 round trip
Schedule: 5:40 AM–11:45 PM (12:45 in summer) from Shelter Island; 6 AM–midnight from Greenport (1 AM in summer)
Credit Cards: None
Reservations: None

SOUTH FERRY

631-749-1200
www.southferry.com
135 South Ferry Rd., Shelter Island, NY 11964
Price: Car and driver $12 one way, $15 same-day round trip; $1 each passenger; bicycles $4 one way, $6 round trip
Schedule: 5:40 AM–1:45 AM from North Haven; 6 AM–1:45 AM from Shelter Island
Credit Cards: None
Reservations: None

Those traveling from New England to the Hamptons generally arrive by Cross Sound Ferry on the North Fork of Long Island at Orient Point and then drive to Greenport. From there they take the North Ferry from Greenport to Shelter Island, drive across Shelter Island, and then take the South Ferry to North Haven, just north of Sag Harbor. These ferries are efficient throwbacks to an earlier age. There are no amenities here, just a drive- or walk-on, open-decked ferry that shuttles back and forth between the island and the North and South Forks. Both ferries operate year-round, but the schedule is more frequent in the summer than the rest of the year.

VIKING FERRY

631-668-5700
www.vikingfleet.com
West Lake Dr., Montauk, NY 11954
Price: Block Island and New London: adults $40 one way, $75 round trip; children $25 one way, $40 round trip; bicycle and/or surfboard $7 one way, $10 round trip; auto parking in Montauk or Block Island $10/day. Martha's Vineyard: adults $75 one way, $120 round trip; children $40 one way, $60 round trip; bicycle and/or surfboard $7 one way, $10 round trip; auto parking Montauk and Martha's Vineyard $10/day
Schedule: Block Island ferries, daily during summer season; depart Montauk 10 AM and 3:30 PM, arrive Block Island 11 AM and 4:30 PM; depart Block Island 11:30 AM and 5 PM, arrive Montauk 12:30 PM and 6 PM. New London ferries, Fri. and Sun. only, depart Montauk 6:30 PM, arrive New London 7:30 PM; depart New London 8 PM, arrive Montauk 9 PM. Martha's Vineyard ferries, very infrequent (one or two trips a summer); depart Montauk 6:30 PM,

Distance and Travel Time to the Hamptons by Car and Ferry

ROUTE	DISTANCE	TRAVEL TIME
Manhattan to . . .		
Westhampton Beach	83 mi	1½ hrs
Southampton	96 mi	2 hrs
East Hampton	106 mi	2½ hrs
Sag Harbor	105 mi	2½ hrs
Montauk	123 mi	3 hrs
Greenport	102 mi	2½ hrs
Boston to Greenport:		
Boston to New London, CT (by car)	141 mi	3 hrs
New London to Orient Point (via Cross Sound Ferry)		1 hr 20 min
Orient Point to Greenport (by car)	10 mi	15 min
Greenport to North Haven (via North Ferry, car across		
Shelter Island, and South Ferry)		1 hr

arrive Martha's Vineyard 11:30 PM; depart Martha's Vineyard 4:30 PM, arrive Montauk 9:30 PM
Reservations: Not required

The Viking Line operates passenger-only ferries in the summer and early fall between
Block Island, Rhode Island; New London, Connecticut; and Martha's Vineyard, Massachusetts, leaving from Montauk. This is a great way to do a one-day or overnight bicycle trip.
These ferries have snack bars and restrooms on board, as well as outside space in which to
relax or read.

By Air

The nearest airport providing scheduled service by major airlines is Long Island/Islip
MacArthur Airport in Ronkonkoma. For recorded information about all airlines, call 631-
467-3210. The following airlines, with their direct reservation numbers, serve MacArthur
Airport.

Southwest Airlines 800-435-9792
U.S. Airways Express 800-428-4322

Several other airlines offer charter services to Montauk, East Hampton, and Suffolk County
Airports (Francis S. Gabreski) in Westhampton Beach, and several operate helicopter service from Manhattan. For information about prices and availability, contact: **Action Airlines
Charter** (800-243-8623); **Air Hamptons** (800-248-4311); **East Hampton Airlines** (631-
537-3737); **Eastway Aviation** (631-737-9911); **Excelaire Service** (631-737-5801); **Executive Fliteways Inc.** (631-588-5454); **New England Airlines** (800-243-2460); and
Shoreline Aviation (800-468-8639). **Sound Aircraft** (800-443-0031 outside 631 or 516
area codes only; 631-537-2202 locally) has shared seaplane commuter service that departs
from Manhattan's Skyport Marina on East 23rd to East Hampton and helicopter service
from Manhattan's East Side Heliport on East 34th or the West Side Heliport on West 30th to
East Hampton Airport. Its fleet includes planes that can land on either land or water. It also

offers charter flights throughout the Northeast. Should you and your friends want to fly directly to your hunting preserve on an isolated island with no airport, these folks can help.

If you own your own plane and wish to wing it, the following airports offer landing and tie-down services, and all can accommodate small jets. Then, just like local luminaries, you can be a true jet-setter.

East Hampton Airport 631-537-1130
Montauk Airport 631-668-3738
Suffolk County Airport–Francis S. Gabreski (in Westhampton Beach) 631-852-8095

GETTING TO AND FROM AIRPORTS

For private limousine and town-car service, please refer to the limousine companies in the preceding section of this chapter. The following companies offer group rides.

Classic Transportation (631-567-5100; 800-666-4949 outside New York State only; www.classictrans.com) Provides door-to-door transportation from all Long Island airports to destinations throughout Long Island. The company's courtesy 24-hour telephones are located at LaGuardia, Kennedy, and Islip airports, and vans will be there to pick you up within 15 minutes. Service is friendly, courteous, and helpful.

Four Ones (631-728-0050; 631-728-0500) Operates Lincoln Town Cars for 1–6 passengers and passenger vans that accommodate 10–14, from all major New York City airports, including Islip and Newark.

Winston Transportation (888-444-4425; 800-424-7767; www.winstontrans.com) Provides door-to-door transportation between your home and Islip, LaGuardia, Kennedy, and Newark airports. Rides are shared, so travel time is longer than with direct service, but the price is lower. The company is efficient and reliable.

GUIDED TOURS

There are several guided tours to the Hamptons from New York. The Long Island Rail Road offers tours from Pennsylvania Station (NYC), and bus companies also offer convenient ways to see the area without the trauma of fighting traffic. Travel agents are the best source of information for bus and town-car tours, and some include overnight accommodations along with the ride.

LONG ISLAND RAIL ROAD
718-558-7498
www.mta.info
Mailing Address: Sales & Promotions Dept. #1424, Jamaica, NY 11435
Departure: Tours leave from Pennsylvania Station (NYC), Brooklyn, Jamaica, and Mineola
Season: Mem. Day–early Nov
Rates: Depending on tour and whether lunch is included; $19–$66 for adults, $10–$57 for children
Credit Cards: AE, D, MC, V

The Long Island Rail Road organizes a series of delightful tours each summer, including many to the Hamptons. Some, such as the Hampton Classic and the Shinnecock Pow Wow, are only offered on the day of the event, but others bring passengers to the Hamptons some 15 times throughout the summer. You can choose from an East End Antiquing trek, a trip to the Montauk Lighthouse, a South Bay cruise that includes lunch, and a Hamptons Hopping tour that includes lunch, a museum tour in Southampton, and a visit to Sag Harbor. Reservations are absolutely necessary.

Specialty Tours

Hampton Jitney (631-283-4600; www.hamptonjitney.com) offers a variety of options for organized tours from the Hamptons, including theater, museum, and shopping trips to New York City, as well as trips to Florida and to the Foxwoods Resort Casino in Connecticut.

Long Island Wine Tours (631-775-8686; www.liwinetours.com) Jim Ferrarie operates an excellent Long Island tour company that offers tours of the wineries and the East End. He has buses and limousines that can accommodate large and small groups, and he's been doing this for 20 years, so he knows where to go for the most enjoyable experience.

Twin Forks Trolley Tours (631-369-3031; www.northforktrolleytours.com; mailing address: P.O. Box 46, Aquebogue, NY 11931) Owners: Tom and Kathie Ingald. Although initially organized to offer winery excursions of the North Fork on their vintage trolley, this company also offers tours of the Hamptons, including stops in Sag Harbor to shop.

Vintage Tours (631-765-4689; www.vintagetour1.com; mailing address: P.O. Box 143, Peconic, NY 11958) Owner: Joann Perry. Joann will take you on an escorted tour of North Fork wineries in her 14-passenger air-conditioned bus, and she also includes a box lunch to be enjoyed at one of the delightful wineries. Yes of course, wine is included.

Viking Fleet (631-668-5700; www.vikingfleet.com) offers several whale watch, offshore bird-watching, and fall foliage trips a year.

GETTING AROUND ONCE YOU'RE HERE

Getting here isn't nearly as much fun as getting around once you arrive. If you prefer to drive someone else's car instead of your own, here are several car-rental options. Be sure to call in advance to reserve. Or, for short-term transportation, the following taxis are reliable and often will deliver packages and make deliveries. Village location doesn't mean that a taxi is restricted to that village.

Car Rentals

Avis Rent A Car (631-283-9111, national reservation number 800-331-1212; 721 County Rd. 39A Southampton, NY 11968) Open May–mid-Sept. only.

Enterprise Rent-A-Car (631-283-0055, Omni, 395 County Rd. 39A, Southampton, NY 11968, next door to Hampton Jitney (you can take the Jitney here and then rent a car); 631-537-4800, East Hampton Airport, 200 Daniels Hole Rd., East Hampton, NY 11937; 631-668-3464, Montauk at 32 Star Island Rd., Montauk Yacht Club; 631-288-8630, Westhampton at Gabreski Airport) Open Mon.–Sat.

Hertz (631-537-8119, national reservation number 800-654-3131; Montauk Hwy., Bridgehampton, NY 11932; 631-537-3987, East Hampton Airport, 200 Daniels Hole Road, East Hampton, 11937; 631-259-3385, 59 Maple St., Southampton, 11963).

Taxis

AMAGANSETT
Amagansett Taxi (631-267-2006 or 267-0111)

EAST HAMPTON
East Hampton Taxi (631-324-9696 or 324-4100)
Ocean Taxi (631-329-0011)

HAMPTON BAYS
Colonial Taxi (631-589-7878)
Four Ones (631-727-0707)
Hampton Coach (631-728-0050, 631-728-0500)

MONTAUK
Lindy's Taxi (631-668-4747)
Pink Tuna Taxi (631-668-3838)

SAG HARBOR
Ocean Taxi (631-725-6969)
Sag Harbor Car Service (631-725-9000)

SOUTHAMPTON
Atlantic Taxi (631-283-1900)
Hampton Coach (631-283-0242)

WESTHAMPTON BEACH
JRs Westhampton Taxi (631-728-5100)
Westhampton Beach Taxi & Limo (631-288-3252)

Public Buses

Suffolk Transit (631-852-5200; www.sct-bus.org; Mon.–Sat. $1.50, with additional charge of $0.25 for each transfer; seniors and handicapped riders $0.50; students 14–21 $1; children under 5 free) This company operates buses that crisscross the Hamptons, from Montauk to Westhampton and beyond, including the North Fork as far as the Orient Point Ferry. For some reason the information numbers are always busy, and they're only in operation Monday to Friday, 8 to 4:30. Your best bet is to pick up the schedule and fare information from local chamber of commerce offices. The schedules are well prepared, with maps that clearly show the routes, transfer points, and just about anything else you need to know. Suffolk Transit buses will stop anywhere along the route if you flag them down. In general, the buses travel each way about every two hours. You must tell the driver when you get on if you want a transfer. Please note: Exact fare is required, as the drivers do not carry change.

3

HOSPITALITY, HAMPTONS STYLE

Lodging

Hamptons residents have been taking in boarders for more than 200 years. In her book *Up and Down Main Street: An Informal History of East Hampton and Its Old Houses* (1968), Jeannette Edwards Rattray states that the Huntting Inn (then the Huntting home) accommodated boarders as early as Revolutionary War times. And it continues to welcome overnight guests today on Main Street in East Hampton. It is said that in the 18th century, the 1770 House (also still an inn on East Hampton's Main Street) was open on Saturday nights to God-fearing churchgoers who came from other villages to attend East Hampton's churches. Rowdy Hall was housing guests when the artists of the Tile Club first discovered the Hamptons in the late 1800s. (This was later moved to Egypt Lane in East Hampton, where it is now a private home. When Jacqueline Kennedy was a little girl, she lived there with her family.) W. L. Osborn and his wife ran a boardinghouse as early as 1858 in "their big house on the little hill overlooking Town Pond," in East Hampton. The Sea Spray Inn in East

Lobby, Montauk Manor

Hampton was legendary (gone now), as was the Irving Hotel in Southampton (also gone).

Duke Fordham's inn on Sag Harbor's main street was certainly in business before the stagecoach route from the Fulton Ferry in Brooklyn to Sag Harbor was established in 1772; it was chosen as the final stop on the three-day stagecoach trip. In 1877 Addison Youngs opened the American Hotel in Sag Harbor. This hotel was one of the most modern hotels on Long Island, with steam heat, electric lights, and indoor bathrooms. (It's still an inn and restaurant.) Sag Harbor's Sea View Hotel was built in 1891 and stood on a hill overlooking Noyack Bay; it was famous for attracting celebrities such as Enrico Caruso. Later called Hill Top Acres, it burned to the ground in 1970.

Ye Olde Canoe Place Inn was built on the small isthmus where native Indians carried their canoes from the Great Peconic Bay to Shinnecock Bay. First constructed in 1750 as a small house, it later became a stagecoach stop. Over the years it was owned by the Buch-müller family, who had previously owned the Waldorf-Astoria Hotel, and by Julius Keller, owner of Maxim's restaurant in Manhattan. The inn was destroyed by fire on July 4, 1921, but was rebuilt to follow the lines of the original. The new structure included 34 bedrooms, 4 banquet rooms, 20 baths, and a gigantic kitchen. It became a favorite watering hole during the Roaring Twenties, and its Saturday-night dances attracted hundreds. Among its famous guests were Governor Al Smith, who made it his summer headquarters for some 30 years, Franklin Roosevelt, John L. Sullivan, Helen Hayes, Albert Einstein, and Cary Grant. The inn is still in operation as a nightclub and disco.

Of the old-time inns, the American Hotel in Sag Harbor, the Huntting Inn, 1770 House, the Hedges Inn, and c/o The Maidstone (formerly Maidstone Arms) in East Hampton are still welcoming guests, but most of the others have long since burned or been demolished. The Irving Hotel in Southampton, for example, survived until the 1970s, only to be demolished. The Irving Annex across the street, however, survives as the main house of the Village Latch Inn.

Innkeeping continues to be a Hamptons tradition today, much as it was some 200 years ago, but with modern comforts. When I first started writing about country inns and bed & breakfasts (I used to write *Country Inns and Back Roads, Recommended Country Inns of the Mid-Atlantic States,* and *Recommended Bed & Breakfasts of the Mid-Atlantic States*), it was rare to find TVs and telephones in the rooms. Today's inns, however, often include flat-screen TVs, Wi-Fi, CD and DVD players, telephones with voicemail, air-conditioning, fluffy down pillows and comforters, and even turn-down service with yummy chocolates on your pillow. Private baths may include whirlpool tubs plus a collection of amenities, from special soaps and shampoos to thick towels and warm robes.

High season in the Hamptons runs from the July 4th weekend through Labor Day. Almost all bed & breakfast establishments, inns, and motels, however, open earlier and close later in the season, and more and more are remaining open year-round. When possible, dates of operation are indicated, but since they may vary from year to year, it is best to call first. Also, in high season inns and motels often require two- and three-night minimum stays on weekends and four-night stays on holidays.

Bed & breakfast establishments are as varied as their owners. Some are elegant and classy, while others are whimsical and humorous, with all the variations in between. Some are decorated with such élan that they belong in *Architectural Digest;* others offer a homey combination of handmade quilts and pillows. Some pride themselves on the complete breakfasts they serve; others lay out a buffet of fruits and breads. The one common thread, however, is that each owner of a bed & breakfast has invested a bit of himself or herself in

A guest room at The Baker House in East Hampton

their establishment; staying in one is often a very personal experience.

Hamptons inns and bed & breakfasts have a limited number of rooms, and it is necessary to reserve the finest rooms well in advance. Therefore, it is advisable to make reservations as soon as you know your plans. A deposit generally will be required, and strict
cancellation policies are followed. Be sure that you understand the policy and abide by it;
otherwise, you may lose your deposit.

Children under the age of 12 and pets are often discouraged in B&Bs in the Hamptons.
Most have strictly enforced no-smoking policies within the house, but some do allow smoking on porches or on the grounds. Although most inns now provide air-conditioning, it used
to be assumed that the balmy ocean breezes make it unnecessary; generally, that is true.

This chapter offers a guide to places to stay from Montauk to Eastport. Please consult
chapters 9 and 10 for places to stay on the North Fork and Shelter Island.

In the block of information printed with each lodging description, you will see price categories rather than specific prices. These categories are based on the average between the
highest and lowest rates per room, double occupancy. If a continental or full breakfast is
included, it will be noted in the information block under "Special Features." The rates
indicated throughout this book are subject to change, so to be safe, confirm prices when
you call for reservations. These rates generally exclude local taxes and any service charges
that may be added to the bill.

Price Categories

Inexpensive	Up to $100
Moderate	$100–$250
Expensive	$250–$400
Very Expensive	$400 and up

Credit Cards

AE: American Express; D: Discover; DC: Diner's Club; MC: MasterCard; V: Visa

The East Hampton and Southampton chambers of commerce operate an excellent accommodation referral service. Each publishes a free book that lists its members, including those who offer lodging. They also have information and telephone numbers of homes, inns, hotels, and motels that have current vacancies.

East Hampton Chamber of Commerce (631-324-0362; www.easthamptonchamber.com; 42 Gingerbread Ln., East Hampton, NY 11937)

Southampton Chamber of Commerce (631-283-0402; www.southamptonchamber.com; 76 Main St., Southampton, NY 11968)

BED & BREAKFASTS, INNS, RESORTS

There are four excellent small hotels to stay in, all of them adapted from East Hampton homes of over a century ago; the "Huntting," which is an expanded version of Reverend Nathaniel Huntting's parsonage of bygone days; the "Maidstone Arms," successor to the former Osborne House of ancient fame; the "Hedges," once a country boardinghouse of the 1870s and in recent years reopened as a delightful country inn with the flavor of an old home and one of the famous hostelries on Long Island. Then, for those who like to be within sight and smell of the ocean, there is the "Sea Spray," also most comfortable and of high repute, standing on the crest of a dune in a bower of flowers.

—From Discovering Long Island *by William Oliver Stevens, 1939*

AMAGANSETT
THE GANSETT GREEN MANOR

631-267-3133
www.gansettgreenmanor.com
273 Main St., Amagansett
Mailing Address: P.O. Box 799, Amagansett, NY 11930
Innkeeper: Chris Koether

Open: June–Sept., on a nightly basis as a B&B; Oct.–May, cottages rented full-time
Price: Moderate–Expensive
Credit Cards: AE, MC, V
Special Features: Spacious landscaped grounds; Wi-Fi Internet access; kitchens; cable TV; children welcome; pets with prior permission; Hampton Jitney stops in front
Directions: On Montauk Hwy. (Rte. 27) in village

The Gansett Green, a fixture of Amagansett life since 1915, is in tip-top shape. What was once a ramshackle collection of cottages has been transformed into a delightful haven. Each weathered-shingle cottage now has crisp white trim, an individual garden or patio, and wainscoted interior walls; the decor is inspired. The Hidden Garden suite is furnished with rare Chinese blackwood pieces, imported by former owner Gary Kalfin, and has a walled garden with a fishpond. Several of the cottages, including the Hampton Classic Horse Room, have furniture hand-painted by artist David Tabor. All 14 units have kitchens, private baths, flagstone terraces, antiques, and so much more. The 2-acre parcel that once was overgrown with weeds and brush held many surprises; Kalfin found an old wooden tandem sled and, beside the big barn, a covered wagon. All such discoveries remain, as well as the fountains and meandering pathways that lead to fanciful lawn sculptures.

THE HERMITAGE
631-267-6151
www.duneresorts.com
2148 Montauk Hwy., Amagansett
Mailing Address: P.O. Box 1127, Amagansett, NY 11930
Manager: Richard Edelstein, Dune Resorts
Open: Mid-Mar.–New Year's
Price: Inexpensive–Expensive
Credit Cards: AE, D, MC, V
Special Features: On ocean; pool; 2 tennis courts; private sun decks; 7 landscaped acres; kitchens; cable TV/VCR; air-conditioning; telephones; laundry; children welcome; no pets
Directions: On Montauk Hwy. (Rte. 27), 5 miles east of Amagansett at Navajo Ln.

Located on the expansive sandy beach of the Napeague stretch, midway between Amagansett village and Montauk, these ultramodern, bleached-wood, two-story buildings rise from the surrounding dunes. Each of the 56 units has two bedrooms, two baths, living room, full kitchen, dining room, and deck for private sunbathing. The decor is the typical Hamptons motif of pale woods and pastel fabrics, although since this is a co-op, they are not all alike. Views from the oceanside rooms are spectacular. The 7 acres of landscaped grounds include two tennis courts and a pool with a lifeguard in attendance. This is a great place for children.

OCEAN COLONY BEACH AND TENNIS CLUB
631-267-3130
www.duneresorts.com
2004 Montauk Hwy., Amagansett
Mailing Address: P.O. Box 1799, Amagansett, NY 11930
Manager: Carl DeGroote, Dune Resorts
Open: Apr.–Oct.
Price: Inexpensive–Expensive
Credit Cards: AE, D, MC, V
Special Features: On ocean; heated pool; 2 tennis courts; kitchens; private terraces; air-conditioning; smoking permitted in rooms; telephones with voicemail; cable TV; on 8 landscaped acres; golf driving range; laundry; clubhouse with Ping-Pong, table games, adults' and children's library; children welcome; no pets.
Directions: On Montauk Hwy. (Rte. 27), 4 miles east of Amagansett

The Ocean Colony Beach and Tennis Club is a three-level, 69-unit, weathered gray co-op resort built in 1983. It is located on an 8-acre site with 400 feet of private oceanfront. Accommodations range in size from studios to three-bedroom units; all contain a living area, sleeping area, kitchenette, and private deck or terrace. Some have ocean views, and all have handsome furnishings, although since this is a co-op, the decor does vary. "Harbor" is a well-designed, three-bedroom unit with a powder room on the first level and a full bath upstairs, but no ocean view. The cottage ("Deuce") has a very private site on the ocean with walls of windows and wraparound decks for direct views of the crashing waves. There are two bedrooms, a bath, and a superb kitchen. The grounds include a pool, two tennis courts, and a clubhouse/game room.

THE REFORM CLUB
631-267-8500
www.reformclubinn.com
23 Windmill Ln., Amagansett
Mailing Address: P.O. Box 800, Amagansett, NY 11930
Owner: Randy Lerner
Manager: Noelle Franey and Erin Harris
Open: Year-round
Price: Very Expensive
Credit Cards: AE, D, MC, V

Designed to encourage guests to slow down and savor a "peaceful rest," the Reform Club in Amagansett is a secluded and romantic retreat.

Special Features: Continental breakfast; fireplaces in rooms; Wi-Fi Internet access; bikes; safes; iPod docking stations; flat-screen TVs; Duxiana beds; exercise room; private gated cottages have individual steam rooms, gyms, and laundry facilities; 2-person maximum per room; no pets
Directions: From Montauk Hwy. (Main St.), go north on Windmill Ln. Inn is on left in 0.25 mile.

No, regardless of the name, this spectacular new inn (2009) is not an exclusive hotel for recent graduates of a rehab program. The name was chosen because the owner wants a stay at his inn to encourage positive change—for guests to slow down and savor a "peaceful rest," take time "to read, to walk, and to breathe in the sea air." And this elegant, secluded, and utterly romantic inn

certainly persuades patrons to do just that. Soaring ceilings, oak floors, and the decor's soothing earth tones, all conspire to provide comfort and relaxation. There are fireplaces, Duxiana king-sized beds made for snuggling, and flat-screen TVs. If you choose one of the cottages, you'll have a private steam room, an exercise room, your own washer and dryer, a private patio or two, and a spacious lawn—all hidden away behind tall fences and hedges. In Cottage One, you'll even have a wonderful covered terrace with an outdoor fireplace in front of an oversized bed-lounge. Although on the site of the former Mill-Garth Country Inn, there's nothing left of the former place except the old windmill, for which the street was named. Without question, this is the most luxurious (and expensive) getaway in the Hamptons.

SEA CREST ON THE OCEAN

631-267-3159, 800-SEA DAYS
www.duneresorts.com
2166 Montauk Hwy., Amagansett
Mailing Address: P.O. Box 7053, Amagansett, NY 11930
Manager: Jan Mackin, Dune Resorts
Open: Year-round
Price: Inexpensive–Expensive
Credit Cards: AE, D, MC, V
Special Features: On ocean; heated pool; 2 tennis courts; playground; basketball, volleyball, handball, shuffleboard; picnic and BBQ area; kitchenettes; cable TV/VCR; telephones with voicemail; air-conditioning; no smoking; children welcome; no pets
Directions: Located on Montauk Hwy. (Rte. 27), 5 miles east of Amagansett

Sea Crest on the Ocean is a co-op set on over 9 acres, with 150 yards of unspoiled beach. The gray-shingled resort contains 74 units, ranging from studios to two-bedroom units. Facilities in buildings named Rapallo, Saint-Tropez, and San Remo have views of the ocean, while those in the other buildings have views of the pool or partial views of the ocean. All, however, have pleasing, well-designed living and sleeping areas, kitchenettes, and private decks or terraces; larger accommodations have two levels with two decks. All units received new kitchens, carpeting, and wallpaper in 2000, but the furniture will vary with the tastes of the co-op owner. The grounds are very well maintained and include abundant flower beds, a heated pool, two tennis courts, and an elevated boardwalk over the dunes to the beach. A variety of activities are also held on the grounds.

BRIDGEHAMPTON
BRIDGEHAMPTON INN

631-537-3660
www.bridgehamptoninn.com
2266 Main Street, Bridgehampton
Mailing Address: P.O. Box 1342, Bridgehampton, NY 11932
Owner/Innkeeper: Anna Pump
Open: Year-round
Price: Moderate–Expensive
Credit Cards: AE, MC, V
Special Features: Full breakfast; gardens; telephones, cable TV, air-conditioning; children welcome; no pets
Directions: On Main St. (Rte. 27), just west of village

This venerable old (1795) colonial home is one of the handsomest in town. Circled by a white picket fence, the white-shingled structure was totally restored in 1993. The decor has a restrained elegance that's punctuated by clever artwork and extravagant floral displays in the common rooms. There's a welcoming fireplace in the living room, with French doors leading to several brick terraces and expansive gardens beyond. The decor in the four guest rooms and two suites is sophisticated, with beige carpeting, handcrafted four-poster beds, antique dressers and tables, and well-designed marble and tile baths that feature unique European fixtures, including mansion-sized showers with a showerhead in the middle of the ceiling rather than on the wall. My favorite is Room 7, which has red-striped twill fabric on a Victorian settee and a polished antique chest with brass pulls; a Victorian table holds the TV. Room 6, a suite, is furnished with a spectacular eight-piece antique Biedermeier suite. The owners also run the popular Loaves & Fishes gourmet take-out and catering company, in Sagaponack, so breakfasts are divine. A full breakfast, which might include Swedish pancakes with fresh blueberry sauce, ham and eggs, and homemade pastries, is included in the price of the room—and on nice summer mornings, you may eat on the covered terrace in back. The Loaves & Fishes Cooking School is also conducted at the inn. It offers a variety of classes from

Breakfast is served in the informal lounge of the Baker House, which also features a fireplace and honor wine bar for guests' enjoyment.

tapas to seafood to breads and desserts. Inquire about packages that combine room and school.

EAST HAMPTON
THE BAKER HOUSE
631-324-4081
www.bakerhouse1650.com
181 Main St. East Hampton, NY 11937
Innkeepers: Antonella and Robert Rosen
Managers: Kathy and Heather McCormack
Open: Year-round
Price: Expensive–Very Expensive
Credit Cards: AE, D, DC, MC, V
Special Features: Full breakfast; afternoon refreshments; flat-screen TVs, air-conditioning, DVDs, Boze radios, minibar, CD players, iPod docks, wireless Internet access, telephones with voicemail; book and video library; masseur available; spa; indoor and outdoor pool (infinity); sauna, steam shower, soaking tub, exercise room; no smoking; children welcome; no pets
Directions: On Montauk Hwy/Main St. (Rte. 27) in center of village

For many years, this distinctive, buff-colored stucco mansion was the home of the owners of 1770 House and served as an adjunct to the rooms in their inn. In 1996, however, the handsome house was purchased by Gary and Rita Reiswig, formerly the owners of the Maidstone Arms, and transformed into the Hamptons' premier bed & breakfast. Every detail of the major restoration was executed to perfection. The original structure dates to the 1650s, and was at that time the home of Thomas Baker, for whom the inn is now named. In the early 1900s Mr. J. Harper Poor created its current appearance, and the Reiswigs restored it to that period. The inn was purchased in 2004 by Antonella and Bob Rosen, and they have continued to expand and improve the inn. In the sunken living room there are bay windows, a carved plaster ceiling, and a massive tile-fronted fireplace. An oak library table graces the library, which has a wall of books. In keeping with the style of the house, the elegant furnishings have an arts and crafts motif. The guest rooms, which have beamed ceilings, are very large, with roomy closets and equally spacious tiled baths; most have fireplaces. My favorite is The Hedges, which has an iron bed, a wood-burning fireplace, hand-hewn beamed ceilings, paneled walls, and a private balcony overlooking Main Street. All the rooms have William Morris–style fabrics and wallpapers imported from England, Frette bed dressings, and fluffy Frette bathrobes. A spa, which was added in 2000, contains a circulating pool, a sauna, exercise equipment, and steam shower. Breakfast is served in the informal lounge, which has wicker chairs, a plumped sofa in front of a woodstove, wooden floors, and a rustic, hand-hewn beamed ceiling. The full breakfast may include Belgian yeast-raised waffles, Swedish pancakes, or a vegetable frittata, accompanied by freshly baked breads, fruit, and juice. In the afternoon, wines (honor bar), homemade lemonade, and hors d'oeuvres are set out in the informal lounge.

EAST HAMPTON HOUSE
631-324-4300, 800-698-9283
www.duneresorts.com
226 Pantigo Rd., East Hampton, NY 11937
Manager: Sarah Malone, Dune Resorts
Open: Year-round
Price: Inexpensive–Expensive
Credit Cards: AE, D, MC, V
Special Features: Heated pool, two tennis courts, exercise room; private sun deck or patio, telephones with voicemail, cable TV/VCR, wireless Internet access (fee), air-conditioning; no smoking; children under two discouraged in summer; no pets
Directions: On Rte. 27, 1 mile east of East Hampton village

From the street, this appears to be merely an attractive, well-maintained motel, but in reality, the two-story white brick buildings are set on 5 parklike acres of flower beds and manicured lawns that include a pool, tennis courts, and a children's play area. This is a co-op, so the decor of the units may vary, but each is superbly maintained and attractively furnished. There are two sizes of rooms: studios and two-room suites, and each of the 52 units has either a private sun deck or a patio. In summer, a light continental breakfast is available, which may be taken to the room. Although the beach is about a mile away, the pool and the lovely landscaping make this one of the most popular motels in the Hamptons.

EAST HAMPTON POINT
631-324-9191
www.easthamptonpoint.com
295 Three Mile Harbor Rd., East Hampton
Mailing address: P.O. Box 847, East Hampton, NY 11937
Owner: Ben Krupinski
Manager: Michael Capoferri
Open: Year-round
Price: Expensive–Very Expensive
Credit Cards: AE, D, MC, V
Special Features: Pool, tennis court, fitness center; telephones with voicemail, air-conditioning, cable TV/VCR; on 5.5 wooded acres, playground, van service to town and beaches in summer; no smoking; children welcome; no pets; fine restaurant and marina on premises
Directions: From Main St. (Rte. 27) turn left just before Hook Windmill onto North Main St. After two traffic lights, road forks. Take left fork onto Three Mile Harbor Rd.; cottages are on left in about 4 miles.

It's hard not to fall in love with these jewel-box cottages. Each has a modern kitchen with a refrigerator and a Jenn-Aire stove, country tile floors, tile baths, and private brick patios or wooden decks. Some of the 13 cottages have duplex bedrooms and skylights. There are both one- and two-bedroom units. Cottage 2 is absolutely stunning: the main floor has a terrific kitchen, large deck, and tiled powder room; upstairs, there's a bedroom and a bathroom that boasts a skylight, country tile floor, and a huge glass shower. As one might imagine, this cottage is especially popular with honeymooners. Cottage 7 has natural colors, a dark gray granite counter in the kitchen, and an upstairs bath with a marble counter. The cottages are connected by brick pathways and are bordered by abundant flower beds, all in a very private, wooded setting. In the midst of it there's a small chapel that's been converted into a fitness center, complete with TV. The Palmer House Suites, a 2004 conversion of a house on the property, added 7 stunning suites offering plasma TVs, wet bars, and, in some cases, a fireplace or a terrace—Suite 5 has both. Although the popular East Hampton Point restaurant (under the same ownership—see listing in chapter 4) is on adjacent property, it's well removed from the cottages, as are the pool and the tennis court. There's a marina down on the harbor and a ship's store where guests can purchase breakfast in the morning and snacks all day.

THE HEDGES INN

631-324-7101
www.thehedgesinn.com
74 James Ln., East Hampton, NY 11937
Innkeeper: Carol Schnittlich
Open: Year-round
Price: Very Expensive
Credit Cards: AE, DC, MC, V
Special Features: Full breakfast; wireless Internet access, air-conditioning, flat-screen TVs, telephones with voicemail, cable TV; no smoking; children welcome; no pets
Directions: Entering town from the west, the inn is straight ahead at the T-junction. Turn right at traffic light by Town Pond, then immediately turn left onto James Ln. Inn's driveway is first road on right.

The Hedges Inn is one of the oldest and most historic inns on the East End. The Hedges family, one of the founding families of East Hampton, began taking in boarders as early as 1870; it is believed that parts of the house date from the mid-1700s, and legend has it that the famous underground wine cellar was once part of the Underground Railroad. The main house became an acclaimed inn in 1935, when Mrs. Harry Hamlin restored it and put her own cook and butler in charge. Later, in the 1950s, it achieved widespread acclaim when it became home to a restaurant owned by famed chef and restaurateur Henri Soulé, who also owned Le Pavillon in Manhattan. Today the Hedges Inn has been fully restored, and all 12 rooms have beautiful private baths. Expect creamy sand or sage walls with white wainscoting, brown carpeting, taupe-colored sofas, and iron beds. The baths are done in sparkling white tile with white marble counters. A buffet breakfast that might include an egg dish or waffles is served in the pretty, airy breakfast room. A side terrace serves as an auxiliary breakfast room in the summer, but it's also a refined place to sip a glass of wine in the afternoon.

THE HUNTTING INN

631-324-0410
www.thepalm.com
94 Main St., East Hampton, NY 11937
Innkeeper: Linda Calder
Open: Year-round
Price: Moderate–Expensive
Credit Cards: AE, DC, MC, V
Special Features: Continental breakfast; air-conditioning, telephones, cable TV; no smoking; children welcome; pets OK with

The Hedges Inn was originally home to one of the founding families of East Hampton. Chris Foster

prior approval; fine restaurant on premises
Directions: On Montauk Hwy./Main St.
(Rte. 27) at Huntting Ln.

This venerable old inn, which has been taking in boarders since Revolutionary War times, has been a prominent fixture on East Hampton's Main Street since 1699, when it was built as a home for Reverend Nathaniel Huntting, the second minister of East Hampton. Over the years, it has grown as it took in more and more boarders, which accounts for the narrow hallways with their quirky twists and turns. The Hampton Jitney stops directly in front of the inn, making it a most convenient place to stay. The tiny lobby of the Huntting bustles at night, when it serves as the greeting place for diners at the Palm restaurant (see listing in chapter 4), which is located on the main

floor. Off the bar, however, there are several parlors where guests can spend quiet time in the afternoon, reading or viewing the gardens. The 19 guest rooms vary in size and are often funky, although each has carpeted floors, a smattering of antiques, pine furniture, and a private bath (often very tiny). The side flower garden is a riot of color from spring to fall.

C/O THE MAIDSTONE

631-324-5006
www.themaidstone.com
207 Main St., East Hampton, NY 11937
Owner: Jenny Ljungberg
General Manager: Alex Eberle
Open: Year-round
Price: Moderate–Very Expensive
Credit Cards: AE, DC, MC, V

An interior featuring lively and colorful prints has given c/o The Maidstone (formerly the Maidstone Arms) a new look.

Special Features: Overlooks Town Pond; full breakfast; flat-screen TVs, Sony Playstation 3 w/DVD and CD player, minibar, iPod dock, Wi-Fi, telephones with voicemail, cable TV, stereos; DVD library; fireplaces in cottages; children welcome; pets welcome $24/night; excellent restaurant on premises

Directions: On Montauk Hwy./Main St. (Rte. 27) across from Town Pond

There's been an inn on this site, looking much as the present c/o The Maidstone does today, since 1750. Located on a knoll across from Town Pond, the inn is a classic beauty, with a white-shingled exterior, a Greek Revival doorway, and blue shutters. The inn was purchased in 2009 by Jenny Ljungberg, whose lifestyle hotel company c/o Hotels specializes in transforming his- toric landmark hotels into destination resorts. She immediately launched an impressive renovation of the common rooms and dining room (see listing for The Living Room restaurant, chapter 4) in a style she calls Scandinavian Cozy, reflecting a mix of Scandinavian designs from the 17th century to today. The clubby Scandinavian Cozy Lounge, just off the lobby, has a bleached pine floor, bead board and shin- gled walls and ceiling, Scandinavian- designed love seats, and chairs dressed in bright floral fabrics that take their cue from vintage Josef Frank designs. The chairs and loveseats overflow with bright pillows, and the walls are decorated with bold modern photographs. This is the perfect place to sip a hot mulled wine in the winter, while watching children ice-skate on Town Pond, or in summer to enjoy the extensive gardens from the adjoining patio. It's also a pleasant place to begin the day while reading your complimentary copy of the *New York Times*. There are 16 guest rooms and 3 cottages, all with private baths. As we went to press, several have been renovated and embellished with bright fabrics and wall and window coverings, but there is a plan to close for several months in the winter of 2009–2010 to renovate the remaining rooms. A full breakfast in the dining room is included for overnight guests.

MILL HOUSE INN

631-324-9766
www.millhouseinn.com;
innkeeper@millhouseinn.com
31 North Main St., East Hampton, NY 11937
Innkeepers: Gary and Sylvia Muller
General Manager: Lee Ellis
Open: Year-round
Price: Expensive–Very Expensive
Credit Cards: AE, D, DC, MC, V
Special Features: Full breakfast; telephones with voicemail, flat-screen TV, DVD players, iPod docks, wireless Internet access; no smoking; children welcome; pets welcome with prior permission $50/night; Graybarn Cottage, a luxurious separate house, for rent on premises
Directions: From Main St., turn left at fork just before Hook Windmill. Inn is on left, across from windmill.

The charming Mill House Inn enjoys a convenient, in-town location and a lovely view of the historic Hook Windmill. Now under the guidance of Gary and Sylvia Muller, the inn, dating to 1790, has been decorated in the arts and crafts style. There are hand-hewn beams in the living room and the breakfast room; the living room has a fireplace with a white mantel, mellow leather sofas and chairs, and a pine cupboard; the breakfast room has soothing sage-green walls, mission-style chairs, and a needle-

point rug. Be sure to take note of the wonderful photos on the wall, as they are the artistry of Sylvia's grandfather, Clarence Kennedy, a best buddy of Ansel Adams. Each of the four rooms and six suites has a private bath—and all have gas fireplaces. Hampton Breezes, for example, has a Shaker-style, handcrafted cherry sleighbed and a bentwood chair upholstered in leather. There's a fireplace, and the large tiled bath has a whirlpool tub. Gary is a chef, so breakfasts here are quite exceptional. You can choose from 15 different egg dishes, as well as pancakes or brioche French toast. Or you might have fresh fruit or Irish oatmeal with dried cherries, blueberries, and strawberries. We love to follow a day at the beach with some quiet time on the screened-in porch or in the beautifully landscaped backyard, sipping a refreshing lemonade. In addition, The Graybarn Cottage, a luxurious full-house cottage, is for rent on the property.

1770 HOUSE

631-324-1770
www.1770house.com;
innkeeper@1770house.com
143 Main St., East Hampton, NY 11937
Owner: Ben Krupinski
Innkeeper: Demi Reichart
Open: Year-round
Price: Expensive–Very Expensive
Credit Cards: AE, MC, V
Special Features: Full breakfast in-season and all weekends, continental breakfast remaining days; air-conditioning, telephones with voicemail, flat-screen cable TV, working fireplaces; no smoking; children over 12 welcome; no pets; fabulous restaurant on premises
Directions: On Montauk Hwy./Main St. (Rte. 27) in center of village

Although 1770 House has been graciously welcoming guests for over 200 years, it doesn't look its age thanks to the loving care of its owners through the years. Located in the heart of the original village, it's put in service as a general store, a dining hall for Clinton Academy, a private home, and a public inn. When new owners took over the helm in April of 2002, they launched a total renovation that closed the inn for three months. It's now better than new, with all-new plumbing, electricity, a foundation, and much more. Guests will recognize some of the original features. The library, with paneled walls, a beamed ceiling, and a fireplace, is a cozy nook where one can contemplate the dinner choices while sipping an aperitif. Some of the extensive collection of clocks still grace the walls. Or you might meander downstairs to the tavern, with its brick walls, to experience an even cozier ambience. All of the guest rooms have private baths. Room 1 is a large room with a paneled wall surrounding a fireplace, a king-sized bed, and elegant silk draperies. Room 6 is tucked away with a private entrance and overlooks the gardens. The finest accommodation, however, is the Carriage House, which is a separate building behind the inn. It is absolutely stunning, as it features a living room with a fireplace, antique French doors with etched glass that lead to a bedroom decorated in soft earth tones, and a carved curving stairway to a second bedroom and bath. The inn also encompasses one of the finest restaurants in the Hamptons—a not-to-be-missed experience (see listing in chapter 4.)

EASTPORT
SEATUCK COVE HOUSE WATERFRONT INN

631-325-3300
www.seatuckcovehouse.com;
info@seatuckcovehouse.com
61 South Bay Ave., Eastport, NY 11941
Owners: Ed and Carol Galvin
Manager: Colleen McGrath
Open: Year-round
Price: Inexpensive–Expensive
Credit Cards: AE, D, MC, V

Special Features: Full breakfast; waterfront; private beach, heated pool, marina across street; air-conditioning, private balconies, wireless Internet access, flat-screen TVs, satellite TV/stereo system, telephones, Jacuzzi tubs; children over 16 welcome; no pets
Directions: From Sunrise Hwy. (Rte. 27), take exit 61 onto Eastport Manor Rd. (Rte. 55). Follow to end at Montauk Hwy. (Rte. 27A). Turn left (east) onto Montauk Hwy. and drive 0.7 mile to South Bay Ave. Turn right and follow to end to #61, down a long driveway on right.

Hugging 900 feet of waterfront, including its own private beach, this is a spectacular inn. You can arrive by boat or by car, and even in the midst of winter you can enjoy the bountiful views of the water from your own private balcony. The stone-and-shingle house was constructed in 1999 specifically to welcome overnight guests. Every comfort has been well planned. There are three spacious common rooms—one has a masculine ambience with leather sofas, a pool table, and a handsome stone fireplace, while the other two are light, sun-filled rooms that offer walls of windows to take full advantage of the view. There are nautical touches throughout, from the ships' models in one room to seascape paintings on the walls. The five spacious guest rooms all have private balconies, beautiful tiled baths, and attractive decorator linens. My favorite is Dune Suite, which is positively enormous. It has a fireplace and breathtaking views of Moriches Bay, which are especially enchanting at sunset. The full breakfast might consist of ginger and carrot scones or orange marmalade corn muffins followed by Chambord French toast, sweet potato pancakes with sautéed apples, or eggs Benedict. This is the place to come for a total chill-out and pampering. You might read a book by the pool or treat yourself to a holistic spa treatment and massage in the privacy of your room.

A Victorian on the Bay offers rooms with water views.

A VICTORIAN ON THE BAY

631-325-1000, 888-449-0620
www.victorianonthebay.com;
info@victorianonthebay.com
57 South Bay Ave., Eastport, NY 11941
Innkeepers: Rosemary Parker
Open: Year-round
Price: Moderate–Expensive
Credit Cards: D, MC, V
Special Features: No-smoking B&B; water views; pool, hot tub; wireless Internet access, air-conditioning, cable TV/VCR; balconies, fireplaces; marina nearby; fitness room; children over 12 welcome; no pets
Directions: From Sunrise Hwy. (Rte. 27), take exit 61 onto Eastport Manor Rd. (Rte. 55). Follow to end at Rte. 27A (Montauk Hwy.). Turn left (east) onto Montauk Hwy. and drive 0.7 mile to South Bay Ave. Turn right and follow almost to end, to #57. B&B is on right.

I'll never forget my amazement when I stumbled across this beautiful Victorian B&B. It's located down a quiet seaside road in a gentle, off-the-beaten-track Hamptons town (but definitely in Southampton township). There are water views galore and a fine restaurant just down the street at water's edge. Rosemary Parker found this fabulous 3.5-acre property and built her dream B&B to enhance it. You drive up a circular driveway and immediately want to linger on the broad, wraparound front porch. Tarry not, as what lies beyond is even better. A handsome living room, with fireplace, is decorated in soft yellows. There's a piano available for tickling the ivories should you be so talented, and shelves of books and videos for borrowing. The guest rooms, which are located on the second floor, all have distant water views and baths with whirlpool tubs. The master suite has a four-poster feather bed, a fireplace, and a porch from which to enjoy the water view. Breakfasts are divine. You might indulge in challah French toast, plus Rosemary's Victorian Sweet Secret—shhhhh, we won't tell.

On the other hand, don't eat too much, as a beautiful pool awaits.

Montauk
MONTAUK HILL HOUSE
631-668-3084
www.montaukhillhouse.com
114 Glenmore Ave., Montauk, NY 11954
Innkeepers: Robert and Karin Padden
Open: Year-round
Price: Moderate
Credit Cards: MC, V
Special Features: Continental breakfast; coffeemakers in room, safe, wireless Internet access; massages available; no smoking; children over 12 welcome; no pets
Directions: From Main St. traveling east, turn left at the Chase Bank and go halfway around the semicircle, then turn left onto Edgemere St. Drive past train station and continue on Flamingo Ave. to N. Farragut Rd. Turn right onto N. Farragut. B&B is eighth house on left.

This new home, completed and opened as a B&B in the spring of 2009, sits high atop the tallest hill in Montauk, offering splendid views of Lake Montauk, the Atlantic Ocean, and Block Island Sound. The hands-on creation of a builder-craftsman and his artist-wife, the home includes beautiful millwork, elegant, hand-made furniture, and walls adorned with striking paintings. There's an entrance foyer with an arched mahogany door and a floor of sandstone imported from Spain. The living room has white oak floors, a stone fireplace, and floor-to-ceiling windows. There's ample deck space outside, where one might eat breakfast, and a stone patio, with table and chairs tucked under a tree. The two rooms, which are on the second floor, feature baths finished with limestone and marble, as well as elegant wood and stone embellishments, all decorated in soft earth tones. "Sunrise" offers views of Lake Montauk, the ocean, and the rising sun, and from "Sunset," guests have an awesome view of the setting sun. The rooms share a common balcony. A continental breakfast of fresh fruit, pastries, cheeses, yogurt, and granola might be eaten outside on the deck on nice days.

MONTAUK MANOR
631-668-4400
www.montaukmanor.com
236 Edgemere St., Montauk
Mailing Address: RD 2, Box 226C, Montauk, NY 11954
Manager: Janice Nessel
Open: Year-round
Price: Inexpensive–Very Expensive
Credit Cards: AE, D, DC, MC, V
Special Features: Wheelchair access; smoking permitted in some rooms/designated no-smoking rooms; heated indoor and outdoor pools; wireless Internet access; flat-screen TVs most rooms, cable TV/VCR, air-conditioning, telephones with voice-mail, kitchens; doorman, maid service; day spa, health club with Jacuzzi and saunas; conference facilities with audiovisual service; seasonal van service; three tennis courts, exercise room, indoor squash court, golf driving range, putting green, bocci court, shuffleboard; BBQ and picnic area; restaurant (Breakwater Café) on premises; children welcome, no pets
Directions: From Main St. traveling east, turn left at the Chase Bank and go halfway around the semicircle, then turn left onto Edgemere St. Travel 1 mile and look for the hotel sign on right. Follow signs to resort, up hill on right.

Montauk Manor was built by Carl Fisher, the developer of Miami Beach, in 1927 as part of his grand scheme to turn Montauk into the Miami of the North. This imposing building, which sits on 12 acres atop Montauk's highest hill, resembles a feudal Tudor castle; it's on the National Register of Historic Places. It boasts spectacular views of the harbor, where Fisher planned to build grand docks for the ocean liners that were going to depart to, and arrive from, Europe. None of that came to pass, however, and for years the hotel sat idle. In 1987 it was converted to 140 condominium apartments (100 are rented on a transient basis) that range in size from studios to three-bedroom units. Half of the units have balconies, and most have views. The lobby, soaring three stories high, has multiple massive fireplaces along its tiled corridor. The rooms are well designed and tasteful, each with a modern kitchen and tile bath. If you are lucky enough to rent Unit 135, you'll find the arched fireplace that once graced the dining room, a sofa bed in the living room, a loft bedroom, and an arched doorway framing French doors to a mammoth terrace. Mirrored walls in the dining and living rooms expand the space.

MONTAUK YACHT CLUB RESORT & MARINA

631-668-3100
www.montaukyachtclub.com
32 Star Island Rd., Montauk
Mailing Address: P.O. Box 5048, Montauk, NY 11954
Owner: Island Global Yachting
General Manager: Lloyd Van Horn
Open: Apr.–Nov.
Price: Moderate–Very Expensive
Credit Cards: AE, DC, MC, V
Special Features: Wheelchair access; waterfront; private beach; full-service spa; concierge; three pools, four tennis courts, seasonal resident pro, sand volleyball court, children's playground, putting green, bocci court; fitness center; conference facilities; 232-slip marina; surf lessons, surf camp; three restaurants on premises; lounge; private terraces or balconies; flat-screen TVs, in-room refrigerators, iPod docks, wireless Internet access, cable TV, air-conditioning, multiple telephone lines with voicemail; no smoking; children welcome; no pets
Directions: Travel east on Montauk Hwy., continuing through Montauk. Turn left onto West Lake Dr., travel 1.8 miles, and turn right onto Star Island Causeway. Yacht Club is on right in about 0.25 mile.

If you're into viewing fabulous big yachts (or arriving in them) then the Montauk Yacht Club Resort & Marina should definitely be your destination. Now under the ownership of Island Global Yachting, the Montauk Yacht Club underwent a multimillion-dollar renovation in 2009 that transformed it into the luxury resort for which it initially became famous. Founded in 1929, the original resort was built by Carl Fisher, the developer of Miami Beach, who had dreams of turning this sleepy little village into the Miami of the North. Although that never came to pass, the Yacht Club is one of the charming and luxurious legacies he left behind. This one-stop retreat, which is located on 35 acres, offers complete lodging, restaurant, and recreational facilities for the entire family. Each of the 84 guest rooms and 23 hideaway villas has been stylishly upgraded with marine blue and white colors and nautical décor. They are equipped with wicker and rattan furniture. Some of the rooms have water views, and all feature individual balconies or terraces, telephones with voicemail, hair dryers, irons and ironing boards, and coffeemakers. The rooms in the former Florenz Ziegfield estate, located a short walk away at the end of the street, have individual charm. Built in the 1920s, the 23 "villas" have interesting little alcoves with pretty patios, and some feature fireplaces and fabulous water views. Restaurants include the Gulf Coast Kitchen, Hurricane Alley, and Barracuda Bar (see listings in chapter 4 for complete descriptions).

SOLÉ EAST

631-668-2105
www.soleeast.com
90 Second House Rd., Montauk, NY 11954
Owner: Dave Ceva
Open: May–Oct.
Price: Moderate–Very Expensive
Credit Cards: AE, D, MC, V
Special Features: Continental breakfast;

heated pool surrounded by oversized lounges with poolside drink and food service; Zen Den (tranquil area); massage room, in-house masseuse; beach badminton/volleyball court; bicycles for rent; wood-burning fire pit; conference facilities; wireless Internet access, flat-screen HD cable TV, iPod docks; no smoking; children welcome; pets welcome
$150–$200/stay; restaurant (Backyard) on premises; sister inn Solé East Beach located in village
Directions: From Montauk Point State Parkway traveling east, turn left onto Second House Rd. before you arrive in the village; the inn is on the right in about 1 mile.

Located in a wonderful 1920s Tudor-style building outside Montauk proper and constructed by Carl Fisher as part of his plan to turn Montauk into a summer destination (formerly called Shepherd's Neck Inn), the 67-room building was totally renovated in 2005. It has been transformed into a sleek, tres chic, hip destination. Never fear, however; it still retains its casual Montauk attitude. This is not a dress-up spot, just a cool place to hang. The pool is surrounded by oversized beds—perfect for lounging in the sun while sipping a cool drink or snacking (yes, there's poolside service). The rooms and cottages are decorated in soothing white with black tile floors, and the baths have white subway tile on the walls, and vessel sinks. Rosy-colored mood lighting illuminates the hallways. The separate little beach-bungalow cottages are decorated in the same style, but offer a bit more privacy. Backyard, the on-site restaurant (see listing in chapter 4), features Mediterranean cuisine. If you'd rather be closer to the beach, an in-village branch has sprouted at Solé East Beach downtown. See "Other Accommodations" at the end of this chapter for details.

THE SURF CLUB
631-668-3800, 800-LASTWAVE
www.duneresorts.com
20 Surfside Ave. and South Essex St., Montauk
Mailing Address: P.O. Box 1174, Montauk, NY 11954

At Montauk's Solé East, guests can relax around the pool on bed-lounges. Aaron Kotowski

The Surf Lodge in Montauk sports a surfing theme throughout, as here in the lobby.

Manager: Bill Keskey, Dune Resorts
Open: Mid-Apr.–mid-Nov.
Price: Moderate–Expensive
Credit Cards: AE, D, MC, V
Special Features: On ocean; private terraces; kitchens; air-conditioning, telephones with voicemail, cable TV/VCR; 2 tennis courts, heated pool; steam baths; workout room; on 8.5 acres; no smoking; children welcome; no pets
Directions: From Montauk's Main St., turn south onto Essex St. Resort is at end.

This luxurious, gray-shingled oceanfront resort, with its 550 feet of private beach, is the classiest resort in downtown Montauk. It has 92 one- and two-bedroom units, each with a modern kitchen, living and dining area, and private terrace for sunbathing; the units in the oceanfront buildings have spectacular views. The resort is located on 8.5 acres that include a pool with brick terraces and wraparound wooden decks, two tennis courts, and landscaped grounds. Most of the units feature a second-story bedroom with a color television in both the living room and bedroom. The decor in the units is attractive and contemporary.

SURF LODGE

631-668-1562
www.surflodge.com
183 Edgemere St., Montauk, NY 11954
General Manager: Nil Erbil
Open: May–Sept.
Price: Very Expensive
Credit Cards: AE, D, MC, V
Special Features: Continental breakfast; some waterside rooms; private sundecks; beach; wireless Internet access, iPod docks, minibars; spa services available; yoga

classes; fitness trainer on staff; live concerts summer weekends; surfing movies in Den and outdoors; lakeside bonfire; surf rafts, kayaks, canoes, bicycles, and stand-up paddleboards for rent; no smoking; children welcome; pets welcome ($100 fee per pet, per stay); shuttle for hotel guests; restaurant with celebrity chef on premises (see listing in chapter 4).

Directions: From Main St. traveling east, turn left at the Chase Bank and go halfway around the semicircle, then turn left onto Edgemere St. Surf Lodge will be on left in 1 mile.

Bonzai Pipeline meets Ditch Plains at this super-cool Hawaiian-surfing-themed party. A sandy beach, a huge deck right at water's edge on Fort Pond, Sunday-night outdoor surfing cinemas, an inside Den running surfing films 24/7, a celebrity chef in the kitchen, and live concerts on the weekends—got the picture? This is a summer happening! Not only that, but if you're looking for waterfront overnight accommodations, the 19 rooms can't be beat. They're romantic, smartly decorated in earth tones with wood floors, sisal rugs, private decks on the water, and with beds facing Fort Pond. The first thing you see in the morning is the gentle, calm water outside your French doors, and the last thing you see at night is the sunset over Fort Pond. What could be more romantic than that?

Quogue
THE INN AT QUOGUE
631-653-6560
www.innatquogue.com
47-52 Quogue St., Quogue
Mailing Address: P.O. Box 521, Quogue, NY 11959
Owner: Rocco and Colette Lettieri
Manager: Julie Czachur
Open: Year-round
Price: Moderate—Very Expensive
Credit Cards: AE, D, MC, V
Special Features: On 5 landscaped acres; pool; spa offering massages; some units

with kitchens; some rooms with flat-screen TVs and wireless Internet access; fine restaurant on premises (see listing in chapter 4); bicycles and beach passes available; no smoking; children welcome; pets permitted in motel-style rooms, but not in main houses; Hampton Jitney stops in front

Directions: From Sunrise Hwy. (Rte. 27), travel south at exit 63 (Rte. 31) to Montauk Hwy. (Rte. 27A), then east to Quogue St. Turn right. Inn is on right in 0.5 mile.

Quogue is known as the "quiet Hampton," and it's so quiet that many don't even consider it a Hampton at all. It's a jewel of a village, composed mostly of gracious old homes on lovely, tree-lined streets. Ideal for walks and bicycling excursions, the streets are wide and flat; there's a bicycle path along Dune Road to the beach. The main building of the Inn at Quogue dates from the early 1800s, but renovations throughout the years, have kept it up to date. All 70 rooms were recently renovated and are now bright and beautiful. Even the former motel rooms, and those in Peconic House, all of which are located across the street from the main inn, have tile baths, pedestal sinks, wainscoted walls, and handsome linens on the beds. My favorites are still the 15 rooms in the main house, however, as they have interesting little nooks and crannies. The Bridal Suite has been decorated in a subdued Ralph Lauren style and has antique painted chests and tables, a fireplace, and a bath with wainscoted walls and whirlpool tub. I also love the one-bedroom cottage, which has a small kitchen, and a private garden in back. There is a nice pool, and guests may use the Quogue village beach and a nearby tennis club. The inn has an attractive restaurant and an inviting bar with a fireplace, where a pianist sometimes performs on weekends. This inn has long been one of my favorites. Hurray for the renovation! It can now be recommended again as an ideal place to truly "get away."

The main building of the Inn at Quogue dates from the 1800s.

SAG HARBOR

AMERICAN HOTEL

631-725-3535

www.theamericanhotel.com

49 Main St., Sag Harbor

Mailing Address: P.O. Box 1349, Sag Harbor, NY 11963

Innkeeper: Ted Conklin

Manager: Tom Allnoch

Open: Year-round

Price: Expensive–Very Expensive

Credit Cards: AE, D, DC, MC, V

Special Features: Continental breakfast; fully stocked minibar; whirlpool tubs; telephones, wireless Internet access, air-conditioning; historic sailboat for charter; fabulous restaurant on premises (see listing in chapter 4); no smoking; children welcome, but rooms accommodate two people only; no pets

Directions: On Main St. in center of village

The American Hotel, that great, early Victorian brick edifice on Sag Harbor's Main Street, dates back to 1846 when Nathan Tinker, a cabinetmaker, made revisions to his building on Main Street to house his cabinet shop. As an adjunct to the shops on the ground floor, he built apartments in back. In 1877 the building was converted to a hotel by Addison Youngs, and with the addition of steam heat, baths, and electric lights, it became one of the most modern hotels on Long Island. Owned by Ted Conklin for more than 35 years, this gem of a hotel retains all of the charm of a fine Victorian inn. The tiny parlor has games of backgammon and checkers awaiting players, and the glass-topped reservation counter displays a selection of fine cigars. The restaurant, considered by many to be the best classical restaurant in the Hamptons, is contained in four main-floor rooms. There are eight spacious and highly distinctive guest rooms in the hotel—all have tall ceilings and are decorated with Victorian and art deco antiques that exude a faded men's-club gentility. There are overstuffed chairs, massive dressers with ornate mirrors, worn antique Oriental rugs, mahogany sleighbeds, Victorian carved-walnut headboards, and brass beds. There are also antique Victorian tables set with

The American Hotel in Sag Harbor has been welcoming guests since 1877. Morgan McGivern

cordials, liquors, and crystal glasses, and accent pieces might include an old manual typewriter or an old radio. All of the baths are private, and each has a tile floor, a Jacuzzi for two, and an impressive array of soaps, shampoos, and lotions. If you have time, definitely inquire about the vintage sailboat that's available to charter.

HARBORWOODS
631-537-6393
www.harborwoodsguesthouse.com
1702 Sag Harbor Tpke., Sag Harbor, NY 11963
Mailing Address: P.O. Box 289, Sagaponack, NY 11962
Innkeeper: Barbro Magnusson
Open: Year-round
Price: Moderate–Expensive
Credit Cards: MC, V
Special Features: Full breakfast; wireless Internet access, air-conditioning; no smoking; children 12 and older welcome; no pets
Directions: Traveling east on Montauk Hwy. (Rte. 27), turn left in Bridgehampton at the traffic light and monument onto Bridgehampton-Sag Harbor Tpke. Go across the RR tracks, and continue for 2–2.5 miles to driveway, which will be on right. Drive around right side of small roadside house to find B&B in back.

Tucked away off a busy road, and in a difficult-to-find but quiet location, Harborwoods is well worth the quest. Barbro Magnusson was born and raised in Sweden, so much of the Old World charm her guests experience in her bed & breakfast is a reflection of her heritage. She and her husband, who is a builder, built this shingled home in 2006. It sits on 0.5 acres adjacent to a nature preserve and Long Pond Greenbelt, so there are numerous nature and hiking trails to explore. Guests love to lounge in the winter in front of the fireplace in the open living-dining room, and in summer to enjoy the peaceful quiet while gazing at the beautiful perennial garden from the screened-in porch. There are four guest rooms and one cottage on the property. Flying Point, the largest of the rooms, has an iron bed and a window seat, as well as a stone-tiled shower in the bathroom. The cottage, the most luxurious of the accommodations, includes a living room with a 46-inch HD flat-screen TV, a small kitchen, and a sleeping loft with a king-sized bed. Barbro serves a full breakfast that may include her popular Swedish pancakes with lingonberries, or a gourmet egg dish.

LIGHTHOUSE ON THE BAY
631-725-7112
59 Mashomack Dr., Sag Harbor, NY 11963
Innkeepers: Regina and Stephen Humanitzki
Open: Year-round
Price: Expensive
Credit Cards: None
Special Features: Full breakfast; water and marsh views; private beach reached by boardwalk; spacious decks; air-conditioning, TVs, robes in rooms; complimentary beach towels and chairs; no smoking; children over eight welcome; no pets
Directions: Provided when reservations made

If you are seeking a wonderfully romantic night in a magical setting, I can't imagine a better place than Lighthouse on the Bay. The panoramic views are positively breath-taking from the living room, dining area, and wraparound decks, as well as from the guest rooms. On one early summer after-noon, I was able to spy on a pair of nesting swans in their marshy habitat nearby. The house was built by Regina and Stephen Humanitzki in 1997 to resemble a light-house (or, more accurately, two lighthouses joined together). "When we bought this property, we had fallen in love with the land and intended renovating a house on the property, but we decided instead to tear it down and start over." The result is a Hamp-tons-style house sheathed in natural shin-gles and on a stone foundation, with flagstone floors, walls of floor-to-ceiling windows, and expansive decks. The Tower Suite, on the second floor, is the premier guest haven. This six-sided room has a fab-ulous view from the bedroom, but the clincher is the observation room reached via a spiral stairway that has a 360-degree water view. There are comfortable sofas up here as well as a TV. The King Room, on the first floor, has a pine sleighbed. My favorite bedroom, however, is the Round Room; it has a round tower of clerestory windows, an expansive view, a private deck (also with a view), a wonderful tile bath with a Jacuzzi enclosed in a mahogany cabinet and a gran-ite surround, and an iron canopy bed draped in gauzy fabric. Regina, who loves to cook, serves a full breakfast that might include fresh fruit, home-baked muffins or bread, and maybe a cheese soufflé or her special French toast.

SOUTHAMPTON
A BUTLER'S MANOR
631-283-8550
www.abutlersmanor.com
244 North Main St., Southampton, NY 11968
Innkeepers: Kimberly and Christopher Allen

Open: Mar.–Dec.
Price: Moderate–Very Expensive
Credit Cards: AE, MC, V
Special Features: On almost 1 acre; pool, gardens; flat-screen TVs with DVD players, MP3 players, wireless Internet access; full breakfast; smoking outside only; children over 12 welcome; no pets
Directions: From County Rd. 59/Rte. 27 traveling east, turn right at traffic light onto North Main St. B&B is seventh house on left.

The gracious, shingled, butter-yellow house on upper Main Street offers extraordinary hospitality. In true upstairs-downstairs tra-dition, guests enjoy the genuine friendli-ness of Chris and Kim Allen, the hands-on owners. Chris is British, you see, and for more than 20 years he worked as a butler at some of the grandest estates in Europe and America. He puts that training to exemplary use as he ministers to the needs of his guests. Best of all, this is one of the prettiest inns around. Built in 1860, it was the manor house of the Jagger family, one of Southampton's early settlers. The spacious, brick-floored living room has maize-col-ored walls enhanced by white trim that includes an entire wall of bookcases. The dining room, on the other hand, has rasp-berry-red walls. The five guest rooms, which all have private baths, are named for estates that Chris managed. Eton Court is reminiscent of the English countryside. It has a king-sized bed, an antique desk and bureau, and a plethora of British crime nov-els, and furthermore, it overlooks the gar-dens. Villefranche is named for a small harbor town on the Côte d'Azur. It has a four-poster rice bed, as well as an antique armoire and writing desk. Oak Knoll, named for an estate on Long Island's gold coast, has a pewter-finished iron bed and an antique mahogany burl armoire. The inn sits on almost an acre that includes a shady lattice-covered arbor, where breakfast is served, weather permitting, and a pool tucked away in a raised secluded spot reached by climbing several stone stairs.

MAINSTAY INN

631-283-4375
www.themainstay.com
579 Hill St., Southampton, NY 11968
Innkeeper: Elizabeth Main
Open: Year-round
Price: Moderate–Very Expensive
Credit Cards: AE, D, MC, V
Special Features: Continental breakfast; pool, gardens; no smoking; well-behaved children welcome; no pets
Directions: About 1 mile west of Southampton on Rte. 27A (Old Montauk Hwy.), also called Hill St.

Elizabeth Main is always doing something new and wonderful to her inn. This 1870s colonial, which began life as a country store, had good "bones" to begin with, including a weathered shingle exterior and white trim. The whimsy of the decor is evident as you enter the foyer, which is sponge-painted in a spring green. The adjacent parlor has dried flowers over the door, a bead board ceiling, and a fireplace. In the kitchen, which is open to guests, a marvelous mural of English climbing roses covers a wall, while in the country dining room, there are sponge-painted ochre walls fancifully painted with grapes, apples, and pears. This room also has wainscoted walls and a great, old woodstove. A country pine cupboard displays a collection of colorful pottery made by Elizabeth that is used for the breakfast meal. Each of the guest rooms is furnished with either an antique iron or a country pine bed. Of the 10 rooms, 7 have private baths, and 3 share a bath. Master Suite (Room 5) has an antique iron bed, a TV, a fireplace, and a wall of books, while Room 6 has a French loveseat and painted hydrangeas climbing the walls in such profusion that the antique iron-and-brass bed seems to be in a garden. In the gardens, iron and wicker furniture provide additional retreats for private breakfasts or afternoon refreshments. There's a secluded pool in the back.

1708 HOUSE

631-287-1708
www.1708house.com
126 Main St., Southampton, NY 11968
Innkeepers: Skip and Lorraine Ralph
Open: Year-round
Price: Moderate–Very Expensive
Credit Cards: AE, MC, V
Special Features: Wine cellar; on 1 acre; continental-plus breakfast; wireless Internet access in some areas; full concierge service; space for small meetings; beach passes provided; no smoking; children over 12 welcome in main house, children under 12 welcome in cottages; no pets
Directions: On Main St., just beyond Saks Fifth Avenue.

I love to see an old building brought back to life. Skeptics had advocated tearing this old house down, but fortunately, Skip and Lorraine Ralph had a better idea. They transformed it into Southampton's finest bed & breakfast. From top to bottom, this inn shines. The house dates to 1648—one of the oldest in Southampton, and remarkably, it has only been owned by three families during that time. The vintage of the house is most evident on the main floor. In the par-

In the heart of Southampton, next door to Saks Fifth Avenue, parts of the 1708 House date to 1648.

lor, for example, there are polished wide-plank pine floors, exposed hand-hewn oak beams, and a wood-manteled fireplace. The elegant antique tables and chairs in the dining room were supplied from the antique shop Lorraine used to own around the corner and are for sale. A small reading room, with tables that may be used for card games in the evening, has another ceiling with hand-hewn beams, a fireplace, and the original paneled walls. Downstairs there's a wine cellar, lined in stone and with another fireplace, where wine and cheese are served as classical music plays in the background. There are 12 guest rooms in the large house and each of them is spacious and luxurious. I love Room #1, a suite in the oldest section, with its beamed ceilings, antique tester bed, and bath with a claw-foot tub. An annex was attached to the house several years ago, which added three beautiful new rooms as well as a spacious private living room with a fireplace for annex guests. There are also three two-bedroom cottages on the property, two with an eat-in kitchen. Gracious flower gardens surround spacious lawns. Guests will enjoy a breakfast of fresh fruit, juice, croissants, bagels, and perhaps a quiche, eaten on fine china and with sterling silver flatware either in the dining room or on the brick terrace.

SOUTHAMPTON COUNTRY HOUSE

631-283-7338
www.shcountryhouse.com
485 North Main St., Southampton, NY 11968
Innkeeper: Colleen D'Italia
Open: May–Aug. daily; Sept., Oct. weekends only; call for availability rest of year
Price: Expensive
Credit Cards: None
Special Features: Full breakfast; heated pool; air-conditioning, flat-screen TVs (no cable); no smoking; children over 12 welcome; no pets
Directions: From Rte. 27/County Rd. 39

traveling east, turn north onto North Main St. at traffic light. B&B is on left in 0.75 mile, just past horse farm.

It's as if Martha, Ralph, and Laura came to play. On the wraparound porch you can sit in pretty wicker chairs or laze away in the hammock, while gazing out at pastures of grazing horses enclosed by neat white fences. This classic Hamptons shingled "cottage" has all the appealing aspects you generally find in larger B&Bs. You enter a beautiful family room/open kitchen with a huge brick fireplace and a pretty window seat dressed in a red-and-white-checked cushion. There's a wonderful collection of flag-related items—birdhouses, painted wooden flags, and more. Beyond, a pool with a brick surround beckons. The King Room has a blue-and-white quilt and is decorated with white wicker; its beautiful black-and-white tile bath has a black marble counter. An entire apartment is the perfect Hamptons hideaway for a family or two couples traveling together. It has a living room, two bedrooms, kitchen, and fully tiled bath. Colleen serves a full country breakfast that might include French toast, pancakes, or an egg dish.

SOUTHAMPTON INN

631-283-6500, 800-832-6500
www.southamptoninn.com
91 Hill St., Southampton, NY 11968
General Manager: Tony Cotignola
Open: Year-round
Price: Moderate–Expensive
Credit Cards: AE, D, DC, MC, V
Special Features: Air-conditioning, wireless Internet service, telephones with voicemail, cable TV, refrigerators; business center; conference facilities; restaurant serving breakfast and dinner; tennis, croquet, volleyball, badminton; heated pool; game room with pool table and children's play area; seasonal shuttle to beach; no smoking; children and pets welcome
Directions: From Main St., turn west onto

The elegant Pondview at Deerfield was built in 2002 specifically to house B& B guests.

Job's Ln. and go through traffic light. Street becomes Hill St. Turn right at first intersection. Hotel is on left.

If you are coming to the Hamptons for a meeting, this would be a terrific spot. Following a total renovation, the Southampton Inn (really a 90-room hotel) is looking better than ever. One enters an elegant lobby and reception area. Beyond, there's a spacious Great Room with a domed ceiling, gas fireplace, and shelves of books for borrowing. It's decorated with classy beige carpeting, sofas, and chairs. French doors open to reveal a grand deck offering views of the abundant flower gardens and lawns. The generous guest rooms have all been updated, and the baths are sparkling with black-and-white tile floors and pedestal sinks. Four of the rooms were decorated by celebrities. Room 18, for example, was designed by Paloma Picasso; it has beige walls, a pine armoire, and terrific artwork on the walls. Ten "romance rooms," located in a separate building, were redesigned in 2002 with luxe Nicole Miller linens. They offer princely, sybaritic retreats. And for those who can't leave home without them, the inn has an exceptional pet program. The pampered pet set is served a continental breakfast of dog or cat food in the library every morning, and dog biscuits and kitty litter are provided free. The lower level of the hotel contains extensive meeting facilities, as well as a restaurant.

WATER MILL
THE PONDVIEW AT DEERFIELD
631-726-7226
www.thepondview.com
1332 Deerfield Road, Water Mill, NY 11976
Innkeeper: Donna Andreassi
Open: Year-round
Price: Moderate–Expensive
Credit Cards: AE, MC, V
Special Features: Full breakfast; on 10

acres; air-conditioning, wireless Internet access, flat-screen TVs, in-room refrigerators stocked with soda and water; exercise room, tennis court, chipping and putting green (clubs provided); beach passes, chairs, and cooler provided; children over 12 welcome; no pets

Directions: Take Long Island Expwy. (I-495) east to exit 70 (Manorville) and follow Rte. 111 south to Sunrise Hwy. (Rte. 27). Follow this east toward Montauk. Go 0.2 mile past the Water Mill traffic light and turn left onto Deerfield Rd. Follow for approx. 2 miles; inn is on the left through two brick pillars. Go across bridge and stop at first door of house.

This elegant new shingle-style Hamptons classic home was designed specifically to accept overnight guests; they have their own entrance, their own exercise room, their own upstairs lounge with a TV and books, and two beautiful rooms, plus a wonderful cottage in the woods in which to luxuriate. "Sunset," the room facing west, is decorated in soothing blues and has oak furniture and a Corian counter in the bath, while "Sunrise" (facing east, obviously) is in sage greens. The shingled cottage is truly fabulous. It has a welcoming front porch filled with wicker furniture and looks out on a peaceful pond. There are two bedrooms, a full kitchen, a living room, and a dining area. You would be comfortable staying here all summer. It has cable TV/VCR, an individual telephone line, and even a washer and dryer. The beautifully landscaped grounds are as lovely as the house and impeccably maintained. This is one of my top choices in the Hamptons.

OTHER ACCOMMODATIONS

There are so many inns, B&Bs, cabins, motels, and resorts in the Hamptons that it is impossible to describe them all. Nevertheless, here are a few additional entries. The codes at the end of each listing indicate whether it is a bed & breakfast (B), a series of cabins (C), a motel (M), or a full-service resort (R).

AMAGANSETT

White Sands Motel on the Ocean (631-267-3350; www.whitesands-resort.com; 28 Shore Rd.; P.O. Box 747, Amagansett, NY 11930) Owners: Bernhard Kiembock and Sara Mendoza. Price: Inexpensive–Expensive. Open mid-Apr.–mid-Oct. Twenty units; on ocean; private location; spotlessly maintained; outdoor grill area; family-operated; no-smoking motel; children welcome; no pets; *highly recommended.* D, MC, V. (M)

BRIDGEHAMPTON

The Enclave Inn (www.enclaveinn.com.; 877-998-0800 or 631-537-2900) The Enclave Inn is not a single destination, but a collection of five lodging establishments, mostly located in former motels. They are: Bridgehampton: 2668 Montauk Hwy.; mailing address P.O. Box 623; Bridgehampton, NY 11932; Southampton: 450 County Rd. 39, Southampton, NY 11968; Southampton: 52 Longview, Southampton, NY 11968; Southampton: 300 Montauk Hwy. Southampton, NY 11968; Wainscott: 380 Montauk Hwy.; mailing address P.O. Box 1301, Wainscott, NY 11975. Owners: Michael and Suzy Wudyka; Manager: Marta Wawrzeniuk. Price: Inexpensive–Expensive. Open year-round. This quintet of neat and trim former motels has been thoroughly renovated and offers clean, well-maintained rooms. Pool; flat-screen TVs; wireless Internet in some locations; cable TV; air-conditioning; children welcome; no-smoking; no pets. AE, MC, V. (M)

EAST HAMPTON

Cove Hollow (631-324-7730 or 212-580-8614 or 917-887-8494; www.covehollow.com; 145 Cove Hollow Rd., East Hampton; mailing address: P.O. Box 2234, East Hampton, NY 11937) Owner: Ann Colonomos. Price: Moderate. Not actually a B&B, this cottage is the perfect alternative for a family or a group of friends, but it's rented by the week only. There are four bedrooms and three full baths in the house, as well as a cozy living room with cable TV, VCR/DVD capability and wireless Internet access. The grounds are beautifully landscaped and there's a pool, hammock, gas grill, outdoor shower, and beach bikes. A beach pass to East Hampton beaches is provided too. (B)

Getaway House (631-324-4622; www.getawayhouse.com; 4 Neighborhood House Dr., East Hampton; Mailing Address: P.O. Box 2609, East Hampton, NY 11937) Owner: Johnny Kelman. Price: Moderate–Expensive. Open: Year-round. Located in a rural wooded setting north of the village, this Hamptons-shingled home offers four guest rooms and one suite. Some rooms share a bath, but there's a pool, a continental breakfast is served, bicycles are available to rent ($15), and beach passes are provided for East Hampton beaches; no smoking; children welcome in suite only; no pets. (B)

HAMPTON BAYS

Bowen's by the Bays (631-728-1158, 800-533-3139; www.bowensbythebays.com; 177 West Montauk Hwy., Hampton Bays, NY 11946) Owners/Managers: Kevin and Eileen Bowen. Price: Inexpensive–Expensive. Open: motel units Apr.–Oct., cottages year-round. 16 units (9 motel rooms, 7 cottages with 1-2 bedrooms); on 3.5 acres; pool; lighted tennis court; playground; putting green; horseshoe pit; shuffleboard; kitchens; cable TV/VCR; air-conditioning; smoking outside only; children welcome; pets permitted with prior permission, $20 fee, per pet, per day; *highly recommended*. AE, D, MC, V. (C) (M)

The Hampton Maid (631-728-4166; www.hamptonmaid.com; 259 Montauk Hwy.; mailing address: P.O. Box 713, Hampton Bays, NY 11946) Owner: The Poulakis family. Price: Moderate–Expensive. Open: Apr.–Oct. 30 units; on 5 acres; pool; antiques and collectibles shop; cable TV; refrigerators; wet bars; air-conditioning; telephones; restaurant (breakfast only); playground; no-smoking; children welcome; no pets. AE, MC, V. (M)

Inn Spot on the Bay (631728-1200; www.theinnspot.com; 32 Lighthouse Road, Hampton Bays, NY 11946) Owners: Colette Connor and Pam Wolfert. Price: Inexpensive–Moderate. Open: Year-round. Four rooms in a charming 1857 house at water's edge, plus eight "villas"; all with cable TV and air-conditioning. Excellent restaurant on premises (see listing in chapter 4); no smoking; children welcome; pets allowed in two of the villas $35/night. AE, MC, V. (I)

MONTAUK

Gurney's Inn Resort & Spa (631-668-2345; www.gurneys-inn.com; 290 Old Montauk Hwy., Montauk, NY 11954) General Manager: Paul Monte. Price: Moderate–Very Expensive. Open year-round. On a high bluff overlooking the ocean, this resort with 109 guest rooms and 5 romantic cottages, as well as a full-service spa, has been welcoming guests for almost 90 years, and was the first spa on the East Coast. There are two restaurants, a pool, tennis, and conference facilities; no smoking; children welcome; no pets. AE, D, MC V (R)

Lenhart Cottages (631-668-2356; www.montauklife.com; 421 Old Montauk Hwy., Montauk, NY 11954) Manager: Ronald Weiss. Price: Moderate–Very Expensive. Open year-round. 12 individual cottages, ranging from studios to two-bedroom units; shingled exterior; ocean view; log-burning fireplaces; kitchens; pool; flat-screen cable TV/VCR; wireless Internet access; CD player; air-conditioning; no smoking requested; children welcome; pets permitted, but inquire first; *highly recommended.* MC, V. (C)

Second House Tavern (631-668-2877; www.secondhousetavern.com; 161 Second House Rd., Montauk, NY 11954) Managing Partner: Addy Monahan. Price: Moderate–Expensive. Open: Mar.–Dec. Eight individual cottages are tucked away on this mostly restaurant property (see listing in chapter 4) and they were all beautifully updated in 2008, with pine floors, whitewashed pine-plank walls, flat-screen TVs, and Wi-Fi. Modern baths have white subway-tiled showers. No smoking; children welcome; pets welcome with a deposit (inquire first).

Snug Harbor Motel and Marina (631-668-2860; www.montauksnugharbor.com; 3 Star Island Rd., Montauk, NY 11954) Manager: Cynthia Brauch. Price: Inexpensive–Expensive. Open Mar.–Thanksgiving. 34 units, ranging from studios to one-bedroom apartments; on lake; some kitchens; pool; marina; playground; bicycles; outdoor grill area; waterskiing; volleyball court; telephones; cable TV; air-conditioning; no-smoking; children welcome; pets with prior permission. AE, D, MC, V. (M)

Solé East Beach (631-668-6700; www.soleeast.com; 107 S. Emerson Ave., Montauk, NY 11954) Owner: Dave Ceva; Price: Inexpensive–Expensive; Open: May–Oct. 26 motel rooms with the same owner as the über chic Solé East, and with many of the same amenities, although the decor was a mix of old and new at press time—upgrades are in the works, however. Across street from beach; wireless Internet access; flat-screen HD cable TV; air-conditioning; no smoking; children welcome; pets welcome with fee of $150–$200 per pet, per stay. (M)

Stone Lion Inn (631-668-7050; www.harvest2000.com; 51 Edgemere Rd., P.O. Box 5028, Montauk, NY 11954) Owner: John Erb. Manager: Laurel Edwards and Walter Tarone. Price: Inexpensive–Moderate. Open year-round. 11 rooms, all with porches overlooking Fort Pond, and with sparkling, newly tiled baths; fine restaurant (East by Northeast, known as ENE—see listing in chapter 4) on premises; cable TV; air-conditioning; coffeemaker; no smoking; children welcome; no pets. MC, V. (M)

SAG HARBOR

Sag Harbor Inn (631-725-2949; www.sagharborinn.com; 45 West Water St.; mailing address: P.O. Box 2661, Sag Harbor, NY 11963) Manager: Erin Jenkins. Price: Inexpensive–Very Expensive. Open year-round. 42 units in a hotel-style building, most with balconies or patios and some overlooking the bay and furnished with reproduction 18th-century pine beds; cable TV; telephones; smoking permitted in some rooms/designated no-smoking rooms; continental breakfast; pool; air-conditioning; children welcome; no pets. AE, MC, V. (M)

SOUTHAMPTON

The Atlantic (631-283-6100; www.hrhresorts.com; 1655 County Rd. 39, Southampton, NY 11968) Owner: David Waksman. Price: Moderate–Very Expensive. Open: year-round. Following a total renovation of a formerly tired motel, this 62-unit inn can now be *highly recommended.* There are tile baths, iron beds, fine linens, and plenty of space. Each unit has a minibar, coffeemakers, hair dryer, iron and ironing board, cable TV/VCR, duel-line telephones with dataports, wireless Internet access, CD players, and much more.

On 5 acres of landscaped grounds, there are a pool and gazebo, two Har-Tru tennis courts, beach parking permits, and hammocks. Continental breakfast served; no smoking; children welcome/under 12 free; pets welcome, $40/night pet fee. AE, MC, V. (M)

The Capri (631-283-6100); www.hrhresorts.com; 281 County Rd. 39A, Southampton, NY 11968) Owner: David Waksman. Price: Very Expensive. Open: Weekends only Mem. Day–Labor Day. This 30-room motel is one of the hottest weekend spots in the Hamptons thanks to the Pink Elephant Night Club and the very cool Day & Night Restaurant located here, so it's not the place to come for a quiet snooze, but the rooms are chic (although small) with plush bed dressings, TV/VCRs, min bars, and CD players; there's a pool and lots of action, so if you're hip and young, this is the place to be; no smoking; adults (21 and older) only; no pets. AE, MC, V. (M)

Village Latch (631-283-2160, 1-800-54-LATCH; www.villagelatch.com; 101 Hill St., Southampton; mailing address: P.O. Box 3000, Southampton, NY 11968) Innkeepers: Martin White and Marta Byer White. Price: Moderate–Very Expensive. Open: Year-round. Located in the center of town, this 65-room inn offers a variety of rooms in a very eclectic setting. There are rooms in the big white building that is the centerpiece of the establishment, as well as rooms in additional buildings scattered throughout the 5-acre property; continental breakfast; heated pool; tennis court; no smoking; children welcome; pets welcome in some rooms. AE, D, MC, V. (I)

WESTHAMPTON BEACH

Dune Deck Beach Resort (631-288-3876; www.dunedeck.com; 379 Dune Rd., Westhampton Beach, NY; mailing address: P.O. Box 1748; Westhampton Beach, NY 11978) Manager: Joanne Clark. Price: Expensive–Very Expensive. Open: Mem. Day–mid-Sept. On the ocean, offering 71 rooms with a laid-back, beachy attitude that includes an outdoor restaurant (Saltwater Grill) with picnic-style tables under canvas roofs, live music on weekends, and a seafood menu; club memberships available; pool; 2 tennis courts; basketball; beach volleyball; no smoking; children welcome; no pets. AE, MC, V.

Westhampton Bath and Tennis Hotel and Marina (631-288-2500; www.bath&tennis .com; 231 Dune Rd.; mailing address: P.O. Box 1727, Westhampton Beach, NY 11978) Price: Expensive–Very Expensive. Open Mem. Day–end of Oct. As we went to press, this hotel and resort were in the midst of an ownership change; all information may not be accurate. On the ocean with private beach and beautiful views; heated pool; five tennis courts; club memberships available; marina across street; fitness center; hair salon; day spa; playground; no smoking; children welcome; no pets. AE, MC, V. (R)

Westhampton Seabreeze Motel (631-288-6886; www.westhamptonseabreeze.com; 19 Seabreeze Ave., Westhampton Beach, NY 11977) Manager: Erlene Wood. Price: Inexpensive–Moderate. Open: Year-round. It's hard to find such an exceptional value in the Hamptons, so this clean motel, tucked away on a side street off Montauk Highway, is a real treasure. There are pine beds and dressers and tile baths with glass-enclosed showers—it's basic but clean, and definitely priced right. No smoking; children welcome; pets allowed for a $50 charge. AE, D, DC, MC, V. (M)

4

FROM THE BOUNTY OF THE LAND

Restaurants & Food Purveyors

Strange to see how a good dinner and feasting reconciles everybody.
—Samuel Pepys, Diary, *November 9, 1660*

When the renowned Manhattan restaurateur Henri Soulé opened his summer restaurant in the village of East Hampton in 1954, he launched a trend. Lured by the abundance of farm-fresh vegetables and fruit, fish from local waters, and duck from nearby duck farms, he created a respect and appreciation for local cuisine that has increased every year. Not only did he attract gourmet diners who couldn't abide a summer away from the elegant cuisine that he had made famous at Le Pavillon, but he also lured other fine chefs to the Hamptons. Pierre Franey, his executive chef in New York, followed him to the area, as did Craig Claiborne, food editor for the *New York Times,* and chef and author Michael Field as well. Soulé had started something. Where fish houses on the docks had once prevailed, appreciation for the finer nuances of food preparation was gaining ground.

Today, Henri Soulé would be proud of Hamptons chefs and the cuisine they are creating; the dishes are inventive, well presented, and, in general, prepared in healthful ways. Butter and cream-based sauces have been replaced by those made of vegetable reductions. Fresh local seafood and produce, the pride of the Hamptons, are used cleverly and well.

Henri Soulé's original restaurant lived on under a variety of names, until 2007, but the building in which it is housed is now strictly a

In summer, the sidewalk tables at Beach Bakery Cafe are filled with happy noshers.

75

B&B called the Hedges Inn. Other long-standing restaurants, such as c/o The Maidstone (formerly the Maidstone Arms), located just down the street, and Sag Harbor's venerable 1846 American Hotel are still recognized for their terrific food and fine wine. For the most part, however, fresh new restaurants set the tone for Hamptons eateries.

Restaurants specializing in American cuisine have surpassed their Italian and French cousins in popularity on the East End, and although high-end gustatory legends still draw appreciative clients, a trend toward casual, more affordable restaurants has taken a firm hold. Naturally, fine seafood restaurants are also in abundance, and fish houses on the docks of Montauk, Hampton Bays, and East Quogue allow diners to watch as the catch of the day is transferred from boat to dock to table.

The decor of choice has developed into what is now recognized as "Hamptons style"—a distinctive blend of spare furnishings, polished wood or tile floors, and white or beige walls, all blending together to offer a subdued, chic backdrop for the cuisine. But these embellishments can't compare to nature's own. The standout restaurants offering dining with spectacular water (and often sunset) views are one of the glories of Hamptons dining. From Westhampton Beach, Southampton, and Hampton Bays, to East Hampton, Sag Harbor, and Montauk, the views are spectacular.

This chapter is not intended to offer a critical review of all of the restaurants in the Hamptons. If a restaurant does not meet the criteria that would allow for its recommendation, it has not been included. Furthermore, there are so many fine restaurants in the Hamptons that space precludes including every single one. Instead, I have incorporated only those that I believe are the very best. I welcome your comments, however.

When deciding which restaurants to include, I considered the same criteria I use for the Zagat Survey—food, decor, and service. The excellence of the cuisine and the expertise of the chef in preparing and presenting it are certainly key factors. But the overall comfort level and inviting appeal of a restaurant are equally important, as are the service and attitude of the staff. Especially in better restaurants, it is imperative that the staff know which ingredients are used in a dish and understand its preparation. It is also important—especially on Long Island's East End, where wine has assumed such a prominent role—to have knowledgeable staff who can make specific wine recommendations and who appreciate the pairing of wines with various appetizers, entrées, and desserts.

A concerted effort has also been made to include the best cafés and budget-priced restaurants. It is my intention to profile the restaurants that offer the best dining experiences in the Hamptons in a broad range of price categories.

As much information as possible about each restaurant has been included. Rather than indicating the exact hours that each restaurant is open, however, I have specified the meals that are served (see "Serving Codes" below). In the information block included with each restaurant, abbreviations are used for accepted credit cards. In addition, price codes, rather than specific prices, are indicated. These codes are based on the average cost of a meal for one person, including appetizer, entrée, and dessert, but not cocktails, wine, tax, or tip. Many Hamptons restaurants offer prix fixe menus at exceptionally low prices off-season. This is a great way to eat out without breaking the bank. Be aware that days and hours of operation change with the season. It's always best to call ahead.

The restaurants are listed alphabetically according to the village in which they are located. If you are not sure in which town a restaurant is located, please refer to the index at the back of the book. Restaurants on the North Fork and on Shelter Island are included in the listings in chapters 9 and 10.

Serving Codes
B: Breakfast; BR: Brunch; D: Dinner; HT: High Tea; L: Lunch; LN: Late Night

Credit Cards
AE: American Express; D: Discover; DC: Diner's Club; MC: MasterCard; V: Visa

Price Categories

Inexpensive	Up to $30	Expensive	$50–$80
Moderate	$30–$50	Very Expensive	$80 or more

RESTAURANTS

AMAGANSETT
INDIAN WELLS TAVERN
631-267-0400
177 Main St., Amagansett
Mailing Address: P.O. Box 1159, Amagansett, NY 11930
Owners: Kevin Boles and Chris Eggert
Chef: Tony Sales
Manager: Patty Sales
Cuisine: American
Serving: B (Sat. and Sun. only) L, D
Open: Year-round
Price: Inexpensive–Moderate
Credit Cards: AE, D, MC, V
Reservations: None
Directions: On Rte. 27 in center of village.

In the space that was formerly occupied by Estia's Cantina, local restaurateurs Kevin Boles and Chris Eggert, who also own Cherrystones in East Hampton, opened this casual, and comfortable, eatery. The restaurant has an open floor plan, with the bar area on one side of a frosted-glass divider and the café on the other. Polished wood floors, brick walls, a pressed-tin ceiling, and black-and-white photos on the walls provide a backdrop for offerings that include burgers, fajitas, fish and chips, and chicken potpie. There are no pretenses here. Jeans are OK, families are welcome, and you don't need to raid the piggy bank.

THE LOBSTER ROLL RESTAURANT
631-267-3740
www.lobsterroll.com
1980 Montauk Hwy., Amagansett
Mailing Address: P.O. Box 1320, Amagansett, NY 11930
Owner/Manager: Andrea Terry
Cuisine: Seafood
Serving: L, D
Open: May–Oct.; daily in summer, weekends-only early and late in season
Price: Inexpensive–Expensive
Credit Cards: MC, V
Special Features: Wheelchair access; outdoor dining; family oriented
Reservations: None
Directions: Located on Rte. 27, about 4 miles east of Amagansett

Everyone knows it as "Lunch" because of the huge red neon sign on the roof, but don't be fooled; dinner is also served. There are no pretensions here. It's a roadside fish shack with paper place-mats on picnic tables, butter in foil, and good, fresh fish at reasonable prices. Most of the fish is caught locally. Fish and chips and the tender, juicy puffers (blowfish) are prepared in a finger-lickin'-good tempura batter, and the creamy tartar sauce is so good we wish it was served in larger cups. A specialty of the house is, of course, the lobster roll, but there's a lot more on the menu, too, including seafood platters, fresh flounder in season, and tuna burgers. The wine and beer list is limited. Desserts include pies made by owner Andrea Terry. The fresh fruit pies, such as peach, raspberry, and blueberry, are fabulous. This is a great place to bring the kids, as plate sharing is approved, and toys are provided.

MEETING HOUSE
631-267-2764
www.meetinghouseamagansett.com
4 Amagansett Sq. Dr., Amagansett, NY
11930
Mailing Address: P.O. Box 266, Amagansett,
NY 11930
Owner: Randy Lerner
Chef: Tim Bando
Cuisine: American
Serving: D
Open: Year-round
Price: Inexpensive–Expensive
Credit Cards: AE, D, MC, V
Special Features: In quaint little shopping
plaza with park in center; porch seating
Reservations: Parties of six or more
Directions: From Main St. in Amagansett
going east, turn right onto Hedges Ln., then
turn right into parking lot.

Randy Lerner, who also owns the Cleveland
Browns football team, as well as the Reform
Club (see listing in chapter 3) in Amagansett, has transformed cute little Amagansett Square into a charming series of
shops and restaurants. There are art galleries, clothing stores, home furnishings
shops, and restaurants, including this
delightful café, all occupying enchanting
restored cottages. This little cottage has a
barn-like open ceiling and paned windows
that give it a light and airy ambience. Dark
wood floors, white walls, and wooden
booths offer an inviting setting for the
American dishes that include a popular mac
'n' cheese and a meatloaf. In warm weather,
the porch is a decidedly alluring place to
enjoy a meal.

BRIDGEHAMPTON
BOBBY VAN'S
631-537-0590
www.bobbyvans.com
2393 Main St., Bridgehampton
Mailing Address: P.O. Box 3055, Bridgehampton, NY 11932
Owners: Joe Hickey and Joseph Smith

Manager: James Phair
Chef: John Stella
Cuisine: American steak house
Serving: D, L, BR
Open: Year-round; D daily; L Mon.–Fri.; BR
Sat. and Sun.
Price: Expensive–Very Expensive; prix fixe
offered Sept.–June.
Credit Cards: AE, D, MC, V
Special Features: Wheelchair access; raw
bar; pianist
Reservations: Recommended
Directions: On Montauk Hwy. (Rte. 27) in
center of village

The venerable name lingers on, but except
for the original bar and its collection of
celebrity photographs, this is a shiny new
version of the old. The dark room with its
quiet, seductive corners has been replaced
with closely packed tables, divided occa-
sionally by floor-to-ceiling potted palms.
There are ceiling fans and bistro chairs; the
piano has been moved to the window, and a
pianist plays all evening. It's a thoroughly
1990s place cloaked in 1960s nostalgia.
Crowds pack the place, even in the winter.
In the summer, the French doors open
directly onto the sidewalk. The menu
includes a good selection of seafood and
pastas, but unless you're a vegetarian, don't
pass up one of Bobby Van's tender, succulent steaks, accompanied by a side of
creamed spinach.

COPA WINE BAR & TAPAS
631-613-6469
www.copawineandtapas.com
95 School St., Bridgehampton
Mailing Address: P.O. Box 1440 Bridge-
hampton, NY 11932
Owner: Cosmo Venneri and Chris
Boudouris
Chef: Eddy Phooprasert
Managers: Abe Versprille and Rudolphe
Siffredi
Cuisine: Spanish
Serving: D, LN

Pierre Weber's vintage Citroen is often parked out in front of his wonderful French restaurant.   Dustin Chase

Open: Year-round
Price: Inexpensive–Very Expensive
Credit Cards: AE, MC, V
Special Features: Windows open to sidewalk; small plates; open late with late-night menu
Reservations: None
Directions: From Main St., turn onto School St. at Community Center; restaurant on left

This new entry into the Hamptons dining scene arrived in the summer of 2009, after a total renovation of the space that used to house 95 School St. and Alison. There's a handsome zinc horseshoe bar in the center of the restaurant that's a popular spot to nosh on one or two (or more) small plates, while sipping and chatting. The handsome wood walls and ceiling are made of poplar, there's a red leather banquette on one side and tall tables on the other, and industrial lighting and venting lend a chic, with-it attitude to the place. Chef Eddy Phooprasert, a graduate of Le Cordon Bleu in Paris, last worked at Steve Wynn's in Las Vegas. The inventive menu gives patrons the opportunity to order as little or as much

Guitars, movie posters, and vintage Mexican postcards line the walls of the Blue Parrot Bar & Grill.

as they want. Most portions are small, so you might enjoy an appetizer and first course before deciding on whether to sample an entrée. Whatever you decide, do place an order for *cocas* (Spanish flatbread) for the table, and heed the suggestions of the knowledgeable waitstaff. And do try one of the unusual desserts, prepared by pastry chef Lori Gilmore, such as the *pera a la Sangria*, a pear poached in Sangria, plated beside a blue cheese cheesecake and served with a rosemary sauce. You'll want more than one.

PIERRE'S
631-537-5110
www.pierresbridgehampton.com
2468 Main St., Bridgehampton
Mailing Address: P.O. Box 2200, Bridge-hampton, NY 11932
Owner/Chef: Pierre Weber
Cuisine: Light seasonal French, with an emphasis on seafood
Serving: L, D, BR
Open: Year-round; D daily; L Mon.–Thurs.; BR Fri.–Sun.
Price: Expensive–Very Expensive; prix fixe offered
Credit Cards: AE, MC, V
Special Features: Patisserie and homemade ice cream on premises; sidewalk dining; late-night bar; live entertainment
Reservations: Recommended
Directions: On Montauk Hwy. (Rte. 27) in center of village

Francophiles unite at this Gallic-inspired eatery, which opened in the summer of 2002. The large bar in front is a natural meeting place for those who like to see and be seen, and the mellow oak floors, ornate tin ceiling, and tables covered with white butcher paper present just the right pseudo-French-bistro setting. In back there are seafoam-green banquettes, white-wainscoted walls, and black-and-white photos of brides on the walls, as well as a little alcove with shelves of books. Owner-chef Pierre Weber buys his ingredients locally, so the menu changes with the seasons. You might start a meal with the luscious tarte *flambée Alsacienne aux lardons et oignons,* a wonderful medley of cheese, onions, and bacon on a thin tart crust, and follow that with Weber's versions of Montauk striped bass. A *crêpe au chocolat chaud* is a wonderful ending. Pastries, which are available for take-out or eat-in, are delectable, as is the ice cream. Tables are set up on the sidewalk in balmy weather and on weekends the bar stays open late, while guest enjoy live music. This is a terrific addition to the Hamptons dining scene.

WORLD PIE
631-537-7999
2402 Main St., Bridgehampton
Mailing Address: P.O. Box 1012, Bridge-
hampton, NY 11932
Owner: Michael Mannino
Chef: Ed Hannibal
Cuisine: Global Italian
Serving: L, D, BR (Sat., Sun.)
Open: Year-round, daily
Price: Moderate
Credit Cards: AE, MC, V
Special Features: Outdoor dining; bocci
court
Reservations: None
Directions: On Main St. near Corwith Ave.

When Bridgehampton's popular eatery Karen Lee's, which had occupied this spot for many years, closed in 1999, Michael Mannino seized the opportunity. Michael has been in the restaurant business for many years (his family owns O'Mally's), so he's definitely not a neophyte. And his "global Italian" menu is unique and ambitious. He features not only wood-oven pizzas, pastas, entrée salads, and panini sandwiches, but also a range of veal and chicken dishes, and there might be an Asian spin on dishes every once in a while. There's an outside patio for summer dining and a bocci court to while away a pleasant afternoon or evening.

EAST HAMPTON
BLUE PARROT BAR & GRILL
631-329-2583
www.blueparroteasthampton.com
33A Main St., East Hampton, NY 11937
Manager: Andrew Chapman and Roland
Eisenberg
Cuisine: Tex-Mex and Regional Mexican
Serving: L, D
Open: Year-round daily
Price: Inexpensive–Moderate
Credit Cards: AE, MC, V
Special Features: Limited wheelchair
access; covered patio
Reservations: None
Directions: From Main St., walk down a
narrow mews (walkway) to the restaurant,
next to Park Pl. parking lot.

If star power alone can ensure the success of a restaurant, then the newly resurrected Blue Parrot is a hands-down winner. Although the restaurant closed in 2006, its demise had been lamented far and wide. To the rescue came Jon Bon Jovi, Renée Zellweger, Ron Perelman, and Larry Gagosian. The doors reopened in the summer of 2009, and it's been packed again ever since. The restaurant is tucked away in a little courtyard between Main Street and the Park Place parking lot, well removed from the hustle and bustle of Main. The hefty "Dirty Bird" margaritas are being served again in mason jars, and the decor is funky, original, and very casual—just like it was before. The floor is painted sky blue, there's a rough-hewn wood bar, and brightly painted walls feature guitars, movie posters, and vintage Mexican postcards. The taquitos (soft tacos) are back with a choice of fillings, the quesadillas come with grilled steak or chicken or cheese, and you can even get a vegetarian burrito. My favorite, however, is the Blue Parrot tortilla pie, a layered dish of tortilla chips, chicken, cheese, and poblano chile sauce. Yummm! It's a very local, casual spot, where on Dirty Bird Tuesdays, local East Hampton residents are offered food and drink specials and the opportunity to purchase a Blue Parrot T-shirt. Who knows, some night, if you're lucky, Jon Bon Jovi might wander in, take a guitar from the wall, and launch into a song or two, just as he did one Fourth of July.

CAFE MAX

631-324-2004
www.unhampton.com
85 Montauk Hwy., East Hampton, NY 11937
Owners/Managers: Max and Nancy Weintraub
Chef: Max Weintraub
Cuisine: New American/Eclectic
Serving: D, BR (Sun. off-season only)
Open: mid-Feb–Dec.; D daily, except closed Tues.; Oct.–Dec. and mid-Feb–May, BR Sun.
Price: Moderate–Expensive; prix fixe offered
Credit Cards: MC, V
Special Features: Limited wheelchair access; award-winning wine list
Reservations: Weekdays for five or more; weekends for three or more.
Directions: On Rte. 27 at Cove Hollow Rd.

The greeting and the decor at Cafe Max are warm and inviting. There are rough-sawn cedar walls, a cathedral ceiling, natural oak floors, and paisley drapes that give the space a country feel. Photographs of Nancy's family line the walls of the bar. We love the food at Cafe Max. The crab cake appetizers are light and fluffy, and the salmon is roasted with honey mustard and dill. The wine list has been winning the Wine Spectator Award of Excellence since 1995. Most of the wines are from California, although there are some excellent Long Island choices—and a nice range is available by the glass every night. There are early-bird and prix fixe options almost every night, making this one of the most affordable restaurants in East Hampton.

CITTANUOVA

631-324-6300
www.cittanuova.com
29 Newtown Ln., East Hampton, NY 11937
Owner: Ben Krupinski
Manager and Sommelier: Carolyn Papetti
Chef: James Gee
Cuisine: Italian
Serving: L, D
Open: Year-round
Price: Moderate
Credit Cards: AE, MC, V
Special Features: Patio and sidewalk seating
Reservations: None
Directions: From Main St. turn north onto Newtown Ln. Restaurant on left.

When local builder Ben Krupinski takes on a project, you can depend on exceptional workmanship and a classy end product— and this trattoria is no exception. He transformed the former Grill into one of the most popular restaurants in East Hampton. Part of Cittanuova's attraction, at least for those who like to see and be seen, lies in its location along busy Newtown Lane. Tables sit at sidewalk-edge, where it's easy to take in all the activity, especially in summer. On the other hand, for those so inclined, there are indoor tables, or you can dine on the patio in back. The main reason it's so popular, however, is the excellent and affordable Italian food. You'll find pastas and pizzas, but the stars are the entrées, such as roasted whole branzino (sea bass) and peppercorn-crusted yellowfin tuna. This is a local hot spot in the off-season, as well, when Italian-wine classes, Italian-language classes, and Monday-night football-trivia contests bring in the crowds.

DELLA FEMINA

631-329-6666
www.dellafemina.com
99 North Main St., East Hampton
Mailing Address: P.O. Box 4215, East Hampton, NY 11937
Owners: Jerry Della Femina and Judy Licht
Manager: Walter Struble
Chef: Michael Rozzi
Cuisine: Globally influenced, seasonal American cuisine
Serving: D, BR (off-season only)
Open: Year-round
Price: Expensive–Very Expensive; prix fixe offered
Credit Cards: AE, DC, MC, V
Special Features: Wheelchair access; fireplace; dining on outside terrace
Reservations: Definitely
Directions: From Main St., continue past traffic light and turn left at fork before windmill. Drive past windmill (on right) and under railroad trestle. Restaurant is on left at first traffic signal.

When Jerry Della Femina opened this restaurant in 1991, it was an immediate hit, and it's continued to be. Everything just runs so smoothly. A profusion of colorful flowers spills from windowboxes in the summer. The bar is light and airy, and it's fun to join the game of seeing how many of the caricatures of local luminaries on the wall you can identify. There's abundant space between tables in the quiet, elegant dining room, which is decorated mostly in subdued, earthy beiges and whites. The food is first-class. One night, for an appetizer, we had a delicious chilled tuna salad with sesame aioli, hearts of palm, avocado, and scallions. Brioche-crusted rack of lamb comes with a potato and onion tart and local vegetables. The wine list is extensive, but you can bring that special bottle from your own cellar, as long as you pay the $30 corkage fee. Definitely save room for the decadent, warm dark chocolate soufflé with caramel sauce and gelato. The desserts, like the entrées, are not just served, but beautifully presented, and worth every calorie.

EAST HAMPTON POINT

631-329-2800
www.easthamptonpoint.com
295 Three Mile Harbor Rd., East Hampton, NY 11937
Owner: Ben Krupinski
Manager: Caroline Scarpinato
Chef: Craig Attwood
Cuisine: New Contemporary American
Serving: L, D, BR (Sun. only)
Open: Mem. Day–Labor Day; D daily, L height of season, BR Sun.
Price: Moderate–Very Expensive; prix fixe offered
Credit Cards: AE, MC, V
Special Features: Wheelchair access; guest cottages on premises; marina on premises; smoking on outside deck; fabulous water and sunset views; outside dining; boat dock
Reservations: Highly recommended
Directions: From Main St., turn left just before Hook Windmill onto North Main St. After two streetlights, road forks. Take left fork onto Three Mile Harbor Rd.; restaurant is on left in about 4 miles.

The outside deck at East Hampton Point is a popular spot for both lunch and dinner.

Were someone unfortunate enough to have time for only one restaurant dinner while in the Hamptons in the summer, I would recommend East Hampton Point. The food and service are excellent, and the sunset view is stunning. Brilliant pink, orange, and red streak across the sky and reflect in the calm waters of Three Mile Harbor, where the slap of sailboat rigging against masts provides soothing background music. Happy memories invariably result. The tiered dining room provides a watery view from every seat by the use of cleverly placed mirrors, and the crisp, marine blue-and-white decor is so subtle that it offers no distractions. Even the bar has a special attraction; a polished mahogany 5.5-liter sloop with a mast that reaches to the cupola in the ceiling, and divides the bar from the restaurant. Even so, the spacious deck is the place to be on a clear, warm night. The entrées are straightforward and expertly prepared. Seared local sea scallops come over sweet corn polenta with a pancetta and watercress salad. One of our favorite desserts is the lemon-lime tart in an almond cookie crust, topped with Italian meringue. A portion of the deck is dedicated to casual dining and cocktails; a lighter menu is available here. Sailors arrive in their yachts from nearby estates with their weekend guests in tow for the generous buffet brunch on Sunday. (See listing in chapter 3 for guest rooms.)

FRESNO

631-324-8700
www.fresnorestaurant.com
8 Fresno Place, East Hampton, NY 11937
Owner: David Loewenberg
Chef: Gretchen Menser
Cuisine: New American
Serving: D
Open: Year-round, but closed Tues.

Price: Moderate–Expensive; early-bird and prix fixe available
Credit Cards: AE, MC, V
Special Features: Zinc-topped bar, outdoor seating
Reservations: Suggested; can eat at bar
Directions: From Main St., turn onto Newtown Ln., then turn left onto Railroad Ave. Drive past train station and straight ahead at traffic light. Turn left at Fresno Pl. Restaurant is on left.

Fresno Street may be an elusive, hard-to-find side street, but over the years it's hosted some of the finer restaurants in East Hampton. In 2004 experienced restaurateur David Loewenberg (Beacon in Sag Harbor, red/bar brasserie in Southampton) opened Fresno on this site (naming it after the street, as well as a former occupant of this space). The cuisine features local produce and seafood. As an appetizer, for example, you might have jumbo lump crabcake with jicama-scallion slaw and mango-curry sauce; your entrée might include a grilled pork chop with peach and cress salad and black mission fig sauce. And for dessert, you may wish to sample the warm Vahlrona chocolate cake with nutella-fluff center and hazelnut gelato. An outdoor patio under a pergola, with a fountain and extensive landscaping, is located beside the restaurant. What a great addition to the local dining scene this has become!

HARBOR BISTRO

631-324-7300
www.harborbistro.com
313 Three Mile Harbor Rd., East Hampton, NY 11937
Owner/chef: Damien O'Donnell
Owner/manager: Nicole O'Donnell
Cuisine: New American with cClassic French touches
Serving: D

Open: May–Oct.

Price: Moderate–Very Expensive; prix fixe available

Credit Cards: MC, V

Special Features: Outdoor dining with marina views; boat dock

Reservations: Recommended

Directions: From Main St., turn left just before Hook Windmill onto North Main St. After two streetlights, road forks. Take left fork onto Three Mile Harbor Rd. Restaurant is on left in about 4 miles.

Chef/owner Damien O'Donnell learned his trade by working side by side with Roy Yamaguchi, the celebrity chef who introduced us to Hawaiian Fusion cuisine. He also put in stints at East Hampton's Palm Restaurant and James Lane Café. In his appetizer of Yellowfin Tuna Poke, which incorporates macadamia nuts and truffle-soy sauce, you can still see a bit of the Hawaiian influence, but for the most part he specializes in creating dishes that use local seafood and produce. A lime-grilled local "catch," for example, is accompanied by local corn and leeks. Overlooking Maidstone Marina, which borders on Three Mile Harbor, this restaurant peers out to the boats bobbing in the harbor. It's a lovely view, although not as breathtaking as East Hampton Point next door. Nevertheless, the large covered outdoor deck is a wonderful place to enjoy the waning light of a summer day, while inside, burnished cherry floors, wainscoted walls, and a sleek black bar entice diners to linger over their desserts and bottles of wine. Do check out the prix fixe menus, as they are excellent bargains.

Located at Maidstone Marina, Harbor Bistro offers diners this tranquil view of the harbor. Photo courtesy Wordhampton Public Relations

C/o The Maidstone (formerly The Maidstone Arms) has been welcoming guests since 1750. Its restaurant, The Living Room, serves Scandinavian-influenced American cuisine.

THE LIVING ROOM AT C/O THE MAIDSTONE

631-324-5006
www.themaidstone.com
207 Main St., East Hampton, NY 11937
Owner: Jenny Ljungberg
Manager: Ro'ee Levi
Chef: James Carpenter; Sous Chef Björn Ericsson
Cuisine: New American; proud participants in the Slow Food movement
Serving: B, L, D, BR (Sun.)
Open: Year-round, daily
Price: Expensive–Very Expensive; prix fixe offered
Credit Cards: AE, D, MC, V
Special Features: Fireplace; outdoor patio in summer; award-winning wine list; guest rooms on premises
Reservations: Recommended
Directions: Overlooks Town Pond on south end of Main St.

Although c/o The Maidstone (formerly the Maidstone Arms) is an inn as well as a restaurant, this is anything but a typical hotel dining room. The inn was purchased in 2009 by Jenny Ljungberg, who owns a lifestyle hotel company that specializes in transforming historic landmark hotels into destination resorts. Based in Sweden, the cuisine incorporates Scandinavian influences into American dishes, and it's absolutely first-class. James Carpenter (formerly of the American Hotel and Della Femina) is a fitting descendant of the Maidstone's previous culinary days of glory in the 1950s, when chef and cookbook author Michael Field presided here. An active participant in the Slow Food movement, Chef Carpenter uses meat from animals that are raised in a healthy manner, and ingredients that are produced organically, thus creating dishes that are good for us to eat. For example, you'll find Satur Farms vegetables and herbs incorporated into such dishes as a pan-roasted halibut accompanied by asparagus, baby carrots, cauliflower purée, and mango chutney, and the popular appetizer tart of flambéed smoked Norwegian salmon and crème fraîche is made with organic farm-raised salmon. The main dining room is elegant and comfortable—with a relaxed manner. It's decorated in soothing earth tones with accents of bright blue and gold on the chair fabrics. The same menu is served in the cozy bar area, which has a beautiful fireplace, and also in the lounge. A light menu is also served between lunch and dinner for famished guests who need something to tide them over until dinnertime.

MICHAEL'S AT MAIDSTONE PARK

631-324-0725
www.michaelsofmaidstone.com

28 Maidstone Park Rd., East Hampton, NY 11937
Chef and General Manager: Luis DeLoera
Cuisine: American
Serving: D
Open: Year-round, daily
Price: Inexpensive–Expensive; prix fixe offered
Credit Cards: AE, MC, V
Reservations: Recommended
Directions: From Main St., turn left just before Hook Windmill onto North Main St. Drive through two traffic lights, take left fork onto Three Mile Harbor Rd., and follow road for 4–5 miles to Flaggy Hole Rd. Turn left onto Flaggy Hole and left again onto Maidstone Park Rd. Restaurant is on left.

Seeking to lure customers beyond the village limits, this out-of-the-way restaurant, located in a residential neighborhood, offers special prices year-round. For example, Sunday through Thursday there's a reasonable prix fixe all night. Consequently, this is a very popular restaurant, especially with local, year-round residents. Few tourists stumble across it. But now you know! Be forewarned, however: you must make reservations. The decor is old-fashioned and romantic; soft candles glow against the knotty pine walls; church pews are used as seats in one of the rooms. Seniors love this place, both for the value and for the food. Michael's serves good, substantial, all-American, home-style fare. The duck is crisp-skinned, and the steak is large. The wine list is OK. Desserts are limited but good.

NICK & TONI'S
631-324-3550
www.nickandtonis.com
136 North Main St., East Hampton, NY 11937
Owner: Toni Ross
Manager: Bonnie Munshin
Executive Chef: Joseph Realmuto
Cuisine: Northern Italian/Mediterranean
Serving: D, BR (off-season: Sun. only)
Open: Year-round; in summer D daily; rest of year closed Mon. and Tues.; BR Sun. off-season only
Price: Moderate–Very Expensive; prix fixe off-season
Credit Cards: AE, MC, V
Special Features: Wheelchair access; tables on covered porch; film and food midweek off-season
Reservations: Highly Recommended
Directions: From Main St., continue past traffic light and turn left at fork before windmill. Drive past windmill (on right) and under railroad trestle. Restaurant is on right, just beyond second traffic light.

There's something so comfortable about Nick & Toni's that one visit is never enough. Casual attire is fine; babies are welcome; seniors love it; this is family. What puts it at the top of the class? Everything just clicks: the food is often sensational; the help is knowledgeable, professional, and friendly; all three rooms are crisp and airy; the wine list is well chosen—and there are no pretensions, and no apologies are needed. It's the kind of place where celebrities eat frequently, because they know they're among friends. Background music leans to progressive and vocal jazz. Hot, thickly sliced Tuscan bread comes to the table in a wooden trough to be dipped in zippy Monini olive oil; the combination is so terrific, it's devoured in a flash. No one should miss the zucchini chips; these little round morsels of paper-thin zucchini are dipped in a chickpea flour batter and deep-fried. A 620-degree wood-burning oven prepares dishes such as whole roasted fish that comes to the table with a crackly crisp skin and tender, juicy meat. The wine list is well chosen and includes Italian, French, and American wines, with some Long Island offerings, and there's a wonderful selection of grappas. Desserts include a chocolate almond torte with crème anglaise that's absolutely fabulous.

THE PALM AT HUNTTING INN
631-324-0411
www.thepalm.com

94 Main St., East Hampton, NY 11937
Manager: Tomas Romano
Chef: Simeon Collado
Cuisine: American
Serving: D
Open: Year-round; daily in summer; rest of year Wed.–Sun.
Price: Expensive–Very Expensive
Credit Cards: AE, D, DC, MC, V
Special Features: Guest rooms on premises
Reservations: Highly recommended
Directions: On Montauk Hwy. (Rte. 27) in center of village

A visit to the Palm is like a trip to New York City with none of the aggravation. This East End brother of the famous Manhattan steakhouse, which has been in the same family for three generations, has established itself as a Hamptons fixture. It's the same formula as the original, but there are no sawdust floors here. Dark wood, booths, pressed-tin ceiling, oak mirrors, and Victorian light fixtures are reminiscent of a pub of yesteryear. The enclosed porch, which is also used for dining, is bright and airy. The food is the same as you'll find at the original. Steaks are thick and cut from the finest meat. Portions are enormous, but split plates are an alternative. The lobster is so large that it spills over the edge of the platter. Take-home portions are so huge they are returned to the table in shopping bags. No vegetables come with the entrées, but the Palm is noted for its creamed spinach. We generally order a combination plate of cottage fries and deep-fried onions; the fries are crisp, and the onions are sliver-thin. The wine list is well chosen and features mostly California and Italian wines. (See listing in chapter 3 for guest rooms.)

1770 HOUSE

631-324-1770
www.1770house.com
143 Main St., East Hampton, NY 11937
Owner: Ben Krupinski
Manager: Michael Cohen
Company Executive Chef: Kevin Penner;
Chef de Cuisine: Matt Birnstill
Cuisine: Seasonal New American
Serving: D
Open: Year-round, daily
Price: Very Expensive
Credit Cards: AE, MC, V
Special Features: Lower-level tavern; guest rooms on premises
Reservations: Highly recommended
Directions: On Rte. 27 in center of village

The 1770 House has long been a local favorite, both for its gracious guest rooms and its fabulous dining room. In 2002 new owner Ben Krupinski put in a sparkling new kitchen and grabbed one of the East End's best chefs to create a world-class dining experience. Kevin Penner first gained acclaim as chef at Della Femina here and in the city, and most recently as chef at the Star Room in Wainscott. For the 40-seat 1770 House, he's created a seasonal New American menu featuring the freshest of ingredients. If he can't find them on the East End, he'll have them flown in. There's also a terrific wine list with more than 100 choices. The dining room still features some of the beautiful clocks and stained glass that we have always loved, as well as antique tables, chairs, and other furniture. The Tavern on the inn's lower level has a brick beehive oven and features a more casual menu than the main restaurant. (See listing in chapter 3 for guest rooms.)

TURTLE CROSSING

631-324-7166
www.turtlecrossing.com
221 Pantigo Rd., East Hampton, NY 11937
Owner/Manager: Stanley and Nancy Singer
Chef: Arthur Wolf
Cuisine: Southwestern/BBQ
Serving: L, D
Open: May–Thanksgiving; in summer L, D daily; rest of season D Thurs.–Mon., L Sat. and Sun.
Price: Inexpensive–Moderate; prix fixe and

special prices available
Credit Cards: AE, MC, V
Special Features: Outside dining; happy hour; live entertainment
Reservations: None
Directions: On Montauk Hwy. (Rte. 27), 1.5 miles east of village

The heady aroma wafting from the hardwood smoker in the kitchen will draw you in, but the juicy, smoky, tender ribs and chicken with their tasty barbecue sauces will keep you coming back. The *New York Times* has called this the best BBQ on Long Island, and this is former president Bill Clinton's favorite local stop. Stanley Singer grew up in Oklahoma City, where BBQ is king. After a stint in Paris at La Varenne, he and his wife Nancy opened this welcome addition to the Hamptons' dining scene. The front room of the restaurant is mostly for take-out, and there's a steady stream of people throughout the day. A small adjacent dining room has a vinyl floor and Naugahyde booths along a wall that has been painted with a huge mural of rodeo riders. Southwestern cow skulls gaze down on the room. You can choose from spit-roasted platters of chicken or smoked BBQ platters of ribs, chicken, brisket, pork, or duck, or a combination of several. With each platter you'll get corn bread and an order of "fixin's," which change nightly and might include black beans, rice, or other side dishes. You can also order a quesadilla or a wrap, or perhaps a jalapeno buttermilk hush puppy. There's a full bar and a selection of Mexican beers, tequila, and frozen drinks.

EASTPORT
TRUMPETS ON THE BAY
631-325-2900
www.trumpetsonthebay.com
58 South Bay Ave., Eastport
Mailing Address: P.O. Box 505, Eastport, NY 11941
Owner: Helen Fehr

Cuisine: Continental
Serving: L and D (Wed.–Mon.), BR (Sun. only)
Open: Year-round; closed Tues.
Price: Expensive
Credit Cards: AE, MC, V
Special Features: Waterside views; fireplace; outside deck; boat dock
Reservations: Recommended
Directions: From Sunrise Hwy. (Rte. 27), take exit 61 and follow service road to Eastport exit. Turn right (south) onto Eastport Manor Rd. Take road to end. Turn left (east) onto Montauk Hwy (Rte. 27A) and drive 0.7 mile to South Bay Ave. Turn right (south) and continue to end. Restaurant is on left.

If you're ready to pop the question, head for this romantic waterside spot on a protected point on Moriches Bay—almost on the Brookhaven Town line. You can even come by boat if you wish. You'll find waterside tables (especially in the back dining room, on the deck, or on the side porch), seductively lighted with candles, as well as sentimental background music and inventive cuisine. What more can you ask for? Even the service is informed and attentive without being overbearing. I had a wonderful entrée one night of macadamia-nut-crusted Chilean sea bass in a light and refreshing mango beurre blanc, sided with a pineapple compote and julienne vegetables. There's a nice wine list, although I would love to see more local wines included.

EAST QUOGUE
DOCKERS WATERSIDE
631-653-0653
www.dockerswaterside.com
94 Dune Rd., East Quogue
Mailing Address: P.O. Box 681, East Quogue, NY 11942
Owner: Larry Hoffman
Manager: Duane Doxey
Executive Chef: Peter Dunlop; Chef: Topher Duprée
Cuisine: Creative American

Serving: D, L
Open: Apr.–mid-Oct.; L and D daily
June–Sept; weekends only rest of season
Price: Moderate–Very Expensive; prix fixe
available
Credit Cards: AE, MC, V
Special Features: Waterside dining; fabulous sunset views; lots of outdoor seating;
live entertainment Fri. and Sat. nights;
happy hour; lobsterbakes; boat dock;
wheelchair access
Reservations: Accepted
Directions: From Montauk Hwy. (Rte. 27A)
in Quogue, turn onto Quogue Main St., then
turn south onto Post Ln. and cross Quogue
Bridge. Turn left at Dune Rd. Restaurant is
on left in 1.5 miles.

It seems as if Dockers has been around
since time began, but the funny little roadside shack—*the* sipping spot for generations
of 20-somethings—has evolved. Starched
white tablecloths, china dishes, and candles
have replaced the paper plates. A total renovation in 2002 created an upscale but still
casual venue. But as much as we laud the
change, we're happy to report that the best
of Dockers' old days remains. The sunset
and water views are still spectacular, and
the menu of lobster, steak, and seafood has
just gotten better and better. The Tuesday-
night lobster special is a bargain, especially
since you get a 1.25 lb. lobster, steamers,
clams, mussels, shrimp, corn on the cob,
and a potato. In 2009 a popular Waterside
Lounge was added, with more terrific water
views, an outdoor living room atmosphere,
and a small-plate menu.

NEW MOON CAFÉ

631-653-4042
www.nmcafe.com
524 Montauk Hwy., East Quogue
Mailing Address: P.O. Box 3028, East
Quogue, NY 11942
Chef/Owners: Ron and Shana Campsey
Cuisine: Texas BBQ and Lone Star Mexican
Serving: D, L, BR

Open: Year-round; D Wed.–Sun., L Sat., BR
Sun; closed Mon. and Tues.
Price: Inexpensive
Credit Cards: AE, D, MC, V
Special Features: Outdoor patio; wheelchair
access
Reservations: Drop-ins encouraged
Directions: On Montauk Hwy. (Rte. 27A) in
center of village

Calling all cowpokes! If you've got a hanker-
in' for good ol' finger-lickin' BBQ beef or
chicken, a sizzlin' plate of chicken fajitas, or
maybe some spicy blackened catfish, head
on down to the New Moon. You'll recognize
this institution (it's been around since 1977)
by the wooden cactus cutouts flanking the
building and the flower-filled windowboxes.
Inside, you'll sit on church pews while you
sip your frozen margarita or piña colada.
And you won't leave until you've had one of
Shana's "handmade" desserts, such as the
luscious banana cream pie, Texas pecan pie,
or rice pudding. Mmmmm; who can resist?

STONE CREEK INN

631-653-6770
www.stonecreekinn.com
405 Montauk Hwy., East Quogue
Mailing Address: P.O. Box 1751, East
Quogue, NY 11942
Owner/Manager: Elaine DiGiacomo
Owner/Chef: Christian Mir
Cuisine: French/Mediterranean
Serving: D
Open: Mar.–Dec.; daily in summer; fewer
days rest of season
Price: Expensive–Very Expensive; prix fixe
offered
Credit Cards: AE, D, MC, V
Special Features: Wheelchair access; fire-
places in dining room and bar
Reservations: Recommended
Directions: On Rte. 27A, 0.5 mile east of
village

This welcome addition to the Hamptons'
dining scene opened in 1996 in the white-
shingled building that used to be the

Ambassador Inn. Following a thorough face-lift, the space has now been voted the prettiest restaurant in the Hamptons by readers of *Dan's Papers*. In the bar, the 1930s carved mahogany back bar is enhanced by a tile floor and a pretty mantel over the fireplace. The two dining rooms have oak floors and tall mullioned windows. Massive palm trees reach toward the tray ceilings, rustling gently in the breeze from the ceiling fans and giving the restaurant a romantic, tropical air. Clever bark vases hold fresh flowers, and lovely Bernardaud china graces the tables. The chef and manager, a husband-and-wife team, met while both were working at Tavern on the Green in New York City. Christian was raised in France, and his dishes exhibit a strong French influence. He uses local, seasonal ingredients; thus the menu changes frequently. An entrée of crispy Scottish salmon is moist and pink inside and is served with whipped potatoes, baby carrots, and several poached shrimp on the side. The outstanding wine list leans heavily toward French wines, although there are a plethora of California and Italians available also, as well as some wonderful Long Island examples. Do not miss the scrumptious desserts. I love the stack of dark and white chocolate mousse layered with phyllo and topped with candied orange peel—all accented by dark and white chocolate sauce and garnished with a sugarcoated strawberry and a white chocolate cigarette.

HAMPTON BAYS
INDIAN COVE
631-728-5366
www.indiancoverestaurantmarina.com
258 Montauk Hwy., Hampton Bays, NY 11946
Owners: Bernard Miny and Rene Peyrat
Chef: Bernard Miny
Cuisine: American-French/fresh local seafood
Serving: D, BR (Sun. only)
Open: Mid-Feb.–Dec.; daily in summer; fewer days rest of season
Price: Inexpensive–Expensive; prix fixe available
Credit Cards: AE, MC, V
Special Features: Water views; happy hour; live entertainment weekends; boat dock
Reservations: Accepted
Directions: From Montauk Hwy. (Rte. 27A), turn south onto Canoe Place Rd. Immediately turn left at restaurant sign and follow signs.

Diners at Indian Cove, located on a high point of land at the southern end of the Shinnecock Canal, get a front-row seat for viewing all the passing yachts. The building is composed of a natural rough cedar exterior with a dining room on the main floor and an indoor/outdoor bar upstairs. Both levels are wrapped with windows or decks. Bernard Miny grew up in Lyons, France, and learned many of his techniques from such luminaries as Paul Bocuse. His prix fixe concept is a fabulous bargain. For $25.00 you can get a choice of appetizers (such as fried goat cheese salad), an entrée (try the grilled salmon) and dessert (perhaps bread pudding or tiramisu). In each category, there are other dishes with supplemental prices, should you wish to splurge, or you can order à la carte—and there's a wonderful wine list, too!

INN SPOT ON THE BAY
631-728-1200
www.theinnspot.com
32 Lighthouse Rd., Hampton Bays, NY 11946
Owners/Cheffes: Colette Connor, Pam Wolfert
Cuisine: Eclectic
Serving: B, L, D, BR (Sun.)
Open: Year-round
Price: Moderate–Expensive
Credit Cards: AE, MC, V
Special Features: On the water; outside dining with views of water; guest rooms on premises

Reservations: Parties of six or more
Directions: From Montauk Hwy. (Rte. 27A) in Hampton Bays, turn south onto Ponquogue Ave. and go to end (about 3 miles). Turn left onto Shinnecock Rd.; at second stop sign, turn right onto Foster Ave., which will become Lighthouse Rd. Inn is on right before bridge.

Colette Connor and Pam Wolfert purchased this charming seaside house in 2004, and it has been a premier dining destination ever since. They arrived with exceptional credentials, having formerly owned The Inn Spot in Quogue, where they served delectable breakfasts and lunches. At their new place, they not only serve breakfast and lunch but full dinners as well. The building is a charming 1857 house perched at water's edge with a wonderful porch for outside dining overlooking the water. Thanks to the herb garden in back, and local farmers offering other fresh ingredients, everything is made from scratch. The menu is extremely inventive and changes frequently; Pam handles the breakfast and lunch duties, while Colette is the dinner toque. Think about these creations, for example: a soup called Cheffe's Elixir, which combines coconut milk and herbs and is garnished with cashews, scallions, and ginger—or croissant-crusted fried oysters, or chocolate fettuccine, or seared local sea scallops topped with candied ginger and citrus glaze and served with a chilled papaya salad. There's an excellent and very affordable wine list, and what I especially love is that it includes a fine selection of Long Island wines. Best of all, you can eat heartily, and quaff as much wine as you want, because there are 12 overnight accommodations to which you can toddle off (see listing in chapter 3).

OAKLAND'S

631-728-6900
www.oaklandsrestaurant.com
365 Dune Rd., Hampton Bays

Mailing Address: P.O. Box 1046, Hampton Bays, NY 11946
Owner: Douglas Oakland
Chef: John Hill
Cuisine: American/Seafood
Serving: L, D
Open: Apr.–Oct.; L and D daily June–Sept.; rest of season open Fri.–Sun.
Price: Moderate
Credit Cards: AE, D, DC, MC, V
Special Features: Fabulous waterside and sunset views; live entertainment some nights; boat dock
Reservations: None
Directions: From Montauk Hwy. (Rte. 27A) in Hampton Bays, go south on Ponquogue Ave. At stop sign turn left onto Shinnecock Rd. At first stop sign, turn right onto Foster Ave. and follow over Ponquogue Bridge. At light turn left onto Dune Rd. and follow to end. Oakland's is on left.

"Sittin' on the dock of the bay" perfectly summarizes a dining experience at Oakland's. Relaxing on the two-tiered deck overlooking the marina as the sun sets over Shinnecock Bay, while dipping into a pile of local Blue Point oysters and sipping a cool one, is one of the finest ways to finish off a day at the beach. The outside tiki bar attracts a young and vibrant crowd who congregate to watch the sun set while waiting for a table (which can take some time, since there's a no-reservation policy). Once you are seated, lobsters—both steamed and stuffed—are the way to go, although there are lots of other seafood choices too, as well as some excellent steaks—and don't forget desserts such as a caramelized banana tart or crisp berry cobbler.

TIDE RUNNERS

631-728-7373
www.tiderunners.com
7 North Rd., Hampton Bays, NY 11946
Owners: Tom Dollard, Justin Dwyer, Chris Glynn
Manager: Chris Glynn

Chef: Justin Dwyer
Cuisine: American/Seafood
Serving: L, D
Open: May–Labor Day
Price: Moderate
Credit Cards: AE, D, MC, V
Special Features: Waterside dining; raw bar; boat dock; live music
Reservations: Accepted
Directions: From Montauk Hwy. (Rte. 27A), turn north onto North Rd. Restaurant is down flight of stairs at water's edge.

The setting is ideal. Diners sit at waterside tables right on the Shinnecock Canal, where they can watch the procession of boats and yachts parade past. A hot spot with hip dot-commers, the lively outside bar features a band Thursday to Sunday nights. The pretty inside dining room has a crisp navy-blue-and-white decor and marine scenes on the walls. The menu is mostly composed of seafood. You can get lobster, salmon, tuna, crab cakes, and mussels, but you really come for the view and the scene.

MONTAUK
BACKYARD AT SOLÉ EAST
631-668-2105
www.soleeast.com
Solé East, 90 Second House Rd., Montauk, NY 11954
Owner: Dave Ceva.
Chef: Larry Kolar
Cuisine: Mediterranean
Serving: D, BR (Sun.) daily in summer; fewer days rest of season
Open: May–Oct.
Price: Moderate–Expensive
Credit Cards: AE, D, MC, V
Special Features: Poolside dining on large lounges; patio; live entertainment and DJs
Reservations: Absolutely
Directions: From Montauk Point State Parkway traveling east, turn left onto Second House Rd. before you arrive in the village; the inn is on right in about 1 mile.

This restaurant, in the very cool and hip

hotel (see listing for Solé East in chapter 3) where the rather fusty Shepherds Neck Inn held forth for many years, has come of age. There's nothing old-fashioned or stodgy about this new place. Just as the promo says, it's all about "good, wholesome, fresh, natural ingredients and sources . . . fresh catch from the local fishermen; organic meat and veggies from the local farmer's markets"—all delivered with panache. Imagine lounging on a big blue mattress, poolside, in your bathing suit, and nibbling on tuna tiradito while a DJ spins Elvis or the Jackson Five. Between courses, you slip off the lounge and take a dip, surfacing as the waitress hands you another Bellini. Is this paradise, or what?

BREAKWATER
631-668-3949
Montauk Manor, 236 Edgemere St., Montauk
Mailing Address: P.O. Box 2272, Montauk, NY 11954
Owners: Yvonne and Conrade Bennett
Chef: Jhonathan Rupchand
Cuisine: Contemporary American
Serving: B, D daily in summer; B Fri. and Sat. off-season, D fewer days also
Open: Year-round; daily in summer; closed Mon. and Tues. rest of year.
Price: Moderate–Expensive; prix fixe offered
Credit Cards: AE, D, MC, V
Reservations: Recommended
Directions: From Main St. traveling east, turn left at the Chase Bank and go halfway around the semicircle, then turn left onto Edgemere St. Travel 1 mile and look for the hotel sign on the right. Follow signs up hill to resort.

Located in Montauk Manor, the grand hotel built in 1927 by Carl Fisher, who had plans to turn Montauk into the Miami of the North (see listing in Chapter 3), this stylish café sits just off the lobby, and has a wonderful big terrace for warm-weather dining (no view, however, except of the manicured lawn). The New American menu features such entrées as Roasted Half Duck Grand Marnier, Classic Shrimp Scampi, and a Grilled Prime Sirloin Steak with crispy onions—there's even a half-pound sirloin burger, for those so inclined. A three-course nightly prix fixe is only $24.99.

DAVE'S GRILL

631-668-9190
www.davesgrill.com
468 West Lake Dr., Montauk
Mailing Address: P.O. Box 1491, Montauk, NY 11954
Owners/Managers: David and Julie Marcley
Chef: David Marcley
Cuisine: American/Seafood
Serving: D
Open: May–Oct; daily July–mid-Sept. except Wed. when closed; May, June, and mid-Sept–Oct. open Thurs.–Sun.
Price: Moderate–Very Expensive; prix fixe offered
Credit Cards: MC, V
Special Features: Outdoor patio in summer
Reservations: Required; taken same day after 4:15 PM only
Directions: From center of village, take Edgemere St. north until it becomes Flamingo Ave. Continue on Flamingo to West Lake Dr., straight ahead after stop sign. Restaurant is on right along docks.

David Marcley, a chef, met Julie Goldstone, a singer, and they fell in love, bought a dockside diner that served breakfast to fishermen all night, and got married in Barbados. As Dave's Grill gained popularity, they started serving dinner instead of breakfast. Now all remnants of the diner have vanished. The restaurant has an interior of dark wood and brass; a pretty and very upscale patio overlooks the harbor for summer dining. Dave selects the fish right off the boats, and the nightly specials reflect his choices. There may be flash-fried Montauk flounder fillet with an onion and potato crust, or Dave's cioppino, a combination of fish, lobster, scallops, clams, shrimp, mussels, and calamari. There's an excellent wine list that includes Long Island whites and reds as well as wines from California, France, Spain, and Italy. Dave is noted for his chocolate bag dessert, a medley of ice cream, crème anglaise, whipped cream, and raspberry sauce in a chocolate bag.

EAST BY NORTHEAST

631-668-2872
www.harvest2000.com
51 Edgemere Rd., Montauk
Mailing Address: P.O. Box 5028, Montauk, NY 11954
Owner: John Erb
Chef: John Weston
Cuisine: Seafood
Serving: D
Open: Feb.–Dec; in summer D daily; fewer days rest of year
Price: Expensive–Very Expensive; prix fixe offered
Credit Cards: MC, V
Special Features: Beautiful waterside and sunset views; raw bar; live music Friday nights
Reservations: Accepted
Directions: From Main St., go north at tower onto Edgemere St. Restaurant is on left in 0.1 mile.

Brought to you by the same people who created such a success at Harvest on Fort Pond, this 2002 newcomer offers panoramic views across Fort Pond, which are especially awesome at sunset. There's a stylish interior with terra-cotta sponged walls and mahogany floors. The predominantly seafood menu has an Asian spin, so for a starter, you might order Peking duck tacos, which come with a hoisin sauce and avocado salsa. The entrées include panko-crusted rare tuna and pan-roasted halibut with a corn and edamame salad, shiitake mushrooms, and green curry coconut milk. Do not, under any circumstances, skip dessert. The pastry chef is a whiz kid who can whip up spectacular concoctions, such as fried tapioca pudding with cinnamon crème anglaise. (See listing for Stone Lion Inn, chapter 3, for guest rooms.)

FISHBAR ON THE LAKE

631-668-6600
www.freshlocalfish.com
Gone Fishing Marina; 467 East Lake Dr., Montauk
Mailing Address: P.O. Box 1357, Montauk, NY 11954
Owner: Montauk Food Works
Chef: Jennifer Meadows
Manager: Daniel Grimm
Cuisine: Seafood
Serving: L, D daily in summer; L Sat. and Sun., D Thurs.–Sun. rest of season.
Open: May–Columbus Day
Price: Moderate–Expensive; early-bird available
Credit Cards: MC, V
Special Features: On water overlooking marina; sunsets; boat dock
Reservations: Parties of eight or more only
Directions: From Montauk Village, take Rte. 27 east toward the Montauk Lighthouse. In approx. 2 miles, turn left onto East Lake Drive. Continue for approx. 1.5 miles to restaurant, on left.

You can't get fish any fresher than this! Straight-from-the-boat fish and shellfish make a short detour through the kitchen and then come straight to your table. Jennifer Meadows is a savvy and knowledgeable chef. She graduated from Johnson & Wales, and has cooked in fine restaurants from California to Hawaii, and now she's in Montauk. Her dishes show creativity and an excellent understanding of the use of our local ingredients. She selects her daily catch right off the boat, and uses her "finds" to create her daily menus. I don't know of any other restaurant that prepares that East End favorite, a true "clam pie"—and hers is fab-

ulous, using local clams, carrots, celery, onions, red potatoes, and fresh thyme, bound together in a thick cream sauce and baked in a puff pastry. Or you can get a seafood feast for two that includes two steamed lobsters, 10 clams, 10 mussels, 10 grilled shrimp, plus chorizo, red potatoes, grilled local corn, and drawn butter. In addition, there's a very nice vegetarian menu, and the wine list includes fine choices of local wines. The restaurant is located on the second floor of a building at the Gone Fishing Marina. The exterior belies its elegant dining room, which has walls of windows that overlook the marina, Lake Montauk, and beautiful sunset views beyond.

GOSMAN'S DOCK

631-668-5330
www.gosmans.com
500 West Lake Dr., Montauk
Mailing Address: P.O. Box 627, Montauk, NY 11954
Owner: The Gosman Family
Chef: Sam Joyce
Cuisine: Seafood
Serving: L, D
Open: Mid-Apr.–mid-Oct. daily except closed on Tues.
Price: Inexpensive–Moderate
Credit Cards: AE, MC, V
Special Features: Waterside views; wheelchair access; outside dining in summer; fish market; clam bar; boat dock
Reservations: None
Directions: From center of village, take Edgemere St. north until it becomes Flamingo Ave. Continue on Flamingo to West Lake Dr. and follow to end.

Gosman's is the ultimate fish house—casual, and noted for its fresh fish. There's a view from the dining room of the fishing fleet entering and leaving the harbor, but because of Gosman's volume, this is not the sort of place that encourages dawdling over coffee. The decor is of the dark, lacquered table, Windsor chair, and paper place mat variety. Nevertheless, the seafood is fresh off the boat. The lobster is always a good choice, and the flakey fillet of fluke comes with a brown butter and lemon sauce. Gosman's is a popular meal stop for families and bus tours—and it's more than a restaurant, it's a little village. In addition to the main restaurant, Topside is located on the roof, offering even better views of the inlet, with a menu of lobster, fish and chips, and sushi; the Inlet Café also has a full menu and sushi, and the clam bar offers a spot for a quick lunch. There are clothing and gift shops to browse in, and a seafood market is impressive for the variety and volume of seafood for sale—right off the boat.

GULF COAST KITCHEN
631-668-3100
www.montaukyachtclub.com
Montauk Yacht Club; 32 Star Island Rd., Montauk, NY 11954
Owner: Island Global Yachting
Chef: Michael Dimitrovich
Cuisine: Southern Coastal
Serving: D
Open: Apr.–Nov.
Price: Expensive—Very Expensive
Credit Cards: AE, C, MC, V
Special Features: Fireplace; boat dock
Reservations: Recommended
Directions: Travel east on Montauk Hwy., continuing through Montauk. Turn left onto West Lake Dr., travel 1.8 miles, and turn right onto Star Island Causeway. Yacht Club is on right in about 0.25 mile.

Following a total renovation, launched by new owners in 2009, this venerable and historic 1929 hotel has a new lease on life—and its restaurants are a reflection of the innovative direction of the management. Gulf Coast Kitchen has stunning décor—a stained glass ceiling, wicker couches, a fireplace, and historic Yacht Club photos on the walls. The food achieves a New Orleans meets Cancun appeal, offering a mix of Southern, Cajun, Cuban, and Mexican dishes. You might start a meal with Fried Oysters Rockefeller, a dish that combines spinach, oysters, and Pernod béchamel and is topped with crisp shallots. For an entrée, there's BBQ shrimp with hominy grits and a Cuban paella. **Hurricane Alley**, another restaurant on the property, serves breakfast, lunch, and dinner in a casual setting, while the **Barracuda Bar and Turtle Lounge** are indoor/outdoor venues for enjoying drinks and light fare, such as fried green tomatoes with Cajun remoulade.

HARVEST ON FORT POND
631-668-5574
11 South Emery St., Montauk
Mailing Address: P.O. Box 473, Montauk, NY 11954
Owner: John Erb
Chef: John Weston
Cuisine: Northern Italian
Serving: D
Open: Year-round; daily in summer; fewer days rest of season
Price: Very Expensive
Credit Cards: AE, D, MC, V
Special Features: Beautiful water view; boat dock; pretty side garden with benches
Reservations: Recommended
Directions: From Main St. (Rte. 27) traveling east, turn left onto South Emery St. before reaching the Plaza in the center of town. Restaurant is on left.

The beautiful garden with its brick pathways and garden benches announce that this is an owner who deeply cares about his customers and his business. I can't imagine a lovelier place to enjoy an after-dinner drink, or a full dinner, on a warm summer evening—and the sunsets are breathtaking! But the inside is equally pleasant. There are wide-plank pine floors and walls of soft, muted earth tones mixed with white. The wraparound, enclosed porch offers fabulous views of the pond (you have the impression of being suspended over it). This is one of

Located in the Montauk Yacht Club, Gulf Coast Kitchen specializes in Southern Coastal cuisine.

the finest places to eat in Montauk. You might start with the mussels steamed in garlic, shallots, and parsley, then move on to pork tenderloin with an apricot-apple chutney and a watercress and pine nut salad. No matter what you choose, you won't be disappointed, and you'll have a selection of great wines to go with it. But be careful! All dishes are made for sharing, so they come in large portions.

INLET SEAFOOD

631-668-4272
www.inletseafood.com
541 East Lake Drive, Montauk
Mailing Address: P.O. Box 2148, Montauk,
NY 11954
Owner: Inlet Seafood
Chef: Wellington Ovando

Cuisine: Seafood
Serving: L, D
Open: Mid-Feb.–Nov.
Price: Inexpensive–Moderate
Credit Cards: AE, MC, V
Special Features: On water with wonderful marine and sunset views; art gallery; wheelchair accessible
Reservations: None
Directions: From Montauk Village, take Rte. 27 east toward the Montauk Lighthouse. In approx. 2 miles, turn left onto East Lake Drive. Continue for approx. 2 miles to restaurant, which is on left.

The Inlet cooperative fishing dock in Montauk, located directly across the inlet that separates Lake Montauk from Block Island Sound and squarely opposite Gosman's Dock, has been the largest commercial

The Grill at Second House Tavern (where Ruschmeyers resided for many years) was built with salvaged wood from a Manhattan building.

operation in New York State for many years, packing and shipping fresh-from-the-boat fish to Manhattan, where it is then shipped throughout the country. Its six fishermen owners eventually decided to open a restaurant themselves—and we're the beneficiaries of that decision. Their motto: "Respect the ocean—Harvest the bounty—Feed the people" is prominently displayed throughout the restaurant, and the shingled two-story building makes a statement also. One enters the ground floor, where a beautiful stone fireplace and reception area is used as an art gallery, displaying photos of the Montauk fishing fleet or other local art. Upstairs, there's a long oak bar and another fireplace on the left, and a dining room with several outside decks on the right. Order any of the seafood dishes, and you'll be happy. There's even a sushi menu. And the views across the water, especially at sunset, are dramatic and exceptional. This is a great new addition to the Montauk dining scene.

SECOND HOUSE TAVERN

631-668-2877
www.secondhousetavern.com
161 Second House Rd., Montauk
Managing Partner: Abby Monahan
Executive Chef: Jeremy Blutstein
Cuisine: New American Bistro
Serving: D
Open: Mar.–Dec. daily in summer; closed Tues. and Wed. off-season
Price: Moderate–Expensive
Credit Cards: MC, V

Special Features: Raw bar; guest rooms on premises; handicapped accessible; view of Fort Pond
Reservations: Recommended
Directions: From Montauk Point State Parkway traveling east, turn left onto Second House Rd. before you arrive in the village; the inn is on left in about 1.5 miles.

This inventive new restaurant opened its doors in 2008 following a total renovation of the former Ruschmeyer's estate. There are soaring vaulted ceilings with exposed trusses in the main dining room, and the original warm wood floors have been scraped and sanded, but still show their character. The white walls hold mirrors and lush photographs of farm-fresh produce. The adjacent and more casual Grill also has interesting décor, as it was almost totally finished with salvaged wood from a demolished Manhattan building. In this room, you might order fish and chips, slow-roasted ribs, or a pizza from the wood-burning oven while watching your favorite game on the flat-screen TVs. The tavern menu, however, provides more serious fare.

Fresh Montauk black bass and local clams celebrate the bounty of local waters, while Long Island duck and herb-roasted rack of lamb satisfy carnivores. The eight cottages on the property have been refurbished also, and offer smart and hip accommodations with luxe bedding, in a secluded spot removed from the hubbub of the restaurant (see listing in Chapter 3 for guest rooms).

SURF LODGE
631-668-1562
www.surflodge.com
183 Edgemere St., Montauk, NY 11954
General Manager: Nil Erbil
Executive Chef: Sam Talbot
Cuisine: New American
Serving: D; BR Sun.
Open: May–Sept.
Price: Moderate–Expensive
Credit Cards: AE, D, MC, V
Special Features: Beach; deck; on the water, with lake and sunset views
Reservations: Accepted Mon.–Thurs.; not accepted Fri. and Sat.
Directions: In the village of Montauk, turn

The outdoor deck and sandy beach at Surf Lodge, which borders Fort Pond, are popular destinations for the hip and chic.

left at the Plaza (five-story brick building on left), and continue on Edgemere St. Surf Lodge is on left in 1 mile.

Summertime is party time at the Surf Lodge, where a surfing theme prevails. There's a beach, with a bonfire glowing in the evening, folks playing beach volleyball, a huge deck where live entertainers hold forth on weekends, and a Den (lounge) with a big screen where classic surfing films play 24/7. In the kitchen, celebrity chef Sam Talbot, who gained fame on *Top Chef,* toils away. Not one to dwell on his celebrity status, however, he's committed to using as many local ingredients as possible, and he's been known to catch fish that he incorporates into his nightly menu. You might try the crispy whole fluke with lotus chips and Vietnamese vinaigrette, or the panko-crusted tuna with succotash and salsa verde. For those not into fish, there's a cheeseburger or a lush mac 'n' cheese with peas and crispy ham. This is a happening place! (See listing in Chapter 3 for guest rooms.)

QUOGUE
RESTAURANT IN THE INN AT QUOGUE
631-653-6800
www.innatquogue.com
The Inn at Quogue; 47 Quogue St., Quogue
Mailing Address: P.O. Box 1705, Quogue, NY 11959
Owner: Rocco and Colette Lettieri; Larry Hoffman
Chef/Manager: Dee Angelo
Cuisine: American
Serving: D, BR
Open: Year-round; in summer D Wed.–Sun.; rest of year D Thurs.–Sun.; BR Sun. only
Price: Expensive–Very Expensive
Credit Cards: AE, D, MC, V
Special Features: Two working fireplaces; guest rooms on premises
Reservations: Accepted
Directions: From Montauk Hwy. (Rte. 27A), turn east onto Quogue St. and follow for 0.5

mile to the Inn at Quogue, in center of village at Jessup Ave.

The beautiful Restaurant in the Inn at Quogue recently experienced yet another change. Under new management, it now sports polished dark walnut floors, white wainscoted walls with grasscloth above, and a polished steely-gray ceiling. Fireplaces in the main dining room, as well as in the bar, offer cuddly warmth on chilly nights, and vintage photographs of Quogue line the walls, reminding us about the roots of this beautiful village. Now under the auspices of Dee Angelo, who also owns a restaurant in downtown Westhampton Beach, the menu is straightforward. There's an excellent mac 'n' cheese appetizer and a wonderful crab and crispy angel-hair pasta dish. Entrées include a roasted pork chop and a fresh catch of the day. It's all fare that's appropriate for an upscale country inn, but with a new-millennium appeal. (See listing in chapter 3 for guest rooms.)

SAGAPONACK
TOWNLINE BBQ
631-537-2271
www.townlinebbq.com
3593 Montauk Hwy., Sagaponack
Mailing Address: 10 Main St., East Hampton, NY 11937
Pitmaster: Sean Rafferty
Cuisine: BBQ
Serving: L, D
Open: Year-round; off-season closed Tues. and Wed.
Price: Inexpensive
Credit Cards: MC, V
Special Features: Outside deck; fireplace in bar
Reservations: None
Directions: On Rte. 27 at Town Line Rd., 2 miles east of Bridgehampton

It's the same owners as the Nick & Toni/Rowdy Hall/La Fondita crowd, so you know it's going to be done right—and it is. It's all about down-home, finger-lickin'-

good BBQ, done up in a super casual, order-at-the-counter-and-wait-for-your number to be called sort of place. You pick up your order, select a table—inside or out?—and just enjoy. Oh, don't forget to pick up your beer too! The Texas chili is great—and so are the ribs—and have you ever had fried mac 'n' cheese? Or pickled jalapenos? Or banana pudding like they make it in Texas? If you're looking for a casual, lots-of-fun atmosphere—and terrific BBQ—this is the place to come.

SAG HARBOR
AMERICAN HOTEL

631-725-3535
www.theamericanhotel.com
49 Main St., Sag Harbor
Mailing Address: P.O. Box 1349, Sag Harbor, NY 11963
Owner: Ted Conklin
Chef: Jonathan Parker
Cuisine: French/American
Serving: L, D
Open: Year-round; D daily, L Sat. and Sun. only
Price: Expensive—Very Expensive; prix fixe available in conjunction with Bay Street Theatre Credit Cards: AE, CB, D, DC, MC, V
Special Features: Exceptional wine list; fireplace; guest rooms on premises; bar; covered porch
Reservations: Highly recommended
Directions: On Main St. in center of village

It was almost 35 years ago that Ted Conklin purchased this 1846 hotel, one of the few remnants of Sag Harbor's glorious whaling days. The charming Victorian rooms have such a European ambience that you feel as if you're eating in a French country inn. The rooms are formal and romantic and range from the dark, convivial bar with its fireplace, to the skylit atrium with its brick wall. Classical music plays gently in the background. An international crowd chatters away in a variety of languages, and the dress is partly New York chic and partly Hamptons casual. The American Hotel has consistently, since 1981, won Wine Spectator's Grand Award for its legendary 85-page, 2,500-selection wine list, which includes some incredible classic French Bordeaux as well as fine wines from less well-known vintners. It also offers a broad range of California and Long Island wines at lower prices. Wines available by the glass are as well selected as those by the bottle. Over the years, the menu has slowly evolved from strictly classical French dishes to some French, some American. Dinner might start with caviar, or fresh sautéed foie gras laced with sauterne. Entrées include fresh local flounder that's sautéed amandine and slow-roasted Long Island Pekin duckling with a citrus ginger sauce. The kitchen is a proud member of Slow Food USA, using meat from animals that are raised in a healthy manner and ingredients produced organically, resulting in dishes that are good for us to eat. There's a lovely selection of after-dinner sauternes and ports. Upstairs, there are eight remarkable guest rooms that are filled with antique furniture and Oriental rugs and have fantastic bathrooms with whirlpools. (See listing in chapter 3 for guest rooms.)

THE BEACON

631-725-7088
www.beaconsagharbor.com
8 West Water St., Sag Harbor
Mailing Address: P.O. Box 2266, Sag Harbor, NY 11963
Owner/Manager: David Loewenberg
Chef: Sam McLelland
Cuisine: French-inspired American
Serving: L in summer Thurs.–Mon.; fewer days rest of season; D nightly
Open: May–Dec. daily in summer; fewer nights rest of season
Price: Moderate—Expensive
Credit Cards: AE, MC, V
Special Features: Fabulous waterside setting and view; boat dock

Reservations: None in summer; accepted rest of season

Directions: From Main St. turn west onto West Water St. Restaurant is on right in about 1 block, near Bridge St.

Although it's tiny, this seaside venture by David Loewenberg (also a part owner of Fresno in East Hampton and red/bar brasserie in Southampton) packs a wallop. For one thing, the restaurant is located on the second floor of a building that offers stunning views of the harbor and marina, especially at sunset. A light and breezy menu has been created to match the casual bistro setting. There's grilled salmon with French lentils, asparagus, and balsamic reduction, and sesame-crusted tuna with napa cabbage, jicama slaw, and Asian glaze. An excellent wine list, incorporating many Long Island wines, is affordable and extensive and, no matter what, desserts should not be missed. As of 2009, Beacon adjusted its season to extend dinner into December—*and* you can reserve a table!

BLUE SKY MEDITERRANEAN LOUNGE

631-725-1810
www.blueskysagharbor.com
63 Main St., Sag Harbor, NY 11963
Owner: Jerry Wawryk
Managing Partner/Executive Chef:
Buiseppe "Beppe" Desiderio
Cuisine: Mediterranean
Serving: L, D, BR (Sun. only)
Open: Year-round
Price: Inexpensive–Expensive
Credit cards: AE, MC, V
Special Features: Indoor patio; art exhibits by local artists
Reservations: Accepted
Directions: On Main St. in center of town

Beppe Desiderio was raised on the island of Capri, where he learned the restaurant business at an early age at his family's various establishments. Bringing his talents to the United States, he has run several suc-

cessful restaurants in New York City, Palm Beach, and on the East End. This new venture, where Spinnakers held forth for many years, features Mediterranean cuisine in a light and airy setting that includes white-washed walls, a pressed-tin ceiling, an indoor brick patio with skylights, lots of big windows, and marine blue cushions on booth and table seating. The menu includes pizzettes, pastas, small plates, and such entrées as brick-oven roasted chicken Saloniki and roasted baccala Romero, which comes with a spinach flan and rosemary buerre blanc. An oven-roasted Tuscan bread may be ordered with truffle mushrooms, goat cheese, and toasted nuts. There's an excellent selection of Italian wines from which to choose, and the restaurant features local artwork on the walls.

B. SMITH'S

631-725-5858
www.bsmith.com
Long Wharf at Bay St., Sag Harbor
Mailing Address: P.O. Box 600, Sag Harbor, NY 11963
Owners: Barbara Smith and Dan Gasby
Executive Chef: John Poon
Cuisine: International/Eclectic
Serving: L, D, BR
Open: May–mid-Oct.; daily in summer; Fri–Sun. rest of season
Price: Moderate–Very Expensive
Credit Cards: AE, D, MC, V
Special Features: Wheelchair access; waterfront dining on spacious decks; bar/lounge area; boat dock
Reservations: Recommended
Directions: Traveling north on Main St., cross over Rte. 114 (Bay St.) and continue down Long Wharf. Restaurant is on right.

Celebrity author, TV hostess, and lifestyle guru B. Smith has operated a popular Manhattan theater-area restaurant for some time, and she also graces the Hamptons in the summer. This location has long been

Named for its lifestyle-celebrity owner, B. Smith's is located directly on the water, offering unbeatable harbor views.

one of the premier sites in the Hamptons, as it overlooks the harbor and marina where huge sailboats and cruisers sit at anchor. B. Smith's strikes just the right note, as the owners have thoughtfully allowed the view and the food to take front seat. Creamy yellow walls are accented with white, marine-blue-and-white-striped banquettes line the wall, huge blue pots hold palm trees, and ceiling fans whir silently overhead. A multitude of French doors open the interior dining room to the outside. Although B. Smith's has been noted for its cuisine with a Southern twist, most recently, with the addition of chef John Poon, who previously cooked at Saloon and America in Manhattan, there's been an introduction of other styles as well. You can still get the BBQ ribs, but now you can also get a grilled rack of lamb, or prime filet of beef Rossini. An excellent and affordable wine list, that includes some local East End wines, is available.

IL CAPUCCINO RISTORANTE

631-725-2747
www.ilcapuccino.com
30 Madison St., Sag Harbor
Mailing Address: P.O. Box 1438, Sag Harbor, NY 11963

Owner: Jack Achille Tagliasacchi
Manager/Chef: Jim Renner
Cuisine: Northern Italian
Serving: D
Open: Year-round; daily, except major holidays
Price: Inexpensive–Expensive; prix fixe available some nights
Credit Cards: AE, MC, V
Special features: Restaurant displays paintings by owner.
Reservations: Parties of four or more
Directions: From Main St. traveling south, bear left at monument onto Madison St. Restaurant is on right.

This rambling old red wooden building has three dining rooms, with tables and chairs tucked into various nooks and crannies. It's a restaurant of red-checkered tablecloths, brown-painted floor, and bentwood chairs. Decorations include original oil paintings by owner Jack Achille Tagliasacchi, raffia-wrapped Chianti bottles hanging from the ceiling and walls, and lace curtains. A tumbling-down storefront next door was torn down and replaced with a new, similar building in 1995; this expanded the seating for summer dinners and for private parties. This is a homey Italian restaurant that could just as easily be located on a street in Naples. Everyone loves the hot, homemade knotted dinner rolls topped with garlic and parsley and dredged with melted butter. It is customary to sop up every drop of the potent garlicky butter from the bottom of the paper-lined basket. For entrées, there are chicken, fish, and pasta winners. Tortelloni al pistacchio is an excellent pasta stuffed with ricotta and served in an Alfredo sauce with Parmesan cheese.

NEW PARADISE CAFE
631-725-6080
126 Main St., Sag Harbor
Mailing Address: P.O. Box 120 Sag Harbor, NY 11963
Owner/Chef: Robert Durkin

General Manager: Eric Peele
Cuisine: New American
Serving: D
Open: Year-round, daily
Price: Moderate–Expensive; prix fixe available
Credit Cards: AE, MC, V
Special Features: Outside seating on deck
Reservations: Accepted
Directions: On Main St. in center of village

Although this terrific restaurant started out as a café behind a bookstore, it never was of the typical Barnes & Noble variety. In fact, the restaurant is so good, it has now taken over the entire space. Black-and-white tile floors, wainscoted walls, and reed chairs give it a French café atmosphere, and there's a little deck in back for outside dining. Chef Robert Durkin (who also owns Robert's in Water Mill) offers a menu of wonderful local favorites. For dinner, try his roasted Long Island duck with walnut wild rice or the grilled local sea scallops on grilled and roasted vegetables. (You see, this is serious food.)

OASIS
631-725-7110
www.oasishamptons.com
3253 Noyac Rd., Sag Harbor, NY 11963
Owners: John and Gina Donnelly and Lou and Kerri Dollinger
Managers: Gina Donnelly and Lou Dollinger
Chef: John Donnelly
Cuisine: Modern American with an emphasis on seafood
Serving: D
Open: Year-round; in summer D nightly; fewer days rest of year
Price: Expensive
Credit Cards: AE, D, MC, V
Special Features: Beautiful water views; boat dock; live jazz Sun. or Mon.
Reservations: Accepted.
Directions: From Sag Harbor Main St. traveling west, turn right onto Noyac Rd. Continue straight ahead (west) at intersection

This local favorite, with its lacy curtains on the windows and raffia-wrapped wine bottles hanging from the ceiling, features Italian comfort food.

with Long Beach Rd. Restaurant is on right in 0.25 mile in Mill Creek Marina.

Opening in 2002, this American restaurant has settled in as one of the most dependable and popular places in the Hamptons. In the first place, it's on the second floor of a building (actually at street level, but the land dips down in back), affording lovely views of Mill Creek and the marina, and the decor, which is in light and airy earth tones, is comfortable and inviting. In the second

place, chef John Donnelly is a graduate of Johnson & Wales and has cooked at some of the best New York hotels, so he really know his stuff. He loves to work with seasonal local ingredients—for example, try his pan-seared scallops on sweet corn risotto with carrot emulsion, or his East End bouilla-baisse. As a starter, we loved the mini tuna tartare tacos with mango and red onion salsa and avocado vinaigrette. And for dessert, both the flourless chocolate cake

An outdoor courtyard expands summer seating at Tutto Il Giorno.

with its mini milkshake, and the angel food cake with fresh blueberry compote and peach sorbet, were memorable.

PHAO THAI KITCHEN

631-725-0101
www.seninthehamptons.com
29 Main St. Sag Harbor
Mailing Address: P.O. Box 3138, Sag Harbor, NY 11963
Owner: Jeff Resnick and Tora Matsuoka
Chef: Deena Chafetz
Cuisine: Thai
Serving: D
Open: Year-round
Price: Moderate–Expensive
Credit Cards: AE, MC, V
Special Features: DJ Fri. and Sat. nights
Reservations: None
Directions: On Main St. in center of town

Although a former incarnation of this restaurant used to reside across the street, its demise had been lamented by locals ever since it closed in 2003. Now, lo and behold, it's emerged again next door to its sister restaurant, Sen. The seductive but rustic post-and-beam decor, booths dressed in bright pillows, and sexy lighting attracts celebs and locals, as well as summer folk. The menu includes both mild and hot choices, as well as vegetarian—there's crispy tamarind duck and Phao drunken noodles with shrimp, as well as traditional pad thai with a choice of shrimp, chicken, or tofu.

SEN

631-725-1774
www.seninthehamptons.com
23 Main St., Sag Harbor
Mailing Address: P.O. Box 3138, Sag Harbor,

NY 11963
Owner: Jeff Resnick and Tora Matsuoka
Sushi Chef: Kai Yoshino
Cuisine: Japanese
Serving: D
Open: Year-round
Price: Expensive–Very Expensive
Credit Cards: AE, MC, V
Special Features: Karaoke Thurs. nights
Reservations: None
Directions: On Main St. in center of village

This extremely popular Japanese standout has won a place in the hearts of Hamptonites. Decorated with rich wood floors, river stone walls, and cushioned seating, it exudes a welcoming atmosphere. But folks don't come for the decor, they come for the gourmet Japanese delights. There are teriyaki and tempura dishes, as well as salads. Or you might choose from one of the extensive superfresh hand-rolled sushi offerings or a sashimi plate. There's a select list of wines, Japanese beers, and sake to accompany the meal.

TUTTO IL GIORNO

631-725-7009
6 Bay St., Sag Harbor, NY 11963
Owner/Chef: Maurizio Marfoglia
Managers: Fabrice Twagriumkiza and Nina Doig
Cuisine: Italian
Serving: L (Fri.–Sun.), D (Tues.–Sun.)
Open: Year-round
Price: Moderate–Very Expensive
Credit Cards: AE, MC, V
Special Features: Patio seating; fireplace
Reservations: Accepted
Directions: From Main St. traveling north, turn right at end onto Bay St. Restaurant is on right in two blocks.

This pretty but tiny little place expands in the summer onto a beautiful brick side patio with cushioned benches and pots of flowers. Inside, there's a fireplace and numerous wood accents. The Italian menu, created by owner/chef Maurizio Marfoglia,

who was executive chef at Barolo in Manhattan for many years, includes some excellent pasta dishes (ravioli with apples, ricotta and braised lamb ragout) as well as a grilled swordfish steak with minted organic cauliflower and micro sprouts salad and wild sea bass poached with white wine and fresh tomato.

SOUTHAMPTON
THE COAST GRILL

631-283-2277
1109 Noyack Rd., Southampton, NY 11968
Owner/Manager: Joseph Luppi
Chef: Brian Cheewing
Cuisine: American Contemporary/Seafood
Serving: D
Open: Year-round; daily mid-June–mid-Sept., rest of year Fri.–Sun.
Price: Moderate; prix fixe available; winter specials
Credit Cards: AE, MC, V
Special Features: Wheelchair access; waterside views; boat dock
Reservations: Accepted
Directions: From Montauk Hwy., drive north on North Sea Rd. to intersection with Noyack Rd. Turn right. Restaurant is 2 miles east on Noyack in Peconic Marina.

This wonderful restaurant has been serving up fresh fish, prepared in a simple, straightforward manner, for many years. Why has it been such a success when so many others have come and gone? Because owner Joseph Luppi knows exactly what he's doing. He was previously the cooking assistant to *New York Times* food editor Craig Claiborne, and also to the late chef and columnist Pierre Franey, so he learned from the best. And the menu isn't confined to seafood. The braised beef short ribs with local corn polenta, wild mushrooms, and horseradish cream is fabulous, as is the crispy roasted chicken. Nevertheless, it's the fish and shellfish that dominate the menu. You might try the local fish stew with shrimp, clams, dayboat fish, and mussels, or the whole roasted fish of the day. As one might expect, the wine list offers excellent accompaniments to the menu, with about 30 whites and 25 reds.

LE CHEF

631-283-8581
www.lechefbistro.com
75 Job's Ln., Southampton, NY 11968
Owner/Chef: Frank Lenihan
Cuisine: French/Continental
Serving: L (Tues.–Sat.), D nightly; BR Sun.
Open: Year-round, daily; closed Thanksgiving, Christmas
Price: Moderate–Very Expensive; prix fixe offered
Credit Cards: AE, MC, V
Special Features: Wheelchair access; sidewalk seating; jazz Thurs. nights
Reservations: Accepted, but not required
Directions: From Main St., go west on Job's Ln. Restaurant is on right across from Agawam Park.

This pretty little restaurant with its tiny, up-front bar serves creative French and continental fare at reasonable prices. There's a $26.95 prix fixe dinner that's offered all night Sunday to Wednesday and until 6 PM Thursday to Saturday. For this price you'll get an appetizer and entrée, or, alternatively, you could order from the à la carte menu. The restaurant is reminiscent of one you might find on a side street on the Left Bank or the Île Saint-Louis, with its maroon carpet and white wainscoting topped by ochre-sponged walls—all adorned with colorful paintings by Nicolai Cikovsky. Songs like "Tennessee Waltz" and "Our Love Is Here to Stay" play in the background. It may be a throwback, but the food is prepared with finesse. There's a local flounder crusted with walnuts and almonds, and a Long Island duckling sauced with a pomegranate and balsamic reduction. For dessert, the selection includes cappuccino mousse, cheesecake, crème caramel, and many more. Naturally, there's a fine wine list.

PLAZA CAFÉ

631-283-9323
www.plazawinedinners.com
61 Hill St., Southampton, NY 11968
Owner/Chef: Douglas Gulija
Cuisine: New American
Serving: D
Open: Year-round; daily in summer, rest of year Tues.–Sun., closed Mon.
Price: Expensive; prix fixe available
Credit Cards: AE, DC, MC, V
Special Features: Fireplace; outdoor seating; Sun. BYO wine—no corkage
Reservations: Highly recommended
Directions: From Hill St., turn north by Southampton Inn. Restaurant is tucked into shopping plaza on right side of street behind 71 Hill St. Plaza.

Enthusiasts rave about this New American restaurant—the caring service, the pretty setting, and the accomplished kitchen. Chef Doug Gulija, who was chef previously at Le Grand Vefour in Paris, has created a distinctive cuisine that somehow manages to be cutting edge without losing a certain comfort level. His signature dish of seafood "shepherd's pie" uses local lobster, shrimp, shiitake mushrooms, and corn in a chive-potato crust, which leaves diners begging for more. One evening I had a perfectly prepared salmon fillet that came on a bed of warm frisée that was napped with a mustard-seed vinaigrette. Its simple preparation offered a subtle melding of flavors. One unique feature of the menu is that Doug offers a wine suggestion with each entrée, allowing diners to sample some of the hard-to-get wines in his cellar. The desserts are equally refined. I had a fabulous dessert one evening of fresh berries marinated in Bedell Cellars raspberry wine accompanied by mascarpone mousse and topped with amaretti crumbs. It's all served in a soothing, rather Mediterranean setting that combines a cathedral-ceilinged room with gold-sponged walls, a massive iron chandelier, and a beautiful, big stucco fireplace.

RED/BAR BRASSERIE

631-283-0704
www.redbarbrasserie.com
210 Hampton Rd., Southampton, NY 11968
Owners: Kirk Basnight and David Loewenberg
Chef: Erik Nodeland
Cuisine: French-inspired American Brasserie
Serving: D
Open: Year-round; daily in summer; rest of year Wed.–Sun.
Price: Expensive; prix fixe available
Credit Cards: AE, MC, V
Reservations: Accepted
Directions: From Main St., drive east on Hampton Rd. Restaurant is on right in about 1 mile.

Romantic and casual, red/bar has become a favorite Southampton destination since its opening in 1998. The setting is crisp, airy, and elegant, highlighted by walls of windows on three sides that suffuse the room with light in daytime and act as reflectors for the candles that light the tables at night. The food is consistently good. One night we had the truffled chicken breast with mushroom risotto, which was wonderful, while another night, the roasted Long Island duckling with sweet potato hash and a plum-cherry sauce won raves. The excellent and affordable wine list wins Wine Spectator awards, and there's a first-rate selection of Long Island wines to choose from. In addition, such desserts as an apricot and almond tart with raspberry coulis and a baked Alaska with tropical fruits and flaming rum offer a fitting finale. This is one restaurant to keep on a favorites list.

SANT AMBROEUS

631-283-1233
www.santambroeus.com
30 Main St., Southampton, NY 11968
Owners: Hans and Francesca Pauli
Chef: Johnny Guidierrez
Cuisine: Northern Italian Ristorante/Pasticceria
Serving: L, D
Open: Year-round; in summer L and D daily; rest of year Fri.–Sun.
Price: Moderate–Very Expensive
Credit Cards: AE, MC, V
Special Features: Wheelchair access; espresso bar; pasticceria; sidewalk and patio seating
Reservations: Accepted
Directions: On Main St. in center of village

Sant Ambroeus, which is named after the patron saint of Milan, has such a Milanese flavor that you feel as if you should speak Italian—and you'll hear many patrons doing just that. It's a spot in which to linger over a cappuccino or espresso, while watching the world march by. This authentic Italian pasticceria, confettieria, and restaurant has glass cases in front where the most remarkable desserts are displayed. The tempting selections include gelati and Italian cakes, pastries, cookies, and chocolates. Midway into the restaurant there's an espresso bar, and behind the bar is a small, white-linen-tablecloth restaurant. Watermelon-colored Ultrasuede banquettes and bentwood chairs offer sophisticated backdrops for the wonderful meat dishes (such as a chicken breast stuffed with mixed mushrooms and provolone), risottos (one with a ragout of sausage and peas, for example), pastas (a fettuccini with shrimp, porcini, and tomato perhaps?), and salads. In addition, in summer the sidewalk seating in front, and on a more secluded patio, has people lined up waiting for tables. There are about 15 selections of both red and white Italian wines to accompany the meal.

SAVANNA'S

631-283-0202
www.savannassouthampton.com
268 Elm St., Southampton, NY 11968
Manager: Tony Fortuna
Cuisine: Contemporary American
Serving: D

Open: May–Sept.; daily in summer; fewer days rest of season
Price: Moderate–Very Expensive; prix fixe offered
Credit Cards: AE, D, DC, MC, V
Special Features: Wheelchair access; happy hour; outdoor dining pavilion; fireplace
Reservations: Recommended
Directions: From traffic light in center of village, travel east on Hampton Rd. Turn left onto Elm St. and follow to end. Restaurant is on right before train station.

In this current transformation of Southampton's old village hall (and later a funky bar/restaurant), the interior walls have been removed, and three exterior walls contain windows, so a beautiful, open, light-filled space now reigns. At night, votive candles line the windowsills, creating a magical effect. There are columns inside the restaurant and a fireplace at one end. In the summer, an outdoor pavilion in the garden in back is a marvelous place to dine; a tentlike structure is supported by Grecian columns. The entrées are presented with flair: there's a crispy wood-oven-roasted Long Island duckling that comes with sweet potatoes and an apricot glaze; a grilled branzino is plated with olives, capers, and tomatoes. The wine list is excellent, both in selections by the glass and by the bottle. There are Long Island wines as well as California and Italian. The exceptional desserts are all house-made and should not be missed. Who could resist a chocolate dulce de leche tart or a "Soltners" chocolate mousse?

75 MAIN STREET
631-283-7575
www.75main.com
75 Main St., Southampton, NY 11968
Owner: June Spira
Chef: David Gerard
Cuisine: American Bistro
Serving: D, BR/L, LN

Open: Year-round, daily
Price: Moderate–Very Expensive
Credit Cards: AE, MC, V
Special Features: Wheelchair access; sidewalk dining; live entertainment
Reservations: Accepted for parties of four or more
Directions: On Main St. in center of village

Attracting a young, upscale crowd, 75 Main is trendy and casual. It has oak floors, daffodil-colored sponged walls and wainscoting, and French doors across the front that open to the sidewalk. The bar area in the front is as large as the restaurant in the back. It's a popular place to see and be seen. Furthermore, the food keeps getting better and better, and the wine list has been winning Wine Spectator awards. The current chef has an interesting background. He grew up on Long Island, but then he cooked in Korea, where he learned to incorporate Asian ingredients and techniques into his repertoire. You might start with Thai spring rolls with Nam Pla, for example, but there are plenty of American and continental dishes on the menu as well, such as the chopped steak dinner and the American bison short ribs.

SILVER'S
631-283-6443
www.silversrestaurant.com
15 Main St., Southampton, NY 11968
Owner/Chef: Garrett Wellins
Cuisine: Eclectic
Serving: L
Open: Year-round except closed Wed. in summer; open Thurs.–Mon. rest of year
Price: Moderate
Credit Cards: AE, MC, V
Special Features: sidewalk seating
Reservations: None
Directions: On Main St. in center of village

Garrett Wellins, thankfully, is carrying on the family tradition at this unconventional little luncheon spot—and he's the third generation to do so. His grandfather opened the first Silver's in 1923, and the black-and-white tile floor, old-fashioned soda-fountain-style counter, vitrines filled with memorabilia, brass chandeliers, beautiful oil paintings filling the walls, and curved exterior windows still lend a Prohibition-era ambience. But the food is anything but old-fashioned, and the lovely selection of wines dispels any memories of Prohibition. Among the soups, the lobster bisque comes with tons of lobster and a bit of cream, plus a dash of cognac and sherry; and a toasted baguette is slathered with truffled foie gras mousse and accompanied by baby pears, grapes, and apples. An entrée might include crab cakes or a roast duck leg confit. Everything is house-made to order, using local ingredients. And yes, there are delectable desserts too—such as the opera cake, a confection of liquor-soaked layers of genoise with hazelnut and mocha buttercream and "glossed" with dark chocolate. Disappointments? Only one. That it's not open for dinner too.

SOUTHAMPTON PUBLICK HOUSE

631-283-2800
www.publick.com
40 Bowden Sq., Southampton, NY 11968
Owner: Donald Sullivan
Cuisine: Contemporary American/Microbrewery
Serving: L, BR, D
Open: Year-round, daily
Price: Inexpensive–Expensive; special lunch and dinner prices daily
Credit Cards: AE, MC, V
Special Features: Wheelchair access; porch dining; fireplaces; live music many nights
Reservations: Accepted
Directions: From traffic light in center of village, travel north on North Sea Rd. to intersection with Bowden Sq. Restaurant is on right.

The enormous stainless-steel vats behind their glass viewing windows dominate one end of the dining room, but that just adds to the charm of this casual restaurant. There are brick walls, oak floors, stenciling on boxed beams, a tin ceiling and tin walls, and fireplaces in the dining room and taproom. On the menu you'll find steaks, roasted rosemary chicken breast, burgers, and lager-battered fish and chips. There are microbrews on tap, and the wine list includes some local wines. There's live entertainment many nights, as well as a happy hour, ladies nights, etc. It's a lively, fun, upbeat place to hang out—everybody has a good time, and a wonderful, broad front porch serves as an outside dining room almost year-round.

TUSCAN HOUSE

631-287-8703
www.thetuscanhouse.com
10 Windmill Ln., Southampton, NY 11968
Owner/ Executive Chef: William Oster
Cuisine: Italian
Serving: L, D
Open: Year-round; L, D daily, BR Sun.
Price: Moderate–Very Expensive
Credit Cards: AE, D, MC, V
Special Features: Wheelchair access
Reservations: Accepted
Directions: On corner of Windmill and Job's Lns.

This restaurant has the fresh, airy feeling of Santa Fe, but the food is strictly northern Italian. Stucco walls, tiled floors, and high ceilings create a casual but upscale atmosphere. The menu offers a good selection of antipasti and pastas, but this is a much more serious restaurant than those dishes suggest. For example, imagine a chicken (bone-in or out) with shallots, prosciutto, mushrooms, peas, and artichoke hearts that's bathed in a brown sherry sauce, or a fresh fish topped with shrimp and roasted tomato on a bed of sautéed spinach with a lemon sherry sauce. The wine list concentrates mostly on Italians, but there are also some California wineries represented. The desserts are made on the premises and include a chocolate ganache cheesecake, a raspberry almond tart, and a cabernet pear tart.

SPEONK

OLDE SPEONK INN

631-325-8400
www.theoldespeonkinn.com
190 Montauk Hwy., Speonk
Mailing address: P.O. Box 177, Speonk, NY 11972
Chef: Kevin Lueck
Cuisine: Classic American
Serving: D, BR (Sun.)
Open: Year-round; daily in summer; rest of year Wed.–Sun.
Price: Moderate; prix fixe available
Credit Cards: MC, V
Special Features: Live music
Reservations: Accepted
Directions: On Montauk Hwy. (Rte. 27A) 0.25 mile east of Speonk village and 2 miles west of Westhampton

Located in a rambling old roadhouse that's been through numerous incarnations, the current version has skylights, a carpeted floor, and wooden shutters. It's been rumored that Elizabeth Taylor and Richard Burton once dined here. You might start the meal with baked local mussels with Pernod-herb butter. Entrées include an herb-crusted swordfish, and a seared yellow fin tuna with wasabi mashed potatoes and grape tomato relish. There's an excellent wine list that includes about 80 wines, and, best of all, they're fairly reasonably priced.

WAINSCOTT

GEORGICA RESTAURANT AND LOUNGE

631-537-5603
108 Montauk Hwy., Wainscott
Owner: Antonio Fuccio
Chefs: Robert Hesse and Seth Levine
Cuisine: Contemporary American
Serving: D
Open: Year-round; nightly in summer; Fri. and Sat. only rest of year
Price: Expensive–Very Expensive
Credit Cards: AE, MC, V
Special Features: Glass-enclosed porch overlooking Georgica Pond; late-night lounge with DJ Fri. and Sat.
Reservations: Accepted
Directions: Located on Montauk Hwy. (Rte. 27) at Wainscott Stone Hwy.

Set in a Tudoresque building on the banks of Georgica Pond, this restaurant offers multilevel dining rooms with seductively peaceful views. An evening on the porch overlooking the pond, where exterior lighting creates a magical mood, illuminating the trees and the calm waters through which the swans glide by, turns a dinner here into an unforgettably romantic experience. Now under new ownership, and with celebrity chefs Robert Hesse and Seth Levine, top contestants on Gordon Ramsey's reality-TV show *Hell's Kitchen,* manning the stoves, this kitchen is anything but hell. You might try a wild Atlantic salmon wellington with boursin cheese and baby spinach in puff pastry and sauced with a dill caper crème, or a macadamia-crusted Chilean sea bass with a coconut risotto cake and a blood orange beurre blanc. Late night, the waiting area in the center of the restaurant turns into a hot lounge spot, with a DJ spinning pulsing tunes. After the summer season, the restaurant is only open Friday and Saturday nights, but then there's still lots of action in the lounge.

RUGOSA

631-604-1550
www.rugosarestaurant.com
290 Montauk Hwy., Wainscott, NY 11975
Owners/Chefs: Bill and Yvette Mammes
Manager and Sommelier: Chimene Visser
Cuisine: New American with French influences

A sophisticated setting is an appropriate backdrop for the outstanding New American cuisine at Rugosa.
Photo courtesy Wordhampton Public Relations

Serving: D
Open: Year-round; D daily in summer; rest of year closed Tues. and Wed.
Price: Moderate–Very Expensive; prix fixe available
Credit Cards: AE, MC, V
Special Features: Wheelchair access; small plates at bar; tasting menu
Reservations: Highly recommended
Directions: On Montauk Hwy., 2.5 miles west of East Hampton village

Bill Mammes grew up on Long Island, graduated from the Culinary Institute of America, and then held some very impressive culinary positions, including sous chef at the Ritz Carlton in New Orleans (where he met Yvette, who was the pastry chef). After marrying and working at major hotels in Las Vegas, the two ventured to Long Island to open their own restaurant. And we are very fortunate they did. Focusing on local ingredients, the menu changes with the ingredients that are in-season. A crab salad in August featured blue claw crab, zucchini, and apples with toasted almonds and crab vinaigrette, as well as an entrée of seared

Long Island duck breast with a curry polenta cake, date chutney, turnips, and five-spice duck jus. Yvette's desserts are unusual and ethereal. A meringue brûlée was unlike any dessert I've ever had—absolutely delicious. The space, which has housed several restaurants before, has an open floor plan, dark wood floors, and ivory walls that hold dramatic paintings—especially notable are those by local artist Scott Hewett.

WATER MILL
DISH
631-726-0246
www.dishhampton.com
760 Montauk Hwy. Water Mill, NY
Owners/Chefs: Peter Robertson and Merrill Indoe
Cuisine: New American
Open: Year-round; in summer Thurs.–Sun. (and sometimes Mon.); rest of year fewer days
Price: Moderate
Credit Cards: AE, D, MC, V
Special Features: BYOB
Reservations: Absolutely necessary
Directions: From Montauk Hwy. (Rte. 27) traveling east, turn left at the traffic light in Water Mill onto Station Rd. and park in the parking lot.

Dish is located in a tiny little space in the Water Mill shopping center, where Peter Robertson and Merrill Indoe, a husband-and-wife team who both graduated from the Culinary Institute of America, dream up a new menu every night based on the availability of local ingredients. With only 12 seats, and communal tables, this is not an intimate, romantic restaurant, rather it's a foody haven, with a relaxed, casual vibe, where you can taste original dishes prepared by two dedicated chefs who are passionate about their work. The decor consists of copper pans on the walls, blue-and-white-checkered napkins, and fresh flowers. One night in autumn, you might

have an entrée of pan-fried local fluke served with potato croquettes, and brussel sprouts with bacon. A dessert could feature a pumpkin cheesecake with a gingersnap topping, served with Chantilly crème. Be sure to bring your own wine.

MIRKO'S RESTAURANT
631-726-4444
www.mirkos.com
Water Mill Square; 670 Montauk Hwy. Water Mill
Mailing Address: P.O. Box 217, Water Mill, NY 11976
Manager/Owner: Eileen Zagar
Chef/Owner: Mirko Zagar
Cuisine: Eclectic
Serving: D
Open: Mar.–Dec.; in summer Thurs.–Mon.; fewer days rest of year
Price: Expensive–Very Expensive
Credit Cards: AE, D, MC, V
Special Features: Wheelchair access; outdoor patio; fireplace
Reservations: Recommended
Directions: From Montauk Hwy. (Rte. 27), turn into Water Mill Sq. opposite the Windmill. Continue past the first parking field and turn left into the second. Restaurant is at end on left.

Tucked away in the back of Water Mill Square, Mirko's is definitely not a place you'd stumble upon by accident. Nevertheless, it's absolutely worth seeking out, as it's consistently ranked among the top restaurants on Long Island by Zagat reviewers. Once there, you'll discover a tranquil setting, far from the traffic noise of Montauk Highway. You'll also find a husband-and-wife team who, for more than 25 years, have been dedicated to making your dining experience so memorable that you'll return again and again. Eileen will greet you at the door and see to your every dining need. Mirko is Croatian-born, and his inventive cooking reflects both eastern European and French influences. Grilled shrimp and

Mirko's has been earning applause for its eclectic cuisine for more than 25 years. Photo courtesy Mirko's Restaurant

bacon is a wonderful appetizer—plump shrimp are wrapped in bacon, grilled, and served in a light lemon, pepper, and white wine sauce laced with coarsely diced shallots. For entrées, the spice-rubbed roasted Long Island duck breast comes with wild-rice griddle cakes, a bing cherry compote, and an orange-honey pomegranate sauce. Mirko and Eileen grow their own herbs and vegetables behind the restaurant, to ensure they're absolutely fresh when brought to your table. There's also a well-chosen wine list, and, of course, the desserts are sublime. Inside the dining room, the fireplace is welcoming on chilly nights, and the elegant ambience is romantic and alluring—muted lighting, exquisite sconces with pretty shades, and wainscoted walls—conspire to transport patrons to Europe. In summer, a very pretty courtyard offers a welcoming place to dine.

MUSE RESTAURANT AND AQUATIC LOUNGE
631-726-2606
760 Montauk Hwy., Water Mill, NY 11976
Owner/Chef: Matthew Guiffrida
Cuisine: New American
Serving: D
Open: Year-round; daily in summer, Thurs.–Sun. rest of year
Price: Moderate–Expensive
Credit Cards: AE, D, MC, V
Special Features: Glass-topped bar with aquarium underneath; water wall behind bar

Reservations: Recommended
Directions: From Montauk Hwy. (Rte. 27) traveling east, turn left at the traffic light onto Station Rd. and park in the parking lot.

Matthew Guiffrida has created a restaurant in the Water Mill shopping center that is original, whimsical, and just plain fun. For example, should you care for a drink prior to dinner, be sure to sit at the clever bar, as it's got a glass top where you can watch colorful fish swimming under your drink in the saltwater aquarium, and you can watch a cascade of water behind the bar. The ceiling of the restaurant is an electric blue, and the gold walls have been splashed with color— although this may sound garish, it's really quite attractive. The menu is as whimsical and tongue-in-cheek as the decor. Tuna Palooza turned out to be tuna in four different guises, and Not Ya Mama's Meatballs is a tasty treat consisting of four varieties of meatballs. Both of these are appetizers, but the entrées are equally inventive. Desserts include such creations as caramel candied apple fritters, and the Fistful of Fosters is a riff on bananas Foster. If you're in the mood for a fun, casual evening of good food, you won't go wrong here.

ROBERT'S

631-726-7171
www.robertshamptons.com
755 Montauk Hwy., Water Mill, NY 11976
Owner/Manager: Robert Durkin
Chef de Cuisine: Natalie Byrnes
Cuisine: Coastal Italian
Serving: D
Open: Year-round; daily in summer; rest of year fewer days
Price: Very Expensive; prix fixe offered
Credit Cards: AE, MC, V
Special Features: Wheelchair access; outside dining; fireplace
Reservations: Highly recommended
Directions: At traffic light in Water Mill

Robert Durkin, also the owner of New Para-
dise Café in Sag Harbor, has been a noted East End restaurateur for many years. His namesake, Robert's, is located in a charming pre–Revolutionary War building with low, beamed ceilings, wide-plank pine floors, and a fireplace. It's very elegant, intimate, and utterly romantic. There are some wonderful pasta dishes, such as orecchiette with gulf shrimp, tomato, broccoli rabe, garlic, and red pepper, and some excellent fish dishes, such as the monkfish piccata with baby artichokes, caperberries, and lemon. Creamy polenta with Gorgonzola is a terrific side. My favorite dessert is a fallen chocolate hazelnut soufflé cake, but the silky smooth panna cotta with biscotti and a glass of vin santo will fill you with reminiscences of your most memorable meal in the heart of Tuscany.

TRATTA EAST

631-726-6200
www.trata.com
1020 Montauk Hwy., Water Mill, NY 11976
Chef: Jose Luis Falcon
Cuisine: Greek
Serving: D
Open: Apr.–Oct.; daily in summer; fewer days rest of season
Price: Expensive–Very Expensive; prix fixe offered
Credit Cards: AE, MC, V
Special Features: Wheelchair access; raw bar; entertainment Thurs.–Sat. in-season
Reservations: Accepted
Directions: On Montauk Hwy. (Rte. 27) just east of town

Although this location has had as many names as the characters in a Russian novel, this incarnation, by the same folk who own Trata Estiatorio in Manhattan and Trata in Roslyn, has definitely struck the right chord. The white and orange walls, wooden floor, and bright pillows transport us to the Greek isles, and the display of fresh fish on ice is a reminder of the Greek bond between sea and table. The specialty of the house is whole fish, which is flown in daily and priced by the pound. It's charcoal grilled with olive oil and lemon, which is absolutely delicious—and light—which means it's easy on the diet too.

WESTHAMPTON BEACH
ANNONA
631-288-7766
www.annona.com
Manhattan Motorcars; 112 Riverhead Rd., Westhampton Beach, NY 11978
Owner: Richard Rubio
Executive Chef: Pietro Bottero
Cuisine: Italian
Serving: D
Open: Year-round; daily in summer; closed Mon. rest of year
Price: Expensive—Very Expensive; prix fixe available off-season
Credit cards: AE, D, MC, V
Special features: Outside dining on rooftop terrace; viewing window overlooking exotic cars and motorcycles
Reservations: Accepted
Directions: From Route 27, take exit 63 south onto Old Riverhead Rd., toward Westhampton Beach. Continue for about 3 miles. Watch for Coachworks/Manhattan Motorcars on left. Park behind building and enter restaurant in back.

If you're in the mood for a nice romantic dinner, and your guy is thinking more along the lines of car shopping, then this is the place for you. He can drool over the Rolls Royces, Bentleys, Lamborghinis, and Ferraris on the showroom floor, while you flirt with the handsome waiter who's bringing your Bentley Bellini. It may seem like an odd combination, but it certainly does work! The restaurant is named for the Roman goddess of the harvest, which is appropriate because the vegetable and herb garden outside the kitchen supplies fresh ingredients for lucky diners every night. Executive chef Pietro Bottero exerts as

much attention and care to the preparation and presentation of his dishes as the Rubios do in marketing fine automobiles. His credentials are impeccable, having formerly worked at some of the finest Manhattan restaurants. You might start a meal, for example, with a comice pear salad, which comes with wild arugula, pecorino tuscano, and aged balsamic. You might have a risotto entrée that includes wild mushrooms, parmigiano and white truffle oil, or seared sea scallops with sunchoke puree, shiitake mushrooms, asparagus, and sweet garlic foam. The Italian wine list includes selections for every taste, and the desserts are to die for—especially the mascarpone cheesecake with maple glaze and crushed walnuts. The sleek and understated decor of the restaurant and bar is comfortable and inviting—and the rooftop terrace, with its overhanging pergola, is the perfect place to dine on a balmy summer evening.

PATIO AT 54 MAIN
631-288-0100
www.thepatiowhb.com
54 Main St., Westhampton Beach, NY 11978
Owner: Dwayne Kirchner
Executive Chef: Katherine Kane
Cuisine: New American Bistro
Serving: D
Open: Year-round
Price: Moderate—Expensive; prix fixe available
Credit Cards: AE, MC, V
Special Features: Raw bar; outside dining; live entertainment on weekends
Reservations: Accepted
Directions: On Main St. between Potunk Ln. and Sunset Ave.

This pretty restaurant has been around for some 75 years, and it's seen its ups and downs, but it's definitely in an up mode at present. Dwayne Kirchner, who has been the owner since 2004, undertook a complete renovation several years ago that turned the old girl into a pretty young maiden. The decor in the multiple dining rooms is bright and cheerful, and the courtyard dining in the summer is secluded from the street. Chef Katherine Kane prepares a menu that's sure to please most tastes. The appetizer of thin-sliced fried zucchini and lemon chips, with its horseradish cream sauce, is a terrific starter, as is the three-onion tart, with its topping of Gorgonzola. A seared salmon fillet comes over a watercress salad, and the hanger steak is marinated and served with sautéed mushrooms and onions.

SALTWATER GRILL

631-288-1485
Dune Deck Resort; 379 Dune Rd., Westhampton Beach
Mailing Address: P.O. Box 1748, Westhampton Beach, NY 11978
Executive Chef: Jack Hekker
Cuisine: Seafood
Serving: L, D
Open: Mid-May–mid-Sept.
Price: Moderate–Expensive
Credit Cards: AE, D, MC, V
Special Features: View; beachside dining; live entertainment; guest rooms on premises Reservations: Accepted
Directions: From Main St., Westhampton Beach, drive south on Jessup Ln. and cross bridge to Dune Rd. Turn right and follow Dune Rd. for 1.2 miles. Restaurant is on left in Dune Deck Resort.

If you have romance on your mind, there are few settings that can compare to this oceanside restaurant in the Dune Deck Resort. The views are spectacular. You might eat inside in the bar area (the once-

You can dine beachside at Saltwater Grill, at the Dune Deck Resort.

elegant dining room that Chef Starr Boggs made a destination was expected to emerge from renovation in time for summer dining in 2010), or outside at picnic tables with bold navy and white ticking covering benches and pretty striped awnings overhead. The entire effect is charming and very casual. And the food's not bad either. There are fish and dips—a deep-fried fish with three dipping sauces—a seafood brochette incorporating tuna, halibut, and tilapia, sandwiches (including the ubiquitous lobster roll), and small plates—but you really come for the outdoor setting of beach, dune grass, and the smell of the ocean. Live bands play frequently, creating a convivial scene, and it's very kid-friendly. (See listing in Chapter 3 for guest rooms.)

STARR BOGGS
631-288-3500
www.starrboggs.com
6 Parlato Dr., Westhampton Beach, NY 11978
Owner/Chef: Starr Boggs
Cuisine: New American
Serving: D
Open: May–Nov.
Price: Expensive–Very Expensive; prix fixe available
Credit Cards: AE, D, MC, V
Special Features: Outside dining; live entertainment; lobster bakes

Reservations: Highly recommended
Directions: From Main St. in Westhampton Beach traveling east, turn right onto Library Ave. Turn right at the first intersection onto Perlato Dr. Restaurant is on right.

Starr Boggs is more than a restaurant; Starr Boggs, the man, is a legend—an institution. This is a chef who cares deeply about his craft, as well as about creating healthy dishes, by using organic ingredients that are produced without harming the environment. He incorporates fresh-from-the-farmer produce and fishermen's daily catch into his nightly menu—and he's been doing so for almost 30 years. You might start with an Exotic Mushroom Sauté that includes a medley of chanterelles, shiitake, and abalone mushrooms with brioche toast and brandy cream, or a salad of local baby beets with frisée, truffled goat cheese, and hazelnuts. In the entrée category, the almond-crusted flounder has become a signature, and it's perfection. But the big, juicy steaks and the seared bigeye tuna are equal hits. The wine list is extensive and impressive. All this drama is presented in a series of light and airy rooms in a historic old house on a back street—away from the hustle of the village. A lovely garden courtyard with a multitude of plants and flowers, as well as a waterfall, makes it a favorite summer venue.

FOOD PURVEYORS

Social events, dinner parties, art-gallery openings, fund-raising benefits, and al fresco picnics consistently give business to Hamptons caterers, bakers, restaurant chefs, confectioners, delis, gourmet shops, and wineshops. Fish markets stock fish fresh from the morning catch, and farmers' markets sell produce straight from the field. Specialty food shops are filled with homemade jams, jellies, chutneys, and breads, as well as with the pungent smell of aging cheeses and freshly brewed coffee. Juice bars offer thick mixtures of fresh strawberries, raspberries, peaches, and other fruits in-season that are cool refreshers after a hot day at the beach. Coffee bars serve cappuccinos, espressos, lattes, and American coffees.

Bakeries and Confectioneries

EAST HAMPTON

Dylan's Mini Candy Bar (631-324-6181; www.dylanscandybar.com; 52 Main St., East Hampton, NY 11937; open year-round, in summer, Mon.–Thurs. 10–10, Fri. and Sat. 9–11, Sun. 10–9; fewer days and shorter hours rest of year.) An offshoot of the big Manhattan store, this "mini" shop carries the scrumptious candy for which Dylan's is famous. You'll find boxed chocolates in a variety of flavors, gummy bears, chocolate-covered pretzels and popcorn, and lots more to satisfy the sweet tooth.

Fat Ass Fudge (631-324-6540; www. fat-assfudge.com; 81 Newtown Road, East Hampton, NY 11937; sold online or through Lucy's Whey (see "Gourmet Food Shops & Markets," this section) in East Hampton.) Owner: Donna McCue. Donna learned fudge making at her mom's apronstrings, but she's perfected her recipe over the years. Using organic goat milk, organic sugar, and Belgian chocolate, she whips up creamy, ethereal confections in milk chocolate, dark chocolate, and a wonderful white chocolate with peppermint flecks during the holidays. She also makes fudge brownies, English toffee, and hot fudge sauce.

SOUTHAMPTON

Blue Duck Bakery Café (631-204-1701; www.blueduckbakerycafe.com; 30 Hampton Rd., Southampton, NY 11968; open year-round Mon.–Sat. 6:30 AM–6 PM; Sun. 6:30 AM–5 PM) Artisanal breads, as well as cakes, pastries, cookies, sandwiches (using house-made breads), are made by Keith Kouris, a graduate of the French Culinary Institute's International Bread Baking Program. You will find his breads at fine restaurants in New York City, and throughout Long Island, as well as at this bakery and another on the North Fork in Southold.

Tate's Bake Shop (631-283-9830; www.tatesbakeshop.com; 43 North Sea Rd., Southampton, NY 11968; open daily year-round 8–6) Kathleen King opened her shop at this location more than 20 years ago, eventually building a distribution network that supplied more than 300 upscale gourmet shops nationwide—so when she resigned following a dispute with out-of-state backers, you could hear the cry of dismay all the way to Manhattan. We're happy to report, however, that Kathleen started over and her business is now bigger than ever, encompassing a distribution network of more than 1,000 outlets nationwide. Her shop and products are called Tate's in honor of Kathleen's father, and the baked goods are fabulous—absolutely yummy crisp chocolate-chip cookies, apple crumb pies, breads, and scones direct from the source—or, if you're not in the neighborhood, from her online store. Best of all, her baked goods are good for you. She uses all-natural products with no preservatives and makes everything herself from scratch, just as our grandmothers used to do.

WAINSCOTT

Breadzilla (631-537-0955; www.breadzilla.com; 84 Wainscott-Northwest Rd., P.O. Box 384, Wainscott, NY 11975; open year-round, Tues.–Sat. 8–4, Sun. 8–3; closed Mon.) Nancy and Brad Thompson have filled their wonderful shop with home-baked breads, cakes, pies, cheesecakes, and individual desserts. The Gruyère bread is crusted with cheese, and the chocolate mousse is divine. Lunch is served from 11:30–2:30 (Sun. until 1:30) and includes such offerings as lemon herb chicken salad, a roasted local corn quesadilla, a super steak melt, or a puttanesca basswich (using locally caught bass).

Kathleen King makes some of the best bakery goods in the Hamptons. You can purchase and sample them at Tate's Bake Shop in Southampton.

Levain Bakery (631-537-8570; www.levainbakery.com; 354 Montauk Hwy., P.O. Box 787, Wainscott, NY 11975; open May–Sept.) Owners: Connie McDonald and Pamela Weekes. This terrific transplant from Manhattan (there's also a shop at 167 West 74th St.) offers breakfast goods in the morning and pizzas and sandwiches in the afternoon; as well as great breads, desserts, and their signature cookies. There are no preservatives or additives in their products, and the hefty 6-ounce cookies could be a meal in themselves. Try the dark-chocolate chocolate chip for a chocolate buzz!

WESTHAMPTON BEACH

Beach Bakery Cafe (631-288-6552; www.beachbakerycafe.com; 112 Main St., Westhampton Beach, NY 11978; open daily in summer 7–midnight; rest of year 7–6) The wonderful aroma wafting from this little bakery is like a magnet, but so are the delicious goodies. Great breads, cookies, cakes, pies, and much more are made by Simon Jorna, the owner, and they are baked on the premises. In summer, he also makes a terrific pizza that he will deliver. Simon tripled the size of his bakery in 1998 to make room for little café tables and rattan chairs, where you can munch on a confection or savor some ice cream right on the premises, and in summer the sidewalk in front is filled with tables of happy families enjoying the luscious fare purchased inside.

Holey Moses Cheesecake (631-288-8088; www.holeymosescheesecake.com; 332 Frances S. Gabreski Airport, Westhampton Beach, NY 11978; open Mon.–Fri. 9–6 ; Sat. noon–4; closed Sun.) Chris Weber's cheesecakes are sold in hundreds of restaurant and food outlets in the tristate region. He'll take orders for a single cheesecake or 1,000. His cheese-cakes, with flavors of pumpkin, Oreo cookie, lime, etc., are so popular that restaurants proudly proclaim "cheesecakes from Holey Moses."

Cafés & Coffeehouses

A restaurant is listed as a café if, in general, dinner is not served. In several of the venues featured here, dinner is indeed served, but the listed establishments are best known and loved as breakfast or lunch spots, and thus have been placed in the café category.

AMAGANSETT

Hampton Chutney Co. (631-267-3131; www.hamptonchutney.com; Amagansett Sq., P.O. Box 273, Amagansett, NY 11930; open in summer 10–7; shorter hours rest of year) Gary and Isabel MacGurn have expanded their terrific chutney company from the Hamptons to two locations in Manhattan, but the Amagansett Square location is definitely the most charming. Here, diners can sit at picnic tables in the grassy square and eat delicious dosas, which are light, thin, crispy crêpes made with rice and lentils and filled with interesting ingredients such as grilled chicken with goat cheese, spinach, roasted tomato, and, of course, chutney. They can also get a tall, refreshing lassi, a smoothie made with yogurt and fresh fruit. Don't leave without a container of cilantro, mango, or tomato chutney.

LaFondita (631-267-8800; www.lafondita.net; 74 Montauk Hwy., Amagansett, NY 11930; open Apr.–mid-Oct.; Wed.–Sun. 11:30–8:00, closed Mon. and Tues.) Brought to us by the same folks who own Nick & Toni's, Rowdy Hall, and Townline BBQ, this Mexican outpost, on the outskirts of Amagansett, provides flavorful burritos, huaraches, tostadas, fish tacos, chile rellenos, quesadillas, and more. Order at the counter and eat at picnic tables on the lawn. Off-season, you can purchase the same great dishes at sister restaurant Townline BBQ in Sagaponack.

BRIDGEHAMPTON

Bridgehampton Candy Kitchen (631-537-9885; Main St., P.O. Box 3011, Bridgehampton, NY 11932; open daily in summer 7 AM–10 PM; daily in fall 7 AM–8 PM; daily in winter 7 AM–7 PM) Owner: Gus Laggis. The spot for breakfast or an afternoon ice-cream treat! This old-fashioned coffee shop and soda fountain has been in business since 1925. It's a legendary star hangout that looks much as it did when it opened. The food hasn't changed much either. Breakfast is of the bacon-and-eggs variety. In the afternoon and evening, there are hamburgers, clubs, and grilled-cheese sandwiches. Milk shakes, ice cream sodas, and egg creams are just as they should be. Sundaes have sauce dripping down the sides, with a mound of whipped cream, chocolate sprinkles, and a cherry. You can also get cherry and lemon Cokes. The ice cream is made on the premises in a wide variety of flavors. There's nothing fancy here, just old-fashioned, good food.

The Golden Pear Café (www.goldenpearcafe.com; 631-537-1100, 2426 Montauk Hwy., Bridgehampton, NY 11932; also 631-329-1600, 34 Newtown Ln., East Hampton, NY 11937; also 631-283-8900, 99 Main St., Southampton, NY 11968; also 631-725-2270, 111 Main St., Sag Harbor, NY 11693; open daily 7:30–5:45) Owner Keith Davis's Golden Pear Cafés, now in four East End locations, offer both eat-in and take-out. Newspapers are on hand, and these bright, welcoming, convivial spots are great for breakfast, lunch, or just relaxing with a friend over a cup of coffee. There's nothing fast-food about the

Golden Pear; each café has its own chef. There are fresh muffins and cookies hot from the oven, excellent salads, and a variety of hot dishes such as pastas, chilis, chicken pot-pies, and pies and cakes available whole or by the slice.

Starbucks (www.starbucks.com; 631-537-5851, 2478 Montauk Hwy., Bridgehampton, NY 11932; also 631-329-8645, 39 Main St., East Hampton, NY 11937; 631-728-7530, 24 W. Montauk Hwy., Hampton Bays, NY 11946; open daily in summer 6 AM–11 PM; shorter hours rest of year) Finally, in 2000, the first Starbucks opened in the Hamptons. Located in the fabulous old Bridgehampton Bank building, right at the monument in the center of the village, it's the classiest Starbucks we've seen. It's all done in gold, brick, and mocha colors, and there's a carpeted area with comfortable chairs and sofas. Since that time, two other Starbucks have opened in the Hamptons, as well as several on the North Fork. No longer is the East End Starbucks-deprived!

EAST HAMPTON

Babette's (631-329-5377; www.babetteseasthampton.com; 66 Newtown Ln., East Hampton, NY 11937; open daily in summer 8 AM–10 PM; fewer days and shorter hours rest of year) Owner: Barbara Layton. Babette's has earned high esteem both with health-conscious celebrities and with nonvegetarians for its interesting and unusual vegetarian and organic dishes. Try the gift-wrapped burritos with grilled tofu, tempeh, tuna,

You'll nosh on creative vegetarian and organic dishes at Babette's in East Hampton. Photo courtesy Wordhampton Public Relations

chicken, or shrimp. If you sip a smoothie at an outside table, you may be sitting next to Meg Ryan or Bernadette Peters.

Cherrystones Clam & Lobster Shack (631-324-1111; www.indianwellstavern.com; 277 Pantigo Rd., East Hampton, NY 11937; open May–Oct., in summer daily noon–10; rest of season open Fri.–Sun. noon–8) Owners: Chris Eggert and Kevin Boles. It seemed like the Snowflake had been here forever. Originally it was an old-fashioned drive-in, but through the efforts of several new owners this local favorite has finally entered the 21st century. Now in the accomplished hands of the team who also own Indian Wells Tavern in Amagansett (and for many years, Bostwick's), it's sure to extend its long life. There's a courtyard for outside dining that's hidden behind a privet hedge, and inside dining that's comfortable and contemporary. The seafood-centric menu includes a raw bar, sandwiches (lobster rolls and fried flounder) and fish and chips, fried oysters, and crab cakes—and there's a full bar.

Sam's (631-324-5900; www.sameasthampton.com; 36 Newtown Ln., East Hampton, NY 11937; open year-round, Mon.–Thurs. 5–10, Fri.–Sun. 5–11) Sam's has been an East Hampton institution since 1947, and it remains a local hangout. There's nothing fancy here, just pizzas that are renowned—they're thin-crusted, and come with piles of great toppings. Yes, you can get pasta and meat entrées, but the pizzas reign supreme.

MONTAUK

Joni's (631-668-3663; 9 S. Edison St., Montauk, NY 11954; open Mar.–Dec., daily in summer 7:30–6; shorter hours and fewer days rest of season) Owner: Joan Huey. This cute little café has standing room only at the counter for fabulous breakfast and lunch dishes that include breakfast wraps (scrambled eggs with perhaps cheddar cheese, smoked apple bacon, and caramelized onions) and jaffles, which are grilled pressed sandwiches (you choose your ingredients). For lunch there's a variety of soups, sandwiches, and wraps, as well as fresh fruit smoothies and blended coffees. There are indoor and outdoor tables.

SAG HARBOR

Bay Burger (631-899-3915; www.bayburger.com; 1742 Bridgehampton/Sag Harbor Tpke., Sag Harbor, 11963; open Mar.–Nov. daily in summer, fewer days rest of season.) Owners: Liza and Joe Tremblay. Joe is a veteran of the top-notch Burger Joint at Le Parker Meridien in Manhattan and Liza is a Culinary Institute of America grad, so, as you would expect, their burgers are not your run-of-the-mill variety. You can pile lots of extras onto their juicy offerings, and in addition, they serve breakfast (green and white eggs = two scrambled eggs with goat cheese and scallions on a toasted croissant), lunch and dinner.

SOUTHAMPTON

Annie's Organic Café & Market (631-377-3607; www.anniesorganiccafe.com; 56 Nugent St., Southampton, NY 11968; open: year-round daily) Owner: Jessica Greenfield. Located on a side street, in the old George Martin space, this cute little café serves organic and vegetarian breakfast and lunch dishes. There's an excellent juice bar, or you can get protein shakes or smoothies. Organic oatmeal and homemade organic muffins, or a scrambled tofu burrito, are on the breakfast list, while for lunch a grilled vegetable or tempeh sandwich is offered. The on-site market provides take-home packaged items not usually found in grocery stores.

WATER MILL

Hampton Coffee Company (631-726-COFE, www.hamptoncoffee.com; 869 Montauk
Hwy., Water Mill, NY 11976; open daily year-round 5:30–6; also 631-288-4480; 194 Mill
Rd., Westhampton Beach, NY 11978; open daily year-round 6–6) Owner: Jason and
Theresa Belkin. If, as far as you're concerned, it's all about the flavor, then you must try
these terrific cafés, where the coffee is roasted on the premises and ground just before
brewing. You won't be disappointed. You will also be able to get bagels, scones, croissants, or breakfast dishes such as huevos rancheros and breakfast burritos. At lunch,
there are sandwiches, soups, and salads, and dinner (Water Mill only) entrées include
broiled salmon and marinated sirloin steak.

WESTHAMPTON BEACH

Sunset Café (631-998- 0372; www.sunsetcafewhb.com; 49 Sunset Ave., Westhampton
Beach, NY 11978; open daily May–mid-Sept.; Sat. and Sun. only rest of year) Owner:
Christine Sparacino. This pretty shingled building, with its welcoming covered brick
front porch, offers an array of breakfast and lunch items (mostly organic and locally
grown.) There are even super-friendly kid items, such as chocolate-bread panini with
peanut butter and sliced bananas. For adults, the selection of stuffed sandwiches and
hot paninis keep them coming back for more. At night, the place turns into a coffee and
liquor bar. Then you can relax, have a drink, feast on tapas before the fireplace, and, on
Saturdays, listen to live music.

Cigar Lounges

Even as restaurants are banning smoking in their dining rooms, the popularity of cigars is
on the increase. In the Hamptons, as in Manhattan, exclusive clubs where one may pull on a
stogie are rising from the smoke. Often these include special rooms, open to members
only, that offer locked, individual humidors and comfortable lounges where cigar smoking
is welcomed. There also may be a Scotch and cordials bar and live entertainment.

SAG HARBOR

The Cigar Bar (631-725-2575; 2 Main St., Sag Harbor, NY 11963; open year-round, in summer noon–4 AM; slightly shorter hours rest of year) Owner: Arlene. This elegant shop
has a fine selection of imported cigars; pick your choice from those in a 12-by-10-foot
walk-in humidor. You can also buy cigar accessories, including an elegant Spanish cedar
humidor. There are overstuffed chairs, Oriental rugs on the floor, and a lounge with
original art on the walls. At the little bar, you can select cognac, single-malt Scotch,
wine, espresso, or cappuccino for sipping. A pianist entertains on weekends.

Eggs & Poultry

EAST HAMPTON

Iacono Farms (631-324-1107; 106 Long Ln., East Hampton, NY 11937; open year-round
Mon. and Wed.–Sat. 8:30–5, Sun. 10–12:30; closed Tues.) The plump, juicy chickens
that Salvadore and Eileen Iacono have been raising since 1948 are deservedly popular,
as are their super fresh eggs. It's often advisable to order in advance on summer weekends, because they sell out early. And you'll also want to take home some of the breads
and cookies made by their daughter. The Iaconos are some of the busiest and nicest

Farm stands along country roads yield fresh-from-the-field produce and flowers.

folks around. No matter how many grouchy, impatient customers are lined up, there's always a pleasant word for each.

SOUTHAMPTON

North Sea Farms (631-283-0735; 1060 Noyac Rd., Southampton, NY 11968; open daily year-round 8–6) Owner: Richie King. This terrific farm raises succulent, fat chickens that are prized for their tenderness, and many restaurateurs come here for their supply. But you don't have to go to a restaurant to sample them. You can pick up a fresh hen here for a tasty summer BBQ at home, and while you're at it, you might pick up some fresh eggs and organic produce.

Farms & Farm Stands

AMAGANSETT

Amagansett Farmers Market (631-267-3894; 367 Main St., Amagansett, NY 11930; open Mem. Day–early Oct., 7 AM–7 PM daily in summer; closed Tues. and Wed. rest of season) Manager: Eli Zabar. After several years in which its future seemed uncertain, this venerable farm stand is now in the secure hands of the Peconic Land Trust, and managed by veteran restaurateur and bread maker Eli Zabar, who owns three restaurants in Manhattan and a wholesale bread business supplying numerous restaurants. The market is, once again, the place to go on a sunny day for the newspaper, coffee, and sticky buns from Eli's bakery. Patrons are encouraged to relax at tables on the lawn or on benches down by the fishpond. The variety of fresh produce and fruit—all from local farmers—is staggering. In addition, the market includes a deli section with salads, pâtés, cheeses, and roast or fried chicken; and a cold section with sodas, egg creams, milk, eggs, and ice cream. In addition to Eli's breads, a line of prepared foods is for sale at the market.

BRIDGEHAMPTON

Hayground Market (631-537-1676; Montauk Hwy., Bridgehampton; mailing address P.O. Box 623, Aquebogue, NY 11931; open Apr.–Nov., daily in summer 8–8, daily in fall 8–7) You'll recognize the Hayground Market by the tall ear of corn at the edge of Montauk Highway or the big cauliflower on the farm wagon. You'll also notice piles of pumpkins attractively displayed in the fall and washtubs full of brilliantly hued zinnias earlier in the season, as well as bountiful displays of produce, fruits, and berries. The 200-acre home farm that supports this large market has been in the Reeve family for many generations, and the farm stand has been operating since the early 1950s.

Mecox Bay Dairy (631-537-0335; www.mecoxbaydairy.com; 855 Mecox Rd., Bridgehampton, NY 11932; no set hours, you must make an appointment to purchase cheese) Owners: Arthur and Stacy Ludlow. Formerly potato farmers, the Ludlows switched to dairy in 2003, and now make outstanding artisanal cheeses. The dairy is located in the former potato-storage barn. The Farmhouse Cheddar is mildly sharp with a creamy finish. Atlantic Mist, on the other hand, is rich and creamy, while Sigit is a flavorful hard cheese with Gruyère characteristics. You can arrange to tour the dairy (call ahead) to see the interesting process of converting milk to cheese: $12/adult, $6/child.

EAST HAMPTON

Round Swamp Farm Country Market (631-324-4438; www.roundswampfarm.com; 184 Three Mile Harbor Rd., East Hampton, NY 11937; open May–Nov., Mon.–Sat. 8–6, Sun. 8–2) Round Swamp Farm, "Farmers of Land and Sea," is supported by the 20-acre Lester Farm, which has been family-owned for 250 years. Carolyn Lester Snyder started selling the family bounty when she was a child, from a tiny roadside stand built for her by her father. Now 16 family members contribute goods to the market. Piles of tender white corn are heaped on a farm wagon; tomatoes, potatoes, and onions fill the bins; and the chilled produce room is stocked with a variety of lettuces, peppers, herbs, fruit, and berries. Baked goods are a family specialty. Cookies, breads, muffins, chutneys, relishes, and cakes are snapped up by loyal customers. (The best cookies I've ever tasted are Lisa's Ultimate Cookies—an incredible confection of chocolate chips, nuts, crunchy toffee, and lots more.) Homemade soups and a small selection of salads are also popular. An adjacent fish market supplies fresh fish daily and also has a refrigerated milk, egg, and cheese section. Freshly cut flowers are also available.

WATER MILL

The Green Thumb (631-726-1900; www.greenthumborganicfarm.com; 829 Montauk Hwy., Water Mill; mailing address 132 Halsey Ln., Water Mill, NY 11976; open May–Dec., daily 8–6, later in midsummer) The 77-acre Halsey Farm, family-owned since 1644, is now in the capable hands of the 11th generation, and it's an award-winning certified-organic farm. For dependable, high-quality produce, this farm stand can't be beat: the Halsey family grows over 15 varieties of lettuce, 12 kinds of salad greens, 19 different herbs, a colorful variety of sweet peppers, red and gold raspberries, beans, tomatoes, squash, pumpkins, flowers, and much, much more. At the Green Thumb, you can buy tiny French green beans (haricots verts) and succulent little yellow pear tomatoes, as well as other, more unusual varieties. In summer there are pony rides for children.

Gourmet Food Shops & Markets

In general, the following shops operate busy catering businesses as well as storefront shops, and they have many more recipes in their culinary repertoire than meet the eye. If planning a party or a catered dinner, be sure to discuss the event with the catering manager, who can plan a menu specifically for you.

AMAGANSETT

Mary's Marvelous! (631-267-8796; www.marysmarvelous.com; 209 Main St., P.O. Box 124; Amagansett, NY 11930; open daily in summer 7–5; rest of year Sun.–Tues. and Thurs. 7–3:30, Fri. and Sat. 7–5, closed Wed.) Owner: Mary Schoenlein. Mary has been working in the food industry for more than 20 years, and she produces and markets her own line of natural, slow-roasted granola. Now she's opened this lovely little shop where she also sells freshly baked muffins and scones, cakes, brownies, sandwiches, and some take-out entrée items.

BRIDGEHAMPTON

Citarella (631-726-3636; www.citarella.com; 2209 Montauk Hwy., Bridgehampton; mailing address: 2135 Broadway, New York, NY 10023; open daily 9:00 AM–7:30 PM) Owner: Joe Gurrera. See full description under Water Mill destination.

The 77-acre Halsey Farm, which has been in the same family since 1644, supplies The Green Thumb market in Water Mill with its organic produce. Morgan McGivern

EAST HAMPTON

Citarella (631-324-9190; 2 Pantigo Rd., East Hampton, open daily 9–7; also Red Horse Market, 74 Montauk Hwy., East Hampton, open daily 11–9; mailing address: 2135 Broadway, New York, NY 10023) Owner Joe Gurrera opened this branch of his terrific Manhattan and Water Mill stores in 2003. See the Water Mill listing for the full story.

Lucy's Whey (631-324-4428; www.lucyswhey.com; 80 North Main St., East Hampton, NY 11937; open: Feb.–Dec., daily in summer, fewer days rest of year.) Owners: Catherine Bodziner and Lucy Kazickas. Growing out of a love of good cheese, this aromatic shop carries a select group of fine artisanal cheeses. In addition, there's a charcuterie, an olive counter, oils, vinegars, freshly baked pies, tarts and cheesecakes, and chocolate (our favorite is Fat Ass Fudge, made with goat cheese). Events throughout the year include Friday-night fondue tastings off-season.

Villa Italian Specialties (631-324-5110; www.villaitalianspecialties.com; 7 Railroad Ave., East Hampton, NY 11937; open year-round Sun.–Thurs. 10–6:30, Fri. and Sat. 9–6:30) Owner: Jerry Geio. This wonderful Italian deli has been in business for almost 20 years, so you know it's doing something right. Although new owners took over in 2002, they kept the same great dishes that had long been staples here. For fresh Parmesan Reggiano or pecorino Romano, real prosciutto, house-made sausage and mozzarella, fresh puttanesca sauce, fresh ravioli or tortellini, and entrées such as eggplant Parmesan and chicken cacciatore, this is definitely the place to come.

QUOGUE

Quogue Country Market (631-653-4191; www.quoguecountrymarket.com; 146 Jessup Ave., P.O. Box 1419, Quogue, NY 11959; open year-round; in summer Mon.–Fri. 7 AM–8 PM, Sat. and Sun. 7 AM–9 PM; rest of year daily 7 AM–6 PM) This large, well-stocked market and deli dates from the 1920s. There's farm-fresh produce, more than 20 kinds of prepared salads, a meat market (no packaged meats), a fresh-fish counter, a large selection of gourmet canned and bottled food products, a fresh bakery with tiny little muffins (very popular), an ample cheese counter, and fresh coffee and cappuccino. An extensive catering menu ranges from baked lasagna to stuffed fresh flounder with herbed cream cheese. The market also sells newspapers, greeting cards, small gift items, and more. Fred Schoenfeld, the owner, is friendly, helpful, and knowledgeable.

SAGAPONACK

Loaves & Fishes (631-537-0555; www.landfcookshop.com; 50 Main St., P.O. Box 318, Sagaponack, NY 11962; open Easter–Christmas, daily 9–5 except Tues. Mem. Day–Labor Day; rest of season fewer days; closed Jan.–Easter) Anna Pump has operated this respected catering and gourmet food shop for more than 15 years. She's earned a deserved reputation for excellence. From her fork-tender beef filet to the chicken curry salad; from condiments such as curried apricot mayonnaise or lemon curd to freshly baked breads and exotic soups—some of the best dinner parties are catered by Loaves & Fishes. You can buy her popular cookbooks here too. (See also listing for Bridgehampton Inn in chapter 3 for Loaves & Fishes Cooking School, and listing in chapter 5 for Loaves & Fishes Cookshop, Bridgehampton.)

Sagg General Store (631-537-0233; www.saggstore.com; 542 Sagg Main St., P.O. Box 433, Sagaponack, NY 11962; open Mar.–Dec., 7–5) Owners: Karen and Richard Thayer. The Sagg General Store is the heart and soul of the hamlet of Sagaponack. The store takes up

one-half of a circa 1880s white clapboard building, and the local post office occupies the other
half. Customers arrive for the mail and a morning paper, and fill their own Sagaponack Main
Store mug with coffee before sitting at a table in
the little courtyard in front to chat. Tom Wolfe,
Kurt Vonnegut, and other notables are as at
home here as you and I. They're open for breakfast, when you might indulge in pancakes,
muffins, or croissants, and for lunch, when you
can nosh on a variety of sandwiches and salads,
as well as cakes, brownies, lemon bars, and
macaroons.

SAG HARBOR

Espresso (631-725-4433; 184 Division St., P.O.
Box 44, Sag Harbor, NY 11963; open year-
round; in summer weekdays 7 AM–9 PM, weekends 7 AM–10 PM; rest of year shorter hours)
Located off the beaten track in the village of Sag
Harbor, Espresso is a great Italian deli/grocery
that just keeps getting better. Richard Cama-
cho's hot focaccia bread, sprinkled with rosemary and garlic and splashed with olive oil, is
heavenly. The packaged Italian specialties
include items that you don't often find at the
finest Italian groceries in Manhattan. Prepared
foods include salads, pastas, and a variety of
entrées. Inventive breakfasts are served in the
morning, and sandwiches are made to order at lunch.

*The owners of this fine gourmet take-out
shop cater some of the best Hamptons
parties.*

SOUTHAMPTON

Village Gourmet Cheese Shop (631-283-6949; 11 Main St., Southampton, NY 11968; open
daily year-round, 7:30–6) Owner: John Grecu. Much more than a cheese shop, this is
the place to come for a newspaper, coffee, and a bagel first thing in the morning or for a
terrific deli sandwich before heading for the beach. You will find prepared hot dishes,
salads, cold drinks, pâtés, charcuterie items, and a good selection of cheeses.

WATER MILL

Citarella (631-726-3636; www.citarella.com; 760 Montauk Hwy. at Citarella Plaza, Water
Mill; mailing address: 2135 Broadway, New York, NY 10023; open year-round
Mon.–Thurs. 9–7:30, Fri.–Sun. 8–7:30) Joe Gurrera has stocked his Water Mill, Bridgehampton, and East Hampton shops just like those in Manhattan, with a fabulous array of
gourmet items. There's a fresh fish and shellfish section that has 10 kinds of oysters and
a tank containing not only live lobsters but also live Dungeness crabs. The meat market
has every imaginable cut of meat, and the cheese section is equally impressive. Of
course, there's a bakery. The prepared-food section includes salads, pasta dishes, veg-

etable napoleons, and prepared meats. Local farms supply the fresh produce. (See listings under East Hampton and Bridgehampton for sister stores.)

WESTHAMPTON BEACH

Sydney's "Taylor" Made Cuisine (631-288-4722; www.sydneyscatering.com; 103 Main St., Westhampton Beach, NY 11978; open daily year-round; 8:00–7:00 in summer, shorter hours rest of year) After operating their terrific take-out business from a building on Mill Road for several years, Erin Finley and David Blydenburgh have moved downtown. You will still find a large selection of cheeses, salads, desserts, pâtés, and rotisserie-baked chickens and ducks. There are also smoked fish, a full bakery selection, and bottled and packaged gourmet foods.

Ice Cream Parlors

BRIDGEHAMPTON

Bridgehampton Ice Cream and Yogurt Company (631-537-0233; 2462 Main St., P.O. Box 1190, Bridgehampton, NY 11932; open July 4–Labor Day, Sun.–Thurs. noon–11, Fri. and Sat. noon–2 AM; May, June, Sept., Oct., fewer days and shorter hours; closed rest of year) The Bridgehampton Ice Cream and Yogurt Company carries Steve's Ice Cream, Columbo Frozen Yogurt, and American Glacé.

EAST HAMPTON

Scoop du Jour (631-329-4883; 35 Newtown Ln., East Hampton, NY 11937; open Mem. Day–Columbus Day, Sun.–Thurs. 10–11, Fri. and Sat. 10–midnight; Columbus Day–Thanksgiving, weekends only and shorter hours) Owner: Lori Zagardo. Great ice cream and an old-fashioned soda fountain make this a very popular spot. They carry Steve's Ice Cream, T & W ice cream, and Columbo and American Glacé yogurt. This is also a coffee bar offering espresso and cappuccino coffees, ice cream sundaes, sodas, and Dreesen's ethereal freshly made doughnuts, in a comfortable, café atmosphere.

MONTAUK

Ben & Jerry's (631-668-9425; www.benjerry.com; 478 West Lake Dr., P.O. Box 667, Montauk, NY 11954; open mid-May–Columbus Day; Jul. and Aug. daily noon–11; call for hours rest of season) Yes, you can get that creamy, rich Ben & Jerry's stuff right here in Montauk.

SAG HARBOR

Ice Cream Club (631-725-2598; www.icecreamclub.com; 7 Main St., Sag Harbor, NY 11963; open year-round, in summer 10–12; shorter hours rest of year) Owner: Daniel Solsedo. Although this is a franchise, the lines generally snake out the door and down the sidewalk for these flavorful scoops.

SOUTHAMPTON

The Fudge Co. (631-283-8108; 67 Main St., Southampton, NY 11968; open Mar.–Dec.; daily in summer 11 AM–midnight; rest of season daily 11 AM–5 PM) From this respected shop, Hugo and John Fudge sell Columbo Soft Yogurt, Cream-of-the-Hamptons ice cream, and their luscious homemade candies.

Sip 'n Soda (631-283-9752; 40 Hampton Rd., Southampton, NY 11968; open daily in sum-

Fresh lobsters, scallops, and fish, much of it grown right here, can be purchased at the fascinating Fish Farm Multi Aquaculture Systems.

mer 7:30 AM–10 PM, shorter hours rest of year) Owner: Jim Parash. Terrific homemade ice cream is served here at a counter. It's good enough to stand in line for.

Seafood Markets and Take-outs

AMAGANSETT

Fish Farm Multi Aquaculture Systems (631-267-3341; 429 Cranberry Hole Rd.; mailing address: P.O. Box 679, Amagansett, NY 11930; open: year-round, daily, 10–6:30) Owners: Bob and Marie Valenti. This is one of the funkiest and most interesting places in the Hamptons. In fact, it's hard to even believe it's *in* the Hamptons. You'll barely see the arrow pointing the way off Montauk Hwy. As you drive up the rutted dirt road (which floods in a hard rain), all you see are dilapidated buildings; pens of geese and chickens; huge drums of growing shellfish, lobster, fluke, and sea bass; and cats and dogs roaming around. But there's a lot going on here. They ship their fish and shellfish throughout the U.S., and you can pick some up here to take home, or you can place an order at the tiny take-out counter and they'll deliver it to the Sea Slug Lounge, a collection of picnic tables right at water's edge. The owner is French, and she really knows how to cook. In addition to the lobster rolls, fish-ka-Bob (get it?) in ponzu, and fish and chips, there are delectable onion tarts, pear and apple tarts, and a chocolate soufflé. Before you leave, be sure to visit the tiny gift shop and perhaps leave with a purchase from the display of Terre E' Provence pottery.

Stuart's Fish Market (631-267-6700; www.stuartsseafood.com; 41 Oak Ln.; mailing address: P.O. Box 1859, Amagansett, NY 11930; open daily year-round 9–6; longer summer hours) Owners: Bruce and Charlotte Sasso. Stuart's Fish Market, on a narrow residential side street between East Hampton and Amagansett, not even close to any water, is definitely not on the beaten track. Nevertheless, the owners are fishermen who catch what they sell. They're in Montauk waters in summer, and off the Florida coast in winter. There's a good seafood selection, with lots of fresh lobster in a watery tank. Several local specialties also are made by Stuart's—the clam chowder (both New England and Manhattan varieties) is thick with chunks of potatoes, carrots, celery, onions, bacon, and clams, and the New England version is made with real cream. You can order a clambake to go, or the best homemade clam pies you'll ever have.

MONTAUK

Duryea's (631-668-2410; www.duryealobsters.com; 65 Tuthill Rd., Montauk, NY 11954; market open daily year-round except Sun., 7–4; deck open May–mid-Oct. daily noon–7) Owner: Perry B. Duryea and Sons. This Montauk institution has absolutely the freshest and best lobster anywhere. You can come here to pick up some whole lobsters to take home, or you can sit on the outside deck and get your lobster roll, lobster dinner, or fish burger to eat on paper plates with plastic utensils. There are no pretensions here. You serve yourself and clean up after yourself. But the view of Fort Pond Bay is dazzling and you absolutely won't find fresher fish anywhere.

Gosman's Fish Market (631-668-5645; 484 West Lake Dr.; mailing address: P.O. Box 2340, Montauk, NY 11954; open Apr.–Nov. daily 10–6) Gosman's Fish Market is located on the Montauk docks near their restaurant. The range of fish and shellfish is one of the largest on the East End. You'll find tanks of clams, oysters, and lobsters, and cases of shrimp, salmon, bass, flounder, tuna, shark, and just about everything else—fresh from the fishing boats. Many locals consider this their favorite fish market.

SOUTHAMPTON

Clamman (631-283-6669; www.clamman.com; 235A North Sea Rd., Southampton, NY 11968; seafood shop open year-round Sun.–Thurs. 9–6, Fri. and Sat. 9–7, lunch pickup 11–3) Owner: Jean MacKenzie. The North Sea Road location is tough to find, but well worth the effort. There are cases of super-fresh fish and shellfish in all varieties, as well as sauces, vinegars, prepared soups, and a case of frozen dishes. You can also get prepared sandwiches, salads, and entrées, and this popular caterer can often be found at the Hamptons' snazziest fund-raisers.

East End Clambakes (631-726-5360; www.clambake.hamptons.com; 590 County Rd. 39, Southampton, NY 11968; open May–early Sept. only) Owner: Captain Phil Gay. This esteemed East End caterer has been creating deluxe clambakes for celebrities and handling fund-raising and corporate events on Hampton beaches since 1981, but in 2003 he opened this take-out storefront. Captain Phil was a bayman himself, fishing for tuna and marlin as well as working on lobster boats, before becoming a caterer, so he understands exactly how to select the highest-quality seafood. You'll find fresh steamers, fried clam and shrimp platters, lobster rolls, and even grilled yellowfin tuna.

You'll get fresh-from-the-sea shellfish and seafood at the Clamman Seafood Market in Southampton.

WAINSCOTT

The Seafood Shop (631-537-0633; www.theseafoodshop.com; 356 Montauk Hwy., P.O. Box 246, Wainscott, NY 11975; open year-round, Sun.–Thurs 8–6, Fri. and Sat. 8–8) Owner: Colin Mather. The Seafood Shop carries a wide array of fresh fish and shellfish. In addition, it has a crew of fishmongers who will fillet a whole fish, cut custom-ordered fish steaks, or prepare just about any other special order you may want. This fish market has been around a long time and has a loyal following of summer and year-round residents.

WESTHAMPTON BEACH

Starr Boggs Fish (631-288-2573; 11 Parlato Pl. Westhampton Beach, NY 11978; Open: May–mid-Sept. daily 10–7) Owners: Beth Dalessio and Starr Boggs. This little take-out cottage, a few feet from Starr Boggs' popular restaurant, features fresh fish, shellfish, veggies, prepared salads, side dishes, and pastries. If you've eaten at the restaurant for six days in a row and would rather chill out in the backyard at home, stop here first. Hey, you know it's the same quality as next door, and for a fraction of the price!

Wineshops

AMAGANSETT

Amagansett Wine & Spirits (631-267-3939; www.amagansettwine.net; 203 Main St.; mailing address: P.O. Box 1060, Amagansett, NY 11930; open year-round Mon.–Thurs. 10–8, Fri. and Sat. 10–10) Amagansett Wine & Spirits rivals the finest shops in Manhattan, both for the depth of its wine collection and for its prices. Owner Michael Cinque buys directly from France and has assembled one of the finest wine cellars on the East

End. If you walk the cool basement recesses with him, you will see rare old Latours and Margaux. He sponsors sophisticated wine tastings in the Hamptons and New York City, as well as wine-appreciation classes. He also carries one of the most complete selections of Long Island wines and a wide variety of affordable, drinkable, light wines. His prices are so popular that he makes two to three delivery trips to Manhattan each week to supply his regular customers.

BRIDGEHAMPTON

DePetris Liquor Store (631-537-0287; 2489 Main St.; mailing address: P.O. Box 3036, Bridgehampton, NY 11932; open year-round, in summer Mon.–Thurs. 9–8, Fri.–Sun. 9–9; rest of year closed Sundays) Owner: Danny DePetris. A good selection of Long Island, California, and European wines is available at this well-stocked store. The Long Island wines, in particular, are well represented, with selections from most East End wineries.

EAST HAMPTON

Domaine Franey (631-324-0906; www.domainefraney.com; 459 Pantigo Rd., East Hampton, NY 11937; open year-round daily, Mon.–Sat. 10–8; Sun. 12–6; longer hours in summer) Owner: Jacques Franey. Raised with an appreciation for fine wine and gourmet cuisine, Jacques had worked in the vineyards of France and in some of New York City's finest wine stores before opening his own shop in East Hampton. (Jacques is the son of the late famed restaurateur Pierre Franey, who was chef at New York City's Le Pavillon, and the longtime author of a cooking column in the *New York Times,* as well as many cookbooks.) In his shop, he carries an incredible number of wines, but he and his staff are particular proponents of Long Island wines. They are extremely knowledgeable and dedicated, and will offer suggestions for wine pairings at the finest dinner parties.

Park Place Wines & Liquors (631-324-2622; 84 Park Pl., East Hampton, NY 11937; open year-round; in summer weekdays 9–8, weekends 9–9; rest of year shorter hours) Owner: Donald T. McDonald. Tucked away off the Park Place parking lot, this shop has a terrific selection of wines, especially those from Long Island.

Wines by Morrell (631-324-1230; 74 Montauk Hwy., East Hampton, NY 11937; open year-round; in summer Mon.–Thurs. 9–8, Fri. and Sat. 9–9; shorter hours rest of year) Located in the Red Horse Market, this branch of the great Manhattan store offers an excellent selection of wines, especially those from Long Island wineries. Throughout the shop, you will find unusual and interesting wines that are not available elsewhere.

EASTPORT

A Grape Pear Wine Boutique (631-801-2790; www.grapepearwine.com; 509 Montauk Hwy., Eastport, NY 11941; open year-round, in summer daily 10–8, rest of year Mon.–Fri. 12–8, Sat. 10–8, Sun. 12–7) Owners: Jim Borruso and Krystle Harb. What's in a name? World travelers and wine aficionados Jim and Krystle, who were married in 2009, are a "great pair." Passionate about wine, they decided to open a wine boutique specializing in wines handcrafted by small producers. In their elegant little shop you'll find about 300 wines from faraway places around the world, as well as several from Long Island and upstate New York. All the artisanal wines they carry are lovingly produced by their winemakers in quantities of no more than 1,000 cases a year. Wine tastings familiarize customers with these rarified brands, and the best part is that most bottles are in the $20–$25 price range.

HAMPTON BAYS

Hampton Bays Wine and Spirits (631-728-8595; 44 East Montauk Hwy., Hampton Bays, NY 11946; open year-round, Mon.–Thurs. 9–7:30, Fri. and Sat. 9–8:30, Sun. 12–6) Owner: Dana Rubin. Located in the Hampton Bays Town Center, this store has an extensive selection of Long Island and New York State wines, as well as those from other regions of the U.S. and other countries.

SAG HARBOR

Long Wharf Wines & Spirits (631-725-2400; www.longwharfwines.com; 12 Bay St.; mailing address: P.O. Box 2443, Sag Harbor, NY 11968; open year-round, Wed.–Mon. 11–8) This well-stocked wineshop is strong on Long Island and California wines. The owner, Sandy DiGennaro, will help you select a casual drinking wine or match courses for a dinner party. The shop holds frequent wine tastings.

Noyac Liquors (631-725-0330; 354 Noyac Rd., Sag Harbor, NY 11963; open year-round Mon.–Thurs. 11–8, Fri. and Sat. 11–9, Sun. 12–6) Owner: Cathy Tice. You will find a nice selection of Long Island wines at this shop, as well as other domestic and foreign selections.

SOUTHAMPTON

Herbert and Rist (631-283-2030; 63 Job's Ln., Southampton, NY 11968; open year-round, Mon.–Thurs. 9–8, Fri. and Sat. 9–9, Sun. 12–5) Owner: Jack Rist. This excellent wineshop carries a good selection of Long Island wines, as well as those from California and Europe. Whether you're looking for a cold bottle to go with a sandwich while sitting on the banks of Agawam Pond or a case for a party, this is the place to find it.

WESTHAMPTON BEACH

Bonnie's Beach Liquors (631-288-1240; 171 Montauk Hwy., Westhampton Beach, NY 11978; open year-round, Mon.–Thurs. 10–8, Fri. and Sat. 10–9) Owner: Bonnie Small. In addition to having a nice selection of local and other wines, this shop offers great discounts. It's worth comparing prices here.

Hamptons Wine Shoppe (631-288-4272; www.hamptonswineshoppe.com; 62 Sunset Ave., Westhampton Beach, NY 11978; open year-round Mon.–Sat. 10–7) Owner: Paul DeVerna. There's a terrific selection of local and imported wines at this outlet.

WINERIES ON THE SOUTH FORK

Viticulture and wine production have become big business on Long Island's East End. One day the region may rival some California areas in quality, if not in production levels. Because most wineries are located on the North Fork, chapter 9 contains extensive information about winemaking on the East End, wineries to tour, wine activities, and much more. Wine production on the South Fork is more recent. Bridgehampton Winery, which is now defunct, began production in 1983, but they bought their grapes from other growers. Wölffer Estate planted the first vineyards intended for wine production on the South Fork in 1987. Their first bottling took place in 1991. It's always interesting to visit wineries dur-

Channing Daughters Winery in Bridgehampton produces fine wine and is a lovely setting for a picnic.

ing the harvest, when overflowing trucks bring the tiny grapes to the winery for processing. The following wineries offer tours, samples, and sales rooms.

CHANNING DAUGHTERS WINERY

631-537-7224
www.channingdaughters.com
1927 Scuttle Hole Rd., Bridgehampton
Mailing Address: P.O. Box 2202, Bridgehampton, NY 11932
Open: Year-round daily 11–5, except closed Wed. off-season
Fee: $6 per person for entire flight of wines

The phenomenal success of the Long Island wine industry has encouraged new ventures. Walter and Molly Channing, who have four daughters, planted 26 acres of grapes on their rather remote property north of Bridgehampton in 1988 in a mixture of Chardonnay and Merlot. They produced their first commercial wine, a 1993 Merlot, in 1995 and a Chardonnay in 1996, but they have branched into much more diverse blends since that time. Larry Perrine, a respected and experienced Long Island vintner, is the CEO, while Christopher Tracy is the winemaker. The winery produced about 10,000 cases in 2008. For a light, refreshing, drinkable wine with no pretensions of grandeur, the Sauvignon Blanc is fabulous, especially with light summer fare, but the rosés and reds are outstanding also. There's a pretty tasting room and a courtyard for outside sipping. Don't miss the interesting and unusual sculptures by Walter Channing surrounding the building.

DUCK WALK VINEYARDS

631-726-7555
www.duckwalk.com
162 Montauk Hwy., Water Mill
Mailing Address: Box 962, Water Mill, NY 11976
Open: Tasting and sales room open daily 11–6; guided tours, Sat. 2 PM
Fee: $4 for five wines

The former Southampton Winery (and also, at one time, Le Reve) was purchased in 1994 by Dr. Herodotos Damianos, who also owns Pindar Vineyards on the North Fork. The magnificent brick château, with its lush lawns and large terrace, was built in 1986, reputedly for $17 million. The winemaker is Jason Damianos; the vineyard manager is Peter Gristina; and the general manager is Alexander Damianos. With the capability of producing 50,000 cases a year, the production was about 35,000 cases in 2008. This stunning building is located on a slight hill overlooking the vineyards. It's worth the trip to visit the vineyards and sample their steadily improving wines, as well as to listen to live music on weekends. In 2008 the family opened a branch, Duck Walk North, in Southold on the North Fork. The spectacular tasting room is one of the largest in the area.

WÖLFFER ESTATE

631-537-5106
www.wolffer.com
139 Sagg Rd., Sagaponack
Mailing Address: P.O. Box 9002, Sagaponack, NY 11962

Wölffer Estate has a beautiful Mediterranean-style winery that also houses an interesting museum of antique wine jugs and elegant wineglasses.

Open: Tasting and sales room open daily summer: Sun.–Wed. 11–6; Thurs.–Sat. 11–7; winter: Sun.–Wed. 11–5; Thurs.–Sat. 11–6
Fee: Four different flights of wine available—Price: $12–$18

Wölffer Estate was the first South Fork winery to produce estate-bottled wines. The first of its 55 acres of grapes was planted in 1987, with two-thirds in Chardonnay and one-third in Merlot. The first Chardonnays were produced in 1991. About 15,000 cases of wine were processed in 2003. The Wölffer Premier Cru Merlot is challenging fine Bordeaux for complexity and finesse. The land and winery were owned by the late Christian Wölffer, who also owned Sagpond Farms, the horse farm next door. Roman Roth is the winemaker and general manager, while the vineyard manager is Richard Pisacano. A lovely winery building was completed in 1997. It is reminiscent of an Italian villa, with ivy climbing the burnt-umber stucco walls, a fountain courtyard, and a covered patio overlooking the vineyards. It contains not only a tasting room, which overlooks the stainless steel vats, but also a wonderful museum of antique faience wine jugs and painted wineglasses, as well as a very classy art gallery. On Twilight Thursdays and Sunset Fridays you can listen to live music. A satellite shop, the Wine Stand, located at 3312 Montauk Highway, is open 11–5 daily. Winemaker Roman Roth launched his own label in 2006, called the Grapes of Roth. He personally selects his grapes from local growers and oversees production from beginning to end. His 2001 Merlot, and subsequent vintages, has been winning rave reviews. His wines can be purchased at www.thegrapesofroth.com.

5

Shop 'Til You Drop

Shopping

Shopping in the Hamptons can be as rewarding as shopping in Manhattan—and every bit as much fun. Many creative people have decided to live here, including a number of designers whose own workrooms are in the Hamptons, although they sell through larger retail outlets in New York City. As a result, you probably will pay less if you buy locally. And, in addition, some designers and entrepreneurs choose to offer their particular brand of artistry only in the Hamptons, priding themselves on bringing a unique flair and personality to their shops that can't be reproduced elsewhere. Manhattan shops have branches here, too. Whether you're choosing clothing or art, the Hamptons are a treasure trove.

The Hamptons offer another boon to treasure seekers. Yard and tag sales abound, and they're unlike those you'll find anywhere else. Many people bring items from their New York City apartments to the Hamptons for their annual yard sale. You'll find everything from priceless antiques to lawn mowers, from china to tools, from artwork to games, and from designer clothes to books. Artists hold home-based sales, book dealers weed out extra stock, and home owners do their spring cleaning in the summer. Savvy shoppers check the local newspaper listings Friday night, hit the sales on Saturday from 8 to 12 noon, and then head for the beach.

In addition, transfer stations have an unofficial recycling center for furniture, rugs, and other large pieces. Especially at the end of the summer, you can find some real treasures discarded there.

There is only one true mall in the Hamptons, although there are numerous shopping plazas. On the North Fork, the huge Tanger Factory Outlet Center in Riverhead has a wonderful array of merchandise at discount prices. For details about Tanger, consult chapter 9.

Bridgehampton Commons, on the South Fork, deserves special mention. In addition to Kmart, King

During the summer, antiques shows and sales take place frequently in the Hamptons. This one is at Mulford Farm in East Hampton. Morgan McGivern

Kullen grocery store, and Rite Aid Pharmacy, the Commons also contains the following shops: American Eagle Outfitters, The Gap, Gap Kids, Williams-Sonoma, Sunglass Hut, Banana Republic, Athlete's Foot, Wild Bird Crossing, Brennan's Bit and Bridle, T. J. Maxx, Radio Shack, Victoria's Secret, and Hampton Photo Arts, among others. In this chapter, rather than attempting to list every gallery, shop, and store, I have generally featured those that offer articles unique to the Hamptons. Although every attempt has been made to verify hours of operation, such information does change frequently. If in doubt, call ahead.

Antiques Dealers & Shops

AMAGANSETT

Balassas House Antiques (631-267-3032; 208 Main St.; mailing address: P.O. Box 711, Amagansett, NY 11930; open year-round, daily in summer 10:30–5; rest of year closed Tues. and Wed.) Owners: George Balassas and Tom Bergmann. From quirky pincushions to elegant marble fireplace mantels, you'll find hundreds—probably thousands—of antiques and reproductions at Balassas. The rambling old house has room after cluttered room of both old and new, ranging from English tables and huge monumental cupboards to rustic furniture, old tools, dishes, and mirrors, plus American and French furniture. When you've finished looking in the house, there are three outbuildings in which to browse.

Decorum (631-267-4040; 248 Main St., Amagansett, NY 11930; open year-round, Thurs.–Mon. in summer 11–6; rest of year Fri.–Sun. 11–5) Owner: Elaine Monroe. Ms. Monroe is a true Francophile. Her shop gives her a reason to travel to France frequently to personally select the beautiful and interesting antique country French furniture she carries in her store. In addition to the furniture, she has beautiful hand-blown imported glass vases in a variety of sizes, French silk floral arrangements, old porcelain and faience, and new and antique chandeliers and lighting fixtures. This store is a treat!

Nellie's of Amagansett (631-267-1000; 230 Main St.; mailing address: P.O. Box 2790, Amagansett, NY 11930; open year-round, in summer Thurs.–Mon. 11–5; rest of year Fri.–Sun. 11–5 or by appt.) Owner Connie Dankmyer has collected an interesting and eclectic array of early American and primitive antiques to sell in her shop. You will find rustic refectory tables, chests, large cupboards, and even a well-used pine workbench.

BRIDGEHAMPTON

The American Wing (631-537-3319; www.theamericanwing.com; 2415 Main St.; mailing address: P.O. Box 1131, Bridgehampton, NY 11932; open year-round, daily in summer 11–5; fewer days rest of year) Owner Mark Olives has assembled a high-quality collection of English and American furniture and decorative objects, as well as toys, wicker and rattan items, and architectural and garden accessories.

Barbara Trujillo (631-537-3838; 2466 Main St.; mailing address: P.O. Box 866, Bridgehampton, NY 11932; open year-round, daily in summer 11–6; fewer days rest of year) Owner: Barbara Trujillo. There's lots of folk art, including vintage American flags, Statue of Liberty miniatures, a detailed dollhouse and furniture, pressed glass, turquoise jewelry, lots of old toys and wooden blocks, and even a wire garden bench in this cute shop.

John Salibello Antiques (631-537-1484; www.johnsalibelloantiques.com; 2309 Montauk Hwy.; mailing address: P.O. Box 98, Bridgehampton, NY 11932; open year-round, daily in summer 11–6; rest of year Thurs.–Mon. 11–5) Owner: John Salibello. John Salibello is noted for his eclectic offerings. In this shop—the East End branch of his Manhattan store—he carries a vast array of antiques, such as elegant crystal chandeliers hanging next to funky lights made from gaudy bunches of glass grapes. There's also jewelry, cast-iron doorstops, and an entire room of vintage cookie jars.

Laurin Copen Antiques (631-537-2802; www.laurincopenantiques.com; 1703 Montauk Hwy.; mailing address: P.O. Box 34, Bridgehampton, NY 11932; open year-round, Wed.–Mon. in summer, 11–5; rest of year Fri.–Sun. 11–5) Owner: Laurin Copen. You'll find an unusual array of French iron and tin furniture here—French café tables and chairs, for example, as well as iron campaign beds, tin cabinets, sconces, and chandeliers. Outside on the lawn are more garden furniture, statuary, and urns.

East Hampton

Architrove (631-329-2229; www.architrove.com; 74 Montauk Hwy., East Hampton, NY 11937; open year-round, daily in summer 10–6; rest of year same hours but closed Tues.) Owner: Gary Kephart. Located in the Red Horse Market, Architrove carries a marvelous selection of elegant, antique marble- and wood-carved fireplace mantels, columns, top-quality furniture (a perfect walnut trestle table, a beautiful marble-topped dresser), crystal chandeliers, sinks, and even doorknobs and hinges. Everything is neatly arranged and very clean. You may run into Christy Brinkley here, as I did just recently.

Butler's Fine Art & Antiques (631-267-0193; 50 Park Pl. East Hampton, NY 11937; open year-round, daily in summer 11–6; rest of year Thurs.–Mon. 11–5) Owners: Mary Butler and Peter von Bartheld. Beautiful, fine-quality 19th- and 20th-century paintings and folk art are displayed on the walls in this tiny shop, as well as on the tops of elegant pieces of furniture such as desks, tables, and chests, which are also for sale.

The Grand Acquisitor (631-324-7272; 12 Pantigo Rd. East Hampton, NY 11937; open by appt.) Owner: Maria O. Brennan. For elegant linen and lace tablecloths, sheets, coverlets, napkins, lacy pillowcases, and charming children's dresses, this marvelous store can't be beat. (This should be your first stop for an antique christening dress.) All the merchandise is neatly boxed and labeled, so items are easy to find even though the store inventories over 200,000 items. Now in a much larger hidden-away location, Maria has expanded her selection of antique furniture, china, and silver, and added elegant rugs as well, but she's still most noted for her incredibly beautiful linens and fabrics.

Montauk

Haven (631-668-4844; www.havenmontauk.com; 83 S. Elmwood St.; mailing address: P.O. Box 2464, Montauk, NY 11954; open year-round, daily in summer 10:30–6; rest of year fewer days and hours) Owner: Kathi Cogen. A little of this and a little of that are what you'll find at this interesting Montauk shop. Vintage fireplace mantels, lots of old tin advertising clocks, canisters, and signs, peely paint furniture, mahogany claw-foot tables, lots of funky pottery (hula girl mugs, etc.) next to elegant new crystal glasses and silver sugar and creamer sets, plus a full range of Shabby Chic fabrics.

Montauk Ice House (631-668-5736 or 516-639-5115; 65 Tuthill Rd.; mailing address: P.O. Box 1164 Montauk, NY 11954; open in summer weekends 11–5; rest of year by chance or appt.) Kenneth Gulnick carries an incredible array of rare Americana. There are old photos of Montauk, paintings, and furniture, but there's also an amazing collection of rare framed American flags. How often do you see an American flag that was made shortly after Oklahoma became a state, for example?

Whoa! Nellie! (631-722-8509 or 631-872-5615; www.whoanellieretro.com; 770 Montauk Hwy. Montauk, NY 11954; open year-round, in summer daily 10–9, rest of year fewer days and hours) Owner: Linda Seaton. Linda Seaton would like us to slow down and smell the roses, so she's gone into the recycling business. Most of the '40s, '50s, and '60s items in her cluttered little shops have been salvaged from yard sales and thrift shops, although she does carry some reproductions as well. There's vintage jewelry, painted furniture, cookie jars, dolls, repro. cast iron trucks and banks, quilts, flags, and lots more.

SAG HARBOR

Carol O'Neill Vintage Linen (631-725-9893; Sage and Division Sts. above Sage Street Antiques, enter from Division St.; mailing address: P.O. Box 2171, Sag Harbor, NY 11963; open year-round, Sat. 11–5, Sun. 1–5) Owner: Carol O'Neill. If you love antique linens, Carol has collected a nice selection that includes tablecloths, lots of napkins, vintage sheets and pillowcases, and even some fabrics, laces, vintage hats, gloves, and more.

Ruby Beets Old & New (631-899-3275; www.rubybeets.com; 25 Washington St.; mailing address: P.O. Box 1174, Sag Harbor, NY 11963; open year round, in summer daily 11–5; rest of year Fri.–Mon.) Owners: Sharone Einhorn and Honey Wolters. When this store was located in Bridgehampton, my car couldn't drive past without turning in—and then it was gone. Now Sharone and Honey have reemerged in Sag Harbor with a shop that combines the best of old and new. The antiques include farmhouse tables, painted furniture, baskets, perhaps a vintage tricycle or hat trunk, while the new includes lighting fixtures, tabletop, glassware, dishes, furniture, and wonderful trompe l'oeil wallpaper (a bookcase full of books).

Sage Street Antiques (631-725-4036; corner Division St., or Rte. 114, and Sage St.; mailing address: P.O. Box 504, Sag Harbor, NY 11963; open year-round, Sat. 11–5, Sun. 1–5) Owner: Eliza Werner. Everything, including the kitchen sink, may be found at this long-established vintage collector's dream. In the yard, there are old doors and shutters, sinks, and tables and chairs; inside you'll find a cluttered array of furniture, dishes, dolls, jewelry, and more. This is not the place to come to furnish your elegant Hamptons mansion, but a great place for affordable stuff for your summer share or rental.

Sag Harbor Antique Shop (631-725-1732; 17 Madison St.; P.O. Box 1500, Sag Harbor NY 11963; open year-round, in summer daily 11–5; fewer days and hours rest of year) Owner: John Krug. This is a bit like browsing through your grandma's attic. You'll find an eclectic mix that includes collectibles and early 18th- and 19th-century furniture.

SOUTHAMPTON

Ann Madonia (631-283-1878, 516-741-1882; www.annmadoniaanatiques.com; 36 Job's Ln., Southampton, NY 11968; open year-round, in summer Fri.–Mon. 11–5, or call and they'll open for you; rest of year Fri.–Sun. 11–5) Owners: Ann and Susan Madonia. This store sells some of the most elegant antiques in the Hamptons, from fine English and French furniture to silver and other accessories—all on two floors in a spacious, refined setting. The enclosed garden in back displays select garden furniture. There's another location in Garden City, if you don't find what you want here.

Another Time Antiques (631-283-6542 or 631-283-6223; www.anothertime antiques.com; 765 Hill St., P.O. Box 1414, Southampton, NY 11968; open year-round, in summer Fri.–Mon. 11–5; rest of year Fri.–Mon. noon–4:30) Owners: Meredith and

Thomas Joyce. The owners have filled their shop, as well as two adjacent buildings, to the rafters with dolls (Madame Alexander, Nancy Ann) and toys, stained glass, old doors, sinks, wicker chairs and desks, oak and mahogany tables, costume jewelry, collectible figurines (Hummel and more), dishes (some Fiestaware), and much more. Don't miss the incredible toy train or the lead soldier collections in a back room. There are treasures to be found here.

Black Swan Antiques (631-377-3012, www.blackswansouthampton.com; 20 Hampton Rd., Southampton, NY 11968; open year-round, summer Mon.–Fri. 10:30–5:30, Sat. 9–8; fewer days and shorter hours rest of year) Owners: Randy and Diana Kolhoff. This expansive antiques store, which is located on two sides of an atrium in a downtown building, is filled with quality paintings, rugs, tables, chairs, highboys, and chests in handsome woods, and accessories.

Croft Antiques (631-283-6445; 11 S. Main St., Southampton, NY 11968; open year-round, daily Thurs.–Tues. in summer, 11–5; rest of year Fri.–Mon. 11–5) Owner: J. Christopher Hines. This tiny shop is filled to the rafters with exotic and dramatic antiques. You'll find very unusual tables stacked on chests that sit on dressers that reach right up to the ceiling.

Morgan MacWhinnie (631-283-3366; 1411 North Sea Rd.; mailing address: 520 North Sea Rd., Southampton, NY 11968; open year-round, daily 11–5) Owner: Morgan MacWhinnie. You won't just wander into this huge antiques shop while you're strolling around town, as it's located far from the crowds. But a special trip is definitely worthwhile. Mr. MacWhinnie stocks his shop with elegant, exceptional pieces of 18th-century American furniture and accessories in 4,000 square feet of space. He's been in business for almost 50 years, so you know he knows what he's doing.

Old Town Crossing (631-283-7740; www.oldtowncrossing.1stdibs.com; 46 Main St., Southampton, NY 11968; open year-round, Mon.–Fri. 10–5:30, Sat. 10–6, Sun. noon–5) Don't let this diminutive shop on Main Street fool you. Although Judith Hadlock displays an impressive array of mirrors, lamps, silver, silk tassels, and elegant, small furniture pieces, the bulk of the inventory is located nearby in a 5,000-square-foot warehouse. Customers are welcome to poke around the collection of 18th-century English beds, tables, dressers, and more.

Renaissance Restoration Workshop (631-287-1119; 224B North Main St.; mailing address: P.O. Box 3114, Southampton, NY 11968; open year-round, Mon.–Sat. 10–6) Owner: Kurt Hardcastle. Although they sell American and Continental furniture and accessories, they are also restoration specialists, so they can repair your beloved antique (even paintings) for you. They've been in business for almost 35 years, so you know you're in good hands.

Yesterday's Treasures (631-283-5591; 1547 County Rd. 39, Southampton, NY 11968; open daily year-round 10–5); also **Galerie Hamptons** (631-288-6888; 185 Montauk Hwy., Westhampton Beach, NY 11978; open year-round, daily in summer 10–5; rest of year Fri.–Sun. 10–5.) Owner: Lawrence Schaeffer. These funky/eclectic shops carry such a variety of items, it's hard to categorize them. You will find beautiful tables with ormolu embellishments, elegant china and glassware, fabulous wood, iron, and tin toys, monumental iron estate gates, fences, lanterns, and lampposts, and also a huge variety of improbable statues—wooden soldiers, pirates, horses, cows, and even a Dick Tracy.

WAINSCOTT

Georgica Creek Antiques (631-537-0333; www.1stdibs@georgicacreekantiques.com; 332

The finest Hamptons homes are outfitted with furnishings from Georgica Creek Antiques. Morgan McGivern

Montauk Hwy.; mailing address: P.O. Box 877, Wainscott, NY 11975; open year-round, Mon.–Sat. 11–5, Sun. 12–5) Jean Sinenberg has collected a marvelous array of unusual and interesting antiques in her spacious white building. On a recent visit I spotted a wonderful carved French dresser, a cache of beautiful antique quilts in perfect condition, lamps, ornate silver candlesticks, a great crystal chandelier, and a set of beautiful gold-rimmed Limoges dishes. In back, there's a garden full of architectural elements such as columns and pillars, as well as wicker and Victorian wire planters and garden furniture. Check out the Web site, as Jean and her daughter Susan also run the finest antiques shows in the Hamptons. You'll find the schedule on the Web.

WATER MILL

Antique Lumber Co. (631-726-7026 or 631-484-5261; www.theantiquelumberco.com; 728 Montauk Hwy., Water Mill; mailing address: P.O. Box 1958, Sag Harbor, NY 11963; open year-round; Mon.–Sat. except Wed., 10–4) Owner: Don Disbrow. This shop specializes in antique lumber, flooring, and millwork that has been salvaged from old buildings. You'll find hand-hewn beams, wide-plank pine flooring, and even some antiques.

Donna Parker's Habitat (631-726-9311; www.habitatltd.com; 710 Montauk Hwy.; mailing address: P.O. Box 1071, Water Mill, NY 11976; open year-round, in summer daily 11–5; fewer days rest of year) Donna Parker sells important and very elegant French and Italian furniture and decorative objects, such as a leafy iron table, a crystal chandelier, marble pedestals holding bronze busts or gilt mirrors, crystal lamps, oyster plates, and much more. You'll pay for these pieces, but you'll have a one-of-a-kind item. Don't miss the barn in back!

Jon Vaccari Antiques (631-283-3313; www.jonvaccaridesign.com; 720 Montauk Hwy.; mailing address: P.O. Box 1405, Water Mill, NY 11976; open Apr.–Dec., Thurs.–Mon., 10–5) Mr. Vaccari has assembled a large selection of 19th- and 20th-century French furniture and lighting fixtures, as well as more modern American pieces from the '40s–'60s. He has a shop in New Orleans also.

Books, Magazines, Music

AMAGANSETT

The BookHampton Corner Store (631-267-5405; www.bookhampton.com; Amagansett Sq., 154 Main St., Amagansett, NY 11930; open: year-round, Sun.–Thurs. 8:30–10; Fri. and Sat. 8:30–11) Owners: Jeremy Nussbaum and Charline Spektor. This latest branch of the BookHampton bookstores, which is located in cute little Amagansett Square, has DVDs and CDs as well as books.

EAST HAMPTON

BookHampton (631-324-4939; www.bookhampton.com; 41 Main St., East Hampton, NY 11937; open: year-round, Sun.–Thurs. 8:30–10; Fri. and Sat. 8:30–11) Owners: Jeremy Nussbaum and Charline Spektor. This is the Hamptons' all-purpose, everything-you-want bookstore. It has a wide selection in every category: best sellers, paperbacks, local history, children's books, travel, cookbooks, videos, and tapes. Local authors often give readings and sign books. Before the movies, after the movies, anytime—this is a great place to shop.

Glenn Horowitz Bookseller (631-324-5511; www.ghbookseller.com; 87 Newtown Ln., East Hampton, NY 11937; open: year-round, Mon.–Sat. 10–5, Sun. 11–4; closed Tues. and Wed. in winter) Owner: Glenn Horowitz. Specializing in fine old books and prints, this shop has an excellent selection. There are a number of books and photographs that relate to local history, as well as some rare, old, leather-bound and first-edition volumes. If what you're looking for isn't here, it may be at their New York branch, or they'll do a search for you.

Harper's Books (631-324-1131; www.harpersbooks.com; 66 Newtown Ln., East Hampton, NY 11937; open year-round, Wed.–Sat. 10–5; Sun. 11–4) Owner: Harper Levine. Dealing in rare books and photographic literature, this exceptional bookstore also features a gallery where photographers exhibit their art.

MONTAUK

The Book Shoppe (631-668-4599; The Plaza; mailing address: P.O. Box 750, Montauk, NY 11954; open year-round, daily in summer 9:30–10; rest of year shorter hours and closed Tues.) Owner: Perry Haberman. This little bookstore may be small, but it's packed with great things. Not only can you purchase or order the latest books, but you can also buy cards and small gifts. (As we went to press, Mr. Haberman, who had just purchased the store, was preparing to close for major renovations. Call for updated hours.)

SAG HARBOR

Black Cat Books (631-725-8654; ww.blackcatbooks.com; 78 Main St., in the Sag Harbor

Shopping Cove; mailing address: P.O. Box 943, Sag Harbor, NY 11963; open year-round, in summer Mon.–Thurs. 10–6, Fri.–Sun. 10–10; rest of year daily 10–6) Owner: Dawn Hedberg. You will find an interesting selection of used, rare, and out-of-print books at this tucked-away little cubbyhole. There are books on art, architecture, poetry, photography, literature, and more.

BookHampton (631-725-8425; www.bookhampton.com; 20 Main St., Sag Harbor, NY 11963; open year-round, Sun.–Thurs. 8:30–9; Fri. and Sat. 8:30–10) Owners: Jeremy Nussbaum and Charline Spektor. This branch of BookHampton opened in 2003 (there had previously been a branch in the New Paradise Café). It has the same terrific selection of books as the stores in East Hampton and Southampton.

Canio's Books (631-725-4926; www.caniosbooks.com; 290 Main St., Sag Harbor, NY 11963; open year-round, daily 10–6) Owners: Maryann Calendrille and Kathryn Szoka. Canio Pavone had always been the literary community's friend, so the new owners had big shoes to fill, but they've done it admirably. Not only is this shop a great place to find out-of-print books and new ones, but on many Saturdays at 6, there are book signings or poetry and book readings. There's also an art gallery and art exhibitions. It's a funky, artsy place that fits right into the Sag Harbor attitude.

Metaphysical Books & Tools (631-725-9393; 83 Main St., Sag Harbor, NY 11963; Open year-round, Mon.–Sat. 10:30–5:30; Sun. 11–5) Owner: Joe Benzola. This is the place to come for spiritual books, candles, incense, tarot cards, or just to mellow out in the friendly atmosphere.

SOUTHAMPTON

BookHampton (631-283-0270; www.bookhampton.com; 91 Main St., Southampton, NY 11968; open year-round, Sun.–Thurs. 8:30–8; Fri. and Sat. 8:30–9) Owners: Jeremy Nussbaum and Charline Spektor. This branch of BookHampton has the same extensive, all-encompassing selection as the others. A great place to shop or browse.

WESTHAMPTON BEACH

The Open Book (631-288-2120; 135 Main St., Westhampton Beach, NY 11978; open year-round, Mem. Day–Labor Day, Mon.–Thurs. 10–7, Fri.–Sun. 10–10; rest of year Thurs.–Tues. 10–5) Owner: Terry Lucas. The Open Book has a good selection of hardbound and softcover books and greeting cards and is especially strong in children's literature, including the classics.

Children's Shops: Clothing

BRIDGEHAMPTON

C & W Mercantile (631-537-7914; Main St.; mailing address: P.O. Box 1275, Bridgehampton, NY 11932; open year-round, daily in summer 10–6; rest of year shorter hours) Owner: Barbara Dutton. Frothy and feminine children's dresses share space in this adorable shop with table linens, gifts, candles, and elegant bed dressings. This shop rivals the finest that the tony Upper East Side has to offer.

Gap Kids and Baby Gap (631-537-2428; www.gap.com; Bridgehampton Commons, Bridgehampton, NY 11932; open year-round, Mon.–Sat. 10–8, Sun. 10–6) Great, stylish play clothes that are comfortable and durable, from T-shirts to jeans. Also check out the Baby Gap and Gap Kids discount shops in the Tanger Mall in Riverhead (see listing chapter 9).

EAST HAMPTON

Bonne Nuit (631-324-7273; 55 Main St., East Hampton, NY 11937; open year-round, in summer Mon.–Thurs. 10–10, Fri. and Sat. 10–11, Sun. 10–6; rest of year daily 10–6) Owners/managers: Ashlyn and Lorna Maloney. This fine lingerie shop carries the most beautiful European children's clothing. Delicate smocked dresses in Liberty of London fabrics, French sundresses made of a Swiss cotton so fine it feels like silk, and frilly pink tulle skirts with wands for flirty fairy princesses are only a few of the offerings. (See also entry under "Clothing, Adult.")

Calypso (631-319-0033; www.calypso-celle.com; 21 Newtown Ln., East Hampton, NY 11937; open year-round, daily in summer 10–7; rest of year shorter hours) Owner: Christiane Celle. If you've got a jazzy kid with a yen for bright, "look at me" clothes, bring her here. There are wonderful little-girl dresses in vivid colors, ornaments for the hair, splendid thongs with flowers over the toe, and lots more. Best of all, these goodies come in mommy sizes, too (see entry under "Clothing, Adult").

The Monogram Shop (631-329-3379; www.themonogramshops.com; 7 Newtown Ln., East Hampton, NY 11937; open year-round, daily 10–6) Owner: Valerie Smith. We love this shop for the exquisite baby and children's clothing and accessories, as well as the wonderful big gingham shirts for moms, and so much more. Yes, they love to monogram items.

Ralph Lauren (631-907-9120; www.ralphlauren.com; 45 Main St., East Hampton, NY 11937; open year-round, in summer Mon.–Thurs. 10–9, Fri. and Sat. 10–10, Sun. 10–6; shorter hours rest of year) This is summer central for Hampton moms. From newborns to teens, the "Lauren look" will take them to the finest events, or just give the little tykes something to lounge around the summerhouse in. From denims to shoes to frilly blouses or cable-knit sweaters—this is the place.

The Red Pony (631-329-6685; 74 Montauk Hwy., East Hampton, NY 11937; open year-round, daily in summer 10–5; rest of year closed Tues. and Wed.) Owner: Robert Ginsberg. Hampton moms need not traipse to Manhattan to elegantly outfit their children. Coats, dresses, and jackets made of the finest fabrics and in the latest designs can be purchased right here at home. Located in the Red Horse Market.

SAG HARBOR

Andrew & Company (631-725-3236; 83 Main St., Sag Harbor, NY 11963; open year-round, daily in summer 9:30 AM–8 PM; rest of year Thurs.–Mon. 10–6) Owner: Cathy Hansen. You'll love the beautiful children's clothing that's assembled here. There are fleecy coats with floral appliqués, pretty dresses in beautiful floral fabrics, sweaters, and adorable little-boys' clothing.

SOUTHAMPTON

Aunt Suzie's Clothes for Kids (631-287-4645; www.auntsuzies.com; 20 Hampton Rd., Southampton, NY 11968; open year-round, Mon.–Fri. 10–5:30, Sat. 10–6, in summer, also open Sun. 11–4.) Owner: Suzanne Reynolds. This large shop for kids has a wide selection of clothing in sizes ranging from newborn to preteen. For summers in the sun or back to school, this can't be beat. Toys, too.

Hatchlings (631-283-4855; www.hatchlingsonline.com; 30 Main St. Southampton, NY 11968; open year-round, daily in summer 11–5; rest of year closed Tues. and Wed.) Owner: Cristina Peffer. Absolutely beautiful Italian and French baby and children's clothing in exquisite fabrics, for children from newborn to 14. The smocked dresses are gorgeous.

WESTHAMPTON BEACH

Shock Kids/Baby Shock (631-288-2522; www.babyshock.com; 99 Main St., Westhampton
   Beach, NY 11978; also at 631-288-1772; 115 Main St. Westhampton Beach, NY 11978;
   open year-round, daily in summer 10–9 or later; shorter hours rest of year) Owner:
   Elyse Richman. Remember your lime-green and shocking-pink capri pants from the
   '60s? You can outfit your pint-sized offspring in '60s retro at this blast-from-the-past
   shop. There are short leather skirts with cropped tops and hand-knit dresses and tops,
   as well as hats and so much more. Once your kid looks oh so cool, you can team up for a
   treat in the ice cream parlor, where there's homemade ice creams, yogurts, and Italian
   ices. It's a great place for a party, too!

Children's Shops: Furniture, Games, & Toys

BRIDGEHAMPTON

Second Star to the Right (631-537-6111; www.2ndstartoys.com; Bridgehampton Commons, 2044 Montauk Hwy., Bridgehampton, NY 11932; open year-round, daily 10–6)
   Now that Marianne Kearns has moved her terrific shop to a larger location (she had
   been at her tiny little place in East Hampton for many years), she's been able to spread
   out. Now you have a much easier time seeing all her wonderful inventory of cars, trucks,
   planes, dolls, dollhouses, puzzles, arts and craft items, and tons of cute stuffed animals.
   Visit her Web site for the full story.

SAG HARBOR

Kites of the Harbor (631-725-9063; 75 Main St., Sag Harbor, NY 11963; open year-round,
   daily in summer 10–10; rest of year fewer days and hours, but open weekends) Owners:
   Mary Ellen Gallagher and Charlene Katz. And now for something really different! There
   are hundreds of colorful kites to purchase at this fun shop. They range from brightly
   colored spirals and cylinders to pinwheels and boxes, as well as traditional kites with
   flapping tails.

The colorful and family-friendly Kites of the Harbor shop in Sag Harbor is a treat for young and old.   Dustin Chase

SOUTHAMPTON

Stevenson's Toys & Games (631-283-2111; www.stevensonstoys.com; 68 Jobs Ln., Southampton, NY 11968; open year-round, in summer Mon.–Thurs. 10–6, Fri. and Sat. 10–7, Sun. 11–6; rest of year closes one hour earlier and sometimes closed Wed.) Owners: Roy and Polly Stevenson. Here, in one of the most complete shops in the Hamptons, you will find a large selection of Madame Alexander dolls, model airplanes and cars, very creative books and games such as "my very own scrapbook," art supplies, toy trains, stuffed animals, and more. It's a very deep store, so just keep looking.

Clothing, Adult

BRIDGEHAMPTON

Anne Moore (631-537-2442; www.annemoore.com; 2468 Main St., P.O. Box 1108, Bridgehampton, NY 11932; open year-round, daily in summer 10–6; rest of year fewer days and shorter hours) Owner: Anne Moore. Easter, Hamptons Classic Horse Show time, or anytime, Anne's hats will be seen covering the prettiest heads. From classic brimmed bonnets to funky and whimsical varieties, you'll find them all here.

Gloria Jewel (631-284-3761; www.gloriajewel.com; 2486 Main St., Bridgehampton, NY 11932; open year-round, daily in summer 10–6; closed Thurs. rest of year.) Owner: Megan Leary. I love this store. The dresses, skirts, and blouses are sophisticated but easy to wear, they come in an array of colors and beautiful fabrics, and they're affordable. There are silk dresses, cashmere sweaters, jewelry, and handbags. There's also a shop in Jamesport.

Out of the Closet (631-537-2470; www.lucyscloset.com; 2401 Main St.; mailing address: P.O. Box 2194, Bridgehampton, NY 11932; open year-round, in summer 11–9, shorter hours rest of year) Specializing in vintage clothing from the Victorian era through the 1970s, Lucille Martin and Ruth von Witenberg Chernaik have assembled an enormous cache of clothing that hang on racks, or on the walls in their rambling old house. There are coats, skirts, blouses, and dresses, as well as petticoats, ties, formals, jewelry, handbags, and shoes. There's even a western section with fringed suede jackets and fancy belts. Come when you have time to browse, as there's lots to see.

tutto bene (631-537-3320; 2414 Main St.; P.O. Box 1156, Bridgehampton, NY 11932; open year-round, in summer Mon.–Sat. 10–6, Sun. 11–5; rest of year same hours but closed Tues. and Wed.) Joanne Kahn and Barbara Remia have filled their store with shoes and accessories to go with wonderful linen shirts and dresses for summer wear and with classy sweaters for fall and winter. Some are imported from Italy, but all of their clothes have a classic, chic Italian style.

Waves (631-537-7767, www.wavesbridgehampton.com; Main St.; mailing address: P.O. Box 1273, Bridgehampton, NY 11932; open year-round, daily in summer 10–6; rest of year closed Tues.) Owner: Linda Li. In summer, Waves has cotton clam diggers, silk flowered slacks, French ballet slippers, and canvas espadrilles, along with Lucy Isaacs and Native American–style turquoise jewelry. In winter, there are chic chenille sweaters and scarves in gem tones, panne velvet dresses, and floral oilcloth umbrellas.

EAST HAMPTON

Bonne Nuit (631-324-7273; 55 Main St., East Hampton, NY 11937; open year-round, in summer Mon.–Thurs. 10–10, Fri. and Sat. 10–11, Sun. 10–6; rest of year daily 10–6) Owners/managers: Lorna and Ashlyn Maloney. Bonne Nuit, owned and operated by sisters, is also located in Manhattan. The stores carry fine lingerie brands, such as Pluto, sexy bustiers, ephemeral slips and nightgowns, chenille bed jackets, hair accessories, and pretty painted ballet slippers (see also entry under "Children's Shops: Clothing").

Brooks Brothers (631-324-3928; www.brooksbrothers.com; 54 Main St., East Hampton, NY 11937; open May–Dec., in summer daily 10–6; rest of season closed Tues. and Wed.) In the summer of 2009, this terrific men's clothing store opened a tiny branch in the village of East Hampton. You'll find classic shirts, polos, sweaters, Bermuda shorts, wallets, and accessories.

Calypso (631-329-0033; www.calypso-celle.com; 21 Newtown Ln., East Hampton, NY 11937; *other locations at* 631-283-4321, 24 Job's Ln., Southampton, NY 11968; 631-668-4999, 99 The Plaza, Montauk, NY 11954; 631-725-1711, 117 Main St., Sag Harbor, NY 11963; 631-288-7208, 123 Main St., Westhampton Beach, NY 11978; all stores open year-round, daily in summer 10–7; rest of year shorter hours) Owner: Christiane Celle. This mini-chain began business in Saint-Barth, showcasing the wonderful, wearable designs of Christiane Celle. Now there are children's shops and home stores, as well as those offering adult clothing throughout the East End. Although the East Hampton store is mostly devoted to spicy women's clothing in brilliant colors, children's clothing takes up space in one corner. For women, there are long silk skirts with ruffled hems, gauzy blouses, drawstring pants, shifts with appliquéd roses on one shoulder, jewelry, and skin care products.

Catherine Malandrino (631-329-6990; www.catherinemalandrino.com; 25 Newtown Ln., East Hampton, NY 11937; open year-round, daily 10–6) This high-end designer has a free and easy style that appeals to women who are carefree and confident. There are bustier-topped dresses with cutouts or embroidered designs, as well as slacks, tops, and skirts.

Collette Designer Resale (631-324-7727; www.colletteconsignment.com; 59 The Circle, East Hampton, NY 11937; open year-round, in summer Mon.–Sat. 10–6, Sun. 11–5; rest of year Sun., Mon., Thurs., and Fri. 11–5, Sat. 10–6) Owner: Tisha Collette. If you're into vintage, you can't beat this mini-chain of select and top-quality designer clothes. You'll find dresses, suits, coats, shoes, bags, and some jewelry. Check out the Sag Harbor or the Southampton stores, if you don't find what you want here.

Côte d'Azure (631-324-5000; 85 Main St., East Hampton, NY 11937; open year-round, daily in summer 10–6; rest of year Thurs.–Sun. 10–5) Owner: Margaret Dictenberg. This is the Hamptons place to go for the most elegant cashmere sweaters and jackets, but these are now supplemented by gorgeous long taffeta skirts (a red one with a red metallic design is stunning), pretty filmy short skirts with uneven hems, ruffled taffeta blouses, a gossamer blouse with balloon sleeves, and beaded skirts and slacks. If you're looking for a smashing, dressy knockout, come here first.

Eileen Fisher (631-324-4111; www.eileenfisher.com; 26 Newtown Ln., East Hampton, NY 11937; open year-round, in summer Mon.–Sat. 10–6, Sun. 10–5; rest of year daily 10–5) In the quirky, old shingled building that was formerly the Odd Fellows Hall, Nancy Goell has assembled a fine collection of svelte women's clothing, mostly in basic black, white, or brown—all designed for comfort as well as style.

Elie Tahari (631-329-8883; www.elietahari.com; 1 Main St., East Hampton, NY 11937; open year-round, in summer Sun.–Thurs. 11–8, Fri. and Sat. 10–8; rest of year Sun., Mon., and Thurs. 11–6, Fri. and Sat. 10–8, closed Tues. and Wed.) Owner: Elie Tahari. Simple, classic cuts of women's slacks, jackets, and coats made from absolutely beautiful fabrics are sold here, as well as unusual sweaters and blouses. Those who gravitate here understand understated elegance—they have no need for flash because they exude confidence already.

Entre Nous (631-324-8636; 37 Newtown Ln., East Hampton, NY 11937; open year-round, daily in summer 10–6; closed Tues.–Thurs. rest of year) Owner: Phyllis Baden. This shop has very elegant European clothing—silk knit sweaters, wool gabardine slacks, exclusive suits, and cocktail dresses. All clothing is imported from France or Italy, and much of it is specially ordered for customers. On a recent visit, I also spotted beautiful, tiny dress handbags covered in flowers, as well as a few accessories for the pampered pooch.

Gucci (631-907-9290; www.gucci.com; 46 Main St., East Hampton, NY 11937; open year-round, in summer Sun.–Fri. 10–6, Sat. 10–7, shorter hours rest of year) Fifth Avenue segues to the Hamptons with the arrival of this international Italian designer. There are beautiful handbags, shoes, men's and women's classic clothing, and leather goods in this very elegant store.

Hermès (631-324-1177; www.hermes.com; 63 Main St., East Hampton, NY 11937; open mid-May–mid-Sept. only; Wed., Thurs., Sun., and Mon. 11–7, Fri. and Sat. 11–8) This legendary international French atelier set up its first Hamptons boutique in the summer of 2009, saving their East End clientele a trip to the city. The impeccable luxury items offered at the store included their famous scarves and ties, leather accessories, jewelry, watches, belts, and shoes—all packaged in their distinctive bright orange boxes. A hand-crafted saddle and equestrian accessories add another dimension. Will they open a summer store every year? Perhaps a call to the New York headquarters (212-759-7585) will reveal future summer plans.

Jill Stuart (631-267-3100; www.jillstuart.com; 62 The Circle, East Hampton, NY 11937; open year-round, Mon.–Fri. 10–6; Sat. 10–8; Sun. 10–7.) Known for her feminine, sexy, sassy, classy clothes, Jill Stuart creates dresses with ruffles and blouses with sheer, billowy sleeves—all in exquisite fabrics, and with the bags and shoes or boots to go with them.

La Perla (631-771-3232; www.laperla.com; 66 Newtown Ln., East Hampton, NY 11937; open May–Dec., in summer 10–6, rest of season closed Tues. and Wed.) The most elegant and interesting swimwear and lingerie will be found in the Hamptons shop of this high-end Italian designer. Silky and lacy lingerie and beachy, innovative swimwear with hand-detailing are included in the collection.

Magaschoni (631-329-8139; www.magaschoni.com; 75 Main St., East Hampton, NY 11937 open year-round, in summer Mon.–Thurs. 10–7, Fri. and Sat. 10–10; rest of year daily 10–6; *also* 631-204-0207, 53C Jobs Ln. Southampton, NY 11968; open daily in summer 10–7; rest of year open Fri.–Sun. only) You'll find smart, classy ladies clothing at this refined store. The fabrics are elegant, such as the little slip of a cashmere sweater with a fringed hem and sleeves, and best of all, the prices are not off the chart.

Polo Country Store (631-324-1222; www.ralphlauren.com; 31-33 Main St., East Hampton, NY 11937; open year-round, in summer Mon.–Thurs. 10–9, Fri. and Sat. 10–10, Sun. 10–6; shorter hours rest of year) In the trademark setting of wooden floors, old resort signs, and leather, Ralph Lauren has done it again. If you've been invited to a garden party and you want something classic and understated to wear, this is the place to come. Men buy white linen slacks and "the blazer," as well as jeans, sweaters, and all of the classically correct Ralph Lauren gear. Women love the long white linen dusters, the soft, supple suede jackets and skirts, and the swingy flowered skirts.

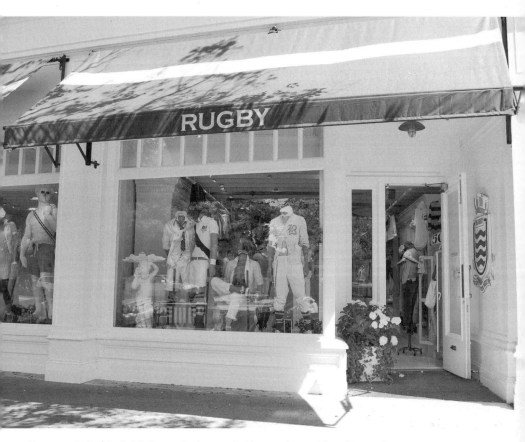

The preppy look of the Ralph Lauren Rugby stores holds special appeal for college students. Dustin Chase

Rugby Ralph Lauren (631-907-0960; www.rugby.com; 34 Main St., East Hampton, NY 11937; open year-round, in summer Mon.–Thurs. 10–9, Fri. and Sat. 10–10, Sun. 10–6; shorter hours rest of year) Just hand over the Black card. This new, very preppy Lauren brand is *the* place for college-aged men and women to shop. Yes, the authentic Rugby shirts are in abundance, but there are also chesterfield and motorcycle jackets, cardigans and sweaters, knee socks and leggings, and lots of shirts.

Shoe-Inn (631-329-4500, 66 Newtown Ln., East Hampton, NY 11937; open daily in summer 10–10, rest of year daily 10–6; *also* 631-288-0999, 123 Main St., Westhampton Beach, NY 11978; open year-round, in summer Sun.–Wed. 10–6, Thurs. 10–8, Fri. and Sat. 10–10, rest of year fewer days and shorter hours) These stores are devoted to shoes designed by fashion designers such as Anne Klein, Calvin Klein, and Ralph Lauren, among many others. The designers often make announced visits to the store to promote their shoes—which is met with a somewhat ho-hum response in the Hamptons, where celebrity sightings are commonplace.

Tommy Hilfiger (631-324-0540; www.tommyhilfiger.com; 69 Main St. East Hampton, NY 11937; open year-round, daily in summer 10–8, shorter hours rest of year) Tommy came to town in the summer of 2009, and he stayed. There's a terrific line of swimwear and sportswear for "summer in the Hamptons," as well as shirts, blazers, knits and sweaters.

SAG HARBOR

Collette Designer Resale (631-725-9300; www.colletteconsignment.com; 78-80 Main St., Sag Harbor, NY 11963; open year-round, daily Sun.–Fri. 9:30–7, Sat. 9:30–9) Owner: Tisha Collette. This very classy pair of shops on Sag Harbor's Main Street mirrors the owner's shops in East Hampton and Southampton. You'll find top-quality women's vintage designer clothing in excellent condition. The selection includes skirts, blouses, shoes, bags, and some jewelry.

Lisa Perry (631-725-7467; www.lisaperrystyle.com; 45 Main St., Sag Harbor, NY 11963; open May–mid-Oct.; June–Sept., Sun.–Thurs. 11–8, Fri. and Sat. 10–10, fewer days and shorter hours rest of season) It's evident that owner Lisa Perry never quite outgrew the '60s. Her use of bold colors blended with sculptured and architectural designs are reminiscent of Courréges. They're fun, young, and very wearable. You'll find A-line dresses in wonderful fabrics with brightly contrasting pockets or stripes, as well as dresses with long sleeves that unzip to become short sleeves. It's all totally clever and original. If this store is closed when you need her, she's got several year-round stores in Manhattan.

Nikki Eve (631-725-4634; Madison St., Sag Harbor, NY 11963; open year-round, daily in summer 11–6; rest of year Sat. and Sun. 11–5) You'll find a wonderful variety of elegant vintage couture garments from designers such as Chanel and Dior, but owner Nikki Aarons also has a lighter side. Her second-floor walk-up includes a nice selection of younger, funkier garments, as well. You'll find clothing by Emilio Pucci, Adolpho, Courréges, Rudy Gernreich, and more, in velvet, lace, and taffeta, as well as sweaters, riding apparel, alligator bags and shoes, and lingerie such as lacy camisoles and elegant, custom-made silk pajamas.

Pailletts (631-899-4070; 78 Main St., Sag Harbor, NY 11963; open Mar.–Dec., daily in summer, fewer days rest of season) Designer Danielle Gisiger has been creating couture ensembles at her atelier in Manhattan for more than a decade, but now she brings her elegant cocktail dresses and pretty cotton frocks to the Hamptons. In addition to dresses, she sells jewelry, handbags, and scarves.

Urban Zen (631-725-6176; www.urbanzen.org; 4 Bay St., Sag Harbor, NY 11963; open May–Dec.; in summer daily 10–7, fewer days and hours rest of season) This store brand, created by Donna Karan, helps raise money for her Urban Zen Foundation, which has three goals: increasing well-being, empowering children, and preserving cultures. You will find casual and relaxed women's wear in natural fabrics, incorporating asymmetrical lines that often include draping, mostly in earth tones of ivory, beige, and brown.

SOUTHAMPTON

Christopher Fischer Cashmere Collections (631-204-9090, www.christopherfischer.com; 52 Job's Ln., Southampton, NY 11968; open year-round, in summer Mon.–Sat. 10–7, Sun. 11–6, rest of year fewer days and hours; *also* 631-907-0900, 67 Main St., East Hampton, NY 11937; open in summer Mon.–Fri. 10–6, Sat. 10–7, Sun. 11–6; rest of year shorter hours and closed Tues. and Wed.) Owner: Christopher Fischer. This pair of cashmere shops carries a huge selection of top-quality cashmere sweaters in a variety of colors and styles, from fancy designs to simple turtlenecks.

Collette Designer Resale (631-204-9511, www.colletteconsignment.com; 89 Job's Ln., Southampton, NY 11968; *also* Collette Country Store, 631-283-1867, 10 Main St., Southampton; open year-round, in summer Mon.–Sat. 10–6, Sun. 11–5; rest of year

Mon. and Wed.–Sat. 10–6, Sun. 11–4, closed Tues.) Owner: Tisha Collette. These designer resale shops take top-notch designer clothes on consignment. You may find a wonderful Calvin Klein suede skirt, or a vintage pair of black Claude Montana tuxedo slacks, or an early Badgely Mischka dress here, as well as shoes, purses, and some jewelry. All are in top-notch condition, and they're beautifully displayed. If you like vintage, this is the crème de la crème. If you don't find what you want here, check out the East Hampton or the Sag Harbor shops. During the summer, she also sells some vintage furniture in the Main Street store. The rest of the year, she sells furniture in her location at 116 North Sea Road, Southampton.

Diane von Furstenberg (631-204-0129; www.DVF.com; 53B Jobs Ln., Southampton, NY 11968; open year-round, Mon.–Sat. 10–6, Sun. 10–5.) We're happy to see that Diane von Furstenberg opened a wonderful boutique just off Job's Lane the summer of 2009—her first in the Hamptons. It's stocked with her signature wrap dress and other designs, all in summer prints, and there are plenty of hats, bags, and jewelry to go with them.

Edward Archer (631-283-2668; 85 Main St., Southampton, NY 11968; open year-round, Mon.–Sat. 9:30–5:30) Owner: Ed Archer. This incredibly elegant men's shop has beautiful wool and silk suits; some are casual, but most are very formal and proper. This is *the* place to come if you don't have time to run over to Savile Row to have a custom suit whipped up.

Hampton & Co. (631-283-2899; www.hamptonandco.com; 60B Jobs Lane, Southampton, NY 11968; open year-round, in summer Mon.–Thurs. 10–6, Fri. and Sat. 10–7, Sun. 11–5; rest of year open Mon., Tues, Fri., and Sat. 10–5, Sun. 11–4, closed Wed. and Thurs.) Owners: Nick Beech and Randi Jacklin. This terrific local company designs and produces elegant handmade silk ties, men's and women's polos, linen shirts, sailcloth bags, drawstring board shorts, and more—all in top-quality fabrics. Best of all, at least 10 percent is donated to local charities.

Ralph Lauren (631-287-6953; www.ralphlauren.com; 41 Jobs Ln. Southampton, NY 11968; open year-round, in summer Mon.–Thurs. 10–9, Fri. and Sat. 10–10, Sun. 10–6; shorter hours rest of year) The look and the attitude of Ralph Lauren are captured here in his distinctive store, styled with distressed wood floors and leather chairs. You'll find the same terrific merchandise as in East Hampton—rugby shirts, cable-knit sweaters, and denims, as well as blazer jackets and elegant evening dresses.

Saks Fifth Avenue (631-283-3500; www.saksfifthavenue.com; 1 Hampton Rd., Southampton, NY 11968; open year-round, Mon.–Sat. 10–6, Sun. noon–6) In this mini-version of its big sister in Manhattan, you can outfit an entire family from jewelry to shoes, handbags to evening gowns.

Wainscott

Bellhaus (631-537-5050; www.bellhaus.net; 328 Montauk Hwy., Wainscott, NY 11975; open year-round, summer Mon. and Wed.–Sat. 10–6, Sun. 11–5; rest of year Thurs.–Sat. 10–6, Sun. 10–5) In this beautiful, modern building with floor-to-ceiling windows and a high-tech ambience, you will find some of the most elegant (and expensive) clothing for men and women in the Hamptons. The fabrics—in gorgeous silks, leathers, and wools—are exquisite, and the designs set them (and anyone wearing them) apart from all others. For men, the style is classic; while for women the offerings range from feathery evening wear to classic suits to zingy, swingy dresses and skirts in bright pinks and oranges.

WESTHAMPTON BEACH

Darbelle (631-288-0292; 88 Main St., Westhampton Beach, NY 11978; open year-round, in summer Mon.–Thurs. 10–10; Fri.–Sun. 10–12; fewer days and hours rest of year) Owner: Anick Darbellay. This classy women's wear shop carries unusual clothing in bright colors and interesting fabrics—a neon-orange leather skirt, for example.

Jimmy's (631-288-7000; 167 Main St., Westhampton Beach, NY 11978; open year-round, in summer Mon.–Sat. 10–6, Sun. 10–5, rest of year fewer days and hours.) Owners: Dominick and Betsy Lepore. You can sit on a plush sofa and ogle the designer clothes that are displayed for you, before you try them on, if you wish. They'll most likely bring out Valentino and Saint Laurent suits and dresses, Roberto Cavellero beaded dresses, elegant Italian suits, and fun furs.

Sweet Anezka's Lingerie (631-288-2612; www.anezkas.com; 120 Main St., Westhampton Beach, NY 11978; open year-round, in summer daily Mon.–Thurs. 11–6, Fri. and Sat. 11–10, Sun. 11–7, rest of year open Thurs.–Mon. 11–6) Who doesn't love lingerie? In her well-stocked store, Anezka Jureckova offers a broad selection of lacy undies and coverups, as well as swimwear. It's hard not to resist.

Decorative Arts, Interior Design, Furniture

BRIDGEHAMPTON

Country Gear (631-537-1032; www.countrygearltd.com; 2408 Main St.; mailing address: P.O. Box 727, Bridgehampton, NY 11932; open year-round, Mon.–Sat. 10–6, Sun. 10–5) Designer Charles DiSapio's unique niche is appreciated by the most discriminating home owners. His shop is filled with fascinating English and Irish country-style antiques that include harvest tables, fireplace mantels, and armoires. Although all of these are for sale, they are also used as models for his custom-designed work. Adapting a molding here or a finish there and using aged pine (generally 150 to 200 years old), he custom-designs libraries, entertainment centers, hutches, and armoires that won't be found anywhere else. Scattered throughout the shop are smaller English antique accessories such as metal bottle caddies, enamel kitchen boxes, mirrors, and birdcages.

English Country Antiques (631-537-0606, www.ecantiques.com; 26 Snake Hollow Rd.; mailing address: P.O. Box 1995, Bridgehampton, NY 11932; also 631-204-0428; 53 North Sea Rd., Southampton, NY 11968; open year-round, Mon.–Sat. 9–5:30, Sun. 10:30–5:30) Chris Mead has assembled an extensive collection in his warehouse-sized showrooms that specialize in English (and some French) antiques and reproductions. Many of the armoires, china cabinets, beds, breakfronts, and tables are in pine. You'll also find birdcages, mirrors, lamps, chandeliers, candlesticks, weather vanes, whirligigs, and much more.

Urban Archaeology (631-537-0124; www.urbanarchaeology.com; 2231 Montauk Hwy.; mailing address: P.O. Box 191, Bridgehampton, NY 11932; open year-round, Mon.–Sat. 9–5) Owner: Gil Shapiro. Urban Archaeology was born because the owner wanted to salvage great architectural elements from buildings about to be demolished. The demand for the great old pieces was so steady, however, that the company now has its own line of reproductions: artisans in Spain make alabaster lamps; in Italy, they create iron pieces; and in Manhattan, they make a variety of objects in the lower recesses of the main store. In their Bridgehampton store, they sell their own items, which include handsome marble Victorian washstands, platform tubs, and beautiful tiles. Knowledgeable designers will help you design a unique bathroom or other interior space.

You can access the Home Furnishings section of the Ralph Lauren store in East Hampton through this charming entry. Dustin Chase

EAST HAMPTON

Calypso Home (631-324-8146; www.calypso-celle.com; 17 Newtown Ln., East Hampton, NY 11937; open year-round, Mon.–Sat. 10-6; Sun. 11–5) Owner: Christiane Celle. This store, showcasing Calypso's home furnishings (for clothing see listings under "Children's Shops; Clothing" and "Clothing, Adult"), features beds dressed with the Calypso line of sheets and coverlets, tables and chairs, rugs, pillows, towels, candles, and more.

Polo Home Country Store (631-324-1222; www.ralphlauren.com; 31-33 Main St., East Hampton, NY 11937; *also* 631-287-6953; 41 Jobs Lane, Southampton, NY 11968; open year-round, Mon.–Thurs. 10–6, Fri. and Sat. 10–7, Sun. 11–5; rest of year weekends 10–6) Located down the alley beside the Ralph Lauren clothing stores (of course, you can also walk through the stores to get to them, although you may be distracted by all the elegant clothes), you'll find his charming cottage-home stores. Rattan chairs are piled with Lauren pillows, and beautiful bedding, bar ware, picture frames, and leather goods are attractively displayed.

Rumrunner (631-725-1379; www.rumrunnerhome.com; 330 Montauk Hwy. Wainscott; mailing address: P.O. Box 222, Wainscott, NY 11937; also 631-287-0583, 62 Hampton

Rd. Southampton, NY 11968; both stores open year-round, daily 10–6) Owners: Regis Waleckl Jr. and Greg Foglia. Rumrunner offers a fabulous selection of furniture, bright Italian and Portuguese dishes, replicas of old signs, mechanical banks, painted tiles, pillows, tabletop items, cards, and so much more. It's the perfect stop for great hostess gifts, as well as terrific accessories for your own home.

SAG HARBOR

Bloom (631-725-5940; 43 Madison St.; mailing address: P.O. Box 897, Sag Harbor, NY 11963; open year-round, daily in summer 11–5; rest of year Thurs.–Mon. 11–5) Owner: Mona Nerenberg. The interesting and unique home and garden furniture and accessories make this shop worth a detour on any shopper's schedule. You'll find white ironstone, linens, china, and much more, all lovingly displayed in a great old Sag Harbor house and garden.

Fisher's Home Furnishings (631-725-0006; www.fishershomefurnishings.com; 144 Main St., P.O. Box 2100, Sag Harbor, NY 11963; *also* Fisher's Annex on Bridge St., Sag Harbor; open year-round, daily 10–5) Owners: Susan and Bob Fisher. This large shop features country pine antiques and reproductions, iron beds, painted and distressed furniture, and a vast selection of interesting and unusual home furnishings. You'll find 1940s flowered tablecloths and napkins, botanical prints, Soleido tablecloths and napkins,

Mecox Gardens in Southampton, with its classic furniture and accessories, garden sculptures, and pavilions, offers you countless ways to enrich your home.

decorative pillows, and china. Pine furniture can be custom-ordered, and there's a restoration studio for repairs and custom finishes.

SOUTHAMPTON

Brambles (631-283-5171; 44 Main St., Southampton, NY 11968; open year-round, Mon.–Sat. 10–5, Sun. 11–5; closed Tues. in Jan. and Feb.) Owners: Anne Ashare and Susan Rimland. This is a one-stop shop for casual, beachy furniture and accessories. There are lots of puffy sofas and boards painted with clever sayings such as "Laugh and the world laughs with you; snore and you sleep alone."

Broken Colour Works (631-259-3612; www.brokencolourworks.com; 27 Hampton Rd., Southampton, NY 11968; open year-round, daily except Wed. 10–5; *also* 631-725-6152; Division and Bay Sts., Sag Harbor, NY 11963; open weekends 10–5) Owner/designer Shannon Willey can faux-paint a wall to make it look like a beach scene, marbleize a table, or paint whimsical characters on a child's dresser. At her shops, she also sells decorative accessories such as candles, metal outdoor furniture, and cute hot-air-balloon pictures for a child's room.

Mecox Gardens (631-287-5015; www.mecoxgardens.com; 257 County Rd. 39A, Southampton, NY 11968; *also* 631-329-9405, 66 Newtown Ln., East Hampton, NY 11937; open year-round, daily 10–5) Owner: McDowell Hoak. Although both sell classic furniture and accessories and provide an array of interior-design services, the Southampton store is much larger than the one in East Hampton. You'll find mirrors, hurricane lamps, chandeliers, sconces, puffy sofas and chairs, and even elegant stationery. Outside, there's an array of garden furniture and various pavilions that can be adapted to your own estate setting—all on three acres. Outside the Hamptons, there are stores in Chicago, Dallas, Houston, Los Angeles, New York City, and Palm Beach.

Simply French (631-283-5115; 18 Job's Ln., Southampton; mailing address: P.O. Box 9000, Bridgehampton, NY 11932; open year-round, in summer Mon.–Sat. 10:30–5:30, Sun. 11–5; fewer days and hours rest of year) Owner: Lynn Buoniconti. This marvelous shop specializes in fine French country items, especially those from Provence. There's 18th- and 19th-century furniture, including iron beds, chandeliers, upholstered chairs, and painted chests, as well as soap from St. Rémy, colorful French fabrics and linens, elegant two-toned cashmere throws, dolls, pottery and faience, art, and more. If you're a Francophile, as I am, you'll return again and again.

WESTHAMPTON BEACH

Excentricities (631-288-0258; 83 Main St., Westhampton Beach, NY 11978; open Mem. Day–Labor Day daily 11–6; Sept.–Oct. same hours but closed Tues. and Wed.; closed Nov.–Mem. Day) Owner: Carol Adams. A summer branch of her shop in North Palm Beach, this one sells beautiful new furniture and accessories. The little candles in shells are unique and make terrific hostess gifts.

WATER MILL

The Furniture Garden (631-726-4647; www.thefurnituregardens.com; 337 Montauk Hwy. Water Mill, NY 11976; open year-round, daily in summer 11–4; fewer days rest of year) Owner: Deanna Annis. This interesting shop includes numerous tables, chairs, Buddhas, and decorative items—most of them made of the finest teak to the owner's specifications in Bali. All of the pieces have a distinctive Asian theme and showcase the beauty of the wood.

Doggone It

SOUTHAMPTON

Pampered pets are welcome at Little Lucy's in Southampton.

Little Lucy's (631-287-2352; 91 Job's Ln., Southampton, NY 11968; open year-round, daily in summer 10–7; rest of year Thurs.– Mon. 11–6, closed Tues. and Wed.) Owner: Patricia Hurley. This adorable shop carries a marvelous selection of couture wear for our best friends, whether of Yorkie or standard poodle size. You can outfit poochie in Cindy Adams's Jazzy Couture line or dress him up in a cowboy hat. There's a full line of beach attire, as well as pajamas, sweaters, terry coats, and all kinds of accessories from carriers to hair ribbons. It's a fun and funky shop. You may meet Miss Lucy herself if you attend one of the trunk shows where she's sure to be modeling.

Factory Outlets

AMAGANSETT

Amagansett Square This very tasteful collection of cottages houses a variety of outlet stores, including Van Heusen, Le Sportsac, Bass, and Sunglass Hut. The prices are much better than retail, especially when sales are under way.

EAST HAMPTON

Coach (631-329-1777; www.coach.com; 50 Newtown Ln., East Hampton, NY 11937; open year-round, daily 10–6) For classic leather handbags, briefcases, and wallets, plus T-shirts, sweats, and shorts, this shop has very reasonable prices.

SOUTHAMPTON

Cashmere Outlet (631-283-1926; www.thecashmereoutlet.com; 43A Job's Ln., Southampton, NY 11968; *also* 631-324-8341; 58 Newtown Ln., East Hampton, NY 11937; open year-round, daily in summer 11–6; rest of year noon–5 but closed Tues.) Owners: Corey and Patty Wielgus. In these shops you'll find interesting and unusual cashmere (Scottish only) sweaters at 30 percent off retail. I loved a cable-stitched number with buttons and fringe.

Villeroy and Boch Factory Outlet (631-283-7172; www.villeroy-boch.com; 35 Main St., Southampton, NY 11968; open year-round, Mon.–Sat. 10–5, Sun. 11–6) This factory outlet store of the well-known German tabletop designer offers porcelain, silver, glassware, and gifts at discounts of 40 to 70 percent off retail.

Galleries

Art galleries abound in the Hamptons and are the site of many art shows. Opening receptions attract glittering crowds of artists, writers, and actors. The gallery scene is such an established institution in the Hamptons that the gallery hopper may attend as many as five or six openings in one night. The following listings represent only a few of the better-known galleries.

AMAGANSETT

Crazy Monkey Gallery (631-267-3627; 136 Main St., P.O. Box 2147, Amagansett, NY 11930; open May–Dec.; daily in summer 11–5; closed several days rest of season) Owner: Andrea McCafferty. Tucked away in a parking lot, this little shop is a treasure trove of interesting things. There's a display case of beautiful jewelry; another of pretty velvet and tapestry satchels; there are pedestals supporting pottery; and oil paintings on the walls.

BRIDGEHAMPTON

Mark Borghi Fine Art (631-537-7245; www.borghi.org; 2426 Main St., Bridgehampton, NY 11932; open year-round, daily in summer 10–5:30; rest of year Fri.–Mon. 10–5 or by appt.) Owner: Mark Borghi. This gallery exhibits extraordinary paintings, watercolors, and drawings by incredible Long Island artists. Among a recent display were works by William Merritt Chase, Emily Nichols Hatch, Fairfield Porter, and Maurice Prendergast. You can also visit their New York gallery.

EAST HAMPTON

Giraffics Gallery (631-329-0803; www.girafficsgallery.com; 79A Newtown Ln., East Hampton, NY 11937; open year-round, daily in summer 1–6; rest of year fewer days and hours, or by appt.) Owner: Peter DeRosa. This interesting gallery specializes in graphics, prints, and lithographs. It provides representation for such artists as Hilary Knight, the renowned illustrator of the Eloise books, and fashion illustrator Rene Bouché. An exhibit might include stage set sketches by well-known theater designers such as Tony Walton, or one featuring vintage film posters. You can buy collector Eloise books here too.

Pritam & Eames (631-324-7111; www.pritameames.com; 29 Race Ln., East Hampton, NY 11937; open year-round, Mon.–Sat. 10–5, except closed Wed., Sun. 12–4) Owner: Bebe Pritam Johnson and Warren Eames Johnson. This gallery has been open since 1981, making it the oldest furniture gallery in the U.S. They specialize in exhibiting the work of artist/craftsmen who create one-of-a-kind studio furniture—often using exotic pieces of wood that are carved and molded into extraordinary pieces of furniture and decorative art.

Spanierman Gallery (631-329-9530; www.spanierman.com; 68 Newtown Ln., East Hampton, NY 11937; open year-round, Thurs.–Mon. 10–6) Owner: Ira Spanierman. The Spanierman Galleries are among the most respected in America. Their exhibitions, especially in their New York gallery at 45 East 58th Street, are on a par with the finest exhibits at our leading art museums, and, in fact, a number of their exhibitions have traveled to leading East Coast museums. The East Hampton branch features art by postwar and contemporary artists from Long Island's East End. You might see Thomas Moran or Jackson Pollock, as well as artists whose names are less well known.

Wallace Gallery in East Hampton specializes in 19th- and 20th-century American art created by Eastern Long Island landscape and maritime artists. This watercolor on paper of the Wainscott Mill, c. 1885, was painted by George Herbert McCord (1848–1909). Photo Courtesy Wallace Gallery, East Hampton

Vered Art Gallery (631-324-3303; www.veredart.com; 68 Park Pl., East Hampton, NY 11937; open year-round, daily in summer 11–11; rest of year closed Tues., Wed., and sometimes Thurs.) Owners: Ruth Vered and Janet Lehr. The Vered Gallery represents and/or sells the work of some of America's and Europe's most prestigious artists— Willem de Kooning, Wolf Kahn, Milton Avery, Pablo Picasso, Henri Matisse, Marc Chagall, Alfonso A. Ossorio, Louise Nevelson, Fairfield Porter, Bert Stern, Man Ray, Thomas Moran, Childe Hassam, Larry Rivers, Alfred Stieglitz, and Andy Warhol, among others.

Wallace Gallery (631-329-4516; www.hamptonsweb.com/wallacegallery; 37A Main St., East Hampton, NY 11937; open year-round, daily in summer 10–7; rest of year closed Tues.–Thurs.) Terry Wallace is an expert in museum-quality 19th- and 20th-century American art; he specializes in art from that period created by eastern Long Island landscape and maritime artists. In his shop, on a mews off Main Street, you'll find fine oil paintings and watercolors, and at one time I saw a tile painted by Thomas Moran, who was one of the members of the Tile Club, a group of 19th-century painters who made East Hampton their home in the summer. Mr. Wallace now shares space with Hollander's, which specializes in fine 19th- and 20th-century European art. It's a great combination.

SAG HARBOR

Grenning Gallery (631-725-8469; www.grenninggallery.com; 17 Washington St., Sag Harbor, NY 11963; open year-round, in summer Sun.–Thurs. 11–6, Fri. and Sat. 11–10; rest of year open Mon., Tues., Thurs.–Sat. 11–6, Sun. 12–5) Owner: Laura Grenning. Dedicated to the work of artists who employ a style and philosophy similar to that of the old masters, this gallery, located at the Sag Harbor Cinema, features realistic still lifes, landscapes, nudes, and portraits that have been painted from life. You will find beautiful paintings worthy of hanging in the most elegant homes.

Tulla Booth Gallery (631-725-3100; www.tullaboothgallery.com; 66 Main St., Sag Harbor, NY 11963; open in summer Fri.–Mon. 12–6, or by appt.) Owner: Tulla Booth. Tulla is a talented photographer who specializes in botanical and floral photographs. She displays her own work and that of other photographers in her gallery.

The Winter Tree Gallery (631-725-0097; www.cucaromley.com; 125 Main St.; mailing address: P.O. Box 1463, Sag Harbor, NY 11963; open year-round, daily in summer, except Tues., 12–6; fewer days rest of year) Owner: Cuca Romley. Cuca Romley is an incredibly gifted artist. She does intricate, detailed etchings of her subjects, which include the Plaza Hotel, the Statue of Liberty, and other familiar landmarks, and then hand-paints them. The results are wonderful. She also sells note cards and other items containing these images. In her gallery she displays the work of other talented artists and collectors, as well. At one time, she had a magnificent collection of handcrafted model ships by a skilled craftsman on display and for sale.

SOUTHAMPTON

Chrysalis Gallery (631-287-1883; 2 Main St., Southampton, NY 11968; open year-round, Mon.–Sat. 10–6, Sun. 11–5) Owner: Agnes Ehrenreich. You'll find original oils, watercolors, and sculptures at this fine arts gallery on a prominent corner of the village, as well as prints by artists such as Michael Delacroix.

RVS Fine Art (631-283-8546; 20 Job's Ln., Southampton, NY 11968; open year-round, daily in summer 12–5; rest of year Fri.–Mon. 1–5) Owner: Roberta von Schlossberg. Ms. von Schlossberg has had a fine art gallery in Southampton for more than 30 years, so she definitely knows what she's doing. She's a proponent of local artists, although she represents other American and international talent as well. She is particularly strong in contemporary art.

Gifts

SAG HARBOR

Blooming Shells (631-725-9504; www.bloomingshells.com; 11 Washington St.; P.O. Box 2024, Sag Harbor, NY 11963; open year-round, in summer daily 10–7; fewer days and hours rest of year. Owner: Debbie-lou Houdek. Debbie-lou has filled her little shop with bin after bin of beautiful shells. There are polished lion paws, whelks, helmuts and mother of pearl, and you can also purchase necklaces, bracelets, and earrings made of shells, and boxes embellished with them.

Romany Kramoris Gallery (631-725-2499; www.kramorisgallery.com; 41 Main St., P.O. Box 2664, Sag Harbor, NY 11963; open year-round, daily in summer 10am–11/12pm; shorter hours rest of year) Owner: Romany Kramoris. This eclectic collection of unusual items is like a blast from the '50s. The gifts range from blown glassware and shell lampshades, to books, cards, and stationery. There are Christmas items, candles, and a garden full of statuary and distressed garden benches.

WESTHAMPTON BEACH

O'Suzanna (631-288-2202; 108 Main St., Westhampton Beach, NY 11978; open year-round, in summer Sun.–Wed. 10–6, Thurs.–Sat. 10–10; rest of year daily 10–6) Owner Suzanne Marchisello travels the back roads of Italy every year, finding new ceramic designers whose work she features in her store. Many of the designs are her own, and most of her pieces won't be seen elsewhere. Come here to find bright, hand-painted Italian platters, vases, dishes, and plaques, as well as Portuguese ceramics, table and bed linens, and fancifully painted dishes by Lynn Chase.

Pine Cone (631-288-8316; 1 Glovers Ln., Westhampton Beach, NY 11978; open year-round, in summer Mon.–Thurs. 10–8, Fri.–Sun. 10–10; rest of year daily 11–5:30, but call for hours Jan.–Apr.) Owner: Judy Garry. This shop has some very interesting pieces tucked into its tiny space. There are large collections of antique lead soldiers and ceramic teapots (some hand-painted). All of the Limoges, Kosta Boda/Orrefors, Wedgwood, and Battersea dishes and figurines, as well as other porcelain lines, are discounted. There are also unusual dolls, picture frames, teddies, teddies, and more teddies, jewelry, brass candlesticks, cobalt glass vases, and more.

Handcrafts

AMAGANSETT

Gone Local (631-267-5315; www.gonelocalamagansett.com; 199 Main St.; mailing address: P.O. Box 1588, Amagansett, NY 11930; open year-round, daily in summer 10–5, closed Wed. rest of year) Owner Susan Seitz-Kulick. If you are looking for something that says "Hamptons," this is the place to come. There are T-shirts and sweatshirts, original paintings, prints of historic Hampton landmarks, books related to the area, weathered-looking Hampton village signs, locally made food products, handmade silk ties, games, and jewelry. You can even arrange to have your pet's portrait painted.

EAST HAMPTON

The Irony (631-329-5567; 53 Sag Harbor Rd., East Hampton, NY 11937; open year-round, Mon.–Fri. 9–5 or by appt.) Owner: Bob Blinker. If you would like a decorative wrought iron fence surrounding your house, just like the ones in New Orleans, or a lacy iron windowbox, or a distinctive light fixture, Bob Blinker will make it for you.

SAG HARBOR

Megna Hot Glass (631-725-1131; www.megnaglass.net; 11 Bridge St., Sag Harbor, NY 11963; open year-round, Wed.–Sat. 10–4, sometimes there longer hours and Sundays) Owner: Martin Megna. Why travel to Seattle when we have our own Dale Chihuly right here? Martin Megna does enormous blown-glass chandeliers and other pieces on commission, but he also makes glass vases, kitchen knobs, faucets, hummingbird feeders, bowls, sculptures, wineglasses, and much more, and sells them around the country to stores, who then sell them to you. But, as we all know, no one is perfect 100 percent of the time, so when a piece doesn't meet his exacting standards, he sells them here in his studio to visitors. You can watch him work and also purchase some of his "rejects" at true factory-outlet prices.

SOUTHAMPTON

Shinnecock Indian Outpost (631-283-8047; www.shinnecocktradingpost.com; Shinnecock Reservation, 1286 Montauk Hwy., Southampton, NY 11968; open year-round, Mon.–Sat. 6:30–9; Sun. 7–8) This interesting shop carries Native American arts and crafts that include pottery, dream catchers, sand paintings, sculptures, beaded belts, glassware, moccasins, and jewelry. The items have been assembled from a variety of American Indian tribes; some especially lovely work comes from the Southwest.

Home: Kitchen, Garden, Linens, Stationery

AMAGANSETT

Charlie Whitmore Gardens (631-267-3182; www.cwhitmoregardens.com; 26 Montauk Hwy.; mailing address: P.O. Box 1380, Amagansett, NY 11930; open year-round, daily 8:30–5, except to 6 Thurs. and Fri.) Owner: Charlie Whitmore. You'll find lovely pots and containers here as well as a wide selection of outdoor furniture. There's a full landscaping and design staff to help plan your outdoor spaces from patios and waterfalls, to gazebos and garden statuary, to privacy hedges, as well as border or perennial gardens—all your landscaping needs.

BRIDGEHAMPTON

Alice B. King Fine Stationery, Ltd. (631-537-5115; 2454 Main St.; mailing address: P.O. Box 475, Bridgehampton, NY 11932; open year-round, daily 11–6, except Wed.) Since we love fine stationery, we were pleased when Alice King opened this stationery shop on Main Street in 2000. There are unusual invitations, pretty pens, and a wide variety of elegant and unusual notecards, and stationery that can be purchased or custom ordered.

Loaves & Fishes Cookshop (631-537-6066; www.landfcookshop.com; 2422 Montauk Hwy.; mailing address: P.O. Box 1342, Bridgehampton, NY 11932; open year-round, in summer Mon.–Thurs. 9–6, Fri. 9–9, Sat. 9–8, Sun. 9:30–5; shorter hours rest of year) Owners: Sybille and Gerrit van Kempen. This wonderful kitchen shop (brought to you by the daughter of the owner of Loaves & Fishes caterers and take-out shop in Sagaponack) burst on the Hamptons scene in 2003, and we're among those convinced it's one of the best things that's happened around here. You can buy a fabulous Viking Range for your kitchen (they're distributors), or some dishes, cookbooks, or tablecloths, or you can hone your cooking skills by attending a wide variety of classes. How about a fish dinner class with freshly caught seafood, or a class featuring a variety of cocktail party dishes? There are classes for kids, too.

Marders (631-537-3700; www.marders.com; 120 Snake Hollow Rd.; mailing address: P.O. Box 1261, Bridgehampton, NY 11932; open year-round, in summer Mon.–Sat. 8–6, Sun. 9–5; rest of year closes one hour earlier) Owner: Charlie Marder. This is the landscaping capital of the Hamptons. Marders can create landscaping designs, install rock walls and walkways, plant huge trees, design a lighting system, and even take care of your lawn and

With everything from fresh flowers to garden furniture, Topiaire Flower Shop in Southampton is inviting and fun.

yard maintenance on a weekly basis. In addition, the garden shop is full of interesting containers, garden furniture, and whatever you might need for your garden.

Williams-Sonoma (631-537-3040; www.williams-sonoma.com; Bridgehampton Commons, 2044 Montauk Hwy.; mailing address: P.O. Box 802, Bridgehampton, NY 11932; open year-round, in summer Mon.–Thurs. 10–7, Fri. and Sat. 10–8., Sun. 11–6; rest of year closes one hour earlier) The addition of a new building at Bridgehampton Commons in 1994 brought this well-known kitchen store to town. Here you'll find terrific pots and pans, dishes, cookbooks, linen, silverware, glassware, knives, and such food staples as garlic oil, vinegars, and coffee beans—cooking classes too.

EAST HAMPTON

Home, James! (631-324-2307; www.homejameseasthampton.com; 55 Main St., East Hampton, NY 11937; open year-round, in summer Mon.–Fri. 10–5, Sat. 10–6, Sun. 11–5; rest of year call for hours) Owners: David Cipperman and Josef Schreick. If you're looking for a wonderful set of antique dishes, perhaps some new Spode, or a delicate French lace or handsome Irish linen tablecloth, you must come here. You will find a wide selection of elegant china, crystal, linens, and small antiques. And if you're looking for expert interior design assistance, that's here, too.

SAG HARBOR

Sylvester & Co. (631-725-5012; 103 Main St.; mailing address: P.O. Box 2069, Sag Harbor, NY 11963; open year-round, daily in summer 8 AM–9 PM; rest of year shorter hours and closed Tues. and Wed.) Owner: Linda Sylvester. This is a kitchenware shop with all the items you'd expect, but it also sells gourmet food items, pottery, china, place mats, gardening baskets, cookbooks and gardening books, fresh coffee, muffins, cookies, and pastries. The coffeepot is on all day, and it's a town gathering spot.

SOUTHAMPTON

Elegant Setting (631-283-4747; www.theelegantsetting.com; 31 Main St., Southampton, NY 11968; open year-round, in summer daily 10–6; fewer days and hours rest of year) Stephanie Finkelstein has created the ultimate hostess shop. She's got vintage, one-of-a-kind crystal, china, silver, and linens, as well as new china, linens, and stationery. You can get monograms put on totes, beach towels, and brightly colored cocktail and dinner napkins—and if you're a weekend guest on an estate, she'll help you find the perfect thank-you.

Privet Cove (631-287-5685; 69 Job's Ln., Southampton, NY 11968; open year-round, daily in summer 10–7; rest of year daily 10–6; may close Tues. and Wed. in winter) Owner: Constantine Patsimas. If you love to surround yourself with white, you can buy it all here. There are white dishes, casual furniture (tables, chairs, painted cupboards), hurricane lamps, shells, candles, and even a wonderful bench made from a Jenny Lind bed.

Topiaire (631-287-3800; 51 Job's Ln., Southampton, NY 11968; open year-round, daily 9:30–6) Owner: Erin Meaney. The exterior of this adorable shop is so whimsical and inviting that you can't resist poking around inside, and it's well worth your while. You'll find lots of cute vintage-looking garden signs, beautiful floral arrangements, and lovely garden furniture.

Jewelry

EAST HAMPTON

Jennifer Miller (631-329-9061; www.jewelsbyjen.com; 55 Main St., East Hampton, NY 11937; open year-round, Mon.–Sat. 10–6, Sun. 10–5; also in Southampton: 631-283-9061; 28C Jobs Ln., Southampton, NY 11968; open May–Sept. only) What woman wouldn't want to wear the elegant baubles created by Jennifer Miller? Combining fine and faux in exquisite designs, she uses diamonds and pearls, as well as precious and semiprecious stones to create pieces that are the envy of all who don't own them.

London Jewelers (631-329-3939; www.londonjewelers.com; 2 Main St., East Hampton, NY 11937; *also in Southampton:* 631-287-4499; 47 Main St., Southampton, NY 11968; open year-round, in summer Mon.–Thurs. 10–5:30, Fri. and Sat. 10–7, Sun. 11–5; rest of year shorter hours) Owners: Mark and Candy Udell. London Jewelers has been in business on Long Island for over 80 years, and they now have five stores—two of them in the Hamptons. After renovating a great old building that was in need of considerable repair, they opened the very elegant East Hampton store in 1996. The Southampton store followed several years later. They both offer a selection of fine jewelry, watches, glassware, and gifts. There's a Tiffany jewelry department, Bulgari jewels, Cartier and Piaget watches, an Alfred Dunhill humidor room where you can select fine cigars, plus a collection of MacKenzie-Childs hand-painted furniture and dishes.

You can buy far more than fine jewelry at London Jewelers. An extensive MacKenzie-Childs shop, an Alfred Dunhill humidor room, and a Tiffany jewelry department are only a few of the pleasures. Morgan McGivern

Mayfair Diamond & Fine Jewelry (631-329-8444; www.mayfairdiamonds.com; 73 Main St., East Hampton, NY 11937; open year-round, daily 10:30–5:30) This respected jeweler has been owned by the same family since 1923, and they really know their diamonds. If you're looking for an engagement ring or an anniversary present, they'll explain all the nuances before you make the investment. The shop also has a full line of watches, as well as men's and women's jewelry.

Tiffany & Co. (631-324-1700; www.tiffany.com; 53 Main St., East Hampton, NY 11937; open year-round, in summer Mon.–Sat. 10–6, Sun. 11–5; rest of year Mon.–Sat. 10–6, Sun. 12–5) This fine jewelry company opened an East End store in 2002 that carries the same fabulous jewelry, vases, china, watches, and elegant diamonds as the Manhattan store—a wonderful addition to the Hamptons shopping scene.

SAG HARBOR

Adornments Fine Jewelry (631-725-0051; 83 Main St., Sag Harbor, NY 11963; open year-round, daily in summer 11–7; fewer days and hours rest of year) Owner: Joseph Maio. Glamorous and elegant jewelry, created by a variety of designers, both established and up and coming, can be purchased at this shop. Each piece is personally selected for the store by the owner.

SOUTHAMPTON

Hollis Reh & Shariff (631-283-6653; www.hollisrehandshariff.com; 2 Job's Ln., Southampton, NY 11968; open year-round, daily in summer 10–6; rest of year call for hours) Owners: Hollis Reh and Sal Shariff. Fine estate jewelry that includes such names as Van Cleef & Arpels and Bucheron can be found at this elegant and very classy shop. Definitely a must for those seeking fine jewels.

Rose Jewelry (631-283-5757; www.rosejewelers.net; 57 Main St., Southampton, NY 11968; open year-round, Mem. Day–Dec. Mon.–Sat. 9:30–5:30, Sun. noon–5; rest of year same hours but closed Sun.) Owner: Jan Rose. This very elegant jewelry shop carries unusual handcrafted rings, bracelets, and other jewelry, and an excellent selection of gifts.

WESTHAMPTON BEACH

Joan Boyce (631-288-1263; www.joanboyce.com; 116 Main St., Westhampton Beach, NY 11978; open Mem. Day–Labor Day, daily 11–6 except Tues.; rest of year open a few weekends, but generally closed) Joan Boyce, who also has shops in Manhattan and in Aspen, is a jewelry designer of international fame. She fashions elegant bracelets, earrings, necklaces, and rings from precious and semiprecious gems in her unmistakably graceful style. Her classy and bold baubles include huge pearls and stones used in unusual ways to create exquisite, but very wearable, works of art.

Old-Fashioned Emporiums

Hildreth's (631-283-2300; www.hildreths.com; 51-55 Main St., Southampton, NY 11968; open year-round, Mon.–Fri. 10–5:30, Sat. 9–6, Sun. 10–5 Hildreth's Home East 631-329-8800; 109 Pantigo Rd., East Hampton, NY 11937; open year-round, Mon.–Fri. 10:30–5:30, Sat. 10–6, Sun. 10–5) Hildreth' Patio Store 631-259-8888, 15 West Main St., Southampton, NY 11968; open year-round, Mon.–Fri. 10:30–5:30, Sat. 10–6, Sun. 10–5) Owner: Henry Hildreth. This is the granddaddy of Hamptons department stores. Established in 1842, it's billed as "America's Oldest Department Store." It's still a general store, but one that sells all of the items necessary for today's home: thread, needles, fabric, furniture, bedding, towels, china, glassware, pots and pans, outdoor furniture, BBQs, and more. Don't miss the end-of-summer sale, when items are sold at a 40 to 80 percent discount.

Sag Harbor Variety Store (631-725-9706; 45 Main St., Sag Harbor, NY 11963; open year-round, July–Aug. Mon.–Sat. 9–9, Sun. 9–5; rest of year Mon.–Sat. 9–6, Sun. 9–3) Remember the old five-and-dime stores—the ones with soda fountains and lunch counters, photo booths where you could have silly pictures taken, and shelves stacked from floor to ceiling with every delight imaginable? That tradition lives on in Sag Harbor. The photo booth and soda fountain may be missing, but how many of the old stores had two cigar-store Indians guarding the entrance, and an old Texaco pump converted to a floor clock? The Sag Harbor Variety Store has been doing what it's been doing for almost 75 years, and that means selling pots and pans, fabric by the yard, sewing notions, candy, hats, cosmetics, jewelry, toys, and much more.

Thayer's Hardware & Patio (631-537-0077; 2434 Montauk Hwy.; mailing address: P.O. Box 790, Bridgehampton NY 11732; open year-round, in summer Mon.–Sat. 9–5:30, Sun. 10–3; rest of year closed Sun.) Owner: Roger Thayer. You can buy garden and household tools, dishes, BBQs, and terrific patio furniture in this great store.

Photo Shops

Many pharmacies, groceries, and shops sell film and handle photo processing. The following listings are camera stores in the Hamptons that specialize in meeting the needs of photographers. These stores not only help with your film and film-developing needs but also sell cameras and accessories.

AMAGANSETT

Reed's Photo Shop (631-324-1067; 4 Amagansett Sq.; mailing address: P.O. Box 484, Amagansett, NY 11930; open year-round, except Wed. and Sun., 8:30–5:30) Owner: Dennis Carr. This excellent photo shop processes film and sells cameras, accessories, and a variety of film. It is the place to bring print film for quick developing, or to have digital photos enlarged etc. The salespeople are accommodating and friendly.

BRIDGEHAMPTON

Hampton Photo Arts, Inc. (631-537-7373; 2044 Montauk Hwy.; mailing address: P.O. Box 1268 Bridgehampton, NY 11932; open year-round, Mon.–Sat. 10–6, Sun. 10–2) Owner: Dave McHugh. Located in Bridgehampton Commons, behind Kmart, this store not only carries a full line of cameras and photographic supplies but also sells art supplies and offers custom framing.

SOUTHAMPTON

The Morris Studio (631-283-0085; 72 Main St., Southampton, NY 11968; open year-round, Mon.–Sat. 9–5:30, Sun. 11–4) Owner: James Thomas. The Morris Studio has been around for over 100 years, and they really know their cameras. A full-service photo shop, they process film; sell cameras, film, and accessories; and also carry artists' supplies.

Thrift Shops

In this area of abundance, the thrift shops truly thrive. You can find fantastic bargains on everything from clothing to furniture and china—even silver—and the proceeds all go to a good cause. You might start your search here.

BRIDGEHAMPTON

St. Ann's Episcopal Church (631-537-5150; Main St. and Hull Ln., Bridgehampton, NY 11932; open year-round, Thurs.–Sat. 10–4) You might find a designer suit or an antique silver bowl hidden away here among other finds.

EAST HAMPTON

Ladies' Village Improvement Society (LVIS) Bargain Box and Bargain Books (631-324-1220; 95 Main St., East Hampton, NY 11937; open Mar.–Jan., Tues.–Sat. 10–4:30) This is the grandmother of them all. Founded in 1895, and located in the Gardiner Brown house, the shop is set well back from Main Street. You may peruse a huge selection of books, designer and not-so-designer clothing, furniture, paintings, housewares, toys, and lots more. Don't miss this!

SAGAPONACK

Animal Rescue Fund Thrift & Treasure Shop (ARF) (631-537-3682; 17 Montauk Hwy. Sagaponack, NY 11962); open year-round, Mon.–Sat. 10–5, Sun. 11–3) This store has lots of books, clothing, housewares, lamps, and much more, all to benefit this wonderful organization that saves endangered animals.

SOUTHAMPTON

Southampton Hospital Thrift Shop (631-204-0526; 40 West Main St. Southampton, NY 11968; open year-round, Mon. and Thurs.–Sat. 9:30–3:45) In my opinion, this is one of the finest thrift shops anywhere, including Manhattan. You can find fine silver, designer clothing, books, furniture, and much more. Donors bring new merchandise to the shop, a favorite Hamptons charity, on donors' days, Tuesday and Wednesday, when it's closed for sales. In anticipation of all that good new "stuff," buyers line up at the door for the Thursday-morning opening bell.

6

DEVELOPING ARTISTRY

Culture

Over the last 100 years, cultural pursuits have played an increasingly important role in the lives of Hamptons residents and visitors, but even as new artistic expression has flourished, appreciation for traditional art has not diminished. Instead, there is renewed and heightened interest in the history and heritage of the Hamptons.

Today, because of an active historic-preservation movement in the Hamptons, 18 historic districts on the South Fork are listed on the National Register of Historic Places—encompassing 29,290 acres that contain 2,079 houses and buildings, 19 structures, and 4 objects. In addition, there are 12 significant individual historic houses, windmills, sites, and even a wrecked ship on the list. This appreciation for the old, combined with the daring thrust of new expression, gives the Hamptons a unique place in history.

We often read about the artistic skill of painters and sculptors from the Hamptons, but we hear less about the skilled craftspeople and artisans, past and present. For instance, the Dominy family lived and worked in East Hampton from around 1750 to 1850. These skilled furniture makers, who were far more than local carpenters, obtained ideas and tools from Europe and Boston and are known for their tall-case clocks, chests, chairs, and the solid windmills scattered across the East End. Their artistry is appreciated as much today as it was in the 1800s, and examples of their work appear in several local museums. Furthermore, the value of their work is nationally recognized—their workshop and the tools they used are now part of the permanent collection at the Winterthur Museum in Delaware.

This dual interest in old and new also exists in the fine arts. Although the works of Thomas Moran, Childe Hassam, Fairfield Porter, and William Merritt Chase continue to be respected, collected, and admired, the Hamptons embraced and nurtured the art of the abstract expressionists in the 1940s and 1950s.

Artists of all genres are attracted to the Hamptons, as much by this spirit of acceptance and encouragement as by the area's natural beauty. Prominent writers and playwrights who have chosen to live in the Hamptons include P. G. Wodehouse, Truman Capote, John Steinbeck, E. L. Doctorow, Ken Auletta, Peter Matthiessen, Linda Bird Francke, Kurt Vonnegut, Tom Wolfe, Wendy Wasserstein, and many more.

Recording artists, entertainers, singers, composers, newscasters, magazine editors, directors, and producers—all artists of a different nature—are also attracted to the Hamptons. A few include Steven Spielberg, Billy Joel, Jerry Seinfeld, Donna Karan, Paul Simon, Kathleen Battle, Chevy Chase, Matt Lauer, Paul McCartney, Chuck Scarborough, Martha Stewart, and Dick Cavett.

The Parrish Art Museum in Southampton has a secluded sculpture garden.

CALENDAR OF EVENTS

The following events take place on Long Island's South Fork every year. The **Long Island Convention and Visitors Bureau** (631-951-3440) publishes an excellent guide to Long Island, but for specific local information you should call the following chambers of commerce on the South Fork, or check their Web sites. Also, please refer to chapter 9 for events taking place on the North Fork.

East Hampton 631-324-0362; www.easthamptonchamber.com
Hampton Bays 631-728-2211; www.hamptonbayschamber.com
Montauk 631-668-2428; www.montaukchamber.com
Sag Harbor 631-725-0011; www.sagharborchamber.com
Southampton 631-283-0402; www.southamptonchamber.com
Westhampton Beach 631-288-3337; www.whbcc.org

October–May

Long Island Traditional Music Association (631-725-9321; Water Mill Community Center, Rte. 27A, Water Mill) Meets first Saturday each month for traditional dances, including a barn dance and contra dancing.

December–May

Seal Watching (631-369-9840) Sponsored by the Riverhead Foundation for Marine Research and Preservation.

January/February

Hikes and walks are sponsored on the South Shore during January and February by several organizations. These include the **Long Island Greenbelt Trail Conference** (631-360-0753); the **Group for the East End** (631-537-1400); the **East Hampton Trails Preservation Society** (631-329-4227); the **Southampton Trails Preservation Society** (631-537-5202); the **Nature Conservancy for the South Fork** (631-329-7689); and the Nature Conservancy's **Mashomack Preserve** on Shelter Island (631-749-1001).

The Naked Stage and other companies (631-324-0806; Guild Hall, East Hampton) A series of theatrical productions take place in January and February.

Long Island Winterfest (631-951-3900, ext. 317) Many East End wineries and restaurants participate in this festival, which runs from mid-February through mid-March and features numerous concerts; the 2009 theme was "Jazz on the Vine."

Seal Watch Walks (631-668-5000; Montauk Point State Park) Walk with a naturalist and observe wintering seals. Sponsored by the NY State Office of Parks, Recreation & Historic Preservation. Adults $5, children $3; parking $6 per vehicle.

Student Arts Festival (631-324-0806; Guild Hall, East Hampton) This professionally curated show features art by students in East Hampton Township schools.

March

Bay Street Theatre (631-725-9500; Bay Street at Long Wharf, Sag Harbor) This wonderful community-minded theater company has a series of events that take place throughout the year, including adult classes, Kidstreet @ Bay Street Theatre, and Picture Show @ Bay Street Theatre, offering screenings of classic movies such as *King Kong*, Garbo classics, and Doris Day/Rock Hudson weekends.

Members Exhibition (631-324-0806; Guild Hall, East Hampton)

Purim Carnival (631-324-9858; Jewish Center of the Hamptons, East Hampton; 631-725-0904; Temple Adas Israel, Sag Harbor)

Saint Patrick's Day Parade (631-668-1578; Main St., Montauk.) This great parade and soup sale has been a tradition for almost 50 years. (Also 631-288-3337, Mill Rd. and Main St., Westhampton Beach)

April

Easter Bonnet Parade & Petting Zoo (631-725-0011; Main Street, Sag Harbor)

Easter Egg Hunts (Amagansett Firehouse, Amagansett; Hampton Library, Bridgehampton; Maidstone Gun Club, East Hampton; Sag Harbor Village; Parrish Art Museum, Southampton)

Hamptons Restaurant Week (631-329-0050) Most restaurants participate in this annual event by offering a prix fixe dinner.

May

Craftsmen's Guild Show (631-726-2777; Bridgehampton Presbyterian Church, Bridgehampton) The South Fork Craftsmen's Guild holds an annual show featuring artists in jewelry, weaving, art, photography and other crafts.

Dan's Papers **Annual Potatohampton Minithon 10K** (631-537-0500; Bridgehampton, Mem. Day weekend)

Guild Hall Artist Members Exhibition (631-324-0806; 158 Main St., East Hampton.) Annual (now in its seventh decade) art exhibition.

Kites for a Cure (Coopers Beach, Southampton) Annual family kite-flying to benefit Uniting Against Lung Cancer.

Memorial Day Parade (631-324-0362; East Hampton)

Montauk Fine Arts Festival (631-421-1590; Village Green, Montauk)

June

Blessing of the Fleet (631-329-0973) Takes place on a Sunday afternoon in Montauk. Fishing craft and private boats parade past a reviewing stand to receive a prayer for safety and a successful fishing season. Sponsored by the Montauk Boatman's Association.

Fresh Air Home Decorators & Dealers Party (631-283-1594) Auction and benefit that includes professionally decorated rooms. Sponsored by Southampton Fresh Air Home.

Greater Westhampton Chamber of Commerce Arts and Craft Show (631-288-3337; Main St., Westhampton Beach) This giant craft fair offers a wide variety of high-quality items.

Hamptons Annual Spring Garden Antiques Show & Sale (631-537-0333; Bridgehampton Community House, Montauk Highway, Bridgehampton)

Jewish Center of the Hamptons (631-324-9858; 44 Woods Lane, East Hampton) Hosts a series of talks relating to religion, the Holocaust, etc.; concerts and other events continuing through the summer.

Landscape Pleasures (631-283-2118; Southampton) Offers a tour of South Fork gardens and a series of seminars. Sponsored by Parrish Art Museum.

Pianofest (631-329-9115) Piano recitals and concerts sponsored by Pianofest, Stony Brook University in Southampton. Through July.

Southampton Rotary 8K Run (631-283-0402; Agawam Park, Southampton)

Taste of the Hamptons (631-427-3700, ext. 255; Wölffer Estate Winery, Sagaponack) Leading chefs, food producers, and wineries showcase their wares and talents; sponsored by Group for the East End.

July

A Day in 1776 (631-324-6850; Mulford Farm, East Hampton) A reenactment of the British invasion of the East End during the Revolutionary War. Sponsored by the East Hampton Historical Society.

All American Picnic and Fireworks (631-283-5847; 1030 Meadow Lane, Southampton) This event, to benefit the Southampton Fresh Air Home, is one of the most anticipated of the summer season. There are balloons, clowns, games, hot dogs, BBQ, ice cream, and, yes, Grucci fireworks!

Artists' Studio Tour East Hampton (631-324-2225; call for locations) Annual tour of up to 30 studios, homes, and gardens of East End artists. This three-day event includes a reception and garden party. Sponsored by the Artists Alliance of East Hampton.

Bridgehampton Polo Club (631-537-3881; Two Trees Stables, 849 Hayground Rd., Bridgehampton.) Annual polo tournament continuing for six consecutive Saturdays. Sponsored by Mercedes-Benz.

Choral Society of the Hamptons (631-204-9402; Presbyterian Church, Bridgehampton) Series of choral concerts taking place each summer.

Concerts in the Parks Free concerts are held in several Hamptons villages in July and

August. You can call the following numbers for schedules: Sag Harbor, Tuesdays, Marine Park (631-725-0011); Southampton in Agawam Park (631-283-4377); Westhampton Beach at the gazebo (631-288-1500).

Parades are plentiful in the Hamptons. Morgan McGivern

East Hampton Antiques Show (631-324-6850; 10 James Ln., Mulford Farm, East Hampton) This annual event includes numerous well-known antiques dealers from Manhattan and across the U.S.

Fireworks Displays (631-324-6868, Main Beach, East Hampton, sponsored by the East Hampton Volunteer Fire Department, at dusk. Also 631-668-2428, Umbrella Beach, Montauk, sponsored by the Montauk Chamber of Commerce; **Great Bonac Fireworks Show** Three Mile Harbor Rd., East Hampton)

Fourth of July Village Parade (631-283-2530, 631-283-1623; Southampton) Sponsored by combined veterans' organizations.

Greater Westhampton Chamber of Commerce 5K Race (631-288-3337; Main St., Westhampton Beach)

Hamptons Antiques Classic & Design Show (631-537-0333; Bridgehampton Community House, Montauk Hwy., Bridgehampton.)

Hampton Designer Showhouse (631-283-4248; Southampton) This event, coordinated by *House and Garden* magazine, is a showcase for major New York interior designers. It generally opens in late July and closes the end of August. Proceeds benefit Southampton Hospital.

Hamptons Greek Festival (631-283-6169; 111 St. Andrews Rd., Southampton) Annual festival featuring traditional Greek food, wine tasting, dancing to live music, children's rides and games.

Ladies' Village Improvement Society Fair (631-324-1220; 95 Main St., East Hampton) Begins at 10 AM. Great for kids—games, contests, rides, home-baked goodies, an evening BBQ, and square dancing.

Mary O. Fritchie Outdoor Art Show (631-288-3337) Sponsored by the Greater Westhampton Chamber of Commerce, late July or early August.

Midsummer Party (631-283-2118) Music, food, and fun to benefit Southampton's Parrish Art Museum.

Montauk Point Lighthouse Triathlon (631-668-2544) This annual event includes a 0.5-mile swim, a 14-mile bike ride, and a 3.3-mile run and ends at the lighthouse.

Music Festival of the Hamptons (631-267-8293; various venues) Fifteen days of classical music, ranging from the Baroque to the Romantic periods, including concerts by a chamber orchestra, a harp concert, numerous piano recitals, children's and senior citizens' concerts, and much more.

Opera of the Hamptons (631-728-8804) A series of operas (*La Bohème* and *Tosca*, for example) are performed at locations on both the North and South Forks.

Perlman Musical Program (631-749-0740; Shelter Island) A series of musical events featuring the exceptional students who are chosen to attend Itzhak Perlman's summer music camp on Shelter Island.

Sag Harbor Historic House Tour (631-725-0049; Sag Harbor) Benefits John Jermain Memorial Library.

Sand Castle Contests (631-324-6250, Atlantic Ave. Beach, Amagansett, sponsored by the Clamshell Foundation; 631-288-7670, Muschutt Beach County Park, Hampton Bays; 631-668-2554, Hither Hills State Park, Montauk Hwy., Montauk; every Sat. in summer) Several sand castle contests take place during the summer. They're fun for all the family, and the prizes are great.

August

Antique Auto Show (631-728-3836; Rogers Mansion, 17 Meeting House Ln., Southampton) Annual antique-auto show, exhibiting cars from Model Ts to 1950s classics.

Antiques & Design in the Hamptons (631-537-1088; 2368 Montauk Hwy, Bridgehampton) Annual antique furniture, lighting, silver, ceramics, rug sale on grounds of Bridgehampton Historical Society.

Antiques at Mulford Farm (631-324-6850; 10 James Lane, Mulford Farm, East Hampton) Numerous antiques dealers set up shop on the grounds of Mulford Farm for this annual event.

Artists and Writers Softball Game (631-324-0362; East Hampton) Well-known writers and artists compete in a very serious softball game.

Arts and Crafts Fair (631-725-0011) Annual juried fair in Sag Harbor.

Atlantic Coast J15 Sailing Championships (631-725-4606; Sag Harbor) Sponsored by the Breakwater Yacht Club.

Authors Night (631-324-0222; East Hampton Library) This event is extremely popular, as each year it includes such local authors as Alec Baldwin, Candace Bushnell, and Jay McInerney. Sponsored by the East Hampton Library.

Bridgehampton Chamber Music Festival (212-741-9403; 631-537-6368 in Aug. only) A series of 10-plus concerts for young and old alike that take place in Bridgehampton.

Chefs & Champagne (212-675-4984; Wölffer Estate, 139 Sagg Rd., Sagaponack) Annual event showcasing chefs and wineries sponsored by James Beard Society.

Dan's Papers Annual Kite Fly (631-537-0500; Sagg Main Beach, Sagaponack) Kites are judged in 24 categories.

Ellen's Run (212-840-0916; 235 Herrick Rd., Southampton)

Fisherman's Fair Held at Ashawagh Hall in Springs, traditionally on the second Saturday in August. Delectable food, annual art show, booths with crafts, children's games, and much more. Sponsored by the Springs Improvement Assn.

Guild Hall in East Hampton is the site of concerts, theatrical productions, art shows, and numerous classes for both adults and children. Here, the annual Clothesline Art Sale is in progress. Morgan McGivern

Guild Hall Clothesline Art Sale (631-324-0806; 158 Main St., East Hampton) A popular
sale of art created by local artists that is both framed and unframed (originally, the
unframed were pinned to clotheslines).

Hampton Classic Horse Show (631-537-3177; 240 Snake Hollow Rd., Bridgehampton)
Held the end of August and beginning of September. Sponsored by the Hampton Classic
Horse Show.

House and Garden Tour (631-537-1527; St. Ann's Episcopal Church, Main St., Bridgehampton) Tour of homes in the Hamptons sponsored by St. Ann's.

Lighthouse Weekend at Montauk Point (631-668-5340) Sponsored by the Montauk Historical Society.

Long Island J80 Sailing Championship (631-725-4604; Sag Harbor) Sponsored by the
Breakwater Yacht Club.

Montauk Fine Art Show on the Green This large event takes place on the Montauk Green
and is sponsored by the Montauk Artists' Assn.—now in its 15th year.

Sag Harbor Cup Sailing Regatta (631-725-4604; Sag Harbor) Sponsored by the Breakwater Yacht Club.

Southampton Hospital Annual Summer Party This event has been held annually for more
than 50 years and is one of the major fund-raising events of the season. Dinner, dancing, silent auction, and a plethora of celebrities raise money for Southampton Hospital.

Super Saturday (Bridgehampton Polo Grounds, 849 Hayground Rd., Bridgehampton)
Sponsored by the Ovarian Cancer Research Foundation, this designer tag sale is in its
13th year. Top-name designers donate clothes that can be purchased at incredible
prices.

Quilt Show and Sale (631-726-4625; Water Mill Museum, Water Mill) Annual quilt show
features new and antique quilts, quilting suppliers, and a quilt raffle.

September

Arf Beach Ball (631-537-0400) Beach benefit to raise money for Animal Rescue Fund of
the Hamptons.

Grand Slam Winners Tennis Exhibition (631-907-5112; Ross School, 26 Goodfriend Dr.,
East Hampton) Celebrity-Pro Match to benefit Ross School scholarships and programs.

Historic Sag Harbor "Harbor Fest" Weekend (631-725-0011) Includes tours, a parade,
whaleboat races, and a concert. Sponsored by Sag Harbor Chamber of Commerce.

Rotary Club Antique Show and Sale (Miss Amelia's Cottage grounds, Amagansett) Annual
antique show and sale held on Labor Day Weekend.

Shinnecock Indian Powwow (631-287-2462) Held on the Indian reservation in
Southampton, this event includes three days of traditional dances, songs, and lots to do,
see, buy, and eat.

Slow Food East End (631-537-7068; 151 Mitchells Ln., Bridgehampton) Annual fair featuring
food that's raised organically and with sustainable methods—pig roast, wine, live music.

October

Architectural House Tour (631-537-0120; several villages) Sponsored by the League of
Women Voters.

Artist and Celebrity Birdhouse Auction (631-726-8715; Southampton) Celebrities and
artists create birdhouses for auction to support Ellen Hermanson Breast Center at
Southampton Hospital.

East Hampton Chamber of Commerce Annual Georgica Jog 5K Run (631-324-0362) Part of the Fall Festival sponsored by the East Hampton Chamber of Commerce.

Fall Family Festival (631-283-2118; Southampton) Parrish Art Museum annual National Circus Project, includes roving circus performers and face painters.

Fall Festival on the Village Green (631-668-2428; Montauk) Includes a Clam Chowder Recipe Competition, hayrides, bike race, and pumpkin decorating. Sponsored by the Montauk Chamber of Commerce.

Halloween Party (631-325-0200; Westhampton) For children and pets. Sponsored by Bide-A-Wee.

Hamptons International Film Festival (631-324-4600) Showings include new and art films. Stars and directors attend.

Montauk Annual Full Moon Bass Tournament (631-668-2428) Bluefish surf-casting contest; striped bass derby.

Pumpkin Trail and Halloween Activities (631-725-0011; Sag Harbor) Annual festivities. Sponsored by the Sag Harbor Chamber of Commerce.

Westhampton Harvest Festival and Street Fair (631-288-3337; on the village green in Westhampton Beach) Sponsored by the Westhampton Chamber of Commerce.

November

Country Christmas (631-283-0402; Southampton) Celebration with Santa coming to town. Sponsored by the Southampton Chamber of Commerce.

Diver's Flea Market (631-283-4000; Stony Brook University, Southampton Campus) Sale of new and used diving equipment.

Sweetpotatohampton (631-537-0500; Bridgehampton) Annual A.T. (after turkey) 8K run. Sponsored by *Dan's Papers.*

Turkey Day Run for Fun (631-324-2417; Montauk) Sponsored by East Hampton Town Recreation Department.

December

Gallery of Trees (631-324-0362; East Hampton) Trees decorated by businesses and celebrities. Sponsored by the East Hampton Chamber of Commerce.

Holiday Historic House and Inn Tour (631-324-0362; East Hampton) Sponsored by the East Hampton Chamber of Commerce.

Sag Harbor Holiday Events (631-725-0011) Annual events include Santa's arrival and outdoor lighting, costumed carolers, and horse-and-carriage rides. Sponsored by the Sag Harbor Chamber of Commerce.

Santa Parade (631-324-0362; East Hampton) Sponsored by the East Hampton Chamber of Commerce. Also, tree lighting (631-283-0402), sponsored by the Southampton Village Decorating Committee.

Santa Visits the Montauk Point Lighthouse (631-668-2544)

ARCHITECTURE

What a wealth of architectural attractions we have! Architectural styles for residential dwellings range from New England saltbox cottages to elegant 1700s manor houses. There are Federal-style buildings, high Greek Revival mansions, ornamented Victorians, and modern award-winning contemporaries.

Today the Hamptons are noted for the distinctive modern houses that seem to rise in geometric curves and angles from the dunes and potato fields, as if from another world. Just as famed artists have left their mark on the East End, so have famed architects. The Hamptons have become a laboratory for innovative new ideas in architecture. George Nelson, Richard Meier, Andrew Geller, Jacquelin Robertson, Gwathmey/Siegel, Norman Jaffe, and Robert A. M. Stern are only a few of the contributors.

Several excellent books describe Hamptons architecture. Architectural critic Paul Goldberger's book, *The Houses of the Hamptons* (1986), is an excellent resource, as is *Hampton Style: Houses, Gardens, Artists* (1993) by John Esten and Rose Bennett Gilbert, with photographs by Susan Wood, which provides an inside look through photographs and text into Hamptons homes.

As Robert B. MacKay said in his introduction to the *AIA Architectural Guide to Nassau and Suffolk Counties, Long Island* (1992):

> Few parts of the country can boast the range and depth of domestic architecture that can be found on Long Island. Perhaps because the Industrial Revolution bypassed the region for lack of falling water to power mill turbines, Long Island's built environment was not seriously affected by subsequent development from the seventeenth century until the post–World War II period, when the G.I. Bill and the growth of the aircraft industry sent thousands eastward on Robert Moses' parkways toward new suburban communities, such as Levittown. As a result, Long Island possesses close to 100 First Period buildings, the greatest concentration of surviving windmills . . . most of its eighteenth-century manorial seats and dozens of relatively intact nineteenth-century villages. . . . Long Island is also significant for its Modern and Post-Modern architecture, the South Fork in particular having served as an incubator for progressive domestic design for over a century.

Art Museums

Some artists claim the light is better in the Hamptons than anywhere else—clearer, with a bluer sky and less haze. In an account of the first visit of the Tile Club to East Hampton, published in *Scribner's Monthly* in 1879 and titled "The Tile Club at Play," the writer claimed the light of the area was ideal. "The afternoon sky was filling with color, and the cumulus clouds that toppled from the horizon were turning to vast chryselephantine statue-galleries, ivory and gold." The area has also been praised for its peace and tranquility—the absence of noise, except for the occasional caw of a crow or the call of geese flying overhead. Whatever the reason, for more than a century, artists have been attracted to Long Island's South Fork.

The rich tapestry of art now enjoyed in the Hamptons can be traced to those first artists who came here in the 1800s and spread the word. When Thomas Moran, Winslow Homer, Childe Hassam, and their friends from the Tile Club made East Hampton their summer home, they set up their easels at the beach, on the village streets, and on the dunes at Montauk. Their paintings not only captured romantic fancy, but also brought more artists and residents to the area every summer. When one of their members penned a *Scribner's Monthly* article, complete with charming sketches, the summer migration to the Hamptons began in earnest.

William Merritt Chase arrived during this time and made Southampton his home. He established an acclaimed art school, where students painted *en plein air,* capturing the sea and dunes on their canvases. Thomas Moran, who painted many of America's national parks, loved East Hampton so much that he also made it his permanent home. The art of Moran and Chase was similar to that of the Barbizon School, which was located just outside Paris—romantic landscapes and sunsets, fields of flowers, and pretty women and children—so the Hamptons were christened "The American Barbizon."

The work of Jackson Pollock, who came to the village of Springs in 1945, was art of a different sort. Full of bold color and raw energy, it looked to some like little more than wild abandon put to canvas, but to others it represented a brilliant new technique—and abstract expressionism assumed new importance. Pollock, as did Moran before him, attracted other artists who appreciated the tranquility of the region as well as its proximity to New York City. Robert Motherwell, Larry Rivers, Willem de Kooning, and Alfonso Ossorio were only a few of those who followed Pollock to the Hamptons. The Museum of Modern Art held summer art classes at Ashawagh Hall in the mid-1950s. Fairfield Porter, who gained increasing stature with a more realistic style, came to Southampton in 1949 and stayed until his death in 1975.

The following list is a representative sampling of exhibition art galleries in the Hamptons. For information about commercial art galleries, see chapter 5, "Shopping."

EAST HAMPTON
GUILD HALL
631-324-0806
www.guildhall.com
158 Main St., East Hampton, NY 11937
Open: Year-round; Mem. Day–Labor Day, daily except Tues. 11–5, rest of year Fri.–Sun. noon–5
Admission: $7

Guild Hall has three large galleries in which art is exhibited throughout the year. This marvelous institution has been encouraging artists in a variety of genres for more than 70 years. In addition to art and sculpture exhibitions, the Clothesline Art Sale, held in August, offers a place for both amateur and professional artists to exhibit and sell their work. There are literary readings by emerging and established writers, as well as the H. R. Hays poetry series, readings by internationally acclaimed poets. Adult and children's art and writing workshops are offered throughout the year, and you can see musical and dance performances, hear cabaret and jazz artists, and attend plays at the John Drew Theatre.

SOUTHAMPTON

FINE ARTS GALLERY
631-283-4000
239 Montauk Hwy., Southampton, NY 11968
Open: Mon.–Fri. 1–5
Admission: None

The Fine Arts Gallery on Stony Brook University's Southampton Campus hosts a variety of art exhibits year-round, ranging from paintings and photography by students and faculty to works by a variety of local painters and sculptors.

THE PARRISH ART MUSEUM

631-283-2118
www.parrishart.com
25 Job's Ln., Southampton, NY 11968
Open: Mid-June–mid-Sept., Mon.–Sat. 11–5, Sun. 1–5; mid-Sept.–mid-June, closed Tues., Wed.
Admission: Suggested: $5 adults, $3 seniors and students

The Parrish Art Museum was established in 1897 when its founder, Samuel Longstreth Parrish, hired architect Grosvenor Atterbury to build an addition to the existing Art Museum. The building, containing exhibition space and a concert hall, is located in the heart of the village beside the old Rogers Memorial Library building. In 2000 the library relocated to Cooper's Farm Road, so the Parrish now uses the library building as an education center. The Parrish collection of American art of the 19th and 20th centuries is especially strong in paintings by William Merritt Chase and Fairfield Porter, who spent much of their working life in the area. This fine museum also has a sculpture garden and an arboretum and offers lectures, concerts, changing exhibits, and children's programs in art and theater. Adult programs are also offered, including films, tours, musical performances, and more.

SOUTHAMPTON CULTURAL CENTER

631-287-4377
www.southamptoncultralcenter.com
2 Pond Ln., Southampton, NY 11968
Open: Depends on exhibit or event
Admission: Depends on exhibit or event

The Southampton Cultural Center, in the heart of the village across from Agawam Lake, exhibits art by members of the Southampton Artists' Association (a group of almost 300 artists) about four times yearly. It also sponsors workshops, seminars, and courses, as well as concerts in Agawam Park in the summer. This is a Village of Southampton facility.

CINEMA

Movie producers, directors, and actors call the Hamptons home (or at least their summer home), and a number of films have been shot on location here, so it's natural for local residents to have an avid interest in movies. As early as 1915, *The Sheik,* which featured Rudolph Valentino galloping across the dunes of Montauk, was filmed here. In 1932 *No Man of Her Own,* starring Clark Gable and Carole Lombard, was shot in Sag Harbor, as was *Sweet Liberty,* with Alan Alda, in 1985. The 1988 movie *Masquerade,* with Meg Tilly and Rob Lowe, was also filmed here. Every summer since 1988, HBO has screened a major television film at the East Hampton Cinema. The event attracts a bevy of stars, directors, and their friends.

In 1993 the Hamptons International Film Festival was inaugurated. This popular event now screens some 150 popular and art films over a five-day period in October. Most of the films are shown at the East Hampton Cinema or Guild Hall, although screenings might also take place at other venues. Stars and directors are often on hand for the screenings and for lectures and symposia held at the Guild Hall.

Hamptons residents thus come by their appreciation of movies quite naturally. We have as much interest in seeing new movies as soon as they come out as do New Yorkers, and our movie theaters don't disappoint us. Movies generally open here the same week they do in New York City. Beware, however: we have often gone to the theater in East Hampton 30 minutes before showtime only to find that the film is sold out. It is advisable to buy the tickets early and then come back.

Hampton Arts (631-288-2600; Brook Rd., Westhampton Beach, NY 11978) A twin movie theater.

The Movie (631-668-2393; 3 Edgemere St., Montauk, NY 11954) A single-movie theater.

Sag Harbor Cinema (631-725-0010; Main St., Sag Harbor, NY 11963) A single-movie theater that specializes in art and foreign films.

United Artists East Hampton Cinema (631-324-0448; 30 Main St., East Hampton, NY 11937) A six-plex movie theater.

United Artists Hampton Bays Theatre (631-728-8251; 119 West Montauk Hwy., Hampton Bays, NY 11946) A five-plex movie theater.

United Artists Southampton Theatre (631-287-2774; 43 Hill St., Southampton, NY 11968) A five-plex movie theater.

CULTURE COURSES

The Hamptons attract some of the finest art teachers, writers, photographers, and craftspeople, who conduct summer and winter workshops, classes, courses, and seminars. Since many of these are arranged on short notice, it is important to watch the local newspapers every week for the list of scheduled events. In addition, posters announcing special courses will often appear in local stores and offices. The courses listed here are taught annually.

The Art Barge (631-267-3172; Victor D'Amico Institute of Art, Napeague Meadow Rd., Napeague, NY 11930; June—end of Sept.) The Art Barge is a great East End resource. It offers innovative, refreshing courses, as envisioned by its founder, Victor D'Amico, who was director of education at the Museum of Modern Art before beaching his unique barge in Napeague Bay. A wide range of classes is offered, especially in painting and drawing, but also in photography, papermaking, ceramics, sculpting, jazz, acting, and writing. There are also frequent play readings.

Bay Street Theatre (631-725-0818; Long Wharf, Sag Harbor, NY 11963) Throughout the year, this fine theater company offers classes in acting and playwriting.

Guild Hall (631-324-0806; 158 Main St., East Hampton, NY 11937) A variety of workshops and classes for adults and children is offered throughout the year, including courses in watercolor, figure drawing, photography, collage, and much more. Call for a complete schedule.

Loaves and Fishes Cookshop (631-537-6066; 2422 Montauk Hwy., Bridgehampton, NY 11932) There's a wonderful array of classes at this terrific cook shop. They range from wedding cake decoration, to a panini sandwich demo, to book signings by very well-known chefs.

Ross Institute Wellness Center (631-907-5555, 4 Goodfriend Dr., East Hampton, NY 11937) Classes, seminars, and lectures are held throughout the year.

Silvia Lehrer's Cookhampton (631-537-7831; Water Mill, NY 11976) Sylvia Lehrer has been writing the cooking column for *Dan's Papers* since 1990; now she's also conducting great cooking classes—but strictly on a request basis. She might teach a series herself on the nuances of regional Italian cooking or the flavors of Provence. In these cases, the classes are hands-on and fully participatory in nature. Other times, she'll invite a well-known cookbook author, such as Giuliano Bugialli or a Hamptons chef, to teach a demonstration class. In either case, the classes are instructional and lots of fun. Call for schedule and location.

Stony Brook University, Southampton Campus (631-283-4000, ext. 8175) A diverse and outstanding selection of courses is offered year-round. The following list represents several of the special workshops offered each summer and does not begin to scratch the surface. Call for a catalog.

Master Workshop in Art A group of renowned artists teach a creative course every summer for artists who have mastered the basic techniques. Studio space is provided for this four-week living and working experience, and enrollment is limited. Interaction among the artists is a valuable component. Call for information.

Photography Workshop This is an annual workshop held by some of the nation's leading photographers, who teach courses as varied as quality black-and-white printing, landscape and architecture in large-format photography, and electronic imagery and scanning photography. Call for a schedule.

Summer Writer's Conference This esteemed conference encompasses a variety of wonderful workshops, lectures, forums, and classes that are conducted by distinguished authors, poets, and playwrights. The workshops and classes include fiction writing, poetry, children's literature, screenwriting, and more. Call for a schedule.

HISTORIC HOUSES, SITES, MUSEUMS & GARDENS

The Hamptons have a progressive and active historic-preservation movement; many historic houses, museums, and sites have been identified and are open to the public. In recognition of its "effective efforts to sustain the beauty of the historic village," the Village of East Hampton was awarded the Pillar of New York Award by the Preservation League of New York State.

The historic houses, sites, museums, and landmarks below are all open to the public. For an excellent history of East Hampton, with walking tours of Sag Harbor, East Hampton, Springs, Wainscott, Amagansett, and Montauk, a nature walk through Napeague, and three suggested bicycle tours, read *East Hampton: A History & Guide* (1985) by Jason Epstein and Elizabeth Barlow. In addition, there are excellent house and garden tours in East Hampton, Sag Harbor, and Southampton every year.

AMAGANSETT
EAST HAMPTON TOWN MARINE MUSEUM
631-324-6850
www.easthamptonhistory.org
301 Bluff Rd., Amagansett
Mailing Address: 101 Main St., East Hampton, NY 11937
Open: Mem. Day–Columbus Day, Sat and Sun. 10–5.
Admission: Adults $4; seniors $3; and students $1

The East Hampton Town Marine Museum, which overlooks the double dunes and Atlantic Avenue beach beyond, contains a fascinating collection of exhibits that describe and illustrate the history of whaling and fishing on the East End. There are dioramas, boats, tools, equipment, and explanations of the baymen's ongoing struggle with nature. An exhibit of haul seining illustrates the difficulty of this type of fishing; other exhibits describe shell-fishing, harpooning, and the evolution of whaling. Outside, a series of displays is devoted to hunting in the Hamptons.

MISS AMELIA'S COTTAGE
631-267-3020
Montauk Hwy. and Windmill Ln., Amagansett
Mailing Address: P.O. Box 7077, Amagansett, NY 11930
Open: Summer and fall only, Fri.–Sun. 10–4
Admission: Adults $2; children $1; Pony rides: $5

This delightful cottage provides a view into the life of Miss Mary Amelia Schellinger, who occupied the cottage from 1841 to 1930. The house was built in 1725 by one of Miss Amelia's ancestors and was moved to its present site in 1794. It contains a collection of furniture made by the Dominy family, as well as other examples of furniture and objects typical of the area. For insight into life in the Hamptons during a very interesting period, *Miss Amelia's Amagansett* (1976) by Madeline Lee and a tour of Miss Amelia's house are highly recommended. The Roy K. Lester Carriage Museum, also located on the property, contains a fascinating collection of 30 carriages (several impeccably restored), including racing sulkies and sleighs and even a surrey with a fringe on top. Pony rides are offered in the summer. The site is operated by the Amagansett Historical Association.

BRIDGEHAMPTON
BRIDGE GARDENS
631-537-7440
www.peconiclandtrust.com
36 Mitchell Lane, Bridgehampton, NY 11932
Open: May–Oct.; in summer Wed.–Sun. approx. noon–5; rest of season weekends
Admission: Adults $10; family $20

This 5-acre garden is a 20-year labor of love for gardeners Jim Kilpatric and Harry Neyens. It is lush with trees, flowers, herbs, and plants. There are two distinct gardens. The Inner Garden includes a trimmed Spanish-styled knot garden with perennial borders, a water garden, hosta and fern room, ivy maze, and hidden bamboo room. The Outer Garden features a collection of 800 antique and modern roses, a walk of lilacs, eight lavender beds, and a bed of 22 variations of thyme. It's managed by the Peconic Land Trust.

CORWITH HOUSE
631-537-1088
www.historicalsociety.hamptons.com
2368 Montauk Hwy., Bridgehampton
Mailing Address: P.O. Box 977, Bridgehampton, NY 11932
Open: Year-round: Mon.–Fri. 10–3; also mid-June–mid-Sept. open Sat. 10–2.
Admission: $5

The Corwith House, an historic 1820s home in Bridgehampton, contains interesting Colonial, Empire, and Victorian furniture and decor, all displayed in room settings. A former kitchen, which is set up as a washroom, reveals the difficulties of keeping all those white lace dresses clean and ironed. Upstairs rooms are devoted to lovely Victorian children's clothing, toys, and dolls. The Tractor Barn displays tractors and farm machinery, including a tall and unwieldy 1921 steam tractor. The Hildreth-Simons Machine Shop, on the same property, includes antique engines—all kept in working order. In the George W. Strong Wheelwright Shop, tools used to make wagons and sleds are displayed. The machine shop and the wheelwright shop are generally open only on special occasions. Operated by the Bridgehampton Historical Society.

SOUTH FORK NATURAL HISTORY MUSEUM AND NATURE CENTER
631-537-9735
www.sofo.org
377 Bridgehampton/Sag Harbor Tpke, P.O. Box 455, Bridgehampton, NY 11932
Open: Year-round; daily 10—4.
Admission: Adults $7; children 3—12 $5; children 2 and under free.

This state-of-the-art natural history museum and nature center offers adventures for young and old alike. There are interactive habitat exhibits, a description of how glaciers created Long Island, an indoor hike with a salt marsh, a freshwater coastal plain pond, a beach—all with live animals. There's also a gallery of live native reptiles and amphibians, and a marine touch tank. Outside, you can stand on a deck to view the 70-acre fields and woodlands that are part of the museum or you can take a nature walk along the Vineyard Nature Trail, which connects to Long Pond Greenbelt. There are nature walks and workshops throughout the year.

EAST HAMPTON
The **East Hampton Historical Society** conducts an award-winning walking tour of East Hampton's historic downtown year-round. Tours are led by Hugh King, who dresses in colonial costume. This knowledgeable guide delivers a spicy historical narrative about East Hampton's colorful past. He also conducts tours of East Hampton's historic South End Cemetery. For information, call 631-324-6850.

CLINTON ACADEMY
631-324-1850, 631-324-6850
www.easthamptonhistory.org
151 Main St., East Hampton
Mailing Address: 101 Main St., East Hampton, NY 11937
Open: Mem. Day—Columbus Day; Sat. 10—5; Sun. noon—5
Admission: Adults $4; seniors $3; students $2

Clinton Academy is a stately, three-story brick and clapboard building that once housed the first chartered secondary school in New York State, established in 1784. Students came from as far away as the West Indies to attend this esteemed school to prepare for college. It was especially notable as it was one of the first schools to offer a coeducational program. Its graduates attended Harvard, Yale, and Princeton. The academy is now one of East Hampton's primary historical museums, housing 12,000 articles that include furniture, clothing, textiles, ceramics, porcelains, tools, books, and photographs. It is operated by the East Hampton Historical Society.

HOME SWEET HOME
631-324-0713, 631-324-4150
www.easthamptonvillage.org
14 James Ln., East Hampton, NY 11937
Open: May–Sept., Mon.–Sat. 10–4 and Sun. 2–4; Oct. and Nov. weekends only; by appt. Dec.–Apr.
Admission: Adults $4; children $2.

Home Sweet Home, a 1650 saltbox house, was the boyhood home of John Howard Payne, author of the famous poem and song, "Home, Sweet Home," which presumably referred to this house. The house and all the furnishings have been impeccably restored. There is a very fine collection of English ceramics, including lusterware and blue Staffordshire china, American furniture, and textiles. The grounds include the 1804 Pantigo Windmill and a lovely garden. Home Sweet Home is operated by the Village of East Hampton.

HOOK WINDMILL
631-324-0713, 631-324-4150
www.easthamptonvillage.org
Montauk Hwy., East Hampton
Mailing Address: 14 James Ln., East Hampton, NY 11937
Open: Under restoration. Please call for information about visits.
Admission: Adults $2; children $1

This is one of the best surviving examples of the windmills that dotted the landscape of the East End for many years, grinding grain and sawing lumber, and ensuring the area's prosperity. Although 11 windmills still remain—more than in any other part of the U.S.—many are not open to the public. The Hook Windmill was built in 1806 by Nathaniel Dominy IV and is one of the finest examples of Dominy workmanship. Among the laborsaving devices constructed here are a sack hoist, a grain elevator, a screener to clean the grain, and bolters to sift the flour and cornmeal. The Hook Windmill is operated by the Village of East Hampton.

LADIES' VILLAGE IMPROVEMENT SOCIETY
631-324-1220
www.lvis.org
95 Main St., East Hampton, NY 11937
Open: Apr.–Dec., Tues.–Sat. 10–5; Jan.–Mar., Fri., Sat. only 10–5.
Admission: None
Special Features: Thrift shop and bargain books for sale.

Affectionately known as LVIS, this venerable organization is dedicated to the beautification and preservation of the parks, gardens, trees, and shrubs of East Hampton. It was founded in 1895, and every year its members supervise the planting of flowers at the entrances to the village; remind home owners to check their elm trees for Dutch elm disease; and maintain the village greens and the trees on village streets. To raise funds for its work, the society holds a perpetual flea market, which includes an enormous selection of used books, as well as an annual fair that families consider one of the highlights of the summer season. LVIS headquarters is located in the Gardiner Brown House, which dates to 1740.

LONGHOUSE RESERVE

631-329-3568
www.longhouse.org
133 Hands Creek Rd., East Hampton
Mailing Address: P.O. Box 2386, East Hampton, NY 11937
Open: July and Aug., Wed.–Sat. 2–5; May, June, Sept., and Oct., Wed. and Sat. only 2–5;
otherwise open only for lectures, tours, and special events.
Admission: Adults $10; seniors $8

This is the laboratory and home of renowned designer Jack Lenor Larson. Events include
tours, seminars, and workshops, as well as visual arts, dance, and musical performances.
Mr. Larson, a textile designer, art collector, gardener, and philanthropist, said, "This is a
dimensional, evolving study in lifestyle, built with the firm belief that we all learn best
when experiencing visual arts in the 'full round' . . . as opposed to the media." Special events
are often held, such as a reading by Edward Albee. Operated by the LongHouse Foundation.

MULFORD FARM

631-324-6869, 631-324-6850
www.easthamptonhistory.org
10 James Ln., East Hampton
Mailing Address: 101 Main St., East Hampton, NY 11937
Open: Mem. Day–Columbus Day; Sat. 10–5, Sun. noon–5.
Admission: Adults $4; seniors $3; students $2

Mulford Farm was settled in 1680, and it remained in the Mulford family from 1712 to 1944.
The farm, located in the heart of East Hampton, has been restored to its 1790s roots and
provides an exceptional view of life on a prosperous, working 18th-century farm. This 4-
acre site includes the farmhouse with its original kitchen, implements, furniture, barn,
and farm tools. Costumed guides give a narrated tour that includes an architectural history
of East Hampton, as well as a look at early decorative arts and interior design. The tour also
includes a living-history exhibition in which guides demonstrate family activities, such as
weaving and churning butter. Even historical properties need restoration and maintenance, however, and that is certainly the case with Mulford Farm. Through a generous contribution by Ralph Lauren, the farm will undergo much-needed improvements starting in
2010. Mulford Farm is operated by the East Hampton Historical Society.

OSBORN-JACKSON HOUSE

631-324-6850
www.easthamptonhistory.org
101 Main St., East Hampton, NY 11937
Open: Year-round, Tues.–Sat. 10–5
Admission: Adults $4; seniors $3; students $2

The Osborn-Jackson House is a handsome 1740 colonial that serves as headquarters for the
East Hampton Historical Society. It has been restored to its 1870s appearance and contains
exhibits that interpret the lives of several generations of men, women, and children who
lived there. Occasional evening lantern tours help visitors re-create the mood and ambience of the period.

The Osborn-Jackson House in East Hampton was built in 1740. Today it serves as the headquarters of the East Hampton Historical Society. Morgan McGivern

TOWN HOUSE

631-324-6850
www.easthamptonhistory.org
149 Main St., East Hampton
Mailing Address: 101 Main St., East Hampton, NY 11937
Open: Mem. Day–Columbus Day; Sat. 10–5, Sun. noon–5
Admission: Free with visit to Clinton Academy

The Town House, a small structure built in 1731, is an excellent example of a one-room schoolhouse. The potbellied stove at the front, old school desks that contain children's scribbled notes, and early books and slates reveal how children were educated. The building, which also served as the town's original meeting hall, was moved several times. It now stands next to Clinton Academy, on Main Street in the heart of the village, and is operated by the East Hampton Historical Society.

MONTAUK
MONTAUK POINT LIGHTHOUSE MUSEUM

631-668-2544
www.montauklighthouse.com

Montauk Hwy., Montauk
Mailing Address: RFD 2, Box 112, Montauk,
NY 11954
Open: Year-round; May–Oct. 10:30–5:30;
later hours Sat. and holidays; weekends only
and shorter hours rest of year; call for sched-
ule
Admission: Adults $8.50; seniors $7; children
$4; parking $6 (administered by NYS Dept. of
Parks, Recreation and Historic Preservation)
Special Features: Gift shop, snack bar

Located at the state's easternmost tip, the
Montauk Point Lighthouse is one of the most
recognizable landmarks in New York State.
More than 100,000 people visit each year. Its
construction was authorized by President
George Washington in 1792 to warn ships of
the large landmass they were approaching.
Although originally built 297 feet from the
steep cliffs, erosion during its 200-year history has eaten away all but the remaining 50
feet. Efforts are under way to stabilize the
cliffs, although the lighthouse remains open.
A museum at the base of the lighthouse contains exhibits and an interesting videotape

The Montauk Lighthouse, on the easternmost tip
of Long Island, is visited by more than 100,000
people a year.

narrated by Dick Cavett that describes the importance and function of lighthouses. Children (must be at least 41 inches tall) and adults can walk to the top of the tower for a spectacular view of the ocean. A snack bar, a large picnic area beside the parking lot, and many
trails lead to the beach and across the bluffs. This landmark is operated by the Montauk
Historical Society.

SECOND HOUSE MUSEUM

631-668-5340
Second House Rd., Montauk
Mailing Address: P.O. Box 81, Montauk, NY 11954
Open: July–Columbus Day, daily 10–4, closed Wed.; Mem. Day–June, weekends only 10–4
Admission: Adults $2; children $1

Second House Museum was the second house built to shelter the cattle and sheep tenders
who spent their summers on the Montauk pasturelands. From 1661 until the 1920s, tenders
herded settlers' cattle each summer to the verdant pastures in Montauk. It is said that cattle
joined these great cattle drives from as far away as Patchogue. Second House was built in
1746 and is now the oldest building in Montauk. It's furnished with artifacts and beautiful
period furniture, including lovely wicker and pine pieces. The original construction using
handmade nails and pegged beams is still visible. It is operated by the Montauk Historical
Society.

THIRD HOUSE MUSEUM
631-852-7878, 631-854-4949
Montauk Hwy., Theodore Roosevelt County Park, Montauk, NY 11954
Open: Mem. Day–Columbus Day, Wed.–Sun. 10–5
Admission: None

Third House Museum was built in 1749. It is the third and final house constructed for the "cowboys" who watched over the cattle, sheep, and horses on the summer pastureland in Montauk. This large, rambling wooden house is where Teddy Roosevelt stayed in 1898 when he and his Rough Riders, as well as 28,000 soldiers, returned sick and injured from the Spanish-American War in Cuba. The house is also headquarters for the Theodore Roosevelt County Park, which surrounds the museum. The Pharaoh Museum, containing Indian artifacts once belonging to the last family of the Montauk tribe to occupy the area, is in a wooden building on a hill behind Third House. Also on display are archaeological tools and exhibits describing digging and dating techniques. Third House is operated by the Suffolk County Parks Department.

QUOGUE
OLD SCHOOLHOUSE MUSEUM
631-653-4224
90 Quogue St. East, Quogue
Mailing Address: P.O. Box 1207, Quogue, NY 11959
Open: July 4–Labor Day, Wed. and Fri. 3–5, Sat. 10–noon
Admission: None

The Old Schoolhouse Museum provides a look at a much larger schoolhouse than the one in East Hampton. When it was built in 1822, it was acclaimed as the "largest and best in Suffolk County." It is in pristine condition, with polished wood floors, a large fireplace, and a weathered-shingle exterior. Used as a school and community meetinghouse until 1893, it now contains artifacts from Quogue's history, including photographs, dolls, toys, furniture, and more. Workshops, lectures, and exhibits are held in the museum in the summer. It is operated by the Quogue Historical Society.

SAGAPONACK
THE MADOO CONSERVANCY
631-537-8200
www.madoo.org
618 Sagg Main St., Sagaponack
Mailing Address: P.O. Box 362, Sagaponack, NY 11962
Open: mid-May–mid-Oct., Fri. and Sat. noon–4
Admission: $10

The Madoo Conservancy was established to perpetuate the unique vision of artist Robert Dash, who created this lush and verdant garden on a two-acre plot of land that also contains his two studios and a wonderful collection of sheds, buildings, and outdoor sculptures. Near the entrance you'll encounter a whimsical gold and purple bench with a huge wheel at one end and wheelbarrow handles at the other, and as you meander along the paths, you discover an Oriental bridge crossing a little stream, a gazebo, arbors, and secret gardens. The gardens are continually in transition as Mr. Dash adds and amends.

SAG HARBOR

Sag Harbor has many interesting old houses and buildings. The Society for the Preservation of Long Island Antiquities has developed a handy walking map to help you find and identify them. The map is on the inside of the brochure for the Old Custom House. Also, the Information Center, located in the old windmill at the entrance to Long Wharf, is a good resource.

THE OLD CUSTOM HOUSE

631-725-0250, 631-692-4664
www.splia.org
Garden St., Sag Harbor
Mailing Address: P.O. Box 148, Cold Spring Harbor, NY 11724
Open: Mem. Day–Columbus Day Sat. and Sun. 1–5; closed rest of year
Admission: Adults $3; seniors and children ages 7–14 $2

The Old Custom House, on the corner of Main and Garden streets across from the Sag Harbor Whaling Museum, was originally the home of Henry Packer Dering, who became the second customs collector of Sag Harbor in 1789. He later became the first postmaster as well, handling both duties from this home. The room that he used as his office is especially interesting. It has interior wooden shields that Mr. Dering could slide across the windows to prevent people from seeing inside when he was counting money. The building contains many pieces of furniture and decorative details that help us understand how a sophisticated family lived in the 18th century. It is operated by the Society for the Preservation of Long Island Antiquities.

SAG HARBOR WHALING MUSEUM

631-725-0770
200 Main St. (corner of Garden St.), Sag Harbor
Mailing Address: Box 1327, Sag Harbor, NY 11963
Open: mid-May–Oct., Mon.–Sat. 10–5, Sun. 1–5
Admission: Adults $5; seniors and students $4

The noble Greek Revival mansion that now houses both the Sag Harbor Whaling Museum and the Sag Harbor Historical Museum was designed by Minard Lafever in 1845 for Benjamin Huntting, one of the earliest of Sag Harbor's whaling scions. The museum is entered through the jaws of a right whale. It features china, dolls, toys, a boat collection, ship models, whaling tools and artifacts, period furnishings, oil paintings, scrimshaw, and documents about Sag Harbor's glorious whaling days.

TEMPLE ADAS ISRAEL

631-725-0904
Atlantic Ave., Sag Harbor, NY 11963

In 1881 Joseph Fahys established a watchcase factory in Sag Harbor (it later became a Bulova watch factory). As his business grew, he expanded his workforce, eventually bringing some 40 Jewish families to Sag Harbor directly from Ellis Island. Finding no place to worship, they built this synagogue in 1900, the first synagogue on Long Island.

THE WHALER'S CHURCH
631-725-0894
Union St., at end of Church St., Sag Harbor, NY 11963

This is the most magnificent church on the South Fork. Designed in 1844 by well-known architect Minard Lafever, it is set back from the street and has a broad platform of stairs that reach to the front door. Its impressive size, dignity, and stature command respect. This is a church that was meant to be noticed. Sadly, the magnificent 185-foot steeple tumbled off in the 1938 hurricane—what is left appears boxy and wanting—but there's good news on the horizon. A fund-raising effort is currently under way to raise money to fully replace the original steeple. One day we'll see it just as it was designed! The interior holds up to 1,000 people, and its soaring, three-story height is truly inspirational. Concerts are often held here, and Presbyterian church services are conducted every Sunday.

SOUTHAMPTON
Conscience Point is the spot on which the first settlers from Lynn, Massachusetts, stepped from their boat in 1640, onto the land that became part of the first English settlement in New York State. A huge boulder set with a brass plaque marks the spot, which is located off North Sea Road in North Sea.

ELIAS PELLETREAU GOLDSMITH SHOP
631-283-2494
www.southamptonhistoricalmuseum.org
78 Main St., Southampton
Mailing Address: P.O. Box 303, Southampton, NY 11968
Open: June 15–Sept. 15, Tues.–Sat. 11-4
Admission: Adults $4

The Elias Pelletreau Goldsmith Shop is one of the few historic buildings still located on its original site, although it now faces in a different direction. Built in 1686, the shop of this famous colonial gold- and silversmith is fully restored, exhibiting a workshop complete with tools. It is operated by the Southampton Historical Museum.

THE THOMAS HALSEY HOMESTEAD
631-283-2494
www.southamptonhistoricalmuseum.org
249 South Main St., Southampton
Mailing Address: P.O. Box 303, Southampton, NY 11968
Open: July–mid-Oct. 11-4
Admission: Adults $4

The Old Halsey House (known as Hollyhocks for many years) is the oldest building in Southampton and one of the oldest saltbox houses in New York State. It dates to 1666. This was a large home for its day, and it is still in excellent condition, with wide-plank floors, many fireplaces, and authentic 17th- and 18th-century furnishings. The acquisition of the furnishings was supervised by Henry Francis duPont, founder of the Winterthur Museum in Delaware, and many of the fine pieces are by well-known craftsmen. The grounds of the homestead contain colorful flower borders, an apple orchard, and an herb garden enclosed by privet hedges, which illustrate how it must have looked when the Halseys were living there. It is operated by the Southampton Historical Museum.

ROGERS MANSION
631-283-2494, 631-283-1612
www.southamptonhistoricalmuseum.org
17 Meeting House Ln., Southampton
Mailing Address: P.O. Box 303, Southampton, NY 11968
Open: Year-round, Tues.–Sat. 11–4; Research Center: Year-round, Tues.–Sat. noon–4
Admission: Adults $4

The Southampton Historical Museum is a collection of 12 buildings and 35 separate exhibits. The main house, a large, white, whaling captain's home, was built by Captain Albert Rogers in 1843. It contains many interesting exhibits, including period china, glassware and tole collections, a Shinnecock Indian exhibit, Revolutionary War artifacts, dolls, toys, and period clothing and furniture. Another building, an old New York schoolhouse (1850), contains the school's original desks, books, and maps. The Red Barn houses the Charles Foster collection of whaling instruments. It is set on a village street with a carriage shed, carpenter shop, blacksmith shop, the Corwith Drug Store, and a cobbler and harness shop. The Country Store is located in the pre–Revolutionary War barn where the British stabled their horses during the occupation of Long Island. It includes an old post office and general store. The complex is operated by the Southampton Historical Museum.

SPRINGS
It's been said of the Green River Cemetery that artists are "dying to get in." Ever since Jackson Pollock was buried here in 1956, other artists have been purchasing plots. Pollock's grave, in the back of the oldest section, is marked by a massive boulder called an erratic, which was deposited here as the glaciers receded some 15,000 years ago. Pollock's wife, Lee Krasner, who was also an artist, is buried in front of him. The cemetery is located on Accabonac Road, almost to Old Stone Highway.

POLLOCK-KRASNER HOUSE AND STUDY CENTER
631-324-4929
830 Fireplace Rd., East Hampton, NY 11937
Open: May–Oct., Thurs., Fri., and Sat. 1–5; guided tours: May, Sept., and Oct., 11–4 on the hour; June, July, and Aug. one tour at noon
Admission: $5; guided tours $10 per person

Jackson Pollock's painting techniques were unique. Instead of using typical artists' paint, he preferred ordinary house paint. Instead of using artists' brushes, he devised several methods of splashing his canvas with color. He placed the canvas on the floor instead of on the wall; he sometimes poured directly from the can, or he spattered, dripped, or dribbled with a large brush, a stick, or a filled basting syringe, or he might apply the paint directly with his bare hands. Although his methods may have been considered primitive, the results that he achieved changed the face of American art; the critics called it abstract expressionism. This first uniquely American art technique gained acclaim and respect for American artists and put them on a par with their European contemporaries.

Pollock's barn studio was so drafty that he filled the wide cracks with rags in the winter, but it was here, between 1946 and 1956, that he created his greatest masterpieces. After Pol-

Jackson Pollock's art studio (and that of his wife, Lee Krasner) in Springs is open to visitors. Courtesy Pollock-Krasner House and Study Center

lock's death in 1956, his wife, Lee Krasner, began using his studio, and she continued to paint here well into the 1980s. The farm on which they lived, overlooking the peaceful marshes and bay of Accabonac Creek, the barn studio, and the grounds are open to the public. The study center, which contains the artists' personal papers and a valuable oral history library, is open year-round, by appointment only. In the summer there are lectures and other events. Operated by the Stony Brook Foundation.

WATER MILL
WATER MILL MUSEUM
631-726-4625
41 Old Mill Rd., Water Mill, NY 11976
Open: Mem. Day–mid-Sept., Mon. and Thurs.–Sat. 11–5, Sun. 1–5
Admission: Adults $3, or donations accepted

The Water Mill Museum is located in Southampton's original mill, which was constructed in 1644. This is a waterwheel mill rather than the more prevalent wind-powered mill. The museum exhibits the fully functional wooden gears, shafts, and restored wheel of this, the oldest operational mill on Long Island. Inside, the museum contains the tools of various local trades, such as farmers, blacksmiths, carpenters, spinners, weavers, and millers. You can watch corn being ground into cornmeal at the mill. The museum is only open in the summer, and arts-and-crafts exhibits by local artists are also held in the summer. It is operated by the Ladies' Auxiliary of Water Mill.

KULTURE FOR KIDS

Summertime in the Hamptons is packed with things for children to do. In addition to walking the nature trails and running on the beach (see chapter 7, "Recreation"), there are musical and art classes and performances geared especially to the younger set.

Bay Street Theatre Kidstreet (631-725-9500 box office; 631-725-0818 office; Bay St., Sag Harbor, NY 11963) A series of concerts for children, ranging from puppet shows to concerts featuring *Sesame Street* songs, attract a bevy of children.

Childhood Memories (917-538-5049) This summer musical program for children ages six months to seven years encourages kids' spontaneous, natural enjoyment of music through movement, fantasy, and play. Instruments from around the world are featured, and there are enchanting child-sized props as well.

Children's Museum of the East End (631-537-8250; 376 Bridgehampton/Sag Harbor Tpke., Bridgehampton) Year-round; Mon., Wed., Thurs., and Sat. 9–6; Fri. 9–7:30; Sun. 10–6. In this fast-moving, technological world, the Children's Museum encourages families to slow down and actively share in their children's growth. The museum provides interactive experiences that foster curiosity through a variety of exhibits. There are art workshops, performances, a "Mad Science" weekend workshop, Pizza and Pajama nights, etc. There is a fee for the workshops and *reservations are required.*

East Hampton Historical Society Summer Camp (631-324-6850) Ages 5 to 11. Children dress in costume and experience life in the 17th, 18th, and 19th centuries in a unique hands-on atmosphere. At the East Hampton Town Marine Museum in Amagansett, 6- to 8-year-olds may participate in a weeklong camp that includes science discoveries, maritime-history classes, games, crafts, and games. A weeklong camp for kids ages 9 through 12 is taught in collaboration with a Cornell Marine program and delves into marine biology, data collection, and environmental sustainability.

Goat on a Boat Puppet Theatre (631-725-4193; 5 Hampton St., Sag Harbor, NY 11963) Puppet group offering shows for children, generally ages 5 and younger.

Guild Hall (631-324-0806; 158 Main St., East Hampton, NY 11937; May–Oct.) Enjoyable workshops are conducted in drawing, sand painting, mosaics, puppetry, soft sculpture, kite making, sculpting, and other artistic endeavors. Guild Hall also has a popular "Kids' Fest" every Wednesday throughout the summer and periodically at other times. In addition, in February March the annual student Art Festival takes place, exhibiting the work of students from K–8th grade. There are also theatrical productions just for children.

Isabella Rupp Documentary Filmmaking Class (631-287-8735) This writer-director offers firsthand instruction to children, in directing, shooting, interviewing, writing, and editing their own documentaries.

Kids on the Green (631-288-3337) Every Tuesday in July and August, the Westhampton Chamber of Commerce sponsors free live performances for children on the village green. They might see a magic show, farm animals, or a rock 'n' roll band.

Kidsummer Art Camp (631-283-2118, ext. 30; www.parrishart.org; 25 Jobs Ln. Southampton, NY 11968) This summer camp for children ages 6 to 11 is taught in five one-week sessions by staff of the Parrish Art Museum. Children's classes include painting, sculpture, drawing, photography, printmaking, and textiles; day trips are also offered.

Le Cercle Français (631-725-2128) A summer program, as well as after-school classes, acquaints students with the French language, culture, theater, cooking, manners, couture, and style. Classes are offered at Stella Maris in Sag Harbor or at the Cultural Center of Southampton for children from kindergarten through high school.

Ross School (631-907-5555; www.ross.org; 18 Goodfriend Park, East Hampton) The Ross School (and Institute Wellness Center) is a terrific local resource. Instruction stresses "inquiry through primary sources and hands-on interpretation and analysis of information." There are a number of mind-stretching summer classes for children ages 7 to 18 that go beyond painting and drama (although they offer those also). There's an eco-adventure class (an exploration of local wetlands, ponds, forests, and the ocean) and a Harry Potter science class (children construct camera obscuras, make a periscope, study air pressure and flight). There are also after-school classes that range from music instruction and photography to Chinese acrobatics and tumbling, the art of magazine and music illustration, crime-scene science, and jazz to hip-hop dance.

Southampton Historical Museum (631-283-2494; 17 Meeting House Ln., Southampton) In the summer the historical museum sponsors a walking tour for children ages 8 to 12 of historic Job's Lane in Southampton.

Suffolk County Farm and Education Center (631-852-4600; www.ccesuffolk.org; 350 Yaphank Ave., Yaphank, NY 11980) The Cornell Cooperative Extension Service has numerous craft classes and day and summer camps for children. Be sure to peruse the Web site for all the many opportunities.

Westhampton Beach Performing Arts Center (631-288-1500) Special Kidsstage productions have included *Cinderella, Pinocchio, Peter Pan, The Wizard of Oz,* and *Sleeping Beauty.* In addition there are puppet shows, a family fun night, comedy acts, and much more.

LIBRARIES

Libraries in the Hamptons are especially rich in local history; the Long Island Collection in the East Hampton Library encompasses one of the finest resources on Long Island for local research. Although the libraries allow unlimited use of historical material on premises, several permit residents to check out books; a nonresident library card can be purchased in some cases.

AMAGANSETT FREE LIBRARY

631-267-3810
215 Main St., Amagansett
Mailing Address: P.O. Box 726, Amagansett, NY 11930
Open: Mon.–Sat., 10–5; Thurs. 10–8; Sun. 1–4
Fee: Library cards free to year-round residents and taxpayers; but honors cards from libraries throughout Suffolk County; temporary card free to summer residents also

The Amagansett Free Library was established in 1916 and is located in a building that dates from 1922. The director emeritus, the late Carleton Kelsey, was noted for his keen sense of local history. His book, *Amagansett: A Pictorial History 1680–1940* (1986), contains valuable photographs and historical material not found elsewhere.

EAST HAMPTON LIBRARY

631-324-0222
www.easthamptonlibrary.org
159 Main St., East Hampton, NY 11937
Open: Mon.–Thurs. 10–7; Fri., Sat. 10–5; Sun. 1–5. Long Island Collection, Mon., Tues., Thurs., and Sat. 1–4:30
Fee: Library cards free to year-round residents and taxpayers of the East Hampton, Springs, and Wainscott school districts; nonresidents $75

The East Hampton Library was established in 1897, and it just keeps growing and getting better. The building is located on a parcel of land that once contained the home of Samuel Buell, East Hampton's third minister. The main building was designed in an Elizabethan style by Aymar Embury II in 1911. It has been expanded several times, in aesthetic and complementary architectural styles—once in 1946 by Embury himself, and again in 2000. It includes a local history and periodical room; a children's library where storytelling takes place; a video, record, tape, and CD lending library; a music listening room; and a large lending library. This is the repository of the Long Island Collection, most of which was donated by Morton Pennypacker, who was at one time historian of Suffolk County. The bequest has been bolstered by additional historic collections over the years, including the Thomas Moran Biographical Art Collection, and it contains an outstanding assemblage of books, prints, newspapers, genealogies, and much more.

HAMPTON BAYS PUBLIC LIBRARY
631-728-6241
52 Ponquogue Ave., Hampton Bays
Mailing Address: P.O. Box 1017, Hampton Bays, NY 11946
Open: Mon.–Thurs. 10–9; Fri. 10–7; Sat. 10–5; Sun. 1–5
Fee: Free to full-time residents and taxpayers of Suffolk County; summer residents library card Mem. Day–Labor Day $5, plus $30 deposit, fully refunded if all books are returned

The Hampton Bays Public Library was established in the 1960s. It has a children's room where storytellers often read to children. You can borrow books, videos, CDs, books on tape, and music tapes, and there is an excellent lending book collection that is strong in art books.

HAMPTON LIBRARY IN BRIDGEHAMPTON
631-537-0015
www.hamptonlibrary.org
2478 Main St., Bridgehampton
Mailing Address: P.O. Box 3025, Bridgehampton, NY 11932
Open: Mon.–Thurs. 9:30–7; Fri. and Sat. 9:30–5; Sun. 1–5
Fee: Library card free to residents of Bridgehampton and Sagaponack school districts; also honors cards from other Suffolk libraries

The Hampton Library is housed in a white-shingled building built in 1876 and expanded in 1982. During the summer, the courtyard is the site of the library's popular Fridays at Five, a discussion series with well-known authors. In addition to lending books, the library has a music room, a children's room, a video library, and a selection of periodicals. Children's story hours are held on Saturdays throughout the year. A major addition to the building was under way in 2009, and although the library moved to a temporary location during construction, it was expected to return to the new/old building by spring 2010.

JOHN JERMAIN MEMORIAL LIBRARY IN SAG HARBOR
631-725-0049
Main St., Sag Harbor
Mailing Address: P.O. Box 569, Sag Harbor, NY 11963

Open: Mon.–Wed. 10–7, Thurs. 10–9; Fri. and Sat. 10–5; Sun. 1-5 (mid-Oct.–Mid-June only)
Fee: Free to residents of Sag Harbor; accepts library cards from other Suffolk County libraries.

The John Jermain Memorial Library was built with funds donated by Mrs. Russell Sage in 1907. This imposing two-story brick building houses a fine collection of books. The former library historian, Dorothy Zaykowski, wrote an excellent book, *Sag Harbor: The Story of an American Beauty* (1991), which chronicles the history of Sag Harbor.

MONTAUK LIBRARY
631-668-3377
871 Montauk Hwy., Montauk
Mailing Address: P.O. Box 700, Montauk, NY 11954
Open: Mon., Tues, Fri. 11–6; Wed. 11–8; Sat. 10–5; Sun. 2–5; closed Thurs.
Fee: Free to year-round residents and taxpayers of the Montauk school district; nonresidents $30/year

The Montauk Library, housed in a building completed in 1991, has bright spaces for reading and an interesting collection that is especially strong on fishing and early Montauk history.

QUOGUE LIBRARY
631-653-4224
90 Quogue St. East, Quogue
Mailing Address: P.O. Box 5036, Quogue, NY 11959
Open: Sun., Mon. 12–5; Tues., Fri., Sat. 10–5; Tues. and Thurs. 10–8
Fee: Free to residents of Quogue and those with library card within Suffolk County

The Quogue Library is located in a charming 1897 building of weathered shingles on the same property as the Old School House Museum. The library sponsors summer programs for children and adults, as well as art events. A popular author-lecture series is held on Sundays in the summer.

ROGERS MEMORIAL LIBRARY IN SOUTHAMPTON
631-283-0774
91 Cooper's Farm Rd., Southampton, NY 11968
Open: Year-round, Mon.–Thurs. 10–9; Fri. 10–7; Sat. 10–5; Sun. 1–5
Fee: Free to year-round residents or taxpayers of Southampton or Tuckahoe school districts; nonresidents $50

The Rogers Memorial Library was established in 1896 through a gift from Harriet Jones Rogers. For many years it resided on Job's Lane in an impressive Victorian redbrick building with an arched entrance, designed in classic R. H. Robertson style. In the fall of 2000 the library moved to its equally impressive, Hamptons-shingle-style building just off Windmill Lane. The new building is light and bright and extremely user-friendly—a wonderful place to peruse the extensive collection of books, as well as videos, tapes, and CDs. A Children's Reading Club sponsors popular storytelling activities. The old library is now being used as an education center by the Parrish Art Museum, which is located next door.

This impressive shingle-style structure is the home of the Rogers Memorial Library in Southampton.

SPRINGS LIBRARY
No telephone
Old Stone Hwy., East Hampton, NY 11937
Open: Mon., Tues., Fri. 10–noon; Wed. 10–noon and 3–5; Sat. 9–noon, evening hours Fri. 6–8
Fee: $10

The Springs Library is located in a small 1700s white clapboard house that is the former home of the Parsons family, one of the oldest Springs families. The library is not open full-time and does not have a telephone, but it is an excellent resource for local Springs history.

WESTHAMPTON FREE LIBRARY
631-288-3335
7 Library Ave., Westhampton, NY 11977
Open: Mon.–Fri. 9:30–9; Fri. and Sat. 9:30–5; Sun. 1–5

Fee: Free to year-round residents and taxpayers of Westhampton school district; accepts library cards from other Suffolk County libraries

The Westhampton Free Library has much more than books. There's a lending library of CDs, audio books, tapes, and videos, as well as activities, such as a Sunday bridge game, storytelling for children, a French club, and a book-discussion group. The library contains an extensive village history collection, and it is fully handicap-accessible.

Music

Many musical events take place in the Hamptons, especially in the summer.

The Art Barge (631-267-3172; Napeague) Musical events, including blues, jazz, dance, and music performances, and much more, are performed at the Victor D'Amico Institute of Art.

The Choral Society of the Hamptons (631-283-0404; Bridgehampton Presbyterian Church) This 100-voice choir performs several concerts during the year with orchestral accompaniment. Their performances are always eagerly anticipated for their mix of classical music, opera, and show tunes.

Music Festival of the Hamptons (631-267-8293, 800-644-4418; www.musicfestivalofthe hamptons.com) This Hamptons festival has grown since its inception in 1995, and offered more than 20 concerts in 2009. These include chamber music, piano recitals, children's concerts, and vocal events. It's under the distinguished leadership of Michael Guttman. Events take place under a festival tent on Snake Hollow Road in Bridgehampton or at Old Whalers Church in Sag Harbor or the Wölffer Estate Vineyards in Sagaponack.

Opera of the Hamptons (631-728-8804) Light opera is performed at dinner theaters, wineries, Agawam Park, and other venues on the North and South Forks. Some concerts are outdoors, and you are encouraged to bring a picnic dinner.

Perlman Music Program (631-749-0740) This wonderful summer music camp, which Itzhak Perlman established in order to teach musically gifted students, is located on Shelter Island (see listing under "Cultural Attractions" in chapter 10 for location and schedule). Concerts take place the last week in June through the first week of August.

Pianofest (631-329-9115; Fine Arts Theatre, Long Island University, Southampton Campus; July–Aug.; concerts $10) This weekly series provides Hamptons residents and visitors with a rare treat. Polished piano artists are selected by nomination and audition to attend a summer residential study program in the Hamptons. Often these students have already won prestigious competitions and are on the verge of launching concert careers.

Sag Harbor Community Band (631-725-9759; American Legion Post 388, Bay St., Sag Harbor; July–Aug.; free) Tuesday-night band concerts might feature blues, jazz, or pop artists. Bring a blanket or lawn chair.

Village of Southampton (631-287-4300; Agawam Park, Southampton; July–Aug.) A variety of musical performances are sponsored by the Southampton Cultural Center.

Westhampton Beach Performing Arts Center (631-288-1500; Westhampton Beach) A variety of musical performances by such entertainers as Marvin Hamlisch, Joan Baez, Joan Rivers, New York City Opera, and Donnie Osmond take place in this restored art deco building, which was formerly a cinema.

NIGHTLIFE

Nightlife in the Hamptons is frenetic in the summer. From bikini contests to ladies' nights, giveaways, and theme parties—the clubs compete for business. The following are only a few of the many nightspots that pack them in. Most stay open until 2 or even 4 AM on weekends, which allows employees of restaurants and sports shops and visitors from New York City to participate. The clubs listed here are noted for their entertainment and their celebrity DJs, and many serve food as well. Although not listed here, many restaurants also offer live music on weekend nights. It's best to check the newspapers.

AMAGANSETT

Stephen Talkhouse (631-267-3117; 161 Main St., Amagansett, NY 11930) This is the place to go for music, music, music. It's been around since 1832, so it's got the formula down pat. The rather small room is intimate. For name entertainers, such as Richie Havens or Kris Kristofferson, the cover charge can climb as high as $100, but most of the time it ranges from $10 to $40, and some evenings it's as low as $5. Stephen Talkhouse is also noted for the stars who drop by unannounced. Paul McCartney, Paul Simon, Billy Joel, Jimmy Buffet, G. E. Smith, and many more have been known to stop in for quick jam sessions with their friends. There's often a waiting line on weekends, so plan ahead.

EAST HAMPTON

Lily Pond (631-324-3332; 44 Three Mile Harbor Rd., East Hampton, NY 11937) This very classy nightclub-*cum*-lounge is *the* place to come for celebrity sightings. There are bed-style lounges and private cabanas for those seeking privacy. In the club, you'll hear music ranging from reggae to hip-hop. Call in advance to get details about the evening entertainment. Sometimes they host celebrity-studded product launches; other times they host parties for gays; other times it's closed for private parties thrown by such celebs as Sean Combs. A high-profile restaurant, Philippe East, will fill the bill before club action picks up.

EAST QUOGUE

Neptune Beach Club (631-653-8737; www.neptunebeachclub.net; 70 Dune Rd., East Quogue, NY 11942) This wild thing is located right on the beach, and it's super popular. There are private VIP cabanas, bed-lounges, and cute young things—but do heed the management warning—"some attire required"! Visit the Web site for parking information.

HAMPTON BAYS

Beach Bar (631-723-3100; www.beachbar.net; 58 Foster Ave., Hampton Bays, NY 11946) There are parties Friday and Saturday nights, seafood, and drink specials, ladies' night parties, TGIF events, bikini contests, and lots of action at this happening place.

Boardy Barn (631-728-9733; www.boardybarn.com; 270 W. Montauk Hwy., Hampton Bays, NY 11946) This place has been on the map for almost 40 years, so you know they know the ropes. It's a casual, don't-get-dressed-up, spot, where the beer flows and the music plays.

Whitehouse (631-728-4121; www.whitehousenightclub.com; 239 E. Montauk Hwy. at Shinnecock Canal, Hampton Bays, NY 11946) This historic spot, known as CPI (Canoe Place Inn), for many years, has an old history and a young crowd. It served as the summer home of New York's Governor Al Smith and bedded, at various times, Franklin Roosevelt, Helen Hayes, Albert Einstein, Cary Grant, and many others. A renovation/transformation took place in 2009, and she's looking pretty good. Whitehouse begins swinging about 10 PM and keeps up a jived pace until the wee hours. It's so large that it can hold 1,000 people in its three distinct lounges. The music ranges from '50s tunes and rock to reggae. Live bands, $1 drinks, cash prizes for winners of bikini contests—it just goes on and on. The VIP lounge features comedy and karaoke!

MONTAUK

Nick's (631-668-4800; 148 South Emerson Ave., Montauk, NY 11954) And now for something different! A restaurant/bar by day, this place turns into a club at 11 PM. Some nights you can perform in a karaoke contest; other nights there might be a *Who Wants to Be a Millionaire*–style game show; the rest of the time there's a DJ spinning discs.

Surf Lodge (631-668-3284; 183 Edgemere St., Montauk, NY 11054) With a surfing theme, and a laid-back attitude, this has become one of the hottest spots in the Hamptons. There are outdoor surfing films, a beach and bonfire, and live music on the deck on weekends.

SAG HARBOR

Oasis (631-725-7110; 3253 Noyac Rd., Sag Harbor) By day this is an elegant seaside restaurant, but Saturday nights it morphs into a party room with a DJ spinning tunes, free hors d'oeuvres, and drink specials.

SOUTHAMPTON

AXE Lounge at Dune (631-283-0808; www.dunesouthampton.com; 1181 North Sea Rd., Southampton, NY 11968; open Mem. Day–Labor Day, Thurs.–Sat.) This East End rendition of the Manhattan and Miami clubs is opulent and ultra elegant, and it's exclusively VIP. You might find Lindsay Lohan or Paris Hilton dropping by, or, some nights, maybe Tommy Hilfiger will be hosting a party (read: lots of supermodels); other nights, there may be a product launch. It helps to arrive with a celeb in tow or to look knockout gorgeous (male or female) to get past the velvet ropes. DJs spin until 4 AM.

THEATER & DANCE

BAY STREET THEATRE FESTIVAL
631-725-9500 (box office); 631-725-0818 (office)
www.baystreet.org
Bay St., Sag Harbor
Mailing Address: P.O. Box 810, Sag Harbor, NY 11963
Open: Mar.–Dec.
Admission: $35–$75 for plays; $10 for spring and fall play readings

The Bay Street Theatre Festival in Sag Harbor opened with a bang in 1992, and it gets better every year. One of the principals is Emma Walton, daughter of Julie Andrews and Tony Walton, although she did decide to retire after the 2009 season, but she will certainly continue to remain involved. On occasion, her mom stars or helps with fund-raising benefits. During the 2003 season she directed *The Boyfriend*. Theatrical performances, play readings, pre–New York City openings, cabaret productions, and much more are presented in an intimate 299-seat professional theater throughout the year. In addition to the Main Stage, there are special performances, such as a concert by Betty Buckley, or there's the Comedy Club, showcasing the performances of well-known comedians, such as Robert Klein. The Picture Show at Bay Street presents classic films on a big screen. The company also sponsors courses in drama, direction, and playwriting, a Kidstreet program of performances for kids, and also a Young Playwrights curriculum in local schools that culminates in a student production.

THE HAMPTON THEATRE COMPANY

631-653-8955
Quogue Village Theatre, Jessup Ln., Quogue, NY 11959
Mailing address: P.O. Box 734, Westhampton Beach, NY 11978
Open: Sept.–June
Fee: $20

The Hampton Theatre Company produces several plays during the fall, winter, and spring seasons. Performances take place either at the Quogue Village Theatre on Jessup Ave. in Quogue or at the Westhampton Beach Performing Arts Center.

JOHN DREW THEATRE OF GUILD HALL

631-324-4050
www.guildhall.org
158 Main St., East Hampton, NY 11937
Open: Year-round
Admission: Varies, depending on performance

The John Drew Theatre of Guild Hall in East Hampton is the oldest playhouse on Long Island and sponsors theatrical productions, cabaret singers, poetry readings, and children's theater. During the summer, it teams up with several New York theater companies to hold readings and premiere performances of productions before they head for the city.

THE PLAYWRIGHTS' THEATRE OF EAST HAMPTON

631-324-5373, 718-434-6566
John Drew Theatre, East Hampton
Mailing Address: 30 Talmadge Farm Ln., East Hampton, NY 11937 (summer); 666 E. 19th St., Brooklyn, NY 11230 (winter)
Open: 4 weeks in late summer
Admission: play readings $15; benefits $25

The Playwrights' Theatre of East Hampton conducts readings of new plays, but these are a far cry from ordinary readings. Here, well-known dramatic artists, such as Tammy Grimes, Ben Gazzara, or Phyllis Newman, might be heard reading plays by Joyce Carol Oates or Lucy Wang that are directed by respected Broadway directors. These events are followed by lively discussions and refreshments.

WESTHAMPTON BEACH PERFORMING ARTS CENTER

631-288-1500 (box office); 631-288-2350 (office); 631-288-8519 (fax)
www.whbpac.org

76 Main St., Westhampton Beach
Mailing Address: P.O. Box 631, Westhampton Beach, NY 11978
Open: Year-round
Admission: $15–$125, depending on performer

Just as the beautiful and spirited old art deco Westhampton Beach Cinema was sliding into a steep decline, a group of public-spirited citizens came to the rescue. After herculean efforts that included fund-raising events and an immense amount of volunteer effort, the ornamented interior now shines, and a full schedule of live performances takes place. You might see a Hamptons version of *Forbidden Broadway* or performances by Claire Bloom, Ben Vereen, Marvin Hamlisch, Leslie Uggams, the Smothers Brothers, Neil Sedaka, the Glenn Miller Orchestra, or Alan King, as well as performances by various ballet companies, blues concerts, Beatlemania, and a film screening series.

7

ONE OF THE LAST
GREAT PLACES

Recreation

The first Hamptons settlers believed that each day was placed before them so that they could accomplish a task—build a barn, till the soil, bake bread, tend a flock. Days were filled with hard work, and the concept of recreation was foreign. And yet, today, recreation is the Hamptons' chief attraction. An early-morning walk along the beach with the spray from the crashing waves rising to meet the mist; a jog along the bay at dusk as the fiery setting sun leaves brilliant streaks of pink, orange, and red; a sail to Block Island, whisked along on bundling breezes; a quiet kayak trip through tall reeds, surprising a crane at its meal—these are only a few of the many joys to be experienced in the Hamptons.

The abundance and bounty of the waters surrounding the Hamptons attract people who know that the best fishing, the best boating, and some of the best beaches in the United States are found right here. Hikers, bicyclists, horseback riders, and birdwatchers also have their favorite haunts, as do canoeists, golfers, tennis enthusiasts, and scuba divers.

Through the enlightened perseverance of the Nature Conservancy, the Peconic Land Trust, and Group for the East End, more land is in the public domain on the East End of Long Island than in almost any other place in America. The Nature Conservancy on Long Island alone is responsible for saving more than 150,000 acres of Long Island bays, beaches, marshes, and land—preserving them for us and our children to enjoy, appreciate, and gently use.

> *Everybody needs beauty as well as bread, places to play in and pray in, where Nature may heal and cheer and give strength to body and soul alike.*
>
> John Muir, Yosemite, 1942

AUTO RACING

Auto racing began in 1915 in Bridgehampton, when European-style road races were conducted along the narrow dirt streets and the adjacent fields. These races continued in one form or another until 1953, when the state banned car races through village streets for safety reasons. Now races take place at the **Long Island Motor Sports Park** (631-288-1555) at 102 Old Country Road in Westhampton. This is the site of drag racing and other exhibi-

Humans aren't the only ones who enjoy the beauty and solitude of Hamptons beaches.

tions on Friday, Saturday, and Sunday in the summer. (See also Riverhead Raceway in chapter 9 for NASCAR races on the North Fork.)

BEACHES

The beaches are the glory of the Hamptons. They are clean, broad stretches of white sand that, in this writer's opinion, are the finest in the world. Unlike the beaches of France or Italy, for example, pesky flies and other bugs stay away. Unlike Hawaiian and other Pacific beaches—often mere slips of sand hidden between rock cliffs or promontories—Long Island beaches stretch from Rockaway Point in Queens to Montauk Point, some 130 miles of sand, interrupted only by inlets and bays.

Don't be fooled into thinking that the best beaches are all on the ocean, however. When the fog hovers near the ocean until noon, head for the secret bay beaches, where you might bask in brilliant sunshine from early morning until late afternoon. In general, the bay beaches are less populated than those on the ocean, so if you seek solitude or prefer a lazy swim in calm waters unaccompanied by the crash of ocean waves, the bay should be your choice. Everyone has their favorite beach, and there are enough to go around, so start your quest now for your own personal choice.

Beach rules are very strict in the Hamptons. Driving on beaches is permitted with a sticker, but generally in the summer it is allowed only when swimmers and sunbathers are not using them. Signs posted at each beach give details about driving and also about when dogs are allowed on the beach (a controversial, ever-evolving issue). Check with town or village officials for the current rules.

Now for the tricky part—getting there. If you live within walking distance, walk! The next best mode of transportation is a bicycle; there's an abundance of bicycle racks at most beaches. If you must drive, be certain that you have the proper parking sticker. This is essential from Memorial Day to Labor Day. A parking sticker from East Hampton Town, for example, will not allow you to park at an East Hampton Village beach or a Southampton Village beach. Qualifications for resident and nonresident status vary from village to village, so check with the appropriate town hall before you go. Parking is available at several beaches on a daily use–fee basis, but generally a sticker is required. Resident and nonresident stickers may be purchased for the following fees. No fee is charged to residents of the villages for use of village beaches, but please note—summer renters are not considered residents by most villages, and they are required to pay the nonresident fee. Also, it's important to obtain your parking permit early in the year, as permits are limited and may be sold out once the season begins. Following are the fees for seasonal stickers.

Resident Parking Sticker Fees

East Hampton Town	$25 primary sticker; $15 each addl. sticker
Southampton Town	$30; seniors $20

Nonresident Parking Permit Sticker Fees

East Hampton Town	$325	631-324-4142
East Hampton Village	$300	631-324-4150
Quogue Village	$200	631-653-4498
Sag Harbor Village	$100	631-725-0222
Southampton Town	$225	631-728-8585
Southampton Village	$350	631-283-0247
Westhampton Beach Village*	$300	631-288-1654

Summer renters in Remsenburg, Quiogue, Westhampton, and Speonk can purchase WHB permits for $600.

The following is by no means a complete list of area beaches, but included here are the most popular choices.

AMAGANSETT

Atlantic Avenue (ocean beach) Restrooms; telephones; parking with East Hampton Town resident or nonresident permit, or $15 per day (weekdays only); no weekend or holiday nonresident daily parking. A broad ocean beach, Atlantic Avenue has a number of addi-

East Hampton's Main Beach is as popular today as it was when this scene was painted by Edward Lamson Henry in the 1880s. C. Frank Dayton Collection, East Hampton Library Historical Collection

tional amenities. The concession stand in the former coast guard station is terrific. You can buy hamburgers, hot dogs, and great marinated-chicken-breast sandwiches, as well as old-fashioned comfort-food desserts, such as ice cream bars and Popsicles; you can also rent beach chairs and umbrellas. Known for years as Asparagus Beach (because so many singles stood in packs, surveying everyone else), this is now a very popular family beach, where you might find numerous volleyball games under way.

Fresh Pond (bay beach) Restrooms; telephone; picnic tables; grills; nature trails; parking with East Hampton Town permit. Fresh Pond is a delightful spot at the end of Fresh Pond Road on Napeague Bay. Breakwaters create a sandy beach, and from a park bench you can contemplate the tranquility of the scene and watch the gulls wheel over the fishing nets in the water. The preferred sun site is the sandy beach surrounding Fresh Pond; small, shallow pools of placid, clean water at the entrance to the larger pond are ideal for families with children.

Indian Wells (ocean beach) Restrooms; telephones; mobile concession stand; parking with East Hampton Town resident permit. Indian Wells is near the spot where the Montauk Indians once came for fresh water. At the end of Indian Wells Highway in the middle of the Atlantic Double Dunes Preserve, the gleaming, white-sand beach stretches as far as the eye can see. Unspoiled by development of any kind, this beach remains a favorite with sun lovers who want to pretend they are on their own beach, on their own private island.

Lazy Point (bay beach) Boat launch; parking with East Hampton Town permit. Lazy Point, a protected point of land jutting into Napeague Harbor, is accessed through Napeague State Park. Surrounded by the tiny fishing cottages of the village of Napeague (no shops, just cottages), this beach is generally deserted, except for wind surfers who have found the bay breezes ideal for skittering across the water. Main Beach (631-537-2716; www.mainbeach.com), a sporting goods shop in Wainscott, rents out wind surfing equipment from a truck on nice summer days.

BRIDGEHAMPTON

Mecox Beach (ocean beach) Parking with Southampton Town resident or nonresident permit only; no daily parking permitted. Mecox Beach is on the ocean at the end of Job's Lane in Bridgehampton. A wooden walkway leads to the beach from the large parking lot. There are no restrooms or food facilities.

W. Scott Cameron Beach (ocean beach) Restrooms; showers; lifeguard; concession stand; parking with Southampton Town resident permit. This beach is on the ocean in Bridgehampton at the end of Dune Road.

EAST HAMPTON VILLAGE

Georgica Beach (ocean beach) Restrooms; showers; lifeguard; parking with East Hampton Village permit only; bicycle racks. Located at the end of Apaquogue Road and Lily Pond Lane in the heart of the estate section of East Hampton, Georgica Beach is one of the preferred ocean-side sun spots. With a backdrop of estates and mansions just beyond the dunes, this sparkling clean beach is underutilized.

Main Beach (ocean beach) Restrooms; telephones; lockers and showers; lifeguards; tidal report; concession stand; beach chair and umbrella rentals; parking with East Hampton Village permit, or $20 per day, weekdays only; no daily parking permitted weekends and holidays. Main Beach, at the end of Ocean Avenue, is consistently rated the number-one beach in Hamptons surveys. This broad expanse of pristine beach has it all, but it's also one of the most crowded. To bask in the glorious sun, to roll over and see the elegant mansions, to sit on the spacious, covered deck and gaze out to sea—this truly is summer heaven. Walk up to the pavilion and select a freshly sliced fruit cup, a tall glass of lemonade, a grilled hamburger, or an ice-cream cone from the Chowder Bowl. If you find that you've forgotten something, there's a shop that sells everything from aspirin and sunscreen to beach chairs.

Two Mile Hollow (ocean beach) Parking with East Hampton Village permit. This beach is located at the end of Two Mile Hollow Road, almost on the village/town line. In the midst of a nature sanctuary, it is preferred by many village residents for its serene and peaceful surroundings. There's none of the mob scene of Main Beach here, but neither are there any facilities.

HAMPTON BAYS

Meschutt Beach (bay beach) Parking with Southampton Town resident or nonresident permit, a $5 fee for Suffolk County residents with a Green Key Card (available for $24 and good for three years) or $12 per day without a card. Meschutt Beach is a Suffolk County park, operated by the Town of Southampton. It is on North Highway where the Shinnecock Canal joins the Great Peconic Bay in Meschutt Park.

Ponquogue Beach (ocean beach) Restrooms; lifeguard; parking with Southampton Town resident or nonresident permit, or $20 per day. Ponquogue Beach is on the ocean, on Dune Road at the end of the Ponquogue Bridge, bordered by Shinnecock County Park East and West.

Road H (ocean beach) Parking with Southampton Town parking permit. Road H, in the Shinnecock Inlet County Park East, is a favorite place for surfers and scuba divers. It's right beside the jetty from the ocean into Shinnecock Bay, where a rich supply of saltwater fish journey into the quiet bays to spawn.

Tiana Beach (ocean beach) Restrooms; lifeguard; parking with Southampton Town permit, or $20 per day. Located on Dune Road, Tiana is on that great expanse of ocean beach sandwiched between Shinnecock Bay and the ocean. The Town of Southampton Parks and Recreation Department conducts a series of classes (swimming, sailing, wind surfing) at Tiana Beach.

MONTAUK

Ditch Plains (ocean beach) Restrooms; showers; lifeguard; mobile concession stand; parking with East Hampton Town permit. Noted for its great surfing, Ditch Plains is off Ditch Plains and DeForest roads. The usual snacks and ice cream can be purchased from the Beach Dog, a mobile concession stand.

Gin Beach (bay beach) Restrooms; lifeguard; mobile concession stand; parking with East Hampton Town permit. Broad and sandy, Gin Beach is at the end of East Lake Drive, near the jetty where boats enter Lake Montauk. It's great for fishing and for watching the boats coming and going in the harbor.

Hither Hills State Park (ocean beach) Camping (631-668-2554; reservations required), parking $8 per day. This park has one of the finest beaches on the ocean—a broad, 2-mile expanse of clean, white sand. You can camp beside the beach and take a swim as soon as you awaken in the morning and the last thing at night. See additional information in "Parks & Nature Preserves," this chapter.

NORTHWEST

Sammy's Beach (bay beach) Parking with East Hampton Town permit. Sammy's is a broad crescent of protected bay beach that overlooks Gardiner's Bay. It's a wonderful place for waterskiing and boating (the boats can come directly to shore), but because of the steep drop-off, it is not a great place for children to swim.

NOYACK

Foster Memorial (bay beach) Restrooms; lifeguard; snack bar/restaurant; parking with Southampton Town permit, or $20 per day. Foster Memorial is on Long Beach, the stretch of land separating the inner harbors of Sag Harbor from Noyack Bay. The small snack bar/restaurant (open in summer only) serves pizza and is a welcome change from the food that you get at most mobile beach concessions. On the Noyack end of the beach, a special section has been reserved for powerboats, and it's a popular spot from which to water-ski.

QUOGUE VILLAGE

Quogue Village Beach (ocean beach) Restrooms; bicycle path; parking with Quogue Village permit only. Located on Dune Road, this beach is accessed by the Post Lane Bridge from the Village of Quogue. Due to erosion, drive-on beach access is no longer permitted.

SAGAPONACK

Sagg Main Beach (ocean beach) Restrooms; showers; mobile concession stand; parking with Southampton Town resident or nonresident permit, or $20 per day weekdays only (but very few daily permits sold; no daily parking weekends or holidays). Sagg Main Beach, on the ocean at the end of Sagaponack Main Road, is reached by passing through the sleepy village of Sagaponack. There are no designer boutiques here, just the local general store, where the food is homemade and excellent. Have the proprietors prepare a picnic lunch and head for the beach for a delightful al fresco repast.

SAG HARBOR VILLAGE

Havens Beach (bay beach) Restrooms; lifeguard; picnic tables and grills; children's play area; parking with Sag Harbor Village permit, or $10 per day. Located on Bay Street in Sag Harbor Village, Havens Beach is part of the former Frank C. Havens estate. There are benches where you can watch the children playing on the sandy beach and the pleasure boats bobbing in the water beyond.

SOUTHAMPTON VILLAGE

Southampton Village beaches stretch from Mecox Bay to the Shinnecock Inlet, an unbroken line of broad, white, splendid sand. The village does not require permits for all of its beaches, but pay close attention to the signs, as the authorities are very strict about where you park. In general, permits are required for all beach access points, including short street ends (an exception is an area near South Main Beach, where a few complimentary parking spots are still available, but read the signs carefully); specific parking spots are clearly marked. The village police patrol the beach parking lots regularly and will definitely give you a ticket or have your car towed if you are parked illegally. My advice is to go early. There are many more street ends than the ones identified here.

Coopers Beach (ocean beach) 268 Meadow Ln. Southampton. Restrooms; concession stand; parking with Southampton Village permit, or $40 per day. Located at the end of

Coopers Neck Lane, this is the main public beach for Southampton Village. It's a favorite with the high school crowd, and an excellent restaurant opened here in the summer of 2009 called Serenity at Coopers Beach, offering lobster bakes for $26.50 and much more.

Dune Beach (ocean beach) Restrooms; handicapped access; parking with Southampton Village permit. Located in Southampton Village, this beach is toward the end of Dune Road, almost to the Shinnecock Inlet. There is a wooden deck for picnics and a board-walk to the ocean over the seagrass-covered dunes.

Old Town Beach (ocean beach) About 30 parking spaces, no permit required. Old Town Beach is uncrowded, perfect for relaxed reading or quiet contemplation. This is not a young person's beach; there are no restrooms or food facilities.

South Main Beach (ocean beach) A small number of spaces (about 15) at the far end of the Agawam parking lot beside Agawam Lake are no-permit-required; permit required for rest of spaces by Southampton Beach Club and Agawam Lake. There's no lifeguard on duty here, and no concession stand, but there are porta-potties, and, best of all, dogs are permitted on the beach and plastic bags are provided for cleanup. This beach is located at the south end of Agawam Lake, next to the Southampton Beach Club.

SPRINGS

Louse Point (bay beach) Boat launch; parking with East Hampton Town permit. At the end of Louse Point Road you will find a two-sided beach separating Napeague Bay from Accabonac Harbor. Locals say, "Please don't tell anyone about Louse Point. The tourists will come." The harborside is picturesque, dotted with marshy islands filled with birds—a favorite place for egrets, cranes, and osprey. At one time, the area fostered a rich oyster bed.

Maidstone Park Beach (bay beach) Restrooms; lifeguard; baseball field; picnic area; pavilion; parking with East Hampton Town permit. Maidstone Park Beach is one of the all-time great places to watch a sunset. The long, broad, sandy beach hugs the jetty into Three Mile Harbor; it is an excellent spot for watching the yachts go by. Anglers find the fish are plentiful off the jetty.

WATER MILL

Flying Point Beach (ocean beach) Restrooms; lifeguard; mobile concession stand; parking with Southampton Town resident or nonresident permit only. One of the most popular beaches in the Hamptons is located on the ocean on Flying Point Road. On the way there, alongside Mecox Bay, you'll see baymen with handheld nets, plucking fish from the rich waters.

WESTHAMPTON BEACH VILLAGE

Westhampton Beach Village maintains some of the finest beaches along the Atlantic Ocean, but village parking permits are required, and they're generally restricted to residents. They're free to taxpayers and can be purchased by residents of Remsenburg, Quiogue, and Speonk. Even those who walk or bicycle to the beach must have a walk-on pass (obtained from the village offices) or a photo ID with a local address.

Lashley Pavilion (ocean beach) Restrooms; showers; mobile concession; parking with Westhampton Beach Village permit only. Lashley Pavilion is located at the western end of Dune Road. This beach generally handles the overflow from Rogers, although some people prefer it for its quieter crowd.

Rogers Pavilion (ocean beach) Restrooms; lifeguard; concession stand; handicapped access; parking with Westhampton Beach Village permit. Rogers Pavilion is located at the end of the Beach Lane Bridge on Village Beach. At the excellent concession stand, they have fresh fruit, and the sandwiches are made with fresh, local produce.

BICYCLING

With miles of flat, paved roads, this is a cyclist's paradise. Although Montauk Highway has a broad, paved shoulder that is frequently used by bicyclists, in-line skaters, and joggers, the back roads offer the least traveled byways for leisurely cycling. The bayside roads tend to be hillier than those near the beach. This writer's favorite short cycling trip is along Dune Road in Southampton, with outrageous mansions on the ocean side and a rich, marshy bird habitat on the bay side. Another favorite trip is to start in Bridgehampton and ride past the potato fields and horse farms of Sagaponack, continuing through the village of Wainscott and then on to East Hampton.

There's an excellent guide to bicycling the Hamptons, *Short Bike Rides on Long Island*, by Phil Angelillo (1998, 5th ed., Globe Pequot Press), which includes about eight trips throughout the Hamptons, with maps and explicit directions. The chambers of commerce in East Hampton and Southampton have maps and information that include several suggested bicycle rides as well.

When bicycling through a village, be sure to observe the signs. In East Hampton Village, for example, bicycling is not permitted on the sidewalks in the main business district, but it is permitted on the street. In Southampton Village, bicycling is not permitted in the main business district, either on the streets or the sidewalks. If you plan to rent a bicycle, remember to call ahead. Shops often run out of rental bicycles early in the day.

Rotations Bicycle Center (631-283-2890) in Southampton sponsors diverse and interesting weekend group bicycle rides for beginners, intermediate cyclists, and racing enthusiasts.

The following shops have bicycles to rent, generally fairly basic models (12 speeds or less), unless otherwise noted.

AMAGANSETT
Amagansett Beach & Bicycle (631-267-6325; www.amagansettbeachco.com; 624 Montauk Hwy. at Cross Hwy.; Mailing Address: P.O. Box 2483, Amagansett, NY 11930; open daily except Wed.) English, hybrid, mountain, and children's bicycles, $15/ hour, $30/ day, $100/ week; road bikes $24/hour; $50/day; $150/week.

EAST HAMPTON
Bermuda Bikes (631-324-6688; www.bermudabikes.com; 36 Gingerbread Ln., East Hampton, NY 11937; open daily except Wed.) Owners: Kent and Pam McDonald. $20/hour, $30/day, $120/week.

MONTAUK
Montauk Bike Shop (631-668-8975; www.montaukbikeshop.com; 725A Montauk Hwy.; mailing address: P.O. Box 2208, Montauk, NY 11954; open daily) Owner: Chris Pfund. $14/ hour, $25/ day; $85/week.
Plaza Surf & Sport (631-668-9300; www.plazasurfnsport.com; 716 Main St./P.O. Box

5087, Montauk, NY 11954; open daily) Owners: Peter and Diane Ferraro. Bicycles: $14/hour; $25/day; $85/week; mopeds: $55/two hours, $75/four hours; $85/ day.

SAG HARBOR

BikeHampton (631-725-7329; www.bikehampton.com; 36 Main St., Sag Harbor, NY 11963; open daily) Owner: Dave Krum. Hybrid bikes: $10/hour, $35/ day; road and mountain bikes $45/day.

SOUTHAMPTON

Rotations (631-283-2890; www.rotationsbicyclecenter.com; 32 Windmill Ln., Southampton, NY 11968; open daily except Wed.) Hybrid bikes: $12/two hours; $19/four hours; $30/day, $120/week; pro road bikes $50/day.

BOATING AND WATER SPORTS

There are more than 80,000 boats on Long Island's network of waterways every year. The quiet, tranquil bays between the North and South Forks or between the sandy barrier bar and the South Fork along the ocean provide many opportunities to fish, sail, participate in a variety of water sports, take a cruise, or just bob quietly while soaking up the sun. Many marinas provide daily, weekly, and monthly moorage. In addition, boats can be rented, either for group charter or on daily, scheduled sails. Fishing charters and excursions are also readily available (see "Fishing & Shellfishing," this chapter).

Boating

Group Excursions

VIKING FLEET
631-668-5700
www.vikingfleet.com
West Lake Dr., Montauk
Mailing Address: RD 1, Box 259, Montauk, NY 11954
Summer excursions to Block Island, Martha's Vineyard, and New London.
Rates: Block Island and New London: adults $40 one way/$75 round trip; children 5–12 $25 one way/$40 round trip; children under 5 free; bicycles $7/$10. Martha's Vineyard: adults $75 one way/$120 round trip; children 5–12 $40 one way/$60 round trip; children under 5 free; bicycles $7/$10. Whale watching $49 adults, $19 children.

The Viking Ferry in Montauk offers several delightful options for boating excursions, including daily trips to Block Island, Rhode Island, on high-speed ferries, which leave every day in summer at 9 and 3:30 and leave Block Island for the return trip at 11:30 and 5:00. This trip takes about an hour each way and allows almost 6 hours on the island (an excellent place for biking and hiking). A less frequent sunset trip to New London, Connecticut, leaves at 7 PM and returns about 9 PM. There are also once-a-year trips to Martha's Vineyard, and whale-watching tours in migrating season.

Launching Ramps & Public Marinas

Towns provide many launching ramps in this boat-oriented area, but they also require permits to use the ramps and to park. Contact town offices for requirements and maps showing locations of launching ramps. In addition, several of the towns provide marinas for transient use, sometimes for a fee and, in other cases, on a complimentary basis.

The **Town of East Hampton** (631-324-4142) has about 100 marina spaces available every season, but seldom on an overnight basis. Applications for space must be made to the Town Trustees, and then space is assigned at various locations throughout the town. Fees vary. Call the East Hampton harbormaster (631-329-3078) for other inquiries.

The **Village of Sag Harbor** (631-725-2368) operates a marina at Marine Park on Bay Street in the village. There are slips for yachts, cruisers, and sailboats, and some of the largest yachts in the world dock here in the summer. Rates are $1.25 per foot for three hours or less or $5 per foot for overnight moorage, plus $15 for electric hookup. No reservations are taken—it's first come, first moored.

The **Shinnecock Canal County Marina** (631-852-8291) is run by the Suffolk County Parks and Recreation Department. It offers approximately 50 slips during the season. Stays are limited to two weeks or less. There are electric hookups, sanitary facilities, and showers. Rates are $40/day on weekdays, $45/day on weekends for Suffolk County residents with a Green Key Card; $60/day on weekdays, $70/day on weekends for nonresidents. The marina is located at the Shinnecock Canal, Hampton Bays.

The **Town of Southampton** (631-283-6000) offers town marina space in several areas, but acceptance is by lottery, and price is about $10/foot.

The **Village of Westhampton Beach** (631-288-9496) maintains Stevens Park Municipal Yacht Basin, on Library Avenue in the village, for public use. There are daily, weekly, monthly, and full-season rates and municipal launching ramps. The fees range from $75/day for less than 25 feet to $150/day for a 50-foot boat, plus $10/day for electric hookup. In addition, there are a limited number of boat parking spaces by the car parking lot behind Main Street. These are complimentary, but are limited to two hours during the day and three hours at night.

Private Marinas

The Hamptons have a variety of private marinas where boats can be moored. The following are only a few of those accepting transient travelers.

EAST HAMPTON

East Hampton Point Marina (631-324-8400; 295 Three Mile Harbor Rd., East Hampton, NY 11937) Restrooms; showers; laundry; pool; tennis; ship store; complimentary continental breakfast; van service. Rental cottages and a fine restaurant on premises with deck for watching spectacular sunsets; other restaurants within walking distance. 58 slips.

Gardiner's Marina (631-324-5666; 35 Three Mile Harbor Rd., East Hampton, NY 11937) Restrooms; showers; electric hookup. 45 slips. Operated by Seacoast Enterprises.

Halsey's Marina (631-324-5666; ; 73 Three Mile Harbor Rd., East Hampton, NY 11937) Restrooms; showers; laundry; electric hookup; wireless Internet access. 40 slips. Operated by Seacoast Enterprises.

The Harbor Marina of East Hampton (631-324-5666; 423 Three Mile Harbor Rd., East Hampton, NY 11937) Restrooms; showers; beach; electric hookup; repair shop; gas; fishing supplies; gift shop; full pumping service "no discharge" marina. Fine restaurant and bar on the premises; spectacular views. 100 slips. Operated by Seacoast Enterprises.

Maidstone Harbor Marina (631-324-2651; 313 Three Mile Harbor Rd., East Hampton, NY

11937) Restrooms; showers; pool. Fine restaurant on premises; other restaurants within walking distance. 100 slips.

HAMPTON BAYS

Hampton Watercraft & Marina (631-728-0922; 44 Newtown Rd., Hampton Bays, NY 11946) Restrooms; electric hookups. 106 slips.

Jackson's Marina (631-728-4220; 6 Tepee St., Hampton Bays, NY 11946) Restrooms; showers; electric hookups; cable TV; fishing supplies; repairs; gas. 200 slips.

MONTAUK

Gone Fishing Marina (631-668-3232; 467 East Lake Dr., Montauk, NY 11954) Small shop on premises. 180 slips; great seafood restaurant on premises.

Montauk Marine Basin (631-668-5900; 426 West Lake Dr.; Mailing Address: P.O. Box 610, Montauk, NY 11954) Restrooms; showers; electric hookups; charter boats; fishing equipment. About 25 slips.

Montauk Yacht Club Resort Marina (631-668-3100; 32 Star Island Rd., Montauk, NY 11954) Restrooms; showers; laundry; three pools; tennis; fully equipped health club, cable TV. Two restaurants, lounge, bar. 232 slips.

Star Island Yacht Club & Marina (631-668-5052; Star Island Rd., Montauk, NY 11954) Restrooms; showers; laundry; pool; picnic area; fishing charters; fishing supplies; bar and grill. Weekend entertainment, including dancing. About 160 slips.

Uihlein's Marina (631-668-3799; 444 West Lake Dr. Ext., Montauk, NY 11954) Showers. Many restaurants and shops within walking distance. 10 slips.

West Lake Fishing Lodge (631-668-5600; 352 West Lake Dr., Montauk, NY 11954) Restrooms; showers; charter boats; fishing supplies. Bar and restaurant. 100 slips.

SAG HARBOR

Sag Harbor Cove Yacht Club East & West (631-725-3939 and 631-725-1605; 50 West Water St., Sag Harbor, NY 11963) Restrooms; showers; laundry; cable TV; access to pool. Many restaurants and shops within walking distance. 84 slips.

Mill Creek Marina (631-725-1351; 3253 Noyac Rd., Sag Harbor, NY 11963) Restrooms; showers; gas; kayak rentals; excellent restaurant on premises. 140 slips.

Waterfront Marina (631-725-3886; 1A Bay St., Sag Harbor, NY 11963) Restrooms; showers. Many shops and restaurants within walking distance. 75 slips.

Canoeing & Kayaking

In a serene pond shaded by overhanging trees, you sit quietly in your canoe as you watch a crane feeding. Suddenly, a graceful osprey swoops to the water, dives, and emerges with a fish in its talons, then departs. This image is the reason that canoeing and kayaking are so popular in the Hamptons. There are hundreds of secluded, interconnecting ponds, streams, and bays in which these and other images appear again and again.

Local groups often sponsor nature trips to visit bird and animal sanctuaries. The trips are educational, interesting, and fun. Check the local newspapers for expeditions sponsored by the Group for the East End and the Nature Conservancy.

Amagansett Beach & Bicycle (631-267-6325; www.amagansettbeachco.com; 624 Montauk Hwy. at Cross Hwy., Amagansett, NY 11930) Rents kayaks: single kayaks $40/half-day, $60/full day; double kayaks $60/half-day, $80/full day.

Mill Creek Kayaks (631-725-4712 or 631-725-1351; Mill Creek Marina, 3253 Noyac Rd., Sag Harbor, NY 11963) In addition to standard kayak rentals, this great company offers ecology, sunset, and kids' kayak tours. A child's tour, for example, features a treasure hunt complete with bandannas, swords, and clues for finding a buried treasure. Single kayaks $16/hour, $35/three hours; double kayaks $20/hour, $42/three hours.

Flying Point Surf School (631-885-6607; www.flyingpointsurfschool.com; 116 North Sea Rd., Southampton, NY 11968; open daily 10 AM–6 PM, rest of the year fewer days and shorter hours) Owner: Shane Dyckman. You can purchase canoes, surfboards, kayaks, and all the beach and boating accessories to go with them at their sister shops in Southampton and Sag Harbor, but for rentals, instruction, and expeditions, this is the place. Rentals: $55/half-day, $85/full day. They offer a number of kayak and stand-up paddleboard excursions to local bays and estuaries. A two-hour expedition is $150.

Main Beach Surf & Sport (631-537-2716; www.mainbeach.com; 352 Montauk Hwy., Wainscott, NY 11975) Owner: Lars Svanberg. Rents canoes and kayaks for individual use or for organized excursions. Main Beach is located across the street from the northern tip of Georgica Pond. The pond provides a delightful paddle past the Creeks, one of the great estates of the Hamptons, as well as many other fabulous estates. The rich, marshy borders of the pond are feeding grounds for a variety of birds. Single kayaks $55/half-day, $85/full day; double kayaks and canoes $70/half-day, $90/full day.

Plaza Surf & Sport (631-668-9300; www.plazasurfnsport.com; 716 Main St., Montauk, NY 11954) Rents kayaks: single kayaks $40/four hours, $50/full day; double kayaks $50/four hours, $60/full day.

Puff & Putt (631-668-4473; 659 Main St., Montauk, NY 11954) Owners: Joe and Peter Cucci. Rents canoes, rowboats, and pedal boats for use on Fort Pond. Canoes, single kayaks, pedal boats $18/half-hour, $30/hour; double kayaks $20/half-hour, $35/hour; stand-up paddleboards are $30/hour.

Windsurfing Hamptons (631-283-9483; www.w-surf.com; 1686 North Hwy. (Rte. 27) Southampton, NY 11968) Not just a wind surfing destination, you can also rent kayaks. Single kayaks $48/two hour; $65/half-day; $90/full day. Double kayaks $60/two hours; $85/half-day; $110/full day. Kayak lesson are available also at $120 for a two-hour lesson.

Sailing

Sailing is as popular in the bays and lakes of the Hamptons as it is in Narragansett and San Francisco bays. Headwinds make the bays ideal for sailboat racing. Favorite local places to sail are Mecox Bay in Bridgehampton, Napeague Bay off Lazy Point, and Quantuck Bay in Quogue.

For sailboat rentals and instruction, there are only a few options available. (It's the insurance, we're told.)

Puff & Putt (631-668-4473; 659 Main St., Montauk, NY 11954) Owners: Joe and Peter Cucci. Rents sailboats, such as Sunfish ($30/hour), Hobie cats ($40/hour), 15-foot Dayfish ($40/hour), for use on Fort Pond; they also rent pedal boats ($30/hour), as well as canoes and kayaks (see entry in above section) and stand-up paddleboards ($30/hour). For landlubbers, there's an 18-hole miniature golf course and a video room.

Sag Harbor Sailing School (631-725-5100; www.sailsagharbor.com; 57 Pine Neck Ave., off Noyac Rd.; mailing address: P.O. Box 899, Sag Harbor, NY 11963) There's a full range of

You can rent pedal boats or sailboats at Puff & Putt in Montauk for use on Fort Pond.

classes at this excellent school, from a four-day beginners' basic keelboat course for young adults 11 to 16, to an adult racing course. Private instruction is $75/hour for one student, $100/hour for two. They also rent a 23-foot, a 27-foot, and a 34-foot Catalina. Weekday rates for the 23-foot sloop run $250/half-day, $350/full day; sunset cruise, $200. The 27-foot Catalina rents for $395/day, and the 34-footer rents for $495/day. Captains are available on a half-day basis for $100 and full day for $150.

Uihlein's (631-668-3799; www.uihleinsmarina.com; 444 West Lake Dr. Ext.; mailing address: P.O. Box 357, Montauk, NY 11954) Rents boats ranging from a 16-foot skiff to a 26-foot fishing boat.

Water Sports

Surfing and Stand-up Paddleboarding

Surfing has emerged as one of the most popular and practiced sports in the Hamptons in the summer—witness the surfers out at 6 AM along Dune Road in Westhampton Beach or at Ditch Plains Beach in Montauk, and the tremendously popular classes that take place on Southampton beaches. (But be aware that no surfing is allowed within 100 feet of public-bathing beaches.) Although the waves may not equal the height or intensity of those pounding Hawaii's shores, they provide challenging and exhilarating rides, especially after storms. Hamptons surfing has gained such acclaim that the U.S. Surfing Association has considered holding the U.S. Amateur Surfing Championships at Ditch Plains.

Stand-up paddleboarding has also captured the hearts of Hamptonites. You can ride the waves on one, or use one to do flatwater touring. It offers an incredible cardio workout. You will find lots of options for renting them and for lessons.

Amagansett Beach & Bicycle (631-267-6325; www.amagansettbeachco.com; 624 Montauk Hwy., Amagansett; mailing address: P.O. Box 2483, Amagansett, NY 11930) Rents surfboards: $25/half-day; $35/full day. Paddleboards: $60/half-day; $80/full day. Boogie boards $15/half-day; $25/full day.

Flying Point Surf School (631-283-1507 or 631-287-7834; www.flyingpointsurfschool.com; 116 North Sea Rd., Southampton, NY 11968) Owner: Shane Dyckman. Experienced and knowledgeable instructors will guide even the most novice beginners in the art of surfing and paddleboarding. Surfboards rent for $40–$50/day, while stand-up paddleboards are $100/day. Private surf classes for all ages start at $125 for a 90-minute class; a paddleboarding lesson runs $150 for a 90-minute class. The school has a summer surf camp ($125/day; $500/four days; $600/five days) and also leads paddleboard expeditions throughout the summer months to such serene spots as Conscience Point, Morton Wildlife Refuge, and Mecox Bay for $150/person for a two-hour trip.

Main Beach (631-537-2716; www.mainbeach.com; 352 Montauk Hwy., Wainscott, NY 11975) Owner: Lars Svanberg. This store provides one-stop shopping for surfers, wind surfers, stand-up paddleboarders and all those who enjoy water-related sports. In addition to providing a daily surf report (631-537-SURF), Main Beach rents and sells surfboards, boogie boards, paddleboards, canoes, and kayaks. Surfboard rentals are $40 or $50/day; bodyboards $25/day; paddleboards $75/day; and stand-up paddleboards $100/day. Surfing instruction runs $150 for 90 minutes and there's a terrific Kids Surf Academy for ages 7–15. A 90-minute stand-up paddleboard class is $150.

Plaza Surf & Sport (631-668-9300; www.plazasurfnsport.com; 716 Main St.; mailing address: P.O. Box 5087, Montauk, NY 11954) Rents surfboards, fins, and a variety of other sporting equipment. Surfboards $20/half-day, $30/day; surfboard and wetsuit combo $40 full or half-day; stand-up paddleboards $35/day; boogie boards $6/day.

Sunrise to Sunset (631-283-2929; 36 Hill St., Southampton, NY 11968) Rents surfboards and boogie boards. Surfboards $50/24-hour day; boogie boards $10/day.

Windsurfing Hamptons (631-283-9483; www.w-surf.com; 1686 North Hwy. (Rte. 27) Southampton, NY 11968) This organization offers surfboard and stand-up paddleboard rental and lessons, as well as wind surfing. Surfboard rental: $30/two hours; $40/half-day; $60/full day; individual one-hour surfing instruction $100. Stand-up paddleboard rental: $35/one hour; $50/two hour; $80/half day; $90/full day; one-hour stand-up paddleboard lesson is $100.

Scuba Diving and Skin Diving

For those who like to dive for sunken treasure or explore shipwrecks, many underwater opportunities quietly await in the waters surrounding the Hamptons. Shipwrecks dot the ocean floor from Amagansett to the Montauk Lighthouse, but some of the finest diving is farther offshore. About 40 miles off Montauk lies the wreck of the *Andrea Doria*, which sank in 1956 after a collision with the *Stockholm*. Because of its depth and poor visibility, however, this is considered a very dangerous dive. Wrecks of numerous other ships, though, are much safer.

There are less hazardous diving sites in Napeague Bay and off Block Island, as well as on the South Shore near the Shinnecock Inlet and the Ponquogue Bridge. Visibility is good along the South Shore, where divers can see tropical fish in the summer and other fish and shellfish year-round.

One must take a course and become certified in order to scuba dive; the course usually takes about four weeks. (For schools on the North Fork, see chapter 9.)

Sea Turtle Dive Charters (631-335-6323 or 631-725-0565; www.seaturtlecharters.com; 76 Swamp Rd., East Hampton, NY 11937) Captain and owner of this charter service, Chuck Wade, and his crew will take experienced divers on a variety of high-drama dives locally and as far away as Block Island. Explore local reef or deep-water wrecks, or, for the truly adventurous, there are shark dives that take place in the warm water near the Gulf Stream (about 15–30 miles away); divers descend in a two-person cage about 3–7 feet below the surface. Overnight trips and shark-and-wreck combos also available. Price: Wreck dives range from $100–$220, depending on distance; shark dives run $200–$300; overnight trips run $300–$450.

Weight-N-Sea Scuba School (631-329-9073) Run by certified PADI instructor Paul Casciotta, this school gives lessons in open-water and rescue diving, either in a group or individually. Lessons generally take place on Fort Pond Bay in Montauk from May to November. Paul is an experienced diver who knows the local waters. He takes people in his small, two-person boat to nearby dive sites, such as the old World War II navy dock in Fort Pond Bay.

Waterskiing, Wind Surfing, & Jet Skiing

Waterskiing is permitted in Noyack Bay at Foster Memorial beach. The Town of East Hampton also has designated a section of Three Mile Harbor, from Settlers Landing at the end of Hands Creek Road to Sammy's Beach, for waterskiing. Within Three Mile Harbor, the water is generally glassy smooth.

Amagansett Beach & Bicycle (631-267-6325; www.amagansettbeachco.com; 624 Montauk Hwy.; mailing address: P.O. Box 2483, Amagansett, NY 11930) You can rent wind surfing equipment here for a terrific trip across Napeague Bay. $60/half-day; $80/full day.

East End Jet Ski (631-728-728-8060 or 631-728-0286; 9 Canoe Place Rd., Hampton Bays, NY 11946; open summer only, Fri.–Mon.) Just off the beaches of Shinnecock Bay in Hampton Bays at the Mariner's Cove Marine, one- or two-person Jet Skis are available for rent. The rate is $75/half-hour and includes instruction and fitted life preserver. Plenty of thrills are available at speeds up to 40 mph.

Main Beach (631-537-2716; www.mainbeach.com; 352 Montauk Hwy., Wainscott, NY 11975; open daily 10-6) Owner: Lars Svanberg. This store provides one-stop shopping for surfers, wind surfers, stand-up paddleboarders and all those who enjoy water-related sports. In the summer, an affiliate (call 808-268-3400 and ask for Luke) sets up a satellite mobile wind surfing shop with rental equipment at Lazy Point Beach on Napeague Harbor.

Uihlein's Marina (631-668-3799; www.uihleinsmarina.com; 444 West Lake Dr. Ext., mailing address: P.O. Box 357, Montauk, NY 11954) Jet Skis can be rented here for $95/half-hour, $160/hour; in addition, ski boats and skis for up to four people can be rented for skiing on Lake Montauk, $175/hour, $275/two hours, $375/three hours, $575/full day. This price includes wakeboards, tubes, life jackets, and other safety equipment—whatever you need to make your time on the water safe and enjoyable.

Windsurfing Hamptons (631-283-9463; www.w-surf.com; 1686 North Hwy. (Rte. 27), Southampton, NY 11968) Wind surf rental $55/two-hour; $80/half-day; $120/full-day; individual wind surfing instruction $185 for two hours. Sunfish rental $150/day, $240/weekend, $300/week; Sunfish instruction $120 for two hours.

EQUESTRIAN ACTIVITIES

Horseback Riding

DEEP HOLLOW RANCH
631-668-2744
www.deephollowranch.com
Montauk Hwy., Montauk
Mailing Address: P.O. Box 835, Montauk, NY 11954
Open: Year-round
Rates: $75/one-and-a-half-hour, 6-mile trail and beach ride; $65 one-hour ride (no beach); $35 half-hour ride (no beach); pony rides $7; ask about riding lessons.
Directions: Montauk Hwy., 3 miles east of Montauk village

The owners claim that this ranch, established in Montauk in 1658, is the oldest cattle ranch in the U.S., and thus it professes to be the home of the first American cowboys. It is still a working cattle ranch, with about 30 head of cattle and numerous horses, and there certainly are cowboys in residence. Rusty Leaver first came to the ranch in 1963 and eventually married the owner's daughter, who is a fifth-generation descendant of the family who has owned it since the 1800s. Now Rusty and Diane run the ranch. Deep Hollow Ranch offers trails on 3,000 acres that include Suffolk County and New York State parklands. You'll enjoy picturesque beach rides along Block Island Sound and rides through a countryside reminiscent of Old West movies. Groups of six to seven people leave the ranch daily on the hour; Western saddles and gear are used. Deep Hollow offers riding lessons, using both English and Western saddles. During the school year, a program called "Living History" helps students understand and appreciate the rich history of the region.

RITA'S STABLES
631-668-5453
3 West Lake Dr., Montauk
Mailing Address: 96 Benson Dr., Montauk, NY 11954
Open: Year-round
Rates: $35/half-hour trail ride, $60/1-hour trail ride; pony rides and petting farm $6
Directions: 1 mile east of Montauk village. Turn left onto West Lake Dr. at Montauk Downs sign and take first right after little white house.

Rita Foster's stable offers trail rides, pony rides, and a petting farm for children that includes sheep, goats, calves, peacocks, rabbits, chickens, ducks, and more. Inquire about group rates and the summer pony camp.

   The above stables are the only ones offering trail rides. For those who want to take lessons, especially in dressage, equitation, hunting, and jumping, the following stables offer instruction.

Deep Hollow Ranch in Montauk has been home to cowboys since 1658. Dustin Chase

Amaryllis Farm Equine Rescue (631-537-7335; www.forrascal.com; 44 Little Fresh Pond Rd., Southampton, NY 11968)

East End Stables (631-324-9568 or 631-324-9802; www.eastendstables.com; 171 Oak View Hwy., East Hampton, NY 11937)

Quantuck Bay Farm (631-288-0303; 607 Main St., Westhampton Beach, NY 11978)

Quogue Horse & Pony Farm (631-875-3042; www.ponyfarm.net; 48 Lewis Rd., East Quogue, NY 11942)

Rose Hill Farm (631-537-1919; 2045 Scuttle Hole Rd., Bridgehampton, NY 11932)

Rosewood Farm (631-287-4775; www.rosewoodfarm-shrc.com; 320 Majors Path, Southampton, NY 11968)

Swan Creek Farms (631-537-0662; 820 Halsey Ln., Bridgehampton, NY 11932)

Topping Riding School (631-537-0948; 58 Daniels Ln., Sagaponack, NY 11962)

Two Trees Stables (631-537-3881; 849 Hayground Rd., Bridgehampton, NY 11932)

Wölffer Estate Stables (631-537-2879; www.wolfferestatestables.com; 41 Narrow Lane East; mailing address: P.O.Box 604, Sagaponack, NY 11962)

Horse Show

Hampton Classic Horse Show (508-698-6810; www.hamptonclassic.com; 240 Snake Hollow Rd., Bridgehampton, NY 11932) Price: general admission, $10/person or $20/car-

load; reserved seats, $20/person bench seats in grandstand; $30/person premium cen-
ter-section. Parking is free. This incredible horse show is more than 30 years old and
has grown to become the largest hunter/jumper show in America. Located on 65 acres,
there are more than 1,500 horses exhibited and more than 60,000 spectators attend.
Equitation, jumping and hunting categories that often include riders who are Olympic
medalists, are included in the competitions in this grand classic exhibition of horse-
manship.

Polo

Bridgehampton Polo Club, Inc. (631-537-1110 or 212-421-1367; Two Trees Farm, 849
Hayground Rd., Bridgehampton, NY 11932; mailing address: c/o RZ Capital LLC, 40 E.
57th St., 23rd Fl., New York, NY 10022) Now in new facilities on the South Fork (it used
to be headquartered at the Big E in Jamesport), this private polo club holds exhibition
games from mid-July to mid-August. The games, which are played on Saturdays at 4 PM,
are open to the public for a $20/car fee (which is a tax-deductible donation to breast
cancer research). This is a terrific place to spread a blanket on the lawn and enjoy a
gourmet picnic with a bottle of Long Island wine while watching the "sport of kings." For
those who want to learn to play, clinics are sometimes offered.

Shops Devoted to Equestrian Activities

Brennan's Bit and Bridle, Inc. (631-537-0635; www.brennansbitandbridle.com; Bridgehampton Common, Plaza East, P.O. Box 1677, Bridgehampton, NY 11932; open daily in
summer 10–5; rest of year fewer days) Owners: David Boot and Lucy Batchelor. Custom
saddle makers, these highly skilled craftsmen make saddles to meet the specific needs
of each horse and rider. In addition, this is the place to come for elegant riding apparel,
including crops, boots, tack, blankets, and bridles. They also carry a good selection of
horsey gift items—a must stop for participants and attendees of the Hamptons Classic
Horse Show, which takes place just down the road.

The Tack Trunk (631-267-2013; 137 Main St., P.O. Box 1247, Amagansett, NY 11930; open
in summer Mon.–Fri. 10–5:30, Sat. 10–6, Sun. 11–4; rest of year fewer days and shorter
hours) Owner: Erica Walters. Everything the serious rider needs to be properly outfitted, including hats, boots, and riding pants, plus there's a nice selection of gifts for
horse lovers and even horse–inspired cards.

FAMILY FUN

Events and activities for children take place year-round in the Hamptons. In the spring,
summer, and fall, hikes along the beaches and nature trails, and bicycle rides along the
back roads, open a world of adventure and ideas to children's inquisitive minds. Also consult chapter 6, "Culture," for music and art classes, as well as chapter 9 for additional activities in the North Fork area. The following are just a few of the planned activities available
to children in the Hamptons.

Pathfinder Country Day Camp at Montauk (631-668-2080; www.pathfinderdaycamp.com;
Second House Rd., Montauk, NY 11954) This camp offers swimming, boating, tennis,
and crafts for children ages 4 to 12 in summer only.

Puff & Putt (631-668-4473; 659 Main St., Montauk, NY 11954) Owners: Joe and Peter

Cucci. Rents sailboats, such as Sunfish ($30/hour), Hobie cats ($40/hour), 15-ft. Day-fish ($40/hour), for use on Fort Pond; they also rent pedal boats ($30/hour), canoes and kayaks (see listing under "Canoeing & Kayaking") and stand-up paddleboards ($30/hour). For landlubbers, there's an 18-hole miniature golf course and a video room.

Quogue Wildlife Refuge (631-653-4771; www.quoguewildliferefuge.com; 3 Old Country Rd., Quogue, NY 11959) Guides lead children on well-marked trails as they explain about the animals, birds, ponds, marshes, and plants along the way. There are tame deer, hundreds of ducks, and several bird species, including an American bald eagle at the refuge. You can go on your own also, as the trails are open dawn to dusk every day. At the Nature Center (open Tuesday and Thursday 2 to 4, and Saturday and Sunday 11 to 4) you can also see rescued animals being nursed back to health.

Suffolk County Farm and Education Center (631-852-4600; www.ccesuffolk.org; 350 Yaphank Ave., Yaphank, NY 11980) The center offers a glimpse of life on a farm 100 years ago. Operated by the Cornell Cooperative Extension Service, this is a fully opera-tional farm with pigs, sheep, goats, beef cattle, and other farm animals. An 1870 hay barn is a typical example of post, beam, and peg construction and is often the starting point for hayrides (by advance reservation for groups of 10 or more). In addition, there are many, many more activities for children and the whole family. Agricultural and hor-ticultural activities and classes, marine-science classes, as well as a children's summer day camp. There are also programs incorporating family arts and crafts projects, animal care, outdoor discovery, etc. Check out all the possibilities on the Web site. If you want to just hang out on the farm, there's a grassy picnic area in the gardens. The center is free to the public and is open seven days a week from 9 AM to 3 PM. There is a fee for the classes and programs.

Fishing & Shellfishing

The Hamptons, and particularly Montauk, which is considered the "sportfishing capital of the world," is noted for outstanding fishing. Over 30 world-record fish (registered in the International Game Fish Association Record Book) have been caught at Montauk. In 1999, for example, a 617-pound bluefin tuna, in 1995 a 560-pound shark, and in 1993 a 321-pound mako were only a few of the prizes, but these were child's play compared to the 1,087-pound tiger shark and the 3,450-pound great white shark caught in 1986. Seasonal tournaments attract anglers from all over the world. Cash prizes, trophies, and world records often reward the dedicated.

Rules are distinctly different when fishing for saltwater fish as opposed to freshwater fish. As we went to press, a new state law requiring an annual $10 saltwater-fishing license was being challenged in some East End towns. Thus it's required in some areas (parts of Montauk), but not in others. Be sure to check before you go. If you're into surfcasting, you may be rewarded with the elusive but remarkable striped bass, bluefish, weakfish, floun-der, or blowfish. Some fishermen enjoy the challenge of bagging a big game fish while fish-ing offshore from a "party boat," with groups as large as 100 people, all vying for the catch of the day; others prefer a charter boat that generally takes six or fewer people; and the rest fish from their own yachts. The offshore lure is for tuna, marlin, mako, swordfish, and shark. Inshore fishing, closer to home base, will net such prizes as bluefish, striped bass, blackfish, cod, flounder, fluke, mackerel, pollack, porgy, sea bass, weakfish, and whiting.

Fishing for freshwater fish in the local ponds is a much more complicated proposition. New York State requires a fishing license, which can be obtained from any of the town offices, but you must be a resident to obtain one. With the license you'll get a state booklet advising where fishing is permitted, if you live in East Hampton Town. If, on the other hand, you want to fish in Southampton Town waters, and you are not a Southampton Town resident, there's one more step to take. Since the town trustees claim ownership over fish in local ponds, you are allowed to fish only if accompanied by a guide licensed by the trustees. Call the trustees for a list of their approved guides. For more information about the license, contact the **Town of East Hampton** (631-324-4142; www.town.east-hampton.ny.us), or **Southampton** (631-283-6000; www.southampton.ny.us). For a list of licensed guides, call the **Southampton Trustees** (631-287-5717). For excellent booklets and maps about freshwater fishing on Long Island, contact the **New York State Department of Environmental Conservation Freshwater Fisheries** (631-444-0280 or www.dec.ny.gov).

A shellfish license is required for harvesting shellfish from Hamptons waters, and the times and quantities are strictly regulated. Contact the appropriate town for a license (see telephone numbers above); you must be a resident to apply. The **New York State Department of Environmental Conservation Shellfish Fisheries** (631-444-0475) maintains a list of prohibited areas. It will also advise about pollution levels and water quality. The department operates a hotline (631-444-0480) that gives recorded information about any areas unsafe for harvesting due to storms or other temporary problems.

At the **Shellfish Hatchery** (631-668-4601), which is located off Edgemere Road in Montauk, clams, oysters, and scallops are cultivated and then seeded in nearby ponds and bays for harvesting. Group tours can be arranged with advance notice. The hatchery is operated by the Town of East Hampton.

Party Boats

Ebb Tide (631-668-2818; www.ebbtidemontauk.com; Salivar's Dock, 470 West Lake Drive, Montauk, NY 11954) *Ebb Tide* is a 65-ft. boat offering two half-day fishing trips daily for about 50 people, and night fishing some nights from 7 PM to 1 AM, for about 30 people. It has enclosed lounges, a sundeck, modern fish-finding equipment, and a knowledgeable crew. Adults $85 night trips; $50 half-day trips.

Flying Cloud (631-668-2026; www.montaukflyingcloud.com; Viking Dock, 470 West Lake Dr., Montauk, NY 11954) Captain Fred E. Bird will take up to 80 fisherpeople on fishing trips on his 70-ft. party boat. The price includes rod, tackle, bait, and anything else you might need. For half-day fishing trips, which are conducted May through July, the fare is $45 for adults, $30 for children; for full-day trips, which take place August through November, the fare is $80/adult; $75/seniors (weekdays only); $60/child. Located behind Dave's Grill.

Lazybones (631-668-5671; www.montauksportfishing.com/lazybones; Johnny Marlin's Dock, 144 Jefferson Ave., Montauk, NY 11954) Capt. Mike Vegessi offers fishing trips twice daily, mid-April through November, on a 55-ft. cruiser. The boat can accommodate 35 people and concentrates on the gentle, inshore waters. Only soda and beer are sold on board. From April to July, they look for flounder and blackfish; from July to September, the catch is fluke; from September to November, the quest is for striped bass. Adults $45: children 12 and younger $30.

Marlin VI Princess (631-668-4700; www.marlin6princess.com; Uhlein's Marina, 444 West

Lake Drive, Montauk, NY 11954) Captain Eddie Beneduci operates an 85-ft. double-deck beauty that is capable of carrying 150 passengers and cruising at speeds of up to 20 knots. Day and night fishing year-round. Winter night fishing for cod, leaving at 3 AM and returning at 4 PM, is $100 per person.

Viking Fishing Fleet (631-668-5700; www.vikingfleet.com; 462 West Lake Dr., Montauk, NY 11954) This is the largest party boat operator in Montauk. The trips range from half-day fishing for fluke, to all-night trips for bluefish and striped bass, to two-day offshore trips. Half-day trips run 8 AM to 12 noon and 1 to 5 PM. Viking boats have full restaurants on board, sun decks, and restrooms. The half-day fare for adults is $45; for children ages 5 to 12 it's $25. Full day trips cost $85 for adults and $40 for children. Fares include rod and reel. Night-fishing trips depart at 7 PM and return at 1 AM. The $85 charge for night fishing includes rod, reel, and bait. Longer fishing trips are offered as well, including a two-day swordfish trek for $600.

Charter Boats
Charter fishing boats are very sophisticated these days. They take a maximum of six passengers and are equipped with fish finders, radar, and satellite navigation. The following charter boats are piloted by experienced captains who know exactly where to find fish.

Abracadabra (631-668-5275; Montauk) Captain Ray Ruddock takes anglers on excursions for shark, tuna, marlin, bass, bluefish, weak, cod, pollack, flounder, and fluke.

Adios (631-668-5760; www.adiosboat.com; Montauk) Captain Skip Rudolph has a fully refitted 36-ft. custom Ensign with all the latest electronic fish-finders and radar; half-day, full day, inshore, and offshore.

Alyssa Ann (631-668-1051; www.alyssaannsportfishing.com; Montauk) Astounding record-sized fish have been caught aboard this beauty, which can cruise at 20 knots. Captain Charlie Mayrer takes customers on inshore and offshore trips, and even offers special long-range trips for giant cod, pollack, and hake, which like to hide in the wrecks of ships.

Blue Fin IV (631-668-9323; www.bluefiniv.com; Montauk) This custom-built 41-ft. Montauk sportfishing boat has sophisticated electronics and a large cabin and is piloted by a second-generation captain, Michael Potts.

Charter Boat Montauk (631-668-2056; www.charterboatmontauk.com; Montauk) Captain

Group fishing trips are fun for the whole family.

Mike Albronda pilots a 42-ft. boat. His customers have secured some of the largest fish off Montauk.

Daybreaker (631-668-5070; www.fishdaybreaker.com; Montauk) Captain Mike Brumm pilots his 38-ft. down-east-style boat, as well as his 28-ft. McKee Craft, from Montauk to the continental shelf.

Fishhooker (631-668-3821; Montauk) Offshore and inshore charters of half-day or full-day duration on this 35-ft. custom-built J/C are captained by Otto Haselman.

Florence B (631-324-6492; Montauk) This new 35-ft. down-easter will take you to the quiet bays or offshore with Captain Jeff Picken.

Lady Grace V (631-842-0237; www.ladygracecharters.com; Montauk) Captain Mario Melito's *Lady Grace* departs from West Lake Fishing Lodge on half- or full-day trips.

Masterpiece **Charters** (631-668-3881; www.masterpiececharters.com; Montauk) This boat sails out of the Montauk Yacht Club Marina and does half- or full-day trips for striped bass and other close-to-shore fish, as well as shark and tuna trips. Captain: Mark Assogna.

Oh, Brother **Charter Boat** (631-668-2707, 800-439-0034; Montauk) Fishing offshore for shark, tuna, and marlin, or inshore for bass and bluefish is offered with Captain Robert Aaronson.

Sea Otter IV (631-668-2669; www.seaotterfishing.com; West Lake Dr. at the mouth of Montauk Harbor; mailing address: P.O. Box 938, Montauk, NY 11954) Captain: Joe Lizza.

Star Island Yacht Club & Marina (631-668-5052; Montauk) A number of fishing boats are chartered out of this marina. They'll be pleased to give you the telephone numbers of several captains.

Susie E (631-523-8862; www.susiee.com; Montauk) Half-day and full-day trips for both inshore and offshore fish.

Venture (631-668-5405; Montauk) Captain Barry Kohlus operates a 41-ft. Hatteras, built for sportfishing.

FLYING, GLIDING, SKYDIVING

Except for the Wright brothers' first flight, most of the historic events in aviation history took place on Long Island. Glenn Curtiss experimented with his "pusher plane" in Garden City in 1909 and steadily expanded his company, building record-breaking racing planes during the 1920s. Charles Lindbergh launched his famous *Spirit of St. Louis* in 1927 from Long Island's Roosevelt Field, giving Long Island the title "the cradle of aviation." In the 1940s Grumman Aircraft Engineering Corporation, headed by Leroy Grumman, who grew up in Huntington watching Curtiss aircraft spiraling through the skies, became a major military-aircraft manufacturer. Today, although little aircraft manufacturing remains on Long Island, flying, gliding, and skydiving are enjoyed as recreational activities.

Flying

Sound Aircraft Flight Enterprises (631-537-2202; East Hampton Airport, Wainscott, NY 11975) Sight-seeing rides for up to three people, $175/ hour; instruction available.

Sky Sailors Glider School (631-288-5858; Francis S. Gabreski Airport, Westhampton Beach, NY 11978) This school will take you on an L-19 Bird Dog ride, where you'll experience the nostalgia of flying in a WWII–Vietnam-era plane. $150 for 20-minute ride.

Gliding

Sky Sailors Glider School (631-288-5858; www.skysailors.com; Francis S. Gabreski Airport, Westhampton Beach, NY 11978) Birds do it and so can you. If you've never taken a glider flight, you are missing a fabulous experience. Half-hour Golden Eagle introductory glider flight (with licensed pilot at the controls), $199/one person, $250/two persons; lesson and ride $250/one person.

Skydiving

Skydive Long Island (631-208-3900, 631-878-5867; www.skydivelongisland.com or www.skydivenewyork.net; Calverton Enterprise Park, off Grumman Blvd., Calverton, NY 11933) This was the first jump center on Long Island. Owner Ray Maynard has made over 3,000 jumps himself and has operated this school for almost 20 years. You can participate in a tandem jump (with an instructor) for $225 on weekends, and if you want it videotaped and photographed, it's $345; or $210 on weekdays and $330 with video. Subsequent tandems with video and still photos are $305.

Sky Sailors Glider School (631-288-5858; www.skysailors.com; Francis S. Gabreski Airport, Westhampton Beach, NY 11978) Sky Sailors has expanded its operation to offer skydiving as well as glider rides. A tandem dive for one person (with instructor) is $250.

GOLF

Much of golf's early history in the U.S. took place in the Hamptons. The first golf course (only six holes) was laid out on a lawn in Yonkers in 1888, but the Hamptons were not far behind. In 1891 the Shinnecock Hills Golf Club in Southampton became the first incorporated golf club in America and the first professionally planned course in the U.S. The 12-hole course was laid out by the Scottish golfer Willie Dunn Jr., who patterned it after those in his native Scotland. In 1931 it was lengthened by William Flynn. The exquisite clubhouse was designed by the renowned firm of McKim, Mead, and White and was completed in 1892—the first clubhouse in America. Furthermore, this was the first golf club in America to admit women to full membership. In 1896 the Shinnecock Hills Golf Club hosted the second U.S. Open and the U.S. Amateur Championship. The Open was held here again in 1986, 1995, and 2004.

Other clubs were not far behind. The Maidstone Club in East Hampton was established in 1890 as a tennis club, but soon had its own 18-hole golf course. The National Golf Links of America, in Southampton, was established in 1908, along the lines of St. Andrew's in Scotland.

Most golf in the Hamptons is still played on private courses. If you're lucky enough to belong to one of the private clubs or have friends who do, have a great time! Otherwise, the following courses are open to the general public. (For courses on the North Fork and Shelter Island, consult the listings in chapters 9 and 10.)

BARCELONA NECK

631-725-2503
683 Barcelona Point Rd. (off Rte. 114), bet. East Hampton and Sag Harbor
Mailing Address: Sag Harbor Golf Club, Golf Club Rd., Sag Harbor, NY 11963
Open: Year-round, dawn to dusk

Size: 9 holes; par 35; 2,475 yards
Rates: $16 weekdays; $24 weekends
Directions: 1 mile south of Sag Harbor on Rte. 114

This course, which is managed by the Sag Harbor Golf Club, has a small clubhouse that sells soft drinks, beer, snacks, and hamburgers and hot dogs. The land is owned by the Nature Conservancy and is also laced with hiking trails. Soft-spike shoes only, please.

MONTAUK DOWNS GOLF COURSE

631-668-5000; golf reservations 631-668-1234
www.montaukdowns.org
50 S. Fairview Ave., Montauk, NY 11954 (in Montauk Downs State Park)
Open: Year-round except Christmas, sunrise–sunset
Size: 18 holes; par 72; 6,860/6,402 yards
Rates: New York State residents: $46 weekends and holidays; $41 weekdays; $27 twilight weekends and holidays; $24 weekdays. New York State seniors: $27 daytime; $18 twilight. Out-of-state residents: $92 weekends and holidays; $82 weekdays; $54 twilight weekends and holidays; $48 weekdays.
Directions: 1 mile east of Montauk village. From Montauk Hwy., turn left onto West Lake Dr. and follow signs to Montauk Downs on left.

The Shinnecock Hills Golf Club hosted the U.S. Open in 1896, 1986, 1995, and again in 2004.

This golf course, within Montauk Downs State Park, is a rare state treasure. Built in the 1920s by Carl Fisher as part of his grand scheme to turn Montauk into the "Miami of the North," the golf course was redesigned in the 1960s by Robert Trent Jones and Rees Jones, and in 2009 it was being redesigned yet again by Rees Jones. This has been rated one of the finest public courses in the U.S. There are four courses, ranging from 5,787 yards to 6,976. You'll find lockers, showers, pro shop, resident pro, and much more; instruction is available. The restaurant, Fairway East (631-668-2089) located in the clubhouse, serves breakfast and lunch. Six tennis courts and two swimming pools (an Olympic-sized and a kiddie pool) complete the facility.

POXABOGUE GOLF COURSE AND DRIVING RANGE

631-537-0025
www.poxgolf.com
Montauk Hwy., Bridgehampton
Mailing Address: P.O. Box 890, Wainscott, NY 11975
Open: Apr.–Sept., 7 AM–6 PM
Size: 9 holes; par 30; 1,706 yards
Rates: Golf course: resident: $20 Mon.–Fri., $30 Sat. and Sun.; nonresident: $30 Mon.–Fri.; $40 Sat. and Sun.; lower fees for seniors and juniors; early-bird and twilight specials; driving range: $8/1 bucket of 55 balls, $15/2 buckets, $20/3 buckets, $25/4 buckets.
Directions: Montauk Hwy., 2 miles east of Bridgehampton.

Poxabogue Golf Course includes a pro shop and a driving range that is especially appreciated by those with limited time; it has six par-3 and three par-4 holes. Now jointly owned by the Towns of East Hampton and Southampton, and operated by Long Island Golf Management, this course, which had an uncertain future a few years ago, seems to be on top of its game now.

HIKING & RUNNING

Hiking trails are described in "Parks and Nature Preserves," below. *Short Nature Walks on Long Island* (2001, 7th ed., Globe Pequot Press), by Rodney and Priscilla Albright, lists 14 walks on the South Fork, with maps and specific directions.

Jogging and running are also favorite pastimes in the Hamptons. Montauk Highway's broad shoulder attracts many joggers, as do the side roads. Local high schools also have running tracks that are available for public use when school is not in session.

PARKS & NATURE PRESERVES

The Hamptons are blessed with an enlightened and environmentally aware population, both among the permanent and the summer residents. The Nature Conservancy, a national environmental organization, owns many areas in the Hamptons, and because of its perseverance, we can walk along trails that skirt marshes and dunes and overlook bays and the ocean, realizing we would not have the privilege had its members not persevered. The Nature Conservancy publishes a pamphlet, *The Nature Conservancy South Fork Shelter Island Preserve Guide* (1990), describing each of its properties; it is available at most bookstores and chamber of commerce offices. The organization owns or manages 26 preserves on the

South Fork and is responsible, along with the Group for the East End and the Peconic Land Trust, for the preservation of some 150,000 acres of open space and farmland on Long Island, including about 8,000 acres on the South Fork.

Because of the sensitive nature of the land and its plant and animal inhabitants, many areas are open to the public only via guided tours. Listed here are a few of the areas in which visitors are welcomed throughout the year. For more areas, watch for announcements in local newspapers or call the **Nature Conservancy** (631-329-7689; www.nature.org), the **Group for the East End** (631-537-1400; www.groupforthesouthfork.org), or the **Long Island Greenbelt Trail Conference** (631-360-0753; www.hike-li.org).

In addition to those within preserves or parks, there are currently five official hiking trails on Long Island, ranging in length from 3.7 to 47 miles, managed by the Long Island Greenbelt Trail Conference. Most meander in a north-south direction across the width of the island, but it has long been a dream of Long Island residents to create a hiking trail from Rocky Point to Montauk Point—one of roughly 125 miles in length that would be the region's version of the Appalachian Trail. Recently that dream came closer to reality. The New York State legislature passed a bill protecting the Pine Barrens region of central Long Island and opening the way for the creation of the **Paumanok Path**. For more information, contact the **Long Island Greenbelt Trail Conference** (631-360-0753; www.hike-li.org) in Hauppague, or on weekends in the summer, stop at the **Pine Barrens Trail Information Center** (631-369-9768) to pick up a map. In addition, the **Southampton Trails Preservation Society** (631-537-5202; www.hike-li.org) and the **East Hampton Trails Preservation Society** (631-329-4227; www.hike-li.org) have constructed a series of trails. Trails that already lie within the two townships are the **Red Creek Trail**, the **Long Pond Greenbelt**, and the 10-mile **Northwest Path**. Organized hikes and walks are sponsored by these organizations—consult their Web sites or local newspapers for the schedule.

Suffolk County residents who wish to camp or to use the county parks should purchase a Green Key Card. The price is $24 for three years and entitles residents to reduced fees for parking, camping, and other activities. The card can be purchased at the entrance to the parks, but be sure to bring proper identification, proving you are a full-time county resident. Call or e-mail Suffolk County (631-854-4949; www.suffolkcountyny.gov/parks) for details.

BRIDGEHAMPTON

Long Pond Greenbelt This is a 6.2-mile trail, threading past a chain of ponds and wetlands. It is in the heart of the Atlantic Flyway, making it rich with bird life. Managed by the Nature Conservancy, trails lead into the area from Sag Harbor's Mashashimuet Park.

EAST HAMPTON

East Hampton Village Nature Trail No fee. The trail is a delightful area in the heart of East Hampton Village and is accessed from David's or Huntting lanes. Ducks and swans, often with their babies, happily paddle about in the tiny pond; birds and small animals hustle in and out of the underbrush along the wooded paths. It's a popular spot for parents and children.

HAMPTON BAYS

Sears Bellows County Park (631-852-8290; www.suffolkcountyny.gov/parks; camping $15/night for county residents with a Green Key Card; $30/noncounty residents) This Suffolk County park has 70 tent and trailer campsites, a bicycle hostel, restrooms, showers, nightly lectures and movies, a picnic area, lake swimming, hiking trails, row-boat rentals, and freshwater pond fishing. Access is from Bellows Pond Road, off Route 24 in Flanders.

MONTAUK

Hither Hills State Park (631-668-2554; www.licamping.com; reservations required for campsites, 800-456-CAMP; $28/night New York State residents; $56 nonresidents; $12 reservation fee, $8 parking) This park has 168 tent and trailer campsites, hiking trails, restrooms, a camp store, a children's play area, and a picnic area. It is situated on 1,700 acres overlooking 2 miles of ocean beach in Montauk. Entertainment can include movies, children's summer theater, concerts, square dancing, games; and always lots of fun. A variety of trails crisscross this vast acreage, making available a wealth of scenic vistas, ponds, dunes (including the walking dunes), and marshes. The state park is adjacent to Hither Woods Preserve and the County Nature Preserve.

Montauk Point State Park (631-668-3781; www.nysparks.com; $6 parking fee) With over 700 acres, hiking and nature trails, and a snack and gift shop, this park adjoins Theodore Roosevelt County Park and includes the Montauk Point Lighthouse (which charges a fee and is under different management). Some trails near the lighthouse are currently closed as efforts are made to stabilize the cliff from ongoing erosion. (See detailed information about the Montauk Point Lighthouse Museum in chapter 6.) Many other hiking and nature trails are open, however, and some overlook the ocean; it's easy to see why so many shipwrecks have taken place here. Surf fishing is a popular sport, especially for striped bass.

Theodore Roosevelt County Park (631-852-7878; www.suffolkcountyny.gov/parks; camping $15/night for county residents with a Green Key Card; $30/non-county residents; also outer beach camping $15/night; $30 nonresident.) On 1,185 acres, the park has picnic areas, campsites, and a hostel for cyclists. The park headquarters and the Pharaoh Indian Museum are located in Third House; the rest of the park is off East Lake Drive in Montauk. There is camping space for about 400 families on the 3 miles of beach, but campers must use four-wheel-drive, self-contained vehicles. A trailer park with access to the beach is also available. A 3-mile nature trail meanders through a wooded, swampy area, offering picturesque views of wildflowers, ferns, and a variety of birds, turtles, and animals.

NORTHWEST

Cedar Point County Park (631-852-7620; reservations 631-244-7275; www.suffolkcounty ny.gov/parks; camping $15/night for county residents with a Green Key Card; $30/non-county residents; rowboat rental $6 first hour and $4 each hour after or $30/day) This park has 190 tent and trailer campsites, restrooms, hot showers, camp store, playground, basketball and volleyball courts, baseball diamond, nature trails, and free movies in summer. It is located on a 608-acre point that juts into Northwest Harbor and points toward Shelter Island and Sag Harbor. The old stone lighthouse on its tip was built in 1868 to guide whaling ships to their home port of Sag Harbor. When built, the light was actually on an island; the landmasses were joined together during the 1938 hurricane. One of the most interesting trails is the beach walk to the lighthouse, where, in early summer, a barrier protects the nesting area of endangered birds, such as terns, plovers, and giant ospreys.

This quiet pavilion on Fort Pond in Montauk is part of Kirk Park.

QUOGUE

Quogue Wildlife Refuge (631-653-4771; www.quoguewildliferefuge.com; 3 Old County Rd.; mailing address: P.O. Box 492; Quogue, NY 11959) Run by the Southampton Township Wildfowl Association, this is a marvelous place to acquaint children with various species of birds. They'll love all the ducks, the turkey that gobbles as they enter, and the tame deer. There's a nature center with exhibits and a sanctuary where staff take care of injured and orphaned animals. Guides lead exploratory walks. A resident population of Canada geese make the refuge their permanent home, and children delight in seeing the baby geese march across the grass in the spring. The 7 miles of trails are well marked, and there are benches along the way. A Nature Center is open Tues. and Thurs., Sat. and Sun. 11–4; the trails and Distressed Wildlife Complex are open daily from sunrise to sunset. Dogs, bicycles, and smoking are not allowed. Access is off Old Main Road, near the Long Island Rail Road tracks in Quogue.

SAG HARBOR

Morton National Wildlife Refuge (631-286-0485) Run by the U.S. Fish and Wildlife Service, this 187-acre preserve is a temporary home to migratory waterbirds. A self-guided nature trail explains what you are viewing; a map may be obtained from the Nature Conservancy (631-329-7689). The entrance is off Noyack Road, west of Sag Harbor.

SPRINGS

Merrill Lake Sanctuary (www.nature.org) The Nature Conservancy owns this property of about 200 acres within the Accabonac Harbor Preserve (one of the primary spots on the East End for bird-watching). You may see ospreys nesting as their young hatch in late June and early July, or graceful herons feeding in the marshy lagoons, as well as a variety of other animal and plant life. The entrance is well marked, off the Springs Fireplace Road.

ROLLERBLADING & SKATEBOARDING

Rollerblading is currently as popular as bicycling. A favorite spot to practice the sport is Long Beach in Sag Harbor, especially in the evening when there's a blazing sunset. Watch the local newspapers for places to freestyle. You can rent equipment at **Amagansett Beach & Bicycle** (631-267-6325; www.amagansettbeachco.com; 624 Montauk Hwy. at Cross Hwy., Amagansett, NY 11930; rollerblade rentals $25/half-day, $35/full-day, including pads and helmet).

And if you think skateboarding has lost its luster, or that it's just for punks, think again. There are now a number of skate parks in the Hamptons that welcome skateboarders and offer lessons and freestyle exhibitions to boot: **East Hampton Skate Park** (16 Abrahams Path, East Hampton; summer daylight hours; school year 2 PM–dusk); **Montauk City Skate Park** (South Essex Street, Montauk; daily 10 AM–dusk); **North Sea Skate Park** (1370A Majors Path, Southampton; daily 10 AM–dusk); **Red Creek Skate Park** (102 Old Riverhead Rd., Hampton Bays; Sept.–June Mon., Wed., and Fri 3–7; Sat. and Sun. noon–7; July and Aug. daily noon–8).

SWIMMING

East Hampton Town and Southampton Town conduct numerous swimming classes, ranging from beginners' classes to lifesaving courses, each summer at the town beaches. Most swimming areas have been listed under "Beaches" in this chapter. Nevertheless, there are several public swimming pools and freshwater ponds in which to swim in the Hamptons also.

Emma Rose Elliston Park (631-283-6000; Big Fresh Pond, off Millstone Brook Rd., North Sea) This park, for Southampton Town residents only, has a tiny beach on Big Fresh Pond with restrooms, lifeguard, and picnic area. It's within a beautifully maintained park.

Montauk Downs State Park (631-668-5000; 50 S. Fairview Ave., Montauk) This park has two pools (one Olympic-sized, the other a kiddie) that are open long hours; an excellent array of classes is also offered every summer. Lifeguard on duty. Adults $5; children $3; seniors $3; season passes available.

Trout Pond Noyack Road This pond, in Noyack, is rated locally as the favorite freshwater swimming spot in the Hamptons, but beware! There are no lifeguards, and signs warning no swimming, posted by the Town of Southampton, are placed there for a reason. The depth of the pond is uneven and hard to predict, but since there's not much beach, children generally paddle about on rafts or in inner tubes.

Tennis & Racquet Sports

The Meadow Club of Southampton, the first tennis club in the Hamptons, was established in 1887. The club now has more grass courts than any other on the East Coast, as well as smooth croquet lawns, all hidden away behind tall privet hedges. The Maidstone Club of East Hampton, not far behind, opened in 1891. Although a golf course was built at Maidstone, tennis continues to be the main interest of many of its members.

In the Hamptons, there are many more courts at private clubs than in public places, and most clubs, private and public, are open primarily in the summer. Several Hamptons villages, though, have public tennis courts, but the fees and access vary from village to village, so check before you go.

Private Clubs

Although the following are membership clubs, they also offer short-term playing opportunities to nonmembers. All stated fees are for nonmembers.

Amagansett

Napeague Tennis Club (631-267-8525; www.gothamtennis.com; 2145 Montauk Hwy. at Napeague, bet. Amagansett and Montauk; Amagansett, NY 11930) Four outdoor courts and one multipurpose court; $75/hour court time; $150 private lesson; adult clinic (90 min.) $110/player. Open to the public Mem. Day–Labor Day.

Sportime (631-267-3460; www.sportimeny.com; 320 Abrahams Path; mailing address: P.O. Box 778; Amagansett, NY 11930; open May–Oct, Sat. and Sun. only) This facility has 34 Har-Tru tennis courts, a 1,500-square-foot outdoor swimming pool, mini-basketball court, outdoor sports fields, children's camp house, tennis pro shop, and snack bar. Court time $30/hour–$68/hour.

East Hampton

Buckskill Tennis Club (631-324-2243; www.buckskilltennis.com; 178 Buckskill Rd., East Hampton, NY 11937) The club has six Har-Tru courts, three grass courts, one Deco-Turf court, a pro shop, and clubhouse. Har-Tru and Deco-Turf: $55/hour AM Sat. Sun., and holidays, $45/hour weekdays and PM Sat., Sun., and holidays; grass court: $50/per person/per court am Sat., Sun., and holidays, $40/per person/per court weekdays, PM Sat, Sun., and holidays.

Southampton

Southampton Racquet Club (631-283-5444; www.southamptonracquetclub.net; 655 Majors Path, Southampton, NY 11968) 10 Har-Tru courts; cardio tennis $55; private lesson $135. Offers instruction and will arrange games with varied-level players. Also runs a summer camp for children that offers tennis combined with classes in painting, pottery and gardening.

Triangle Tennis Club (631-287-3052; www.triangletennis.com; 411 Hampton Rd., Southampton, NY 11968) Three all-weather courts; prices: $60/court/hour AM Sat., Sun., and holidays; $50/court/hour weekdays and PM Sat., Sun., and holidays.

Westhampton Beach

East Side Tennis Club (631-288-1540; www.westhamptontennis.net; 142 Montauk Hwy., Westhampton Beach, NY 11978) 12 Har-Tru courts; $25/hour AM, $15/hour PM. Primarily a teaching academy. Game room; clubhouse; volleyball.

Westhampton Tennis & Sport Club (631-288-6060; www.whbtennisandsport.com; 86 Depot Rd., Westhampton Beach, NY 11978) 24 Har-Tru courts and 7 all-weather courts under a bubble. Court rental is $20–$30/hour.

Public Tennis Courts

AMAGANSETT

Abrahams Path Park (631-324-2417; Abrahams Path, Amagansett, NY 11930) Four courts; $8/hour; restrooms; attendant on duty; reservation required day of play.

BRIDGEHAMPTON

Bridgehampton High School (631-537-0271; Montauk Hwy., Bridgehampton, NY 11932) Two courts for public use; no fee, first come, first served.

EAST HAMPTON

East Hampton High School (631-329-4143; 2 Long Ln., East Hampton, NY 11937) Six courts; no fee, first come, first served.

Herrick Park (631-329-4143; Park Pl., East Hampton, NY 11937) Three courts; no fee, first come, first served. Easily accessed from Park Place (parking lot behind shops on Main Street and Newtown Lane).

MONTAUK

Lions Park (631-324-2417; Essex St., Montauk, NY 11954) Three courts for public use; no charge; first come, first served.

Montauk Downs State Park (631-668-6264; 50 S. Fairview, Montauk, NY 11954; off West Lake Dr.) Six Har-Tru courts; $18/court/hour; seniors $10/court/hour. Attendant on duty; restrooms; showers; lockers; golf course; two swimming pools; restaurant.

SAG HARBOR

Mashashimuet (631-725-4018; Main St., Sag Harbor, NY 11963) Ten courts for public use (two all-weather and eight clay); hard courts $20/hour; clay courts $25/hour; attendant on duty. Although this is a membership organization, sometimes courts are available on an hourly basis, and seasonal memberships are reasonable. Managed by Sag Harbor Tennis Company for the Parks and Recreation Association of Sag Harbor.

SOUTHAMPTON

Sandy Hollow Tennis Club (631-283-3422; 125 Sandy Hollow Rd., Southampton, NY 11968) 14 Har-Tru courts; $40/hour.

Southampton High School (631-591-4600; Leland Ln., Southampton, NY 11968) Five courts for public use; no fee, first-come, first-served.

Southampton Village (631-283-0247; Ann's Ln., Southampton) One court. Permit required for use; $10/person or $30/family for the season.

SPRINGS

Springs Recreation Area (631-324-2417; off Old Stone Hwy., Springs, NY 11937) Three courts for public use; no fee, first come, first served.

WESTHAMPTON BEACH

Westhampton Beach High School (631-288-3800; Oneck Ln., Westhampton Beach, NY 11978) Eight courts for public use; no fee; first come, first served.

WHALE WATCHING

The Viking Fleet (631-668-5709; www.vikingfleet.com) offers whale-watch cruises during the summer, departing from the Viking Dock in Montauk. A naturalist is always on board to explain what you are seeing. The schedule is different every year. Sometimes there are three or four trips a week, and other times there are only two overnight offshore trips a summer. They take place in July and August, as that is when the whales are migrating. There's often a bonus sighting of turtles, dolphins, seabirds, sharks, tuna, and other marine life. The price of the daylong trips is $49/adult and $19/child; the price of an overnight trip to the Great South Channel off Martha's Vineyard (there are 65 navy-style bunks and you are asked to bring a sleeping bag and pillow) is $310. The cruise is long, and it is not recommended for children under 5. Reservations are required.

WINTER SPORTS

We don't think of the Hamptons as a center for winter sports, but there are numerous activities that take place during the colder months, nevertheless. The **Group for the East End** (631-537-1400; www.groupforthesouthfork.org), the **Long Island Greenbelt Trail Conference** (631-360-0753; www.hike-li.org), the **Southampton Trails Preservation Society** (631-537-5202; www.hike-li.org) and the **East Hampton Trails Preservation Society** (631-329-4227; www.hike-li.org) organize hikes and exploratory adventures all winter. Look for their schedules in local newspapers, or on their Web sites.

Buckskill Winter Club (631-324-2243; www.buckskillwinterclub.com; 178 Buckskill Rd., mailing address: P.O. Box 1417, East Hampton, NY 11937) Beginning its sixth season in 2010, this club offers a full roster of figure skating and hockey lessons from about Thanksgiving to the end of March on a rink that's conditioned regularly with high-tech equipment. Seasonal memberships are available, but you can skate even if you aren't a member or taking a class. There are numerous public skating times, especially in the afternoons and evenings, as well as drop-in hockey sessions. Public skating: weekdays adults $12/hour; children $8/hour; seniors $9/hour; weekends and holidays adults $18/hour; children $12/hour; seniors $14/hour; skate rental is $5/adult; $3/child. Drop-in hockey: weekdays $20/session; weekends and holidays $30/session. Skate sharpening: adults $18; kids $15. Skate profiling: adults $35; kids $30.

8

Practical Matters

Information

A complete guide to the Hamptons wouldn't live up to its name without the following basic, though essential, information. We hope that, whether you are a longtime resident or a tourist, you will turn first to this guide for accurate and complete information.

Insider's tip: In East Hampton, people with a 324 telephone prefix often give their telephone number using the last four digits only.

For local time, call 631-976-1616.

For local weather, call 631-976-1212.

For extended weather forecast, call 631-976-8888.

AMBULANCE, FIRE, POLICE

Throughout Suffolk County the emergency number is 911, but most small villages have their own fire and police departments that can be reached at the following local numbers. (*Area code for all is 631.*)

Town	Fire	Ambulance	Police
Amagansett	267-3300		
Bridgehampton	324-4477		
East Hampton Town	324-0124	324-6767	324-0024
East Hampton Village	324-0124	324-0777	
Hampton Bays	924-5252	728-3400	
Montauk	911	668-3709	
North Sea	283-3629		
Quogue	o	653-4175	
Sag Harbor	324-6550	725-0058	725-0058
Southampton Town	283-1250	728-3400	728-3400
Southampton Village	283-0072	287-0558	283-0056
Westhampton Beach	o	288-3444	

Coast Guard Search and Rescue

Group Moriches: 631-878-0320
Montauk Station: 631-668-2716
Shinnicock Station: 631-728-1171

The Sag Harbor Information Booth is located in a windmill.

For other emergency and contact numbers, please consult the following list or your telephone directory.

Emergency: 911
AIDS Hot Line: 631-385-2437
AL-ANON: 631-669-2827
Alcohol and Substance Abuse Hot Line: 516-504-0244
Alcoholics Anonymous: 631-654-1150
American Red Cross, Emergency: 631-924-6911
Child Abuse Hot Line: 800-342-3720
Coast Guard (South Shore): 631-878-9320
Domestic Violence Hot Line: 800-942-6906
FBI: 631-501-8600
Gas Emergency: 800-490-0045
General Fire, Rescue, and Emergency Number: 631-924-5252
LIPA (electric company) Emergency: 631-755-6900
NYS Terrorism Tip Line: 866-SAFE-NYS
Poison Control: 516-542-2323
Pregnancy Information and Referral: 631-243-0066
Rape Hot Line: 631-360-3606
Runaway Hot Line: 800-231-6946
Southampton Hospital: 631-726-8200
State Police (in Hampton Bays): 631-728-3000
Suicide and Crisis Counseling: 631-751-7500
West Nile Virus Hot Line: 631-853-3055

AREA CODES

The area code for all of Suffolk County is 631. Frequently called nearby area codes are as follows:

New York
Nassau County: 516
Manhattan: 212, 646, 917
Brooklyn, Bronx, Queens, Staten Island: 718, 917
Westchester County: 914

Connecticut
Western Coastal Connecticut: 203
Eastern and Northern Connecticut: 860

CHAMBERS OF COMMERCE

East Hampton Chamber of Commerce (631-324-0362; www.easthamptonchamber.com; 42 Gingerbread Ln., East Hampton, NY 11937) Open May–Dec. 10–4; Jan.–Apr. fewer days, usually Wed.–Sat. 10–4.

Greater Westhampton Chamber of Commerce (631-288-3337; www.whbcc.org; 7 Glovers Ln.; mailing address: P.O. Box 1228, Westhampton Beach, NY 11978) Open in summer, Mon.–Sat. 10–4; in winter, Mon.–Fri. 10–2.

Hampton Bays Chamber of Commerce (631-728-2211; www.hamptonbayschamber.com; 140 West Main St.; mailing address: P.O. Box 64, Hampton Bays, NY 11946) Open Fri., Sat. 10–5.

Montauk Chamber of Commerce (631-668-2428; www.montaukchamber.com; Main St., The Plaza, Montauk, NY 11954) Open May–Oct., Mon.–Fri. 10–5, Sat. 10–3, Sun. 10–2; Oct.–Apr., Mon.–Fri. 10–4.

Sag Harbor Chamber of Commerce (631-725-0011; www.sagharborchamber.com; 55 Main St.; mailing address: P.O. Box 2810, Sag Harbor, NY 11963) Open July–Aug., daily 9–5; rest of year by telephone or mail.

Southampton Chamber of Commerce (631-283-0402; www.southamptonchamber.com; 76 Main St., Southampton, NY 11968) Open Mon.–Fri. 10–4, Sat. 11–4.

TOWN GOVERNMENT

On the East End, town government is the predominant local lawmaking and enforcement agency, but within each town, individual incorporated villages and even smaller hamlets are self-governing. The incorporated villages generally have legal and law-enforcement influence within their boundaries (and this includes maintaining their own police force), but the hamlets depend upon the town for these services. Most villages have a village hall where local business is conducted. Beach permits for village beaches, for example, are issued by the village, while permits for the town beaches are issued at the town office.

Town Offices

East Hampton Town Office (631-324-4143; www.town.east-hampton.ny.us; 159 Pantigo Rd., East Hampton, NY 11937)

East Hampton Town Satellite Office (631-668-5081; Main St., Montauk, NY 11954)

Southampton Town Hall (631-283-6000; www.town.southampton.ny.us; 116 Hampton Rd., Southampton, NY 11968)

Village Offices

East Hampton Village Office (631-324-4150; www.easthamptonvillage.org; 86 Main St., East Hampton, NY 11937)

North Haven Village Office (631-725-1378; www.northhavenny.us; 335 Ferry Rd., Sag Harbor, NY 11963)

Quogue Village Office (631-653-4498; www.villageofquogue.com; 123 Jessup Ave.; mailing address: P.O. Box 926, Quogue, NY 11959)

Sag Harbor Village Office (631-725-0222; www.sagharborny.gov; 55 Main St.; mailing address: P.O. Box 660, Sag Harbor, NY 11963)

Southampton Village Office (631-283-0247; www.southampton village.org; 23 Main St., Southampton, NY 11968)

Westhampton Beach Village Office (631-288-1654; www.westhampton beach.org; 106 Sunset Ave.; mailing address: P.O. Box 991, Westhampton Beach, NY 11978)

East Hampton's village hall is located in a house formerly occupied by Lyman Beecher and his family when he was minister of East Hampton. (Harriet Beecher Stowe had not been born yet, however.)
Morgan McGivern

Westhampton Dunes Village (631-288-6571; www.whdunes.org; 4 Arthur St., Westhampton Dunes, NY 11978)

Zip Codes

Town/Village/Hamlet	Zip Code	Town/Village/Hamlet	Zip Code
Amagansett	11930	Remsenburg	11960
Bridgehampton	11932	Sagaponack	11962
East Hampton	11937	Sag Harbor	11963
Eastport	11941	Southampton	11968
East Quogue	11942	Speonk	11972
Hampton Bays	11946	Wainscott	11975
Montauk	11954	Water Mill	11976
North Haven	11963	Westhampton	11977
Quogue	11959	Westhampton Beach	11978

BANKS, FOREIGN EXCHANGE, 24-HOUR ATMS

If you arrive in the Hamptons with currency from another country, be assured that you will not be stranded. Most banks will cash traveler's checks, and Cook Travel converts foreign money into American traveler's checks. In addition, Chase Manhattan Bank in Southampton has a foreign money exchange and will be able to convert most currencies.

Cook Travel, Inc./American Express (631-324-8430; 20 Main St., East Hampton, NY 11937. Also 631-283-1740; 71 Hill St., Southampton, NY 11968.) Open Mon.–Fri. 9:30–5:30, Sat. 10–5.
JP Morgan Chase (631-283-6742; 60 Main St., Southampton, NY 11968) Open Mon.–Thurs. 9–3, Fri. 9–6.

Why is it that we seem to run out of cash at the most inopportune times? Fortunately, in this electronic age, most area banks have Automatic Teller Machines, and they accept almost every credit card, so we're never far from our money when we need it. The following stores have ATMs as well, so if you can't find a bank, perhaps one of these stores can be of assistance.

BRIDGEHAMPTON
King Kullen (631-537-8103; Bridgehampton Shopping Plaza, Bridgehampton, NY 11932) Available during store hours.

EAST HAMPTON
Waldbaums (631-324-6215; 67 Newtown Ln., East Hampton, NY 11937) Available during store hours.

HAMPTON BAYS
King Kullen (631-728-6482; 52 East Montauk Hwy., Hampton Bays, NY 11946) Available during store hours.

SOUTHAMPTON
Southampton Hospital (631-726-8200; 240 Meeting House Ln., Southampton, NY 11968)
Southampton Town Hall (631-283-6000; 116 Hampton Rd., Southampton, NY 11968)
Waldbaums (631-283-0045; 168 Jagger Ln. (at Main St.), Southampton, NY 11968)

CLIMATE, WEATHER, TIDES

The climate in the Hamptons is generally moderate and mild, with cooling ocean breezes in the summer and brisk winds in the winter. For the **daily weather report**, call 631-976-1212; for the **extended local forecast**, call 631-976-8888. The following are average temperature and precipitation figures (from information collected by the National Oceanic and Atmospheric Administration in Bridgehampton).

Month	Ave. Temp.	Ave. Precip. (in inches)	Month	Ave. Temp.	Ave. Precip. (in inches)
January	29.9	4.18	July	71.5	3.00
February	31.1	3.85	August	71.0	3.45
March	38.2	4.11	September	64.1	3.46
April	46.5	3.97	October	54.0	3.39
May	56.2	3.82	November	45.0	4.53
June	65.5	3.59	December	35.2	4.31

Tidal information along the ocean and, to a lesser extent, in the bays is essential to a relaxed, enjoyable day. If you're sunning by the ocean, the beach generally is wide enough so that you can just move farther back if the water starts to lap your toes. If, on the other hand, you are hiking or picnicking, you will not want to be stranded on a sandbar; and if you are boating, you will want to know the time of high and low tides in order to successfully navigate your way back to the dock. The Coast Guard can inform you of coastal weather conditions and give you tidal information; it's wise to call before heading out to sea. Also, you can get tidal information online at www.tidesandcurrents.noaa.gov. Three Coast Guard stations serve the Hamptons and can give you weather and tidal reports.

Coast Guard Group Moriches (631-395-4400) Remsenburg and Westhampton Beach.
Coast Guard Station Montauk (631-668-2773) Eastern tip of the South Fork.
Coast Guard Station Shinnecock (631-728-0343) Westhampton Beach to about 15 miles east of the Shinnecock Canal.

COMPUTER, INTERNET, FAX, & BUSINESS SERVICES

You're in the Hamptons on vacation, but someone from the office calls with an emergency. Your expertise is needed. Generally, you'll have your wireless computer with you, and there will be Wi-Fi wherever you need it. If that's not the case, however, instead of returning to the office, perhaps the work can be accomplished right here. The following businesses specialize in organizing and doing the routine jobs so that you can concentrate on what you do best.

The Boating Channel (631-725-4440; www.boatingchannel.com; 2615 Deerfield Rd., Sag Harbor, NY 11963) This is an Internet channel for boaters.

Computer Professionals (631-537-9888; www.computer-professionals.net; 41 Industrial Rd., P.O. Box 910, Wainscott, NY 11975) Owner John Charde and his staff are experts in advising about network design, security, remote access, upgrades, removing bugs, and giving computer lessons.

East Hampton Business Service (631-324-0405; 20 Park Pl., East Hampton, NY 11937) This is a one-stop shop for all business needs, including typing, word processing, typesetting, developing mailing lists, creating printouts from floppy disks, copying (including color), blueprints, fulfillment and mailing house services, fax service, bookkeeping, accounting, and mailboxes. (This book has relied on their invaluable help.)

Hamptons Online (631-287-6630; www.hamptons.com; 39 Windmill Ln., P.O. Box 299, Southampton, NY) This is a Hamptons online service, providing Internet and World Wide Web access, Web site design, hosting, e-commerce, and a regional Web site that offers local news and a directory of events, dining, lodging, and services.

HamptonsWeb.com (www.hamptonsweb.com)(631-267-8288; e-mail sagal@sagal.com) This very sophisticated and flashy Web site, created by William Sagal of Sagal Computer Systems as a service to his clients (he is a system consultant, Web site developer, and Internet adviser), has an incredible array of information about the Hamptons. There's everything from dining and lodging to a calendar of events. Check it out for the latest information about what's going on.

Montauk Printing and Graphics (631-329-1270; 78 Park Pl., East Hampton, NY 11937; 631-668-3333; 771 Main St., Montauk, NY 11954o) You can have great printing and graphics done here, as well as color and black-and-white copies.

South Shore Computer Works (631-324-7794; 41 Pantigo Rd., East Hampton, NY 11937) Expert advice on upgrades, plus they have rental computers; they will do on-site service calls for installation and repairs.

HANDICAPPED SERVICES

Suffolk County publishes a brochure describing accessibility to its county parks and golf courses. Also, a Suffolk County Green Key Card with a handicapped designation entitles its holder to free weekday admission to all county parks and reduced fees for activities. Contact the **Suffolk County Office of Handicapped Services** (631-853-8333 voice; 631-853-5658 TTY; www.suffolkcountyny.gov).

HOSPITALS & MEDICAL SERVICES

Prime Care (631-728-4500; 240 West Montauk Hwy., Hampton Bays, NY 11946) Open Mon., Tues., Thurs., Fri. 8–5, Sat. 8–12; closed Wed., Sun. Walk-in medical office.

Southampton Hospital (631-726-8200; www.southamptonhospital.org; 240 Meeting House Ln., Southampton, NY 11968) 194 beds; 115 doctors on staff; 550 full-time employees; surgical, maternity, pediatrics, ambulatory, outpatient, and emergency departments; radiology; full laboratory services. Hampton Eye Physicians and Surgeons also use the hospital's operating facilities.

Southampton Urgent Medical Care (631-204-9600; 609 Hampton Rd., Southampton, NY 11968) A walk-in medical office.

Wainscott Walk-In Medical Care (631-537-1892; 83 Wainscott Northwest Rd. Wainscott, NY 11975) A walk-in medical center in a shopping plaza behind Wainscott Windows and Walls.

KENNELS & ANIMAL WELFARE

You've been invited to a country house for the party of the season, and you find that your host is allergic to pets. Yet, you never leave your darling behind. What to do? If a Hamptons kennel is the answer for you, here are several suggestions. Remember, however, that advance reservations are a must.

East Hampton Veterinary Group (631-324-0282, 800-287-3484; 22 Montauk Hwy., East Hampton, NY 11937) Boarding and full veterinary services. Kennels are sized to the dog, and cats are kept in their own facility.

Hampton Veterinary Hospital (631-325-1611; 176 Montauk Hwy., Speonk, NY 11972) Traditional medical treatment as well as acupuncture and herbal remedies; boarding in individually sized cages.

Olde Towne Animal Hospital (631-283-0611; 380 County Rd. 39, Southampton, NY 11968) Full-service veterinary hospital that also boards pets.

Not a kennel but an animal rescue agency, the **Animal Rescue Fund** (631-537-0400; 90 Daniel's Hole Rd., Wainscott, NY 11975) rescues and cares for injured and abandoned animals; they also have an adoption service. Should you find a stray animal, take it to the ARF. If you feel like taking a walk, you could also stop by at ARF, and they will lend you a dog who would love the companionship. You can both stroll along ARF's dog-walking trail.

Bide-A-Wee (631-325-0200; 118 Old Country Rd., Westhampton, NY 11977) operates both an animal shelter/adoption service and a clinic, offering a full range of veterinary services. They also provide pet training and pet therapy. There's a pet cemetery, and they'll arrange a memorial service and/or bereavement counseling as well.

LATE-NIGHT FOOD SERVICES

Groceries

Brent's Amagansett General Store (631-267-3113; Montauk Hwy. at Cross Hwy., Amagansett, NY 11930) Open until 11 PM or 12 AM in summer.

King Kullen (631-537-8103, Bridgehampton Common, Montauk Hwy., Bridgehampton, NY 11932; 631-325-9698, 25 Eastport Manor Rd., Eastport, NY 11941; 631-728-9621, 260 West Montauk Hwy. and Terrace Rd., Hampton Bays, NY 11946) Open 24 hours in summer, except Sun.

7-Eleven (631-653-9889, 397 Montauk Hwy., East Quogue, NY 11942; 631-728-5130, 53 West Montauk Hwy., Hampton Bays, NY 11946; 631-725-3931, Main and Water Sts., Sag Harbor, NY 11963; 631-283-8511, 10 County Rd. 39, Southampton, NY 11968; 631-288-9755, 61 Sunset Ave., Westhampton Beach, NY 11978; 631-288-3446, 410 Mill Rd. at Montauk Hwy., Westhampton Beach, NY 11978) Open 24 hours year-round.

Restaurants

East Hampton Bowl (631-324-1950; 71 Montauk Hwy., East Hampton, NY 11937) Open weekdays 10 AM–midnight, weekends 10 AM–3 AM. Snack bar serves pizza, nachos, etc.

Hampton Bays Diner and Restaurant (631-728-0840; 157 West Montauk Hwy., Hampton Bays, NY 11946) Open 24 hours in summer; Oct.–Apr., Sun.–Thurs. 6 AM–midnight, Fri., Sat. 24 hours.

McDonald's (631-283-6777; 307 North Sea Rd., Southampton, NY 11968) 7 AM–11 PM.

Salivar's (631-668-2555; 470 West Lake Dr., Montauk, NY 11954) Open 24 hours in-season; open 11 PM–3 PM off-season. This diner has never changed, either in decor or in the food that it offers. Late-night partygoers and early-morning anglers can get burgers, chili, or breakfast.

LATE-NIGHT FUEL & AUTO SERVICES

Should you find yourself stranded, either because of car trouble or lack of gas, the following numbers may help.

For AAA members, the emergency number is 800-AAA-HELP day or night. For those who are not members of AAA, the following garages and gas stations are open late (and early in the morning) to provide fuel and road service.

B & B Auto Service (631-668-1195 days, 631-668-2217 nights; 213 Edgemere Rd., Montauk, NY 11954)

Bays Auto Repairs (631-728-0650; 192 West Montauk Hwy., Hampton Bays, NY 11946)

Joe's Garage (631-283-2098; 1426 North Sea Rd., Southampton, NY 11968)

North Main Street Citgo (631-324-8671; 72 Harborview Ave., East Hampton, NY 11937)
Village Auto Body (631-728-1500; 82 Old Riverhead Rd., Hampton Bays, NY 11946)

Laundromats

When you're on vacation, washing machines and dryers are not always readily available. The following laundromats have been selected because they are clean, well maintained, and conveniently located.

Montauk Laundromat (631-668-4349; 5 Elmwood Ave., Montauk, NY 11954)
Sag Harbor Launderette (631-725-5830; 20 Main St., Sag Harbor, NY 11963) Large, very clean, well lit; attendant on duty.
Tony's Tubs (631-728-1046; 218 West Montauk Hwy., Hampton Bays, NY 11946) Very clean, new; attendant on duty who will help carry laundry to and from your car.

Media

Newspapers & Magazines

Dan's Papers (631-537-0500; www.danshamptons.com; 2221 Montauk Hwy.; mailing address: P.O. Box 630, Bridgehampton, NY 11932) An irreverent, tongue-in-cheek, tabloid-style paper, carrying current local news and unabashedly plump with the editorial opinions of its owner, Dan Rattiner. It's over 30 years old and they claim it has the largest circulation in the Hamptons. Free and available throughout the area.

East Hampton Star (631-324-0002; www.easthamptonstar.com; 153 Main St., East Hampton, NY 11937) A venerable newspaper that's been in business since 1885, mostly in the able hands of the Rattray family, who still steer the ship. It covers business and events in a no-nonsense, professional manner for the Town of East Hampton and beyond.

Edible East End (631-537-4637; www.edibleeastend.com; Sag Harbor, NY 11963) This terrific magazine-style publication features the bounty of the fields and land in the Hamptons. There's information about chefs, winemakers, growers, farmers, and much more.

Hamptons Magazine (631-283-7125; www.hamptons-magazine.com; 67 Hampton Rd. Suite 5, Southampton, NY 11968) Free, glossy, upscale, full-color magazine, published in the summer only. Fashion news, what's happening at the clubs, and gossip.

H C & G (Hamptons Cottages & Gardens) (631-537-6710; www.hcandg.com) With offices in Connecticut and New York City, this oversized and beautiful architecture and garden magazine is free, and is published every summer. Similar magazines published for Connecticut, Westchester, and Palm Beach.

The Independent (631-324-2500; www.indyeastend.com; 74 Montauk Hwy., Ste. 19, at Cove Hollow Rd. in the Red Horse Market; mailing address: P.O. Box 5032, East Hampton, NY 11937) and *Southampton Independent* (631-287-2525; 33 Flying Point Rd., Suite 218, Southampton, NY 11968) Tabloid-style paper that was launched in 1993 and reports local news and views. Now also publishing Westhampton Beach and Riverhead/North Fork editions.

Sag Harbor Express (631-725-1700; www.sagharboronline.com; Main St., P.O. Box 1620, Sag Harbor, NY 11963) The first newspaper on Long Island, the *Long Island Herald* was established in Sag Harbor in 1791. Although the *Sag Harbor Express* is not a direct descen-

Egrets, ibis, and herons enjoy their home in the marshy Hamptons bays.

dant, it's certainly close, and it recently celebrated its 175th year.

Southampton Press (631-283-4100; www.27east.com; 135 Windmill Ln., Southampton, NY 11968) Established in 1897, this newspaper offers complete news, business, and events coverage in Southampton Town, and beyond.

Wine Press (631-298-3200; www.liwinepress.com; Times/Review Newspapers. This publication is the official magazine of the Long Island Wine Council. It contains information about the vineyards and wineries, as well as Wine Country happenings.

Radio

WBAB-FM 102.3 and WHFM-FM 95.3 (631-587-1023; 555 Sunrise Hwy. W. Babylon, NY 11704) Popular and rock music.

WBAZ-FM 102.3, WBSQ 102.3, Light, adult, contemporary music ("Z-Lite on the Bays"). WBEA BEACH-FM 104.7, top-40 adult contemporary; WEHM-FM 96.7, progressive rock (631-267-7800, 249 Montauk Hwy., P.O. Box 7162, Amagansett, NY 11930)

WBLI-FM 106.1 (631-669-9254; 555 Sunrise Hwy., West Babylon, NY 11704) Popular music.

WLNG-AM 1600 and WLNG-FM 92.1 (631-725-2300; 1692 Redwood Causeway; mailing address: P.O. Box 2000, Sag Harbor, NY 11963) Popular music, local news, and information.

WLIU-FM 88.3 (631-591-7000; 239 Montauk Hwy., Long Island University, Southampton Campus, Southampton, NY 11968) Classical, jazz, and progressive music.

Television

LTV, CH 23 (631-537-2777; 75 Industrial Rd., Wainscott, NY 11975) Community-access cable for the East End.

WLIG CH 55 (631-727-1741; Wading River Hollow Rd., Middle Island, NY 11953)

WVVH, CH 58, UHF CH 23 (631-537-0273; 75 Industrial Rd., Wainscott, NY 11975) Commercial TV for the East End.

POST OFFICES

For information about all post offices, you can call 1-800-275-8777.

Amagansett (631-267-2804; 501 Montauk Hwy., Amagansett, NY 11930)
Bridgehampton (631-537-9322; 2322 Main St., Bridgehampton, NY 11932)
East Hampton (631-324-6320; 12 Gay Ln., East Hampton, NY 11937)
East Quogue (631-653-5247; 6 Bay Ave., East Quogue, NY 11942)
Hampton Bays (631-728-6994; 16 Ponquogue Rd., Hampton Bays, NY 11946)
Montauk (631-668-7043; 73 South Euclid Ave., Montauk, NY 11954)
Quogue (631-653-6427; 6 Midland Ave., Quogue, NY 11959)
Remsenburg (631-325-5937; 137 Main St., Remsenburg, NY 11960)
Sagaponack (631-537-9346; 542 Sagg Main St., Sagaponack, NY 11962)
Sag Harbor (631-725-8968; 21 Long Island Ave., Sag Harbor, NY 11963)
Southampton (631-204-9822; 29 Nugent St., Southampton, NY 11968)
Speonk (631-325-1741; 323 Montauk Hwy., Speonk, NY 11972)
Wainscott (631-537-8943; 357 Montauk Hwy., Wainscott, NY 11975)
Water Mill (631-726-6310; 670 Montauk Hwy., Water Mill, NY 11976)
Westhampton (631-288-4081; 408 Mill Rd., Westhampton, NY 11977)
Westhampton Beach (631-288-4093; 170 Main St., Westhampton Beach, NY 11978)

REAL ESTATE

If you've come to the Hamptons for a visit and just can't bear to return home, you may wish to consult one of the following real estate firms, which will be pleased to assist you with either the rental or purchase of a home. These are some of the area's top househunters.

Brown Harris Stevens (631-537-2727; www.brownharrisstevens.com; 2408 Main St., Bridgehampton, NY 11932; 631-324-6400, 37 Newtown Ln., East Hampton, NY 11937; 631-725-5555, 76 Main St., Sag Harbor, NY 11963; 631-283-0209, 24 Main St., Southampton, NY 11968; 631-288-5500, 70 Main St., Westhampton Beach, NY 11978)

Corcoran Group (631-267-7700; www.corcoran.com; 140 Main St., Amagansett, NY 11930; 631-537-3900, 1936 Montauk Hwy. Bridgehampton, NY 11932; 631-537-4106; 2405 Main St., Bridgehampton, NY 11932; 631-324-3900, 51 Main St., East Hampton, NY 11937; 631-725-1500, Main St. at Madison, Sag Harbor, NY 11963; 631-283-7300, 88 Main St., Southampton, NY 11968; 631-288-6900; 92 Main St., Westhampton Beach, NY 11978, plus many more locations)

Prudential Douglas Elliman Real Estate (631-267-9700; www.prudentialelliman.com
/HamptonsNorthFork; 216 Main St., Amagansett, NY 11930; 631-537-5900, 2488 Main
St., Bridgehampton, NY 11932; 631-329-9400, 83 Main St., East Hampton, NY 11937;
631-668-6565, 752 Montauk Hwy., Montauk, NY 11954; 631-653-6700, 134 Jessup Ave.,
Quogue, NY 11959; 631-283-4343, 70 Jobs Lane, Southampton, NY 11968; 631-288-
6244, 104 Main St., Westhampton, NY 11978, and more)

Sotheby's International Realty (631-537-6000; www.sothebyshomes.com/hamptons;
2446 Main St., Bridgehampton, NY 11932; 631-324-6000, 6 Main St., East Hampton,
NY 11937; 631-283-0600; 50 Nugent St., Southampton, NY 11968)

Tina Fredericks (631-324-4418; www.tinafredericks.com; 76 Georgica Rd.; mailing
address: P.O. Box 532, East Hampton, NY 11937)

9

FROM VINES TO WINES

The North Fork

Although the North Fork of Long Island is not part of the Hamptons and is distinctly different in character, it has a fascinating history and numerous attractions of its own. Its burgeoning wine industry leads to comparisons with the early days of the Napa Valley. And as the wine industry grows, so do the tourist facilities. Old, established restaurants are thriving, and chefs in new restaurants are testing new ground. Interesting bed & breakfasts and inns are housed in gingerbread Victorian homes—remnants of the North Fork's days as a whaling port and transportation hub.

The North Fork is approximately 20 miles shorter than the South Fork, with the tip, Orient Point, approximately 120 miles from New York City. The trip from Manhattan can be completed in 2.5 hours and in less time from Connecticut. In general, the North Fork has a more permanent, year-round population than the Hamptons, although as travelers learn about the beautiful beaches, the variety of activities, and the number of shops and restaurants that are open year-round, a larger summer population is enjoying the pleasures of the North Fork. Visit the North Fork and you'll be pleasantly surprised. It's a trip you'll undoubtedly want to repeat over and over again.

Although this chapter cannot identify all of the North Fork's many attractions, I have attempted to include the very best.

HISTORY

My manner of living is plain, and I do not mean to be put out of it. A glass of wine and a bit of mutton are always ready.

—*George Washington*

The early history of the North Fork is closely tied to that of the South Fork. Yet, although the South Fork has now acquired a cachet of social prominence, with large homes replacing potato fields and duck farms, the North Fork remains stubbornly rural, clinging to its water and land resources for sustenance. The winds, however, are shifting. As the local wine industry gains recognition, so does the region. Where scattered, homegrown restaurants once lured folks out for dinner after church on Sunday, a variety of fine gourmet restaurants now beckon a sophisticated clientele. Where boardinghouses and seaside motels prevailed, we now find high-class inns and B&Bs.

Raphael opened this spectacular visitors' center and winery in 2001.

Southold's history is almost as old as Southampton's. They were both settled in 1640, probably only a few months apart. Actually, a friendly rivalry exists over which was settled first. The truth lies buried in the records, or the absence of them—Southold's are not as complete as Southampton's. It is established, however, that Southold's settlers organized the first church society in New York State.

It's also true that the intrepid traveler George Washington came through Greenport in 1757, bound for Boston to secure his commission as commander in chief of the Virginia troops from Governor Shirley of Massachusetts prior to the American Revolution. Already recognized as a fine seaport, Greenport offered the most desirable route to Boston from Virginia. Fortunately, Governor Shirley fully concurred with Washington's appointment and made his trip worthwhile. After journeying to Greenport, Washington and his entourage stayed at a country house owned by Lieutenant Constant Booth and took the ferry the next day to New London, Connecticut. He thereby avoided crossing 18 rivers on horseback in the freezing winter months. The house where Washington stayed was moved from Greenport some years ago to the nearby hamlet of Orient, where it is maintained today by the Oysterponds Historical Society.

Almost 100 years after George Washington's trip, there were still few bridges across the rivers that separated New York from Boston, the United States' two great northern cities, and travel by water was preferred to the bumpy, dusty stagecoaches. Greenport thus became an important transportation hub. In 1844 the Long Island Rail Road established its northern terminus in Greenport, thereby making the journey even shorter. Following along George Washington's path, travelers came to Greenport by railroad. They then boarded steamers for an overnight trip to Boston, complete with dinner, dancing, and gambling.

Because of its water orientation, the North Fork's commercial enterprises traditionally have been linked to the water—fishing, shipping, and boatbuilding. Jamesport had a thriving commercial fishing industry in the mid-1800s, and the first submarines purchased by the U.S. Navy were built in New Suffolk in 1900.

The whaling and shipbuilding industries flourished in Greenport, where many large sailing ships were built. By the late 1800s, 286 sailing vessels and 73 fishing boats made Greenport their home. As merchants and shipbuilders grew wealthy, they built grand Victorian homes, many of which still remain.

The advent of Prohibition didn't slow down the North Fork. It's said that the coastal villages of the East End prospered substantially during this time, not only from the moonshine itself but also from servicing and repairing the boats of both bootleggers and revenuers, which often were repaired side by side.

In the 1930s, Greenport gained distinction of another type. The sailing master for three successful America's Cup defenders lived in Greenport. Although the ships were headquartered in Newport, Rhode Island, Captain George Monsell brought all of the crews to Greenport to sign their contracts. One of the skippers and a first mate lived here as well. Those were heady days when the *Enterprise* won the race in 1930, the *Rainbow* in 1934, and the *Ranger* in 1937.

As William Oliver Stevens wrote in *Discovering Long Island*, in 1939:

> *What is most tempting about Greenport is the waterfront, that long, ragged fringe of wharves, boatbuilder's yards, and sail lofts from which one looks out across the harbor to the wooded bluffs of Shelter Island. Of course, the whalers in these waters have long since become completely extinct, and those square-rigged ships that sailed from here direct to the West Indies for molasses are also long since dead and gone.*

Even if whaling ships no longer docked in Greenport, it was still an important shipbuilding center, and other North Fork villages had developed thriving oyster and scallop industries. Peconic Bay scallops are still considered sweeter and more tender than those harvested elsewhere, making them prized by chefs around the world.

The beauty of the North Fork cannot be denied. Pure, unspoiled bays, inlets, and creeks to the south and majestic Long Island Sound to the north are linked together by miles of flat, rich farmland. Villages remain true to their New England roots with treasured old houses and buildings looking much as they did a century ago.

Fortunately for us, community-spirited citizens recognized the importance of preserving some of the oldest and most historic buildings. In Mattituck, Cutchogue, Southold, and Orient, buildings have been moved from locations where they were endangered and settled into clusters around a village green where they are open to the public. In Greenport, the Stirling Historical Society also maintains several buildings, and there's an interesting walking tour past historic old homes. There are now three historic districts on the North Fork included on the National Register of Historic Places. They comprise 1,448 acres that include 342 buildings and 4 structures.

TRANSPORTATION

This chapter does not repeat the information contained in chapter 2, "Transportation," but it does identify specific ways to reach the North Fork.

The Cross Sound Ferry runs between Orient Point on the North Fork and New London, Connecticut, in about 90 minutes.

By Bus

Hampton Jitney (631-283-4600; www.hamptonjitney.com; mailing address: The Omni, 395 County Rd. 39A, Southampton, NY 11968. Fare: $22 one-way; $40 round trip) This bus company provides a full schedule of bus service from Manhattan to the North Fork. Buses leave from stops on Lexington Avenue and make stops from the Tanger Outlet in Riverhead to Orient Point. Buses leave Manhattan from 7:20 AM to 7:50 PM, and leave the North Fork from 4:45 AM to 7:45 PM. On Fridays there are nonstop buses from Manhattan to Southold and Greenport, with return nonstop service on Sundays.

Suffolk Transit (631-852-5200; www.sct-bus.org; Mon.–Sat. $1.50, with additional charge of $0.25 for each transfer; seniors and handicapped riders $0.50; students 14–21 $1; children under 5 free) Operates buses throughout Suffolk County, including the North Fork as far as the Orient Point Ferry. For some reason the information numbers are always busy, and they're only in operation Monday to Friday, 8 to 4:30. Your best bet is to pick up the schedule and fare information from local chamber of commerce offices. The schedules are well prepared, with maps that clearly show the routes, transfer points, and just about anything else you need to know. Suffolk Transit buses will stop anywhere along the route if you flag them down. In general, the buses travel each way about every two hours. You must tell the driver when you get on if you want a transfer. Please note: exact fare is required, as the drivers do not carry change.

By Car

From Manhattan, the trip to the North Fork is infinitely easier than to the Hamptons. The Long Island Expressway (I-495) terminates in Riverhead, the gateway to the North Fork. It is from this point that two fingers of land—one reaching north and east and the other south and east—separate to enclose Peconic Bay. Furthermore, there are two auto routes along the North Fork, giving travelers the option of traveling through each village or taking a four-lane highway to reach the eastern villages more quickly. The first of the North Fork wineries is no more than 15 minutes from the end of the Long Island Expressway.

By Ferry

A pleasant way to travel from Connecticut is via the **Cross Sound Ferry** (www.longisland ferry.com) from New London, Connecticut, to Orient Point, on the eastern tip of the North Fork. For information and reservations, call 631-323-2525 in New York, or 860-443-5281 in Connecticut. Another route is via the **Bridgeport/Port Jefferson Steamboat Company** (www.bpjferry.com) ferry to Port Jefferson on the North Shore of Long Island, followed by a drive along Route 25A to the North Fork, less than an hour's trip along a meandering, rural road. For reservations and information, call 631-473-0286. The third ferry route is from the South Fork. You can drive to North Haven and take the ferry to Shelter Island, drive or bicycle across Shelter Island, and then take a second ferry from Shelter Island to Green-port: **North Ferry** (631-749-0139;www.northferry.com) and **South Ferry** (631-749-1200;www.southferry.com). All of these routes are described in detail in chapter 2.

By Train

The **Long Island Rail Road** (718-217-5477 in New York; 631-231-5477 in Suffolk County; 516-822-5477 in Nassau County; www.mta.info) runs trains to the North Fork on its North Shore branch, although travel is rather infrequent. During the week, there are four trains daily leaving Penn Station for Greenport, which is the termination point on the North Fork, and four trains make the return trip. Departure times from Penn Station are: 7:39 AM—9:16 PM; trains from Greenport are: 5:30 AM—9:44 PM. On weekends, there are two trains. Those leave Penn Station at 9:16 AM and 2:16 PM; trains leave Greenport at 1:11 PM and 6:11 PM. If someone can pick you up in Ronkonkoma, however, the options are increased to over 20 trains per day. The fare is $23 one way during peak hours and $16.75 off-peak times to both Riverhead and Greenport.

By Group Tour

Long Island Rail Road (718-558-7498; www.lirr.org) The Long Island Rail Road offers a variety of tours to the North Fork in the summer. Among them are one to the Mattituck Strawberry Festival in June ($42 for adults, $33 for children), one to an Orchard Harvest (includes visits to a farm stand, a winery, and Greenport; $47/adult, $34/child ages 5–11), one to Splish Splash Water Park in Riverhead ($58.75/adult, $46/child ages 4–11), and several during the summer to the vineyards.

Long Island Wine Tours (631-775-8686; www.liwinetours.com) Jim Ferrarie operates an excellent Long Island tour company that provides tours of the wineries and the East End. He has buses and limousines that can accommodate large and small groups, and he's been doing this for 20 years, so he knows where to go for the most enjoyable experience.

Twin Forks Trolley Tours (631-369-3031; www.northforktrolleytours.com; mailing address: P.O. Box 46, Aquebogue, NY 11931) Owners: Tom and Kathie Ingald. Although initially organized to offer winery excursions of the North Fork on their vintage trolley, this company also offers tours of the Hamptons, including stops in Sag Harbor to shop. Or, you can combine a visit to a winery with lunch and a trip to the Tanger Outlet Mall, and they'll customize tours for groups also.

Vintage Tours (631-765-4689; www.vintagetour1.com; mailing address: P.O. Box 143, Peconic, NY 11958) Owner: Joann Perry. Joann will take you on an escorted tour of North Fork wineries in her 14-passenger air-conditioned bus, and she also includes a box lunch to be enjoyed at one of the delightful wineries. Yes, of course, wine is included.

Rental Cars

Most national car-rental companies have offices at Long Island Islip/MacArthur Airport, approximately 25 miles from Riverhead. In addition, the following companies are located on the North Fork.

Enterprise Rent-A-Car (631-369-6300; 1076 Rte. 58, Riverhead, NY 11901)

Hertz (631-727-7892; Riverhead Best Western; 1830 West Main St., Riverhead, NY 11901)

Taxis & Limousines

Taxi service on the North Fork is very limited. To avoid disappointment, you should either make arrangements to rent a car or hire one of the following car services.

Islander Limousine (631-765-5834) has 6- and 8-passenger town cars and a 10-passenger limousine. Call for rates and details.

Moonlight Classic Limo and Taxi (631-727-5800; 135 Railroad Ave., Riverhead, NY 11901) Will do airport runs as well as taxi trips between towns—and yes, they will handle transportation for weddings.

WINERIES

When men drink, then they are rich and successful and win lawsuits and are happy and help their friends.
Quickly, bring me a beaker of wine, so that I may wet my mind and say something clever.

—Aristophanes

People in California, New York, and Europe are talking about Long Island's East End wines. There hasn't been this much excitement in the wine world since the Napa, Sonoma, and Alexander valleys of California began serious production. In the 30 years of East End wine production, the number of wineries has grown to 46 on the North Fork and 3 on the South Fork. As the awards for the wines accumulate, the number of visitors to the tasting rooms increases, and so do the sales. That's good news for other businesses, too. New gourmet restaurants, caterers, motels, bed & breakfast establishments, gift shops, and wine shops are flourishing. Therefore it seems natural to begin this chapter with a description of the wineries.

It all started when a local farmer, John Wickham, planted the first grapes on the North Fork in the early 1960s; he sold them at his farm stand to home winemakers. Alex and Louisa Hargrave, who recognized the climate and soil similarities of the region to those of Bordeaux, were the first commercial pioneers. They planted vinifera vines in 1973 and pro-

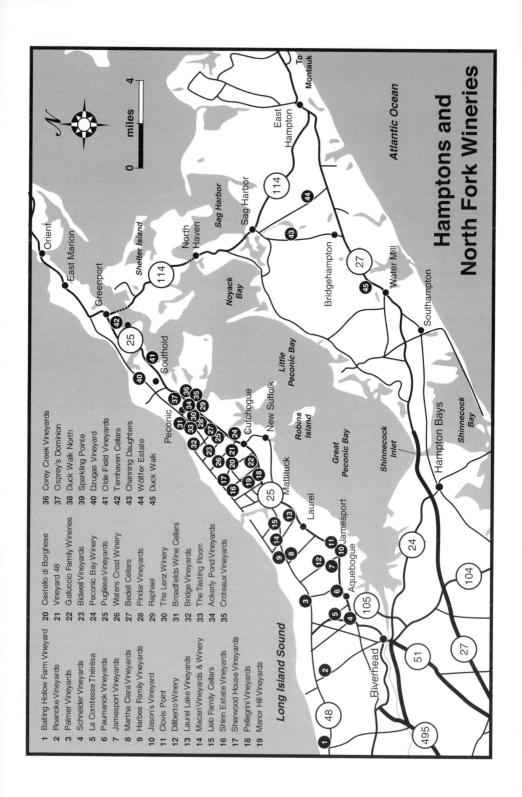

Hamptons and North Fork Wineries

1 Baiting Hollow Farm Vineyard
2 Roanoke Vineyards
3 Palmer Vineyards
4 Schneider Vineyards
5 La Comtesse Thérèsa
6 Paumanok Vineyards
7 Jamesport Vineyards
8 Martha Clara Vineyards
9 Harbes Family Vineyards
10 Jason's Vineyard
11 Clovis Point
12 Diliberto Winery
13 Laurel Lake Vineyards
14 Macari Vineyards & Winery
15 Lieb Family Cellars
16 Shinn Estate Vineyards
17 Sherwood House Vineyards
18 Pellegrini Vineyards
19 Manor Hill Vineyards

20 Castello di Borghese
21 Vineyard 48
22 Galluccio Family Wineries
23 Bidwell Vineyards
24 Peconic Bay Winery
25 Pugliese Vineyards
26 Waters Crest Winery
27 Bedell Cellars
28 Pindar Vineyards
29 Raphael
30 The Lenz Winery
31 Broadfields Wine Cellars
32 Bridge Vineyards
33 The Tasting Room
34 Ackerly Pond Vineyards
35 Croteaux Vineyards

36 Corey Creek Vineyards
37 Osprey's Dominion
38 Duck Walk North
39 Sparkling Pointe
40 Dzugas Vineyard
41 Olde Field Vineyards
42 Ternhaven Cellars
43 Channing Daughters
44 Wölffer Estate
45 Duck Walk

duced their first wines (then called Hargrave Vineyards, now Castello di Borghese) in 1977. Modern, award-winning wineries that rival those of Napa Valley are now the sites of guided tours and tastings as well as musical events, poetry readings, cooking classes and demonstrations, and much, much more.

Wine production for some wineries, however, is still so small that they have opted to join Russell Hearn, the winemaker at Pellegrini, in a custom-crush operation that he and his partners completed in Mattituck. First reported by Frank Prial in the *New York Times* (July 26, 2000), Premium Wine Group is patterned after the highly successful Napa Wine Company. Lieb Family Cellars, which partnered with Mr. Hearn, for example, now produces, ages, bottles, and labels its wines here instead of building its own winery. The stature and respect that Mr. Hearn has earned on the North Fork gives these growers confidence that their wines will be produced with the same integrity as if they were doing all the work themselves. Other small wineries have sought the expertise of Eric Fry, the tremendously respected winemaker at Lenz Vineyards, to handle the processing for them.

To put the production in perspective, in 2000 there were still only 2,200 acres of land planted in grapes on the East End, while more than 6,000 acres were planted in potatoes, the North Fork's largest crop. Ten years later, the numbers have changed dramatically—the number of acres planted in grapes has increased to nearly 3,000, while the acreage in potatoes has diminished to about the same. In 2000 wine production was estimated at 300,000 cases, about the same as for one medium-sized California winery. Ten years later, case production has increased to 500,000 annually—still not a rival in quantity to California (which some estimates put at 200 million cases annually), but certainly in quality.

The world is taking note of the quality of Long Island wine, as local wineries are racking up an impressive array of international awards. The Old Vine series of Lenz cabernet sauvignon and merlots consistently rank among those from the finest French chateaux, including Latour and Petrus. Lieb Cellars wins gold medals for its Reserve Pinot Blanc and Bridge Lane Chardonnay.

For anyone interested in wines, now is the time to visit. The enthusiasm and excitement are contagious. When you visit an East End winery, you're likely to meet the owner and the winemaker, who are sometimes the same person. You'll find that most of today's wineries are family enterprises run by hardworking vintners who are absolutely serious about their wines. They will share their belief in the region, their dreams for their vineyards, and their growth objectives for their winery. In a few years, as demand and production grow, some of this personal contact inevitably will be lost.

In fact, the times are already changing. The wine world has taken note! In 1998 and 1999, investors with deep pockets purchased several of the wineries and have now completed major expansions. Raphael Vineyards opened a spectacular Mediterranean-style winery in 2001, which rivals the finest in California. Martha Clara has now opened its own tasting room, as has Lieb Cellars. In 2007 Duck Walk opened a North Fork branch of its South Fork winery. In addition, in 2003 the Tasting Room, a sales and sampling outlet that showcases the fare of some of the smaller wineries, opened in Peconic.

When I first started writing this book, I was able to include all the wineries on the North Fork. Unfortunately, now that there are 46, there just isn't room to describe every one. This is a guidebook to the region and not a book about the wineries, although they are an important reason to visit. There are books, however, strictly about the wineries. An excellent book about North Fork wines, *Long Island Wine Country* (2009) by Jane Taylor Starwood, offers a current perspective on the origins of Long Island as a wine region, as well as an introduction to the owners, the wineries, and their products. *The Story of North Fork Wine* (2009) by John Ross, gives a first-person account of the launch of the North Fork as a wine region, as well as offering profiles of winery owners, vineyard managers, winemakers, and providing wine country recipes. As the chef/owner of the leading North Fork restaurant in the 1970s–1990s, he witnessed the origins of the wine industry and played a pivotal role by championing Long Island wines in his restaurant. *The Wines of Long Island, Birth of a Region* (2nd ed., 2000) by Philip F. Palmedo and Edward Beltrami, is recommended reading for anyone visiting East End wineries. It is a comprehensive guide to the history of winemaking on the East End and includes profiles of the wineries, the owners, and the winemakers. Another guide to East Coast wines, including an analysis of those from Long Island, is *Touring East Coast Wine Country: A Guide to the Finest Wineries* (2002) by Marguerite Thomas. This book highlights some of the region's wineries and includes interviews with winemakers and ratings for the wines. For up-to-the-minute information about local wines, call the Long Island Wine Council (631-369-5887; www.liwines.com).

Should you wish to take a guided tour of the wineries, several services are available. Vintage Tours (631-765-4689; www.vintagetour1.com), and Long Island Wine Tours (631-775-8686; www.liwinetours.com) both offer winery excursions. See "Group Tour" section above for complete listings.

If you still haven't had your fill of North Fork wineries after one of these tours, you might consider attending the **North Fork Wine Camp** (631-495-9744; www.winecamp.us), a truly wonderful immersion course. Organized by some of the leading wineries and by several bed & breakfasts, the camp is a four-day adventure offering an in-depth education in winemaking, as well as dinner at one of the outstanding North Fork restaurants, three nights in a B&B, lunches (wine, of course, included) in several vineyards, and a private dinner at one of the wineries, as well as breakfast every morning in your B&B.

Vine Time (631-477-0654; 800-551-0654; www.longislandvinetime.com) offers another excellent bed & breakfast plus winery option. You'll get a two-night stay at one of several outstanding B&Bs, including full breakfasts, dinner at leading North Fork restaurants, an all-day tour of participating wineries in a luxury van with an excellent guide, opportunities to talk directly to the winemaker, have a barrel tasting, or watch the harvest, depending on the season, plus a gourmet lunch at one of the wineries. (Ask about summer tours of several of the leading farms, coordinated with B&B stays.)

This section is not a comprehensive guide to the wineries, nor does it analyze the wines. Instead I hope to enhance your visit to this very special place by describing the settings as well as suggesting lodgings, restaurants, and cultural and recreational attractions. So buy some cheese, a baguette, perhaps some pâté, and plan a day of wine tasting. Actually, you should plan several days, with a leisurely stop for lunch at a winery, perhaps on a deck overlooking the vineyards.

(For the three excellent wineries located on the South Fork, see listings in chapter 4.)

ACKERLY POND

631-765-6861
www.ackerlypondvineyards.com
1375 Peconic Lane, Peconic
Mailing Address: P.O. Box 151, Peconic, NY 11958
Open: Mid-June–Sept., Wed.–Mon. 12–5; Oct.–May, Sat. and Sun. 12–5
Fee: $7 for six wines

Bedell Cellars

Ray Blum was one of the earliest proponents of wine production on the North Fork, where he planted his first grapes in 1979 and produced his first Peconic Bay wines in 1984. So even though he sold his winery in 1999, he just couldn't abandon the business he had done so much to foster. Therefore, that same year, he purchased 85 acres, planted 58 of them in grapevines, and started over again. Although Ray passed away in 2007, his widow, Jill, has hired a team who are as dedicated as she is to maintaining Ray's dream. Eric Fry is the winemaker; the enterprise produces approximately 500 cases a year. The tiny tasting room is located in a cedar-shake-sided 100-year-old barn on Peconic Lane.

BAITING HOLLOW FARM VINEYARD
631-369-0100
www.baitinghollowfarmvineyard.com
2114 Sound Ave., Baiting Hollow, 11901
Open: Year-round, Mon., Wed., and Thurs. 11–5; Fri. 11–6; Sat. and Sun. 11–7
Fee: $6 for three demi-tastes; $8 for four demi-tastes; $10 for five demi-tastes; $7/glass
Special Features: Live music weekends

The inviting farmhouse on Sound Avenue in Baiting Hollow, with its wraparound porch and vineyards is a family enterprise. Patriarch Sam Rubin purchased the land in 1988 and planted produce he farmed organically, but in the 1990s he decided to plant a few grapevines too. Obviously, one thing led to another and now the Rubin clan, including son Richard and daughter Sharon, are making wine at Premium Wine Group, with the assistance of winemaker Tom Drozd. They've got 11 of their 17-acre farm planted in grapevines, and they produce over 2,000 cases a year. The big old farmhouse, with its welcoming front porch, has been meticulously restored, and there's a large brick patio on which to enjoy the samplings of red table wine, rosé, and Merlot. In addition to the winery, the family farm includes stables and paddocks in which they care for rescued horses.

BEDELL CELLARS
631-734-7537
www.bedellcellars.com
36225 Main Rd. (Rte. 25), Cutchogue, NY 11935
Open: May–Oct., daily 11–6; Nov.–Apr., 11–5
Fee: $8 five table wines; $12 five reserve or premium wines
Special Features: Extraordinary contemporary art collection; VIP tours and tastings weekends at 12 and 3 $35/person; VIP tour including gardens $50

Kip Bedell planted his first grapes in 1980 and sold his first wines in 1985. By 1998 he had 32 acres planted, but in 2000 he got an offer he couldn't refuse from Michael Lynne, co-CEO of New Line Cinema and executive producer of the *Lord of the Rings* trilogy. Lynne is now the owner, and he's absolutely as serious about his wine business as Mr. Bedell was. He hired Pascal Marty, formerly with Chateau Mouton Rothschild, as his consulting oenologist, and Kelly Urbanik, whose background spans the globe from California to France, as winemaker. Dave Thompson is the vineyard manager, and Kip Bedell is often still consulted as well. Lynne also owns Corey Creek Vineyards, and he now has approximately 60 acres planted. The annual production for both Bedell and Corey Creek ranges from 12,000 to 15,000 cases. An enthusiastic collector of contemporary art, Lynne commissioned well-known artists to design the labels. Consistently winning awards, especially for Merlot, Chardonnay, and several blends, this winery is modern and efficient. Lynne renovated and expanded it in 2005, installing exceptional state-of-the-art equipment and French oak barrels. The tasting room resides in a beautiful beige shingled building with a two-level lounge, one of which contains a fireplace. Some of Lynne's extraordinary contemporary art collection is displayed on the walls, and VIP tours, which include a winery tour, tasting, and discussion of the artwork, can be arranged. A wonderful 4,000-square-foot covered outdoor tasting pavilion offers a serene place to sip while enjoying a sweeping view of the vineyards.

CASTELLO DI BORGHESE
631-734-5111
www.borghesevineyard.com
17150 North Rd. (Rte. 48) between Alvah's and Depot Lns., Cutchogue
Mailing Address: P.O. Box 957, Cutchogue, NY 11935
Open: May–Dec., Mon.–Fri. 11–5:30; Sat. 11–6; Sun. 11:30–6; Jan.–Apr., Thurs.–Mon. 11–5
Fee: $9 for five estate wines; $12 for five reserve wines
Special Features: Art gallery; gift shop; Winemaker's Walk (tour of winery and tasting) $20

This is where it all began. Alex and Louisa Hargrave were the first to believe that Long Island's North Fork could produce great wines, and they were right. Planting their first vines in 1973, they achieved tremendous success. After many years of hard work, however, they sold their winery in 1999 to Marco and Ann Marie Borghese, an Italian couple with a royal pedigree. The winery currently has 85 acres of vines planted and it produces 8,500–10,000 cases a year in a variety of wines. Castello di Borghese is particularly noted for its red wines—Cabernet Franc, Pinot Noir, and Reserve Merlot, but it's also been winning awards for its Sauvignon Blanc and Chardonnay. The tasting room incorporates a gift shop featuring wine and cookbooks, hand-painted glasses, and Castello di Borghese olives and olive oils from the family estate in Calabria, Italy, among other goodies, and there's also a pergola where guests can enjoy al fresco tastings and picnics. In a former barn, there's a rotating art exhibit, where opera and musicales are sometimes held.

CLOVIS POINT

631-722-4222
www.clovispointwines.com
1935 Main Rd. (Rte. 25), Jamesport, NY 11947
Open: year-round, Thurs.–Sun. 11–6
Fee: $7 for four wines; $12 for six wines plus cheese; $18 for six wines, cheese, and a tour of the vineyard (groups of six only)
Special Features: Live music, cooking demonstrations, book signings

Hal Ginsburg and Nasrallah Misk, along with several friends, purchased a plot of land containing a great old potato barn on the North Fork in 2001, and then in 2002 they supplemented it with the purchase of an existing vineyard. Next, they put together a top-flight team. John Leo is winemaker, and he oversees production at Premium Wine Group; Peter Gristina is the vineyard consultant. Of the 10-acre parcel, 8.5 acres are planted with Merlot, Cabernet Franc, Cabernet Sauvignon, Chardonnay, and Syrah vines. The aim of the winery is to produce highly drinkable blended wines. The wines can be tasted in a spectacular renovated potato barn opened in 2007. The soaring ceiling is supported by massive cedar posts, which were cleverly surrounded at the base with wine barrels and topped by a table to hold wineglasses. Stools are made of barrel staves. There's a bluestone floor, rough-hewn cedar walls, and a tasting bar that extends the length of the room, illuminated by massive brass hanging lamps. The entire effect is masculine and rustic. Beyond sets of mahogany French doors, a covered patio offers al fresco sipping. The winery produces about 3,000 cases annually.

COREY CREEK VINEYARDS

631-765-4168
www.bedellcellars.com
45470 Main Rd. (Rte. 25), Southold
Mailing Address: The Bedell North Fork, 36225 Main Rd., Cutchogue, NY 11935
Open: Year-round, daily Mem. Day–Oct., 11–6; rest of year 11–5
Fee: $5 for three wines; $8 for four wines; $12 for five wines

The 30 acres in Southold that Joel and Peggy Lauber called Corey Creek Vineyards were planted with vines in 1981, but the grapes were originally sold to local wineries. Now these mature vines are yielding grapes for estate-bottled wines. In 1999 the Laubers sold the winery to Michael Lynne, co-CEO of New Line Cinema, who also owns Bedell Cellars. Corey Creek produced its first estate bottles of Chardonnay in 1993, which immediately earned

This charming outdoor tasting room is an inviting place to sample the rosé wines of Croteaux Vineyards.

rave reviews. Its Chardonnays, in particular, continue to shine, and its Gewürztraminer has been winning awards as well. The wines are produced at Bedell. A beautiful, natural-sided wood building was completed in 1997 to house a handsome tasting and sales room. This is a great spot for a picnic, as a huge deck overlooks the vineyards.

CROTEAUX
631-765-6099
www.croteaux.com
1450 South Harbor Rd., Southold, NY 11971
Open: Fri.–Sun. 12–5
Fee: $7 for three rosés and one sparkling wine
Special Features: You can sit at tables in a charming courtyard or on Adirondack chairs on the lawn with views of the vineyard, for tastings; children's playroom.

This vineyard produces only rosé wines, making it unique on the East End, and perhaps across the U.S. As they say here, it's "rosé on purpose," meaning they grow their Merlot grapes specifically to make rosé. The vineyard was planted in 2003 on 10.5 acres of Paula and Michael Croteaux's 14-acre property, and their first vintage was produced in 2006. Although they oversee production, the wines are made by Richard Olsen-Harbich at Raphael in Peconic. Annual production ranges from 500 to 800 cases annually. This land had been farmed for many years, and the courtyard behind the tiny little sales room and gift shop is charming—bordered on both sides by preserved old barns that date to the 1700s. Should you wish to taste the wines while sitting in Adirondack chairs on the lawn, you will have views of row after row of grapevines. Paula is also the proprietor of a cooking and baking school, offering lessons in her restored farmhouse that range from olive oil tastings, to selecting and cooking with peaches, to bread baking, to the cuisine of Ireland.

DILIBERTO WINERY
631-722-3416
www.dilibertowinery.com
250 Manor Lane, Jamesport, NY 11947
Open: June–Oct., Thurs.–Mon. 11–6; Nov.–May, Sat. and Sun. 11–6
Fee: $8 for five wines
Special features: Live music on weekends; charming tasting room with Italian village mural
on wall.

Salvatore Diliberto began making wine in his home in Queens, but once he started buying
the grapes from Ray Blum at Peconic Bay Winery, he was hooked on the North Fork. He and
his wife, Maryann, purchased their farm in 1991 and eventually planted their first grapevines in 1998. And lo and behold, their first Merlot won a gold medal in a New York State
wine contest. They make food-friendly red wines that are meant to be drunk young, so they
can go directly from the tasting room to the table. The Dilibertos have a 4-acre vineyard.
Sal is the winemaker, and he produces about 1,000–1,200 cases a year. The tasting room
offers far more than your average quick sampling stop. Enter the door, and you're transported to Ristorante Benevento, a café in an Italian piazza that's made realistic by a fabulous
trompe l'oeil mural painted on the back wall. There may be live music, or Italian opera on
the sound system. Should you decide to sit outdoors, there's a spacious patio as well.

JAMESPORT VINEYARDS
631-722-5256
www.jamesportwines.com
1216 Main Rd. (Rte. 25), Jamesport
Mailing Address: P.O. Box 842, Jamesport, NY 11947
Open: Daily 10–6
Fee: $10 for five estate wines; $13 for five premier wines

This winery is partly new and partly old. Rising from the ashes of the defunct North Fork
winery and with grapes from a Cutchogue vineyard planted in 1981 by Ronald Goerler Sr.
and his son, Jamesport Vineyards produced its first wines in 1987. Jamesport has been
noted for years for its Sauvignon Blanc and Merlot wines, but a Late-Harvest Riesling
recently won high ratings at a *Wine Spectator* tasting. This winery uses only its own grapes,
making it a true estate winery. All 60 acres of the estate are now planted, and the annual
production is approximately 8,000 cases. The general manager is Ron Goerler Jr. The winery and tasting room are located in a 150-year-old cedar-shake potato and hay barn with
soaring ceilings.

LAUREL LAKE VINEYARDS
631-298-1420
www.llwines.com
3165 Main Rd. (Rte 25), Laurel, NY 11948
Open: Apr.–Dec., daily 11–6; Jan.–Mar., daily 11–5
Fee: $4 for three wines

In 1993 Michael McGoldrick purchased 35 acres that had been partially planted in
Chardonnay vines in 1980, and he bottled his first Laurel Lake Vineyards wines in 1994.
But that was just the beginning. In 1997 he built a beautiful gray wooden winery with dorm-

ers and front and side porches that offer spots for quiet relaxation and picnics. Inside there's a tall ceiling with a skylight, a window for viewing the stainless steel tanks and barrels, and a hospitality area for tastings and sales. In 1999 Mr. McGoldrick sold the winery to Juan Esteban Sepulveda, Francisco Gillmore, and Alejandro Parot—all with deep roots in the wine business in Chile. In addition to Chardonnay, the winery is now producing Cabernet Sauvignon, Merlot, several blends, Riesling, an Ice Wine, and a Meritage. Twenty-four acres of the vineyard are now planted, and the winery has been proudly garnering awards, especially for its Chardonnays and Cabernet Sauvignons. Current production is approximately 5,500 cases annually.

LENZ VINEYARDS

631-734-6010
www.lenzwine.com
Main Rd. (Rte. 25), Peconic
Mailing Address: P.O. Box 28, Peconic, NY 11958
Open: Mem. Day–Columbus Day, daily 10–6; Nov.–May, daily 10–5
Fee: $5 tasting of 7 estate wines; $10 tasting of premium old cuvées
Special Features: Merlot tastings, winter wine tour and tasting with winemaker Eric Fry, $25/person.

The handsome tasting room for Laurel Lake Vineyards has multiple decks overlooking the vineyards.

Lenz, which is located in a rose-stained wooden building, has an interesting entrance that is shaped somewhat like a hopper. The property is surrounded by a split-rail fence, and grapevines cover the rustic, colonnaded porch. Although the first vines were planted in 1980, the current winemaking team—owners Peter and Deborah Carroll, winemaker Eric Fry, vineyard manager Sam McCullough, and general manager Tom Morgan—was assembled in 1990. They are an exceptional team, making Lenz one of the most respected wineries on Long Island. They are absolutely dedicated to producing the highest-quality product on the 68-acre vineyard estate where they produce an average of 9,500 cases annually. The Lenz Old Vine Merlots and Cabernet Sauvignons consistently win scores that equal or excel the finest French wines in competitions. They should be treasured, especially when the prices are compared to their French counterparts. For example, in a 2008 blind tasting, a 2002 Lenz Old Vines Cabernet at $40 a bottle tied a 2002 Chateau Latour at $495 a bottle with 90 points each, and a 2002 Lenz Old Vines Merlot at $55 a bottle received a score of 92 compared to a 2002 Chateau Petrus at $900 a bottle, which received a score of 93.

LIEB FAMILY CELLARS

631-298-1942
www.liebcellars.com
35 Cox Neck Rd. at North Rd. (Rte. 48), Mattituck
Mailing Address: P.O. Box 907, Cutchogue, NY 11935
Open: Sun.–Fri. 11–5; Sat. 11–6
Fee: $8 for four wines
Special Features: Special release wines for charity

Lieb Family Cellars is an excellent example of the next generation of wines that we can expect to see produced on Long Island. Mark and Kathy Lieb purchased a 20-acre farm in Cutchogue in 1992 that had been partially planted in 1982 with Pinot Blanc grapes, making it one of the oldest vineyards on the North Fork. Over the years, they added more acreage and more grapes to bring their holdings to 50. Until 1997 they sold all their grapes to other wineries, but in that year they began making their own wines. When they released their 1997 Merlot in 2000, it had been made with such finesse that it immediately won rave reviews, and since that time, the Pinot Blanc Reserve and the Chardonnay Reserve have as well. Their intention is to remain small and to concentrate on producing only fine reserve wines. Always on the cutting edge, in 2008 they produced their first release of a White Merlot, made with 90 percent Merlot and 10 percent Sauvignon Blanc grapes and fermented without the skin. Rather than building their own winery, they are partners with Russell Hearn in the Premium Wine Group custom-crush winery, which opened in the fall of 2000. Their wines are produced there, but they have their own tasting room next door. The general manager is Gary Madden. They are producing 7,500 cases annually.

MACARI VINEYARDS AND WINERY

631-298-0100
www.macariwines.com
150 Bergen Ave. (just off Rte. 48), Mattituck
Mailing Address: P.O. Box 2, Mattituck, NY 11952
Open: Mon.–Fri. 9–5; Sat. and Sun. 11–5:30
Also: 631-734-7070

Macari Vineyards and Winery is located on one of the largest farms on the North Fork.

24385 Main Rd. (Rte. 25), Cutchogue
Open: Mon.–Fri. 11–5; Sat. and Sun. 11–5:30
Fee: $6 for a variety of four wines; $7 for four all white wines; $12 for five premier white wines; $12 for five premier red wines

In 1995, 105 acres of former potato fields were planted by the Macari family on their 500-acre waterfront estate, in a combination of Merlot, Chardonnay, Cabernet Franc, and Viognier. Several years later, they purchased an adjacent 5 acres of mature vines on acreage that had belonged to the former Mattituck Hills winery, and since that time they have continued to plant, bringing their planted acreage to 180 acres. By 1998 they had opened an impressive, natural cedar-sided building in Mattituck, with a stone foundation and a spacious covered deck. This is a great place to hold an event or to just sit at the black wrought-iron tables overlooking the vineyards and sip the wine. This thoroughly modern winery is fully computerized, yet the vines are tended with the utmost concern for the environment. The Macari family (father Joe Macari Sr. and son Joe Macari Jr.) use only organic and sustainable methods in their vineyards—rich composts and no pesticides. The first wines were offered in 1997, and current production is about 12,000 to 14,000 cases annually. This team is committed to producing the very highest-quality wines. The Macaris have one of the largest farms on the North Fork, and there are plans to continue to plant them with grapes. The winemakers are Paola Valverde and Helmut Gangl.

MARTHA CLARA VINEYARDS

631-298-0075
www.marthaclaravineyards.com
6025 Sound Ave. (Rte. 48), Riverhead, NY 11952
Open: Mon., Wed., Thurs. 11–6; Tues. 11–11; Fri. and Sat. 11–7
Fee: $6 for three red or white wines; $7 for three sparkling wines

Special Features: Horse-and-carriage rides, cooking demos; live music weekends; art shows; patio; deck; excellent gift shop that includes unique items

When a friend of mine moved to Seattle, she made me promise to send her a care package of Entenmann bakery products once a month. Now folks are making similar requests for his wines. Robert Entenmann planted a broad selection of red and white grapes on 106 acres of his 200-acre former thoroughbred horse farm in 1995. In 1999 his first wines were released. They are getting rave reviews and winning prestigious awards. The Viognier, Sauvignon Blanc, Merlot, and Ciel, a lush dessert wine, are particularly fine. The wine-maker is Juan Eduardo Micieli-Martinez, the vineyard manager is Wojtek Majewski, and the proprietor and owner is Entenmann's daughter Jacqueline Entenmann Damianos (yes, she's married to Jason Damianos, winemaker at Duck Walk and Pindar and proprietor of Jason's Vineyard). They use the facilities at Premium Wine Group to make their wines, and their annual production is about 15,000 cases annually. There's a large tasting room with an out-door pavilion, and two historic barns on the property have been converted to art galleries and special-event spaces. In the tasting room, in addition to the wines, you can also pur-chase jams (peach, raspberry, and currant) that are house-made, as well as salad dressings. Both the tasting room and the gallery/barn include demonstration kitchens equipped for TV coverage. Numerous cooking demonstrations and celebrity-chef events take place here.

THE OLD FIELD
631-765-0004
www.theoldfield.com
59600 Main Rd. (Rte.25), Southold
Mailing Address: P.O. Box 726, Southold, NY 11971
Open: Daily Thurs.–Mon., 11–5
Fee: $1 per wine or $7 for all seven wines
Special Features: Sustainable Agriculture Tour and Historical Tour, both $10

There's evidence the Old Field land was farmed long before the arrival of the first English settlers. Apparently when the English arrived in 1640, they found a flourishing Indian pop-ulation who, appreciating the rich alluvial soil, had established this area as their primary farmland. It's been farmed in some fashion ever since. Christian Baiz is the fourth genera-tion of his family to farm this land. One of his ancestors planted the first grapevines in 1974, and now Chris and his wife, Ros, are preserving the land that's been in his family since World War I, by producing premium table wines. Approximately 10 acres are planted in Chardonnay, Pinot Noir, Merlot and Cabernet Franc. Old Field grapes are processed at Lenz Winery, where they are overseen by winemaker Eric Fry, but Ros and daughter Perry Weiss assist in the winemaking, and the wines are sold right here on the farm at a tiny little tasting room. This is a wonderful place to bring a picnic lunch and sit down by the icehouse and pond with a bottle of Merlot and some tasty bread, cheese, and pâté. Current produc-tion ranges from 1,300 to 1,800 cases annually.

OSPREY'S DOMINION WINERY
631-765-6188
www.ospreysdominion.com
44075 Main Rd., Peconic
Mailing Address: P.O. Box 198, Peconic, NY 11958

Open: Mem. Day–Labor Day, Sun.–Thurs. 11–6, Fri. and Sat. 11–9; rest of year, Sun.–Fri. 11–6; Sat. 11–7.
Fee: $5 for five wines; $7 for five award-winning wines.
Special Features: Live entertainment weekends

When Bud Koehler and Bill Tyree purchased 70 acres in Peconic that had been planted with grapevines in the 1980s (and sold to other wineries), they acquired mature vines that allowed them to offer their own estate wines. They subsequently added an additional 20 acres, and now the winery's annual production ranges from 12,000 to 16,000 cases. A handsome yellow stucco retail and tasting outlet was built in 1996, where such classics as Sauvignon Blanc, Pinot Noir, Cabernet Franc, and Gewürztraminer are award winning. Winemaker Adam Suprenant also makes a hot-spiced wine, similar to a mulled wine, and light, crisp peach and strawberry wines (they call it "strawberry shortcake in a glass"). The latter was created for the annual Mattituck Strawberry Festival. The general manager is Bud Koehler, and the vineyard manager is Tom Stevenson. Osprey's Dominion also makes excellent grape jellies and vinegars, and you can buy sweatshirts, books, picnic backpacks (perfect for bicyclists), and gift baskets. A pretty patio overlooks the vineyards. Additional weekend attractions include hayrides and art shows.

PALMER VINEYARDS

631-722-9463
www.palmervineyards.com
5120 Sound Ave. (Rte. 48), Riverhead, NY 11901
Mailing Address: P.O. Box 2125, Aquebogue, NY 11931
Open: June–Oct., daily 11–6; Nov.–May, daily 11–5; self-guided tour
Fee: $6 for three estate wines; $8 for three premium wines
Special Features: Victorian pub tasting room; self-guided tour; live music weekends; hayrides

Robert Palmer was in advertising before he became a winery owner, so promotion was his forte. (He passed away in 2009.) Because of his expertise, Palmer wines are the most widely distributed of Long Island wines, appearing in restaurants in 23 states and 5 foreign countries. Palmer Vineyards, with 125 acres planted, is one of the largest North Fork producers, bottling 15,000 cases annually. Winemaker Miguel Martin produces outstanding wines. One of the finest is a reserve Chardonnay, but the Cabernet Franc, Gewürztraminer, and White Riesling are also excellent. Visitors (there can be as many as 500 a day) love the look and feel of this user-friendly winery. Clear, informative signs lead visitors on a self-guided tour past windows for viewing the tank, cask, and bottling rooms. The tasting and sales room contains an oak bar, Tiffany-style stained-glass lights, and several oak and wrought-iron Victorian booths that were once part of an authentic 18th-century pub in England. An inviting deck overlooking the vineyards is made for relaxing. There's even a small gift shop where T-shirts, caps, and books are sold. In the summer, there are live concerts, hayrides, and festivals on weekends.

PAUMANOK VINEYARDS

631-722-8800
www.paumanok.com
1074 Main Rd. (Rte. 25), Aquebogue

Mailing Address: P.O. Box 741, Aquebogue, NY 11931
Open: Apr.–Oct., daily 11–6; Nov.–Mar., daily 11–5
Fee: $3 for three wines; $4 for four wines; $8 for four reserve and Grand Vintage wines
Special Features: Self-guided tour; guided tour $5/person; Proprietor's Tour with one of the
owners, including wine tasting $20/person; guided tours by advance appointment only

The vines for Paumanok Vineyards, which is owned by Charles and Ursula Massoud and
their sons, were first planted in 1983, and the first vintage was bottled in 1991. Kareem
Massoud is the winemaker, and sons Salim and Nabeel work on the estate also. The winery
currently produces 8,000 to 9,000 cases annually from 72 acres of vines on the 103-acre
estate. This is one of the most award-winning wineries on the North Fork; all wines are
made strictly from estate-grown grapes. The Cabernet Sauvignon Grand Vintage, in particular, but also Chardonnay, Chenin Blanc, Merlot, and Sauvignon Blanc are all best bets. The
tasting room is spacious, with a glass viewing window overlooking the tank and barrel
rooms below. Guided tours are offered by advance appointment only. The large outdoor
deck is a wonderful place for picnics.

PECONIC BAY WINERY
631-734-7361
www.peconicbaywinery.com
31320 Main Rd. (Rte. 25), Cutchogue
Mailing Address: P.O. Box 818, Cutchogue, NY 11935
Open: Sun.–Fri. 11–5, Sat. 11–6
Fee: $7 for five wines; $9 for six wines; $12 for six reserve wines; or $3 a tasting; $6.50–$15
by the glass
Special Features: Tours Mem. Day–Labor Day 11 AM and 12 PM; $16 by appt.; bonfire Fridays
with live music; live music Sat. and Sun., art shows

Ray Blum, the original owner of Peconic Bay, planted his first grapes in 1979 and produced
his first wines in 1984, so he was one of the first winemakers to discover the region. He
sold the winery in 1999 to Paul and Ursula Lowerre, and it continues to produce a fine
selection of wines. There are now about 55 acres in production on the 200-acre estate, and
the winery bottles around 8,000 cases a year. The winemaker is Greg Gove, Charles Hargrave is the vineyard manager, and the general manager is Matthew Gillies. A pretty patio
covered by an awning has been added to the tasting room by the new owners, and there is
also a small gift shop. Summer concerts include folk and pop singers as well as jazz, and
there's a huge Thanksgiving barrel tasting.

PELLEGRINI VINEYARDS
631-734-4111
www.pellegrinivineyards.com
23005 Main Rd. (Rte. 25), Cutchogue, NY 11935
Open: Daily 11–5; self-guided tour
Fee: $4 for three 1 oz. pours; $8 for three 2 oz. pours, including current releases and Vintner's Pride

It's always an advantage if you can purchase land that is planted with mature grapevines.
Bob and Joyce Pellegrini bought 30 acres in 1988 that had been planted in 1982, enabling
them to produce their first wines in 1992, and they've been adding additional acreage ever

This distinctive landmark gazebo sits amidst the Pellegrini vineyards.

since. In 2000 they purchased an additional 70 to 80 acres, bringing their total acreage to approximately 98, with 70 planted in grapes, which allows them to grow all their own grapes and produce estate wines. Production now ranges from 10,000 to 12,000 cases annually. The winemaker is Russell Hearn. The Pellegrini winery opened in 1993 in a sensational building; it's shaped like a cloister, with a grassy inner courtyard circled by a brick-and-flagstone walkway. Inside, vaulted ceilings and a multitude of windows create a light-filled space. There's a tasting counter on one side and tables and chairs by the windows; outside there's a deck for picnics or lounging. A loft overlooking the room could be used for musicians or as another place to sip and gaze out across the vineyards. This is a winery built for visitors. Self-guided tours may be taken throughout the day, or visitors may watch the winery workers from a balcony above the tank and barrel rooms. Special events often take place in this wonderful space, and the Pellegrini gazebo is a local landmark.

PINDAR VINEYARDS

631-734-6200
www.pindar.net
37645 Main Rd. (Rte. 25), Peconic
Mailing Address: P.O. Box 332, Peconic, NY 11958

Open: Daily 11–5:30; seasonal tours, call for schedule

Fee: $4 for five wines

Special Features: Live music weekends in summer; vineyard tours daily in summer

Dr. Herodotus Damianos, who also owns Duck Walk Vineyards on the North and South Forks, is of Greek descent (Pindar was an ancient Greek poet), and the distinctive labels on his bottles are derived from Greek mythology. The first vines on Pindar's 667-acre spread were planted in 1979, and the first release was bottled in 1983. When the winery first opened, the huge white stucco building seemed to rise from the neat rows of vines like a mirage in the desert, but over the years we've gotten used to it. This is the largest winery on the North Fork, with some 100,000 cases produced annually, and the tasting and sales room is built to accommodate visitors. There are scheduled tours of the winery, and there can be as many as 2,000 visitors a day in the summer and up to 50 people per tour, but the tasting room was recently expanded to handle the crowds and to make room for a large gift shop. Pindar's Mythology, a Meritage, has received much praise and is a must for sampling, as are the Merlot, Viognier, Cabernet Sauvignon, Chardonnay, and a refreshing Summer Blush that includes cranberry juice. Jason Damianos is the winemaker, and his brother, Pindar, is the vineyard manager (another brother, Alexander, manages Duck Walk Vineyards, North and South). A delightful outside pavilion makes a terrific place for a picnic or summer sipping. Lots of events take place here, including the popular Champagne, Chopin, and Caviar—a chance to learn how sparkling wines are made, followed by a sampling, with hors d'oeuvres and background music. Following a distinctive sojourn in France where he learned the benefits of closer spacing of grapevines, Jason Damianos planted his own vineyard on Main Rd. in Jamesport. His wines are sold under the Jason's Vineyard label and he now has his own tasting room in a large, distinctive wooden building with a spacious porch in Jamesport.

PUGLIESE VINEYARDS

631-734-4057

www.pugliesevineyards.com

34515 Main Rd. (Rte. 25), Cutchogue

Mailing Address: P.O. Box 467, Cutchogue, NY 11935

Open: Daily 11–6

Fee: $5 for any four wines, including champagne

The Puglieses planted their first vines in 1980 and made their first wines in 1986. They now have 53 acres planted and produce 8,000–10,000 cases of wine annually, including Chardonnay, Merlot, and a sparkling wine. If packaging can sell a product, the Puglieses will sell a lot of wine. Lovely, hand-painted bottles are decorated by Patricia Pugliese, who owns the winery with her husband, Ralph. But then, the wine is exceptional also. Their son Peter is the winemaker, and Lawrence is the vineyard manager. Their Blanc de Blanc Champagne, made of 100 percent Chardonnay, is outstanding. Tastings are proudly offered at the winery. Rows of gift baskets with hand-painted bottles and glasses line tables in a room adjacent to the tasting room, ready to be given as house gifts to lucky East End hosts. (Call in advance to order a personalized gift basket.) On the wall, spectacular landscape photographs by son Ralph Jr. are for sale. Picnic tables are set up under a grape arbor overlooking a pond and offer one of the most appealing places to sip and relax on the North Fork.

The spectacular visitors' center and winery at Raphael includes a large gift shop and event space.

RAPHAEL
631-765-1100
www.raphaelwine.com
39390 Main Rd., Peconic
Mailing Address: P.O. Box 17, Peconic, NY 11958
Open: Daily, May–Dec. 12–5; Fri.–Mon., Jan.–Apr. 12–5
Fee: $6 for three estate wines; $9 for three full-bodied red wines; or $2–$5 per taste
Special Features: Late-night Thurs. live music in summer

Throughout 2000, those of us who drove down Main Road in Peconic were fascinated by the mammoth Italianate-style building rising from a roadside field—with its warm umber stucco walls and tile roof, it looked somewhat like a Tuscan monastery. Turns out it's the $6 million tasting room and winery of Raphael, an enterprise of John Petrocelli, a New York commercial builder, and his wife, Joan. This winery now rivals the finest in California. But it's not all show—this is a well-conceived venture. Several years ago, Petrocelli planted 42 of his 60 acres in mostly merlot grapes, and he intended initially to produce only a merlot wine. Merlot is still the signature wine, but the remaining 18 acres have been planted with other grapes, and they now produce some Cabernet Franc and Sauvignon Blanc. For his winemaker, he hired Richard Olsen-Harbich, who has been making wines on Long Island since the early 1980s, and he also hired Paul Pontallier, the managing director of Château Margaux, as his consulting winemaker. All three men are banking on the similarities of the North Fork's climate and soil to those of Bordeaux. Production now ranges from 4,000 to 6,000 cases annually. The fabulous visitors' center/winery, which opened in 2001, includes a handsome tasting room, winery, and large gift shop, as well as test kitchens and rooms where official wine comparisons can take place. It's become an extremely popular event locale.

ROANOKE VINEYARDS
631-727-4161
www.roanokevineyards.com
3543 Sound Avenue, Riverhead, NY 11901
Open: Year-round; in summer Sun.–Thurs. 11–6, Fri. 11–7, Sat. 11–9; rest of year Sun.–Fri. 11–6; Sat. 11–9
Fee: $8 for four wines
Special Features: Tasting room with fireplace; art gallery

Richard Pisacano has been involved in the North Fork wine business almost from its start, learning the business, literally, from the ground up. He started more than 30 years ago by apprenticing to Dave and Steve Mudd, who were among the earliest planters and vineyard managers, and he's been vineyard manager at Wölffer Estate Vineyards for more than 10 years. Now the winery that Richard and his wife, Soraya, own, produces elegant artisanal, limited-production, handcrafted wines from grapes grown in their seven-acre vineyard. Roman Roth is the winemaker, and the wines are produced at Wölffer. The handsome tasting room, which has a vaulted ceiling and a fireplace, is the only place the wines are sold. Production ranges from 1,500–3,000 cases a year.

SHERWOOD HOUSE VINEYARDS
631-298-1396
www.sherwoodhousevineyards.com
2600 Oregon Rd., Mattituck, NY 11952
Tasting Room: Elijah's Lane, north of Rte. 48; addl. tasting room scheduled to open at 1291 Main Rd. Jamesport in 2010.
Open: daily 12–6. Wines also available at the Tasting Room, 2885 Peconic Ln., Peconic; 631-765-6404. Open: Summer, Fri.–Sun. 11–6; rest of year, Fri.–Sun. 11–5
Fee: $8 for six wines, $10 for 6 premium wines, $12 for five reserve wines; at Tasting Room, $6 for six wines

Charles and Barbara Smithen traveled the French wine route for many years—always dreaming of owning a winery of their own. Eventually the dream became reality, when they planted their first grapes in 1996 on their own farm in Mattituck. Today they have 38 acres on which mostly Chardonnay and Merlot grapes are planted. Their wines are winning rave reviews as well as gold awards. Gilles Martin is the winemaker, and they produce their wines in the custom-crush winery of Premium Wine Group. Annual production ranges from 1,200 to 3,000 cases. There's a small tasting cottage on Elijah's Lane in Mattituck, but the Smithens are also opening a tasting room on Main Road in Jamesport in 2010. Wines can also be tasted and purchased at the Tasting Room in Peconic.

SHINN VINEYARDS
631-804-0367
www.shinnestatevineyards.com
2000 Oregon Rd., Mattituck, NY 11952

Open: daily, Mon.–Thurs. 11–5; Fri.–Sun. 11–6
Fee: $6.50 for three wines; $8.50 for four wines; $10.50 for five wines
Special Features: Vineyard tours with the owners Sat. and Sun. afternoons at 1:30, $8.50; guest rooms on premises

Barbara Shinn and David Page owned Home Restaurant in New York City, which was noted for its strictly homemade cuisine and its East Coast–only wine list, which for several years included some of their own vintages (they subsequently sold the restaurant and now devote themselves strictly to their winery and bed & breakfast.) In 2000 the couple planted 15 of their 21 acres—mostly in Merlot grapes, but they supplemented these with Cabernet Sauvignon, Sauvignon Blanc, and a few other varietals. They now have all 21 acres planted. Their first harvest was in 2002, and the first Merlot was released in 2004. The couple are adamant proponents of farm sustainability—farming without the use of chemicals—and they even irrigate with a liquid compost. They have their own winery, where they work with winemaker Anthony Nappa, to produce approximately 4,500 cases annually. Their intention is to remain rather small, enabling them to continue their hands-on day-to-day attention to their vineyards and winery, so that they can produce nothing but the highest-quality wines. At the entrance to the estate, before even approaching the tasting room, you'll see the wonderful old farmhouse they've converted into an enchanting bed & breakfast. As you can imagine, David will treat you to terrific breakfasts (see listing under "Lodging," this chapter).

SPARKLING POINTE

631-316-0530
www.sparklingpointe.com
39750 Route 48, Southold, NY 11971
Open: Year-round; daily in summer 12–6; rest of year open Sat., Sun., and holidays 12–6
Fee: $12 for flight of three wines
Special Features: Entertainment events held throughout year—check Web site for dates and entertainer

Tom and Cynthia Rosicki have created one of the few wineries in the United States devoted strictly to sparkling wines, or those created via the traditional *méthod champenoise*. They purchased their 12-acre piece of land (a former nursery) in 2002 and knew right away that they wanted to specialize in sparkling wines. They hired Steve Mudd to prepare the soil, planted their fields in Chardonnay, Pinot Noir, and Pinot Meunier grapes, and hired Gilles Martin, who had previously worked at a major French Champagne house, as their winemaker. Then in 2009, they opened a handsome gray stucco tasting room, with a very impressive interior. There are vaulted ceilings, crystal chandeliers, a fireplace, and a VIP lounge with white leather sofas and another fireplace. Approximately 3,000 cases are produced a year.

TASTING ROOM

631-765-6404
www.tastingroomli.com
2885 Peconic Lane, Peconic
Mailing Address: P.O. Box 2799, Aquebogue, NY 11931
Open: Summer, Fri.–Sun. 11–6; rest of year, Fri.–Sun. 11–5
Fee: $6 for six wines

The Tasting Room offers a venue for smaller boutique wineries to showcase their wines and acquaint the public with them. In general, the vineyards represented by the Tasting Room have limited production, and many do not have their own wineries; their grapes are processed either at Premium Wine Group or another winery. The following wineries are represented by the Tasting Room.

Bouké Wines (877-877-0527; www.boukewines.com; 35 Cox Neck Rd., Mattituck, NY 11952) With grapes selected from local growers and produced at Premium Wine Group, Lisa Donneson's wines are easy sipping and drinkable now. The name is a play on the word "bouquet."

Bridge Vineyards (631-734-6147; www.bridgevineyards.com; 8850 Bridge Ln., Cutchogue, NY 11935) Co-owners: Paul Wegimont and Greg Sandor. Winemaker Eric Fry collaborates with the owners in processing these wines at Premium Wine Group. In addition to samplings at the Tasting Room, you can taste these wines, as well as other New York State offerings, at their terrific wine bar in Brooklyn, while nibbling on sandwiches, salads, and excellent cheese plates.

Christiano Family Vineyards (www.christianowines.com; mailing address: P.O. Box 934, Remsenburg, NY 11960)

La Comtesse Thérèse (631-871-9194; www.comtessetherese.com; Union Ave. & Rte. 105, Aquebogue; mailing address: P.O. Box 1185, Mattituck, NY 11952) Theresa Dilworth is an international tax attorney for Pfizer during the week and an owner, winemaker, and vineyard manager on the weekends. Her wines are produced at the Premium Wine Group in Mattituck. Theresa is also the guiding hand behind the Tasting Room.

Medolla Vineyards (631-334-3059; www.medollavineyards.com; Main Rd., Peconic; mailing address: P.O. Box 008, Peconic, NY 11958) Owned by John and Denise Medolla, this winery may have a small (500 case) annual production, but it has been garnering awards ever since its first wine was produced, in 2002. The grapes (mostly Merlot) are purchased from local growers and made with the assistance of winemaker Eric Fry.

Onabay (917-725-0605; www.onabayvineyards.com; P.O. Box 476, Southold, NY 11971) This winery is located on 180 acres of land on a bay (thus the name) close to Long Island Sound. Owners Brad and Francesca Anderson planted some of their acreage with Chardonnay and Merlot grapes. With the assistance of consultant Bruce Schneider and viticulturist Steve Mudd, they are now producing wines that are being sold in leading restaurants on Long Island and in New York City. The elegant labels, which feature a heron, are designed by Francesca, who is an artist; poems by their daughter Mia are also found on the labels.

Schneider Vineyards (www.schneidervineyards.com) Bruce Schneider apprenticed in Burgundy vineyards, so he's very knowledgeable about wines, and he currently serves as a consultant to several other wineries on the North Fork. He and his wife produce about 2,000 cases annually, including an unfiltered Chardonnay and the popular blended wines Potato Barn White and Potato Barn Red.

Sherwood House (see listing above)

Sparkling Pointe (see listing above)

VINEYARD 48
631-734-5200
www.vineyard48winery.com

18910 North Rd. (Rte. 48), Cutchogue, NY 11935
General Manager: Joseph Pipia
Open: Summer, Sun.–Thurs. 10–6, Fri. and Sat. 10–7; rest of year, daily 11–5
Fee: $9 five wines; $2/glass
Special Features: Live music Mar.–Nov.; Sat. and Sun. 2–5; cigar factory; picnic area

Bidwell, the ancestor of Vineyard 48, bottled its first wines in 1986. Today there are about 30 acres planted, and the winery produces 10,500 cases annually. So this is not a new winery—it's just under new ownership. The Bidwell family sold the winery in 2004 to the Metz, Lamanna, and Bartone families, who run it now, and they're having a grand time. The handsome two-story, green-shingled tasting room, with its elevated ceilings, tiled floors, and art on the walls, was built in 1998. Tables and chairs in the tasting room provide places to sip the wines, and to play chess, and there's also a grassy picnic area outside. You can purchase a variety of items at the gift shop, and if you go on the Web site, you'll see the full list of weekend performers. Events here include dance contests, free food, and lots of fun. Also, don't miss the Little Cigar Factory, which is just across the courtyard from the tasting room. If you've never watched cigars being rolled, it's fascinating. Take some home with you.

WATERS CREST WINERY

631-734-5065
www.waterscrestwinery.com
22355 Rte. 48, Cutchogue, NY 11935
Open: Mon.–Thurs. 10:30–5, Fri.–Sun. 10:30–6
Fee: $12 for eight wines, includes an etched wineglass

Newly opened in 2003, this boutique winery is a must-stop for wine enthusiasts who want to see a wine operation "up close and personal." Bruce and Christiane Baker Schneider were the first on the East End to make fine wine by handpicking the grapes from the finest vineyards, but then they hired expert winemakers to handcraft their wines for them. Jim and Linda Waters have taken this approach a step further. They have their own winery, but because they have no vineyards of their own, they personally select their grapes from local growers. The winery is located in an 1,800-square-foot building in a little strip mall, where they do all the work themselves. When you visit the tasting room, you can take a tour to watch the processing of grapes from harvest to bottle, and you'll see the French oak barrels they use for aging. Among the wines they produce are Merlots, Chardonnays, Rosés, Cabernet Francs, and Meritage. Total annual production is 1,000 cases.

DINING

So many new, wonderful dining establishments have opened on the North Fork that it makes sense to divide them into two categories: restaurants and cafés, bakeries, pubs, and other eateries. All the establishments listed here are of superior quality, but those included in the restaurant section have a bit more to offer—perhaps a larger selection of Long Island wines, or a classier setting.

John Ross, the owner of the first truly gourmet restaurant on the North Fork (Ross's, listed in previous editions of this guide) has written a book about the North Fork, its restaurants and its wines, titled *The Food and Wine of the North Fork* (2005). When Mr. Ross owned his restaurant, the North Fork's wine industry was in its infancy and he was an absolute advocate for Long Island wines. As you entered his restaurant, you were greeted by a floor-to-ceiling rack of local wines, which he recommended with each meal. In this book, he offers numerous recipes, and also describes the demise of a number of North Fork restaurants.

As this book went to press, Nello Balan, noted Manhattan restaurateur and owner of a Southampton summer hotel and restaurant, was working to complete another restaurant in Greenport as well as a small café in Bego, a boutique hotel across the street. Since they were not completed, however, they have not been included here.

Restaurants

A MANO OSTERIA & WINE BAR

631-298-4800
www.amanorestaurant.com
13550 Main Rd. (Rte.25), Mattituck, NY 11952
Owner/Chef: Tom Schaudel
Cuisine: Italian
Open: Year-round; D nightly; L Sat. and Sun.
Price: Moderate–Expensive
Credit Cards: AE, MC, V
Special Features: Outside dining
Reservations: Accepted
Directions: On Main Rd. (Rte. 25) two blocks west of Love Ln.

When Tom Schaudel opens a restaurant, you know it's going to be done right, and A Mano is no exception. Celebrating the bounty of the North Fork, this restaurant showcases the products of local farmers, winemakers, cheesemakers, fishermen, shellfish farms, and local livestock growers to create a menu similar to one that might be found in the Tuscan countryside. The smart but casual space features dark wood floors and earth-toned walls. A patio framed by stone pillars affords outside dining. Among the entrées, you might enjoy a grilled swordfish with herbed polenta or grilled scallops with a lemon-artichoke risotto. The desserts, such as a warm peach crisp with peach gelato, feature local farm ingredients.

AMARELLE

631-886-2242
www.amarelle.net
2028 North Country Rd., Wading River, NY 11792
Owners/Chefs: Lia Fallon and Steve Biscari Amaral
Cuisine: Contemporary Country
Serving: D
Open: Year-round; daily except Mon.
Price: Inexpensive–Expensive
Credit Cards: AE, D, DC, MC, V
Special Features: Patio; fireplace; view of duck pond
Reservations: Highly recommended
Directions: From Long Island Expressway (I-495), take exit 68 to the William Floyd Parkway north. Travel to the end and then turn right onto Rte. 25A. Turn left at second street onto Randall Rd. At end turn right onto North Country Rd. Restaurant is on left.

Although there have been a series of restaurants in this charming building over the years, this one is a keeper. A flagstone pathway leads from the parking area to a gabled entrance flanked by columns and pots of flowers—a welcoming terrace offers outside dining in warm weather. Across the little country road, ducks paddle about in a pond. Inside, there's a bar to the left, and to the right, the dining room is stunning—offering a setting that includes soaring ceilings, wainscoting, walls of windows with views of the pond, and a dramatic free-standing stone fireplace. The setting is delightful, but what you really come for is the outstanding cuisine prepared by owners Lia Fallon and Steve Biscari-Amaral. Steve is a graduate of Johnson & Wales, and has cooked in fine restaurants all over the world, and as joint owners of Black Tie Caterers, the team are top toques at the finest Manhattan and Hampton parties. Now the rest of us can enjoy their expertise too. The menu offers a clever combination of small- and large-plate options and it changes with the seasons, depending on what's available at the local farms. In fall, for example, you might start with a baby pumpkin filled with risotto served with caramelized onion and Romano cheese. Entrées include local fish (perhaps striped bass) plated with creamed butter beans, oven-roasted tomatoes, and a Champagne beurre blanc, or perhaps a suckling pig fixed three ways. Desserts are equally inventive. You might choose a poached pear with a port wine reduction, served with candied walnuts and a local Camembert cheese, or the Amarelle, an almond-cherry financier with vanilla bean yogurt mousse, and cherry coulis. There's a nice wine list that includes local wines. Come here once, and I guarantee you'll put it at the top of your favorites list.

BAYVIEW INN & RESTAURANT
631-722-2659
www.northforkmotels.com
10 Front St., South Jamesport
Mailing Address: P.O. Box 137, South Jamesport, NY 11970
Owner: Scott and Greg Patchell
Chef: Tom Lopez
Cuisine: New American/Continental
Serving: L, D
Open: Year-round; daily except Mon.
Price: Moderate–Expensive
Credit Cards: AE, D, MC, V
Special Features: Deck dining; fireplace; guest rooms on premises

Reservations: Accepted
Directions: From Main Rd. (Rte. 25) in Jamesport, turn south onto S. Jamesport Ave. This takes you to South Jamesport. Restaurant is on the corner of S. Jamesport Ave. and Front St.

The sleepy little village of South Jamesport was once a bustling and popular summer beach community with huge hotel/boardinghouses lining the beach. The little Victorian gem that houses the Bayview Inn was built in 1860 and did its fair share of entertaining in its day. Eventually the large hotels either burned or were torn down, and this little remnant degenerated and eventually closed as well. But fortunately for us, Scott and Greg came to the rescue before it was too late. After a two-year renovation, the Bayview reopened in November 2002. There's a very pretty carpeted dining room with a fireplace and an outside deck, as well as a separate bar and bar deck (there's a pub menu for the bar). Be sure to take time to look at the photos of old South Jamesport on the walls. The food is excellent. For the main course, the Crescent Farm duck (right down the road, so you know it's fresh) is crispy and served with raspberries and a bigarde sauce. Breads and desserts are made on the premises. The banana bread pudding and the flourless chocolate cake are marvelous.

BLACKWELLS
631-929-1800
www.blackwellsrestaurant.com
Great Rock Golf Club; 141 Fairway Dr., Wading River, NY 11792
Executive Chef: Chris Gerdes
Cuisine: Steak house
Serving: L, D
Open: Daily in summer; may close Mon. and Tues. in winter
Price: Expensive; prix fixe and early bird available
Credit Cards: AE, D, MC, V
Special Features: Happy hour Thurs. and

Fri.; outside dining
Reservations: Accepted
Directions: From Long Island Expressway
(I-495), take exit 71 and follow Edwards
Ave. north. Turn left onto Middle Country
Rd. Turn right onto Parker Rd. (Rte. 25A)
and follow this for 2 miles to Sound Ave.
Turn right onto Sound and then turn left
onto Fairway Dr. Restaurant is on left.

Located in the clubhouse of Great Rock Golf
Club, a public course, this beautiful steak
house incorporates mahogany and burgundy into its decor, creating a masculine,
"men's club" appearance. You'll find an
excellent wine list, including some Long
Island selections to complement the steak
and seafood menu, and at lunch duffers
might treat themselves to a four-cheese
macaroni-and-cheese dish that incorporates Italian sausage and grilled chicken, as
well as fish and chips. On balmy days,
there's patio seating.

CLAUDIO'S RESTAURANT

631-477-0627
www.claudios.com
111 Main St., Greenport, NY 11944
Manager: Bill Claudio Jr.
Cuisine: Seafood
Serving: L, D, BR (Sun.)
Open: Daily Mid-Apr.–Nov.
Price: Moderate–Expensive
Credit Cards: MC, V
Special Features: Water views; boat dock;
dockside dining; live music on weekends
Reservations: Accepted
Directions: From Front St. (Rte. 25) turn
right at traffic light onto Main St. Restau-
rant is at end on right.

In 1870 Manuel Claudio opened Claudio's
Tavern. The restaurant has been in the same
family ever since (Bill Claudio Jr. manages
it now), making it the oldest restaurant in
America to be owned continuously by the
same family. The incredible 10-foot-high
Victorian bar was salvaged from an old hotel
in New York in 1885 and brought to the tav-

ern by barge. The decor is a riot of beveled
mirrors, stained glass, and carved wood.
Claudio's history includes interesting inter-
ludes with bootleggers, who incorporated
trapdoors and dumbwaiters in their opera-
tions, as well as the glory days of transcon-
tinental sailboat racing, when captains and
crews of the America's Cup winners called
Greenport home. The food is as fresh as
seafood can be and includes lobster,
shrimp, scallops, and sometimes sea bass.
In the summer, Crabby Jerry's and the Clam
Bar (both at the end of nearby piers) offer al
fresco dining and hot, hot music that brings
out a tumble of wild things.

COOPERAGE INN

631-727-8994
www.cooperageinn.com
2218 Sound Ave. (Rte. 48), Baiting Hollow,
NY 11933
Owner/Chef: Jonathan Perkins
Owner/Manager: Rene Perkins
Executive Chef : Michael Hegeman
Cuisine: Traditional American with eclectic
overtones
Serving: L, D, BR (Sun. only)
Open: Daily year-round except Christmas
and Easter
Price: Moderate; early bird offered
Credit Cards: AE, D, DC, MC, V
Special Features: Events throughout the
year, e.g., Harvest Festival, Comedy Night,
Holiday Festivities
Reservations: Recommended
Directions: From Long Island Expressway
(I-495), take exit 71 north onto Edwards
Ave. Continue on Edwards for about 4 miles
to Sound Ave. Turn right. Restaurant is on
left in about 0.25 mile.

I remember when this was just a tiny roadside café, but even then they served great
food. Then, in 2002, it was suddenly more
than twice its original size, with a very
impressive entrance and plenty of parking
space. The inside is cute, cute, cute—filled
with country charm. There's definitely a

wine and grape theme, from the name of the restaurant to its very grapey decor, which includes grape-colored tablecloths, garlands of vines and grapes swathing the walls, and grape-colored upholstery and curtains. It's a family-oriented spot, with classic traditional American food. You will find chicken potpie and meatloaf, alongside rosemary and pesto-rubbed rack of lamb and potato-and-onion-crusted fresh fluke. For dessert, you'll love the s'mores, the coconut cream pie, and the white chocolate raspberry cheesecake. The Sunday Country Buffet Brunch includes a huge amount of food that's very reasonably priced.

FRISKY OYSTER

631-477-4265
www.thefriskyoyster.com
27 Front St., Greenport, NY 11944
Owner: Dennis McDermott
Chef: Hank Tomashevski
Cuisine: Eclectic American
Serving: D
Open: Year-round; daily in summer; rest of year closed Mon. and Tues.
Price: Expensive
Credit Cards: AE, D, DC, MC, V
Reservations: Highly Recommended
Directions: Rte. 25 becomes Front St. in village. Restaurant is on right in center of town.

This wonderful staple in the North Fork dining scene wins tremendous applause and respect. The decor is avant-garde: poppy red fabric on some walls, others painted celadon, plush red banquettes, and Japanese lanterns hanging from the tall ceiling. There's a white oak and stainless steel bar in front, separated from the dining room by gauzy curtains. Chef Tomashevski is extremely accomplished. You might start with crispy Satur Farms (local) zucchini blossoms stuffed with jumbo lump crab, corn, and goat cheese. For an entrée, you might have pork chops with Dijon mustard spaetzle and asparagus, along with a side of

Parmesan potato spring rolls. One evening for dessert, I had the most remarkable chocolate soufflé cake. It was dense, with multiple chocolate layers, but somehow also very light, served in a pool of crème anglaise. Service is professional and knowledgeable. Best of all, there's a very nice wine list that includes some North Fork wines.

GREENPORT TEA COMPANY

631-477-8744
www.greenportteacompany.com
119A Main St., Greenport, NY 11944
Owners: Jan Kirwan and Jenette Holloway
Cuisine: American Continental
Serving: L, HT
Open: Feb.–Dec.; closed Mon. and Tues.
Price: Inexpensive
Credit Cards: AE, D, DC, MC, V
Special Features: Wheelchair access; sidewalk seating; tea accoutrements for sale
Reservations: Accepted
Directions: From Front St. (Rte. 25) turn right at traffic light onto Main St. Restaurant is on right in middle of block.

There's nothing like the Greenport Tea Company, either in the Hamptons or Manhattan. The Victorian building, with its high ceilings, is an enchanting spot. Shelves on one wall hold teacups and saucers, teapots, and gourmet food products, which are all available for purchase. Tea is served in china cups and from antique teapots—each one different. For lunch you might get a soup and a quiche, or a BBLT (bacon, melted Brie, lettuce, and tomato, with honey-mustard mayo) sandwich or a salad. You can also get a glass of local wine or a beer to wash it all down. Best of all, however, is high tea, served from tiered serving trays laden with the best fresh scones you'll ever eat; an old Irish recipe is responsible for these moist and tender morsels. A variety of finger sandwiches change with the season; there may be salmon, tomato, or cucumber, but they're always made to order and finished with freshly chopped parsley

The charming Greenport Tea Company is the perfect place for afternoon high tea, which includes wonderful scones.

garnishing the edges. The bottom tier is reserved for luscious fresh lemon tarts, minipastries, and fresh fruit. It's the sort of place our grandmothers took our mothers after a day of shopping.

JAMESPORT COUNTRY KITCHEN
631-722-3537
1601 Main Rd. (Rte. 25), Jamesport, NY 11947
Owner/Chef: Matthew Kar
Chef: Larry Hofer
Cuisine: American
Serving: L, D
Open: Year-round; closed Tues.
Price: Moderate
Credit Cards: AE, MC, V
Special Features: Excellent selection of local wines
Reservations: Highly recommended

Directions: On Main Rd. (Rte. 25) in village of Jamesport

Matthew Kar prides himself on featuring the wines and produce of the North Fork in his cuisine. In fact, from the time he first opened his restaurant, he has featured nothing but Long Island wines. His four-page wine list now contains almost 150 varieties, and most are extremely afford-able. This is an excellent place to sample local wines paired with local food. The menu is well priced and changes every week to reflect the freshest local provender. It relies on simple, straightforward dishes, but with fresh, interesting twists. For example, a Caesar salad can be ordered with grilled shrimp or with thinly sliced, grilled filet mignon. Long Island duckling comes with a cranberry-pear relish. Reservations are absolutely necessary at this popular restaurant. Even though the casual country decor doesn't match the sophistication of the food, the wines, or the knowledgeable service, this restaurant is a real sleeper.

JAMESPORT MANOR INN
631-722-0500
www.jamesportmanorinn.com
370 Manor Ln., Jamesport, NY 11947
Owner: Matthew Kar
Executive Chef: David Intonato
Cuisine: New American with Mediterranean flair
Serving: L, D, BR (Sun.)
Open: Year-round, dinner daily except Tues., lunch daily except Tues. and Sun. (when there's BR)
Price: Expensive
Credit Cards: AE, MC, V
Special Features: Fireplaces
Reservations: Highly recommended
Directions: From Main Rd. (Rte. 25) going east, turn left in Jamesport village onto Manor Ln. Restaurant is on right in 0.8 mile.

We remember eating at this old favorite over the years, and watching sadly as it became more and more derelict until, eventually, its doors were shut. Then, lo and behold, Matthew Kar, who also owns Jamesport Country Kitchen, stepped in and began a major renovation project—only to have the building entirely swept away in a fire in the fall of 2005. Never one to give up easily, however, Matthew and his crew went back to work, re-creating the original 1850s building, including its slate mansard roof, ornate corbels, and charming gabled entrance, as well as its elaborate interior featuring a carved wooden bar, fireplace mantels, and carved woodwork. What you see today looks almost identical to the original building. But the best part is that chef David Intonato is equal to the task of creating memorable meals to match the opulence of the building. Although he trained under leading local and European chefs, David's inspiration comes from the bounty of the local fields and waters. Raised on the East End, he knows where to source the finest ingredients; his menu is market driven. You'll find Crescent Farms duck breast with jasmine rice risotto, baby bok choy, and pomegranate jus, for example. And desserts might feature, in season, Lewin's Farm Peach Bread Pudding. One who eats here, in other words, gets the whole package—beautiful surroundings and top-notch cuisine.

LA CUVÉE WINE BAR & BISTRO
631-477-0066
www.thegreenporter.com
326 Front St., Greenport, NY 11944
Owner/Executive Chef: Deborah Rivera Pittorino
Cuisine: French Bistro
Serving: B, L, D
Open: Year-round; daily in summer for all meals; rest of year, D Fri. and Sat.; L Sat.; B Sat. and Sun.
Price: Moderate–Expensive
Credit Cards: AE, MC, V
Special Features: Outside dining; fireplace; guest rooms on premises
Reservations: Accepted
Directions: Rte. 25 becomes Front St. in village. Restaurant is located in the Greenporter, on corner of Fourth St.

Tribeca of the East End, this high-tech dining room pops and sizzles with energy. There's a maple floor, a fireplace fronted by Danish steel in the corner, three walls of windows, a large U-shaped zinc bar, and an elevated deck for outside dining. You'll find chartreuse walls and silver trim—a very chic and sophisticated setting. The menu consists of French bistro fare, and most entrées have local wine suggestions. The cheese selections are outstanding. For lunch you might sample a croque monsieur or a salade niçoise, while for dinner there might be a *saumon du jour,* served *en croute,* with a champagne sauce, and there is sure to be *steak frites*. Best of all, there are more than 60 local wines to taste by the glass or bottle, so this is the perfect place to sample the local juice with food.

LA PLAGE
631-744-9200
www.laplagerestaurant.com
131 Creek Rd., Wading River, NY 11792
Owner/Chef: Wayne Wadington
Cuisine: Eclectic
Serving: L, D
Open: Year-round; daily in summer; rest of year closed Mon. and Tues.
Price: Expensive; lunch prix fixe
Credit Cards: AE, MC, V
Special Features: Outside dining; view of marsh; special events throughout the year; BYO wine nights
Reservations: Highly recommended
Directions: On Rte. 25A coming from the west, turn north onto Wading River-Manorville Rd. At fork, bear left onto North Country Rd. (Coming from the east, follow signs for North Country Rd.) In Wading River village, turn north onto Sound Rd. Restaurant is at end on corner of Creek Rd.

It's an unlikely spot in which to find such fabulous food, but here it is. This restaurant is one of the most highly rated on Long Island, yet the setting is casual. There are a few tables on a patio that have rather distant views of the beach (and better views of a parking lot), but the best views are from the tables in the back dining room, which overlooks a marshy wetlands. All the effort and expertise have been poured into the extraordinary cuisine. You might start your meal with a tart green apple, Danish blue cheese, walnuts, and mâche salad drizzled with a black sesame Jerez vinaigrette. Then try the pan-roasted monkfish with creamed spinach and roasted parsnips. Desserts are equally intriguing. The warm chocolate banana bread pudding is heavenly, but so is the Tahitian vanilla crème brûlée. The wine

list includes an extensive array of Long Island wines. Frankly, no matter what you have here, you'll make a reservation for a return trip before leaving.

LEGENDS
631-734-5123
www.legends-restaurant.com
835 First St., New Suffolk
Mailing Address: P.O. Box 321, New Suffolk, NY 11956
Owners: Dennis and Diane Harkoff
Chef: Ralph Foulkes
Cuisine: Eclectic
Serving: L, D, LN.
Open: Year-round
Price: Inexpensive–Expensive
Credit Cards: AE, D, MC, V
Special Features: Best sports bar on the East End
Reservations: Accepted for dining room only
Directions: From Rte. 25 in Cutchogue, turn south at light onto New Suffolk Rd. and drive 1.5 miles to blinking light. Turn left onto Main St., then left onto First St. Restaurant is on left.

Divided into two sections, Legends has a sophisticated, upscale restaurant on one side with fresh flowers, candles gracing the linen tablecloths, and soft music playing. Sports memorabilia (such as an auto-graphed Mickey Mantle uniform) and pictures of sports figures line the walls, and a polished racing scull hangs from the cathedral ceiling. On the other side, the pub has tables along the windows and a raised sports bar that includes many television monitors. You can actually watch both figure skating and football at the same time without so much as craning your neck. The menu is broad, encompassing steaks and braised short ribs, seafood, and chicken. Most of the wines are from the North Fork and are available both by the glass and by the bottle; there's also a vast selection of more than 200 beers from 34 countries.

Desserts include a chocolate peanut-butter pie and a walnut roll. This lively, happy place is located in the out-of-the-way village of New Suffolk, but the journey down country roads is well worth it.

LOVE LANE KITCHEN

631-298-8989
www.lovelanekitchen.com
240 Love Lane, Mattituck
Mailing address: P.O. Box 131, Mattituck, NY 11952
Owner: Michael Avella
Chef: Ben Warner
Cuisine: New American
Serving: B, L, D
Open: Year-round daily B and L; D served Wed.–Sun.
Price: Inexpensive–Moderate
Credit Cards: AE, D, MC, V
Special Features: Microroast their own coffee
Reservations: Accepted dinner only
Directions: Traveling east on Main Rd. (Rte. 25) in village, turn left onto Love Ln. Restaurant is in middle of first block.

This little storefront café, with its crisp black-and-white-hexagon tile floor, is a popular stop for breakfast and lunch, or for a cup of microroasted brew. But on Wednesday to Sunday nights it segues into a charming little French bistro where you might feast on a double-cut marinated and grilled lamb chop served with a charred eggplant salad, or pan-fried local fluke with Asian-style noodle cakes. The owner's philosophy, which is printed on Love Lane's Web site, describes the café's attitude succinctly: "Source locally, prepare from scratch and price fairly"—and that's just what you get here: fresh, locally grown ingredients that are blended into a very fairly priced evening meal.

LUCE & HAWKINS

631-722-2900
www.jedediahhawkinsinn.com
400 S. Jamesport Ave., Jamesport, NY 11947

Venue: Jedediah Hawkins Inn
Owner: Jeff Hallock
Chef/Proprietor: Keith Luce
Cuisine: New American
Serving: D nightly; L, BR (Sat. and Sun. only)
Open: Year-round
Price: Moderate–Expensive
Credit Cards: AE, D, MC, V
Special Features: Guest rooms available; extensive list of Long Island wines; fireplaces; patios
Reservations: Highly recommended
Directions: Traveling east on Main Road (Rte. 25), turn right onto S. Jamesport Rd. in Jamesport. Restaurant on left in 0.25 mile.

Following a fabulous renovation of this exuberant Victorian home, which is on the National Register of Historic Places, and a stint as a decorator showhouse, the doors opened on this fine country inn and restaurant. Guests are greeted in the living room of the magnificent building. They may be seated in one of several formal dining rooms, or perhaps on the covered terrace or in the open-air courtyard. As we went to press, the dining rooms were being renovated to offer an elegant but subdued backdrop for the exceptional cusine of new top toque and co-owner Keith Luce, who plans to provide "good, wholesome food, prepared with care and sourced sustainably, delivered in a comfortable, unpretentious setting with a focus on value to quality." The ideal chef for this venue, Keith was raised on a farm on the North Fork within minutes of the restaurant. Shortly after high school, however, he began working in noteworthy New York restaurants, such as Le Cirque and La Côte Basque, and eventually at three-star restaurants in France and Italy. Returning to the United States, he became sous chef at the Clinton White House—at age 23!—and soon received the James Beard Award as Rising Star Chef of the U.S. Most recently, Luce has been executive chef at

The Herbfarm outside Seattle, a restaurant that has been called the number one destination restaurant in the world. (Also see listing under "Lodging," this chapter, for room information.)

MICHAEL ANTHONY'S FOOD BAR

631-929-8800
www.michaelanthonysrestaurant.com
2925 N. Wading River Rd., Wading River, NY 11792
Owner/Chef: Michael Anthony Toscano
Cuisine: Eclectic
Serving: D
Open: Year-round, in summer Wed.–Mon. 5–9; rest of year Wed.–Sun. 5–9
Price: Moderate–Expensive; prix fixe available
Credit cards: AE, D, MC, V
Special Features: Patio; fireplace; live entertainment; specialty dinners; outside dining on patio
Reservations: Accepted
Directions: From Long Island Expressway, take exit 71 and follow Edwards Ave. north. Turn left onto Middle Country Rd. Turn right onto Parker Rd. (Rte. 25A) and follow this to Hulse Landing Rd. Turn right onto Hulse Landing Rd. and follow for about 3 miles to N. Wading River Rd. Turn left. Restaurant is on left.

Located in a rural setting on a less traveled road, Michael Anthony's has nevertheless collected a dedicated following of culinary admirers. And no wonder. Chef Toscano's cuisine is inventive and prepared with expertise. He's had a summer restaurant on Shelter Island for a number of years, but this new location (opened in 2006) is open year round. The restaurant is light and airy, with classy muted gray-and-white decor that includes a fireplace and French doors leading to a patio for outside dining. You might have bacon-wrapped monkfish with a leek cassoulette, or perhaps a crispy pork shank with sweet-and-sour red cabbage. As befits a restaurant close to Long Island wine country, a nice selection of local wines is offered, and if you bring your own from one of the vineyards, there's no corkage fee.

NORTH FORK TABLE AND INN

631-765-0177
www.northforktableandinn.com
57225 Main Rd. (Rte. 25), Southold, NY 11971
Owners/Chefs: Gerry Hayden and Claudia Fleming
Cuisine: American
Serving: L, D
Open: Feb.–Dec., Thurs.–Mon. for D; Sat. and Sun. for L
Price: Expensive–Very Expensive
Credit Cards: AE, D, DC, MC, V
Special Features: Guest rooms on premises; extensive list of Long Island wines
Reservations: Highly recommended
Directions: Traveling east on Main Rd. (Rte. 25), pass through Southold. Restaurant and inn are on left.

North Fork Table and Inn is recognized as one of the top restaurants on Long Island, and no wonder. Owners/Chefs Gerry Hayden and Claudia Fleming have been garnering accolades for years—Gerry was formerly at Aureole in New York City and Claudia was pastry chef at Gramercy Tavern. Now they bring their oversized talent to their own country manor. Taking full advantage of their location in the heart of wine country, and next to farmland that yields abundant fresh produce, seas and bays yielding daily catches of fish and shellfish, dairy farmers making artisanal cheeses, and duck and chicken farmers raising free-range poultry, their menu reflects this bounty. Depending on the season, you may find pan-roasted Shinnecock monkfish or crispy-skin Eberly Farms chicken. Claudia's desserts include a milk chocolate hazelnut-crusted napoleon or melt-in-your-mouth warm sugar-and-spice doughnuts. There's an extensive international wine list, laced with local bottles. The backdrop for all this superlative food is a country inn with intimate dining rooms that are smartly dressed for the occasion—simply and elegant.

OLD MILL INN

631-298-8080
www.theoldmillinn.net
5775 West Mill Rd., Mattituck, NY 11952
Owners: Elaine Lafferty, Bia Lowe, Barbara Pepe
Chef: John Nordin
Cuisine: American; seafood
Serving: L, D
Open: Apr.–Nov., in summer L and D Wed.–Mon.; fewer days rest of season
Price: Moderate–Expensive
Credit Cards: AE, MC, V
Special Features: Outdoor waterfront dining; water views from inside dining room; fireplace; boat dock; live music
Reservations: Recommended
Directions: From Rte. 48, travel north on Cox Neck Rd. to West Mill Rd. Follow West Mill Rd. to end.

Down by Mattituck Creek, a little inlet that feeds into Long Island Sound, stands a historic 1821 mill that is built on pilings suspending it over the creek. With its red-shingled exterior and attractive deck filled with tables overlooking the tiny, local fishing fleet, there is little hint of its bawdy Prohibition days, when rumrunners stealthily paddled underneath by night to hoist their bounty through trapdoors into the kitchen. The old beams, posts, barnwood walls, and bare wood floors in the pub look much as they did originally, and the huge brick fireplace continues to warm pub inhabitants. The dining room, however, is much more refined, as it has been beautifully renovated to take full advantage of the watery views from its large windows. Now owned by a high-powered group of friends, with national media ties, they have ramped the cuisine up a notch too. This is serious food—offering small and large plates of fresh clams, oysters, or mussels, steamed

local lobster, a local catch of the day, all of which is purchased from local fishermen, and meat that includes Long Island duck with a Grand Marnier glaze. There's a good selection of Long Island wines, plus wines from California and Europe.

PORTO BELLO

631-477-1515
www.portobellonorthfork.com.
1410 Manhanset Ave. (in Stirling Harbor Marina), Greenport, NY 11944
Owner/Manager: Diana DiVello
Chef: Robert Howie
Cuisine: Northern Italian
Serving: L, D
Open: Apr.–Dec.; daily July 4th–Labor Day; fewer days rest of season
Price: Expensive
Credit Cards: D, MC, V
Special Features: Wheelchair access; fireplace; boat dock
Reservations: Recommended
Directions: From Main St. in Greenport (Rte. 25), turn right onto Champlin Pl. At end, turn right onto Manhanset Ave. Stirling Harbor Marina is on right in 0.25 mile.

Porto Bello, a North Fork favorite since 1991, is now back in the beautiful waterfront space in the Stirling Harbor Marina it occupied in the 1990s. It sits at water's edge surrounded by manicured lawns with views of the harbor filled with classy yachts and with the village lights of Greenport beyond. You're greeted by a large bar area, but the white-topped tables, with their marine blue napkins, beckon beyond. Broad windows offer panoramic views of the water. The menu offers straightforward entrées— grilled veal chop, veal Milanese, broiled flounder, chicken parmigiana. When we visited, they were hoping to add a patio for outside dining.

RED ROOSTER BISTRO

631-734-8267
4805 Depot Ln. Cutchogue, NY 11935

Roosters are the theme inside and out at this cute roadside roost.

Owner/chef: Nick Nickolov
Cuisine: American Bistro
Serving: L, D
Open: Year-round daily
Price: Moderate
Credit Cards: AE, D, MC, V
Special Features: Patio dining
Reservations: Not accepted
Directions: From Route 48, turn right onto Depot Ln. Restaurant is on right in about 0.25 mile.

A proud red rooster sits in front of this cute roadside cottage, greeting guests to his namesake trough. Inside, there are more roosters in a variety of guises, and one afternoon when I was there, a woman drove up in an SUV with yet another load. It's more cute than corny, however—a farmhouse theme offered in a tongue-in-cheek manner. The food is certainly no joke. A Portobello crab cake is stuffed with jumbo crabmeat, a pot roast is slow-roasted, and there are turkey and beef burgers, as well as a nice selection of local wines. Best of all, as the place proclaims, it's "food worth crowing about at chicken feed prices." If you've done the wine trail, and just want to relax, the pretty brick patio in front, under the trees, is a great place to sip one more local wine.

SCRIMSHAW

631-477-8882
www.scrimshawrestaurant.com
102 Main St. (Preston's Wharf), Greenport, NY 11944
Owner/Chef: Rosa Ross
Cuisine: New American
Serving: L, D
Open: Year-round; in summer D daily, L Sat.–Mon.; rest of year D Thurs.–Sun., L Sat. and Sun.
Price: Expensive; prix fixe available
Credit Cards: AE, D, DC, MC, V

Special Features: waterfront dining on a pier; boat dock
Reservation: Recommended
Directions: From Front Street (Rte. 25) turn right (toward the wharfs) onto Main St. Go to end and park in parking lot. Restaurant is to the left on a pier.

Rosa Ross is an amazing woman: a cookbook author, lecturer, cooking teacher, and caterer—she brings her many talents to delight us in her little seaside restaurant. Located on a pier at Preston's Wharf, Scrimshaw gives you the option of eating inside, where you have views of the water through large windows on three sides, or outside, at tables on the pier. Either way, you'll be glad you came. You might start with a green salad with crispy Pipe's Cove oysters (local), and then move on to her Crescent Farm duck breast with cherry sauce and sweet potato fries. Should you wish to just mellow out for a while, you can sit in Adirondack chairs beside the restaurant with a glass of wine and watch the activity on the water.

STONEWALLS
631-208-3510
www.stonewalls-restaurant.com
967 Reeves Ave. (Woods at Cherry Creek Golf Club), Riverhead, NY, 11901
Chef: Gui Peuch
Cuisine: New American–French
Serving: L, D, BR (Sun. only)
Open: Year-round, L daily, D daily except closed Tues., BR Sun., may be closed more days in winter and a few weeks in Feb.
Price: Expensive; prix fixe available
Credit Cards: AE, MC, V
Special Features: Patio for outside dining; view of grounds
Reservations: Recommended
Directions: From Long Island Expressway (I-495) take exit 73, continue on Old Country Rd. (Rte. 58) for 3 miles to traffic circle. Go three-quarters of the way around circle and continue north on Roanoke Ave. for 1.5

miles. Turn right onto Reeves Ave. Restaurant is on right in 0.75 mile.

Located at the Woods at Cherry Creek Golf Club, this fine-dining restaurant is definitely not a typical golf course eatery. The setting, with its panoramic views of the golf course, is pleasant, and the dining room decor is low-key and elegant, although a bit institutional in feel, but you really come here for the food, which is excellent. You might start with frog legs Provençale, for example, and then have an entrée of Dover sole almondine. The wine list is extensive and reasonably priced. Best of all, there's a nice selection of local wines.

A TOUCH OF VENICE
631-298-5851
www.touchofvenice.com
2255 Wickham Ave. (in the Matt-A-Mar Marina), Mattituck, NY 11952
Owner: Ettore Pennacchia
Chef: Brian Pennacchia
Cuisine: Classic Italian
Serving: L, D
Open: Year-round; L and D daily Mem. Day–Columbus Day; rest of year D only; may close midweek in winter
Price: Expensive; prix fixe available
Credit Cards: AE, D, MC, V
Special Features: Water views; fireplace; live music weekends; patio dining; boat dock
Reservations: Accepted
Directions: From the Long Island Expressway (I-495), take exit 73 and continue on Old Country Rd. (Rte. 58) to traffic circle. Go three-quarters of the way around circle and then go north on Roanoke Ave. Continue for 2.5 miles to Sound Ave./North Rd. (Rte. 48) Turn right and continue for 5 miles to fourth traffic light. Turn left onto Wickham Ave. Turn left into Matt-A-Mar Marina. Restaurant is on right.

Tucked away down a pathway from a parking lot, this is not a restaurant that you would stumble on by chance, but it's definitely one to seek out. You enter a bar area and there is a dining room on the left (beautiful water views) and one on the right. The specials can really be excellent. You might start with Chittari, incorporating local littleneck clams, sopressata, olive oil, and gremolata, and then continue with veal rollatini—veal with prosciutto, mozzarella, and pecorino in a porcini-marsala wine sauce with a rice ball on the side. For dessert, peaches that had been marinated in a local merlot and served in a crêpe shell with ice cream were wonderful.

TWEED'S RESTAURANT
AND BUFFALO BAR

631-208-3151
17 East Main St., Riverhead, NY 11901
Owner: Edwin Fishel Tuccio
Executive Chef: Jeffrey Trujillo
Cuisine: New American
Serving: BR, L, D
Open: Year-round; L, D daily, BR Sat. and Sun.
Price: Moderate
Credit Cards: AE, D, MC, V
Special Features: Historic old Riverhead atmosphere; fireplace
Reservations: Accepted
Directions: From the Long Island Expressway (I-495) take exit 72 onto River Rd. (Rte. 25) and continue east to Riverhead. Rte. 25 becomes Main St. in Riverhead. Restaurant is on right, opposite Roanoke Ave.

Located in the John J. Sullivan Hotel, which dates to 1896, this historic restaurant oozes with atmosphere. You can see a bison head on the wall that supposedly was shot by Theodore Roosevelt and stand in the footsteps of Tammany Hall cronies John J. Sullivan and Boss Tweed at the stunning mahogany and marble brass-railed bar that was made for the 1893 Columbian Exposition in Chicago. The tin ceiling is original, as is the warming fireplace, and fascinating photos from Riverhead's heyday line the walls. Tuccio raises buffalo on a 500-acre spread on the North Fork, and bison is a specialty of the house, so you might try a grilled bison steak or attend one of the seasonal game dinners. Or try a fish dish, as it may have been caught that very day by the owner.

Cafés, Bakeries, Pubs, and Other Eateries

Birchwood Tap Room (631-727-4449; 512 Pulaski St., Riverhead NY 11901; open year-round; L, D daily 11:30–10) Owner: James Loo. If you're looking for a pub with its heart in America and its soul in Poland, then come to the Birchwood. You'll find an atmospheric pub complete with lots of beautiful stained glass, an ornate tin ceiling, blue-and-white-checkered tablecloths, and a menu of sandwiches, meatloaf, Yankee pot roast, and Polish specialties including kielbasa, kraut, and a pierogi platter—all in the heart of Riverhead's Polish Town.

Blue Duck Bakery Café (631-629-4123; www.blueduckbakerycafe.com; 56275 Main Rd. (Rte. 25), Southold, NY 11971; open year-round daily 6:30 AM–6 PM) Keith Kouris, a graduate of the French Culinary Institute's International Bread Baking Program, and a fabulous baker, prepares artisanal breads, as well as cakes, pastries, cookies, and sandwiches, at this offshoot of his Southampton bakery. His breads are found in the breadbasket at many fine New York City and Long Island restaurants.

Bruce's Cafe/Cheese Emporium (631-477-0023; 208 Main St., Greenport, NY 11944; open daily in summer 8–6; rest of year closed several days a week) Owner: Bruce Bollman. Choose from over 30 varieties of coffee and a gourmet array of cheeses and pâtés as well as fudge from the Greenport Fudge Factory in a variety of flavors. This little café, with its tin ceiling, tile floor, Victorian fretwork, and marble-topped tables, is a popular local spot. For breakfast, you can have freshly baked pear-raisin muffins, or perhaps an omelette; in the afternoon, there are salads, sandwiches on homemade bread, and ice cream concoctions that can be eaten at tables outside under the awning. Naturally, cappuccino and espresso are available, and this is the ideal place to put together a winery-tour picnic.

Butta' Cakes (631-477-6666; http://buttacakes.com; 119 Main St., Greenport, NY 11944; open year-round June–Sept. Sun.–Thurs. 9–8; Fri. and Sat. 9–11; shorter hours and perhaps fewer days rest of year) Owner: Marc Lamaina. A refugee from corporate America, and a Greenport native, Marc has returned to his roots. He learned to bake while attending college in Charleston, so he's decided to put his talent to use, and we're glad he did. In his bright and cheerful café, you can get a variety of velvety, luscious cupcakes, as well as cakes, cookies, and breads such as olive ciabatta and focaccia. Sandwiches, soups, chocolate, and cheese fondue are served as well—stay tuned! He's applied for a liquor license too.

Do Little's (631-298-4000; Rte. 25, Mattituck Plaza; mailing address: P.O. Box 685, Mattituck, NY 11952; open year-round, daily, lounge from noon on, D served starting at 4.) Owners: Sharon and Dave Sailor. This cute spot has a tin ceiling, old wooden advertising signs on the walls, and a large dining room with Victorian-style booths. Dinner entrées include burgers, fish and chips, apple-sausage-stuffed loin of pork, and pineapple teriyaki chicken. There's a large sports bar adjacent to the dining room with a movie-size TV screen.

Farm Country Kitchen (631-369-6311; www.farmcountrykitchen.net; 513 West Main St., Riverhead, NY 11901; open year round Mon.–Sat. B, L; Wed.–Sat. D) Owners: Tom and Maria Carson. If it's summertime, and you want a waterside lunch or dinner, head for this little café on the banks of the Peconic River. You'll find very caring owners who shop for their ingredients locally and prepare soups, salads, paninis, sandwiches, and entrées

Claudia Helinski continues to whip up delectable goodies, including fabulous fried chicken, just as she used to at the Salamander Café.

such as pan-seared sea scallops served with yellow rice with tomato salsa and French beans.

Lobster Roll Northside (631-369-3039; www.lobsterroll.com; 3225 Sound Ave. (Rte. 48), Baiting Hollow, NY 11901; open mid-Mar.–mid-Dec.; in summer Wed.–Mon. 11:30–8; rest of year Fri.–Sun. same hours) Owner: Fred Terry. Lobster Roll ("Lunch") on the Napeague Stretch on the South Fork has long been a summer destination. Now Fred has opened a North Fork branch in a cute little shopping plaza. It's the same terrific lobster roll and fresh fish and chips, but in a prettier setting.

The Loft at Harbourfront (631-477-3080; www.harbourfrontdeli.com; 48 Front St., Greenport, NY, 11944; open year-round; daily in summer noon–11; rest of year Fri.–Tues., same hours) Owner: Perry and Melina Angelson. The longtime Harbourfront Deli put on a hat in 2002 by opening an upstairs section and turning it into a lovely, fine-dining restaurant. They added a deck that offers views of the harbor and serve entrées such as cedar plank salmon and slow-roasted duck. It's a wonderful addition to the Greenport dining scene.

Meeting House Creek Inn (631-722-4220; 177 Meeting House Creek Rd., Aquebogue; mailing address: P.O. Box 10, Aquebogue, NY 11931; open year-round; L, D daily, BR Sun.) Owner: Tom Drake. If you're looking for a waterfront restaurant, this venerable old-timer has been welcoming water lovers for 14 years under the current management (it was previously the Poop Deck). There's nothing fancy here. You'll find good, hearty, stick-to-the-ribs fare like chicken Jarlsberg, jumbo shrimp française, and a fresh bay-man's platter, and the prices are extremely reasonable. It's a pleasant place to watch the ships bob in the marina or to arrive by boat.

Modern Snack Bar (631-722-3655; www.modernsnackbar.com; 628 Main Rd. (Rte. 25), P.O. Box 930, Aquebogue, NY 11931; open Apr.–Nov.; Tues.–Thurs. 11–9, Fri. and Sat. 11–10, Sun. noon–9, closed Mon.) Owners: Otto and John Wittmeier. Far more than a snack bar, this North Fork institution offers humble decor but terrific food. You can get Long Island duck or bay scallops accompanied by mashed turnips (a signature dish) and Long Island wines. Or you can stop as you drive by to pick up one of their incredible mile-high homemade meringue pies. This is a throwback to another era, but one that has maintained its high standards and welcomes back generations of loyal followers.

Salamander General Store (631-477-3711; 414 First St., Greenport, NY 11944; open Feb.–Dec., daily 10–6) Owner: Claudia Helinski. Claudia first charmed us with her restaurant in Brewer's Yacht Yard (where Antares Tiki is now located), but now she's tak-ing it easier (maybe). You can get her fabulous fried chicken or a variety of sandwiches and salads to eat in (two small tables in the cafe, more outside on the deck) or to go. Don't miss her desserts either.

Spicy's BBQ (631-727-2781; 225 W. Main St., Riverhead, NY 11901; open daily year-round 11–9) Owner: Terance Stoner. It's really just a little diner, but oh my! What food it turns out! Finger-lickin'-good BBQ, fish and chips, sandwiches, and corn bread, plus great little sweet corn poppers—little nuggets of sweet corn batter that are deep-fried and are the best little morsels you're likely to ever have. And don't miss the sweet potato pie, either. This is soul food at its best.

Star Confectionery (631-727-9873; 4 East Main St., Riverhead, NY 11901; open Mon.–Sat. 7–3, Sun. 7–11:30) Owners: the Meras family. You can step back to circa 1911 in this wonderful, old-fashioned soda fountain and luncheonette—all in perfect condition. The elaborate stained glass over the front windows, the tin ceiling, the hexagon-tiled floor,

The Star Confectionery, with its ornate tin ceiling, beautiful Victorian lighting fixtures, oak booths, and hexagon-tiled floor offers a wonderful journey into yesteryear—and you can still get an old-fashioned ice-cream soda at the counter.

the old soda counter with its tiny stools, and the oak booths are all exactly as they were when this place was an ice cream parlor in 1911. Remarkably, it's remained in the same family since 1920, and they obviously take great pride in its beauty and eats. You can get a banana split made with homemade ice cream, juicy hamburgers, or a grilled-cheese sandwich, among other old favorites. There's a candy counter stocked with homemade candies (for the holidays they even make their own chocolates). This is a treasure not to be missed.

FOOD PURVEYORS AND FARM STANDS

A trip to the North Fork in June yields U-pick, farm-fresh strawberries; in the fall, pumpkins, corn, and apples. Throughout the summer, farm stands are filled with fresh fruit, flowers, and vegetables. The following are only a few of the excellent resources on the North Fork that frequently lure restaurateurs and food shop owners from Manhattan.

Bayview Farms (631-722-3077; 891 Main Rd. (Rte.25), Aquebogue, NY 11931; open Apr.–Dec.; daily in summer 8–7; shorter hours rest of season) Brad and Lorraine Reeve and their sons have been operating Hayground Market in Bridgehampton for many years, but the family has been farming on the North Fork since the 1600s. So, in 2003, they built a beautiful shingled farm stand on their land and now offer the same great produce and flowers here as they do on the South Fork.

Briermere Farm (631-722-3931; 4414 Sound Ave. (Rte. 48), Riverhead, NY 11901; open daily in summer 8–6; shorter hours in winter) The fresh vegetables and fruits from the farm are displayed on a covered porch at this roadside stand, but those in the know never stop here without also going inside to the bakery. This is where you can buy the same fabulous pies that are served in several fine local restaurants. All of the cream pies are to die for, but I can never resist the raspberry cream pie or the blueberry-peach cream pie. I usually call to reserve one in advance if I know I'm going that way, because they quickly sell out. Also, if you've ordered in advance, you don't need to stand in the long line—just tell the clerk at the produce counter, and he or she will fetch it for you.

Catapano Dairy Farm (631-765-8042; www.catapanodairyfarm.com; 33705 North Rd. (Rte. 48), Peconic, NY 11958; open Apr.–Dec., daily 9–6) Owners: Karen and Michael Catapano. This lovely little goat farm supplies super creamy and delicious goat cheese either plain or rolled in a variety of flavors, such as sun-dried tomato and basil. You can also get feta cheese and a North Fork rustic that sells out quickly, plus a variety of goat milk soaps, hand and body creams, and baskets. If you have a hankering off-season, you can order from the Web site.

Crescent Duck Farm (631-722-8700; Edgar Ave.; mailing address: P.O. Box 1150, Aquebogue, NY 11931) Owners: The Corwin Family. This 140-acre farm raises a million ducks a year in its 30 barns, which accounts for 4.5 percent of the nation's entire production, according to a 2003 article by Richard Jay Scholem in the *New York Times*. The farm has no retail outlet, but call in advance and they'll have ducks ready for you. At one time in the 1960s, there were 80 duck farms on Long Island, and Long Island duckling gained a nationwide reputation. Now Crescent Duck Farm and Massey Duck Farm in Eastport are the only ones remaining on both the North and South Forks. Crescent Duck Farm has been in the Corwin family since the 1600s, and they have been raising ducks used in the finest East Coast restaurants since 1908.

George Braun Oyster Co. (631-734-6700; www.braunseafood.com; 30840 Main Rd. (Rte. 25), P.O. Box 971, Cutchogue, NY 11935; open daily 8–5) Owner: Ken Homan. George Braun is often rated the best fish market on the East End by local residents. Founded in 1928, the company is the Cadillac of seafood markets, offering homemade clam and lobster pies and a wide selection of fresh fish and shellfish. Most local restaurants and many restaurants in Manhattan are supplied by George Braun. For the freshest Peconic Bay scallops, striped bass, flounder, oysters, and clams, this is the place to come. They also have the largest seafood-distribution network on the East End.

Garden of Eve Organic Farm (631-680-1699; www.gardenofevefarm.com; 4558 Sound Ave. (Rte. 48), Riverhead; mailing address: P.O. Box 216, Aquebogue, NY 11931; open mid-Apr.–Oct. daily Mem. Day–Oct., Fri.–Sun. rest of season) Owners: Chris and Eve Kaplan-Walbrecht. This certified-organic farm grows a variety of vegetables, without the use of pesticides or herbicides, passing the healthful produce on to us at their farmstand. They also grow flowers, raise chickens (you can gather your own eggs), turkeys, goats, and sheep, and they have beehives. Throughout the season, they hold cooking classes, have musical events including a storytelling concert, and in September they hold a Garlic Festival, with music, crafts, and contests for the best garlic recipes.

Golden Earthworm Organic Farm (631-722-3302; www.goldenearthworm.com; 633

For fresh-from-the-farm produce and flowers, head for Bayview Farms.

Peconic Bay Blvd., South Jamesport; mailing address: P.O. Box 871, Jamesport, NY 11947; open during growing season, end of May–mid-Nov., Fri. and Sat. 9:30–5) Owners: Matthew Kurek and James Russo. This 20-acre farm is certified 100 percent organic (no synthetic fertilizers or pesticides or genetically modified organisms), so what they grow is good for the soil and good for you. Throughout the season you will find the freshest produce grown (tomatoes, mesclun, apples, berries, onions, potatoes), and it comes direct from the field. You can also get handmade soaps and several other locally made products here. In addition, for an annual fee, you can become a member of the Community Support Agriculture program, and receive shares of produce throughout the growing season.

Harbes Family Farm (631-722-8546, www.harbesfamilyfarm.com, Main Rd. (Rte. 25), Jamesport; open May or June–Oct., 9–6; also 631-298-0800, 247 Sound Ave. (Rte. 48), Mattituck; mailing address: P.O. Box 1524, Mattituck, NY 11952; open May or June–Oct., 9–6) Owners: Ed and Monica Harbes. The Harbes family (which includes eight children) have farmed their land for three generations, but their transition from potato and cabbage farming to raising super-sweet corn and pumpkins, plus opening a retail outlet that offers a wide array of fruit, vegetables, and flowers, took place in the 1980s. This is the best spot on the East End to bring children, as there are baby animals to pet, pony rides, hayrides, and, in fall, an incredible, huge corn maze. You can pick your own strawberries and pumpkins. You can also enjoy a variety of live musical events throughout the summer and fall, from American bluegrass to light jazz to a New Orleans–style Dixieland band. But that's not all. In 2003 the family planted grapevines on a 5-acre parcel of land and they're now bottling Harbes Wines. Their tasting room is located in Jamesport on Main Rd. (Rte. 25). It's open Tues.–Thurs. 12–6 and Fri.–Mon. 11–6. You can either taste one wine for $1–$2, or seven wines for $9.95.

Krupski's Vegetable & Pumpkin Farm (631-734-6847; 38030 Main Rd. (Rte. 25), Peconic, NY 11958; open June–Nov. daily) The Krupski family have tended their North Fork farm for four generations, mostly growing potatoes, and it's a great source for fresh-from-the-field vegetables and fruit all summer, but it's especially popular in fall, when you can pick out your own pumpkin and take the kids on a hayride, or through the haunted barn or the corn maze.

Lavender by the Bay (631-477-1019; www.lavenderbythebay.com; 7540 Main Rd. (Rte. 25) East Marion, NY 11939; open Apr.–Nov.; daily May–Sept. 9–5; Thurs.–Mon. in Oct.; Sat. and Sun. in Apr. and Nov.) Owner: Susan Rozenbaum. The beautiful fields of purple are an instant draw to this unique farm and farm stand. The fields of lavender stretch for 7 acres—offering 20 different varieties and yielding over 40,000 plants. You can purchase plants in various sizes, as well as fresh-cut and dried lavender, sachets, and even lavender honey from their beehives.

Orient Country Store (631-323-2580; 930 Village Ln., P.O. Box 387, Orient, NY 11957; open Mon.–Sat. 7:30–5:30, Sun. 8:30–5) Owner: Linton Duell. This quaint store is a throwback to another era. It has its original wooden floors and a three-stool counter in the back for coffee or a sandwich. The prices are old-fashioned, too. A huge Reuben sandwich, for example, is still $2.50. The store is next door to the old post office, where wooden floors, old-fashioned brass stamp windows, and brass mailboxes with combination locks still prevail.

Sang Lee Farms (631-734-7001; www.sangleefarms.com; 25180 Rte. 48, Peconic, NY 11958; open year-round; Apr.–Dec., daily 9–6; Jan.–Mar., Thurs.–Sun) Owners: Fred and Karen Lee. The North Fork has great growing conditions not only for grapes, but also for other produce. In 1999 this roadside stand opened to sell the Asian and other vegetables and produce grown on this farm. You can get fresh mesclun (I love their petal mesclun, which comes with flower petals), bok choy, napa cabbage, guy lon, a wide variety of herbs, and more. They also have beautiful flowers, both potted and cut, as well as freshly made pesto, dressings, breads, and more.

A Taste of the North Fork (631-765-8760; www.atasteofthenorthfork.com; 2885 Peconic Ln., Peconic, NY 11958; open year-round, in summer daily 11–5, may close some days rest of year) Jeri Woodhouse and Jayne McCahill use the bounty of the North Fork to create natural and organic products, making them in small batches and with no preservatives. In their storefront in Peconic, and online, you can purchase jams and jellies (North Fork white and red wine, for example) vinegars, olive oils, glazes (apricot BBQ glaze), gourmet salts, spices, mustards, and chutneys, among other products.

Village Cheese Shop (631-298-8556; www.thevillagecheeseshop.com; 105 Love Ln., Mattituck, NY 11952; open year-round; Mon.–Thurs. 10–6, Fri. and Sat. 9–6:30, Sun. 10–5; closed Mon. and Tues. Jan.–Apr.) Owner: Rosemary Batcheller. This terrific cheese shop opened originally as a branch of the popular Southampton store by the same name. Now under different ownership, however, this store continues to offer an excellent selection of cheeses, sandwiches, and imported and domestic condiments. Furthermore, there are tables in a pretty greenhouse-style setting at which to sit and rest as you nibble.

Wickham's Fruit Farm (631-734-6441; www.wickhamsfruitfarm.com; Main Rd. (Rte. 25), Cutchogue, NY 11935; open May.–Dec., Mon.–Sat. 9–5) Owners: the Wickham family. It was John Wickham who first experimented with grape growing in the 1950s, providing the start of the North Fork's prized industry. Today the family grows a variety of fruit that includes apples, peaches, nectarines, pears, apricots, cherries, grapes, raspberries, strawberries, and melons. Call the farm to find out about U-pick days for apples, black-berries, raspberries, strawberries, and cherries. You also can buy delicious fruit pies, fruit breads, jams and jellies, cheeses, and apple cider at the farm stand in season, as well as fresh-from-the-fryer doughnuts.

Will Miloski's Poultry Farm (631-727-0239; 4418 Rte. 25, Calverton, NY 11933; open Feb.–Dec., Wed.–Mon. 8:30–5:30; closed Tues.) Will Miloski raises free-range chick-ens, ducks, geese, and turkeys, and he also supplies venison, pheasants, and buffalo. This is where many local restaurants get their meats. You can get homemade frozen chicken and turkey potpies, fruit pies, and fresh eggs, as well as ready-to-go rotisserie chickens and BBQ meats.

Wineshops

Claudio's Wines and Liquor (631-477-1035; www.claudioswinesandliquors.com; 219 Main St., Greenport, NY 11944; open year-round; Mon.–Thurs. 9:30–6, Fri. and Sat. 9:30–6:30) An excellent selection of Long Island wines as well as wines from around the world.

Michael's Wines & Liquors (631-727-7410; 802 E. Main. St., Riverhead, NY 11901; open Mon.–Thurs. 9–8; Fri. and Sat. 9–10; Sun. 12–6) Owner: Kenny Demchak. This out-of-the-way liquor store is one of the staunchest supporters of Long Island wines in the region. They really understand and appreciate the nuances of the local vineyards, as they've watched the region grow from its nascent beginnings. They appreciate the vari-ous wines produced by individual vintners, and they understand the philosophy of the individual winemakers. Furthermore, they buy in bulk and pass the savings on to the consumer.

Peconic Liquors (631-734-5859; 31425 Main Rd.; mailing address: P.O. Box 901, Cutchogue, NY 11935; open year-round; Mon.–Sat. 9–8) Owners: Beverly Cierach and Cindy Richards. Located in King Kullen Shopping Plaza, this shop features an outstand-ing selection of local wines. Drop by for a friendly chat and guidance in making your selections from the knowledgeable owners.

Showcase Wine & Liquor (631-765-2222; 46455 Rte. 48, Southold, NY 11971; open year-round; Mon.–Sat. 9–7) Owner: Corinne Ferdenzi. This very attractive and well-organ-ized shop offers one of the largest selections of Long Island wines on the North Fork.

LODGING

As we were going to press, Nello Balan, a noted Manhattan restaurateur, and owner and operator of a summer hotel and restau-rant in Southampton, was completing work on a 14-room boutique hotel in Greenport, called Belo. The new building will have a small café on the lower level, and very posh guest rooms above.

BARTLETT HOUSE INN B&B
631-477-0371
www.bartletthouseinn.com
503 Front St., Greenport, NY 11944
Innkeepers: Jack and Diane Gilmore

Open: Year-round
Price: Moderate–Expensive
Credit Cards: MC, V
Special Features: Buffet breakfast; wireless Internet access; air-conditioning; flat-screen cable TVs; children over 10 years welcome; no pets
Directions: Traveling east on Main Rd. (Rte. 25), which becomes Front St. in the village of Greenport, the B&B is on the right, on the corner of Front and Fifth Sts.

John Bartlett was a New York State assemblyman and a delegate to both the 1904 and the 1908 presidential conventions. A leader of his day, he needed a grand home in which to entertain, and in 1908 he completed construction of this handsome Colonial. He installed elaborate moldings, paneling, columns, inlaid floors, stained-glass windows, fireplaces, and a grand staircase. The Bartlett House Inn B&B retains all the embellishments Bartlett incorporated into his house so elegantly, but it now also includes the beautiful bathrooms and modern accoutrements we expect in a fine B&B today. Diane and Jack Gilmore completed the renovation of the inn in 2009 and today we not only enjoy handsome bathrooms, but also wireless Internet access and flat-screen TVs. World travelers, they have included beautiful antiques in the common rooms and bedrooms, and the broad front porch has ceiling fans and wicker chairs in which to relax. Of the ten guest rooms eight have private baths; the other two share a bath between them. Room #2, the former master bedroom, has a mahogany four-poster king bed, a working fireplace, and a stained-glass window. A buffet breakfast includes a quiche, a variety of fresh fruits, home-baked fruit breads, bagels, salmon, ham, and much more.

BLUE IRIS BED & BREAKFAST

631-734-7126
www.blueirisbedandbreakfast.com
1100 Skunk Ln., Cutchogue, NY 11935

Innkeepers: Jerry and Lorry Siani
Open: Year-round
Price: Expensive
Credit Cards: MC, V
Special Features: On 2 landscaped acres; wraparound porch; smoking outside only; air-conditioning; wireless Internet access; gas fireplaces; cable TV; whirlpool tubs; spa treatments and massages available; full breakfast; not appropriate for children; no pets
Directions: Traveling east on Main Rd. (Rte. 25) from Riverhead, continue for about 7 miles to Cutchogue. Go through village and turn right onto Skunk Ln. Go about 800 feet and turn right to inn through a white picket fence.

There's something to be said for a brand-new inn: everything is perfect! In this case, you can add the innkeepers to that equation. Friendly and welcoming, Jerry and Lorry make you feel right at home. You'll notice a parlor with a huge gas fireplace and a baby grand piano waiting to be played. Be sure to take note of the picture of drummer Howie Mann, who was Lorry's father, and also a caricature of him done by the late Al Hirschfeld. Upstairs, you should also note the glamour poster of Lorry's aunt, Louise Hirschfeld, who was married to Al and was a stunning actress/model. The guest rooms are absolutely beautiful. My favorite is the Hollyhock Room, which has a red, white, and blue theme and a four-poster bed. Every room has a beautiful private bath, a gas fireplace, cable TV, and Internet access. There's a wonderful porch from which to enjoy the perennial gardens. A full breakfast might include freshly baked muffins or scones and fresh fruit, followed by an entrée of perhaps an herb-egg torte accompanied by homemade corn bread. This may be followed by a baked apple steeped in Grand Marnier or another sweet finale. And this is for the girls: check out the Pajama Party package, which includes chocolates, wine, continental breakfast, and perhaps massages, facials, and a "chick flick" on the 52-inch TV.

BY THE BLUFF BED AND BREAKFAST

631-477-6155
www.bythebluff.com
5405 Rocky Point Rd., East Marion, NY
11939
Innkeepers: Patricia and Maurice Scannell
Open: Year-round
Price: Moderate–Expensive
Credit Cards: AE, MC, V
Special Features: Full breakfast; TV/DVD
combos; beach towels and chairs; wine
cooler, opener, and glasses; wireless Internet access; spa services and massages available; not suitable for children; no pets (two
Saint Bernards, Daisy and McDuff, on
premises)
Directions: From the Long Island Expressway (I-495) take exit 71 and go north at stop
sign on Edwards Ave. for 3.9 miles to Sound
Ave. Turn right (east) and travel 26 miles to
Rocky Point Rd. Turn left and continue 1
mile to sign for By the Bluff, on left.

For those of us who love the serenity of a
rural setting, By the Bluff is a marvelous
antidote to the hustle and bustle of the city.
Not only will you be able to laze an afternoon away on a private nearby beach (towels, chairs, and wine cooler provided), but
you will experience glorious sunset vistas
from this hillside perch. Furthermore, the
four suites (each with a private en suite
bath) are among the most luxurious on Long
Island. The Galway Suite has a pretty
antique queen-sized bed and a gabled ceiling. Aunt Kate's Master Suite, which is
located on the main floor, is the most opulent. It has a four-poster king-sized bed, a
42-inch flat-screen TV, a bath with a claw-
foot tub, a shower with a rainfall showerhead, and French doors to a patio. It's
tranquil and elegant and gets a 10 on the
romantic rating. A full breakfast is served in
the dining room on elegant china and with
silver utensils. You might feast on an Irish
potato frittata, or baked French toast, or
baked eggs on English muffins, and you will
certainly also have fresh fruit and/or
berries, muffins, and beverages.

FREDDY'S HOUSE

631-734-4180
www.hydrangeafarmandgardens.com
1535 New Suffolk Rd., Cutchogue, NY 11935
Innkeeper: Dan and Prudence Heston
Open: Feb.–Dec.
Price: Moderate
Credit Cards: None
Special Features: On 300-acre farm with
private hiking trails; 0.5 mile of private
beach; gourmet tea breakfast; children over
age 12 welcome; no pets
Directions: Traveling east on Main Rd. (Rte.
25) from Riverhead, continue for about 7
miles to Cutchogue. Turn right onto New
Suffolk Rd. Inn is on left.

This 1798 farmhouse (formerly a Tuthill
homestead; Freddy, Alice, and Flora Tuthill
were siblings) has been artistically restored
to perfection, and it's listed on both the
state and the national Register of Historic
Places. There are polished wide-plank
(King's boards) pine floors, hand-hewn
beams, and a multitude of fireplaces. The
giant hearth in the kitchen is especially
impressive. There are two guest rooms.
Alice's Room, a second-floor hideaway, has
a king-sized bed, air-conditioning, and a
beautiful, modern bath with a claw-foot tub
and separate shower. Flora's Room is a bit
smaller, but it also has a thoroughly modern
bath with a shower. There's a charming sitting room for the guests' use. As a guest, you
have the run of the farm, including picking
your own fruit from the cherry, peach, apple
and apricot trees, or sampling fresh raspberries or strawberries right from the field.
Or you might inspect the overloaded plants
in the hydrangea garden (or purchase one to
plant at home), hike a private trail, laze
away an afternoon on the private sandy
beach, or meander about the 82-acre
wildlife preserve. Either way, you won't
want to miss the gourmet tea breakfast,
which includes fresh fruit or berries from
the farm, fruit breads and coffee cakes, tea
and coffee.

Freddy's House is located on the Wickham Farm in Cutchogue.

THE GREENPORTER HOTEL AND SPA
631-477-0066
www.thegreenporter.com
326 Front St., Greenport, NY 11944
Innkeeper: Deborah Rivera Pittorino
Open: Year-round
Price: Inexpensive–Moderate
Credit Cards: AE, MC, V
Special Features: Pool; hot tub; continental breakfast; restaurant on premises (La Cuvée); minibar; AC; cable TV; two phone lines; wireless Internet access; safe in room; children under 12 free in parents room; pets welcome $69/night/pet
Directions: Rte. 25 is called Front St. in village. Traveling west, Greenporter is on left, on corner of Fourth St.

If you're tired of the cutesy Victorian frills of most bed & breakfasts, then you should definitely give this place a try. It's ultra-high-tech, retro '50s, jazzy, and sophisticated—just what the North Fork has needed. For example, the floors are large polished squares of custom maplewood tile. Clothes hang from an exposed water pipe in the room, and the desk is formed from an undulating two-foot-wide strip of aluminum that curves down to land on a teakwood desktop. In the bath, there's a hand-cut slate countertop with a sink sitting on top and a separate room with an extra large soaking tub. A pool and hot tub are in the central courtyard. There are 30 guest rooms in the hotel, all with queen- or king-sized beds dressed in luxury linens. Breakfast is served in the attached restaurant.

HARBORFRONT INN

631-477-0707
www.theharborfrontinn.com
209 Front St., Greenport, NY 11944
Manager: Jacqueline Dubé
Open: Year-round.
Price: Moderate–Very Expensive
Credit Cards: AE, D, MC, V
Special Features: Water views from many
rooms; pool; private decks and balconies;
flat-screen LCD TVs, CD players, wireless
Internet access, refrigerators, safes, complimentary continental breakfast
Directions: From Main Rd. (Rte. 25) travel
east to Greenport village, where Main Rd.
becomes Front St. Hotel is on right in village.

This handsome, gray-shingled hotel, which
is the first hotel on the North Fork, was
built in 2004. There are 35 units ranging
from standard rooms overlooking the village to a luxurious 700-square-foot Terrace
Suite, located on the third floor, that offers
panoramic views of Peconic Bay and Greenport Harbor, especially from its private
800-square-foot deck. Many of the other
rooms have water views as well. There's no
on-site restaurant, but a continental
breakfast is provided every morning, and
Greenport has several fine restaurants.
The hotel also has meeting and conference facilities.

HARBOR KNOLL

631-477-2352
www.harborknoll.com
424 Fourth St., Greenport, NY 11944
Innkeeper: Leueen Miller
Open: Year-round
Price: Moderate–Expensive
Credit Cards: AE, MC, V
Special Features: Full breakfast; cable TV;
air-conditioning; private dock; basketball
court; pool; waterfront; water views; telephones; flat-screen TVs; wireless Internet
access; children over age of 12 welcome;
no pets
Directions: From Main Rd. (Rte. 25) travel

east to Greenport village, where Main Rd.
becomes Front St. Turn right onto Fourth
St. and cross RR tracks, then take first left
onto a private road. Go to end of road to
Harbor Knoll sign, on right (white picket
fence).

This wonderful, big, 1800s white mansion
sits on manicured lawns that fringe Greenport Harbor. The Shelter Island ferry putt-
putts effortlessly back and forth just beyond
the inn's private dock, and guests can sit out
on the dock to watch the water traffic, rest
in Adirondack chairs on the lawn, or snug-
gle up in wicker chairs on the porch. Wherever you look, you'll see elegant antiques,
an abundance of books, and working fireplaces. This is one of Greenport's most gracious mansions. The ambience is enhanced
by the love and care the Millers have given
the house during their 30+ years of stew-
ardship. But Leueen recently retired from
her diplomatic position with the United
Nations, and although Gordon continues to
practice law in New York City and on Long
Island, Leueen decided to put the house to

*Guests at Harbor Knoll in Greenport enjoy this
spectacular view across Greenport Harbor.*

Harvest Inn Bed & Breakfast in Peconic was built to house guests in 2001.

work. The Lighthouse Room, on the second floor, has fabulous views of the water and Shelter Island. There's a sleighbed, blue-and-white-striped paper, and red-checkered drapes on the windows. A flag covers a chair and the bath is decorated in blue-and-white toile. It's a charming, delightful room, as are the rest of the accommodations, which include an "enchanted cottage" tucked away in the gardens. All of the baths are en suite and have recently been updated. Breakfast might include homemade scones and croissants, fresh fruit in season, and perhaps a quiche or scrambled eggs and sausage or French toast.

HARVEST INN BED & BREAKFAST
631-765-9412
www.harvestinnbandb.com
40300 Main Rd. (Rte. 25), Peconic, NY 11958
Innkeepers: Darolyn and Christopher Augusta
Open: Year-round
Price: Moderate–Expensive
Credit Cards: AE, MC, V
Special Features: Full breakfast; CD players; wireless Internet access; air-conditioning; children over age 16 welcome; no pets
Directions: On Main Rd. (Rte. 25), travel east to Peconic. Inn is on right, just beyond Raphael Vineyards.

This newly built (2001), welcoming inn is a beauty. From the gracious circular driveway to the shingled exterior and broad covered front porch, it was designed for guest comfort. There are polished pine floors, a sitting room with huge windows letting in lots of light, and a gracious dining room with Tuscan red walls and a big iron chandelier, where breakfast is served. Upstairs, there are six guest rooms, all with their own en suite baths. Syracuse has yellow walls, an iron bed, and a braided rug; the Bridal Suite, which is the largest room, has a sofa as well as a four-poster bed and a whirlpool tub in the bath. All of the baths are luxurious. Chris is an excellent chef who trained at the Culinary Institute of America. A typical breakfast might consist of a baked local apple and freshly baked banana-nut bread, plus French toast with pepper-cured bacon or perhaps a fresh vegetable frittata with roasted tomatoes and Florentine pesto bread. Anyone who is interested in learning more about wine should definitely inquire about the North Fork Wine Camp (631-495-9744; www.winecamp.us) in which this and several other B&Bs, and a number of wineries, participate. It's an in-depth course that includes tours of wineries, discussions with vintners, wonderful dinners (one at a winery) accompanied by wines, and overnight accommodations.

JEDEDIAH HAWKINS INN

631-722-2900
www.jedediahhawkinsinn.com
400 S. Jamesport Ave., Jamesport
Mailing Address: P.O. Box 634, Jamesport, NY 11947
Owner: Jeff Hallock
Innkeeper: Debbie Bowen
Open: Year-round
Price: Expensive–Very Expensive
Credit Cards: AE, D, MC, V
Special Features: Fine dining restaurant on premises (see listing under "Restaurants," Luce & Hawkins this chapter); buffet breakfast with hot and cold items; gas fireplaces in rooms; flat-screen TVs; wireless Internet access; fitness room; spa services available; children over 12 welcome; no pets.
Directions: Traveling east on Main Road (Rte. 25), turn right onto S. Jamesport Rd. in Jamesport. Inn is on left in 0.25 mile.

For years, we passed this derelict, but

grand, mansion and yearned for someone to rescue it, but in 2004 it was scheduled for demolition. Then along came Jeff Hallock, who not only rescued it, but spent many years restoring it to its former grandeur. The restoration won the 2008 New York State Historic Preservation Award. The interior and exterior woodwork of this 1860s mansion is stunning, as are the fireplaces. Some of the decor is the result of a North Fork Designer Showhouse (take a peek in the first-floor powder room.) The guest rooms have a sophisticated demeanor and are named for their predominant color. The most dramatic is Cocoa, which has deep, rich brown walls with white trim, hung with black-and-white photos. Indigo features a blue-and-white color scheme and nautical decor. Belvedere is the largest, offering an exposed brick wall, a gabled roof, and access to the belvedere, where you can see for miles through the arched windows. A hot and cold buffet breakfast is served on the first floor, and you can either eat on the covered patio or the terrace, or perhaps in one of the Adirondack chairs down by the pond. There's a fitness center in a separate cottage, and guests can amuse themselves with games of bocce ball or croquet, or perhaps have a glass of wine in the gazebo bar.

THE MORNING GLORY
BED & BREAKFAST

631-477-3324
www.themorningglory.com
912 Main St., Greenport, NY 11944
Innkeepers: Renate and Klaus Wilhelm
Open: Year-round
Price: Moderate–Expensive
Credit Cards: AE, MC, V
Special Features: Full breakfast; wireless Internet access; cable TV; air-conditioning; children over 12 welcome; no pets
Directions: On Main Rd. (Rte. 25), travel east to Greenport village, where Main Rd. becomes Front St. At end of Front St., turn

left onto Main St. Inn is on right in 0.5 mile.

New owners Renate and Klaus Wilhelm, who hail from one of the North Frisian Islands off the coast of Germany, purchased this inn in 2004 and undertook a total renovation. The result is a charming and romantic inn offering both sophistication and enchanting appeal. The Wilhelms are dedicated to making each of their guest's stays memorable, as the quote featured on their Web site reveals: "The value of life lies not in the length of days, but in the use we make of them," by Michel de Montaigne. Each of the three rooms (which all have en suite baths) is named for a sentiment. "Love Deeply" has a king-sized four-poster bed, a sofa, and a beautiful bath with a pedestal sink. "Laugh Out Loud" has a king-sized bed with a wooden head and footboard, and "Live with Passion" includes a queen-sized brass and iron bed and a claw-foot tub in the bathroom. The inn is decorated in soft, muted colors, and all of the rooms have flat-screen TVs with DVD capability. There's a DVD library, chocolates, fresh flowers, and a garden for guests to enjoy. A full breakfast is prepared and served in the dining room. You might have apple pancakes, and homemade pastries.

ORIENT INN

631-323-2300
www.orientinn-ny.com
25-500 Main Rd. (Rte. 25), Orient, NY 11957
Innkeeper Joan Turturro
Open: Year-round
Price: Moderate
Credit Cards: AE, D, MC, V
Special Features: No smoking; full breakfast; air-conditioning; children over age five welcome; pets welcome in one room $50/stay
Directions: From the Long Island Expressway (I-495), take exit 71 and turn left (north) at the stop sign onto Edwards Ave.

Travel 3.9 miles to Sound Ave. Turn right (east) and continue for about 24 miles to Greenport, where it ends and becomes Rte. 25 at a blinking light. Continue east for another 3 miles. Inn will be on right.

Take one circa-1906 gray-shingled house on about an acre and add wicker and rocking chairs on a broad covered porch, beautiful paneling in the entryway, a fabulous columned fireplace mantel, oak pocket doors, and you have the Orient Inn. This charming inn has five bedrooms, all with tall ceilings and private baths. Room 6 has a wonderful four-poster bed and an antique chest. There's a beautiful bath with a pedestal sink and a glass-enclosed shower. Room 7 is pet friendly. A typical breakfast, prepared by Joan, who is a graduate of the French Culinary Institute, might include freshly baked muffins, an egg dish or French toast, and fresh fruit. Cookies and fruit are also available in the afternoon.

SHINN ESTATE FARMHOUSE

631-804-0367
www.shinnestatevineyards.com
2000 Oregon Rd., Mattituck, NY 11952
Innkeepers: Barbara Shinn and David Page
Open: Year-round
Price: Moderate
Credit Cards: AE, MC, V
Special Features: Flat-screen TV; wireless Internet access
Directions: From the Long Island Expressway (I-495), take exit 71. Turn left (north) at stop sign onto Edwards Ave. Continue for 3.9 miles and then turn right (east) onto Sound Ave. (Rte. 48). Continue for 13.7 miles and turn left onto Elijah's Ln. Go 1 mile and turn left onto Oregon Rd. The B&B is on the left in 0.125 mile.

If you want the luxury of waking to absolute quiet in a bucolic country setting, with nothing but acre after acre of farmland for miles around, this is the place. Oregon Road is definitely the "road less traveled" as it meanders through pastures, vineyards, and farmland. Furthermore, you have the added benefit at Barbara Shinn and David Page's beautifully restored farmhouse of seeing a working winery in operation. The four spacious guest rooms, each with a four-poster queen-sized bed, have private baths with classy tiled floors, although one is across the hall. Wine and cheese is set out every afternoon to be enjoyed on the wrap-around porch or in the common room, which has a woodstove, and a complimentary wine tasting in the tasting room is offered to B&B guests. David and Barbara owned Home restaurant in New York City for a number of years, and David prepares a full breakfast for his B&B guests. It may include an omelette with fresh produce from the farm, and maybe some smoked duck hash topped with a duck egg or Catapano Farms goat cheese.

SHORECREST

631-765-1570
www.shorecrestbedandbreakfast.com
54300 North Rd., Southold, NY 11971
Innkeeper: Marilyn Ann Marks
Open: Year-round
Price: Moderate–Very Expensive
Credit Cards: AE, MC, V
Special Features: Full breakfast; one block from beach; beautiful gardens; flat-screen TV in some rooms; wireless Internet access; children over 12 welcome; no pets
Directions: From the Long Island Expressway (I-495), take exit 71. Turn left (north) at stop sign onto Edwards Ave. Continue for 3.9 miles and then turn right (east) onto Sound Ave. (Rte.48). Continue for about 16 miles until you pass Southold Town Beach. Inn is on right about 300 feet beyond beach, behind tall hedge.

This elegant B&B, which opened in 1999, has some of the most beautiful woodwork of any inn on the East End. On the outside, it appears to be a typical weathered-shingle cottage with white trim, but inside, the wide crown and door moldings, 10.5-foot ceil-

ings, and elaborate detailing over the doors and windows mark it as very special. The living room contains a massive fireplace mantel, antique love seats, a pretty lady's writing desk, and a sofa; original paintings hang on the walls. The library, which is lined with bookcases, offers comfortable chairs for reading or watching TV, and the sunroom features antique wicker furniture in a sunny setting that overlooks the beautiful gardens. The Rose Room, located on the first floor, contains a four-poster bed, with a crocheted canopy, a fireplace, and a beautiful tiled bath. Four additional rooms are located upstairs. The East Room has a queen-sized mahogany sleighbed and an antique dresser, while the West Room has a bed with a blue-and-white quilt and framed antique French drawings on the walls. All rooms have private, en suite, updated baths.

A full breakfast, presented on elegant antique or period china, is served in the formal dining room by candlelight. The breakfast features local produce and products and might include fresh fruit or berries with local peach or strawberry wine, cinnamon-raisin toast with local jams, freshly baked scones, and an herb-cheese omelette with local eggs and bacon.

STIRLING HOUSE BED & BREAKFAST

631-477-0654, 800-551-0654
www.thestirlinghouse.com
104 Bay Ave. Greenport, NY 11944
Innkeepers: Frank King and Clayton Sauer
Open: Year-round
Price: Moderate
Credit Cards: MC, V
Special Features: Full breakfast; spacious porch overlooking water; gardens; koi pond; wireless Internet access; flat-screen TVs; iPod docking station; fireplaces; children over age 12 welcome; no pets
Directions: Follow Rte. 25 (Main Rd.) east beyond Riverhead for about 24 miles to Greenport. In Greenport Rte. 25 becomes Front St. At end of Front (traffic light), turn

Vintage Bed & Breakfast is located in the heart of North Fork wine country and has its own vineyard.

left onto Main St. Turn right at first street onto Bay Ave. B&B is on left.

This eclectic 1879 Victorian B&B is decorated with taste, style, and a touch of whimsy. The music parlor has some lovely French antiques including a Victorian love seat and an 1880 Chickering square grand piano. The breakfast room, on the other hand, is a counterpoint to all this elegance. Here you'll find wicker furniture, a glass-topped table, chairs with animal cutouts on the backs, and a variety of antique toys. A popcorn machine sits near the beverage station. The guest rooms are equally eclectic. In the sunny yellow-and-blue Shelter Island Room, there's a picket-fence headboard and a remnant of fence along one wall, suggestive of a garden. The Greenport Room has an elaborate carved oak fireplace mantel as a headboard. I believe my favorite is the French Room. It is quite masculine in character, with an iron bed and French lithographs on the walls. A full breakfast is served at French café tables on the breakfast porch overlooking the water. Clayton

learned to cook in France, and he attended the French Culinary Institute. He makes all of the breads himself. The meal may include a fresh fruit parfait, an herb and cheese frittata, croissants, and much more. He sometimes offers baking classes off-season.

VINTAGE BED AND BREAKFAST
631-734-2053
www.northfork.com/vintagebnb
580 Skunk Ln., Cutchogue, NY 11935
Innkeepers: Jeanne Genovese
Open: Year-round
Price: Moderate—Expensive
Credit Cards: AE, D, MC, V
Special Features: On 2.65 wooded acres; vineyard; full breakfast; CD players; wireless Internet access; not appropriate for children; no pets
Directions: Traveling east on Rte. 25 from Riverhead, continue for about 7 miles to Cutchogue. Go through village and turn right onto Skunk Ln. The B&B is seventh house on right.

This lovely Victorian was built strictly to welcome guests, so everything is new and fresh. There's a wonderful porch across the front, or you might sit in the private vineyard or on one of the patios. The inn's decor reflects the wine country. There's a cherry-wine dining room, where a bountiful gourmet breakfast is served each morning. You might start with rosemary popovers or zucchini bread, followed by a fresh fruit course. Next, you might be served a pesto Parmesan ham strata with sausage on the side, and then a sweet course of perhaps a baked pear with chocolate. The three guest rooms all have beautiful, private, en suite tiled baths with Jacuzzis. They are each named for grape varietals. "Merlot" has purple walls and a canopy bed; "Zinfandel" has a red carpet, red walls, and a crown canopy bed; and "Chardonnay" has a beige carpet and a wrought-iron bed. There's a refrigerator on an upstairs landing and a high pub table designed specifically for intimate wine tastings. The Genovese family make their own wines, and the inn's wines are complimentary. On the lower level you'll find a pool table and lots of exercise equipment. What more could you want? Well…should you be interested in a massage, that can be arranged, too.

SHOPPING

The **Tanger Factory Outlet Center** just keeps growing (631-369-2732 or 800-4-TANGER; www.tangeroutlet.com; 1770 West Main Rd., Riverhead, NY 11901; on Rte. 25 at end of Long Island Expressway (I-495); open Mon.–Sat. 9–9, Sun. 10–8). This giant outlet center opened in 1994 and by 1996 boasted almost 70 outlet stores. In 1997 a new section opened, and now the number of stores has escalated to about 175. The shops currently range from The Gap and Reebok to Bose, Brooks Brothers, Barney's, Lenox, Movado, Pottery Barn, Polo Ralph Lauren, Restoration Hardware, Ann Taylor, and Williams-Sonoma.

Antiques & Furniture

Antiques and Old Lace (631-734-6462; 31935 Main Rd. (Rte. 25), Cutchogue, NY 11935; open year-round; Fri.–Mon. 11–4:30) Owners: Gene and Pat Mott. You'll find 5,000 square feet of space in this shop filled with interesting furniture (especially oak) that ranges from an old telephone booth from a hotel in Maine to rolltop desks. There are old kitchen utensils (irons, egg beaters), tons of chairs, toys, clocks, baskets, art glass, and more.

Beall & Bell Antiques (631-477-8239; 430 Main St. Greenport, NY 11944; open year-round; in summer Fri.–Sun. 10–5; rest of year Sat. and Sun. 10–5) Owners: Ken and Ginger Ludaker. Located in an old two-story house on a side street, this antiques shop features lots of twig, pine, and oak furniture in a shabby-chic sort of style; plus mirrors, lamps, china, and more.

The Clearing House eXchange (631-477-6262 or 631-477-3484; www.tchx.net; 414 First St. and 419 Main St., Greenport, NY 11944; open year-round; Mem. Day–Labor Day daily 11–5, fewer days rest of year) Owners: Nick Nicolino and Victoria Collett. This couple specialize in holding tag sales and auctions, taking items on consignment, and handling business liquidations. In Greenport, they have a storefront, as well as a huge warehouse building *filled* with furniture, rugs, tabletop, lighting, and also a smattering of antiques and collectibles. In general, prices are quite reasonable.

The Furniture Store Antiques (631-477-2980; 214 Front St., Greenport, NY 11944; open year-round; daily noon–6) Owners: Jay and Miz Thomson. Vintage clothing and linen, china and glassware, jewelry, and furniture are all sold here. Don't miss the hallway with all the old tools and books, or the back room that may have an old woodstove or some stained glass.

Gallery 429 (631-477-3070; 429 Main St., Greenport, NY 11944; open year round; Wed.–Mon. in summer 9–5; rest of year daily Wed.–Mon. 11–5) Owner: Barbara Bartoloni. This is a very interesting shop. You'll find excellent European-style oil and watercolor paintings on the walls, lots of furniture, and a whole section of dolls and toys.

Jan Davis Antiques/L. I. Doll Hospital (631-765-2379; www.jandavisantiques.com; 45395 Main Rd. (Rte. 25), P.O. Box 1604, Southold, NY 11971; open year-round; Thurs.–Mon. 12–5) Owner: Jan Davis. This quality roadside shop was built as a country store in 1856. Today, you'll find Victorian furniture, lighting fixtures, sterling silver candlesticks, glassware, and dolls that range from bisque to Madame Alexander. Jan expertly repairs dolls, so you'll find several in the back room being elegantly coiffed or gowned.

Kapell Antiques (631-477-0100; www.kapells.com; 400 Front St.; mailing address: P.O. Box 463, Greenport, NY 11944; open year-round; daily 9–5) Owner: David Kapell. This shop is located in a great old building that houses a real estate agency run by Mr. Kapell, who is also the mayor of Greenport. The antiques are of the highest quality and include massive desks, dining room tables, a giant old scale, lots of pianos, ship models, paintings, folk art, early tools, and more.

Lydia's Antiques and Stained Glass (631-477-1414; 215 Main St., Greenport, NY 11944; open year-round; Thurs.–Mon. 11–5) Owner: Lydia Abatelli. This huge store has a magnificent array of restored and new stained glass (Lydia repairs old glass and customizes new pieces), plus lots of furniture, china, glassware, and so much more.

Shearer Shop (631-477-1357; 425 Main St., Greenport, NY 11944; open year-round; daily in summer except Wed. 10–4:30; rest of year Sat. and Sun. same hours) Owners: Bill and Helen Shearer. This funny little shop, located in a charming old building, is packed on both floors with old "stuff." There are lots of old tools, tons of cups and saucers, old bottles, furniture, jewelry, a lovely old iron umbrella stand, and some beautiful Jadite.

ThistleBees (631-734-5362; 27850 Main Rd. (Rte. 25), Cutchogue, NY 11935; open daily year-round except Tues. 10–4) Owner: Pat Gyscek. You'll find an eclectic array of things in this shop, from old oak furniture and vintage tablecloths to new lacy hand-knit sweaters and christening dresses—some are vintage and others are made from vintage or bridal fabrics.

Three Sisters Antiques (631-722-5980; 1550 Main Rd. (Rte. 25); mailing address: P.O. Box 985, Jamesport, NY 11947; open year-round; Thurs.–Mon. 12–5) Owners: Alice Amrhein, Barbara Amrhein, and Diane Boone. This shop is filled with an unbelievable array of "smalls." You'll find toys, dishes, postcards, dolls, little figurines, and much more.

White Flower Farmhouse (631-765-2353; www.whiteflowerfarmhouse.com; 2845 Peconic Ln., Peconic, NY 11958; open year round; June–Sept. daily 11–5; rest of year fewer days) Owner: Lori Guyer. Prowling the byways, farmhouses, tag sales, and old barns of the North Fork, Lori finds and repairs or refurbishes cast-off furniture and decorative items, turning them into cherished furnishings for the country-style houses of today. You may find wicker, rustic garden furniture, vases, linens, and much more. She's got some true gems waiting in her small shop.

Willow Hill Antiques (631-765-4124; 48405 Main Rd. (Rte. 25); mailing address: P.O. Box

1048, Southold, NY 11971; open year-round; Thurs.–Mon. 11–5) Owner: Richard Sahm.
There are two floors of oak and walnut chests, dressers, and chairs, fireplace mantels,
and lighting fixtures. You'll even find lead soldiers and some dishes.

Books

Burton's Bookstore (631-477-1161; 43 Front St., Greenport, NY 11944; open year-round;
in summer Mon.–Sat. 10–5, Sun. 12:30–4:30; closed Sun. in winter) Owner: George
Maaiki. This complete bookstore carries a wide selection of hardbound and paperback
books, greeting cards, and calendars.

Clothing

b.b.balsam (631-477-2897; 127A Adams St., Greenport, NY 11944; open year-round;
Thurs.–Tues. 12–6) Owner: Barbara Balsam. This sleek, mod shop would be equally at
home in Soho. Tucked away on a side street that parallels Front Street (read: difficult to
find), it offers sassy, classy, youthful ladies' clothing that includes fur-trimmed
sweaters, short-short skirts, and jackets with leather fringe.

Calypso (631-477-2780; www.calypso-celle.com; 15 Front St., Greenport, NY 11944; open
in summer daily 10–6; fewer days and shorter hours rest of year; may close several
months in winter) In 2007 this terrific chain opened its first North Fork shop. Now the
perky and wearable designs of Christiane Celle, who opened her first store in Saint-
Barth, can be purchased here too. There are women's separates in brilliant colors,
including long silky skirts with ruffled hems, gauzy blouses, drawstring pants, and shifts
with appliquéd roses. Jewelry and skin care products are also here.

Gloria Jewel (631-284-3761; www.gloriajewel.com; 1560 Main Rd. (Rte. 25), Jamesport,
NY 11947; open daily 10–6 in summer; fewer days in winter) Owner: Megan Leary. I love
this store. The dresses, skirts, and blouses are sophisticated but easy to wear, they come
in an array of colors and beautiful fabrics, and they're affordable. There are silk dresses,
cashmere sweaters, jewelry, and handbags. There's also a shop in Bridgehampton.

Impulse (631-477-2181; 423 Main St., Greenport, NY 11944; open year round; Mem.
Day–Labor Day daily 10–5; fewer days remainder of year) Owner: Cheryl Feld. This
classy little shop has excellent prices for cute, bright clothes, including dresses, jeweled
thongs, shoes, skirts, blouses, handbags, jewelry, and much more.

Galleries, Crafts, & Gifts

Claudia Lowry Fine Art (631-477-2968; 3 Front St., Greenport, NY 11944; open Apr.–Nov.
daily except Mon. 11–6; rest of year by appt.) Owner: Claudia Lowry. Claudia paints big,
bold, brightly hued oils featuring flowers, flags, and dragonflies, and she's also a sculptress. In addition, in a back room, she exhibits the photography and drawings of her
daughter, Amanda Lowry, and the watercolors of M. P. Bowker.

The Doofpot (631-477-0344; 308 Main St., Greenport, NY 11944; open May–Dec. daily
except Tues. and Wed. 10–5; Jan.–Apr. Sat. and Sun. same hours) Owners: Mary Ann
Zovko and Jaap Hilbrand. Located in Stirling Square, this unique shop carries a marvelous array of brilliant, hand-painted ceramic vases, cachepots, urns, wall frescoes,
and tables, selected by the owner and imported from Italy and Spain. You'll also find
luminous Venetian glass and chandeliers.

The Down Home Store (631-734-6565; 37070 Main Rd. (Rte. 25), Cutchogue, NY 11935;

The colorful window displays of imported hand-painted ceramic vases, urns, and cachepots lure you irresistibly into the Doofpot in Greenport.

open Mar.–Dec. Mon.–Sat. 10–5, Sun. 11–4; Jan. and Feb. Fri.–Mon. same hours)
Owner: P. C. Rueckwald. Once you see the marvelous array of handcrafted items in this
shop, you will come back again and again. You will find elegantly painted furniture in
faux finishes, plus vintage pieces such as an oak buffet, an ornate iron cradle, and an oak
Hoosier. There are small rugs, sailboat models, candles, cards, dried-herb wreaths,
hammocks, teddy bears, birdhouses, china, and splatterware.

Fiedler Gallery (631-477-4242; www.fiedlergallery.com; 207 Main St., Greenport, NY
11944; open year-round; daily in summer 10–5; rest of year Wed.–Sun. 11–4) Owner:
Rich Fiedler. This fine-art gallery, located on two floors of a nice old building, displays
the work of a variety of artists. On the first floor, Rich Fiedler displays his own paintings, which are mostly of local scenes, and are very impressive. Upstairs, you'll find
beautiful watercolors by North Fork artist Tony Scarmato, and sensitive paintings by
Olive Reich, among others. This is definitely the place to come for fine art.

Freda's Fancy (631-477-0020; 1-800-451-0078; www.fredas-fancy.com; 213 E. Front St.,
Greenport, NY 11944; open year-round Thurs.–Mon. 12–4) Owner: Freda Jaycox. For all
your dollhouse needs, from furniture to wallpaper to lighting fixtures to Victorian and
log cabin kits, this is the source.

Gallery M (631-477-9496; www.gallerym.biz; 407 Main St., Greenport, NY 11944; open daily in summer 11–5; rest of year call for hours) Owner: Myra Eisenberg. This contemporary art shop features beautiful art glass, inlaid wooden tables and boxes, paintings, sculptures, jewelry, fabulous silver animals attached to wooden napkin rings, scarves, and gold and silver jewelry by the owner.

Gazebo Gallery (631-477-1410; 124 Main St.; mailing address: P.O. Box 474, Greenport, NY 11944; open daily in summer 9–5; rest of season closed Tues. and Wed.; closed Jan.–Mar.) Owners: Jana Heffernan and Joy Harvey. Jane Schumacher was one of the North Fork's most distinguished artists. She specialized in oil and watercolor paintings of flowers and seascapes. When she passed away in 2001, literally with a paintbrush in her hand, her daughters took over her gallery. Now, in addition to prints of some of Jane's most beloved paintings, you can also buy handmade jackets, hooked rugs, quilted pillows, scarves, and jewelry.

Greenport Art & Design (631-477-2380; www.greenportartanddesign.com; 117 Main St., Greenport, NY 11944; open year-round; June–Labor Day 10–8, fewer days and shorter hours rest of year) Owner: Elizabeth Karsch. In this wonderful paint-your-own pottery studio, you will learn the art of pottery painting, glazing, and firing from the owner, who is an expert at the craft. The shop also features a gallery of contemporary art, where local artists are exhibited, and there's a boutique where you can purchase paintings, pottery, handmade jewelry, toys, handmade children's clothes, and more.

Jamesport Country Store (631-722-8048; 1299 Main Rd. (Rte. 25), Jamesport, NY 11947; open daily year-round 10–5:30) Owner: Howard Woldman. This great old brick building with wooden floors houses a terrific little country store that carries such items as beach plum jam and honey, wicker, baskets, candles, and most other things that you think a country store should carry, except groceries.

La Ferme de la Mer (631-298-4646; www.lafermedelamer.com; 95 Love Lane, Mattituck, NY 11952; open Mon.–Sat. 10:30–6, Sun. 12–5) Owner: Joan Bischoff van Heemskerck. This factory outlet store has a marvelous selection of French and Mediterranean Provincial home furnishings. There are Soleido fabrics, faience dishes, iron tables with mosaic tile tops, wallpapers, rugs, pottery, vases, rattan bistro furniture, French soaps, herbs and spices, all mixed in with local art.

Old Town Arts & Crafts Guild (631-734-6382; www.oldtownguild.com; 28265 Main Rd.; (Rte. 25); mailing address: P.O. Box 392, Cutchogue, NY 11935; open May–Dec.; Mon.–Wed., Fri. and Sat. 10–5, Sun. noon–5) This co-op of North Fork artists was founded in 1948 and displays and sells members' high-quality art that includes knit work, patchwork quilts, jewelry, oil and watercolor paintings, toys, dolls and doll clothes, stained glass, lots of Christmas decorations, carved wooden items, ceramics, and pottery.

Peggy Mach (www.peggymachsplace.homestead.com) For many years sculptress Peggy Mach lived and worked on Shelter Island, where she had a gallery. As her renown increased, however, she found she needed to concentrate on individual commissions and eventually moved off the island to the North Fork. You can still see and purchase her work through her Web site. Her subjects—children, dancers, clowns, lovers—are so lyrical and poignant that you almost feel as if you can talk to them, and they certainly "talk to you." She sculpts in clay and stone and then casts in bronze, using a "lost wax method." Her work is included in important private and museum collections throughout the world.

Preston's Outfitters and Preston's Ship and Sea Gallery (631-477-1990; 1-800-836-

Artist Jane Schumacher's daughters now run the Gazebo Gallery in Greenport, where you can still purchase prints of Jane's luminous floral and landscape paintings.

1165; www.prestons.com; 102 Main St., Greenport, NY 11944; open Mon.–Sat. 10–5, Sun. 11–5) Owner: George Rowsom. Located on Preston's Wharf, Preston's Ships Chandlery has been outfitting ships and their sailing crews since 1883. Today, nautical needs are still supplied, as well as clothing. In addition, a marvelous shop full of nautical gifts brings shoppers from miles around. There are ship models, hundreds of paintings and prints, scrimshaw, Nantucket baskets, shells, and so much more. If it's a nautical object, it's likely Preston's will have it. If you can't get here in person, call to receive the catalog, or order on the Web.

Southold Historical Society Gift Shop (631-765-5500; www.southoldhistoricalsociety.org; 54325 Main Rd., (Rte. 25) Southold, NY 11971; open Mem. Day–Christmas; Mon.–Wed. 11–3, Thurs.–Sat. 10–4) You'll find interesting items here that you won't find elsewhere: pretty white lace parasols, lovely lined baskets, T-shirts, books, quilts, pottery, and antiques, such as a roll-armed wicker rocker. Many of the items are new, but the antiques are in excellent condition. The Treasure Exchange (631-765-1550), a consignment shop across the street, sells items such as antique furniture, silver, and china.

Sweet Indulgences (631-477-8250; www.sweet-indulgences.com; 200 Main St., Greenport, NY 11944; open daily in summer 10–6, except Fri., Sat. 10–9; shorter hours rest of year) Don't let the name fool you! This is so much more than a candy store. Angela Oliv-

Sweet Indulgences in Greenport is filled to the brim with outstanding gift items and decor for the home.

eri has filled her charming shop with wonderful gifts and craft items, including collectible Santas, a huge array of Easter, Halloween, and Thanksgiving decorations, candles, and much more. And yes, there is a counter of Godiva chocolates and other
candies.

Taste (631-477-3357; www.tasteshoppes.com; 409 Main St., Greenport, NY 11944; open
daily in summer except Tues. 11–5; rest of year same hours, closed Tues. and Wed.; Jan.
and Feb. open weekends only) Owner: Charles Marks. This lovely shop has a selection of
some of the most beautiful porcelain trays, cups, saucers, and teaspoons that you'll ever
see. The handles are shaped into fanciful dragonflies, butterflies, and bees. In addition,
there are beautiful pieces of creamware, interesting distressed-iron door knockers and
plant stands, and jewelry. This is a must-stop shop.

Winter Harbor Gallery (631-477-0010; www.winterharborgallery.com; 211 Main St.,
Greenport, NY 11944; open year-round; June–Sept. daily Mon.–Thurs. 10–5, Fri. and
Sat. 10–9, Sun. 10–6, fewer days and hours rest of year) Amy Martin has filled her
gallery with the art and craft of 30 artists—most of whom are local. You'll find original
oil, acrylic, and watercolor paintings, photography, fabric and fiber art, and wood crafts,
as well as jewelry, gifts, and cards.

Housewares

Cookery Dock (631-477-0059; 132 Main St., Greenport, NY 11944; open year-round; daily in summer 10–5; rest of year daily 11–5) Owner: Arlene Marvin. This fine cooking shop has all the things we need to be great cooks, including pots and pans, pot holders, cookbooks, and much more.

Complement the Chef (631-765-3261; www.complementthechef.com; 53740 Main Rd., Southold, NY 11971; open year-round; daily in summer 10–6; rest of year closed Tues. or Mon. and Tues.) Owner: Kevin and Joan Shannon. Not only is this cookware shop stylish and handsome, it carries a wide variety of dishes, pots and pans, accessories, and more.

CULTURE

Calendar of Events

In the summer and fall especially, the wineries hold events that range from wine dinners to concerts, and from theatrical productions to poetry readings and murder mystery events. They take place every weekend, and are so numerous that they are not detailed here. The Long Island Wine Council (631-369-5887; www.liwines.com) has a complete list of events on its Web site. You can also check local newspapers or call the wineries for their individual schedules. In addition, the North Fork Promotion Council (631-298-5757; www.north fork.org; mailing address: P.O. Box 1865, Southold, NY 11971) includes a complete list of events on its Web site, and also publishes a print guide to events, shops, restaurants, lodging, recreation, and cultural institutions once a year. Call for your copy.

February

Presidents' Day Parade The Greenport Fire Department has been sponsoring a parade on Presidents' Day for almost 160 years. More than 50 fire departments from New York and Connecticut participate.

Winterfest—Jazz on the Vine (631-727-0900) Series of concerts at the wineries performed by renowned musicians. East End Arts Council.

March

Easter Egg Hunt (631-298-5248) Every year on the Saturday before Easter, Mattituck Historical Society holds its popular Easter Egg Hunt.

May

Antique and Classic Boat Show (631-477-2100) For 20 years, Greenport has featured more than 40 wooden boats of all styles in its Classic Boat Show. Call the East End Seaport Maritime Museum for information.

Memorial Day Parade (631-765-5500) Southold Historical Society holds a Founder's Day weekend that includes a parade and Civil War encampment.

Mosaic Street Painting Festival (631-727-0966) This annual event, which is held in Riverhead, attracts professional artists and craftspeople, who sell their work at booths, as well as amateurs who wish to paint a street square. Sponsored by the East End Arts Council.

June

Garden Tour (631-765-5262 or 631-734-5223) This annual garden tour is sponsored by the Cutchogue/New Suffolk Chamber of Commerce.

The Mattituck Strawberry Festival (631-298-2222) Eagerly awaited each year, this festival is sponsored by the Mattituck Lions Club. There are over 250 booths featuring arts and crafts, as well as strawberry shortcake for everyone.

Orient & East Marion Spring House Tour (631-323-3501) This annual house tour is sponsored by the Oysterponds Historical Society.

Trawler Fest (www.passagemaker.com) This festival is held at Mitchell Park and Marina, focusing on the cruising-under-power lifestyle. Sponsored by *PassageMaker* magazine.

July

Antiques Show and Sale Sponsored by Cutchogue/New Suffolk Historical Council, this show (which has been held 40+ years) takes place on the village green in Cutchogue. There are almost 100 dealers.

Croquet Tournament (631-323-2480) Held in late July or early August in Orient, this annual event is sponsored by the Oysterponds Historical Society.

Fourth of July Parades There are parades in New Suffolk and Southold.

Gem, Mineral, and Jewelry Show (631-722-4161) This annual event, which has been held for almost 30 years, is held at Mattituck High School on the last weekend in July.

Greenport Carnival This carnival ends with a fireworks display on both Saturday and Sunday of Independence Day weekend.

July 4th Music Festival (631-727-0900) This annual all-day event in Riverhead has featured such national artists as the Benny Goodman Orchestra and Richie Havens. Sponsored by the East End Arts Council.

Mattituck Historical Society Antiques Show (631-868-2751) Now in its 22nd year, this large antiques show draws a distinguished group of dealers.

Mattituck Street Fair (631-298-1452) The village of Mattituck has a street fair on historic Love Lane the second Saturday in July. Sponsored by the Mattituck Chamber of Commerce.

Opera in the Hamptons (631-728-8804) A series of opera performances (*La Bohème* and *Tosca,* for example) are performed on both the North and South Forks.

***Wine Press* Summer Concert Series** (631-722-2220) A series of summer concerts at the wineries. Sponsored by *Wine Press* and the East End Arts Council.

August

Cutchogue Library Annual Book Sale (631-734-6360) Once a year Friends of the Cutchogue Free Library holds a book sale.

Douglas Moore Memorial Music Festival (631-734-6507) 25th annual festival in Cutchogue celebrating the sounds of summer, combined with a community picnic.

Ice Cream Social (631-765-5500) The Southold Historical Society holds an ice cream social that includes hayrides, face painting, and, of course, ice cream.

Outdoor Arts & Crafts Show (631-734-6382) Now almost 55 years old, this event takes place on the village green in Cutchogue. Members of the Old Town Arts and Crafts Guild display and sell their work, using snow fences as props.

Polish Festival Riverhead has been noted for this two-day festival for a number of years.

Booths serve kielbasa and funnel cakes. Polish crafts abound, and the Polka Festival attracts hundreds of avid dancers.

September

Craft Fair (631-765-3161) Local crafts are displayed and sold. Sponsored by the Greenport/Southold Chamber of Commerce.

Garlic Festival (631-680-1699) A celebration of garlic, including music, crafts, and a garlic cookoff. Garden of Eve, Riverhead.

Harvest Festival The Mattituck Chamber of Commerce holds an annual Harvest Festival and Clam Chowder Contest in September.

Historic Seaport Regatta (631-477-2121) An annual sailing event in early September between Greenport and Sag Harbor.

Jazz Festival (631-744-7697) Sponsored by The Arts in Southold town and held at Southold High School.

Maritime Festival and Fishing Tournament (631-477-0004) This festival is held annually in Greenport Harbor and includes a wooden boat parade and regatta, wine and seafood tasting, and much more. Sponsored by the East End Seaport and Maritime Foundation of Greenport.

October

Annual Pig Roast (631-734-7089) This lively event at the Galluccio Winery in Cutchogue includes live music and entertainment.

Corn Maze (631-722-8546; www.harbesfamilyfarm.com) In addition to an incredible corn maze, there are lots of activities for children at the Harbes Family Farm in Cutchogue.

Fall Harvest Festivals Most wineries on the North Fork sponsor a fall festival.

Hallockville Fall Festival and Craft Fair (631-298-5292) An annual event that attracts a variety of craftsmen; also includes games and rides. Sponsored by Hallockville Museum Farm.

November

Christmas Open House (631-323-2655) In late November, the Old Town Arts and Crafts Guild holds this annual event in Cutchogue.

Southold Village Merchants Annual Christmas Parade (631-765-4100) Held the Saturday after Thanksgiving.

December

Caroling on the Green Caroling and refreshments in Cutchogue, sponsored by the Cutchogue/New Suffolk Historical Council.

Christmas House Tour (631-323-2480) In Orient, sponsored yearly by the Oysterponds Historical Society.

First Night Celebration Music, art exhibits, parades, and countdown to midnight, in Greenport.

Holiday House Tour & Progressive Food and Wine Tasting This popular event, which offers a tour of local B&Bs decorated for the holidays, and samplings of food and wine from area restaurants and wineries, is sponsored by the North Fork Bed & Breakfast Association.

Movies

Mattituck Cinemas (631-298-4400; Main Rd. (Rte. 25), Mattituck, NY 11952; open every night year-round) Located in the Mattituck Plaza near the A&P, this is an eight-plex theater showing first-run movies.

Village Cinema Greenport (631-477-8600; 211 Front St., Greenport, NY 11944; open Apr.–Sept. every night, with matinees on weekends; Oct.–Mar. may be open weekends, but call for schedule.) This is a four-plex theater showing first-run movies.

Museums & Galleries

CUTCHOGUE

CUTCHOGUE–NEW SUFFOLK HISTORICAL COUNCIL

631-734-7122
www.cutchoguenewsuffolkhistory.org
Main Rd., Cutchogue, NY 11935
Open: July–Labor Day, Sat.–Mon. 1–4; shorter hours rest of year
Fee: None

Located on the village green, this interesting collection of historic buildings was assembled through a community effort that began in 1959 with a query from the Smithsonian Institution about North Fork Indians. Mounting one of the finest historic-preservation efforts on the East End, community-spirited citizens moved and restored the buildings now included in this complex. The oldest building is the circa 1649 Old House, which is one of the oldest houses in New York State. It is furnished with handcrafted furniture and accessories of the period and is a unique example of how early East End settlers lived. The Wickham Farmhouse, which dates to 1704, served as a Wickham family home for more than 250 years. It is a double Cape Cod–style farmhouse, furnished with a variety of 18th-, 19th, and -20th-century antiques. The Old Schoolhouse was built in 1840 and served as a one-room school until 1903. The Carriage House dates to the early 19th century and now contains an old carriage and the council's information center.

GREENPORT

EAST END SEAPORT & MARITIME MUSEUM

631-477-2100
www.eastendseaport.org
Third St., Greenport
Mailing Address: P.O. Box 624, Greenport, NY 11944
Open: Mid-May–Sept.; Mid-May–June and Sept. weekends 11–5, July and Aug. Mon. and Wed.–Fri. 11–5, Sat. and Sun. 9:30–5. Blacksmith Shop: June–Sept. Sat. and Sun. 11–5
Fee: Adults and children over 12 $2; children under 12 $1

Located at the end of Third Street beside the Shelter Island Ferry terminal, this interesting museum captures the maritime history of Greenport in a series of photographs, artifacts, navigational instruments, ship models, and drawings. You'll learn about the shipbuilding, lighthouses, and fishing and yachting history of the village. The museum members were responsible for restoring the "Bug Light," or Long Beach Bar Lighthouse in 1990, a beloved landmark that had been destroyed by fire in 1963. It is now maintained by the museum and by the Coast Guard. You can also join **East End Lighthouses** (www.eastendlighthouses.org) for cruises from June through September to see the Bug Light and other lighthouses up close, as well as Gardiner's Island and Plum Island. The museum also maintains a Village Blacksmith Shop, located near the dock west of Claudio's. Here, you can watch a real blacksmith at work on weekends in summer.

RAILROAD MUSEUM OF LONG ISLAND
631-727-7920
www.rmli.us
416 Griffing Ave., Riverhead, NY 11901
Open: Mem. Day–Columbus Day, Sat., Sun., and holidays 11–4; rest of season Sat. 10–4
Second location: 631-477-0439
440 Fourth St., Greenport, NY 11944
Open: Mem. Day–Columbus Day, Sat., Sun., and holidays 11–4
Fee: Adults $5, children ages 5–12 $3, children under 5 free

The old train station in Greenport, which became the easternmost terminus of the Long Island Rail Road in 1844, is now the site of an interesting railroad museum. Actually, the primary site of the museum is in Riverhead, and this smaller version is a satellite location. You will learn all about the East End's relationship with the railroad at these museums, as well as the importance of the Long Island Rail Road to progress on the East End. In Riverhead, children can take a ride on a World's Fair miniature train. Call for information about special events, such as the arrival of Santa on the noon train in early December.

STIRLING HISTORICAL SOCIETY
631-477-3026
319 Main St. (in Monsell Park), Greenport, NY 11944
Open: July and Aug., Sat. and Sun. 1–4
Fee: Donations accepted

This little 1831 house, located in the parking lot behind Main Street, is the headquarters of the Stirling Historical Society. You can see art exhibits here in the summer, as well as tour the interior of the house.

ORIENT
OYSTERPONDS HISTORICAL SOCIETY
631-323-2480
www.oysterpondshistoricalsociety.org
1555 Village Ln., Orient
Mailing Address: P.O. Box 70, Orient, NY 11957
Open: June–Sept., Thurs., Sat., Sun. 2–5, or by appt.
Fee: Adults $5, children $1

The Oysterponds Historical Society is in the delightful hamlet of Orient, a designated National Historic District. The museum encompasses a variety of 19th-century buildings. In the former village inn, the parlors, dining room, and kitchen are furnished in a style that reflects a range of periods from 1790 to 1940; there is also a marvelous toy and train collection. The Old Point Schoolhouse was built in 1873 and contains a library of historical documents. The Amanda Brown Schoolhouse serves as the Beach Plum Museum Shop, where society members sell craft items. One of the most interesting buildings in the collection, the Webb House, is an authentic "George Washington Slept Here" structure—Washington rested in the house in 1757 when traveling to Boston to receive his commission to lead the Virginia troops into battle prior to the American Revolution. The house was then owned by Lt. Constant Booth and was located in Greenport. This beautiful building was later moved to this site and expertly restored. The society sponsors frequent walking tours of the village, a holiday house tour, an annual croquet tournament, and numerous cultural events, such as Gilbert and Sullivan musicals and plays.

RIVERHEAD
ATLANTIS MARINE WORLD
631-208-9200
www.atlantismarineworld.com
431 East Main St., Riverhead, NY 11901
Open: Year-round, 10–5
Fee: Adults $21.50; seniors over 62 $18.50; children 3–17 $18.50

In partnership with the Riverhead Foundation for Marine Research and Preservation (631-369-9840) and the Cornell Cooperative Extension's Marine Division (631-727-7850), Atlantis Marine World opened in 2000. It includes a live coral reef, tanks of sharks, seals (there's a show), and several touch tanks. The setting is designed to conjure visions of the lost city of Atlantis, so you walk through passageways that look like coral reefs with colorful fish tanks on either side. There's a little cylinder of sea horses, a submarine simulator, and more. Atlantis also operates the *Atlantis Explorer,* an excursion boat that takes participants on a 2.5-hour environmental tour of the Peconic River and Flanders Bay. A naturalist explains the ecosystem, and guests participate in trap pulls, plankton tows, and more. The cost for adults is $19, for seniors 62+ $17, children 3–17 $17, and children under 2 $5. You can also walk in a salt marsh, or participate in a shark dive. In the latter, eight participants, accompanied by a trained divemaster, are immersed inside a cage into the shark tank. The cost is $140, and it's done once a day only. The mission of the foundation is to treat and release wounded or stranded marine life, and you can view the turtles, dolphins, whales, porpoises, and seals they are assisting. This is a wonderful place for children to become acquainted with the fragility of the sea and sea creatures, as well as environmental concerns associated with the ocean.

THE BIG DUCK
631-852-8292
1012 Flanders Rd., (Rte. 24), Flanders, NY 11901
Mailing Address: P.O. Box 144, West Sayville, NY 11796
Open: Mid-Apr.–mid Sept., daily except Mon. 10–5; mid-Sept.–Christmas, Fri.–Sun. same hours; closed Jan.–mid Apr.
Admission: None

Recognized as one of the most famous examples of roadside art in America, this gigantic white cement duck measures 30 feet long and 20 feet high, and weighs 16,500 pounds. It was built in 1931 by duck farmers Martin and Jeule Maurer to set them apart from their competitors. And it must have been quite a magnet to their Big Duck Ranch. The inside was a sales room where clients could purchase Peking duck, otherwise known as Long Island duckling. Today it's a tourist information center, where Long Island gifts and "duck-a-bilia" are sold. Operated by the Friends for Long Island's Heritage.

This former village inn serves as the headquarters of the Oysterponds Historical Society in Orient. Dustin Chase

EAST END ARTS COUNCIL
631-727-0900
www.eastendarts.org
141 East Main St., Riverhead, NY 11901
Gallery open: Year-round, Tues.–Sat. 10–4
Admission: Free

The East End Arts Council was founded in 1972 to promote the arts on the East End of Long Island. It's located in two historic buildings on Riverhead's Main Street, where it operates a gallery, with changing exhibits, and a gift shop offering original art by local artisans. Through the Community School of the Arts (631-369-2171) there are art classes for adults and children, private and group music lessons, grant-writing workshops, and numerous resources for artists. Throughout the year, the council sponsors workshops, lectures, and presentations.

HALLOCKVILLE MUSEUM FARM AND FOLKLIFE CENTER
631-298-5292
www.hallockville.com
6038 Sound Ave. (Rte. 48), Riverhead, NY 11901
Open: Apr.–mid-Dec., Tues.–Sat. 11–4; by appt. rest of year
Fee: Adults $7; children 6–16 and seniors $4; children under 6 free

Ezra Hallock was one of the first settlers on the North Fork, and this was his family homestead. The farm, which is on the National Register of Historic Places, was in the Hallock family for almost 200 years, and it's remained virtually intact. Children and adults will see how a turn-of-the-20th-century farm operated. Included are the 1765 Hallock Homestead, furnished as it would have been from 1880 to 1910, a shoemaker's shop, a smokehouse, workshops, a large English-style barn, and an outhouse. The Museum Farm is also home to the Suffolk County Folklife Center. Craft demonstrations, festivals, school programs, and special summer camps take place here; they might include decoy carving, whittling, quill-pen making, fishnet mending, or horseshoeing. The Hallock family still gathers at the family farm once a year for their annual reunion and picnic.

SUFFOLK COUNTY HISTORICAL SOCIETY
631-727-2881
www.suffolkcountyhistoricalsociety.org
300 West Main St., Riverhead, NY 11901
Open: Tues.–Sat. 12:30–4:30; research library open Wed.–Sat.
Fee: $2 donation requested for nonmembers to use library

The Suffolk County Historical Society is the second-oldest historical society on Long Island. The museum, research library, archives, and education programs offer a glimpse into the rich life of Suffolk County. In addition, the Weathervane Gift Shop has unusual gift items that include historical books, maps, and genealogical supplies.

Southold
CUSTER INSTITUTE
631-765-2626
www.custerobservatory.org
1115 Main Bayview Rd., Southold, NY 11971
Open: Year-round, every Sat. dusk–midnight; or call Barbara Latuna (516-722-3850) for appt. and schedule of events.
Fee: Members free; nonmembers recommended minimum donation, $5 adults, $3 children under 14.

The Custer Institute is an astronomical observatory with an auditorium, library, and small museum. It is open to the public every Saturday night to observe stars, planets, and meteors from various telescopes. Concerts, classic films, art exhibits, lectures, and other cultural events are held year-round, and an astronomy jamboree, which includes lectures, solar viewing, and stargazing, is held every fall.

HORTON POINT LIGHTHOUSE AND NAUTICAL MUSEUM
631-765-2101
www.southoldhistoricalsociety.org
Lighthouse Rd. at Long Island Sound, Southold
Mailing Address: P.O. Box 1, Southold, NY 11971
Open: Mem. Day–Columbus Day, Sat., Sun., and holidays 11:30–4
Fee: Adults $3; free for children under 12

The Horton Point Lighthouse was commissioned by President George Washington in 1790, although construction was not completed until 1857. It served as one of the links in the chain of lighthouses that guided ships through the treacherous inlets and rocky points of Long Island Sound. The light was removed from the lighthouse in 1933 and installed on a tower nearby, but it was reinstalled in 1990 as part of the renovation of the lighthouse. Although the light continues to serve its original function and is maintained by the U.S. Coast Guard, the museum in the base is operated by the Southold Historical Society. The Nautical Museum contains sea chests, paintings, maps, ships' logs, and other remnants of the active North Fork shipping trade. A climb up the stairs to the tower to see

The Horton Point Lighthouse was built in 1857 and continues to protect ships from the hazardous shoreline.

the light will be rewarded by a fine view of Long Island Sound. You can join East End Light-houses (www.eastendlighthouses.org) for summer cruises to see many of Long Island's East End lighthouses up close, and also to cruise past Gardiner's and Plum islands.

SOUTHOLD HISTORICAL SOCIETY

631-765-5500
www.southoldhistoricalsociety.org
54325 Main Rd. (at Maple Ln.), Southold
Mailing Address: P.O. Box 1, Southold, NY 11971
Open: In summer only, Wed., Sat., Sun. 1–4; gift shop in Prince Bldg. on Main St., May–Christmas, Thurs.–Sat. 10–4; Treasure Exchange consignment shop, May–Nov., Thurs.–Sat. 10–4
Fee: $2 donation suggested

The Southold Historical Society maintains and operates a collection of 12 buildings in the center of Southold that includes the 1900 Ann Currie Bell Hallock House and Buttery, 1750 Thomas Moore House, 1842 Cleveland Grover Gagen Blacksmith Shop, Downs Carriage House circa 1840, 18th-century Pine Neck Barn, and Bay View School circa 1822. There's a wonderful millinery display of 19th- and 20th-century hats and fabrics, and you'll learn about spinning and weaving, scrimshaw, old ovens and fireplaces, and so much more. The society maintains its headquarters in the ornate Prince Building on Main Street, where its delightful gift shop is located. The Treasure Exchange, a consignment shop, is located on the museum grounds, where you can buy antique furniture, silverware, and china. Events such as garden tours, ice cream socials, and a winter lecture series are also sponsored.

SOUTHOLD INDIAN MUSEUM

631-765-5577
www.southoldindianmuseum.org
1080 Main Bayview Rd., Southold
Mailing Address: P.O. Box 268, Southold, NY 11971
Open: Mem. Day–Labor Day, Sat. and Sun. 1:30–4:30; rest of year Sun. only
Fee: Adults $2; children $0.50

The Southold Indian Museum was organized in 1925 and is now incorporated by the Long Island Chapter of the New York State Archaeological Association. The museum is noted for its extensive collection of local Algonquin Indian artifacts, many of which were found on the North Fork. There are several items that date to more than 10,000 years ago. The collection includes not only arrowheads and spears but also many pieces of pottery unearthed nearby. In a dramatic illustration of how advanced this agrarian society was when the first English settlers arrived in 1640, an exhibit of various corn types highlights the farming techniques used.

Music, Theater, Cultural Events

The North Fork made musical history with the **Greenport Brass Band**, which was formed initially in 1851 as part of the New York State Militia. It was so popular in the early 1900s that folks would come to Greenport on a steamer from New York City just to attend the concerts. Concerts are still held every Friday at 8 PM in the summer and continue to draw crowds.

The wineries sponsor a number of interesting cultural activities during the summer also. Palmer Vineyard, for instance, sometimes has a **Victorian Murder Mystery**, performed by the Wild Thyme Players; a winery tour is included. At other times, a popular poetry series called **Voices on the Vine** is held. **Summer Showcase Outdoor Concerts** take place weekly throughout the summer at the Silversmiths Corner on Town Green in Southold. Past events have included performances by the Bay Chamber Players, North Fork Fiddler and Friends, Barber Shop Harmony, and the Clinton Church Gospel Choir.

The **North Fork Community Theatre** presents summer theatrical productions in a church in Mattituck, and **Opera of the Hamptons** features opera performances in July.

RECREATION

Auto Racing

Riverhead Raceway (631-842-RACE (7223); www.riverheadraceway.com; Rte. 58, Riverhead; mailing address: P.O. Box 148, Lindenhurst, NY 11757; open Apr.–Sept. Sat. and Sun.; adults $16–$30, children 5–12 $5, under 5 free) Rev your engines, because every Saturday night, there's a NASCAR race on this 0.25-mile asphalt, high-banked oval with a figure 8. You can also see demolition derbies, school bus races, monster truck events, and more. On Sundays you might participate in an automotive swap shop or a hot rod show.

Beaches, Parks, Nature Preserves, Hikes, & Walks

Just as on the South Fork, car parking permit stickers are required at all town and village beaches. In Riverhead Town, which includes Aquebogue and Jamesport, a parking permit sticker is $35/day and $200/year for nonresidents. In Southold Town, a resident parking permit is $6/year. A nonresident daily permit is $25/day and a season pass can be obtained for $150.

Dam Pond Marine Reserve In this nature preserve, which is accessed from the East Marion Orient Park on Rte. 25 before crossing the causeway to Orient, you will find scenic walking trails overlooking Long Island Sound and Dam Pond. It's one of the most interesting and beautiful walks on the North Fork.

Indian Island County Park (631-852-3232; www.co.suffolk.ny.us; Riverside Dr. (Rte. 105), Riverhead; mailing address: P.O. Box 144, West Sayville, NY 11796) This 274-acre Suffolk County Park at the mouth of the Peconic River is rich with birds and wildlife that nest among the trees and marshes. The park contains 150 campsites, which cost $14/night for county residents with a Suffolk County Green Key Card ($20, good for three years) and $24 for nonresidents. There are also group camping areas, picnic areas, hiking trails, long stretches of sandy beach (no lifeguard), and a playground for children. In addition, canoeing, fishing, and bird-watching are encouraged.

North Fork Audubon Society Nature Center (www.northforkaudubon.org; 65275 North Rd. (Rte. 48), Greenport, NY 11944) This is the location of the society's Nature Center in Inlet Pond County Park, and the place from which most of their walks depart. There are numerous walks throughout the year to observe birds either during their migrations or in their natural habitat, and lectures also take place in the Little Red House. Check online to get the schedule. The cost is $3 for members of the society and $5 for nonmembers. The Little Red House also has exhibits that are interesting to view. It is open for viewing on Saturdays 10–4.

Orient Beach State Park (631-323-2440; http://nysparks.state.ny.us; Rte. 25, Orient, NY 11957; $6 parking June, $8 July–Labor Day, $6 Labor Day–Columbus Day) Consistently rated the best beach on the North Fork, this is far more than just a beach. There's a concession stand at which local seafood is served and where you can participate in BBQs on the weekends, a bathhouse with showers and restrooms, a playground, and a picnic area with grills. This long spit of land, jutting 4 miles out into Gardiner's Bay, is packed with swimmers and picnickers in summer. For those who like to walk, a hike from the parking lot along Long Beach out to the point passes ponds, marshes, and numerous birds (sometimes osprey on nests on high poles, and sometimes terns or plovers in cordoned-off beach areas). The walk ends near the Long Beach Bar Lighthouse ("Bug Light").

Bicycling & Skateboarding

Bicycling on the North Fork is a pleasure. The land is flat, and the road shoulders are wide. There are relatively few cars, and lots of roads to explore and sites to see. Sound Avenue (Rte. 48) has wide shoulders and makes a nice, flat route on which to travel. Or call the North Fork Promotion Council (631-298-5757) and obtain a copy of its bicycle map for other ideas. Unfortunately, as we go to press, there are no bicycle rental shops on the North Fork that we are aware of.

Skateboarding has taken on new dimensions in many East End towns, and to give the kids a place to skate safely, towns have developed skate parks. Riverhead is no exception. The Town of Riverhead Skate Park is located in Stowsky Park, 101 Pulaski St., Riverhead; 631-208-3826; open Mar.–Dec. daily 2–10 PM.

Boating, Canoeing, Fishing

Eagle's Neck Paddling Company (631-765-3502; www.eaglesneck.com; 49295 Main Rd., Southold; mailing address: P.O. Box 83, Peconic, NY 11958) This company has kayaks and canoes for sale and to rent and provides paddling instructions. It also conducts guided kayak tours that include instructional lectures about the surrounding wildlife, geology, or stargazing. In addition, it offers a 2.5-hour sunset tour every Friday and Saturday. Rental fees: recreational single kayaks $30/2 hours, $45/half-day, $50/full day, $75 2 days. Double kayaks and canoes $40/2 hours, $50/half-day, $60/full day, $100 2 days.

Glory, **Greenport Harbor Tours** (631-477-2515; www.greenportlaunch.com; Preston's
Dock, Greenport; mailing address: 508 Sterling St., Greenport NY 11944; open Mem.
Day–Oct., 12–6) Owners: Andrew Rowsom and David Berson. This sleek, 30-foot solar-
powered mahogany fantail launch is a replica of a turn-of-the-century vessel, complete
with gold-plated trim. Captain David Berson can accommodate up to 13 passengers on
45-minute cruises through the quiet bays near Greenport. Adults $15, seniors $12, children $5.

Marinas

Brewer/Stirling Harbor Marina (631-477-0828; www.byy.com; 1410 Manhanset Ave.,
Greenport, NY 11944) This is an exceptional marina and includes a full gym, aerobics
classes, manicurist, masseuse, pedicurist, delivery of the *New York Times,* full laundry
facilities (will do laundry for you and deliver to your boat), restrooms, electric and cable
hookup, and full repair services. There's also a fine Italian restaurant, Porto Bello (see
listing under "Restaurants," this chapter), which is open year-round.

Brewer Yacht Yard (631-477-9594; www.byy.com; 500 Beach Ave., Greenport, NY 11944)
Part of the Brewer Yacht Marina network, a series of fine marinas located throughout
New England and Long Island, Greenport has 200 slips and provides electric hookup,
laundry, swimming pool, showers and restrooms. The highly acclaimed Long Island
Sailing School employs an instructor certified by the American Sailing Association who
teaches classes to beginning and advanced sailors on a variety of sailboats. The marina
sponsors races, regattas, and trips to other member marinas. This is also the home of
Antaras Tiki Cafe (see listing under "Restaurants," this chapter), which is open year-
round.

Children's Activities

Frank Field's Miniature Railroad (For location, call or stop by North Fork Promotion
Council, 631-477-2433; Third and Webb Sts., Greenport, NY 11944; railroad open
Mother's Day–Halloween, Sun. and holidays 1–4) On a wooded piece of land on Third
and Webb streets in Greenport, Frank Field gives complimentary rides to children on
his marvelous 15-gauge private miniature railroad. This is a treat for children of all ages.

Greenport Carousel (631-477-1383; Front St.; Greenport, NY 11944; in Mitchell Park;
open Fri. 4–9, Sat., Sun., and school holidays 11–6) When Grumman Aerospace Corporation employed thousands of people on Long Island, it maintained a lovely park on the
North Shore where summer picnics, baseball games, and other recreation took place.
The centerpiece of the park was a handsomely carved carousel. After the park closed, the
ornate carousel sat idle for many years, its future sometimes debated but often forgot-
ten, until the village of Greenport obtained it. Today's children can now ride the
carousel in a handsome new domed pavilion that was completed in 2001 as part of the
wonderful new Greenport Waterfront Park. A competition to design the park, which has
a boardwalk, promenades, and much more, attracted submissions from more than 300
recognized architects from around the world.

Long Island Game Farm (631-878-6644; www.longislandgamefarm.com; Chapman Blvd.,
P.O. Box 97, Manorville, NY 11949; open mid-May–mid Oct.; high-season Mem. Day–
Labor Day daily 10–6; adults $17.45, seniors 60+ $15.45, children 3–11 $13.45, children
under 3 free; lower rates rest of season.) Open since 1970, this 300-acre game park has

The marvelous Greenport Carousel is the centerpiece of the new Greenport Waterfront Park.

both exotic and domestic animals. You can walk the nature trails to see more than 75 species, from "big cats" to buffalo and alligators. There are train rides on a restored 1860s train, more rides on a restored antique carousel, pony rides, an in-the-wild animal show, and a petting Bambiland. Call for special events.

Peconic Dunes (631-727-7850; www.ccesuffolk.org) A camp operated by Cornell Cooperative Extension of Suffolk County teaches children about local natural resources and the great outdoors.

Splish Splash Water Park (631-727-3600; 2549 Splish Splash Dr., Calverton, NY 11933. open Mem. Day–Labor Day; July–Aug., daily 9:30–7; weekends only rest of season; adults $35.99, seniors 62+ and children under 48 inches $26.99, parking $12) There are lockers ($8 /day), showers, and food facilities at this 40-acre water park, and the rides range from screechers to tame thrills safe for small fry. There's a wave pool, a cliff-diver ride, a giant twister, Dr. Von Darks Tunnel of Terror, shotgun falls, a mammoth river rapids, soak city, and a lazy river ride. Be sure to come in bathing attire that has no buckles or other decor that might get caught. In addition, there are diving shows, bird shows, and more.

Golf

Cherry Creek Golf Links/The Woods at Cherry Creek (631-369-8983; 888-455-0300 reservations only; www.cherrycreeklinks.com; 900 Reeves Ave., Riverhead, NY 11901)

And now there are two courses at this location. The original "Links" is an 18-hole, par-73, 7,187-yard course that opened in 1996. It includes a driving range, practice bunker, putting green, and pro shop, as well as a restaurant (Stonewalls). It has the only par-6 hole on Long Island. "The Woods" opened in 2003. It is an 18-hole, par-71, 6,565-yard course across the street from the Links. Summer fees are: $60/weekdays with cart, $70/weekends with cart for 18 holes; rest of year $40 weekdays, $50 weekends with cart. If you wish to walk the course, you can do so on weekdays for $15 less.

Great Rock Golf Club (631-929-1200; www.greatrockgolfclub.com; 141 Fairway Dr., Wading River, NY 11792) This beautiful course, which offers distinctive boulder outcroppings as well as supreme views, has a 71-par 6,193-yard course. It's a semiprivate club where for a nominal fee members receive priority tee times, but nonmembers can play as well. An excellent restaurant, Blackwells, is on premises. Green fees for nonmembers in the summer are: weekends, $89 before 11 am, $65 between 11 and 2 PM, $49 after 2 PM; weekdays, $69 before 11 AM, $55 between 11 and 2 PM, $39 after 2 PM; lower rates rest of year.

Indian Island Country Club and Golf Course (631-727-7776; 631-727-0788 restaurant; www.indianislandcountryclub.com; 661 Riverside Dr. (Rte. 105) Riverhead, NY 11901) Manicured greens and a gated entrance make this look more like an exclusive private club than a public golf course. Beautifully maintained by the Suffolk County Department of Parks, Recreation, and Conservation, it's an 18-hole, par-72, 6,508/6,055-yard course with pro shop, clubhouse, driving range, putting green, lockers, showers, rental clubs and carts, and a restaurant serving breakfast, lunch, and dinner. The club and course are part of Indian Island County Park. Non–Suffolk County residents $38/weekdays, $45 weekends to 2 PM, then $30; Suffolk County residents with three-year Green Card ($20) $28/weekdays, $30/weekends to 2 PM, then $18. Seniors and disabled: $17 to 2 PM, then $11; juniors (17 and under) $10 to 2 PM, then $9. Carts are an additional $16.

Island's End Golf & Country Club (631-477-0777; www.islandsendgolf.com; 5025 Main Rd. (Rte. 25), P.O. Box 2066, Greenport, NY 11944) This golf course is actually part of a private club, but nonmembers can play for a fee. It's an 18-hole, par-72, 6,700-yard course with a driving range, pro shop, clubhouse, snack bar, restaurant, and rental clubs and carts. Summer rates are: $45/weekdays and $55 weekends for nonmembers; carts additional $18. Lower rates prevail the rest of the year.

Long Island National Golf Club (631-727-4653; www.longislandnationalgc.com; 1793 Northville Tpke., Riverhead, NY 11901) Opened in 1999, this dramatic course, which was designed by Robert Trent Jones Jr., features a spectacular natural-shingled clubhouse faced with massive white columns in a style similar to that of the clubhouse designed by Stanford White for Shinnecock Hills. There's a lovely restaurant and bar, and an extensive golf shop. The course is challenging, to say the least, as it includes rolling hills with roughs similar to those at St. Andrews and three large lakes. It features 18 holes with a par 71 and extends over 6,800 yards. Rates: $69 Fri.–Sun. and holidays, $59 weekdays; senior rate Mon.–Fri. $39; twilight rate daily $39; all rates include cart.

Horseback Riding

Hedgewood Farm (631-298-9181; www.hedgewoodfarm.org; 4000 Main Rd., Laurel; P.O. Box 566, Laurel, NY 11948) This farm has a 12-acre riding facility where hunt seat equitation and western pleasure riding are taught. They have a lighted indoor arena that permits year-round lessons, conduct escorted trail rides if given advance notice, and offer pony rides, and you can also board your horse here.

Hidden Lake Farms Riding School (631-765-9896; County Rd. 48, Southold; mailing address P.O. Box 269, Peconic, NY 11958; open daily 8–5) On this 30-acre spread, riders can learn to ride English-style and to fox hunt ("riding to the hounds"). Three large outdoor rings, a pony camp, a cross-country course, trails to the beach, and a lighted indoor arena make this a very versatile school. Group and individual lessons as well as escorted trail rides can be arranged.

Hillcrest Sport Stable (631-369-7821; www.hillcreststable.com; 1219 Middle Rd., Riverhead, NY 11901) This excellent facility offers lessons to adults and children in jumping, equitation, and dressage. They are located on 38 acres and have an indoor arena, a jumping ring, and a hunt course. You can board your horse here, too.

Scuba Diving

Hampton Dive Center (631-727-7578; www.hamptondive.com; 369 Flanders Rd. (Rte. 24), Riverhead, NY 11901; open year-round; daily in summer, Mon.–Fri. 8–7, Sat. 8–6, Sun. 8–3; rest of year Mon.–Fri. 11–7, Sat. 11–5) Hampton Dive Center is a scuba-diving school that offers courses leading to scuba-diving certification; courses are taught twice a week for four weeks and cost $299; or, complete with diving gear, it's $449. These prices are for group classes. Inquire about private classes also, as they have a wide variety, including in patrons' own pools, as well as in open water. Once certification is earned, they regularly take members on dives. Generally, the dives are nearby, either off the jetties on the South Fork or off boats nearby in the ocean, but they also sponsor diving trips to the Caribbean and other spots. You can rent scuba equipment, and they allow nonmembers to accompany them on local dives, which generally cost about $50/dive/person for group dives; $85/dive/person for private dives.

Soundview Scuba Center (631-765-9515; www.soundviewscuba.com; 46770 County Rd. 48, Southold, NY 11971; open Mon.–Fri. except Wed. 9–7, Sat. 9–5, Sun. 9–3) This full-service, year-round company offers sales of scuba diving equipment as well as instruction leading to certification (cost $325). The group package includes all rental gear and diver's manual, log book, etc. Private lessons can be arranged for $600. They have a full complement of scuba rental gear and they conduct tours to distant places such as Curacao also. They also sell and rent kayaks (single kayaks $45/day, tandem kayaks $55/day, triple kayaks $75/day).

INFORMATION

Emergency Numbers
In both Riverhead and Southold Towns, the Police and Fire Emergency Number is 911.

Area Codes
The area code for all Suffolk County is 631. Frequently called nearby areas are as follows:

New York

Manhattan: 212, 646
Brooklyn, Bronx, Queens, Staten Island: 718
Nassau County: 516
Westchester County: 914

Connecticut

Western Coastal Connecticut: 203
Eastern Connecticut: 860

Chambers of Commerce

North Fork Promotion Council This promotion organization operates two information centers on the North Fork. (631-477-1383, www.northfork.org, 72250 Main Rd. (Rte. 25), P.O. Box 186, Greenport, NY 11944; also 631-298-5757, 4995 Main Rd. (Rte. 25), Mattituck, NY 11952; open May–Columbus Day; July and Aug., daily 10–4, rest of season fewer days) These centers are excellent sources for information on wineries and places to eat, stay, and shop. They publish an extensive guide to the North Fork every summer.

Riverhead Chamber of Commerce (631-727-7600; 540 East Main Rd., Riverhead, NY 11901; open year-round, Mon.–Fri. 10–4, Sat. 9–5)

Town & Village Offices

Greenport Village Office (631-477-0248 or 631-477-2385; www.greenportvillage.com; 236 Third St., Greenport, NY 11944)

Riverhead Town Office (631-727-3200; www.riverheadli.com; 200 Howell Ave., Riverhead, NY 11901)

Southold Town Office (631-765-1800; www.southoldtown.northfork.net; 53095 Main Rd., Southold, NY 11971)

Zip Codes

Town/Village/Hamlet	Zip Code	Town/Village/Hamlet	Zip Code
Aquebogue	11931	New Suffolk	11956
Calverton	11933	Orient	11957
Cutchogue	11935	Peconic	11958
East Marion	11939	Riverhead	11901
Greenport	11944	South Jamesport	11970
Jamesport	11947	Southold	11971
Laurel	11948	Wading River	11792
Mattituck	11952		

Business Solutions

The Ink Spot (631-765-3625; www.inkspotpcc.com; 175 Boisseau Ave., Southold, NY 11971; open Mon.–Thurs. 8–5, Fri. 8–4:30) For color or black-and-white printing, fax service, blueprints, typesetting and design, or four-color printing, this is the place.

Hospitals

Peconic Bay Medical Center (631-548-6000; www.peconicbaymedicalcenter.org; 1300 Roanoke Ave., Riverhead, NY 11901) Full-service, large regional hospital.

Eastern Long Island Hospital (631-477-1000; www.elih.org; 201 Manor Pl., Greenport, NY 11944) Small 80-bed full-service hospital.

Media

Radio

WRIV-AM 1390 (631-727-1390; 40 West Main St., Riverhead, NY 11901) Local news, local football, and adult contemporary music.

Newspapers

Newsday (631-727-7333; 633 East Main St., Riverhead, NY 11901) This is the East End news
bureau for Long Island's newspaper.

Times/Review Newspapers (631-298-3200; www.timesreview.com; 7785 Main Rd. (Rte.
25), P.O. Box 1500, Mattituck, NY 11952) This local company is publisher of the *Suffolk
Times* (covering Southold Township) and the *News-Review* (covering Riverhead Township), as well as the *North Fork Vacation Guide*, the *Shelter Island Vacation Guide*, the *Wine
Press* (see below), and *Tanger Times*.

Wine Press (631-298-3200; P.O. Box 1500, Mattituck, NY 11952) Published by Times
Review Newspapers, this is the official magazine of the Long Island Wine Council. It
offers a complete guide to the wineries, as well as winery events, restaurants, and more.
Free.

Post Offices

The general number for all post offices is 800-275-8777. Local numbers and addresses are
as follows:

Aquebogue 631-722-4368; 212 Linda Ave., Aquebogue, NY 11931.
Calverton 631-727-0067; 3690 Middle County Rd., Calverton, NY 11933.
Cutchogue 631-734-6032; 240 Griffin St., Cutchogue, NY 11935.
East Marion 631-477-1668; 9165 Main Rd. (Rte. 25), East Marion, NY 11939.
Greenport 631-477-1493; 131 Front St., Greenport, NY 11944.
Jamesport 631-722-5946; 1451 Main Rd. (Rte. 25), Jamesport, NY 11947.
Laurel 631-298-1672; 2168 Main Rd. (Rte. 25), Laurel, NY 11948.
Mattituck 631-298-1364; 140 Love Ln., Mattituck, NY 11952.
New Suffolk 631-734-6271; 375 First St., New Suffolk, NY 11956.
Orient 631-323-9760; 980 Village Ln., Orient, NY 11957.
Peconic 631-765-9348; 2575 Peconic Ln., Peconic, NY 11958.
Riverhead 631-727-1019; 1210 West Main St., Riverhead, NY 11901.
South Jamesport 631-722-4317; 70 Second St., South Jamesport, NY 11970.
Southold 631-765-4027; 710 Traveler St., Southold, NY 11971.
Wading River 631-929-0219; 1816 Wading River Manor Rd., Wading River, NY 11792.

Real Estate

Brown Harris Stevens (631-734-5657, www.bhshamptons.com; 31855 Main Rd.,
Cutchogue, NY 11935; also 631-477-0551, 120 Front St., P.O. Box 744, Greenport, NY
11944)
The Corcoran Group (631-765-1300; www.corcoran.com; 53795 Main Rd. (Rte. 25); mail-
ing address: P.O. Box 235, Southold, NY 11971)
Daniel Gale Sotheby's International Realty (631-734-5439; www.danielgale.com; 29950
Main Rd. (Rte. 25), Cutchogue, NY 11935; also 631-765-6656, 50300 Main Rd. (Rte. 25),
Southold, NY 11971) This is the North Fork Sotheby affiliate, also located on Shelter Island.

10

A CHARMING
GREEN-CLAD ISLAND

Shelter Island

Shelter Island is actually a well-kept local secret. Merely 0.5 mile from the South Fork and 1 mile from the North Fork of the eastern end of Long Island, it is nevertheless remote and secluded—an ideal haven. It's quiet (no movie theaters or discos, please), peaceful, low-key, uncomplicated, and insular. In fact, most people who regularly come here hope that the rest of the world will never hear about Shelter Island's charms. Covering an area of approximately 8,000 acres, Shelter Island is 6 miles long and 4 miles wide. Many families have been summering here for generations, and they plan to pass along the summer manse to the next generation, and the next, although now the old-money families are mingling with famous artists, writers, and performers, who also came here seeking privacy in a beautiful setting.

HISTORY

> As Long Island stretches out her arms to the Atlantic, she gathers within her embrace a little group of islands. Largest and fairest among them, fertile and beautifully wooded, is Shelter Island, lying in the waters of Gardner's [sic] and Peconic Bays, separated from Greenport and the northern arm of Long Island Sound by about a mile of sunny water, and on its southern side looking across Sag Harbor, and the long, low line which stretches away to Montauk.
> —From an 1889 brochure for Prospect House, reprinted in
> The Grapevine of Shelter Island Heights, 1987

Shelter Island's history includes a mixture of entrepreneurial enterprise, independence, and tolerance. This island was chosen by James Farrett, the personal representative of the Earl of Stirling, as his own land grant. It appears that he inspected it as early as 1638, but he never actually occupied the island. In 1641 he sold Shelter Island to a merchant, Stephen Goodyear, who subsequently sold it in 1651 to four businessmen with interests in the Barbados sugar industry.

Nathaniel Sylvester was one of those businessmen. After returning to England and marrying, he sailed with his bride in 1652 to their new home. Although they suffered shipwreck and lost many of their possessions, the manor house they built on Shelter Island, along

Secluded Shelter Island retains a wealth of handsome mansions with spectacular water views.

with its surrounding gardens, must have been as fine as many in England. The Sylvester Manor House, although changed over the years, is still owned by members of the Sylvester family.

Prior to the Sylvesters' arrival, the Manhanset tribe, led by their sachem, Pogatticut (brother to the sachems of the Montauks of East Hampton, the Shinnecocks of Southampton, and the Corchaugs of the North Fork) ruled Shelter Island. Pogatticut and his people voluntarily left the island shortly after the Sylvesters arrived.

It was apparent from the beginning that the Sylvesters were peaceable people with open minds. For about five years in the mid-1600s, persecution of members of the Society of Friends (Quakers) was particularly severe in Massachusetts. Many were imprisoned, whipped, tortured, branded with hot irons, and banished from their homes. Those fortunate few who found their way to Shelter Island were treated by the Sylvesters with sympathy and understanding. They were given food, protection, clothing, and permission to practice their religion. Quaker church services are still held weekly on Shelter Island.

From 1660 to 1673, a tug-of-war took place between the British and the Dutch over Long Island. Eventually Shelter Island, not immune to the conflict, was confiscated by the Dutch. It was regained later by Nathaniel Sylvester, at a cost of 500 pounds, but only after the Dutch landed on the island with 500 men, surrounded his house, and demanded payment, merely days before they again surrendered the territory to the British.

Other families of importance soon joined the Sylvesters. William Nicoll became the first supervisor of Shelter Island in 1726 and occupied the estate left to him by his father. The Havens family came shortly thereafter in 1742 and purchased an estate of 1,000 acres from Nathaniel Sylvester. By 1769, the house that James Havens's father, William, had built was used as a school by day and a tavern by night, as well as a home, serving such concoctions as a mug of flip, a brandy sling, and a nip of grog to wayfarers. In 1795 Jonathan Havens was elected to serve in the new Congress of the United States, representing the district that contained Shelter Island.

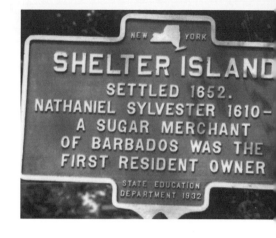

The Dering name emerges in 1760 when Mary Sylvester, who had married Thomas Dering in 1756, inherited Sylvester Manor from her father and consequently moved her family into the manor house. The Sylvester, Nicoll, Havens, and Dering families were cultured people who cherished family life on the island. In 1743 the first church was built, and by 1791 a school had been established.

Around 1800, Timothy Dwight, president of Yale College, journeyed the length of Long Island and included Shelter Island in his travels. He observed, "To the credit of the inhabitants, especially of the principal proprietors, it ought to be observed that they have customarily made considerable exertions to support schools and obtain the preaching of the gospel."

Shelter Island (along with Gardiner's Island) had one of the finest stands of white oak found on the East Coast. These trees were especially prized after the magnificent forests of Connecticut and Massachusetts were exhausted. In the mid-1800s, a shipyard was established on Shelter Island; the massive trunks necessary for keels and masts were cut from the area known as the Great Woods.

Throughout Shelter Island's history, religion has played an important role. In 1871 the highest point of land on the island became the home of the Shelter Island Grove and Camp Meeting Association of the Methodist Episcopal Church. They called the area Prospect, and summer visitors began arriving in numbers. The handsome Prospect House, a colonnaded Victorian hotel with a piazza encircling the building, overlooked the harbor toward Greenport and accommodated up to 300 guests. Although the hotel is gone, the restaurant, where communal meals were held, is the nucleus of the present Chequit Inn. Some of the charming Victorian cottages and the fine houses built by the prominent citizens of the day now form the delightful village of Shelter Island Heights. Due to its unique charm, Shelter Island Heights is registered in the National Register of Historic Places. It encompasses 1,050 acres and includes 141 buildings, as well as one structure.

TRANSPORTATION

Shelter Island remains a quiet, peaceful retreat, secluded and hidden and yet accessible to both the North and South Forks by a 10-minute ferry ride. Although the grand Victorian hotels are no longer here, newer, smaller hotels and inns now provide lodging. You'll find excellent restaurants, interesting shops, and an abundance of recreational options.

Part of the delight of Shelter Island is its island status and the necessity of reaching it by boat. The ferries that ply back and forth are efficient throwbacks to an earlier age. There are no amenities here, just a drive- or walk-on, open-decked ferry that shuttles between the island and the North or South Forks. Both ferries operate year-round, but trips are much more frequent in the summer.

North Ferry (631-749-0139; www.northferry.com) From Shelter Island 5:40 AM–11:45 PM (12:45 AM summer weekends). From Greenport 6 AM–midnight (1 AM summer weekends). Car and driver $9 one way, $13.00 same-day round trip; each passenger or walk-on $2; bicycle and rider $3 one way, $5 same-day round trip; motorcycle and driver $6 one way, $8 same-day round trip.

South Ferry (631-749-1200; www.southferry.com) From North Haven 5:40 AM–1:45 AM. From Shelter Island 6 AM–1:45 AM. Car, driver, and passengers $12 one way, $15 same-day round trip; walk-ons $1; bicycle and rider $4 one way, $6 round trip; motorcycle and driver $7 one-way; $8 same-day round trip.

For those traveling to Shelter Island from Manhattan, the North Shore branch of the **Long Island Rail Road** (631-231-5477) may be an option, although its schedule is limited. There are generally three or four trains each way during the week and two trains on the weekends. The fares range from $16.75 to $23 each way depending on the time of day you travel. The Greenport station is merely steps from the Shelter Island ferry dock, and after a short water ride, you'll be in Shelter Island Heights.

For taxi service, contact **Shelter Island Go'Fors Taxi** (631-749-4252; 1 Thomas Ave., Shelter Island, NY 11964).

The North Ferry on its way to Shelter Island.

LODGING

CHEQUIT INN AND RESTAURANTS
631-749-0018
www.shelterislandinns.com
23 Grand Ave., Shelter Island Heights
Mailing Address: P.O. Box 292, Shelter
Island Heights, NY 11965
Innkeepers: Linda and James Eklund
General Manager: Eric Solomon
Chef: Jose Valentine
Cuisine: Classic American with international influences
Serving: B, L, D
Open: Year-round
Price: Inexpensive–Expensive
Credit Cards: AE, MC, V
Special Features *Inn*: Continental buffet
breakfast; telephones; TV available
Special Features *Restaurant*: Dining room
has porch with view; terrace under the
trees; Chequit Lounge has TVs, live entertainment Sat. nights, and a pool table
Directions: From South Ferry, travel north
on Rte. 114, following signs to North Ferry.
After crossing bridge to Shelter Island
Heights, take Chase Ave. up hill. Inn is
straight ahead. From North Ferry, inn is on
right, about 4 blocks after exiting ferry.

This large, white, 1872 Victorian inn sits
proudly on the only commercial street in
Shelter Island Heights. In 1994 Linda and
James Eklund, also owners of the Ram's
Head Inn, purchased the venerable old inn.
The lobby is filled with old wicker, plus a
huge oak library table. There's a wood-
burning fireplace and a spacious porch that
overlooks the village. There are 35 rooms
(all with private baths). Those on the third
floor of the main building are bright and
cheerful and have carpeted floors, painted
furniture, and such whimsical touches as
old sleds used for coffee tables. Rooms in
the weathered gray Summer Cottage behind
the main building have endearing quirks.
Suite 7–8, for example, has an interesting
little room with a sink and a wicker chair
(sort of a sitting room/bath), and the rest of
the bathroom is located between this room
and the bedroom. The furniture in the bedroom is painted white (some has stenciling), and there are antique beds. There are
more rooms in Cedar House across the
street.

The dining room, on the second floor of
the hotel, overlooks the village and has a
broad porch that is used for dining in the
summer. It's a romantic restaurant with
excellent food. When weather permits,
lunch is served on an outside terrace under
the trees. The Chequit Lounge is a renovated bistro on the inn's lower level. It
offers a relaxed, casual spot for lunch and
dinner, where you can watch a sporting
event on the 55-inch TV, play pool, and listen to the jukebox; there's also live music
Saturday nights in summer.

DERING HARBOR INN
631-749-0900
www.deringharborinn.net
13 Winthrop Rd., Shelter Island
Mailing Address: P.O. Box 3028, Shelter
Island Heights, NY 11965
Manager: John M. King III
Open: May–Oct
Price: Moderate–Very Expensive
Credit Cards: AE, MC, V
Special Features: Limited wheelchair
access; saltwater pool; fireplaces in some
rooms; tennis, volleyball, basketball, badminton; air-conditioning; nonsmoking
rooms; wireless Internet access; cable TV;
kitchenettes in most rooms; fitness center
on premises; children welcome; no pets
Directions: From Rte. 114, travel east on
Winthrop Rd. Inn is on left.

The Dering Harbor Inn sits high on the
bluff overlooking Dering Harbor and the
boats in the marinas. It's a 1960s-style
building, with a massive, double-sided
stone fireplace dividing the stylish, cathedral-ceilinged lobby. Rooms are located in
one- and two-story, gray-stained buildings

with decks overlooking Dering Harbor. This is a co-op, so all of the suites and villas have kitchens. Decor will vary, but most rooms are spacious and well appointed in a Caribbean-meets-the-Hamptons style. Room 7, for example, is a single-level unit with a fireplace, screened-in porch, full kitchen, and lovely view; steps from the deck lead to a private stretch of lawn. In all, there are 21 rooms available for rent and all have private baths. The grounds are lovely, with two tennis courts and a saltwater pool that appears to be suspended over the bay.

HOUSE ON CHASE CREEK

631-749-4379
www.chasecreek.com
3 Locust Ave., Shelter Island Heights
Mailing Address: P.O. Box 364, Shelter Island Heights, NY 11965
Innkeepers: Bill and Sharon Cummings
Open: Year-round
Price: Inexpensive–Moderate
Credit Cards: AE, MC, V
Special Features: Overlooking water; continental breakfast; nonsmoking B&B; wireless Internet access; not appropriate for children under 12
Directions: From Rte. 114 in Shelter Island Heights, turn onto Locust Ave. by little bridge. Inn is on right in about two blocks, on corner of Locust Ave. and Meadow Pl.

This little gem of a B&B is located in the heart of Shelter Island Heights, but it's on a superbly quiet street that even in the height of summer offers a peaceful and quiet refuge. You might relax on the wicker porch swing or on the park bench down by Chase Creek (a wide body of water that resembles a pond more than a creek). When you enter the parlor of the inn, you won't fail to admire the antique sofa and chairs, which have backs inlaid with mother of pearl. There are three guest rooms, and a suite, and they all have private baths. There are iron beds, an antique pedestal tub, wood floors, and marble vanities. The suite

includes a fireplace and a TV. Should you wish larger accommodations, or utter privacy, you might inquire about the Burns House, an entire house that is also offered for rent. A continental breakfast is served on a sunny, wicker-filled porch.

OLDE COUNTRY INN AND RESTAURANT

631-749-1633
www.oldecountryinn.com
11 Stearns Point Rd., Shelter Island Heights
Mailing Address: P.O. Box 1209, Shelter Island Heights, NY 11965
Innkeepers: Jeanne and Franz Fenkl
Chef: Marcel Iattoni
Cuisine: Classic French
Serving: D
Open: Inn open year-round; restaurant open Apr.–mid-Feb.
Price: Moderate–Expensive; prix fixe available
Credit Cards: AE, D, MC, V
Special Features *Inn:* Wheelchair access; wireless Internet access; full breakfast; library with fireplace; piano; intimate bar; not recommended for children under 14; no pets
Special Features *Restaurant:* Fireplaces; outdoor dining; pavilion
Directions: From Shelter Island Heights, take New York Ave. to West Neck Rd., turning right toward Crescent Beach. In 0.2 mile, continue straight ahead onto Shore Rd. when West Neck Rd. turns left. Turn left onto Stearns Point Rd. at second street. Inn is on left.

The historic Shelter Island House, which was built as a hotel in 1886 and sits high on a cliff above Crescent Beach, was renovated and opened as a bed & breakfast inn by innkeepers Jeanne and Franz Fenkl in 1994. Polished oak floors are a crisp backdrop for lovely Victorian furniture, especially in the back lounge, which has a fireplace. The tiny Victorian pub has another fireplace and doubles as an evening dining room. The guest rooms feature iron and brass beds, an exquisite old Victorian coatrack, marble-topped dressers, and upholstered Victorian chairs. Each of the rooms has a private bath with a pedestal sink, built-in shelves, and a tiled tub surround. Two of the rooms have Jacuzzis, and one has a soaking tub. There's also a separate cottage.

Breakfast, eaten either in the pretty breakfast room or on one of the decks, might include crêpes with orange liqueur, omelettes, or waffles with sour cream and fresh berries. After a hiatus of several years, the Fenkls teamed up with Chef Marcel Iattoni again in 2009 (he had been chef previously for 10 years) to serve dinner. Now the restaurant is open most of the year, and the food is so good that reservations are an absolute must. You will dine on such treats as crispy duck confit with blueberry sauce, or in-season, soft shell crabs meuniére. Desserts are made by a local baker and include a tangy and sweet lime coconut cake. Only dinner is served, but it's served with panache and style, and there's a nice wine list that includes local wines to accompany it. Don't miss it!

PRIDWIN BEACH HOTEL & COTTAGES

631-749-0476 or 800-273-4297
www.pridwin.com
81 Shore Road, Shelter Island
P.O. Box 2009, Shelter Island, NY 11964
Owner: Richard Petry
Chef: Keith Marty
Cuisine: New American
Serving: B, L, D (July 4th–Labor Day only)
Open: *Hotel:* May–Oct.; *Restaurant:* July 4th–Labor Day
Price: Moderate–Expensive
Credit Cards: AE, MC, V
Special Features *Inn:* Full breakfast when restaurant open; continental breakfast weekends rest of season; air-conditioning; TVs, wireless Internet access in lobby; telephones; boat docking; beach; pool; DJ some nights; "Kids' Movies" while parents dine; game room; sailing; paddle boats; masseuse on staff; bicycling; Ping-Pong; tennis; billiards; children welcome; no pets
Special Features *Restaurant:* View of water; fish on menu is caught by owner and son; outdoor cookouts; meal plans (breakfast or breakfast and dinner) offered with room rate
Reservations: Accepted
Directions: From Rte. 114 north or south turn west onto West Neck Rd., which will become Shore Rd. As you reach the water, the road turns sharply left. Continue on Shore Rd.; the hotel is on left in 0.5 mile.

The Pridwin, which sits on a hillside gazing out across Crescent Beach and the water to the North Fork, has been around since the 1920s. Commanding impressive views from the restaurant and common rooms, this venerable old lady has been in the loving care of the Petry family since the 1960s. There are 40 guest rooms in the main building, and these are supplemented by several cottages—some with waterviews, and others, nestled among the trees, that have fireplaces. All of the cottages have either kitchenettes or full kitchens, and some were recently redesigned by Fred Bernstein, a local interior designer. This is a summer adventure only—accepting guests from May to October and offering meal service basically from July 4th to Labor Day. And it's a very family-friendly place: kids can attend the resident tennis camp, or venture out in a canoe, or swim in the pool, or make sand castles on the beach. Adults appreciate the evening respite when they dine *à deux* while the youngsters are entertained at supervised "Kids' Movies," and every Wednesday night there's a family cookout. Cuisine at the restaurant is unique, in that most of the fish has been caught either by Frank Petry or his son Gregg. Not only do they fish in local waters for fluke, flounder, bluefish, and bass, but they make weekly expeditions to deeper waters for cod, tuna, and swordfish. The Pridwin is a throwback to an earlier era—a

The Ram's Head Inn, located on remote Ram Island overlooking Coecles Harbor, has lovely guest rooms and a gracious dining room. In summer, guests can also dine on the terrace.

place where families have been coming for several generations.

RAM'S HEAD INN AND RESTAURANT

631-749-0811
www.shelterislandinns.com
108 Ram Island Dr., Shelter Island
Mailing Address: P.O. Box 638, Shelter
Island Heights, NY 11965
Owners: James and Linda Eklund
General Manager: Eric Solomon
Chef: Christopher Meehan
Cuisine: American with international influences
Serving: L (Sat. in summer), D, BR (Sun. in summer)
Open: May–Oct.
Price: Inexpensive–Moderate
Credit Cards: AE, MC, V
Reservations: Recommended

Special Features *Inn*: Nonsmoking inn; overlooks water; telephones; wireless Internet access; TV available; tennis; boating; sauna; exercise room; continental buffet breakfast; room service; children OK, no pets
Special Features *Restaurant*: Fireplace; terrace dining in summer; jazz Sun. evening in summer.
Directions: From South Ferry, travel north on Rte. 114 for 1.3 miles to Cartwright Rd.; Rte. 114 makes sharp left turn, but Cartwright Rd. continues straight ahead. In 1.5 miles, turn right onto Ram Island Rd. at stop sign. In 0.7 mile, turn right onto Ram Island Dr. and continue for almost 2 miles to Ram's Head Inn, on right.

For the ultimate getaway, nothing compares to the Ram's Head Inn, which stands on a bluff overlooking Coecles Harbor. The fireplace in the lobby offers a warm welcome in

Sunset Beach attracts a chic and lively crowd who love its beachside setting and the Mediterranean cuisine served in the waterside restaurant.

the winter, and the pretty sunporch, with its woodstove, green wicker furniture with floral cushions, brick floor, and games at the ready, make this a year-round retreat. The broad, outside terrace overlooks 4.5 acres of manicured lawns that slope to the tennis court and beyond to 800 feet of private beach. There are Adirondack lawn chairs, small boats for guests to use, an old-fashioned swing hanging from a tree, an elaborate children's sandbox, a jungle gym, and hammocks strategically placed in shady groves. The exercise room is equipped with bicycle and step equipment and a sauna. The 17 rooms are fresh and bright, with wicker and white-painted furniture interspersed with antiques; colorful fabrics are used for bedspreads and curtains. At present, only 9 rooms have private baths.

The buffet breakfast includes muffins, sweet rolls, cereal, juice, fruit, and beverages. The wonderful restaurant is the most romantic on Shelter Island. There are polished oak floors topped with Oriental rugs, a fireplace, and handsome oil paintings that softly glow in the candlelight. It's magical. In the summer, French doors open to a terrace for outside dining. You'll find a menu that changes daily. The chef is a proponent of the Slow Food movement, and his menu features such delicious entrées as Long Island duck with fresh cherries (in-season) or grilled swordfish with beet and orange relish. There's an excellent wine list with a fine sampling of Long Island wines, and the inn frequently plays host to wine tastings and local winemakers' dinners.

SUNSET BEACH RESORT
AND RESTAURANT

631-749-2001; *restaurant* 631-749-3000
www.sunsetbeachli.com
35 Shore Rd., Shelter Island
Mailing Address: P.O. Box 278, Shelter
Island Heights, NY 11965
Owner: Andre Balazs
Cuisine: French seaside bistro
Serving: B, L, D
Open: Mid-May–mid-Sept.
Price: Moderate–Very Expensive
Credit Cards: AE, MC, V
Reservations: Recommended
Special Features *Resort*: Beach across street;
pond; sundecks; LCD TVs; DVD players;
stereos with CD players; minibars; tele-
phones; wireless Internet access; bicycles;
paddleboats; children welcome; pets wel-
come ($125/pet/stay)
Special Features *Restaurant*: Spectacular
water views; a beachy boutique
Directions: From Rte. 114, travel west on
West Neck Rd. toward Crescent Beach.
When West Neck Rd. turns left, continue
straight ahead on Shore Rd. to beach.
Resort is on left.

This neat little motel has occupied its prestigious spot across from Shelter Island's
premier beach for many years, but it used to
be furnished with old-fashioned vinyl
chairs and Formica-topped tables. All that
changed in 1997 when André Balazs added
this outpost to his collection of posh and
sophisticated boutique hotels. (He is also
the owner of L.A.'s Château Marmont, the
Standard boutique hotels, and the Mercer in
Manhattan.) Following a thorough
makeover, the outside has been transformed from dull brown to a lively combination of white, marine blue, and yellow.
Best of all, the 20 rooms are bright and
inviting, decorated in a beachy/casual min-
imalist style with white walls, carpeted
floors, and private baths. In every room
you'll find a TV and DVD player, robes, air-
conditioning, telephone, and a minibar
stocked with drinks. But what you'll love
most are the enormous private decks with
beautiful water views (the beach is about
200 feet away). There are pretty gardens on
the property with a little pond as a centerpiece, and there are paddleboats and
mountain bikes for guests to use, as well as
a sandy beach across the street. The French
waterfront bistro and bar is located on three
levels (two are covered and one is open-
air). There are white linen tablecloths,
strings of tiny lights, and wonderful food.
In the beachy bar, you can remove your flip-
flops and sink your toes into the sand-cov-
ered floor. Sunset Beach has a beach-party
friendly and convivial atmosphere with a
South Beach vibe, where star- and beautiful-
people-gazing is de rigueur.

Additional Bed & Breakfast Establishments

When I wrote the first edition of this book in 1994, there were very few inns and bed &
breakfasts on Shelter Island that I felt I could positively recommend. Happily that condition has changed. Today, in addition to the places listed above, which are distinguished by
the quality of their guest rooms, as well as their general ambience, setting, and the profes-
sionalism of their innkeepers, the following B&Bs are also taking guests. These establishments are, in general, more basic than those profiled above, and they may have baths
across the hallway instead of en suite. Nevertheless, they are clean and bright and offer
additional lodging alternatives on Shelter Island.

Beach House (631-749-0264; www.shelterislandgetaways.com; address and directions
given when reservation is made; mailing address: P.O. Box 648, Shelter Island Heights,

NY 11965) Owner Jan Carlson offers four guest rooms with private baths in her contemporary waterfront home. There are antique beds and spectacular sunset views from the beach. Moderate; no credit cards; continental breakfast; nonsmoking inn; children over 14 welcome; no pets.

Candlelite Inn (631-749-0676; www.thecandleliteinn.com; 3 South Ferry Rd. (Rte. 114); mailing address: P.O. Box 237, Shelter Island, NY 11964) Owners John Sieni and Michael Bartholomew have created a thoroughly unique bed & breakfast in the pretty yellow-and-white Victorian they laboriously restored in 1999, and redecorated with stylish contemporary flair in 2009. Most of the main floor is devoted to their hair salon (although there is a living room with TV for guests to use and a kitchen where breakfast is served), but on the second floor there are five bedrooms: two have bathrooms en suite; three have private baths just across the hall. The baths are terrific—all done in tile. But the finest accommodation is the private cottage in back, which has a spacious bedroom and a tiled bath with a whirlpool tub. The B&B is only open to overnight guests Wednesday through Saturday nights. Moderate–Expensive; AE, MC, V; continental breakfast; nonsmoking B&B; wireless Internet access; air-conditioning; not appropriate for children or pets.

Stearns Point House (631-749-4162; www.shelterislandgetaways.com; 7 Stearns Point Rd.; mailing address: P.O. Box 648, Shelter Island Heights, NY 11965) This former farmhouse has a front porch with a ceiling fan and polished pine floors inside. All four bedrooms have private baths. Owner Jan Carlson has decorated it with wicker and floral chintz. Moderate; no credit cards; continental breakfast; nonsmoking B&B; air-conditioning; children welcome; inquire about pets.

Two South Ferry (631-749-3208; 2 South Ferry (Rte. 114); mailing address: P.O. Box 714, Shelter Island, NY 11964) Owner: Chris Gross. A wing was added to this hospitable 1930s farmhouse to create four bedrooms with private baths. A spacious common room offers ample seating, as well as a breakfast table that is supplied with homemade breads for the continental breakfast in the morning and other goodies for snacking the rest of the day. Coffee and tea are ready for sipping. Inexpensive–Moderate; air-conditioning; no credit cards.

RESTAURANTS

THE DORY

631-749-4300
www.doryrestaurant.com
185 North Ferry Rd., Shelter Island
Mailing Address: P.O. Box 3040, Shelter Island Heights, NY 11965
Owner: Jack Kiffer
Chef/Co-owner: Milan Planas
Cuisine: American/seafood, specializing in the local catch
Serving: L, D, BR (Sun. only)
Open: Apr.–mid-Dec., daily
Price: Moderate

Credit Cards: AE, MC, V
Special Features: Beautiful covered deck on Chase Creek; live music summer weekends
Directions: On Route 114 at bridge across Chase Creek

The Dory has been a fixture on Shelter Island since 1925—an old standby that was as beloved as a great-aunt, but it had become a bit frumpy and down at the heels by 2002. Nevertheless, that deck jutting out into Chase Creek offered a terrific outside dining venue, so we forgave its tired demeanor and forgettable food. But its attitude made a 180-degree turnabout in the summer of 2003, when new owner Jack Kif-

Newly refurbished, the Dory has a terrific outdoor deck for summer dining on Chase Creek.

fer tore into the old place and transformed it into a stylish waterfront destination. There's lots of wainscoting, a beautiful bar with a flagstone floor and a stone fireplace, a rustic back bar with stained-glass panels, restaurant dividers made of old oars, and that wonderful deck out over the waters of Chase Creek—now covered with a snappy red-and-white awning. What was once dark and uninviting is now bright, light, and very stylish and chic. The American menu emphasizes local seafood. You might sample fresh stuffed flounder or seared local bay scallops and end the meal with key lime pie.

PLANET BLISS EATERY & MARKET

631-749-0053
www.planet-bliss.com
23 North Ferry Rd., Rte. 114, Shelter Island
Mailing Address: P.O. Box 611, Shelter

Island Heights, NY 11965
Owners: Julie O'Neill and Sebastian Bliss
Chef: Sebastian Bliss
Manager: Julie O'Neill
Cuisine: American regional
Serving: BR (Sun. summer only), L, D
Open: Year-round; Thurs.–Tues. in summer; Fri. and Sat. in winter
Price: Inexpensive–Moderate; prix fixe available
Credit Cards: AE, D, MC, V
Special Features: Broad porch and small patio for outside dining; wine and beer served; juice bar; natural foods market
Reservations: Accepted
Directions: On Rte. 114 at Duvall St.

This building once served both as Shelter Island's first general store and a post office. The funky decor still includes the old wooden meat cases and counters that have settled into the well-trod floors, plus stained-glass windows and antique furniture—it's a comfortable, homey, even kitschy atmosphere—all spiced up with bright orange wainscot walls. Sebastian and Julie Bliss have owned the restaurant since 2000, and from the first week, people have clamored for the chef's delicate crab cakes, as well as his grilled chicken, which he marinates for four days in a rosemary/thyme/lemon broth. There's a lovely wine list that includes some interesting local wines as well as some organic varieties, and the selection of smoothies and juices is terrific. If you'd rather prepare your own meal, stop here anyway to pick up some of the natural foods they sell in the grocery section.

SWEET TOMATO'S

631-749-4114
www.pomodorodolce.com
15 Grand Ave., Shelter Island Heights, NY 11965
Owners: James and Mary Rando

General Manager: Jimmy Rando
Chef: Anthony James Rando
Cuisine: Italian/Continental
Serving: L, D
Open: Year-round; daily in summer; fewer days rest of year
Price: Moderate–Expensive
Credit Cards: AE, MC, V
Special Features: Summer dining on a pretty front porch; fireplace in winter
Reservations: Recommended
Directions: In the heart of Shelter Island Heights village

The space had been vacant for more years than we like to remember, but the wait was well worthwhile. In 2003 this handsome, newly renovated restaurant in an old Victorian house opened, featuring walls with white paneling marching halfway up and butter-yellow paint covering the rest, all creating a stylish backdrop for color blowups of old Shelter Island scenes. Oak chairs, a hardwood floor, brass chandeliers,

Sleek and sophisticated, Sweet Tomato's serves up Italian/continental fare.

crisp white tablecloths, and floral fabric softly draped above the windows finish the look. In the summer, it's a treat to sit on the porch overlooking the quiet street scene. You might start your meal with an appetizer of radicchio stuffed with local goat cheese au gratin and served on a bed of cucumber, and then perhaps select an entrée of pan-seared local striped bass, topped with a light tomato sauce, black olives and capers, and served with a saffron risotto. The elegant, separate bar features a tin ceiling and a black-and-white tile floor.

VINE STREET CAFE

631-749-3210
www.vinestreetcafe.com
41 South Ferry Rd., Shelter Island, NY 11964
Owners/Chefs: Lisa and Terry Harwood
Cuisine: American bistro, specializing in local seafood and produce
Serving: BR (Sun. only), D
Open: Year-round; daily in summer; fewer days rest of year
Price: Expensive; prix fixe available
Credit Cards: AE, D, MC, V
Special Features: Covered porch dining
Reservations: Recommended
Directions: On Route 114, 1.6 miles from South Ferry

In the summer of 2003 Lisa and Terry Harwood (she's the pastry chef), who met while cooking at Union Square Café in New York City and worked together for several years at Sunset Beach, opened this tiny but stylish café in the former Schmidts bakery building, along the road between North and South Ferries. They decorated it with wainscoted walls and white tablecloths covered with white butcher paper, creating a smart and trendy bistro setting. As the fame of this family-run enterprise grew, it became apparent they needed to expand, so in 2009 they tripled the size of the dining rooms and added a separate bar/waiting area. It's a comfortable, convivial spot, where residents and visitors come to sample great cuisine. Specializing in local, organic, farm-fresh ingredients, the menu changes with the seasons. In summer it features traditional bistro items such as miso-glazed salmon and steak frites, as well as regular nightly specials like bouillabaisse on Mondays and crispy duck confit on Saturdays. Don't miss Lisa's signature pineapple tarte tatin or strawberry shortcake, topped with homemade ice cream, for dessert. And you won't be disappointed with the small but very well chosen wine list either.

FOOD PURVEYORS

The Tuck Shop (631-749-1548; 75 Menantic Rd. (corner West Neck Rd.) Shelter Island, NY 11964; open Mem. Day–Labor Day) Owner: Patricia Sulahian. You can tuck into more than 30 flavors of hard and soft ice cream at this nice little ice creamery.

SHOPPING

Boltax Gallery (631-749-4062; www.boltaxgallery.com; 21 North Ferry Rd. (Rte. 114), Shelter Island, NY 11964; open Fri.–Mon. 11–6) Owner: Karen Boltax. You can peruse this gallery for contemporary paintings, glass in vivid colors, modern jewelry, ceramics, photography—some of it by local artists. The smallworks exhibit is especially interesting, as preselected artists are each asked to submit three original works of art. Proceeds from this event benefit the Shelter Island Historical Society.

Celadon Home (631-749-5429; 21 North Ferry Rd. (Rte. 114), Shelter Island, NY 11964;

open year-round, daily in summer; weekends rest of year) Owner: Susan W. Simm. This delightful shop carries beautiful and practical accessories for the home, including trays, tableware, throws, candles, and fragrances. You'll find items by Jonathan Adler, Le Cadeaux, 8 Knots, and Barbara Cosgrove lamps.

Coastal Cottage Home Store (631-749-2544; 11 Grand Ave. Shelter Island Heights, NY 11965) Owner: Patricia McGrath. This lovely shop in a charming building in the heart of Shelter Island Heights features new and vintage furnishings, as well as design services and upholstering. The owner also sells linens, gifts, accessories, and bedding.

Cornucopia (631-749-0171; 27 West Neck Rd., Shelter Island, NY 11964; open year-round) Owner: Marylou Eichhorn. You'll find an array of gifts at this little spot, ranging from baby things and Christmas ornaments to stained glass, lighthouses, jewelry, toys, games, cards, and candy.

Dworkin & Daughter Antiques (631-749-3499; 57B North Ferry Rd. (Rte. 114), Shelter Island, NY 11964) Owner: Leslie Dworkin. Although she's been around for almost 35 years, her move to a new location near the Chase Bank in 2009 offers much more room for her beautiful furniture, china, artwork, etc. Visit and you'll see.

Fallen Angel Antiques (631-749-0243; 631-749-7801, messages only; Washington St., Shelter Island Heights, NY 11965; open Mem. Day–Columbus Day) Owner: Joan Markell. Located in the Chequit Annex, known as Cedar House, this shop is a delightful little treasure trove of quilts, silver, prints, wearable art, and other specialty items.

Hap's Iron Works (631-749-0200; 3 Midway Rd. South, P.O. Box 730, Shelter Island, NY 11964; call for hours) Hap Bowditch Jr. is a man of many talents, but today his interests lie with metal crafting. You cannot fail to recognize his domain, as you will see a field invaded by a mermaid and a whaling vessel furiously being rowed as it tilts in a storm,

Hap Bowditch Jr. designed this iron sculpture he's titled "Ancestors of the Sea" in memory of his seafaring family.

among other metalworks. He also makes smaller garden sculptures. You can buy his work at his gallery, or he will create iron sculptures to your specifications.

Home 114 (631-749-1811; 21 North Ferry Rd., Shelter Island, NY 11964) Owner: Fred Bernstein. This Shelter Island interior designer offers a nice selection of furniture and home furnishings in his shop, and also provides decorating services.

Home Port Antiques & Collectibles (631-749-2373; 9 South Midway Rd., Shelter Island, NY 11064; generally open weekends 12–5) Owner: Janet Hansen. Antiques purchased, refinished, and sold at this catch-as-catch-can Shelter Island antiques shop.

Marie Eiffel (631-749-0707; www.marieeiffel.com; 9 Grand Ave., Shelter Island Heights; mailing address: P.O. Box 1815, Shelter Island, NY 11964) Like a breath of fresh air, this women's designer shop blew into town in 2008 offering bright, interesting designs with international flair. Evoking memories of the colors of southern France, there are dresses in bright prints, long, gauzy shirts, carved wooden rings, and necklaces.

Marika's (631-749-1168; www.marikasantiques.com; 6 South Ferry Rd (Rte. 114).; mailing address: P.O. Box 1586, Shelter Island, NY 11964; open year-round, weekends only) Owner: Tina Marika Kaasik. You could furnish your entire house from this large and eclectic shop, which includes a house, a barn, and stuff all over the yard. You'll find wicker, oak furniture, china cabinets, lots of china to put in them, lots of jewelry, and much more—and the prices are pre-hip Hamptons.

Shelter Island Pottery (631-749-1904; Manwaring Rd., Shelter Island, NY 11964) Owner: Barbara Wright. Drive down a long driveway to this pottery studio where original stoneware and pottery are made and sold by the artist.

Summer Place (631-749-2374; 181 North Ferry Rd. (Rte. 114) 2nd Fl, Shelter Island, NY 11964; open in summer daily 10–6, Apr.–June and Sept.–Nov. weekends only; closed Jan.–Mar.) Owner: Denise Hallock. A clothing store offering women's and children's clothing for summer and winter (some Lilly Pulitzer and Calvin Klein, and Jack Rogers sandals) in a wonderful array of bright prints. The collection ranges from swimwear to sweaters, dresses to separates, as well as jewelry, belts, and accessories.

Wish Rock Studio (631-749-5200; www.wishrockstudio.com; 17 Grand Ave., Shelter Island Heights, NY 11965; open year-round, but more days in summer than winter) Owners: Sandra and Peter Waldner. A lovely gallery in the heart of Shelter Island Heights that includes original paintings, sculptures (they even have several of Peggy Mach's for sale), stained glass, jewelry, a frame shop, and a selection of books—some by local authors.

CULTURE

Calendar of Events

January

Tea & Tree: A Tenth Night Includes carols, cider, music, storytelling; re-creating an old Shelter Island tradition. Sylvester Manor.

April

Easter Egg Hunt (631-749-0107) Held at St. Gabriel's, sponsored by the Shelter Island Heights Fire Department Auxiliary.

Easter Sunrise Service Sponsored by all Shelter Island churches.

May

Memorial Day Parade Sponsored by the Shelter Island American Legion Post.

June

Shelter Island 10K Run (631-749-RUNN) Annual event begins at 5:30 PM, but music, food booths, etc., lead up to the event all afternoon; BBQ at night.

July

Fireworks Show (631-749-0399) Sponsored by Shelter Island Chamber of Commerce.
House Tour (631-749-0025) Sponsored by Shelter Island Historical Society.
One Day in History (631-749-0025) Sponsored by Shelter Island Historical Society.
Perlman Music Program (631-749-0740; Shelter Island) A series of musical events featuring the exceptional students who are chosen to attend Itzhak Perlman's summer music camp on Shelter Island.

August

Annual Arts and Crafts Show (631-749-0399) Sponsored by the Shelter Island Chamber of Commerce and Fire Department Country Fair, Shelter Island.
Annual Shelter Island Heights Firemen's Chicken BBQ (631-749-0107). Held at St. Gabriel's.
King of the Bays Regatta (631-298-9755) Sailing race in Noyack and Gardiner's bays.

September

Beach Blast This event takes place every year on the weekend after Labor Day. Bands from all over the country play at Wades Beach, food and drinks are served, all to benefit the Gift of Life Foundation and Camp Quinipet.
Historical Society Fall Harvest Festival (631-749-0025) At Haven's House, sponsored by the Shelter Island Historical Society.

October

5K Co-ed Run (631-749-0399) Sponsored by the Shelter Island Chamber of Commerce.
Halloween Party and Parade (631-749-0184) Sponsored annually by the Shelter Island Fire Department.
Plant & Sing Weekend, Sylvester Manor. Meet to plant in community garden, listen to fiddle and banjo music, and enjoy potluck supper, ends with contra dance.
Scallop Dinner This event has been going on for more than 50 years. Fresh local scallops are served up in style. Sponsored by the Shelter Island Lion's Club.
Sunset-Moonrise Cruise An annual cruise sponsored by the Shelter Island Lion's Club includes live music.

December

Christmas Tree Lighting (631-749-0399) Town Hall, Shelter Island.

Cultural Attractions

Haven's House and Barn and Manhanset Chapel Museums (631-749-0025; www.shelter

islandhistory.org; Havens House, 16 South Ferry Rd., Shelter Island, NY 11964; open Mem. Day–Labor Day, daily 10–2; rest of year, Mon.–Fri. 10–2) Operated by the Shelter Island Historical Society, the Havens House has period rooms, and is the repository of many items chronicling the fascinating history of Shelter Island. The on-premises shop sells collectibles and antiques (china, silver) donated by members.

Perlman Music Program (631-749-0740; www.perlmanmusicprogram.org; 73 Shore Rd., Shelter Island; mailing address: P.O. Box 838, Shelter Island Heights, NY 11965) As an outgrowth of the Hamptons Summer Music Festival, Itzhak Perlman has developed a summer program for musically gifted students of the violin, viola, cello, and piano. Students are individually selected by Mr. Perlman, and they participate in extensive one-on-one classes. The public is encouraged to attend the rehearsals and performances (where Peconic Lodge used to be), which include full orchestras and a choral component. The performances are held mid-June through mid-Aug. Call for schedule. Don't miss this chance to hear budding Itzhaks and Midoris before they become famous.

Shelter Island Friends of Music (631-749-1488; Presbyterian Church; 32 North Ferry Rd., Shelter Island, NY 11964) A series of summer classical concerts performed by leading musicians.

Shelter Island Public Library (631-749-0042; State Rd., Shelter Island, NY 11964) In this lovely local library circa 1886, there is a children's room, in which a story hour is held every Tuesday, and a library of local history books. An "Author Luncheon" in June attracts interested readers, and there's a summer-long book sale. Call for hours.

Sylvester Manor (80 North Ferry Rd., mailing address: P.O. Box 2029, Shelter Island, NY 11964) Sylvester Manor is unique—it's one of the only remaining manors (Gardiner's Island is another) given to a British family in colonial times that still remain in the same family. Acquired by the Sylvester family in 1652, the 243 acres are now devoted to an educational farm. In the summer volunteers are recruited to tend the farm, while a summer architectural dig takes place under the sponsorship of the University of Massachusetts. The property includes numerous barns, sheds, etc., as well as the current manor house, which dates to 1753, and a wind-powered gristmill dating to 1810. Summer visitors may help on the farm or attend one of the events. To reach the manor, from Rte. 114 going north, continue straight ahead through the white gates after passing the IGA store on the left. Go 300 yards, then turn left through a second set of white gates. You will see the large yellow manor house ahead.

RECREATION

Bicycling

Shelter Island is an especially popular destination for cyclists. The minimal amount of traffic makes the roads relatively safe, even though there are no shoulders. The roads are fairly level—with several significant exceptions, such as Shelter Island Heights. Many people ferry their own bicycles over to the island, but if you prefer to rent a bicycle, the following firm has bicycles for rent.

Piccozzi's Bike Shop (631-749-0045; Bridge Rd., Shelter Island Heights, NY 11965) Hybrid bicycles. $25/full day, $20/half-day.

Boating

Boat Charters and Rentals

Island Yacht Charters (516-647-7298; www.siyachtcharters.com) Owner: Bill Caccese. Operating the 1962 *Andrea*, a luxury Bermuda 40 designed by William Tripp, this company will take you on a half-day cruise for $650, or a full-day for $950. Wednesday evenings, they will do a racing charter for $350. This is a sleek and beautiful sailboat, with sleeping accommodations for six and a galley and head.

Shelter Island Kayak Tours (631-749-1990; www.kayaksi.com; Rte. 114 at Duvall's Rd., Shelter Island, NY 11964) Owner: Jay Damuck. This company provides kayak rentals and guided tours of the abundant waters surrounding Shelter Island, including nature areas that contain a wealth of bird and fish life. They offer a two-hour tour for $60 per person; children 12 and under are half-price. You can also rent a kayak for your own tour, and meander along the Coecles Harbor Marine Water Trail: $30/single kayak two hours; $45/single kayak four hours; $50/double kayak two hours; $70/double kayak four hours.

Tubby **Charters** (631-834-5921; www.tubbycharters.com) Owner: John Tehan. Offers fishing charters and three-hour sunset cruises on Peconic Bay on the 34-foot Marine Trader trawler *Tubby*. Their video system allows fishermen to watch the fish underwater. Half-day fishing $69.95/person; sunset cruise $39.95/person.

Marinas

Coecles Harbor Marina & Boatyard (631-749-0700; www.chmb.net; 18 Hudson Ave.; on Coecles Harbor; mailing address: P.O. Box 1670, Shelter Island, NY 11964) Owners: Needham family. This full-service marina and repair shop has 40 slips, a ship's store, snack bar, BBQ and picnic area, and a swimming pool, and offers sailboat, electric car, and bicycle rentals. The yacht-building division here is the place where Billy Joel builds his 38-foot Downeast-style boats, the Shelter Island Runabouts.

Island Boatyard and Marina (631-749-3333; 63 South Menantic Rd., Shelter Island, NY 11964) This full-service marina has 75 slips for boats measuring 16 feet to 50 feet. It's on 20 acres of wooded grounds that include a swimming pool, the Port Tavern & Restaurant; BBQs, volleyball, game room, and Laundromat.

Piccozzi's Dering Harbor Marina (631-749-0045; Bridge St., Shelter Island Heights, NY 11965) Docking is provided in 35 slips for boats up to 160 feet in length. There are restrooms, hot showers, electric hookups, BBQ, Laundromat, grocery store, game room, and bicycles for rent.

Golf

Shelter Island Country Club (631-749-0416, 631-749-8841; Goat Hill, Shelter Island Heights, NY 11965) 9 holes; par-35; 2,900 yards; clubhouse open to the public; small pro shop; resident pro; full-service restaurant. This is one of the most challenging courses on the East End; it meanders over steep hillsides near the lovely community of Shelter Island Heights. The classy clubhouse with broad porches was built in 1898 and is set high on a hill with a commanding view of the bays. The course opened in 1902, making this the sixth-oldest continuously operating golf course in the U.S. It was a private club until 1940.

Horseback Riding

Hampshire Farms & Equestrian Center (631-749-0156 or 631-749-1093; Bowditch Rd., Shelter Island, NY 11964) This 85-acre center offers riding instruction on an individual or group basis in hunting, jumping, and dressage, as well as summer youth programs. A large, lighted indoor arena permits lessons year-round. The four outside rings and a cross-country course provide experience for hunters and riders. The center also offers escorted trail rides if requested in advance.

Paard Hill Farms (631-749-9462; www.paardhillfarms.com; 41 Ram Island Rd., Shelter Island, NY 11964) Owners: Ellen Lear and Peter Ruig. Located on 36 acres of farmland, this horse farm offers instruction in dressage and jumping, and includes both indoor and outdoor arenas. There's a summer day camp for girls and boys ages seven and above, which includes tacking, washing and brushing horses, as well as daily rides. Scholarships are offered through a foundation founded by the owners.

Miniature Golf

Whale's Tale (631-749-1839; 3 Ram Island Rd., corner Manwaring; mailing address: P.O. Box 1607, Shelter Island, NY 11964; open daily May–Sept.) Owners: Erich and Heidi Inzerillo. Thirsty for an authentic espresso or cappuccino? Come here and pair it with a freshly stuffed homemade cannoli, or a piece of cake or pie. Better yet, how about a yummy ice cream cone? You'll have more than 30 flavors to choose from, which will be especially enjoyable after completing a game of 18-hole miniature golf on their lighted course that stays open till 11 PM in summer.

Parks & Nature Preserves

Mashomack Preserve (631-749-1001; www.shelter-island.org/mashomack; entrance about 1 mile from South Ferry) In the late 1970s, the Nature Conservancy successfully launched the largest fund-raising effort in its history, to save this huge piece of land for us to enjoy. They took title to the property, which occupies almost one-third of Shelter Island, in January 1980. Referred to as the Jewel of the Peconic, this preserve encompasses over 2,000 acres of woods, marshes, freshwater ponds, and tidal creeks. It is also home to one of the largest concentrations of nesting osprey, which, until recently, were almost extinct, as well as a wide variety of other birds, animals, and plants. Excellent maps and brochures are available at the visitors' center for the nature trails and hikes, which range from 1.5 miles to an 11-mile loop. Educational and recreational activities are provided, from canoe trips to bird-watching expeditions, and there's a children's program. The old Nicoll Manor House, a 10-bedroom Victorian mansion with four fireplaces, is used primarily by staff for preserve programs, fund-raising events, and environmental meetings. Group hikes and programs are held most of the year. Call for schedule.

Tennis

Heights Tennis Courts (631-749-8897, Grand Ave., Shelter Island Heights) These public tennis courts are on a pay-as-you-use basis—first come, first served.

Moussa Dramé Tennis Club (631-749-0799; 81 Shore Rd., Shelter Island; open: Mem. Day–Labor Day) Located on the grounds of the Pridwin Beach Hotel and Cottages, this popular summer tennis camp is led by Moussa Dramé, a tennis champion from the country of Mali in West Africa. He'll show students ages 3–20 about how to become future Roger Federers.

INFORMATION

Emergency Numbers

In case of emergency, dial 911.
Police: 631-749-0600
Fire: 631-749-0184 Shelter Island; 631-749-0107 Shelter Island Heights

Towns & Villages

Shelter Island Chamber of Commerce (631-749-0399; www.shelterislandchamber.com;
   47 West Neck Rd.; mailing address: P.O.Box 598, Shelter Island, NY 11964)
Shelter Island Town (631-749-0291; www.shelterislandtown.us; 38 North Ferry Rd., Shel-
   ter Island, NY 11964)
Village of Dering Harbor (631-749-0020; 232 Locust Point Rd., Shelter Island Heights,
   NY 11965)

Post Offices

For general information for all post offices, you can call 1-800-275-8777.

Services are still held in the summer at the Quaker Meeting Ground on the Sylvester property.

Shelter Island Heights Post Office (800-275-8777; 6 Grand Ave., Shelter Island Heights, NY 11965) Open weekdays 8–5, Sat. 9–1.

Shelter Island Post Office (800-275-8777; 45 North Ferry Rd., Shelter Island, NY 11964) Open weekdays 8–5, Sat. 9–1.

Churches

Our Lady of the Isle Roman Catholic Church (631-749-0001; 5 Prospect Ave., Shelter Island, NY 11964)

St. Mary's Episcopal Church (631-749-0770; 26 St. Mary's Rd., Shelter Island, NY 11964)

Shelter Island Friends Meeting (631-749-1603; 116 North Ferry Rd. (Rte. 114), Shelter Island, NY 11964) In the summer, meetings take place at 10 am in the woods at Quaker Martyr's Monument, Sylvester Manor, Shelter Island; in inclement weather and from November 1 to April 30, meetings are held at 9 Heron Lane, Shelter Island.

Shelter Island Presbyterian Church (631-749-0805, 631-749-0642; 32 North Ferry Rd., Shelter Island, NY 11964)

Union Chapel in the Grove (631-749-8938; Shelter Island Heights, NY 11965) Interdenominational services, Sunday 10 am (mid-June through September only).

Business Services

Shillingburg & Associates (631-749-3028; 4 West Neck Rd., Shelter Island, NY 11964) These computer folks design Web sites and offer computer lessons and training.

Late-Night Car Repair

Piccozzi's Service Station & Garage (631-749-0045; Bridge Rd., Shelter Island, NY 11964)

Newspapers

Shelter Island Reporter (631-749-1000; 50 North Ferry Rd., P.O. Box 756, Shelter Island, NY 11964) Weekly newspaper reporting the news of Shelter Island.

Real Estate Companies

The Corcoran Group (631-749-1600; www.corcoran.com; 181 Bridge Street, Shelter Island Heights, NY 11965)

Daniel Gale Sotheby's Intl. Realty (631-749-1155; www.danielgale.com; 40 South Ferry Rd.; mailing dadress: P.O. Box 646, Shelter Island, NY 11964) This is the Sotheby affiliate for Shelter Island. Also located on the North Fork.

If Time Is Short

In my opinion, every trip to New York City, especially in the summer, should include a visit to the Hamptons. I love the energy of the city, the can-do attitude, the feeling that anything is possible. But I also appreciate the slower pace, the tranquility, and the beauty of the Hamptons. I admit to a certain prejudice, however, about both places, and I know it's difficult for many people who live beyond New Jersey to believe that such a profound contrast to Manhattan's hurried pace and masses of people is so close at hand. So, come and see for yourself. A day in the Hamptons will convince you to come again and to stay longer.

History

If you're a history buff, a walk through most of the Hamptons' villages will include seeing buildings that date to the early 17th century. The Rogers Mansion, just off Main Street in Southampton, is made up of 12 buildings and 35 individual exhibits that range from an authentic village store to Revolutionary War artifacts. In East Hampton, Mulford Farm provides a glimpse of life on a working farm in the 17th century. Throughout the villages, picturesque windmills offer poignant reminders of the area's agricultural origins.

Recreation

Traveling through the Hamptons by bicycle is an excellent way to see the countryside. The roads are relatively flat, and major highways have wide shoulders. In addition, opportunities for nature lovers abound. The Long Pond Greenbelt (a 6.2-mile trail) in Bridgehampton threads its way along a chain of ponds and wetlands in the heart of the Atlantic Flyway, making it a rich resource for bird-watching. In Montauk, Hither Hills State Park, a 1,700-acre preserve, includes 2 miles of ocean beach. There are campgrounds, picnic sites, nightly entertainment, movies, and a vast network of hiking trails.

Beaches

The beaches of the Hamptons are glorious—broad, wide strips of fine, clean, white sand that stretch for miles, bordered on one side by the relentlessly steady surge of the ocean and on the other either by sandy dunes covered with sea grass or magnificent mansions. If you can only go to one beach, I suggest Main Beach in East Hampton. It's within walking and bicycling distance of town, and if you have a car, there's a parking lot where you can park for a fee. (But be sure to call 631-324-4150 to find out if parking is permitted on the day you want to go.) In addition, there are bathrooms, changing facilities, and a fine snack bar.

The North Fork

The North Fork of Long Island is a sleeper. This is where most of the East End wineries are located, and it's an easy two-hour drive from Manhattan. Furthermore, as the popularity of the wineries has increased, sophisticated bed & breakfasts and restaurants have opened to accommodate a more demanding class of tourist. I highly recommend a trip to Long Island's North Fork now, before it becomes as overcrowded as the South Fork.

If there is only time for a day trip, my suggestion would be to leave early enough to have time to visit two wineries, have lunch, and then visit two more wineries before heading back to the city. Start the tour at **Palmer Vineyards** in *Aquebogue*. The self-guided tour is interesting, and the tasting room includes remnants of an authentic British pub. Musical events often take place on the weekends. Next, stop at **Raphael** in *Peconic*, which has a spectacular winery building—as nice as most in California—and also excellent wines, plus a beautiful gift shop. You might have lunch at either **Jamesport Country Kitchen** (casual, 631-722-3537) or the **Jamesport Manor Inn** (elegant, 631-722-0500) in Jamesport, both of which serve terrific locally sourced dishes accompanied by local wines. If you long to eat on the water, you should try the atmospheric **Old Mill Inn** (631-298-8080) in *Mattituck,* and if you're further east, you might eat at the **Greenport Tea Company** (631-477-8744) in *Greenport,* where you can get great soups and meat pies or partake of a high English tea. As an alternative, I highly recommend a picnic lunch with a local vintage on the deck of one of the wineries. **Bedell Cellars** in *Cutchogue* is an excellent place for that. It has a beautiful deck that overlooks the vineyards. Heading back to Manhattan, you might stop at **Martha Clara Vineyards** in *Riverhead,* where you'll find excellent wines, a modern tasting room, and two restored barns that often hold art exhibits.

If there's time for an overnight stay, I highly recommend three B&Bs: the **Jedediah Hawkins Inn** (631-722-2900) in *Jamesport,* a recently restored Victorian mansion with an excellent restaurant, the **Morning Glory Bed and Breakfast** (631-477-3324), and **Bartlett House Inn B&B** (631-477-0371), both elegantly restored houses in *Greenport.* Also, if you are able to stay overnight, you must book a table at one of Long Island's finest restaurants. Everything that's been written about **North Fork Table and Inn** (631-765-0177) in *Southold* is true. It's equal to the finest restaurants in the U.S., so a meal here should be on every North Fork tour. Also, the **Luce & Hawkins** restaurant in the Jedediah Hawkins Inn in *Jamesport* holds great promise under new chef Keith Luce. Try it now before there's a six-month waiting list for a reservation.

The South Fork

Lodging

If there's time for just one night in the Hamptons, I would suggest one of the following inns, although the choice was difficult. Please note that I have included only inns that are open year-round; there are many wonderful places to stay that are closed during the winter months.

EAST HAMPTON

East Hampton Point (631-324-9191; 295 Three Mile Harbor Rd., East Hampton, NY 11937) For those who seek total privacy, these charming cottages are the solution. Each is an individual suite, often on two levels, that includes a kitchen and a private deck. Baths are spacious, and most have skylights and Jacuzzis. The cottages are connected by brick pathways and bordered by abundant flower beds. There's a pool, marina, restaurant with a spectacular harbor view, tennis court, and an exercise facility located in a former chapel.

The Baker House (631-324-4081; 181 Main St., East Hampton, NY 11937) This East Hampton Main Street mansion has been transformed into a very elegant bed & breakfast. The architecture and decor are in the arts and crafts style, and the fabrics and wallpapers were imported from England. Each of the five guest rooms is generously proportioned and has elegant tiled baths (several with Jacuzzis) and fireplaces. There's a lovely court-yard in back that overlooks an expansive formal garden with an infinity pool, and there's an in-house spa.

SOUTHAMPTON

1708 House (631-287-1708; 126 Main St., Southampton, NY 11968) The owners spent sev-eral years creating a historically accurate restoration of an old mansion that had fallen on sad days, resulting in this handsome inn. Each of the nine guest rooms and three cot-tages is spacious and luxurious. All are furnished with antiques from the owner's antiques shop and decorated with Ralph Lauren fabrics. In the brick-floored wine cel-lar, wine and cheese are served in the evening.

Restaurants

Selecting a few restaurants from the many excellent choices was almost as difficult as choosing a few places to stay. I have selected the following partly to offer choices in loca-tion, cuisine, and setting.

EAST HAMPTON

Della Femina (631-329-6666; 99 North Main St., East Hampton) This sophisticated restaurant, which is owned by advertising exec Jerry Della Femina and his wife, TV per-sonality Judith Licht, just keeps getting better and better. The food, service, and setting are among the best on the East End. Don't miss this!

The Laundry (631-324-3199; 341 Pantigo Rd., East Hampton, NY 11937) The setting is relaxed, attractive, and cosmopolitan; the food is consistently good. The menu includes a wide variety of options, allowing diners to choose an appetizer, salad, or three- or four-course dinner. This restaurant is a local favorite.

Nick & Toni's (631-324-3550; 136 North Main St., East Hampton, NY 11937) Lights! Cam-era! Action! It's always a "scene" at Nick & Toni's. Sophisticated but charming, this out-standing restaurant is so popular that summer reservations should be made weeks in advance. A star-studded, svelte clientele likes to nosh on chewy Tuscan bread, juicy, fla-vorful meats from the wood-burning oven, and luscious desserts. It's worth every penny.

Turtle Crossing (631-324-7166; 221 Pantigo Rd., East Hampton, NY 11937) Here you'll get great BBQ in an unpretentious little café. You can order an overflowing platter of spit-roasted chicken or smoked ribs, doused in delicious sauces; the *New York Times* has acclaimed it as the best BBQ on Long Island. Don't leave without having a fat square of warm bread pudding with Jack Daniel's sauce.

EAST QUOGUE

Stone Creek Inn (631-653-6770; 405 Montauk Hwy., East Quogue, NY 11942) This elegant and romantic restaurant, in a pretty, white-shingled building, serves French/Mediterranean cuisine. The chef was raised in France, and although he uses fresh local ingredients, he adds a dash of France to each of his dishes. Several fireplaces heighten the sense of romance.

MONTAUK
Dave's Grill (631-668-9190; 468 Flamingo Rd., Montauk, NY 11954) For fresh-from-the-boat seafood, Dave's can't be beat. This is a casual and engaging restaurant with an enclosed patio for summer dockside dining. Don't miss the desserts. The chocolate bag is an outrageous combination of chocolate and caramel sauces, ice cream, and bananas, enclosed in a chocolate crust shaped like a bag.

SAG HARBOR
American Hotel (631-725-3535; 49 Main St., Sag Harbor, NY 11963) This is the Hamptons' most celebrated French restaurant. Fine French/American cuisine is served in an elegant setting that includes a fireplace in one room and a glass ceiling in another. An exceptional wine list has won the highest awards year after year, and the selection of cigars was renowned long before cigar smoking became chic.

WAINSCOTT
Rugosa (631-604-1550; 290 Montauk Hwy., Wainscott, NY 11975) This newcomer (2009) to the Hamptons dining scene delivers on all fronts. The chef/owner husband-and-wife team have put together an exceptional New American menu (and they're both wonderful chefs), they've hired a top-notch team, and they decorated their restaurant in an elegant, subdued fashion, making the dining experience so memorable, you'll want to come back over and over.

WATER MILL
Mirko's Restaurant (631-726-4444; Water Mill Sq., Water Mill, NY 11976) Mirko and Eileen Zagar have been winning rave reviews for their hideaway restaurant for more years than they would like to admit, but their longevity attests to their total dedication to offering a memorable dining experience to their guests. The continental cuisine reflects Mirko's Croatian background.

Robert's (631-726-7171; 755 Montauk Hwy., Water Mill, NY 11976) Robert Durkin won our hearts years ago with his Bridgehampton restaurant and wine bar called Karen Lee's. But in 1999 he closed that restaurant and opened this new, chic spot in a charming pre–Revolutionary War building. His coastal Italian menu is terrific.

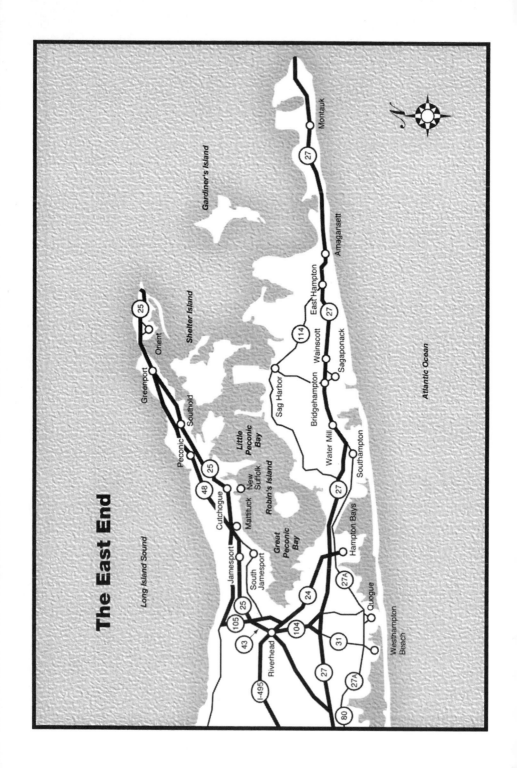

The East End

Long Island Sound

Gardiner's Island

Shelter Island

Atlantic Ocean

Montauk
27
Amagansett
East Hampton
27
Wainscott
114
Sagaponack
Bridgehampton
Sag Harbor
Water Mill
Southampton
27
Orient
25
Greenport
Southold
Peconic
25
Little Peconic Bay
Cutchogue
48
New Suffolk
Robin's Island
Mattituck
Great Peconic Bay
Jamesport
South Jamesport
105
25
43
I-495
Riverhead
27
24
104
31
80
27A
27A
Hampton Bays
Quogue
Westhampton Beach

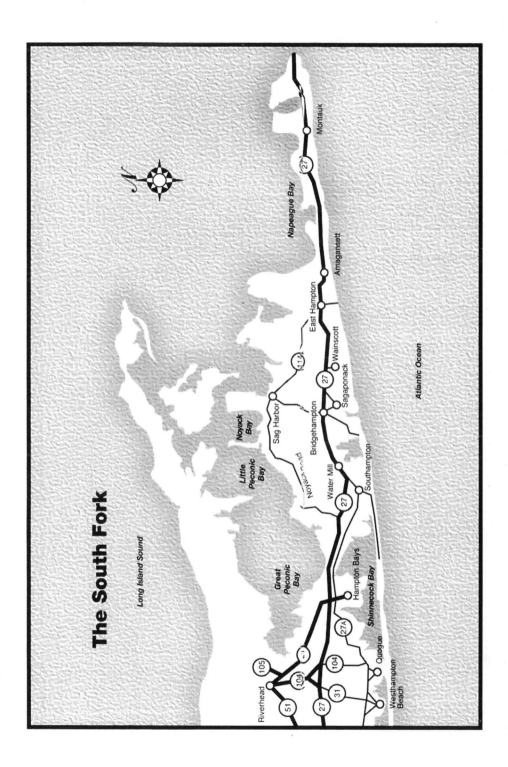

The South Fork

Long Island Sound

Montauk

27

Napeague Bay

Amagansett

East Hampton

Wainscott

114

27

Sagaponack

Sag Harbor

Noyack Bay

Bridgehampton

Little Peconic Bay

Noyac Road

Water Mill

Southampton

27

Great Peconic Bay

Atlantic Ocean

Hampton Bays

Shinnecock Bay

27A

Quogue

Riverhead

105

1

104

104

51

27

31

104

Westhampton Beach

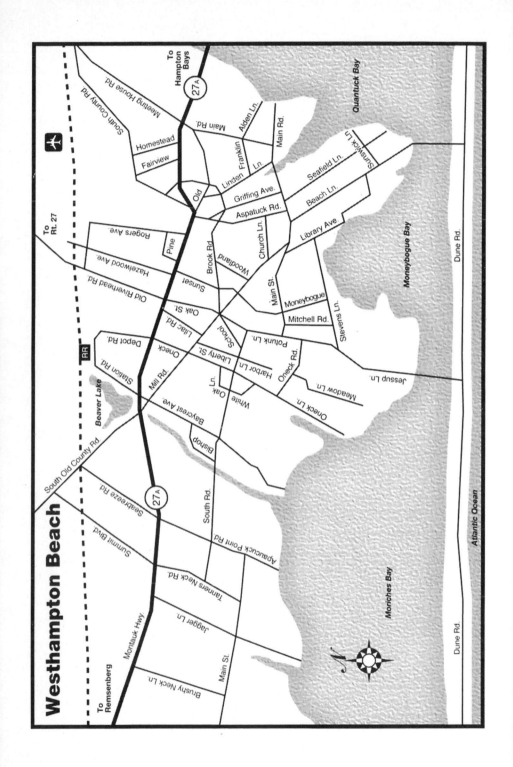

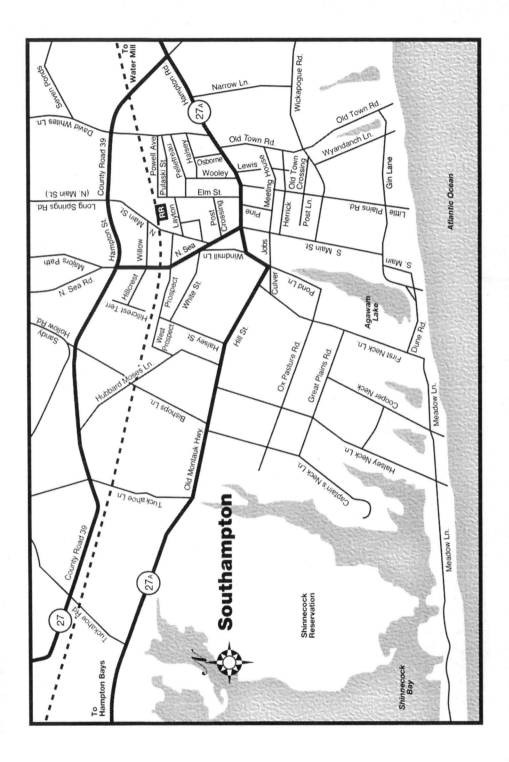

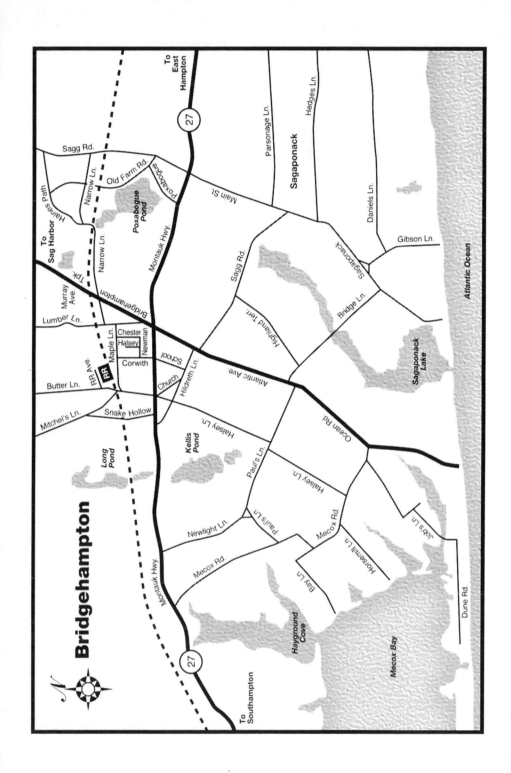

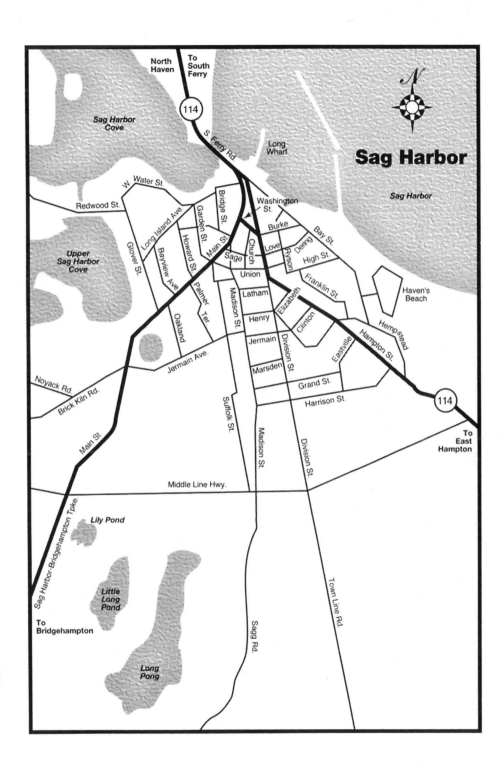

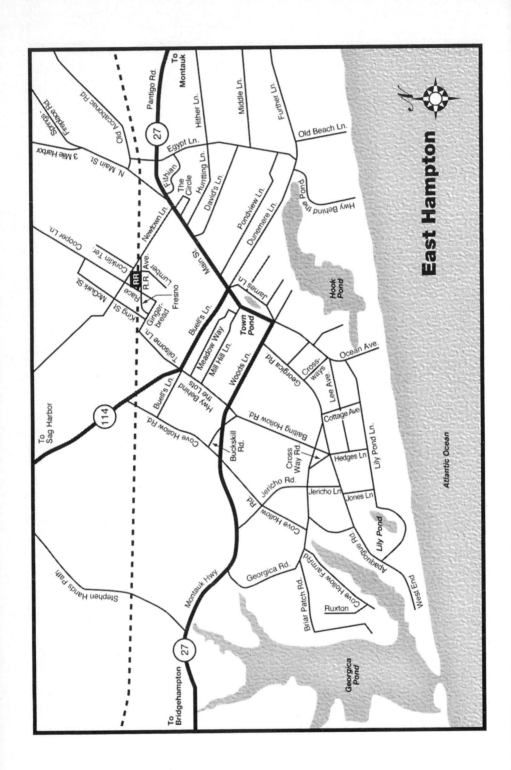

East Hampton

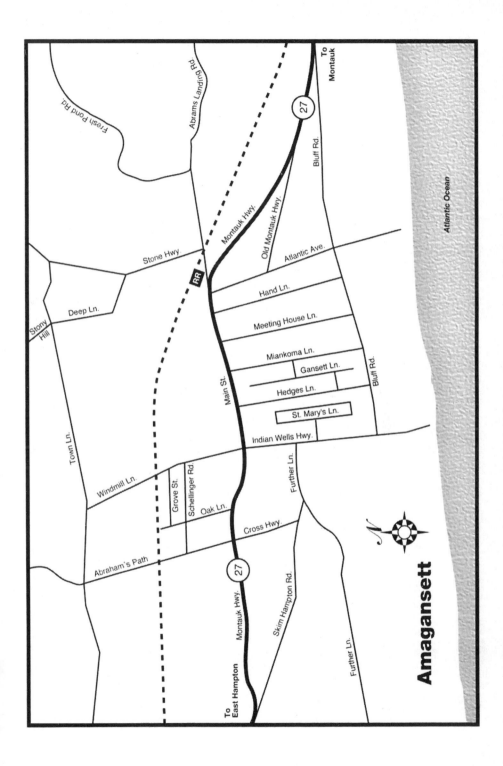

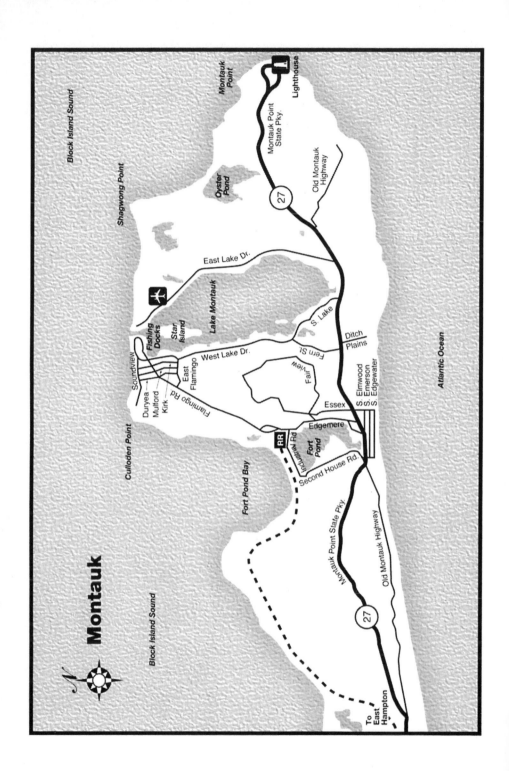

Montauk

Block Island Sound

Block Island Sound

Shagwong Point

Montauk Point

Montauk Point

Lighthouse

Montauk Point State Pky.

Old Montauk Highway

27

Oyster Pond

East Lake Dr.

Lake Montauk

S. Lake

Ditch Plains

Fern St.

Star Island

West Lake Dr.

Fairview

Elmwood

Emerson

Edgewater

Essex

Edgemere

Soundview

Duryea

Mulford

Kirk

East Flamingo

Flamingo Rd.

Culloden Point

Fort Pond Bay

RR

Industrial Rd.

Fort Pond

Second House Rd.

Montauk Point State Pky.

Old Montauk Highway

27

To East Hampton

Atlantic Ocean

Fishing Docks

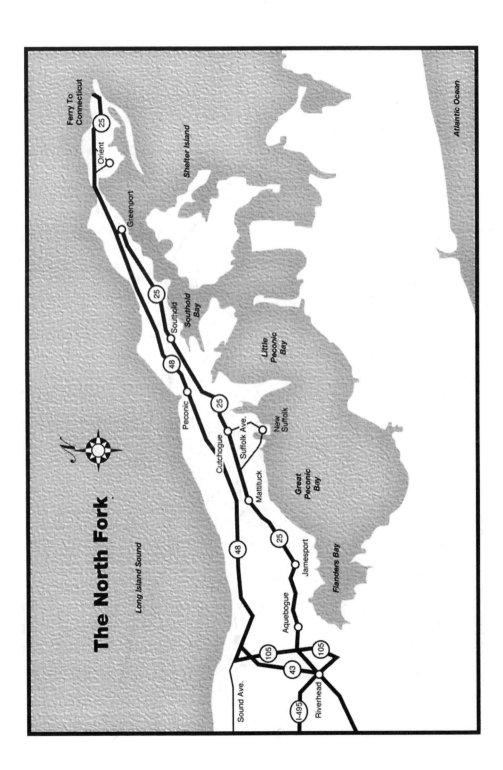

The North Fork

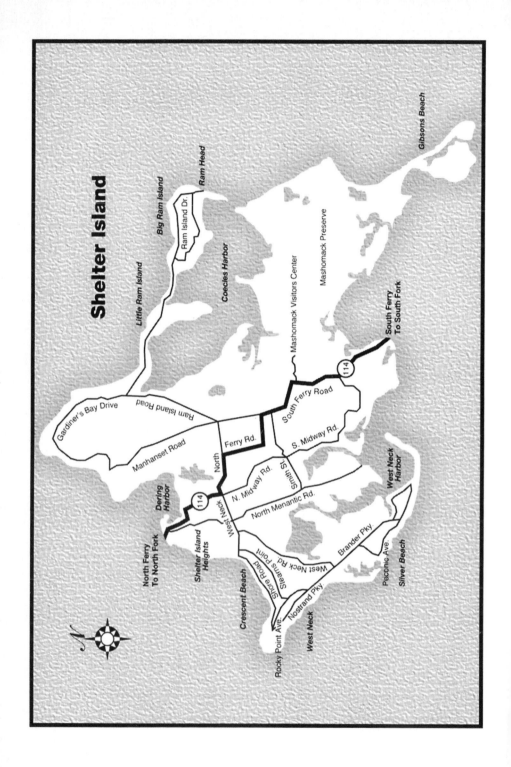

Shelter Island

General Index

A

Abracadabra, 226
Abrahams Path Park, 236
A Butler's Manor (Southampton), 67–68
Ackerly Pond Vineyard, 258–59
acting courses, 183–84
Action Airlines Charter, 41
Adios, 226
Adornments Fine Jewelry, 168
after-school programs for children in French, 196
A Grape Pear Wine Boutique, 135
Air Hamptons, 41
air travel, 41–42
Alice B. King Fine Stationery, 165
All America Picnic and Fireworks, 175
Alyssa Ann, 226
Amagansett
    beaches, 208
    bicycling, 213
    cafés & coffeehouses, 122
    farms & farm stands, 126–27
    gourmet food shops, 128
    libraries, 197
    lodging, 48–51, 71
    map, 363
    museums, 184–85
    nightlife, 202
    restaurants, 77–78
    seafood markets, 132–33
    shopping (see Shopping Index)
    take-out food, 132–33
    taxis, 44
    tennis, 235, 236
Amagansett Beach & Bicycle, 213, 216, 219, 220, 234
Amagansett Farmers Market, 126–27
Amagansett Free Library, 197
Amagansett Square, 160
Amagansett Taxi, 44
Amagansett Wine & Spirits, 134–35
A Mano Osteria & Wine Bar (North Fork), 277
Amarelle (North Fork), 277–78
Amaryllis Farm Equine Rescue, 222
ambulance service, 238

American Hotel, 355
American Hotel (Sag Harbor), 65–66, 101
The American Wing, 141
Amtrak, 38
Andrew & Company, 148
Animal Rescue Fund, 244–45
Animal Rescue Fund Thrift & Treasure Shop, 170
animal welfare, 244–45
Anne Moore hats, 150
Annie's Organic Café & Market, 124
Ann Madonia antiques, 143
Annona (West Hampton Beach), 117
Annual Arts and Crafts Show, 346
Annual Pig Roast, 315
Annual Shelter Island Heights Firemen's Chicken BBQ, 346
Another Time Antiques, 143–44
Antique and Classic Boat Show, 313
antique automobile shows, 177
Antique Auto Show, 177
Antique Lumber Co., 145
Antiques and Old Lace, 306
Antiques at Mulford Farm, 177
Antiques & Design in the Hamptons, 177
antique shopping, 141–46, 306–8. *see also* antique shows
antique shows, 175, 176, 177, 178. *see also* antique shopping
Antiques Show and Sale, 314
Aquebogue wineries, 268–69
Archer (Edward) clothing, 155
Archer Town Car, 35
Architectural House Tour, 178
architecture, 178, 179–80
Architrove antiques, 142
area codes, 240, 327
Arf Beach Ball, 178
art
    artists, 28–29, 172
    camps, 196
    children's programs, 196–97
    courses, 183–84
    galleries, 161–63, 308–12, 316–22
    museums, 180–81, 194–95
    shows, 174, 175, 177, 178

tours, 175
The Art Barge, 183, 201
Artist and Celebrity Birdhouse Auction, 178
artists, 28–29, 172
Artists and Writers Softball Game, 177
Artists' Studio Tour East Hampton, 175
art museums, 180–81, 194–95
Arts and Crafts Fair, 177
A Taste of the North Fork, 295
Atlantic Avenue beach, 208
Atlantic Coast J15 Sailing Championships, 177
Atlantic Taxi, 44
The Atlantic (Southampton), 73–74
Atlantis Marine World, 318
ATMs, 242
A Touch of Venice (North Fork), 288–89
Aunt Suzie's Clothes for Kids, 148
Authors Night, 177
auto racing, 206, 322
auto services, 245–46, 351
auto shows, 177
A Victorian on the Bay (East Port), 59–60
AXE Lounge at Dune nightclub-lounge, 203

B

Babette's, 123–24
Baby Gap, 147
Backyard at Solé East (Montauk), 93
Baiting Hollow Farm Vineyard, 259–60
Baiting Hollow wineries, 259–60
The Baker House, 353–54
The Baker House (East Hampton), 52–53
bakeries, 289–92
Balassas House Antiques, 141
banks, 242
Barbara Trujillo, 141
Barcelona Neck, 228
Bartlett House Inn B & B (North Fork), 296–97, 353
Bay Burger, 124
baymen, 26
Bays Auto Repairs, 245
Bay Street Theatre, 174, 183
Bay Street Theatre Festival, 203–4
Bay Street Theatre Kidstreet, 196
Bayview Farms, 292–93
Bayview Inn & Restaurant (North Fork), 278
B & B Auto Service, 245
b.b.balsam, 308
Beach Bakery Cafe, 121

Beach Bar club-lounge, 202
Beach Blast, 346
beaches
Amagansett, 208
Bridgehampton, 209
East Hampton Village, 209
Hampton Bays, 210
Montauk, 210
North Fork, 322–23
Northwest, 211
Noyack, 211
Quogue Village, 211
Sagaponack, 211
Sag Harbor Village, 211
Southampton Village, 211
Springs, 212
Water Mill, 212
Westhampton Beach Village, 212–13
Beach House (Shelter Island), 339–40
Beach Limousine, 35
The Beacon (Sag Harbor), 101–2
Beall & Bell Antiques, 306
bed & breakfasts, inns, resorts. see also Lodging Index
Amagansett, 48–51
Bridgehampton, 51–52
East Hampton, 52–59
East Port, 58–60
Montauk, 60–61
Shelter Island, 339–40
Water Mill, 70–71
Bedell Cellars, 260, 353
Bellhaus, 155
Ben & Jerry's, 131
Bermuda Bikes, 213
bicycling
Amagansett, 213
East Hampton, 213
Montauk, 213
North Fork, 323
Sag Harbor, 214
Shelter Island, 347
Southampton, 214
tours, 184
Bide-A-Wee, 245
The Big Duck, 318
Birchwood Tap Room, 289
Black Swan Antiques, 144
Blackwells (North Fork), 278–79
Blessing of the Fleet boat parade, 175

Bloom home furnishings, 158
Blooming Shells, 163
Blue Duck Bakery Café, 120, 289
Blue Fin IV, 226
Blue Iris Bed & Breakfast (North Fork), 297
Blue Parrot Bar & Grill (East Hampton), 81–82
Blue Sky Mediterranean Lounge (Sag Harbor), 102
Boardy Barn beer hall, 202
boating
    canoeing, 216–17, 323–24
    charter boats, 226–27
    Group Excursions, 214
    kayaking, 216–17
    marinas, 215, 324, 348
    North Fork, 323–24
    parades, 175
    party boats, 225–26
    sailing, 177, 178, 217–18
    Shelter Island, 348
    and water sports, 214–21
The Boating Channel, 243
Bobby Van's (Bridgehampton), 78
Boltax Gallery, 343
Bonakerland, 31
Bonne Nuit clothing, 148, 150–51
Bonnie's Beach Liquors, 137
BookHampton, Sag Harbor, 146
BookHampton, Southampton, 147
The BookHampton Corner Store, 146
The Book Shoppe, 146
book stores, 146–47, 308
Booth (Tulla) Gallery, 163
bootleggers, 26
Borghi (Mark) Fine Art, 161
Bouké Wines, 275
Bowen's by the Bays (Hamptons Bays), 72
Boyce (Joan) jewelry, 169
Brambles, 159
Breadzilla, 120
Breakwater (Montauk), 93–94
Brennan's Bit and Bridle, Inc., 223
Brent's Amagansett General Store, 245
Brewer/Stirling Harbor Marina, 324
Brewer Yacht Yard, 324
Bridge Gardens, 185
Bridgehampton
    banking, 242
    beaches, 209
    cafés & coffeehouses, 122–23

    farms & farm stands, 127
    gardens, 185
    gourmet food shops, 128
    historic houses, 185–86
    ice cream parlors, 131
    libraries, 198
    lodging, 51–52, 71
    map, 360
    museums, 185–86
    parks & nature, 230
    shopping (see Shopping Index)
    tennis courts, 236
    wineries, 138
Bridgehampton Candy Kitchen, 122
Bridgehampton Chamber Music Festival, 177
Bridgehampton High School, 236
Bridgehampton Ice Cream and Yogurt Company, 131
Bridgehampton Inn (Bridgehampton), 51–52
Bridgehampton Polo Club, Inc., 223
Bridgehampton Polo Club polo tournament, 175
Bridgeport & Port Jefferson Steamboat Company, 38
Bridgeport/Port Jefferson Steamboat Company, 254
Bridge Vineyards, 275
Briermere Farm, 293
Broken Colour Works, 159
Brooks Brothers, 151
Brown Harris Stevens, 248, 329
Bruce's Cafe/Cheese Emporium, 289–90
B. Smith's (Sag Harbor), 102–3
Buckskill Tennis Club, 235
Buckskill Winter Club, 237
Burton's Bookstore, 308
buses, 35–37, 44, 253
business services, 243–44, 328, 351
Butler's Fine Art and Antiques, 142
Butta' Cakes, 290
By The Bluff Bed and Breakfast (North Fork), 298

C

Cafe Max (East Hampton), 82
cafés & coffeehouses. *see also* Restaurant Index
    Bridgehampton, 122–23
    East Hampton, 123–24
    Montauk, 124
    North Fork, 289–92

Sag Harbor, 124
Southampton, 124
Water Mill, 125
Westhampton Beach, 125
Calypso clothing, 148, 151, 308
Calypso Home, 157
Candlelite Inn (Shelter Island), 340
Canio's Books, 147
canoeing, 216–17, 323–24
The Capri (Southampton), 74
Caroling on the Green, 315
Carol O'Neill Vintage Linen, 143
car rentals, 35, 42, 43, 255
Cashmere Outlet, 160
Castello di Borghese, 260–61
Catapano Dairy Farm, 293
Catherine Malandrino clothing, 151
Cedar Point County Park, 232
Celadon Home, 343–44
celebrity birdhouse auctions, 178
celebrity decorated Christmas trees, 179
celebrity residents, 172
celebrity softball games, 177
celebrity tennis exhibition games, 178
cemeteries, 194
chambers of commerce
    East Hampton, 48, 240
    North Fork, 328
    Sag Harbor, 240
    Shelter Island, 350
    South Hampton, 48, 240
Channing Daughters Winery, 138
charity designer clothing sales, 178
Charlie Whitmore Gardens, 165
Charter Boat Montauk, 226–27
charter boats, 226–27
Chefs & Champagne, 177
Chequit Inn and Restaurant (Shelter Island), 334
Cherry Creek Golf Links/The Woods at Cherry Creek, 325–26
Cherrystones Clam & Lobster Shack, 124
Childhood Memories children's music program, 196
children's activities
    after school programs, 196
    art programs, 196–97
    circus programs, 196–97
    concerts, 196
    craft classes, 197
    cultural activities, 195–97

dance programs, 196–97
family fun, 223–24
filmmaking programs, 196
French camp, 196
magic shows, 196
museums, 196
music programs, 196–97
North Fork, 324–25
puppet theaters, 196
science programs, 196–97
summer camps, 196–97, 197
theater, 197
walking tours, 197
Children's Museum of the East End, 196
choral concerts, 175, 201
Choral Society of the Hamptons choral concerts, 175
The Choral Society of the Hamptons choral concerts, 201
Christiano Family Vineyards, 275
Christmas House Tour, 315
Christmas Open House, 315
Christmas Tree Lighting, 346
Christopher Fischer Cashmere Collections, 154
Chrysalis Gallery art gallery, 163
churches, 193
cigar lounges, 125
The Cigar Bar, 125
cinema, 182–83, 316
circus festivals, 179
circus programs, 196–97
Citarella, 128, 129, 130–31
Cittanuova (East Hampton), 82–83
Clamman, 133
classes, cultural, 183–84
Classic Coach and Hamptons Luxury Liner, 35
Classic Transportation, 42
Claudia Lowry Fine Art, 308
Claudio's Restaurant (North Fork), 279
Claudio's Wines and Liquor, 296
The Clearing House eXchange, 306
climate, 242–43
Clinton Academy museum, 186
Clothesline Art Sale, 177
clothing stores, 148–56, 178, 308
Clovis Point Wines, 261
Coach factory outlet, 160
Coastal Cottage Home Store, 344
Coast Guard Group Moriches, 243
Coast Guard Search and Rescue, 238–39
Coast Guard Station Montauk, 243

Coast Guard Station Shinnecock, 243
The Coast Grill (Southampton), 107–8
Coecles Harbor Marina & Boatyard, 348
coffeehouses. *see* cafés & coffeehouses
Collette Designer Resale, East Hampton, 151
Collette Designer Resale, Sag Harbor, 154
Collette Designer Resale, Southampton,
  154–55
Colonial Limousine, 35
Colonial Taxi, 44
Complement the Chef, 313
Computer Professionals, 243
computer services, 243–44
concerts, 175, 176–77
concerts for children, 196
Concerts in the Parks, 175–76
Connecticut area codes, 240, 327
Cookery Dock, 313
cooking courses, 183–84
Cook Travel, Inc./American Express, 242
Cooperage Inn (North Fork), 279–80
Coopers Beach, 211–12
Copa Wine Bar & Tapas (Bridgehampton),
  78–79
Copen (Laurin) Antiques, 142
Corcoran Group, 248
The Corcoran Group, 329, 351
Corey Creek Vineyards, 261–62
Corn Maze, 315
Cornucopia, 344
Corwith House museum, 185–86
Côte d'Azure, 151
c/o The Maidstone (East Hampton), 55–57
Country Christmas, 179
Country Gear, 156
Cove Hollow (East Hampton), 72
Craft Fair, 315
crafts, 164–65, 172, 174, 177, 197, 308–12
Craftsmen's Guild Show, 174
Crazy Monkey Gallery, 161
Crescent Duck Farm, 293
Croft Antiques, 144
Croquet Tournament, 314
Cross Sound Ferry, 39, 254
Croteaux winery, 262
cultural activities. *see also* historic houses
  courses, 183–84
  historical reenactments, 175
  North Fork, 313–15
  powwows, 178

Shelter Island, 345–47
Custer Institute, 320
Cutchogue
  antiques, 307
  museums & galleries, 316
  wineries, 260–61, 269–71, 275–76
Cutchogue Library Annual Book Sale, 314
Cutchogue-New Suffolk Historical Council, 316
C & W Mercantile, 147

D

Dam Pond Marine Reserve, 322–23
dancing, 196–97, 203–5
Daniel Gale Sotheby's International Realty,
  329, 351
Dan's Papers, 174, 177, 246
Darbelle clothing, 156
Dave's Grill (Montauk), 94, 355
Daybreaker, 227
A Day in 1776, 175
Decorum antiques, 141
Deep Hollow Ranch, 221
Della Femina (East Hampton), 83, 354
DePetris Liquor Store, 135
Dering Harbor Inn (Shelter Island), 334–35
designer clothing, 178
Diliberto Winery, 263
dining. *see* Restaurant Index
Dish (Water Mill), 114
Ditch Plains beach, 210
Divers Flea Market diving equipment, 179
Dockers Waterside (Quogue), 89–90
Do Little's, 290
Domaine Franey, 135
Donna Parker's Habitat, 145–46
The Doofpot, 308
The Dory (Shelter Island), 340–41
Douglas Moore Memorial Music Festival, 314
The Down Home Store, 308–9
Drew (John) Theatre of Guild Hall, 204
Duck Walk Vineyards, 138
Dune Beach, 212
Dune Deck Beach Resort (Westhampton
  Beach), 74
Duryea's, 133
Dworkin & Daughter Antiques, 344
Dylan's Mini Candy Bar, 120

E

Eagle's Neck Paddling Company, 323

East by Northeast (Montauk), 94–95
East End Arts Council, 319
East End Clambakes, 133
East End Jet Ski, 220
East End map, 356
East End Seaport & Maritime Museum, 316–17
East End Stables, 222
Easter Bonnet Parade & Petting Zoo, 174
Easter Egg Hunt, 174, 313, 345
Eastern Long Island Hospital, 328
Easter Sunrise Service, 345
East Hampton
   art galleries, 181
   art museums, 181, 194–95
   bakeries & confectioneries, 120
   banking, 242
   bed & breakfasts, 52–59
   bicycling, 213
   cafés & coffeehouses, 123–24
   eggs & poultry, 125–26
   events, 173
   farms & farm stands, 127
   fishing, 225
   gourmet food shops, 129
   ice cream parlors, 131
   libraries, 197–98, 200
   lodging, 52–59, 72
   map, 362
   marinas, 215
   museums, 186–89
   nightlife, 202
   parks & nature, 231
   restaurants, 81–89, 354
   shopping (see Shopping Index)
   short trips, 353–54
   taxis, 44
   tennis, 235, 236
   walking tours, 186
East Hampton Airlines, 41
East Hampton Airport, 42
East Hampton Antiques Show, 176
East Hampton Bowl, 245
East Hampton Business Service, 243
East Hampton Chamber of Commerce, 48, 179, 240
East Hampton High School, 236
East Hampton Historical Society, 186, 196
East Hampton House (East Hampton), 53
East Hampton Library, 197–98
East Hampton Point, 353

East Hampton Point (East Hampton), 53–54, 83–84, 353
East Hampton Point Marina, 215
East Hampton Skate Park, 234
East Hampton Star, 246
East Hampton Taxi, 44
East Hampton Town Marine Museum, 184, 196
East Hampton Town Office, 241
East Hampton Town Satellite Office, 241
East Hampton Trails Preservation Society, 174, 231, 237
East Hampton Veterinary Group, 244
East Hampton Village beaches, 209
East Hampton Village Nature Trail, 231
East Hampton Village Office, 241
Eastport
   bed & breakfasts, 58–60
   restaurants, 89, 245
   wine shops, 135
East Quogue. *see also* Quogue
   equestrian, 222
   library, 199
   museums, 191
   nightlife, 202
   restaurants, 89–91, 354
East Side Tennis Club, 235
Eastway Aviation, 41
Ebb Tide, 225
Edible East End, 246
Edward Archer clothing, 155
eggs & poultry, 125–26
Eileen Fisher clothing, 151
Elegant Setting, 167
Elias Pelletreau Goldsmith Shop, 193
Elie Tahari clothing, 151–52
Ellen's Run, 177
emergencies
   fire service, 238
   medical services, 244, 328
   phone numbers, 239, 327, 350
   police service, 238
Emma Rose Elliston Park, 234
The Enclave Inn (Bridgehamtpon), 71
English Country Antiques, 156
English settlers, 18–22
Enterprise Rent-A-Car, 255
Entre Nous, 152
equestrian activities
   horseback riding, 221–22, 326–27
   horse shows, 178, 222–23

shops, 223
Espresso, 130
events, by month, 173–79, 345–47
Excelaire Service, 41
Excentricities, 159
Executive Fliteways Inc., 41

F

F, 324
factory outlets, 160
Fallen Angel Antiques, 344
Fall Family Festival, 179
Fall Festival on the Village Green, 179
Fall Harvest Festivals, 315
family activities, 223–24
famous residents, 172
Farm Country Kitchen, 290–91
farming history, 29–30
farms & farm stands, 126–28, 292–96
Fat Ass Fudge, 120
fax services, 243–44
ferries, 38–41, 254, 333
Fiedler Gallery, 309
Field's (Frank) Miniature Railroad, 324
film festivals, 179
filmmaking programs, 196
Fine Arts Gallery, 181
fire service, 238
fireworks, 175, 176
Fireworks Displays, 176
Fireworks Show, 346
First Night Celebration, 315
Fischer (Christopher) Cashmere Collections, 154
Fishbar on the Lake (Montauk), 95
Fisherman's Fair, 177
Fisher's Home Furnishings, 158
Fish Farm Multi Aquaculture Systems, 132–33
Fishhooker, 227
fishing
    East Hampton, 225
    festivals, 177, 179
    North Fork, 323–24
    shellfishing, 224–25
    Southampton, 225
5K Co-ed Run, 346
Florence B, 227
Flying Cloud, 225
flying, gliding, skydiving, 227–28
Flying Point Beach, 212

Flying Point Surf School, 217, 219
food stores. *see also* Restaurant Index
    bakeries, 120–22, 289–92
    confectioneries, 120–22
    farms & farm stands, 126–28, 292–96
    gourmet food, 128–31
    grocery stores, 245
    late-night, 245
    purveyors, 119–34, 120, 292–96, 343
    seafood markets, 132–34
    take-out, 132–34
    and wine festivals, 174, 175, 177, 178
foreign exchange, 242
Foster Memorial beach, 211
Four Ones, 42, 44
Fourth of July Parades, 314
Fourth of July Village Parade, 176
Frank Field's Miniature Railroad, 324
Freda's Fancy, 309
Freddy's House (North Fork), 298
Tina Fredericks, 249
French camp and after-school programs for children, 196
Fresh Air Home Decorators & Dealers Party, 175
Fresh Pond beach, 209
Fresno (East Hampton), 84
Frisky Oyster (North Fork), 280
Fritchie (Mary O.) Outdoor Art Show, 176
The Fudge Co., 131
fuel, late-night, 245–46
The Furniture Garden, 159
furniture shopping, 306–8
The Furniture Store Antiques, 306–7

G

galleries, art, 161–63, 308–12, 316–22
Gallery 429, 307
Gallery M, 309–10
Gallery of Trees, 179
The Gansett Green Manor (Amagansett), 48–49
Gap Kids, Bridgehampton, 147
Garden of Eve Organic Farm, 293
gardens. *see also* parks & nature
    and landscaping stores, 165–67
    overview, 184
    tours, 175, 178
Garden Tour, 314
Gardiner's Marina, 215

Garlic Festival, 315
Gazebo Gallery, 310
Gem, Mineral, and Jewelry Show, 314
George Braun Oyster Co., 293
Georgica Beach, 209
Georgica Creek Antiques, 145
Georgica Restaurant and Lounge (Wainscott), 112
Getaway House (East Hampton), 72
gift shops, 163–64, 308–12
Gin Beach, 210
Giraffics Gallery, 161
Glenn Horowitz Bookseller, 146
gliding, flying, skydiving, 227–28
Gloria Jewel, 150, 308
Goat on a Boat Puppet Theatre, 196
Golden Earthworm Organic Farm, 293–94
The Golden Pear Café, 122
golf, 228–30, 325–26, 348
Gone Fishing Marina, 216
Gone Local, 164
Gosman's Dock (Montauk), 95–96
Gosman's Fish Market, 133
gourmet food shops, 128–31
government, local, 240
Grand Slam Winners Tennis Exhibition, 178
Great Bonac Fireworks Show, 176
Greater Westhampton Chamber of Commerce, 176, 240
Greater Westhampton Chamber of Commerce Arts and Craft Show, 175
Great Rock Golf Club, 326
Greenport, 306–7, 316–17
Greenport Brass Band, 322
Greenport Carnival, 314
Greenport Carousel, 324
The Greenporter Hotel and Spa (North Fork), 299
Greenport Harbor Tours, 324
Greenport Tea Company, 353
Greenport Tea Company (North Fork), 280–81, 353
Greenport Village Office, 328
The Green Thumb, 127–28
Grenning Gallery, 163
grocery stores, 245
Group for the East End, 174, 231, 237
group tours, 254–55
Gucci, 152
guided tours, 42–43

Guild Hall art courses, 183
Guild Hall Artist Members Exhibition, 175
Guild Hall art programs, 181, 196
Guild Hall Clothesline Art Sale, 178
Gulf Coast Kitchen (Montauk), 96
Gurney's Inn Resort & Spa (Montauk), 72

H

Hallockville Fall Festival and Craft Fair, 315
Hallockville Museum Farm and Folklife Center, 319–20
Halloween Party, 179, 346
Halsey's Marina, 215
Hampshire Farms & Equestrian Center, 349
Hampton Arts movie theater, 183
Hampton Bays
    banking, 242
    beaches, 210
    events, 173
    libraries, 198
    lodging, 72
    marinas, 216
    nightlife, 202–3
    parks & nature, 231
    restaurants, 91–93
    shopping (see Shopping Index)
    taxis, 44
    wine shops, 136
Hampton Bays Chamber of Commerce, 240
Hampton Bays Diner and Restaurant, 245
Hampton Bays Public Library, 198
Hampton Bays Wine and Spirits, 136
Hampton Chutney Co., 122
Hampton Classic Horse Show, 178, 222–23
Hampton Coach, 44
Hampton & Co. clothing, 155
Hampton Coffee Company, 125
Hampton Designer Showhouse, 176
Hampton Dive Center, 327
Hampton Jitney, 35, 36, 43, 253
Hampton Jitney (limousines), 35
Hampton Library in Bridgehampton, 198
Hampton Luxury Liner, 36
The Hampton Maid (Hampton Bays), 72
Hampton Photo Arts, Inc., 170
Hamptons Annual Spring Garden Antiques Show & Sale, 175
Hamptons Antiques Classic & Design Show, 176
Hamptons Greek Festival, 176

Hamptons International Film Festival, 179
Hamptons Magazine, 246
Hamptons Online, 243
Hamptons Restaurant Week, 174
HamptonsWeb.com, 243
Hamptons Wine Shoppe, 137
The Hampton Theatre Company live theater, 204
Hampton Veterinary Hospital, 244
Hampton Watercraft & Marina, 216
handcraft stores, 164–65
handicapped services, 244
Hap's Iron Works, 344
Harbes Family Farm, 294–95
Harbor Bistro (East Hampton), 84–85
Harborfront Inn (North Fork), 300
Harbor Knoll (North Fork), 300–301
Harbor Marina of East Hampton, 215
Harborwoods (Sag Harbor), 66
Harper's Books, 146
Harvest Festival, 315
Harvest Inn Bed & Breakfast (North Fork), 301–2
Harvest on Ford Road (Montauk), 96–97
Hatchlings children's clothing, 148
Haven antiques, 142
Havens Beach, 211
Haven's House and Barn and Manhanset Chapel Museums, 346–47
Hayground Market, 127
H C & G (Hamptons Cottages & Gardens), 246
The Hedges Inn (East Hampton), 54
Hedgewood Farm, 326–27
Heights Tennis Courts, 349
Herbert and Rist, 136–37
Hermès, 152
The Hermitage (Amagansett), 49
Herrick Park, 236
Hertz rental cars, 255
Hidden Lake Farms Riding School, 327
hiking, 174, 230
Hildreth's, 169
Hilfiger, Tommy, 152
Hillcrest Sport Stable, 327
historical reenactments, 175
Historical Society Fall Harvest Festival, 346
historic houses, 172, 179, 184–89, 194
Historic Sag Harbor "Harbor Fest" Weekend, 178
Historic Seaport Regatta, 315

history. *see also* historic houses
  farming, 29–30
  manufacturing, 24–26
  natural, 14
  The North Fork, 250–52
  reenactments, 175
  Shelter Island, 330–32, 352
  social, 14–32
Hither Hills State Park beach, 210
Holey Moses Cheesecake, 121–22
Holiday Historic House and Inn Tour, 179
Holiday House Tour & Progressive Food and Wine Tasting, 315
Hollis Reh & Shariff, 168
Home 114, 345
Home, James!, 166
Home Port Antiques & Collectibles, 345
Home Sweet Home museum, 187
home tours, 178
Hook Windmill museum, 187
Horowitz (Glenn) Bookseller, 146
horseback riding, 221–22, 326–27
horse shows, 178, 222–23
Horton Point Lighthouse and Nautical Museum, 320–21
hospitals, 244, 328
House and Garden Tour, 178
House on Chase Creek (Shelter Island), 335
House Tour, 346
housewares stores, 165–67, 313
The Huntting Inn (East Hampton), 54–55

I

Iacono Farms, 125–26
Ice Cream Club, 131
ice cream parlors, 131–32
Ice Cream Social, 314
Il Capuccino Ristorante (Sag Harbor), 103–4
Impulse, 308
The Independent, 246
Indian Cove (Hampton Bays), 91
Indian Island Country Club and Golf Course, 326
Indian Island County Park, 323
Indian Wells beach, 209
Indian Wells Tavern (Amagansett), 77
The Ink Spot, 328
Inlet Seafood (Montauk), 97–98
Inn at Quogue (Quogue), 100
The Inn at Quogue (Quogue), 64

Inn Spot on the Bay (Hampton Bays), 72, 91–92
interior design shows, 175, 176
internet access, 243–44
The Irony handcrafts, 164
Isabella Rump Documentary Filmmaking Class, 196
Island Boatyard and Marina, 348
Islander Limousine, 255
Island's End Golf & Country Club, 326
Island Yacht Charters, 348

J

Jackson's Marina, 216
Jamesport Country Kitchen (North Fork), 281–82, 353
Jamesport Country Store, 310
Jamesport Manor Inn (North Fork), 282, 353
Jamesport Vineyards, 263
Jamesport wineries, 261, 263
Jan Davis Antiques/L. I. Doll Hospital, 307
Jazz Festival, 315
Jedediah Hawkins Inn (North Fork), 302, 353
Jennifer Miller jewelry, 167
Jermain (John) Memorial Library in Sag Harbor, 198–99
jet skiing, 220–21
jewelry stores, 167–69
Jewish Center of the Hamptons, 175
Jill Stuart clothing, 152
Jimmy's clothing, 156
Joan Boyce jewelry, 169
Joe's Garage, 245
John Drew Theatre of Guild Hall live theater, 204
John Jermain Memorial Library in Sag Harbor, 198–99
John Salibello Antiques, 141–42
Joni's, 124
Jon Vaccari Antiques, 146
JP Morgan Chase, 242
JRs Westhampton Taxi, 44
July 4th Music Festival, 314

K

Kapell Antiques, 307
kayaking, 216–17
kennels, pet, 244–45
Kids on the Green, 196
Kidsummer Art Camp, 196
King (Alice B.) Fine Stationery, 165

King Kullen, 242, 245
King of the Bays Regatta, 346
kitchenware stores, 165–67
kite festivals, 177
Kites for a Cure, 175
Kites of the Harbor, 149
Kramoris (Romany) Gallery, 164
Krasner, Lee, 194–95
Krupski's Vegetable & Pumpkin Farm, 295

L

La Comtesse Thérèse, 275
La Cuvée Wine Bar & Bistro (North Fork), 282–83
Ladies' Village Improvement Society, 170, 176, 187
Lady Grace V, 227
La Ferme de la Mer, 310
LaFondita, 122
Landscape Pleasures, 175
La Perla, 152
La Plage (North Fork), 283
Lashley Pavilion beach, 212
late-night food services, 245
late-night fuel, 245–46
laundromats, 246
The Laundry, 354
Laurel Lake Vineyards, 263–64
Laurel wineries, 263–64
Laurin Copen Antiques, 142
Lavender by the Bay, 295
Lazybones, 225
Lazy Point beach, 209
Le Cercle Français, 196
Le Chef (Southampton), 108
Legends (North Fork), 283–84
Lenhart Cottages (Montauk), 72–73
Lenz Vineyards, 264–65
Levain Bakery, 121
libraries, 197–201
Lieb Family Cellars, 265
Lighthouse on the Bay (Sag Harbor), 66–67
Lighthouse Weekend at Montauk Point, 178
Lily Pond nightclub-lounge, 202
limousines, 255
Lindy's Taxi, 44
Lions Park, 236
Lisa Perry clothing, 154
Little Lucy's, 160
The Living Room at c/o The Maidstone (East

Hampton), 86
Loaves and Fishes Cookshop cooking courses, 183
Loaves & Fishes, 129
Loaves & Fishes Cookshop, 129, 165, 183
Lobster Roll Northside, 291
The Loft at Harbourfront, 291
London Jewelers, 167
Longhouse Reserve arts and music, 188
Long Island Convention and Visitors Bureau, 173
Long Island Game Farm, 324–25
Long Island Greenbelt Trail Conference, 174, 231, 237
Long Island J80 Sailing Championship, 178
Long Island Motor Sports Park, 206
Long Island National Golf Club, 326
Long Island Rail Road, 37–38, 42, 254, 333
Long Island Traditional Music Association, 173
Long Island Wine Council, 258, 313
Long Island Wine Tours, 43, 254
Long Island Winterfest, 174
Long Pond Greenbelt, 231
Long Wharf Wines & Spirits, 136
Louse Point beach, 212
Love Lane Kitchen (North Fork), 284
Lowry (Claudia) Fine Art, 308
Lucie & Hawkins (North Fork), 284–85, 353
Lucy's Whey, 129
Lydia's Antiques and Stained Glass, 307

M

Macari Vineyards and Winery, 265–66
Mach, Peggy, 310
MacWhinnie (Morgan) antiques, 144
Madonia (Ann) antiques, 143
The Madoo Conservancy gardens, 191
Magaschoni, 152
magazines, 146–47, 246–47
magic shows, 196
Maidstone Harbor Marina, 215–16
Maidstone Park Beach, 212
Main Beach, 209, 219, 220
Main Beach Surf & Sport, 217
Mainstay Inn (Southampton), 68
manufacturing history, 24–26
maps
    Amagansett, 363
    Bridgehampton, 360
    East End, 356

East Hampton, 362
Montauk, 364
North Fork, 365
Sag Harbor, 361
Shelter Island, 366
Southampton, 359
South Fork, 357
Westhampton Beach, 358
Marders, 165–66
Marie Eiffel, 345
Marika's, 345
marinas
    East Hampton, 215
    North Fork, 324
    private, 215–16
    Sag Harbor, 215
    Shelter Island, 348
    Southhampton, 215
    Westhampton Beach, 215
Maritime Festival and Fishing Tournament, 315
Mark Borghi Fine Art, 161
Marlin VI Princess, 225–26
Martha Clara Vineyards, 266–67
Mary O. Fritchie Outdoor Art Show, 176
Mary's Marvelous!, 128
Mashashimuet, 236
Mashomack Preserve, 174, 349
Masterpiece Charters, 227
Master Workshop in Art art courses, 184
Mattituck Cinemas, 316
Mattituck Historical Society Antiques Show, 314
Mattituck Street Fair, 314
The Mattituck Strawberry Festival, 314
Mattituck wineries, 265–66, 273–74
Mayfair Diamond & Fine Jewelry, 168
McDonald's restaurants, 245
Mecox Bay Dairy, 127
Mecox Beach, 209
Mecox Gardens, Southampton, 159
media, 246–48, 328
medical services, 244, 328
Medolla Vineyards, 275
Meeting House (Amagansett), 78
Meeting House Creek Inn, 291
Megna Hot Glass, 164–65
Members Exhibition art show, 174
Memorial Day Parade, 175, 313, 346
Merrill Lake Sanctuary, 234
Meschutt Beach, 210

Metaphysical Books & Tools, 147
Michael Anthony's Food Bar (North Fork), 285
Michael's at Maidstone Park (East Hampton), 86–87
Michael's Wines & Liquors, 296
Midsummer Party music festival, 176
Mill Creek Kayaks, 217
Mill Creek Marina, 216
Mill House Inn (East Hampton), 57
miniature golf, 349
Mirko's Restaurant (Water Mill), 114–15, 355
Miss Amelia's Cottage museum, 185
Modern Snack Bar, 291
The Monogram Shop, 148
Montauk
    beaches, 210
    bed & breakfasts, 60–61
    bicycling, 213
    cafés & coffeehouses, 124
    events, 173
    history, 30–32
    ice cream parlors, 131
    libraries, 199
    lodging, 60–61, 72–73
    map, 364
    marinas, 216
    museums, 189–91
    nightlife, 203
    parks & nature, 231
    restaurants, 93–100, 124, 355
    seafood markets, 133
    shopping (see Shopping Index)
    take-out food, 133
    taxis, 44
    tennis courts, 236
Montauk Airport, 42
Mantauk Annual Full Moon Bass Tournament, 179
Montauk Bike Shop, 213
Montauk Chamber of Commerce, 240
Montauk City Skate Park, 234
Montauk Downs Golf Course, 229
Montauk Downs State Park, 234, 236
Montauk Fine Arts Festival, 175
Montauk Fine Art Show on the Green, 178
Montauk Hill House (Montauk), 60
Montauk Ice House, 142
Montauk Laundromat, 246
Montauk Library, 199
Montauk Manor (Montauk), 60–61

Montauk Marine Basin, 216
Montauk Point Lighthouse, 190
Montauk Point Lighthouse Museum, 189–90
Montauk Point Lighthouse Triathlon, 176
Montauk Printing and Graphics, 243
Montauk Yacht Club Resort & Marina (Montauk), 61, 216
Moonlight Classic Limo and Taxi, 255
Moore (Anne) hats, 150
Morgan MacWhinnie antiques, 144
The Morning Glory Bed & Breakfast (North Fork), 302–3
The Morris Studio, 170
Morton National Wildlife Refuge, 233
Mosaic Street Painting Festival, 313
Moussa Dramé Tennis Club, 349
movies, 316
The Movie theater, 183
Mulford Farm museum, 188
Muse Restaurant and Aquatic Lounge (Water Mill), 115–16
museums, 184–96, 186, 196, 316–22
music
    children's programs, 196
    choral concerts, 175, 201
    concerts, 201
    events, 176, 201, 322
    festivals, 173, 175, 176, 177
    operas, 201
    rock concerts, 196
    stores, 146–47
Music Festival of the Hamptons, 176, 201

N

The Naked Stage theatre company, 174
Napeague Tennis Club, 235
natural history, 14
natural history museums, 186
Nature Conservancy, 231
Nature Conservancy for the South Fork, 174
nature preserves, 230–34, 349
Nellie's of Amagansett, 141
Neptune Beach Club club-lounge, 202
New England Airlines, 41
New Moon Café (Quogue), 90
New Paradise Cafe (Sag Harbor), 104
Newsday, 329
newspapers, 246–47, 329, 351
New York area codes, 240, 327
New York State Department of Environmental

Conservation Fisheries, 225
Nick's nightclub and restaurant, 203
Nick & Toni's (East Hampton), 87, 354
nightclubs-lounges, 202–3
nightlife, 202–3
Nikki Eve clothing, 154
North Ferry, 40, 254, 333
North Fork
    art galleries, 316–22
    bicycling, 323
    boating, 323–24
    cafés, bakeries and pubs, 289–92
    canoeing, 323–24
    car travel, 254
    chambers of commerce, 328
    children's activities, 324–25
    emergency numbers, 327
    ferries, 254
    fishing, 323–24
    food purveyors, 292–96
    golf, 325–26
    group tours, 254–55
    history, 250–52
    horseback riding, 326–27
    limousines, 255
    lodging, 296–306
    map, 365
    marinas, 324
    movies, 316
    museums, 316–22
    music events, 322
    parks & nature, 322–23
    recreation, 322–27
    restaurants, 276–89, 276–92, 289–92
    scuba diving, 327
    shopping (see Shopping Index)
    short trips, 352–53
    skateboarding, 323
    taxis, 255
    theater, 322
    train travel, 254
    transportation, 252–55
    visitor information, 327–28
    wine, 296
    wineries, 255–76
wineries map, 256
North Fork Audubon Society Nature Center, 323
The North Fork Community Theatre, 322
North Fork Promotion Council, 313, 323, 328

North Fork Table and Inn (North Fork), 285–86, 353
North Fork Wine Camp, 258
North Haven Village Office, 241
North Main Street Citgo, 246
North Sea Skate Park, 234
Northwest beaches & parks, 211, 231
Northwest parks & nature preserves, 231
Noyack beaches, 211
Noyac Liquors, 136

O

Oakland's (Hampton Bays), 92
Oasis nightclub and restaurant, 203
Oasis (Sag Harbor), 104–5, 203
Ocean Colony Beach and Tennis Club (Amagansett), 49
Ocean Taxi, 44
Oh, Brother Charter Boat, 227
The Old Custom House museum, 192
Olde Country Inn and Restaurant (Shelter Island), 335–36
Olde Speonk Inn (Speonk), 112
Olde Towne Animal Hospital, 244
old-fashioned emporiums, 169
The Old Field, 267
Old Mill Inn (North Fork), 286, 353
Old Schoolhouse Museum, 191
Old Town Arts & Crafts Guild, 310
Old Town Beach, 212
Old Town Crossing, 144
Onabay Vineyards, 275
One Day in History, 346
O'Neill (Carol) Vintage Linen, 143
opera concerts, 201
opera festivals, 176
Opera in the Hamptons, 176, 201, 314, 322
Orient Beach State Park, 323
Orient Country Store, 295
Orient & East Marion Spring House Tour, 314
Orient Inn (North Fork), 303
Orient museums & galleries, 317–18
Osborn-Jackson House museum, 188
Osprey's Dominion Winery, 267–68
O'Suzanna, 164
Our Lady of the Isle Roman Catholic Church, 351
Outdoor Arts & Crafts Show, 314
outdoor recreation. see also beaches; bicycling; boating; equestrian activities; fishing

auto racing, 206, 322
auto shows, 177
flying, gliding, skydiving, 227–28
golf, 228–30, 325–26, 348
hiking, 174, 230
jet skiing, 220–21
kite festivals, 177
paddleboarding, 218–19
parks & nature, 230–34, 349
rollerblading, 234
sand castle contests, 177
seal watching, 173
skateboarding, 323
surfing, 218–19
swimming, 234
tennis, 178, 235–36
watersports, 214–21
whale watching, 237
wind surfing, 220–21
winter sports, 237
Out of the Closet, 150
Oysterponds Historical Society, 317–18

P

Paard Hill Farms, 349
paddleboarding, 218–19
Pailletts, 154
The Palm at Huntting Inn (East Hampton), 87–88
Palmer Vineyards, 268, 353
parades, 174, 175, 176, 179
Parker's (Donna) Habitat, 145–46
parking permit fees, 208
Park Place Wines & Liquors, 134, 135
parks & nature, 230–34, 349
The Parrish Art Museum, 173, 182
party boats, 225–26
Pathfinder Country Day Camp at Montauk, 223
Patio at 54 Main (West Hampton Beach), 117–18
Paumanok Vineyards, 268–69
Peconic antiques, 307
Peconic Bay Medical Center, 328
Peconic Bay Winery, 269
Peconic Dunes, 325
Peconic Liquors, 296
Peconic wineries, 138–39, 258–59, 264–65, 267–68, 270–75
Pellegrini Vineyards, 269–70
Pelletreau (Elias) Goldsmith Shop, 193

Perlman Music Program, 176–77, 201, 346, 347
Perlman Music Program, 347
Perlman Music Program concerts, 201
Phao Thai Kitchen (Sag Harbor), 106
phone numbers, emergency, 239, 327, 350
photography courses, 183–84
Photography Workshop, 184
photo shops, 169–70
Pianofest, 175
Pianofest concerts, 201
Piccozzi's Bike Shop, 347
Piccozzi's Dering Harbor Marina, 348
Piccozzi's Service Station & Garage, 351
Pierre's (Bridgehampton), 80–81
Pindar Vineyards, 270–71
Pine Barrens Trail Information Center, 231
Pine Cone gifts, 164
Pink Tuna Taxi, 44
The P, 87
Planet Bliss Eatery & Market (Shelter Island), 341–42
Plant & Sing Weekend, Sylvester Manor, 346
The Playwrights' Theatre of East Hampton live theater, 204
Plaza Café (Southampton), 108
Plaza Surf & Sport, 213, 214, 217, 219
police service, 238
Polish Festival Riverhead, 314–15
Pollock, Jackson, 194–95
Pollock-Krasner House and Study Center, 194–95, 195
Polo, 223
Polo Country Store, 152
Polo Home Country Store, 157
polo tournaments, 175
The Pondview at Deerfield (Water Mill), 70–71
Ponquogue Beach, 210
Porto Bello (North Fork), 286
post offices, 248, 329, 350–51
powwows, 178
Poxabogue Golf Course and Driving Range, 230
Presidents' Day Parade, 313
Preston's Outfitters and Preston's Ship and Sea Gallery, 310–11
Pridwin Beach Hotel & Cottages (Shelter Island), 336–37
Prime Care, 244
Pritam & Eames, 161
Privet Cove, 167
Prudential Douglas Elliman Real Estate, 249

public buses, 44
public tennis courts, 236
pubs, 289–92
Puff & Putt, 217, 223–24
Puggliese Vineyards, 271
Pumpkin Trail and Halloween Activities, 179
puppet theaters, 196
Purim Carnival, 174

Q

Quantuck Bay Farm, 222
quilt shows, 178
Quogue. *see also* East Quogue
    beaches, 211
    bed & breakfasts, 64
    gourmet food shops, 129
    libraries, 199
    lodging, 64
    museums, 191
    parks & nature, 224, 233
    restaurants, 89–91, 100
Quogue Country Market, 129
Quogue Horse & Pony Farm, 222
Quogue Library, 199
Quogue Village Beach, 211
Quogue Village Office, 241
Quogue Wildlife Refuge, 224, 233

R

radio stations, 247–48, 328
Railroad Museum of Long Island, 317
Ralph Lauren, 148, 155
Ralph Lauren, Rugby, 152
Ram's Head Inn and Restaurant (Shelter
    Island), 337–38
Raphael, 353
Raphael wine, 272–73
real estate services, 248–49, 329–30, 351
Red/Bar Brasserie (Southampton), 109
Red Creek Skate Park, 234
Red Rooster Bistro (North Fork), 286–87
The Red Pony, 148
Reed's Photo Shop, 170
The Reform Club (Amagansett), 49–50
Renaissance Restoration Workshop, 144
rental cars. *see* car rentals
residents, famous, 172
Restaurant in the Inn at Quogue (Quogue), 100
revolutionaries, 22–24
Rita's Stables, 221

Riverhead
    museums & galleries, 318–20
    wineries, 266–67, 268, 273
Riverhead Chamber of Commerce, 328
Riverhead Raceway, 322
Riverhead Skate Park, 323
Riverhead Town Office, 328
Road H beach, 210
Roanoke Vineyards, 273
Robert's restaurant, 355
Robert's (Water Mill), 116
rock concerts, 196
Rogers Mansion museum, 194
Rogers Memorial Library, 199
Rogers Pavilion, 213
rollerblading, 234
Romany Kramoris Gallery, 164
Rose Hill Farm, 222
Rose Jewelry, 169
Rosewood Farm, 222
Ross Institute Wellness Center courses, 183
Ross School children's cultural programs,
    196–97
Rotary Club Antique Show and Sale, 178
Rotations, 214
Rotations Bicycle Center, 213
Round Swamp Farm Country Market, 127
Ruby Beets Old & New, 143
Rugosa (Wainscott), 112–13, 355
Rupp (Isabella) Documentary Filmmaking
    Class, 196
Rumrunner, 157
running-races, 174, 175, 176, 177, 179, 230
RVS Fine Art, 163

S

Sagaponack
    beaches, 211
    gardens, 191
    gourmet food shops, 129–30
    restaurants, 100–101
    thrift shops, 170
    wineries, 138–39
Sage Harbor Antique Shop, 143
Sage Street Antiques, 143
Sagg General Store, 129–30
Sagg Main Beach, 211
Sag Harbor
    beaches, 211
    bicycling, 214

cafés & coffeehouses, 124
cigar lounges, 125
events, 173
gourmet food shops, 130
ice cream parlors, 131
libraries, 198–99
lodging, 65–67, 73
map, 361
marina, 215
marinas, 216
museums, 192–93
nightlife, 203
parks & nature, 233
restaurants, 101–7, 355
shopping (see Shopping Index)
taxis, 42
tennis courts, 236
Sag Harbor Car Service, 44
Sag Harbor Chamber of Commerce, 240
Sag Harbor Cinema, 183
Sag Harbor Community Band concerts, 201
Sag Harbor Cove Yacht Club East & West, 216
Sag Harbor Cup Sailing Regatta, 178
Sag Harbor Express, 246
Sag Harbor Historic House Tour, 177
Sag Harbor Holiday Events (Christmas), 179
Sag Harbor Inn (Sag Harbor), 73
Sag Harbor Launderette, 246
Sag Harbor Sailing School, 217–18
Sag Harbor Variety Store, 169
Sag Harbor Village Office, 241
Sag Harbor Whaling Museum, 192
sailing, 177, 178, 217–18
Saint Patrick's Day Parade, 174
Saks Fifth Avenue, 155
Salamander General Store, 291
Salibello (John) Antiques, 141–42
Salivar's, 245
Saltwater Grill (West Hampton Beach), 118–19
Sammy's Beach, 211
Sam's, 124
sand castle contests, 177
Sandy Hollow Tennis Club, 236
Sang Lee Farms, 295
Sant Ambroeus (Southampton), 109
Santa Parade, 179
Santa Visits the Montauk Point Lighthouse, 179
Savanna's (Southampton), 109–10
Scallop Dinner, 346
Schneider Vineyards, 275

science classes for children, 196–97
Scoop du Jour, 131
Scrimshaw (North Fork), 287–88
scuba diving, 219–20, 327
Sea Crest on the Ocean (Amagansett), 51
seafood markets, 132–34
The Seafood Shop, 134
seal watching, 173
Seal Watch Walks, 174
Sea Otter IV, 227
Sears Bellows County Park, 231
Seatuck Cove House Waterfront Inn (East Port), 58
Sea Turtle Dive Charters, 220
Second House Museum, 190
Second House Tavern (Montauk), 73
Second Star to the Right, 149
Sen (Sag Harbor), 106–7
7-Eleven, 245
1708 House (Southampton), 68–69, 354
1770 House (East Hampton), 57–58, 88
75 Main Street (Southampton), 110
Shearer Shop, 307
Shellfish Hatchery, 225
Shelter Island
   auto repair, 351
   bed & breakfasts, 339–40
   bicycling, 347
   boating, 348
   business services, 351
   chambers of commerce, 350
   cultural activities, 345–47
   emergency numbers, 350
   events, 345–47
   food purveyors, 343
   golf, 348
   history, 330–32, 352
   lodging, 334–40
   map, 366
   marinas, 348
   miniature golf, 349
   newspapers, 351
   parks & nature, 349
   post offices, 350–51
   real estate services, 351
   recreation, 347–49
   restaurants, 340–43
   shopping (see Shopping Index)
   tennis, 349
   town offices, 350

transportation, 332–33
village offices, 350
visitor information, 350–51
Shelter Island 10K Run, 346
Shelter Island Chamber of Commerce, 350
Shelter Island Country Club, 348
Shelter Island Friends Meeting, 351
Shelter Island Friends of Music, 347
Shelter Island Go'Fors Taxi, 333
Shelter Island Heights Post Office, 351
Shelter Island Kayak Tours, 348
Shelter Island Post Office, 351
Shelter Island Pottery, 345
Shelter Island Presbyterian Church, 351
Shelter Island Public Library, 347
Shelter Island Reporter, 351
Shelter Island Town, 350
Sherwood House Vineyards, 273
Shillingburg & Associates, 351
Shinnecock Canal County Marina, 215
Shinnecock Indian Outpost, 165
Shinnecock Indian Powwow, 178
Shinn Estate Farmhouse (North Fork), 303–4
Shinn Vineyards, 273–74
shipping history, 24–26
Shock Kids/Baby Shock, 149
shopping. *see also* food stores; Shopping Index
  for shopping by location
  antiques, 141–46, 306–8
  art galleries, 161–63
  books, 146–47, 308
  children's clothing, 147–50
  children's furniture, 149–50
  clothing, 148–56, 178, 308
  crafts, 164–65, 172, 174, 177, 178, 197,
    308–12
  equestrian, 223
  factory outlets, 160
  furniture, 156–59, 306–8
  gardening & landscaping, 165–67
  gifts, 163–64, 308–12
  handcrafts, 164–65
  home furnishings, 156–59
  housewares, 165–67, 313
  interior design, 156–59
  jewelry, 167–69
  kitchenware, 165–67
  late-night, 245
  lingerie, 150–51, 156
  magazines, 146–47, 246–47

men's clothing, 151, 155
music, 146–47
old-fashioned emporiums, 169
pet clothing and accessories, 160
photos, 169–70
stationery, 165–67
thrift shops, 170–71
toys, 149–50
wine, 133–37, 134–37, 296
Shorecrest (North Fork), 304
Shoreline Aviation, 41
short trips, 352–55
Showcase Wine & Liquor, 296
Silver's (Southampton), 110–11
Silvia Lehrer's Cookhampton, 183–84
Simply French, 159
Sip 'n Soda, 131–32
skateboarding, 323
Skydive Long Island, 228
skydiving, flying, gliding, 227–28
Sky Sailors Glider School, 227, 228
Slow Food East End, 178
Snug Harbor Motel and Marina (Montauk), 73
social history, 14–32
Solé East (Montauk), 61–62, 73
Sotheby's International Realty (Daniel Gale),
  249, 351
Sound Aircraft Flight Enterprises, 41, 227
Soundview Scuba Center, 327
Southampton
  art galleries, 181–82
  bakeries & confectioneries, 120
  banking, 242
  beaches, 211
  bicycling, 214
  cafés & coffeehouses, 124
  events, 173
  fishing, 225
  gourmet food shops, 130
  ice cream parlors, 131–32
  lodging, 67–70, 73–74
  map, 359
  marinas, 215
  museums, 193–94
  music concerts, 201
  restaurants, 107–12
  seafood markets, 133
  shopping (see Shopping Index)
  short trips, 354
  taxis, 44

tennis, 235, 236
Southampton Chamber of Commerce, 48, 240
Southampton Country House (Southampton), 69
Southampton Cultural Center arts and music, 182
Southampton High School, 236
Southampton Historical Museum children's walking tour, 197
Southampton Hospital, 242, 244
Southampton Hospital Annual Summer Party, 178
Southampton Hospital Thrift Shop, 171
Southampton Inn (Southampton), 69–70
Southampton Limousine, Ltd., 35
Southampton Press, 247
Southampton Publick House (Southampton), 111
Southampton Racquet Club, 235
Southampton Rotary 8K Run, 175
Southampton Town Hall, 241, 242
Southampton Trails Preservation Society, 231, 237
Southampton Trustees, 225
Southampton Urgent Medical Care, 244
Southampton Village Office, 241
South Ferry, 40, 254, 333
South Fork
    map, 357
    short trips, 353–55
    wineries, 137–39
South Fork Natural History Museum and Nature Center, 186
South Hampton eggs & poultry, 126
South Main Beach, 212
Southold
    antiques, 307, 308
    museums & galleries, 320–22
    wineries, 261–62, 262, 267, 274
Southold Historical Society, 311–12, 321
Southold Indian Museum, 321–22
Southold Town Office, 328
Southold Village Merchants Annual Christmas Parade, 315
South Shore Computer Works, 244
Southwest Airlines, 41
Spanierman Gallery, 161
Sparkling Pointe winery, 274
specialty tours, 43
Speonk restaurants, 112

Spicy's BBQ, 291
Splish Splash Water Park, 325
Sportime, 235
Springs
    beaches, 212
    cemeteries, 194
    parks & nature, 234
    tennis courts, 236
Springs Library, 200
Springs Recreation Area, 236
St. Ann's Episcopal Church, 170
Starbucks, 123
Star Confectionery, 291–92
Star Island Yacht Club & Marina, 216, 227
Starr Boggs (West Hampton Beach), 119, 134
stationery stores, 165–67
Stearns Point House (Shelter Island), 340
Stephen Talkhouse nightclub, 202
Stevenson's Toys and Games, 150
Stirling Historical Society, 317
Stirling House Bed & Breakfast (North Fork), 304–5
St. Mary's Episcopal Church, 351
Stone Creek Inn (Quogue), 90–91, 354
Stone Lion Inn (Montauk), 73
Stonewalls (North Fork), 288
Stony Brook University, Southampton Campus, courses, 184
Stuart's Fish Market, 133
Student Arts Festival, 174
Suffolk County Airport–Francis S. Gabreski, 42
Suffolk County Farm and Education Center, 197, 224
Suffolk County Historical Society, 320
Suffolk County Office of Handicapped Services, 244
Suffolk Transit, 37, 44, 253
Summer Place, 345
Summer Showcase Outdoor Concerts, 322
Summer Writer's Conference writing courses, 184
Sunrise to Sunset, 219
Sunset Beach Resort and Restaurant (Shelter Island), 339
Sunset Café, 125
Sunset-Moonrise Cruise, 346
Super Saturday charity designer clothing sale, 178
surfing, 218–19
Surf Lodge (Montauk), 63–64, 99–100

Surf's Lodge club, 203
The Surf Club (Montauk), 62–63
Susie E, 227
Swan Creek Farms, 222
Sweet Anezka's Lingerie, 156
Sweetpotatohampton run, 179
Sweet Tomato's (Shelter Island), 342–43
swimming, 234
Sydney's "Taylor" Made Cuisine, 131
Sylvester & Co., 167
Sylvester Manor, 347
synagogues, 192

T

tablewares stores, 166–67
The Tack Trunk, 223
take-out food, 132–34
Taste of the Hamptons food and wine festival, 175
Taste shop, 312
Tasting Room, 274–75
Tate's Bake Shop, 120
taxis, 44, 255
Tea & Tree: A Tenth Night, 345
television stations, 248
Temple Adas Israel, 192
temples, 192
tennis, 178, 235–36
Thayer's Hardware & Patio, 169
theaters, 174, 196, 203–5, 322
Third House Museum, 191
ThistleBees, 307
The Thomas Halsey Homestead museum, 193–94
Three Sisters Antiques, 307
thrift shops, 170–71
Tiana Beach, 210
Tide Runners (Hampton Bays), 92–93
tides, 242–43
Tiffany & Co., 168
Times/Review Newspapers, 329
Tina Fredericks, 249
Tommy Hilfiger, 152
Tony's Tubs, 246
Topiaire, 167
Topping Riding School, 222
tours
    group, 254–55
    guided, 42–43
    home, 178

Long Island Rail Road, 42
    North Fork, 254–55
town government, 240
Town House museum, 189
Townline BBQ (Sagaponack), 100–101
town offices, 241, 328, 350
trading history, 15–16
train travel, 37–38, 254
transportation
    airport, 42
    buses, 35–37, 44, 253
    car, 34–35, 42, 43, 255
    limousines, 255
    The North Fork, 252–55
    parking permit fees, 208
    Shelter Island, 332–33
    taxis, 44, 255
    train travel, 37–38, 254
Tratta East (Water Mill), 116–17
travelers, types of, 26–28
Trawler Fest, 314
trawlers, 26
Triangle Tennis Club, 235
Trout Pond Noyack Road, 234
Trumpets on the Bay (Eastport), 89
Tubby Charters, 348
The Tuck Shop, 343
Tulla Booth Gallery, 163
Turkey Day Run for Fun, 179
Turtle Crossing (East Hampton), 88–89
Tuscan House (Southampton), 111–12
tutto bene, 150
Tutto Il Giorno (Sag Harbor), 107
Tweed's Restaurant and Buffalo Bar (North Fork), 289
Twin Forks Trolley Tours, 43, 254–55
Two Mile Hollow beach, 210
Two South Ferry (Shelter Island), 340
Two Trees Stables, 222

U

Uihlein's Marina, 216, 218, 220
Union Chapel in the Grove, 351
United Artists East Hampton Cinema, 183
United Artists Hampton Bays Theatre, 183
Urban Archaeology, 156
Urban Zen, 154
U.S. Airways Express, 41

V

Vaccari (Jon) Antiques, 146
Venture, 227
Vered Art Gallery, 162
Victorian Murder Mystery, 322
Viking Fleet, 40, 43, 214, 226
Viking Line, 237
Village Auto Body, 246
Village Cheese Shop, 295
Village Cinema Greenport, 316
Village Gourmet Cheese Shop, 130
Village Latch (Southampton), 74
Village of Dering Harbor, 350
village offices, 241, 328, 350
Villa Italian Specialties, 129
Villeroy and Boch Factory Outlet, 160
Vine Street Cafe (Shelter Island), 343
Vine Time, 258
Vineyard 48, 275–76
Vintage Bed and Breakfast (North Fork), 305–6
Vintage Tours, 43, 255
visitor information
    North Fork, 327–28
    Shelter Island, 350–51
Voices on the Vine, 322

W

Wainscott
    bakeries & confectioneries, 120–21
    restaurants, 112–14, 133, 355
    seafood markets, 133
    shopping (see Shopping Index)
    take-out food, 133
Wainscott Walk-In Medical Care, 244
Waldbauns, 242
walking tours, 174, 186, 197
Wallace Gallery, 162
Waterfront Marina, 216
Water Mill
    beaches, 212
    bed & breakfasts, 70–71
    cafés & coffeehouses, 125
    farms & farm stands, 127–28
    gourmet food shops, 130–31
    lodging, 70–71
    museums, 195
    restaurants, 114–17, 355
    shopping (see Shopping Index)
    wineries, 138
Water Mill Museum, 195

Waters Crest Winery, 276
watersports, 214–21
Waves clothing, 150
weather, 242–43
Weight-N-Sea Scuba School, 220
Westhampton
    bakeries & confectioneries, 121–22
    beaches, 212–13
    cafés & coffeehouses, 125
    events, 173
    gourmet food shops, 131
    libraries, 200–201
    lodging, 74
    map, 358
    marina, 215
    restaurants, 117–19
    seafood markets, 133
    shopping (see Shopping Index)
    take-out food, 133
    taxis, 44
    tennis, 235
Westhampton Bath and Tennis Hotel and
    Marina (Westhampton Beach), 74
Westhampton Beach High School, 236
Westhampton Beach Performing Arts Center,
    197, 201, 204–5
Westhampton Beach Taxi & Limo, 44
Westhampton Beach Village Office, 241
Westhampton Dunes Village, 241
Westhampton Free Library, 200–201
Westhampton Harvest Festival and Street Fair,
    179
Westhampton Seabreeze Motel (Westhampton
    Beach), 74
Westhampton Tennis & Sport Club, 236
West Lake Fishing Lodge, 216
The Whaler's Church, 193
Whale's Tale, 349
whale watching, 237
whaling history, 24–26
White Flower Farmhouse, 307
Whitehorse nightclub, 202–3
White Sands Motel on the Ocean (Amagansett),
    71
Whitmore (Charlie) Gardens, 165
Whoa! Nellie!, 143
Wickham's Fruit Farm, 296
Williams-Sonoma, 166
Will Miloski's Poultry Farm, 296
Willow Hill Antiques, 307–8
windmills, 187

wind surfing, 220–21
Windsurfing Hamptons, 217, 219, 221
wine and food festivals, 174, 175, 177, 178
Wine Press, 247, 314, 329
wineries
  Aquebogue, 268–69, 353
  Baiting Hollow, 259–60
  Bridgehampton, 138
  Clovis Point, 261
  Cutchogue, 260–61, 266, 269–71, 275, 276
  Jamesport, 261, 263
  Laurel, 263–64
  map, 256
  Mattituck, 265–66, 273–74, 275
  North Fork, 255–76, 275
  Peconic, 138–39, 258–59, 264–65, 267–68, 270–75
  Remsenburg, 275
  Riverhead, 266, 268, 273
  Sagaponack, 138–39
  South Fork, 137–39
  Southold, 261–62, 267, 275

Water Mill, 138
Wines by Morrell, 135
wine shops, 134–37, 296
Winston Limousine, 35
Winston Transportation, 42
Winterfest—Jazz on the Vine, 313
Winter Harbor Gallery, 312–13
winter sports, 237
The Winter Tree Gallery, 163
Wish Rock Studio, 345
Wölffer Estate, 138–39, 222
World Pie (Bridgehampton), 81
writers' events, 177
writing courses, 183–84
W. Scott Cameron Beach, 209

Y

Yesterday's Treasures, 144

Z

zip codes, 241, 328

Lodging by Price

Inexpensive:	up to $100
Moderate:	$100 to $250
Expensive:	$250 to 400
Very Expensive:	$400 and up

Amagansett

Inexpensive–Expensive
The Hermitage, 49
Ocean Colony Beach and Tennis Club, 49
Sea Crest on the Ocean, 51
White Sands Motel on the Ocean, 71

Moderate–Expensive
The Gansett Green Manor, 48–49

Very Expensive
The Reform Club, 49–50

Bridgehampton

Inexpensive–Expensive
The Enclave Inn, 71

Moderate–Expensive
Bridgehampton Inn, 51–52

East Hampton

Inexpensive–Expensive
East Hampton House, 53

Moderate
Cove Hollow, 72

Moderate–Expensive
The Huntting Inn, 54–55
Getaway House, 72

Moderate–Very Expensive
C/O The Maidstone, 55–57

Expensive–Very Expensive
The Baker House, 52–53
1770 House, 57–58
East Hampton Point, 53–54
Mill House Inn, 57

Very Expensive
The Hedges Inn, 54

East Port

Inexpensive–Expensive
Seatuck Cove House Waterfront Inn, 58

Moderate–Expensive
A Victorian on the Bay, 59–60

Hampton Bays

Inexpensive–Moderate
Inn Spot on the Bay, 72

Inexpensive–Expensive
Bowen's by the Bays, 72

Moderate–Expensive
The Hampton Maid, 72

Montauk

Inexpensive–Moderate
Stone Lion Inn, 73

Inexpensive–Expensive
The Enclave Inn, 71
Snug Harbor Motel and Marina, 73
Solé East Beach, 73

Inexpensive–Very Expensive
Montauk Manor, 60–61

Moderate
Montauk Hill House, 60

Moderate–Expensive
The Surf Club, 62–63
Second House Tavern, 73

Moderate–Very Expensive
Gurney's Inn Resort & Spa, 72
Lenhart Cottages, 72–73
Montauk Yacht Club Resort & Marina, 61
Solé East, 61–62

Very Expensive
Surf Lodge (Montauk), 63–64

North Fork

Inexpensive–Moderate
The Greenporter Hotel and Spa, 299

Moderate
Freddy's House, 298
Orient Inn, 303
Shinn Estate Farmhouse, 303–304
Stirling House Bed & Breakfast, 304–305

Moderate–Expensive
The Morning Glory Bed & Breakfast, 302–303
Bartlett House Inn B & B, 296–297
By The Bluff Bed and Breakfast, 298
Harbor Knoll, 300–301
Harvest Inn Bed & Breakfast, 301–302
Vintage Bed and Breakfast, 305–306

Moderate–Very Expensive
Harborfront Inn, 300
Shorecrest, 304

Expensive
Blue Iris Bed & Breakfast, 297

Expensive–Very Expensive
Jedediah Hawkins Inn, 302

Quogue
Moderate–Very Expensive
The Inn at Quogue, 64

Sag Harbor
Inexpensive–Very Expensive
Sag Harbor Inn, 73

Moderate–Expensive
Harborwoods, 66

Expensive
Lighthouse on the Bay, 66–67

Expensive–Very Expensive
American Hotel, 65–66

Shelter Island
Inexpensive–Moderate
House on Chase Creek, 335
Ram's Head Inn and Restaurant, 337–338

Inexpensive–Expensive
Chequit Inn and Restaurant, 334

Moderate–Expensive
Olde Country Inn and Restaurant, 335–336
Pridwin Beach Hotel & Cottages, 336–337

Moderate–Very Expensive
Dering Harbor Inn, 334–335
Sunset Beach Resort and Restaurant, 339

Southampton
Inexpensive–Expensive
The Enclave Inn, 71

Moderate–Expensive
Southampton Inn, 69–70

Moderate–Very Expensive
The Atlantic, 73–74
1708 House, 68–69
A Butler's Manor, 67–68
Mainstay Inn, 68
Village Latch, 74

Expensive
Southampton Country House, 69

Very Expensive
The Capri, 74

Wainscott
Inexpensive–Expensive
The Enclave Inn, 71

Water Mill
Moderate–Expensive
The Pondview at Deerfield, 70–71

Westhampton
Inexpensive–Moderate
Westhampton Seabreeze Motel, 74

Expensive–Very Expensive
Dune Deck Beach Resort, 74
Westhampton Bath and Tennis Hotel and Marina, 74

Dining by Price

Inexpensive: up to $30
Moderate: $30 to 50
Expensive: $50 to 80
Very Expensive: $80 or more

Amagansett

Inexpensive–Moderate
Indian Wells Tavern, 77

Inexpensive–Expensive
The Lobster Roll Restaurant, 77
Meeting House, 78

Bridgehampton

Inexpensive–Very Expensive
Copa Wine Bar & Tapas, 78–79

Moderate
World Pie, 81

Expensive–Very Expensive
Bobby Van's, 78
Pierre's, 80–81

East Hampton

Inexpensive–Moderate
Blue Parrot Bar & Grill, 81–82
Turtle Crossing, 88–89

Inexpensive–Expensive
   Michael's at Maidstone Park, 86–87

Moderate
Cittanuova, 82–83

Moderate–Expensive
The Laundry, 85–86
Cafe Max, 82
Fresno, 84

Moderate–Very Expensive
East Hampton Point, 83–84
Harbor Bistro, 84–85
Nick & Toni's, 87

Expensive–Very Expensive
The Living Room at C/O The Maidstone, 86
The Palm at Huntting Inn, 87–88
Della Femina, 83

Very Expensive
1770 House, 88

Eastport

Expensive
Trumpets on the Bay, 89

Hampton Bays

Inexpensive–Expensive
Indian Cove, 91

Moderate
Oakland's, 92
Tide Runners, 92–93

Moderate–Expensive
Inn Spot on the Bay, 91–92

Montauk

Inexpensive–Moderate
Gosman's Dock, 95–96
Inlet Seafood, 97–98

Moderate–Expensive
Backyard at Solé East, 93
Breakwater, 93–94
Fishbar on the Lake, 95
Surf Lodge, 99–100

Moderate–Very Expensive
Dave's Grill, 94

Expensive–Very Expensive
East by Northeast, 94–95
Gulf Coast Kitchen, 96

Very Expensive
Harvest on Ford Road, 96–97

North Fork

Inexpensive
Greenport Tea Company, 280–281

Inexpensive–Moderate
Love Lane Kitchen, 284

Inexpensive–Expensive
Amarelle, 277–278
Legends, 283–284

Moderate
Cooperage Inn, 279–280
Jamesport Country Kitchen, 281–282
Red Rooster Bistro, 286–287
Tweed's Restaurant and Buffalo Bar, 289

Moderate–Expensive
A Mano Osteria & Wine Bar, 277
Bayview Inn & Restaurant, 278
Claudio's Restaurant, 279
La Cuvée Wine Bar & Bistro, 282–283
Lucie & Hawkins, 284–285
Michael Anthony's Food Bar, 285
Old Mill Inn, 286

Expensive
A Touch of Venice, 288–289

Blackwells, 278–279
Frisky Oyster, 280
Jamesport Manor Inn, 282
La Plage, 283
Porto Bello, 286
Scrimshaw, 287–288
Stonewalls, 288

Expensive–Very Expensive
North Fork Table and Inn, 285–286

Quogue
Inexpensive
New Moon Café, 90

Moderate–Very Expensive
Dockers Waterside, 89–90

Expensive–Very Expensive
Inn at Quogue, 100
Restaurant in the Inn at Quogue, 100
Stone Creek Inn, 90–91

Sag Harbor
Inexpensive–Expensive
Blue Sky Mediterranean Lounge, 102
Il Capuccino Ristorante, 103–104

Moderate–Expensive
The Beacon, 101–102
New Paradise Cafe, 104
Phao Thai Kitchen, 106

Moderate–Very Expensive
B. Smith's, 102–103
Tutto Il Giorno, 107

Expensive
Oasis, 104–105

Expensive–Very Expensive
American Hotel, 101
Sen, 106–107

Sagaponack
Inexpensive
Townline BBQ, 100–101

Shelter Island
Inexpensive–Moderate
Planet Bliss Eatery & Market, 341–342

Moderate
The Dory, 340–341

Moderate–Expensive
Sweet Tomato's, 342–343

Expensive
Vine Street Cafe, 343

Southampton
Inexpensive–Expensive
Southampton Publick House, 111

Moderate
The Coast Grill, 107–108
Silver's, 110–111

Moderate–Very Expensive
75 Main Street, 110
Le Chef, 108
Sant Ambroeus, 109
Savanna's, 109–110
Tuscan House, 111–112

Expensive
Plaza Café, 108
Red/Bar Brasserie, 109

Speonk
Moderate
Olde Speonk Inn, 112

Wainscott
Moderate–Very Expensive
Rugosa, 112–113

Expensive–Very Expensive
Georgica Restaurant and Lounge, 112

Water Mill
Moderate
Dish, 114

Moderate–Expensive
Muse Restaurant and Aquatic Lounge, 115–116

Expensive–Very Expensive
Mirko's Restaurant, 114–115
Tratta East, 116–117

Very Expensive
Robert's, 116

West Hampton Beach
Moderate–Expensive
Patio at 54 Main, 117–118
Saltwater Grill, 118–119

Expensive–Very Expensive
Annona, 117
Starr Boggs, 119

Dining by Cuisine

Amagansett

American
Indian Wells Tavern, 77
Meeting House, 78

Seafood
The Lobster Roll Restaurant, 77

Bridgehampton

American Steakhouse
Bobby Van's, 78

French
Pierre's, 80–81

Italian, Global
World Pie, 81

Spanish
Copa Wine Bar & Tapas, 78–79

East Hampton

American
The Palm at Huntting Inn, 87–88
Michael's at Maidstone Park, 86–87

American, Global/Seasonal
Della Femina, 83

American/Mediterranean
The Laundry, 85–86

Italian
Cittanuova, 82–83

Italian, Northern/Mediterranean
Nick & Toni's, 87

New American
Fresno, 84

New American/Classic French
Harbor Bistro, 84–85

New American/Seasonal
1770 House, 88

New American/Eclectic
Cafe Max, 82

New American/Slow Food
The Living Room at C/O The Maidstone, 86

New Contemporary American
East Hampton Point, 83–84

Southwestern/BBQ
Turtle Crossing, 88–89

Tex–Mex–Regional Mexican
Blue Parrot Bar & Grill, 81–82

Eastport

Continental
Trumpets on the Bay, 89

Hampton Bays

American/French
Indian Cove, 91

American/Seafood
Oakland's, 92
Tide Runners, 92–93

Eclectic
Inn Spot on the Bay, 91–92

Montauk

American/Contemporary
Breakwater, 93–94

American/Seafood
Dave's Grill, 94

Italian, Northern
Harvest on Ford Road, 96–97

Mediterranean
Backyard at Solé East, 93

New American
Surf Lodge, 99–100

Seafood
East by Northeast, 94–95
Fishbar on the Lake, 95
Gosman's Dock, 95–96
Inlet Seafood, 97–98

Southern Coastal
Gulf Coast Kitchen, 96

North Fork

American
Jamesport Country Kitchen, 281–282
North Fork Table and Inn, 285–286

American Bistro
Red Rooster Bistro, 286–287

American Continental
Greenport Tea Company, 280–281

American/Seafood
Old Mill Inn, 286

Classic Italian
A Touch of Venice, 288–289

Contemporary Country
Amarelle, 277–278

Eclectic
La Plage, 283
Legends, 283–284
Michael Anthony's Food Bar, 285

Eclectic/American
Frisky Oyster, 280

French Bistro
La Cuvée Wine Bar & Bistro, 282–283

Italian
A Mano Osteria & Wine Bar, 277
A Touch of Venice, 288–289
Porto Bello, 286

New American
Jamesport Manor Inn, 282
Love Lane Kitchen, 284
Lucie & Hawkins, 284–285
Scrimshaw, 287–288
Tweed's Restaurant and Buffalo Bar, 289

New American/French
Stonewalls, 288

New American/Continental
Bayview Inn & Restaurant, 278

Northern Italian
Porto Bello, 286

Seafood
Claudio's Restaurant, 279

Steakhouse
Blackwells, 278–279

Traditional American
Cooperage Inn, 279–280

Quogue

American
Inn at Quogue, 100
Restaurant in the Inn at Quogue, 100

American/Creative
Dockers Waterside, 89–90

Texas BBQ/Lone Star Mexican
New Moon Café, 90

Sag Harbor

American/French inspired
The Beacon, 101–102

American/Seafood
Oasis, 104–105

French/American
American Hotel, 101

International/Eclectic
B. Smith's, 102–103

Italian
Tutto Il Giorno, 107

Italian, Northern
Il Cappuccino Ristorante, 103–104

Mediterranean
Blue Sky Mediterranean Lounge, 102

New American
New Paradise Cafe, 104

Thai
Phao Thai Kitchen, 106

Sagaponack

BBQ
Townline BBQ, 100–101

Shelter Island

American Bistro
Vine Street Cafe, 343

American/Regional
Planet Bliss Eatery & Market, 341–342

American/Seafood
The Dory, 340–341

Italian/Continental
Sweet Tomato's 342–343

Southampton

American Bistro
75 Main Street, 110

American Contemporary/Seafood
The Coast Grill, 107–108

American/French inspired
Red/Bar Brasserie, 109

Contemporary American
Savanna's, 109–110

Contemporary American/Microbrewery
Southampton Publick House, 111

Eclectic
Silver's, 110–111

French/Continental
Le Chef (Southampton), 108

Italian, Northern
Sant Ambroeus, 109
Tuscan House, 111–112

New American
Plaza Café, 108

Speonk

American/Classic
Olde Speonk Inn, 112

Wainscott

American/Contemporary
Georgica Restaurant and Lounge, 112

New American/French inspired
Rugosa, 112–113

Water Mill

Eclectic
Mirko's Restaurant, 114–115

Greek
Tratta East, 116–117

Italian, Coastal
Robert's, 116

New American
Dish, 114
Muse Restaurant and Aquatic Lounge, 115–116

West Hampton Beach

Italian
Annona, 117

New American
Starr Boggs, 119

New American Bistro
Patio at 54 Main, 117–118

Seafood
Saltwater Grill, 118–119

Shopping by Destination

Amagansett

antiques
Decorum, 141
Nellie's of Amagansett, 141

books, magazines, music
The BookHampton Corner Store, 146

factory outlets
Amagansett Square, 160

farms & farm stands
Amagansett Farmers Market, 126–127

galleries
Crazy Monkey Gallery, 161

gourmet food shops & markets
Mary's Marvelous!, 128

handcrafts
Gone Local, 164

housewares
Charlie Whitmore Gardens, 165

photos
Reed's Photo Shop, 170

seafood markets & take-outs
Fish Farm Multi Aquaculture Systems, 132–133
Stuart's Fish Market, 133

wine shops
Amagansett Wine & Spirits, 134–135

Aquebogue

farms & farm stands
Bayview Farms, 292
Crescent Duck Farm, 293

Bridgehampton

antiques
John Salibello Antiques, 141
Laurin Copen Antiques, 142
The American Wing, 141

children's clothing
C & W Mercantile, 147
Gap Kids and Baby Gap, 147

clothing
Anne Moore, 150
Gloria Jewel, 150
Out of the Closet, 150
tutto bene, 150
Waves, 150

farms & farm stands
Hayground Market, 127
Mecox Bay Dairy, 127

furniture
Country Gear, 156
English Country Antiques, 156
Urban Archaeology, 156

galleries
Mark Borghi Fine Art, 161

gourmet food shops & markets
Citarella, 128–129

housewares
Alice B. King Fine Stationery, Ltd., 165
Loaves & Fishes Cookshop, 165
Marders, 165
Williams-Sonoma, 166

old–fashioned emporiums
Thayer's Hardware & Patio, 169

photos
Hampton Photo Arts, Inc., 170

thrift shops
St. Ann's Episcopal Church, 170

toys
Second Star to the Right, 149

wine shops
DePetris Liquor Store, 135

Calverton

farm & farm stands
Will Miloski's Poultry Farm, 296

Cutchogue

antiques
Antiques and Old Lace, 306
ThistleBees, 307

farms & farm stands
Wickham's Fruit Farm, 296

food purveyors
George Braun Oyster Co., 293

galleries, crafts & gifts
The Down Home Store, 308–309
Old Town Arts & Crafts Guild, 310

wine
Peconic Liquors, 296

East Hampton

antiques
Architrove, 142
Butler's Fine Art & Antiques, 142
The Grand Acquisitor, 142

bakeries & confectioneries
Dylan's Mini Candy Bar, 120
Fat Ass Fudge, 120

books, magazines, music
BookHampton, 146
Glenn Horowitz Bookseller, 146
Harper's Books, 146

children's clothing
Bonne Nuit, 148
Calypso, 148
Monogram Shop, 148
Ralph Lauren, 148
Red Pony, 148

clothing
Bonne Nuit, 150
Brooks Brothers, 151
Calypso, 151
Catherine Malandrino, 151
Collette Designer Resale, 151
Côte d'Azure, 151
Eileen Fisher, 151
Elie Tahari, 151
Entre Nous, 152
Gucci, 152
Hermès, 152
Jill Stuart, 152
La Perla, 152
Polo Country Store, 152
Rugby Ralph Lauren, 153
Shoe-Inn, 153
Tommy Hilfiger, 153

factory outlets
Coach, 160

farms & farm stands
Iacono Farms, 125–126
Round Swamp Farm Country Market, 127

furniture
Calypso Home, 157
Polo Home Country Store, 157
Rumrunner, 157

galleries
Giraffics Gallery, 161
Pritam & Eames, 161
Spanierman Gallery, 161
Vered Art Gallery, 162
Wallace Gallery, 162

gourmet food shops & markets
Citarella, 129
Lucy's Whey, 129
Villa Italian Specialties, 129

handcrafts
Irony, 164

housewares
Home, James!, 166

jewelry
Jennifer Miller, 167

London Jewelers, 167
Mayfair Diamond & Fine Jewelry, 168
Tiffany & Co., 168

thrift shops
Ladies' Village Improvement Society (LVIS) Bargain
  Box and Bargain Books, 170

wine shops
Domaine Franey, 135
Park Place Wines & Liquors, 135
Wines by Morrell, 135

East Marion

farms & farm stands
Lavender by the Bay, 295

Eastport

wine shops
A Grape Pear Wine Boutique, 135

Greenport

antiques
Beall & Bell Antiques, 306
The Clearing House eXchange, 306
The Furniture Store Antiques, 306–307
Gallery 429, 307
Kapell Antiques, 307
Lydia's Antiques and Stained Glass, 307
Shearer Shop, 307

books
Burton's Bookstore, 308

clothing
b.b.balsam, 308
Calypso, 308
Impulse, 308

galleries, crafts & gifts
The Doofpot, 308
Claudia Lowry Fine Art, 308
Fiedler Gallery, 309
Freda's Fancy, 309
Gallery M, 309–310
Gazebo Gallery, 310
Greenport Art & Design, 310
Preston's Outfitters and Preston's Ship and Sea
  Gallery, 310–311
Sweet Indulgences, 311–312
Taste, 312
Winter Harbor Gallery, 312

housewares
Cookery Dock, 313

wine
Claudio's Wines and Liquor, 296

Hampton Bays

wine shops
Hampton Bays Wine and Spirits, 136

Jamesport

antiques
Three Sisters Antiques, 307

clothing
Gloria Jewel, 308

farms & farm stands
Golden Earthworm Organic Farm, 293–294
Harbes Family Farm, 294

galleries, crafts & gifts
Jamesport Country Store, 310

Mattituck

food purveyors
Village Cheese Shop, 295

galleries, crafts & gifts
La Ferme de la Mer, 310

Montauk

antiques
Haven, 142
The Grand Acquisitor, 142
Whoa! Nellie!, 143

books, magazines, music
The Book Shoppe, 146

Orient

farms & farm stands
Orient Country Store, 295

Peconic

antiques
White Flower Farmhouse, 307

farms & farm stands
Catapano Dairy Farm, 293
Krupski's Vegetable & Pumpkin Farm, 295
Sang Lee Farms, 295

food purveyors
A Taste of the North Fork, 295

Quogue

gourmet food shops & markets
Quogue Country Market, 129

Riverhead

farm & farm stands
Briermere Farm, 293
Garden of Eve Organic Farm, 293

wine
Michael's Wines & Liquors, 296

Sag Harbor

antiques
Carol O'Neill Vintage Linen, 143

Sag Harbor Antique Shop, 143
Sage Street Antiques, 143

books, magazines, music
Black Cat Books, 147
BookHampton, 147
Canio's Books, 147
Metaphysical Books & Tools, 147

children's clothing
Andrew & Company, 148

clothing
Collette Designer Resale, 154
Lisa Perry, 154
Nikki Eve, 154
Pailletts, 154
Urban Zen, 154

furniture
Bloom, 158
Fisher's Home Furnishings, 158

galleries
Grenning Gallery, 163
Tulla Booth Gallery, 163
Winter Tree Gallery, 163

gifts
Blooming Shells, 163
Romany Kramoris Gallery, 164

gourmet food shops & markets
Espresso, 130

handcrafts
Megna Hot Glass, 164

housewares
Sylvester & Co., 167

ice cream parlors
Ice Cream Club, 131

jewelry
Adornments Fine Jewelry, 168

old–fashioned emporiums
Sag Harbor Variety Store, 169

toys
Kites of the Harbor, 149

wine shops
Long Wharf Wines & Spirits, 136
Noyac Liquors, 136

Sagaponack

gourmet food shops & markets
Loaves & Fishes, 129
Sagg General Store, 129–130

thrift shops
Animal Rescue Fund Thrift & Treasure Shop (ARF), 170

Shelter Island

antiques
Dworkin & Daughter Antiques, 344
Fallen Angel Antiques, 344
Home Port Antiques & Collectibles, 345

art
Hap's Iron Works, 344–345
Shelter Island Pottery, 345

clothing
Marie Eiffel, 345
Summer Place, 345

food purveyors
The Tuck Shop, 343

galleries
Boltax Gallery, 343
Wish Rock Studio, 345

gifts
Cornucopia, 344

housewares
Celadon Home, 343–344
Coastal Cottage Home Store, 344

housewares & furniture
Home 114, 345
Marika's, 345

Southampton
antiques
Ann Madonia, 143
Another Time Antiques, 143
Black Swan Antiques, 144
Croft Antiques, 144
Galerie Hamptons, 144
Morgan MacWhinnie, 144
Old Town Crossing, 144
Renaissance Restoration Workshop, 144
Yesterday's Treasures, 144

bakeries & confectioneries
Blue Duck Bakery Café, 120
Tate's Bake Shop, 120

books, magazines, music
BookHampton, 147

children's clothing
Aunt Suzie's Clothes for Kids, 148
Hatchlings, 148

clothing
Christopher Fischer Cashmere Collections, 154
Collette Designer Resale, 154
Diane von Furstenberg, 155
Edward Archer, 155
Hampton & Co., 155
Ralph Lauren, 155
Saks Fifth Avenue, 155

factory outlets
Cashmere Outlet, 160
Villeroy and Boch Factory Outlet, 160

farms & farm stands
North Sea Farms, 126

furniture
Brambles, 159
Broken Colour Works, 159
Mecox Gardens, 159
Simply French, 159

galleries
Chrysalis Gallery, 163
RVS Fine Art, 163

gourmet food shops & markets
Village Gourmet Cheese Shop, 130

handcrafts
Shinnecock Indian Outpost, 165

housewares
Elegant Setting, 167
Privet Cove, 167
Topiaire, 167

jewelry
Hollis Reh & Shariff, 168
Rose Jewelry, 169

old–fashioned emporiums
Hildreth's, 169

pet clothing and accessories
Little Lucy's, 160

photos
Morris Studio, 170

thrift shops
Southampton Hospital Thrift Shop, 171

toys
Stevenson's Toys & Games, 150

wine shops
Herbert and Rist, 136–137

Southold
antiques
Jan Davis Antiques/L. I. Doll Hospital, 307
Willow Hill Antiques, 307–308

galleries, crafts & gifts
Southold Historical Society Gift Shop, 311

housewares
Complement the Chef, 313

wine
Showcase Wine & Liquor, 296

Wainscott
antiques
Georgica Creek Antiques, 145

bakeries & confectioneries
Breadzilla, 120
Levain Bakery, 121

clothing
Bellhaus, 155

seafood markets & take-outs
The Seafood Shop, 134

Water Mill

antiques
Antique Lumber Co., 145
Donna Parker's Habitat, 145
Jon Vaccari Antiques, 146

farms & farm stands, 127–128
The Green Thumb, 127–128

furniture
Furniture Garden, 159

gourmet food shops & markets
Citarella, 130–131

Westhampton

bakeries & confectioneries
Beach Bakery Cafe, 121
Holey Moses Cheesecake, 121–122

books, magazines, music
The Open Book, 147

children's clothing
Shock Kids/Baby Shock, 149

clothing
Darbelle, 156
Jimmy's, 156
Sweet Anezka's Lingerie, 156

furniture
Excentricities, 159

gifts
O'Suzanna, 164
Pine Cone, 164

gourmet food shops & markets
Sydney's "Taylor" Made Cuisine, 131

jewelry
Joan Boyce, 169

seafood markets & take-outs
Starr Boggs Fish, 134

wine shops
Bonnie's Beach Liquors, 137
Hamptons Wine Shoppe, 137